I love Taya.

Appreciating Shakespeare

Appreciating Shakespeare

by Gideon Rappaport

One Mind Good Press
San Diego, California

One Mind Good Press
San Diego, CA 92117

ISBN: 978-0-578-35165-0

Preface

A fundamental principle of life is that human beings will not live without meaning. It is the deepest need we have. And Shakespeare's plays and sonnets make up one of the richest treasuries of meaning there is. My students in high school, college, graduate school, adult education classes, and professional theatrical companies have agreed. One year, students in my Shakespeare course asked why I had not written a book about Shakespeare for people who were not my students. I could give them no good reason, so here it is.

Appreciating Shakespeare is written to make easily available the essential tools for understanding and enjoying Shakespeare's plays and poems, which means, in practice, experiencing the thrilling meaning of his works. Part 1 offers the background knowledge that you should have in order to appreciate Shakespeare's works (plus a bit more). Part 2 offers short essays on twenty-two of the plays, each meant to help you get to the thematic and dramatic heart of a particular play. These essays are not substitutes for reading and seeing the plays but offer insights intended to deepen your appreciation of the meaning in plays you have already read or seen. Each essay is followed by two sections varying in size—a) Key Lines, and b) Specific Notes to Help in Your Reading—which supplement the body of the essay with some significant points not included there. Part 2 also has a chapter on a selection of the Sonnets.

If there is more here than you need, skip it. If there is less, check out the suggestions for further reading in Appendix 1. Questions about Shakespeare's plays and poems may have brought you to this book. Its aim is to send you back to the plays and poems with the tools you need to find the answers there.

Acknowledgements

This book is a distillation of what I have learned in studying and teaching Shakespeare for forty-five years. Much of it is original; much of it comes through me from and through those who have taught me. They include my own teachers and friends, Mary Holmes, Philip Thompson, John Hazel Smith, Jonathan Saville, Michael Warren, J.V. Cunningham, and Alan Levitan, and generations of scholars (some of whom are cited in the book) to whom all of us owe debts of gratitude. In addition, I am grateful to the producer Craig Noel, the dramaturge Diana Maddox, the actor Jonathan McMurtry, and the directors with whom I have worked as Shakespearean dramaturge: Jack O'Brien and Joe Hardy at the Old Globe Theatre; Joe Vincent at the California Shakespeare Festival; Philip Sneed; Robert Shampain at the British-American Youth Festival Theatre (Bayfest); Sam Woodhouse and Todd Salovey at the San Diego Repertory Theatre; Christy Yael-Cox and Sean Cox at the Intrepid Theatre Company; David Ellenstein at the North Coast Repertory Theatre; Richard Baird at the New Fortune Theatre Company; Thomas Haine and Sam Young at the Coronado Community Theatre; Joe Sofranko, director of the film *Complete Works*; and Scott Feldsher at La Jolla Country Day School. I am also grateful to the producer Nathan Agin of The Working Actor's Journey and the directors with whom I have worked online in scenes from Shakespeare on Zoom—Gigi Bermingham, Brendon Fox, Jamie Newcomb, Elizabeth Swain, and Geoffrey Wade. And I am particularly grateful to the many professional and student actors with whom it has been my privilege to collaborate in bringing Shakespeare's works to life on the stage.

Special thanks go to Courtney Flanagan, my friend and former colleague at The Bishop's School, masterful high school drama teacher and director, with whom I have had the very good fortune to collaborate on countless productions of Shakespeare's plays. I would also like to thank my copyeditor/proofreader, Mark Hussey, and my book designer, Chuck Eng.

I am deeply grateful for my late parents' unfailing support and fruitful criticism, my sisters' moral support and practical ministrations, and the immeasurable devotion of Bruce Cantz, Christopher Maron, and Stan Bui.

Finally, I want to express my gratitude to my students of all ages, whose reception of my teaching and enthusiastic response to Shakespeare have immeasurably enriched both this book and my life.

A Note on Line References

All quotations from the plays and poems of Shakespeare are taken from G. Blakemore Evans, ed., *The Riverside Shakespeare*, Second Edition (Boston: Houghton Mifflin, 1997). For the reader's ease a few words have been silently emended (e.g., *vild* to *vile*) along with an occasional punctuation mark. Line references are indicated as follows:

1 Henry IV, II.ii.4 = *Henry IV, Part 1*, Act II, Scene ii, Line 4.

A slash mark (/) within a quotation indicates the beginning of a new line of verse.

Contents

Part 1: The Background You Need

How Did Shakespeare Become So Great?
The Elements of Shakespeare's Mastery
Subjects
Vitality
Unity
Variety
Freshness of Wit
Characters
Poetic Language
Sound and Sense
Action
Universal Realism

Who Wrote Shakespeare's Plays?
Who Was Shakespeare?
What Kind of Person Was Shakespeare?
Did Shakespeare Go to School?
What Religion Was Shakespeare?
How Could One Person Have Written All Those Plays?
How Long Did It Take Him to Write a Play?
Where Did Shakespeare Get His Ideas?—Sources

Hearing a Play
The Building and the Stage

Judgments of Art
What Does the Work of Art Mean?—Talking about Art
What Makes a Work of Art Great?

Part 2: Plays and Sonnets

Selected Sonnets

Part 1:
The Background You Need

1

What's So Great about Shakespeare?

Shakespeare is the most universally appreciated and admired poet in the history of the world, revered by people from nearly all backgrounds, cultures, nations, languages, and walks of life. But he is not great because he is popular. He is popular because he is great.

Shakespeare is great *not* because he invented new plots; though he rearranged them, his plots were mostly borrowed. He is great not because his plays are long, or complex, or weighty, or old, or written in poetry; many lesser contemporaries of Shakespeare wrote verse plays equally long or complex or weighty. He is great not because he was an original psychologist or political theorist or theologian or educator; most of his ideas in these areas, though often profound, were not originally his own. Nor is he great because of his huge vocabulary, his ability to make up new words, his vast memory, his natural writing ability, or his good ear; he had all those, but they aren't in themselves what make his achievement uniquely great.

Shakespeare is great because his works move people with their breadth and depth of meaning, their truth to life, their ability to evoke intense emotion and deep insight in response to the comedy and tragedy and mystery of what it means to be a human being, and to do so with luminous clarity, vitality, and authenticity. In Shakespeare's works, we experience revelations of the truth of our own personal world and of *the* world. What is so great about Shakespeare is that he provides a variety of deep, authentic, meaningful, and hugely entertaining experiences of reality.

HOW DID SHAKESPEARE BECOME SO GREAT?

This question is easy to answer: nobody knows. Human beings simply don't know where genius comes from or why it appears in this person and not in that, in this age and not in that. The source of artistic greatness is a mystery, even to the artist.

The quality that gives a work of art its greatness comes from a combination of all the talents and gifts the artist brings to the work *plus* something else that he or she cannot command, something that comes according to a schedule he or she cannot control. The artist can prepare a place for that extra something by mastering his art. But its crowning grace—the moving power and depth that make a work what we call "great"—is a gift.

From whom? Modern people might say nature or chance or the unconscious. Or they might more refreshingly say "we don't know." A Christian poet like Milton would say it is inspired by the Holy Spirit—it comes from God. To the ancient Greeks, the givers of these gifts were called the Muses. They were the nine goddesses, daughters of Zeus and Mnemosyne (her name means "memory"), eventually associated with nine established forms of art: epic or heroic poetry, history, love poetry, lyric poetry, tragedy, hymns in praise of the gods, dance, comedy, and astronomy (that is, poetry about cosmology). From them we get the term "music."

Every epic poem in the Western literary tradition begins with an invocation of the muse. This is because the great poets—in fact all great artists, if they are honest—know that if it were merely up to them alone, a work might get made but greatness would not appear in it. The poet invokes "the muse" to acknowledge and call upon the mysterious giver of that special gift of greatness, who gives it if and when she wills or not at all. All the poet can do is to receive it with gratitude; if the muse doesn't give it, it isn't there.

So the only answer to the question of where Shakespeare got his particular ability to join qualities of intellect and feeling, knowledge and belief, memory and invention, language and sound into plays and poems that bear the stamp of true greatness is what the poets call the muse. It's the only useful explanation we have. But though we may not know exactly what "the muse" is, we certainly do know one thing about her: Shakespeare was her darling.

THE ELEMENTS OF SHAKESPEARE'S MASTERY

As little as we can know about where greatness comes from, we can observe the forms that it inhabits when it is present. None of the following elements is the *cause* of Shakespeare's greatness. The cause is hidden. Only the effects of that cause are revealed in the elements discussed below. But in discerning those elements, we can see how richly the muse has stamped Shakespeare's writing with her gift.

Subjects

The first and fundamental element in which we recognize Shakespeare's greatness is the subjects of his plays.

Subject is the element of drama that has been least honored in the last century of literary criticism. For about that long we have been told that not content but only formal qualities matter in judging works of art, that a poem should not *mean* but *be*, as if these were opposites. The phrase appears in the poem called "Ars Poetica" (the art of poetry) by Archibald MacLeish, but it later became a prescription. Of course it is true that bad artists can try to tackle great themes and end up producing bad art, and that great artists can raise into greatness themes once thought trivial. It is important to attend to the formal qualities of any work as well as to its content. But so long as human beings are human beings, what something is *about* will matter. A poem must *both* mean *and* be. In truth, no one honestly cares much for poems that exist for the sake only of their formal qualities but don't say anything significant.

Whatever your own feelings about recent poetry, it is important to know that Shakespeare lived in an age in which the subject of a work of art mattered. In his plays there are thousands of lines and images whose subjects, taken out of context, are trivial. But they all exist to give verisimilitude to the whole play, which, even in the comedies, is about something invariably important and usually profound. In *The Two Gentlemen of Verona*, for example, a young girl writes a love letter, then tears it up, then regrets doing so and tries to put the pieces back together—not an earthshaking event. But the play in which it happens is about betrayal and forgiveness in love and friendship, and the girl's fancy about the torn words on a sheet of paper exists to help develop and dramatize those larger themes.

When we look at Shakespeare's greatest plays, we will be focusing on the most important subjects human beings ever face: lust and love, separation and reunion, pride and humility, power hunger and self-sacrifice, crimes (like murder, rape, and suicide) and their consequences (like punishment and despair, repentance and forgiveness), war and peace, political chaos and political order, injustice and justice, famous historical events and mythical tales, free will and fate, the meaning of life and the meaning of death. In a Shakespeare play nothing is trivial because everything is part of the larger subject, which is almost always a great one.

What form did these important subjects take? Above all, the form of story.

Living long before America's freedom of speech became an ideal, Renaissance playwrights could not without danger explicitly treat the political and religious controversies of the day. In England the Master of the Revels, working for the monarch, made sure nothing went public that would compromise the stability of the regime or the religious establishment.

But apart from those limitations, almost any story was fair game: Ancient Greek and Roman mythology, history, epic poetry, romance, and drama, medieval epics and romances, English history, Italian farce, and stories of the falls of famous men of all periods. Shakespeare took his plots from all these kinds of published works and sometimes reworked older plays that had fallen out of fashion. Sometimes the audiences already knew the stories: In *Julius Caesar* and in *Antony and Cleopatra* Shakespeare stuck very close to his sources (mainly Plutarch's *Lives*) in telling the world-shaking actions of his world-famous characters. Sometimes the audience *thought* they knew a plot but were in for a big fat Shakespearean surprise: In *The Winter's Tale*, which was based on a very popular romance of the time by Robert Greene, Shakespeare changed the ending entirely, no doubt much to the delighted surprise of those who had read the book. Only in *The Tempest* does Shakespeare seem to have made up his own plot entirely. (See Appendix 2 for a list of the works from which Shakespeare took his stories.)

Vitality

This is one of the most precious qualities we can name in works of art. But it is also elusive, almost impossible to define. It is some combination of inventiveness, authenticity, and vividness. As the word implies, a work with vitality has life in it. This quality is not tied to any particular form, whether comedy or tragedy, word choice or syntax, action or contemplation, or any other particular element of poetry. And yet it is the most immediate and discernible quality in any work of art. When it is present, we know it because we feel it. Characters come alive, words scintillate, meaning dances into our consciousness—*we* come alive. And we love that. By contrast, a work of art that lacks vitality we experience as drab, unmoving, humdrum. We may feel and understand it, even value it, but without the thrill that vitality evokes in us.

This vitality is present in Shakespeare almost without measure. When Shakespeare says, in Sonnet 130, "My mistress' eyes are nothing like the sun," we snap to attention. Here's a man talking about his girlfriend in an unexpectedly honest way, forcing us to keep reading to find out how he's going to get away with a compliment that sounds like an insult. He goes on to give a litany of the ideal things his beloved is not, but then ends by saying he thinks she's as "rare" (meaning as rare a beauty) as any woman the earlier poets have lied about to prove their love. He asserts her beauty and loves her after all. And we buy it because his unexpected honesty has taken us off guard and sets up the power of his conclusion, and the invention vibrates with life.

Or take the scene when Prince Hal asks Falstaff, "how long is't ago, Jack, since thou sawest thine own knee?" (*1 Henry IV*, II.iv.327–28). What more lifelike way could there be of evoking the fatness of Falstaff's body and the self-indulgence in his character? It's a verbal trick to plant the image of a huge belly and the idea of fatness in our minds, but the trick has such life to it that when we hear it said we cannot resist its authenticity.

Unity

Every work of art strives to convey meaning on some subject. That meaning cannot be put into a sentence or a paragraph. If it could, the work would not need to exist. In fact, the greater the work of art, the less expressible that meaning will be in any other way than the work of art itself. Only the work as a whole can get that meaning into our experience, and that's what it exists to do.

Shakespeare's imagination is such that each of his plays—some more profoundly than others—achieves this unity of intention. Each play as a whole focuses all its variety of character, action, place, time, and language into a single experience of meaning. *Twelfth Night*, for example, is focused on the difference between self-serving sentimentality and authentic submission to love. *Henry IV, Part 1*, is unified by the attempt to define—not *in* words, but *through* words—the true nature of honor in personal and political life. The vast complexity of *Hamlet* is unified by the main character's spiritual growth from vengeful self-will into submission to the will of the divine.

One way of expressing this element of Shakespeare's greatness is to say that every detail in a Shakespeare play points to the center, and the whole is revealed in all its parts. But when you try to name that whole (as I've just tried to do for three of the plays), you find that the naming is not sufficient to describe the thing. My three examples are true, but they are unsatisfactory, as you'll know when you read or see the plays themselves.

You'll get the unity from the plays, and then you'll see that my phrases are only vague approximations of the real unity in each. It's the unity itself, not its name or description, that is so deeply satisfying in Shakespeare's work. (See the story about Beethoven in Chapter 15 under "What Does the Work of Art Mean?—Talking about Art.") The unified meaning of a Shakespeare play is *in* the experience of it.

Variety

Shakespeare carries us to heights of sublime love, to depths of deserved or undeserved anguish, to hilarious funhouses of wit and silliness, to peaks of power, to the awesomeness of self-renunciation, the solidity of true friendship, the wilderness of betrayal, the torture chambers of evil, the Elysian Fields of virtue. He commands every tone of voice, mood of the heart, and trick of the mind. He takes us to the palaces of the rich and powerful, the town houses of the middle class, and the hovels of the poor; to places next door and far away; to ancient cities we've read about in books and fantastic places that never existed; to islands, forests, and caves; to sheepcotes, prisons, and ships at sea. He writes mostly in blank verse but also in rhymed pentameter and tetrameter couplets, ballad meters, and formal and informal prose. He uses big words, small words, made-up words, Latin, Italian, French, German, and Welsh words, and more English words than any other writer in the language (29,000 of them), including jargon words from the king's court and the law courts, from sailing, warfare, weaving, cooking, medicine, farming, taverns, bear-baiting, and, of course, theater. He portrays rulers, intellectuals, and artists, lovers, parents, and children, kings and queens, nobles and their ladies, knights and warriors, tyrants and senators, doctors, lawyers, soothsayers, traders, sailors, teachers, nurses, peasants, hangmen, pirates, thieves, and gravediggers. Above all, he gives us variety of personalities: brilliant and stupid, quick and plodding, funny and dull, beautiful and ugly, virtuous and vicious, fat and thin, well-shaped and gawky, leaders and followers, kind and callous, and, importantly, mixtures of them all. There seems to be no limit to the variety of character, place, feeling, idea, and language Shakespeare can call upon to fill his made-up worlds with empathy-evoking particulars.

Freshness of Wit

Here's another quality that cannot be defined but only experienced. No matter how familiar you are with a particular speech by Shakespeare, the clever play of wit, whether startling or troubling or funny, always strikes you as new, sudden, fresh, and alive. Check out the prologue to the mechanicals' play of Pyramus and Thisbe in *A Midsummer Night's Dream* (V.i.108-117), where Shakespeare produces hilarity through intentionally faulty punctuation. Or the lying Falstaff's complaint about liars (*1 Henry IV*, V.iv.144–46). Or the gravedigger's quibbling answers to Hamlet's question, "Whose grave's this, sirrah?" (*Hamlet*, V.i.118ff.). Or the villain King Richard III's seduction of the Lady Anne, whose husband and father-in-law he has just killed (*Richard III*, I.ii).

Characters

We know Shakespeare's characters. Once we've seen or read the play in which they appear, we know them almost as if they lived in our house. Sometimes they are more alive in our imaginations than living people we know. This is in part because of Shakespeare's vast emotional range, his profound empathic gift for entering into the psyches of human beings who are not himself. At the same time, his characters are also meaningful. From the major characters like Romeo, Juliet, Falstaff, Hamlet, Othello, Iago, King Lear, Lady Macbeth, Hermione, Prospero, and the rest, down to the minor characters like the jailer in *Cymbeline* or Siward's son in *Macbeth*, Shakespeare's characters come alive as both real and significant. For how this works see "Universal Realism" below and Chapter 5.

Poetic Language

Perhaps the most obvious way in which Shakespeare's greatness reveals itself is through his language. He commands the biggest vocabulary of any writer in English, even adding words to the language when he needs to. More importantly, he puts words together to convey meaning in ways that are masterfully precise, satisfying, clear, and entertaining. Watch him portraying Macbeth attacked by his conscience when he sees his own hands covered in the blood of the good king he has just murdered:

> What hands are here? Hah! they pluck out mine eyes.
> Will all great Neptune's ocean wash this blood
> Clean from my hand? No; this my hand will rather
> The multitudinous seas incarnadine,
> Making the green one red.   (II.ii.56–60)

Here's a partial list of what Shakespeare is doing with language in this speech:

1. Simple common speech ("What hands are here?"), conveying the idea that Macbeth is now looking down and noticing his blood-covered hands.
2. Non-verbal grunt or groan ("Hah!"), giving natural realism and believability.
3. Metaphor ("they pluck out mine eyes"), making a physical picture of someone's hands plucking out someone's eyes—or, more horribly, someone's hands plucking out his own eyes—to convey Macbeth's inner shock at the sight of his bloody hands. Through this metaphor we experience his deed attacking his conscience.
4. Classical allusion ("Neptune"), giving mythic seriousness to the situation; also perhaps implying that the ancient gods have not the power to redeem from guilt.
5. Rhetorical question ("Will all great Neptune's ocean wash this blood / Clean from my hand?") challenging the audience to come up with the answer. Is it possible?
6. Argument from comparison of greater to lesser and lesser to greater ("all great Neptune's ocean . . . my hand . . . my hand . . . multitudinous seas").
7. Metaphor ("Will all great Neptune's ocean wash this blood / Clean from my hand?") of a vast quantity of water trying to alter guilt, implying the question whether anything in the physical world can change a moral condition.
8. Biblical allusion ("Will all great Neptune's ocean wash this blood/ Clean from my hand?") to Isaiah 1:18: "Come now, and let us reason together, saith the Lord: though your sins be as scarlet, they shall be as white as snow; though they be red like crimson, they shall be as wool." (Compare *Hamlet*, III.iii.43–46, "What if this cursed hand / Were thicker than itself with brother's blood, / Is there not rain enough in the sweet heavens / To wash it white as snow?")
9. Interior dialogue ("No"): the rhetorical question is answered.
10. Moral implication ("No"): only a change of will can alter one's moral condition.
11. Double sense of a word ("Clean" can mean both "not dirty" and "completely" or "entirely").
12. Metaphor ("this my hand will rather / The multitudinous seas

incarnadine"—"incarnadine" is a verb here), expressing that the power and extent of moral guilt is greater than that of the greatest physical body, namely the ocean. An additional implication: the water of baptism, or holy water, can wash clean of sin because it is not merely physical water but a sacramental vehicle of spiritual purification. By contrast, no amount of merely physical water can wash away a spiritual sin. (Compare to Lady Macbeth's "A little water clears us of this deed" six lines later.)

13. Combination of words from Latin roots and words from Anglo-Saxon roots. The multi-syllable Latinate words ("multitudinous" "incarnadine") suggest importance, the weight of Rome, Christian theology, and the past. The one-syllable Anglo-Saxon words ("seas . . . the green one red") suggest simple home truth. Their combination here implies that the awful reality of his situation is one, whether seen from the universal perspective or from the intimate and personal perspective.

14. Invention of words: before Shakespeare "incarnadine" was a noun, meaning "the color of flesh" or "carnation color," from the root "carn-" meaning flesh. Shakespeare here uses it as a verb for the first time, altering its implied color. Because of this speech, everyone who has used the word since has used it to mean "to turn (something) the color of blood."

15. Synonyms ("incarnadine" and "making . . . red").

16. Rhythmic meaningfulness—meaning conveyed by the way the natural rhythm of the phrases plays upon the meter (see Chapter 4).

All these language elements are woven into a single speech that works upon us with exactly the effect Shakespeare is trying to achieve. We experience Macbeth's inner condition with perfect comprehension while being largely unconscious of how Shakespeare is getting us to do so. (For the answer to the question "Are we supposed to get all this when we hear those lines?" see "Did Shakespeare's Audience Get It All?" in Chapter 4.)

Sound and Sense

Shakespeare has a great genius for harmonizing sound and sense. That means making the sounds of words reflect (or rather *become*) the meaning of the line in which they are being said. Below are three of my favorite examples. The first two happen both to use the letter *s*, though in different ways; one comes from the sonnets and one from *Macbeth*.

But first a caution: Except for onomatopoeia—i.e., using words that sound like what they mean, for example "buzz"—the meaning of the sounds of words depends on the context. Except in words and sentences, the sounds of letters don't have specific meanings. For example, the sound of "s" means totally different things in the words "hiss," "bliss," "fuss," and "gas." The American poet J.V. Cunningham cautions us that "The glory that was Greece" has a totally different effect if we spell it "The glory that was grease." When we talk about Shakespeare's meaningful use of sounds, we're always talking about the *relation* of sounds to the meanings of the words and phrases in which they appear.

Example 1: When Lady Macbeth is persuading her husband to kill the good king Duncan, she says,

> To beguile the time,
> Look like the time; bear welcome in your eye,
> Your hand, your tongue; look like th'innocent flower,
> But be the serpent under't. He that's coming
> Must be provided for; and you shall put
> This night's great business into my dispatch,
> Which shall to all our nights and days to come
> Give solely sovereign sway and masterdom.   (I.v.63–70)

Notice first the meanings of the words in the last line. They all imply that she wants herself and her husband to have absolute power and control: "solely," "sovereign," "sway" (="control" or "rule"), and "masterdom." Next, notice that all these words have s's in them. Because of this, in saying these words Lady Macbeth begins to sound as if she is hissing. And we are meant to feel her line as hissing (rather than, say, deflating and melting, like the Wicked Witch of the West in *The Wizard of Oz*, or smoldering, like the glowing fire in the next example) because Shakespeare has already planted the idea of a serpent into our minds four lines above ("be the serpent under't"), and serpents traditionally hiss. But there's more. Which is the serpent best known to Shakespeare's audience? Satan, who takes the form of a serpent in the Garden of Eden. And what was he doing there? Tempting Eve and Adam to disobey God, just as Lady Macbeth is tempting Macbeth to disobey God by killing the king. And what was it that Satan ultimately wanted that made him evil? He wanted to be God, just as Lady Macbeth and Macbeth want to be queen and king—that is, he wanted to have "Solely sovereign sway and masterdom"! Do you see how through these words and their *s*'s, Shakespeare associates Lady Macbeth with the satanically tempting serpent not only to our minds but to our ears? The words and their sounds join in our empathic response to become a single unified experience of meaning.

Example 2: Line 8 of Sonnet 73 reads,

Death's second self that seals up all in rest.

The poem is about the feelings involved in the awareness of approaching endings, especially the ending of life. In the previous line, night ("death's second self") encloses into sleep everything that was awake during the day. But notice how many times the letter *s* is used in this line. That sibilant sound keeps going through the line until the *t* in the word "rest" puts an end to it. So the *concept* of day ending in night and awareness ending in sleep is carried, like a soul in a body, within the *sound* of six *s*'s ending in a *t*: sssssst. This is also tied to the hissing sound of the dying fire in the next quatrain of the sonnet. By Shakespeare's artistry, our empathic response to the sounds and our empathic response to the meaning become *one*. And that's the point. That's part of what makes it stick and gives us the thrill.

Example 3: Here we are talking not about consonants but about the sound structure of the lines. In *King Lear* there's a scene in which the good King of France, finding that England's King has angrily and foolishly banished his youngest daughter, Cordelia, with no dowry, announces his intention to marry the girl anyway:

> Gods, gods! 'tis strange that from their cold'st neglect
> My love should kindle to inflam'd respect.
> Thy dow'rless daughter, King, thrown to my chance,
> Is queen of us, of ours, and our fair France.
> Not all the dukes of wat'rish Burgundy
> Can buy this unpriz'd precious maid of me.
> Bid them farewell, Cordelia, though unkind,
> Thou losest here, a better where to find.   (I.i.254–61)

He speaks this speech in rhymed couplets (pairs of rhyming lines), suggesting formality, orderliness, coherence of purpose. He is announcing his betrothal to the rejected daughter of a king and publicly making her, by his words, the Queen of France.

Now, here is King Lear's response:

> Thou hast her, France, let her be thine, for we
> Have no such daughter, nor shall ever see
> That face of hers again. [*To Cordelia*] Therefore be gone,
> Without our grace, our love, our benison.

What has happened to the mood? It sounds as if Lear's anger has banished the orderliness of rhymed couplets. The pauses come in the middles of lines, not at the ends, as in France's speech. (Technically, Lear's speech is enjambed instead of end-stopped—see Rhetorical Devices in Chapter 4.) But look again at the end words: *we/see, gone/benison*. The rhymed couplets are still there, though they seem to have been battered at by chaos.

What has actually happened is that Shakespeare has given us rhymed couplets at war with themselves. Externally and formally, the rhymes are there. But they do not convey the balanced harmony that the rhymed couplets of the King of France convey. The movement from France's calm and orderly phrases to Lear's wild ones feels like order collapsing into chaos, which is exactly what is happening within the mind of King Lear. Though externally he is a king formally giving his daughter in marriage to a king, and therefore remains within the outward form of rhymed couplets, internally he is in a foolish, egotistical rage, and the disorder-within-order of the lines conveys that. Sound and sense are one.[1]

Action

Shakespeare is able to weave action into his web of meaning as if it were a language in itself. Not only sword fights, murders, suicides, and other violence, but subtle actions, too, pack a dramatic punch in Shakespeare. Jaques' famous speech in *As You Like It* on the seven ages of man, beginning "All the world's a stage," ends with a melancholy image.

> Last scene of all,
> That ends this strange eventful history,
> Is second childishness, and mere oblivion,
> Sans teeth, sans eyes, sans taste, sans every thing.
>
> (II.vii.163–66)

(In French "sans" means "without.") It is an ending fitting the melancholy

Jaques. But though it is the final word in Jaques' story of life, it is not the play's final statement. For the next thing that happens is that the young hero, Orlando, enters carrying his weakened old servant, Adam. (We know this because after the stage direction "Enter Orlando with Adam," the Duke says, "Welcome. Set down your venerable burden / And let him feed"—ll.167-68.) The physical action refutes the despairing melancholy of Jaques' verbal conclusion. That the loyal old servant Adam is carried in by his virtuous young master demonstrates that where there is love, an old man, even at the point of death, is *not* "sans every thing."

For other examples of action conveying layers of meaning, study the scene in *King Lear* when Gloucester tries to jump off what he thinks is a cliff (IV.vi.) or the statue scene in *The Winter's Tale* (V.iii). In combination with speech, action in Shakespeare becomes eloquent language.

Universal Realism

Shakespeare's plays represent a remarkable union of two modes of drama. For convenience we can call the first mode realism and the second allegory. As mentioned above, Shakespeare has found a way to make completely believable particulars convey completely meaningful ideas. The effect is that the audience experiences his characters, actions, situations, and speeches as real and believable and at the same time universally significant. Most writers who are good at one of these modes of drama are less effective at the other. Shakespeare is great at both, and at both at the same time. In achieving this marriage of naturalistic realism and abstract allegory, he comes as close to imitating life truly seen as any artist we can name.[2]

Shakespeare achieves this combination, as C.S. Lewis argues, partly through the use of the technique of variation, which will be discussed under "Variation in Speech" in Chapter 4. Another way of looking at this combination is to think about Shakespeare's position in the history of drama.

Briefly, the history of European drama from medieval times to the present is generally (with exceptions, of course) a movement from the more allegorical forms of depicting reality (mystery, miracle, and morality plays) to more realistic modes (what we call "slice of life" realism, which is common in modern plays, films, and TV dramas).

The dramatic forms of our modern age began in the churches with stories that everyone knew and that applied to everyone: Bible stories, like those about Adam and Eve in the Garden of Eden, Noah's flood, and the birth of Jesus; stories about the lives of saints; morality tales like *Everyman*, a play about the fact that every human being dies and goes to judgment. In that allegorical play, characters have the names of abstract concepts, like "Knowledge," "Good Deeds," and "Death," and the main character, Everyman, is neither short nor tall, fat nor thin, unusually good nor unusually bad. He has no *particular* qualities at all except that of being a mortal man. Therefore, he stands for all of us.

Now fast forward to the present day and think of the movies and TV shows you've watched. The vast majority of them are about specific people with specific names and ages and in specific places and situations. They even drink specific drinks: the Coca Cola Bottling Company, for example, pays a lot of money to get the hero of the latest popular film to be seen drinking a Coke instead of water, let alone a Pepsi. We tend to take far more seriously a movie or TV show that might begin, for example, with a boy named Joe Morgan driving along Chicago's outer drive in his father's silver Honda and talking on a cell phone to a girlfriend named Cindy than one that begins "once upon a time there was a boy who lived in a big city."

Shakespeare's ancestors went for the more abstract or allegorical. We go for the more particular or realistic. But Shakespeare came right in the middle of the historical movement from the one mode toward the other, and he and his audience (partly instructed by him) went for both together. We could draw a schematic of this historical movement from the abstract-allegorical modes toward the particular-realistic modes as follows:

→ Time (roughly) ↓ Abstract-Allegorical to Particular-Realistic

church liturgy
  mystery plays (Bible stories)
    morality plays (like *Everyman*)
      miracle plays (lives of saints)
        early Renaissance histories, tragedies, and comedies
        SHAKESPEARE
          Restoration comedies and 18th C. satires and tragedies
          19th C. melodrama
            20th–21st C. drama, film, TV
              docudramas
                news and documentaries
                  reality TV
                    live video and webcams

The causes of this movement from the abstract to the particular are complex and mysterious, having to do with the ways in which human civilization and its styles develop. This movement is significantly influenced by Shakespeare's work itself. But what is important here is to see that Shakespeare comes at the center or pivot point of this historical development. Both in terms of his place in the history of drama and in terms of the qualities of his plays themselves, the union of modes we've been talking about—realistic particulars and universal significance—is the essence of Shakespeare's drama.

One play where this combination of modes is easily visible is *Othello*. But before we look at that play, have you ever seen the old Disney cartoons in which Donald Duck has to make a decision and two mini-versions of Donald appear on his shoulders? The one on the left is red with a pitchfork and a long, pointed tail and horns; the one on the right is white, and he's wearing halo and carrying a small harp. The devil Donald would try to persuade Donald Duck to be bad, and the angel Donald would try to persuade him to be good. This is a modern version of a medieval allegorical device called the *psychomachia*, or war within the psyche (*psyche* means "soul," *machē* means "fight"). In a *psychomachia*, a good angel and an evil angel, or perhaps two figures representing opposing qualities, like courage and fear, or wisdom and folly, stand on the shoulders of a man and debate. Each is trying to persuade the man's free will, and they are trying to pull him in opposite directions. This allegorical debate exists as a way of representing a moral conflict within the mind.

In *Othello*, Shakespeare has portrayed a *psychomachia*. Othello is every man who is caught between trusting a good angel and trusting a lying devil. But here's the magic of Shakespeare: The everyman whose mind is the arena of this terrible choice is *at the same time* a particular man. He is a general named Othello; he is a great and heroic fighter with royal ancestors and a noble bearing; he is a new convert to Christianity; he is a "blackamoor" (i.e., a central African with dark skin); his past life includes very specific experiences; and so on. The good angel, the incarnation of loving patience, is *at the same time* a particular white Venetian lady named Desdemona, daughter of a senator, virtuous, loving, a bit naïve, and Othello's faithful wife. And the devil, an incarnation of jealousy itself, is *at the same time* a particular white Venetian soldier, twenty-eight years old, named Iago, who is a lying villain plotting to destroy his master.

The magic lies in the fact that we experience these two kinds of beings, the abstract (angel, devil, everyman) and the particular (Desdemona, Iago,

Othello), at once, in the same words and situations. Notice: They are not sometimes people and sometimes abstractions; they are both individual particular people *and* abstract figures at every point. The result of this Shakespearean magic is that we experience the play as both completely meaningful and completely believable, both universally significant and convincingly real.

Take one more example: Sir John Falstaff in *Henry IV, Part 1*, is a hilariously witty, self-indulgent, old, fat man whose rank as a knight is entirely at odds with his character. He is devoted to his own comfort and pleasure, eating, drinking, sleeping, thieving, whoring, and joking around, and has lots of fun pretending to be virtuous and brave when he definitely isn't, providing us some of the best laughs in the history of drama. He is one of Shakespeare's most completely convincing achievements in realism. We know Falstaff perfectly and would never mistake him for anyone else in all fiction or reality. At the same time, in the context of the play, Falstaff *also* represents that part in every human being that is attached to the pleasures of the body and the selfish ego, the part that would be perfectly happy to see truth, loyalty, and honor tossed away in favor of fun and pleasure. To our utter delight, Falstaff is both his own utterly believable self and an incarnation of, in Renaissance physiological terms, the sanguine complexion—that is, fat, jolly, and red-faced, like Santa Claus—in Plato's terms, the vegetable soul, and in Christian terms, complete worldliness—"banish plump Jack," he says of himself, "and banish all the world" (II.iv.479–80).

Recognition of this universal realism, this *both-in-one*-ness, realistic particulars united with abstract universals, reveals Shakespeare at his greatest. It is one of the most valuable keys to unlocking the wonders of Shakespeare's drama.

The central purpose of this book is to enable you to access the great experiences of meaning that Shakespeare provides us through the medium of his works. Those meanings cannot be stated in sentences that try to state "the meaning of the play." They can, however, be found if you let Shakespeare guide you to each play's center. All that is needed is a willingness to study the author's language and to become familiar with the author's assumptions, to adopt them for a little while as you read or see his work. If you do so, you will come to the center of each play and there find its meaning for yourself. Then you can decide whether the reward has been worth the effort.

1   This remarkable instance of Shakespeare's artistry was first pointed out to me by Prof. Alan Levitan of Brandeis University.

2   C. S. Lewis puts this unique Shakespearean combination as follows: "[T]he mark of Shakespeare . . . is simply this: to have combined two species of excellence which are not, in a remarkable degree, combined by any other artist, namely the imaginative splendour of the highest type of lyric and the realistic presentation of human life and character"—in C.S. Lewis, "Variation in Shakespeare and Others" in *Selected Literary Essays*, ed. Walter Hooper (Cambridge: Cambridge University Press, 1969, repr. 1980), p. 81. Northrop Frye calls this Shakespearean combination the "high mimetic mode"—in Northrop Frye, *Anatomy of Criticism* (Princeton, NJ: Princeton University Press, 1957), pp. 33-34—and Graham Hough calls it "incarnational"—in Graham Hough, *A Preface to "The Faerie Queene"* (New York: W.W. Norton, 1963), p. 107.

2

Shakespeare the Man

WHO WROTE SHAKESPEARE'S PLAYS?

Shakespeare did. (End of discussion.)

But just so you know, various people have argued, using mostly irrelevant or spurious evidence, that Shakespeare did not write the works of Shakespeare, that they were written by someone else. By whom? Some say Christopher Marlowe, some Sir Francis Bacon, some Edward de Vere, seventeenth earl of Oxford, some Queen Elizabeth herself. Every important writer of Shakespeare's age has at least one would-be scholar defending his favorite's title to the authorship of Shakespeare's plays. Some even argue the plays were written by several authors working together—an Elizabethan committee.

But as a wit once said, "If Bacon wrote Shakespeare, who wrote Bacon?"[1]— meaning that every work of art bears the stamp of the style of its author, and no unprejudiced reader could mistake the best plays and poems we call Shakespeare's for the work of anyone else whose writing we know.

The reasons people have raised this authorship question have little to do with evidence.

One reason is envy. Some people simply cannot bear it that a writer like Shakespeare should exist. His unique greatness, one of the world's great mysteries of art, is an affront to them because they cannot explain it. Hence, consciously or not, they would love to cut him down to their own size. And they feel that if they can ascribe his work to someone else, they have "explained" Shakespeare.

Another reason is intellectual snobbery. Because there is no evidence that Shakespeare attended a university, some people assume the man Shakespeare must have been a country bumpkin who could not have written works of poetic genius. They ignore one important fact and one important bit of logic. The fact is that capable country bumpkins might have got a remarkably good education in local schools like that which

Shakespeare probably attended in Stratford. (See "Did Shakespeare Go to School?" below.) The bit of logic is that if higher education were the key to Shakespeare's greatness, what would account for there being no one else of Shakespeare's caliber among the Elizabethan playwrights who *did* go to a university, like Greene, Marlowe, and Nashe (Cambridge) and Lyly, Peele, and Lodge (Oxford)?

A third reason for the authorship question's even being a question is some people's attraction to conspiracy theories. Many pseudo-scholars produce elaborate and serpentine theories to explain away the hard evidence that appears to refute their claims. This, along with the pleasure of perpetrating a hoax, is most evident in the so-called Oxfordians, who want us to believe that Shakespeare's plays were written by the Earl of Oxford despite the fact that the earl died before Shakespeare's last ten plays were written.

In response to these fancies, only two points need to be made. First, all the solid evidence we have indicates that William Shakespeare of Stratford-upon-Avon is the author of Shakespeare's works,[2] and almost all reputable Shakespeare scholars believe so. Second, whoever wrote the works we ascribe to Shakespeare wrote the greatest works in the English language. Even if his name were not "Shakespeare," it would make no difference to our appreciation of the works themselves. (Actual end of discussion.)

WHO WAS SHAKESPEARE?

The facts that we know about Shakespeare's life include the following: He was born on or about April 23, 1564, the third child and first son of John Shakespeare, a glover and commodities trader who was a yeoman (meaning "a man of substance under the degree [i.e., rank] of gentleman"[3]) and Mary Arden. He grew up in the small town of Stratford-upon-Avon and probably went to grammar school there (see "Did Shakespeare Go to School?" below). He married a woman named Anne Hathaway and had three children: a daughter named Susanna and twins, a son named Hamnet (who died at age 11) and a daughter named Judith. Whether he ever traveled abroad is unknown.

By 1594, at age 30, Shakespeare was living in London, acting in plays, writing plays, and owning shares in the theater company called The Chamberlain's Men, which, with the accession of James I in 1603, became The King's Men. By 1599 he owned shares in the Globe, a public theatre, and by 1608 owned shares in the Blackfriars, a private theatre (see Chapter 3). The last evidence we have of his acting in plays was his performance in Ben Jonson's *Sejanus* in 1603. It is likely that the epilogue to *The Tempest*, written in 1611–12, implies Shakespeare's farewell to the theater. He then retired to Stratford, though he had yet to collaborate on a few more plays (see Chapter 13) and to write his last complete play, *Henry VIII*, in 1612. It was during the performance of that play, on June 29, 1613, that the Globe Theater burned down.

Shakespeare died at the age of 52 on April 23, 1616, on or about his own birthday, and was buried in the chancel of Holy Trinity Church in Stratford. Sometime before 1623 a monument was built, probably by Gheerart Janssen (Gerard Johnson), a Southwark stone-mason and sculptor,[4] which shows a bust of Shakespeare holding a pen. The inscriptions on the memorial plaque read:

IVDICIO PYLIVM, GENIO SOCRATEM, ARTE MARONEM,
TERRA TEGIT, POPVLVS MÆRET, OLYMPVS HABET
[In judgement a Nestor, in genius a Socrates, in art a Virgil:
The earth covers him, the people mourn him, Olympus has him.]

STAY PASSENGER, WHY GOEST THOV BY SO FAST,
READ IF THOV CANST, WHOM ENVIOVS DEATH HATH PLAST
WITH IN THIS MONVMENT SHAKSPEARE: WITH WHOME,
QVICK NATVRE DIDE: WHOSE NAME, DOTH DECK Y^S TOMBE,
FAR MORE, THEN COST: SIEH ALL, Y^T HE HATH WRITT,
LEAVES LIVING ART, BVT PAGE, TO SERVE HIS WITT.

This inscription, though its syntax is complicated and cryptic, asserts that though the man Shakespeare has died, his art lives on to honor him more than any tomb could do.

On April 10, 1693, a Mr. Dowdall, visiting Stratford, wrote in a letter that at Stratford-upon-Avon "I saw the Effigies of our English tragedian, mr Shakspeare . . . Neare the Wall where his monument is Erected Lyeth a plaine free stone, underneath wch his bodie is Buried with this Epitaph, made by himselfe a little before his Death:

Good friend, for Jesus sake forbeare
To dig the dust inclosed here.
Bles't be the man that spares these stones
And Curs't be he that moves my bones!

The Clarke that shew'd me this Church is aboue 80 yrs old." That stone remains in place. Dowdall is probably not correct that Shakespeare wrote that quatrain himself, but the fear of the curse appears to have kept the grave relatively undisturbed ever since. (Rumors to the contrary are not substantiated.)

WHAT KIND OF PERSON WAS SHAKESPEARE?

The printer Henry Chettle reports that Shakespeare was civil in demeanor, upright in his dealings, and honest. To the playwright Ben Jonson he was "My gentle Shakespeare"; Jonson writes, "I loved the man and do honor his memory (on this side idolatry) as much as any. He was indeed honest and of an open and free nature, had an excellent fancy [i.e., imagination], brave [i.e., worthy, excellent, fine] notions, and gentle expressions." The writer John Davies of Hereford calls him "good Will," "generous . . . in mind and mood," a sower of honesty, worthy to be companion to a king. The minor playwright William Barksted called him "so dear loved a neighbor." John Hemming and Henry Condell, the members of Shakespeare's acting company who gathered and published the first collected edition of his plays in 1623, called him a worthy friend and fellow. As did many others, the translator Leonard Digges called him affectionately "Our Shakespeare."

Over and over again people use about Shakespeare the adjective "gentle," meaning not only what we mean by *gentle* but also "of the gentility, gentlemanly, refined, civilized, respectable, admirable, exemplary." And that, apart from what we can gather from the writings, is about all we know of his character. Most of the rest is speculation.

DID SHAKESPEARE GO TO SCHOOL?

So far as we know, Shakespeare did not attend a university. But the universities then existed to train professionals in law, medicine, and divinity, not in literature. On the other hand, hundreds of passages in his work suggest that he had in Stratford the standard grammar school education of his day, offered to the few brightest boys in any town that had such a school, in which case Shakespeare's literary training was extensive. (In the characters of Holofernes in *Love's Labor's Lost* and Sir Hugh Evans in *The Merry Wives of Windsor*, Shakespeare portrays the kind of pedant who might have been his first teacher.) Here is a brief picture of the curriculum offered in the grammar schools of Shakespeare's day, including the one in Stratford-upon-Avon:

PETTY SCHOOL: Two years (starting about age 5) of reading, writing, and possibly counting—students learned under the assistant teacher, called an usher, from three books:

1. a hornbook—"a leaf of paper or parchment framed in wood and covered, for protection, with a thin layer of transparent horn."[5] Written on the paper were the alphabet (small letters and capitals), combinations of the vowels with the three consonants b, c, and d to teach syllables, and the "Our Father" prayer;

2. *The ABC with the Catechism*—which contained the hornbook page, the catechism (questions and answers about the Christian faith) from the Book of Common Prayer, several forms of grace to be said before and after meals, and the nine numerical figures plus a zero (called a "cipher");

3. *The Primer and Catechism*—which contained a calendar, an almanac, seven penitential psalms, and other religious texts.

LOWER SCHOOL: Three or four years (starting about age 7) of grammar, including Latin declensions and conjugations, writing, and speaking. Studies, still under an usher, consisted of the following:

1. Students learned the principles of grammar by memorizing the whole of William Lily's *Short Introduction of Grammar*, whose two parts were devoted to English grammar (in English) and Latin grammar (in Latin). (In Act IV, Scene i, of *The Merry Wives of Windsor* the boy William recites verbatim from the Latin section.)

2. They learned Latin sentences from a collection of Latin moral maxims and Erasmus's *Cato* and read Aesop's fables and the plays of Terence and Plautus in Latin. (In some schools they enacted scenes from those Roman playwrights.)

3. They read texts of more recent Latin moral poets and increased their vocabularies by memorizing a short dictionary.

4. They translated passages of the Bible into Latin from English.

5. They learned to speak in Latin from the texts of the continental humanist writers like Erasmus.

UPPER SCHOOL: Three or four years (from age 10 or 11) of rhetoric, prose composition, verse composition, Latin poets, moral history, moral philosophy, and Greek—students learned, now from the master, the following, all but the last in Latin:

- Rhetoric: Cicero's Ad Herennium (for general rhetorical informa-

tion); Cicero's Topica (for invention and development of rhetorical methods); Cicero, Quintilian, and Susenbrotus (for figures of speech); and Erasmus's Copia (for application of figures of speech);
- Prose composition of letters, formal themes, orations, and declamations;
- Verse composition;
- Latin poetry: Ovid, Virgil, Horace, Juvenal, Persius, and possibly Lucan, Martial, Catullus, and Seneca;
- Roman history: Sallust, Caesar, possibly Livy;
- Roman moral philosophy: Cicero's *De Officiis*;
- Greek: grammar and translation of sentences from the Greek New Testament.

This training included memorizing and being able to use over two hundred figures of speech, the foundation of Shakespeare's poetic art.[6]

About Shakespeare's formal education between the ages of 5 and 15 or so, T.W. Baldwin concludes, "If William Shakespeare had the grammar school training of his day—or its equivalent—he had as good a formal literary training as had any of his contemporaries."[7] (How does this compare to the curriculum of the school you attended?)

WHAT RELIGION WAS SHAKESPEARE?

Shakespeare grew up in a Christian world and absorbed the Christian outlook. Among his very first reading was the catechism (a series of simple questions and answers used to teach Christian doctrines to children), and, like his neighbors, he was required to attend church on certain days of the year.

He was likely to have known some secretly practicing Catholics as well as Protestants, but nowhere in his plays is there clear evidence that he concerned himself with sectarian partisanship except that he avoided running afoul of the censors. It would have been legally, politically, and financially dangerous to take a partisan position even if he had wanted to do so. But in this matter his practical self-interest and the direction of his imagination seem to have been in harmony. In any case, he mostly kept to the realms of religious thought where Catholics and most varieties of Protestants would agree.

The religious dogmas we find implied in Shakespeare's writing are the fundamental and universally shared ones among all Christian believers. A good parallel in the last century is C.S. Lewis, whose writing studiously avoids the areas of doctrinal conflict between Protestants and

Catholics, though he would not have been in political or legal danger in arguing for one or the other set of views. In fact he was not interested in doing so. Like Shakespeare, he stuck to the shared fundamentals. Both seem to have found that there was plenty to say about those shared ideas without getting into sectarian conflicts.

For Shakespeare's stance toward Jews, see the chapter on *The Merchant of Venice*. For his stance toward Muslims and Turks and toward dark-skinned Africans, see the chapter on *Othello*. Important elements of Shakespeare's attitude toward religion will be found in Chapter 7.

HOW COULD ONE PERSON HAVE WRITTEN ALL THOSE PLAYS?

The answer is, if you could write *one* play like Shakespeare's, then, given the time, you could write them all. If Shakespeare had written only one of his plays—almost any of them—we would still consider him to be the greatest of playwrights. Considering that he was able to write one such play, and that he spent most of his adult life writing plays, the number is not so surprising. The miracle is not in the quantity but in the quality of his plays.

HOW LONG DID IT TAKE SHAKESPEARE TO WRITE A PLAY?

We know that one of Shakespeare's earliest plays, *Henry VI, Part 3*, was performed in 1592. *Henry VI, Part 1*, was probably written in 1589–90. His last play, *Henry VIII*, was first performed in 1613. That amounts to thirty-nine plays (or forty, if we count the lost *Cardenio* and collaborations) in about twenty-four years, an average of a little less than two plays a year. Of course in some years he wrote more and in others fewer.

Ben Jonson says, "I remember the Players have often mentioned it as an honour to Shakespeare that in his writing (whatsoever he penned) he never blotted out line." He adds that Shakespeare's imagination, ideas, and expressions flowed with facility (in Jonson's opinion too much facility). So the implication is that Shakespeare worked rather quickly.

Considering that he was also an actor and a shareholder in the theater company, and that he had a family and property in Stratford, to which he traveled from time to time, we can estimate that it took him perhaps one to four months to write a play.

WHERE DID SHAKESPEARE GET HIS IDEAS?—SOURCES

Shakespeare seems to have read everything he could get his hands on, and it appears that he remembered everything he read and could call upon it all, whether for major plot ideas or for the smallest descriptive details. It is difficult to know for sure every work that went into the making of any particular play, but scholars have discovered plenty of evidence, both of major and of minor influences.

The major sources Shakespeare used include

- the Bible (most probably in the Geneva edition);
- ancient Greek epics, philosophy (especially Aristotle), and tragedy and later Greek romances—all in later versions, translations, or retellings;
- Roman tragedies, comedies, historical chronicles, and poems, especially Ovid's *Metamorphoses* (Shakespeare's most often referred-to source), and Plutarch's *Lives*;
- Medieval works on philosophy (like Boethius' *Consolation of Philosophy*, probably in Chaucer's translation) and rhetoric;
- Medieval epics and romances;
- Renaissance moral works (like *Mirror for Magistrates*, giving examples of the rise and fall of famous princes), essays (like those of Erasmus of Rotterdam and Montaigne), and romances (possibly the first part of Cervantes' *Don Quixote*);
- English chronicle histories (mainly those of Hall and Holinshed), poems (like Chaucer's *Canterbury Tales* and *Troilus and Criseyde* and Spenser's *Faerie Queene*), prose romances (like Sidney's *Arcadia*), essays, and every kind of old play.

In the nineteenth century it was common to think of Shakespeare as an untutored natural genius. But, as suggested above, though there is no evidence that Shakespeare went to a university of his time, there is plenty of evidence that he had a top-notch education. For a list of some of the works Shakespeare must have read and perhaps had in his own library, see Appendix 2.

---

1 I have seen this quip ascribed both to the Shakespeare scholar George Lyman Kittredge and to Albert H. Tolman of the University of Chicago.

2 The book to read on the subject of Shakespeare's life is S. Schoenbaum, *William Shakespeare: A Compact Documentary Life* (Oxford: Oxford University Press, 1978). On the various contenders against Shakespeare's authorship, see S. Schoenbaum, *Shakespeare's Lives* (Oxford: Clarendon Press, 1991), especially Part VI: Deviations, pp. 385ff.

3 F.E. Halliday, *A Shakespeare Companion: 1564–1964* (Harmondsworth, Middlesex, England: Penguin, 1964), p. 441.

4 Halliday, p. 322.

[5] Quotations in this section are from S. Schoenbaum, *Compact Documentary Life*, pp. 63–64.

[6] See Sister Miriam Joseph, *Shakespeare's Use of the Arts of Language* (Philadelphia: Paul Dry Books, 2005).

[7] T.W. Baldwin, *William Shakspere's Small Latine and Lesse Greeke* (Urbana, Il: University of Illinois Press, 1944), II.663. This is the monumental authoritative work on the subject of Elizabethan grammar school education.

3

What Was the State of the Art in Shakespeare's Theater?

None of the theaters of Shakespeare's time still stands, so we cannot be certain about many details of their form and operation. But many scholars have worked at recovering information about them based on documents, drawings, and a lot of conjecture. Here we'll address the main points, agreed upon by most scholars, that are essential to understanding the plays themselves.

HEARING A PLAY

The most important single fact to remember about Shakespeare's theater is that people did not then say "let's go see a play," as we would say "let's go see a movie." They usually said, "Let's go *hear* a play." Why? Because the main medium of experience for the plays of Shakespeare's time was speech, not sight.

When the dying Hamlet says to the shocked courtiers "You that look pale, and tremble at this chance" (*Hamlet*, V.ii.334), he is telling the actors how to play the moment, but he is also telling us what we are to imagine the courtiers doing, whether or not the actors playing them are in fact trembling and looking pale. Because of Hamlet's words, the audience members feel the courtiers to be shocked and frightened at the sudden deaths they have just witnessed (as the audience itself is). In today's theater, and even more in a movie, we usually require the actors playing shocked people to look pale and tremble. If they don't, we accuse the production of lacking realism. But in Shakespeare's time that literalism was achieved mostly through the words. Of course, if the actors could actually tremble and look pale, so much the better.

All the non-verbal workings of Shakespeare's theater—sets, props, movement, sounds, and so on—were additions and supports to the speeches. Though Shakespeare's theater often provided the spectacle and loud noises and fireworks that the Elizabethans loved, the greatest special effects of his theater happened in the words, which were enough to do the trick. That's why there are so many speeches in a Shakespeare play and so few stage directions.

THE BUILDING AND THE STAGE

Plays in Shakespeare's day were performed in three kinds of theaters.

The first kind was the various banquet halls belonging to the court, to houses of the nobility, to the universities, and to the four Inns of Court (the law colleges of London): Gray's Inn, Middle Temple, Inner Temple, and Lincoln's Inn. (Shakespeare's *Comedy of Errors* was performed at Gray's Inn in 1594 and *Twelfth Night* at Middle Temple in 1602.)

The second kind was the private theaters in London proper (Blackfriars, Whitefriars, Paul's, Phoenix, and Porter's Hall). These were large rooms indoors, set up with stages and lit with candles and lamps. Their actors and singers were boys rather than adult professional men, and the plays they performed tended to be of an academic sort. (You can get an idea of the rivalry between the private and public theater companies from Hamlet's conversation with Rosencrantz and Guildenstern in the First Folio version of *Hamlet*, II.ii.)

Shakespeare mostly wrote for the third kind of theater, the public theaters. These were large, open air, round or polygonal buildings made of timber and finished with lime and plaster. (In *Henry V*, the Chorus in the Prologue to Act I describes the physical theater as "this wooden O" and "this cockpit," meaning not an airplane pilot's seat, obviously, but an arena for gamecock fighting.) They were located in areas called "the liberties," outside the jurisdiction of the City of London. The Theatre and the Curtain were north of the city; the Rose, the Swan, and the Globe were on the south bank of the Thames. The actors in these theaters were adult professional men. There was seating in galleries for audience members who could afford it and a large open space in the center, called the pit, where the groundlings stood to hear the play. The (probably) three stories of galleries were covered with a thatched roof, but the pit was open to the sky. Sunshine (or lack of it) was all the lighting.

The stage was a wooden platform, about five feet off the ground and about twenty-seven feet deep and over forty feet wide, thrust out into the center of the pit from one edge of the circle or polygon and resting on pillars or scaffolding underneath. Behind it was a dressing area called a tiring house (*cf.* the word *attire*), and the players made their exits and entrances through doors to the right and left at the back of the stage or through a curtain opening to the inner stage at the center back. There was a trapdoor opening into the space under the stage that Hamlet metaphorically calls the "cellarage" (I.v.151), the literal name for the place where the actor playing the ghost, supposed to be moving within the earth, would have said "Swear." In some of the theaters the galleries above the stage at the back may have been used for spectators, for musicians, or for upper-story scenes, like the balcony scene in *Romeo and Juliet*. Above the stage, resting on the back wall and on two pillars or columns toward the front of the stage, was a roof, called the heavens, whose underside was painted blue (for the sky), with images of the sun, the moon, stars, and the signs of the zodiac.

Above the heavens (and possibly above the tiring house too) was a room with a trap door and machinery for lowering things or people to the stage or raising them from it. This room could also be used for storing props and for sound effects—a cannon ball dropped and rolled across its floor made thunder. The overall size of the theater isn't known for sure, but according to Johannes de Witt, the Swan theatre could hold three thousand people.[1] (Arend van Buchell's copy of Johannes de Witt's drawing of the Swan theater in 1596 is our best visual source of authentic information about the Elizabethan public theater.)[2]

From the contract to build the Fortune theatre, which was to be square but based upon the Globe, we infer that the latter too was more elaborate than the drawing of the Swan would suggest, perhaps including baroque arches, pilasters, trompe l'oeil painting, and bright cloth hangings—all to satisfy the Elizabethans' love of spectacle.

SETS

Except for a black curtain at the back for tragedy and a multi-colored one for comedy, the decorated architecture of the theater was the only set. Various movable set pieces could be brought on, such as a bed to indicate a bedroom or some potted plants to indicate a forest. One of the columns might serve for a hiding place. The curtain covering a rear entrance could be pulled back to reveal the stabbed Polonius in *Hamlet* or the snoring Falstaff in *Henry IV, Part 1*. The realism of the setting, once again, was created through the words.

PROPS

Properties, on the other hand, were numbered among the most valuable possessions of any theater company, along with their plays and their costumes. Shakespeare's props included a lion skin (for Snug to wear in the Pyramus and Thisbe scene in *A Midsummer Night's Dream*), a skull (for Hamlet to contemplate), dishes and utensils (for Petruchio to toss about in *The Taming of the Shrew*), a vial (for Juliet to drink from), a map (for King Lear to point to in carving up England), a chess set (for Ferdinand and Miranda to play with in *The Tempest*), swords, daggers, shields, an imitation royal crown, a few movable trees or shrubs for garden or forest scenes, and assorted baskets, chests, cloths, and musical instruments. There was also a throne, a great chair probably fixed upon a platform, to indicate the "seat" or "chair of state" of the ruler.

COSTUMES

By far the greatest expense of the public theater company was its costumes, which were as striking and colorful as possible, including some hand-me-downs from court. Elizabethan costumes were generally contemporary in style, not what we would call historically accurate. However, they could be elaborately decorated with symbolic or allegorical elements corresponding to conventional Elizabethan ideas about the type of character wearing them, whether historical or imaginary. A Roman soldier or hero would wear a breastplate and a plumed helmet and carry a sword or spear. An Oriental potentate would be dressed in baggy pants and carry a curved sword called a scimitar. A monk would be dressed in a robe and hood (called a "cowl"). The airy spirit Ariel might have worn a blue costume decorated with feathers.

ACTORS

Actors in Shakespeare's company were professionals. Some, when they were young, had worked in private theaters (where all the actors were boys). Others might have got their start in children's roles or female roles in the public theater. In either case, they made their living by performing on the stage, some for pay and some, like Shakespeare himself, as partners in the acting company, who earned a share of the profits.

Acting companies were associations of actors under the patronage either of royalty or of a member of the nobility. Actors who invested money in the company (to buy costumes, props, and plays) became "sharers" or shareholders. Some owned whole shares and some partial shares. The shareholders would pick one of their company to serve as business manager and would hire additional actors and apprentices, a book-keeper (who served as prompter and holder of the prompt-book—see below), a tireman (in charge of costumes and props), a stage-keeper (the janitor), and musicians. The shareholding actors themselves were in charge of play production: buying or commissioning plays, casting, tutoring hired actors and apprentices, and so on.[3]

The style of acting was conventional. Though Shakespeare's actors strove to be as convincing as they could, they were not trained in the much later Stanislavsky-style method acting, trying to "feel" the part or "become" the character in some personally emotional way. Their job was to learn the words and gestures and movements and to make them clear. Once again it was mainly the words, more than the physical expression of realistic emotions or movements, that carried the meaning to the audience. To us Shakespeare's actors would probably have sounded like speechmakers instead of living people. What his audience would have considered effective dramatic speech we would probably find too declamatory, stilted, or histrionic. Of course, his audience might find modern realistic actors to be the opposite—mumbling, artless, and prosaic, not more interesting than a gabby neighbor. These differences are functions of the differences in stage conventions of realism that were discussed under Universal Realism in Chapter 1.

But though what seems appropriate to one age might seem overdone or underdone to another, actors in every age are expected to seem natural according to the customs of the time. Even given the more formal acting conventions of Shakespeare's day, there would have been big differences between good and bad actors. Hamlet's speech to the players gives the ideal goal for an actor: He needed to be neither too exaggerated nor too tame but to "Suit the action to the word, the word to the action" in order "to hold as 'twere the mirror up to nature" (*Hamlet*, III.ii.17–22). Despite the more formal conventions, the best actors of the time would have struck the best critics as being thoroughly natural and convincing.

All actors in Shakespeare's time were men or boys. All audience members, male and female, worldly or puritanical, would have considered it shockingly immodest and inappropriate for a woman to show herself on a stage in public. As in the high periods of ancient Greek and Japanese drama, so in the high period of European drama, it was just not done. This means that all Shakespeare's female roles—Juliet, Rosalind, Ophelia, Cleopatra, Hermione, and the rest—were played by boy actors.

Because the acting of women's parts by boys was simply a given of the theater, it would have caused no resentment, gender confusion, or embarrassed tittering in the audience. It was a stage convention, assumed and therefore immediately forgotten when the play began, just as we forget in a movie that the screen is really only two-dimensional, or that a character is being portrayed by an actor whom we have recently seen portraying someone else. In *A Midsummer Night's Dream* Shakespeare has Flute, the bellows-mender, say about playing the role of Thisbe, "Nay, faith; let not me play a woman; I have a beard coming" (I.ii.47–48). No longer a boy, he feels too old to play a woman's part. He fears that his age and beard would compromise the realism of the performance. In any case, his reluctance has nothing to do with worry about his masculinity, as is confirmed when the still more mature Bottom jumps in with "let me play Thisbe too." For the Elizabethan audiences, a boy actor's playing a female role was normal; it was therefore, for the purposes of the plays' meanings, a non-issue. Jokes could be made about it, as in the epilogue of *As You Like It*, where coming out of character the boy actor says "if I were a woman," but such jokes did not imply what we would call gender-bending sexual innuendos.

PLAY DIRECTION

There were no directors in Shakespeare's theater. In fact, the direction of plays by a single individual did not occur until the late nineteenth century with Georg II, Duke of Saxe-Meiningen (1826–1914). It is difficult for us to imagine the absence of a guiding mind in the effective production of such complex works as Shakespeare's plays because since the birth of Romanticism in the late eighteenth century and its spread through the nineteenth, we have become so used to the idea of art proceeding from an individual person's imagination. Even in the collaborative world of theater and film, we believe in the necessity of a director to interpret the script and to make the final product correspond to his or her idea.

But in Shakespeare's day, as in other times and places, collaborators on play productions (as in many other arts) were in such thorough agreement about the conventions and the essential meanings of the works they were producing that they would have found the notion of needing a director ridiculous. They would have felt about a play director the way we might feel at a baseball game if a "director" tried to tell each of us how to sing the National Anthem, or the way an experienced surfer might feel if someone suggested that a "director" on the shore should tell him when to catch a wave and how long to ride it. The actors (or at least the shareholders) knew what they were doing. Any of them might correct a young actor who was sawing the air too much, to which behavior Hamlet objects (*Hamlet*, III.ii.4). But the words of the play and the stage directions seem to have given them all the essential direction they needed.

We have two Shakespearean examples of how a shareholder of the theater company might instruct his fellow actors. One occurs in the passage from *Hamlet* quoted above (III.ii), and the other in *A Midsummer Night's Dream* in the scenes in which the so-called "mechanicals" (physical laborers) of the city, including Flute, quoted above, are rehearsing the Pyramus and Thisbe play-within-the-play. Hamlet gives a lecture on the nature of acting and tries to inspire the actors to make their performance as realistic as possible. He speaks with authority not because he is "directing" the play, but because he is their superior both in rank and in education. (He himself recognizes their superiority in moving audiences with the power of speech.) In *A Midsummer Night's Dream* Peter Quince the Carpenter gives out parts and tries to rein in one actor who wants to do everything and encourage another who is shy about doing anything. Neither Hamlet nor Peter Quince thinks he has to interpret the play for the actors. Part of the hilarity of the *Midsummer Night's Dream* scenes lies in the mechanicals' ignorance of the stage conventions that the real actors and the real audience of Shakespeare's play all took for granted.

PROMPT-BOOK AND BOOK-KEEPER

The prompt-book, then and still in our time called simply "the book," was a fair (meaning a final draft) copy of the play used for rehearsals and probably kept in the tiring house during performances. It was the theater-ready version of the play in which the book-keeper would have written additions to the minimal stage directions of the playwright, noted cuts, revisions, or additions to the speeches, clarified speech headings where necessary, and made notations about which actors were doubling in which roles, where props were called for, etc. It was also the version of the play that was submitted to the Master of the Revels to be censored before the play was finally "allowed" for performance.[4]

The book-keeper was in charge of the prompt-book and served as the prompter, making sure the actors were where they needed to be with the right props at the right time and, if necessary, prompting them with forgotten lines. And since no actor would have a full script of the play, the book-keeper was also responsible for providing each actor the long scroll containing all his own lines and cue lines (still today called a "side").[5]

MUSIC AND DANCE

"That Shakespeare knew a great deal about music is certain. . . . Not only does he make dramatic use of vocal and instrumental music, but his plays are full of musical references and images."[6] Instrumental music and songs sung to musical accompaniment are called for in many of the plays. A few of the melodies have survived, including two composed for *The Tempest* by Robert Johnson, royal court lutenist and composer. Instruments used in plays might include lute, viol, recorder, and virginal, trumpets for the appearance of royalty, drums and pipes for marching armies, horns for hunting scenes.[7]

In addition to specific dances called for by the text of a play as part of the play itself (as in *Romeo and Juliet, Much Ado about Nothing, The Winter's Tale,* and *The Tempest*) or at the end (as in *A Midsummer Night's Dream* and *Much Ado about Nothing*), "It was customary to finish the performance of [any] play with a dance. . . . The music for these dances would be in the form either of the stately pavan or of the sprightly galliard."[8]

AUDIENCE

Who made up Shakespeare's audience? Occasionally royalty, when Queen Elizabeth and later King James ordered performances to be presented at court. In the public theaters, the audience might include nobility, gentility, and commoners. There were lawyers, court functionaries, churchmen, tradesmen, craftsmen, farmers, soldiers, sailors, tailors, innkeepers, purveyors of goods, servants, and so on. For the comfort of the audience there were hawkers of food and drinks, and there were also prostitutes and pimps and the occasional pickpocket, which they would have called a cut-purse.

Not only was Shakespeare's audience made up of a variety of sorts of people, but those people could all be entertained in a variety of ways. In our time we tend to think of the audiences for different kinds of shows as generally different sorts of people: We imagine that those who attend rock concerts don't generally attend the opera and those who watch reality TV don't tune in to Masterpiece Theater, and vice versa. But on any given day, not only was Shakespeare's audience very mixed in itself, but any member of it might just as soon choose to attend a cock-fight or a bear-baiting (a short walk away) as to attend a play. (In the bear-baiting ring, a wild bear was tied to a stake by the neck and bull mastiff dogs were set to attack it. People bet on whether the bear would kill the dogs before the dogs could kill the bear.) We might see Shakespeare's plays as highbrow entertainment and bear-baiting as definitely low-brow, but apart from differences in individual personal taste, Elizabethan audiences in general might be just as pleased to attend a bear-baiting or a bull-baiting or a public hanging as *A Midsummer Night's Dream* or *Hamlet*.

This variety in the audience partly explains why the same play might contain all kinds of content (intellectual argumentation, deep spiritual insight, romance, low physical comedy) and all levels of language (formal poetry, barbs of wit, coarse prose). There was something for everyone. Yet overarching the variety of particular appeals to particular groups, the whole play also managed to appeal to everyone in the audience.

There was one group that was not pleased with any public entertainments, including plays. They were the Puritans. We have a variety of examples of Puritan preachers petitioning the government to close down the theaters, which they accused of presenting immoral plays and of being hotbeds of lewdness, drunkenness, prostitution, impiety, and heresy. For religious and political reasons, they were supported in this by the city government. Hence the public theaters were not allowed within the city limits of London but were forced to locate outside in the "liberties" mentioned above. Fortunately for us, the theaters were defended by the Queen and her Privy Council, and many playwrights got away with satirizing the Puritans.[9] As usual, Shakespeare avoided direct criticism, even of the Puritans, but you can get a sense of his opinion of the hypocritical moralism and austerity that many associated with them in his characterization of Malvolio in *Twelfth Night*. Ben Jonson more directly satirized the type in a character in *Bartholomew Fair* called Zeal-of-the-Land Busy. So far as we know Shakespeare, unlike Jonson, never spent time in jail for seditious writing.

In general, performances were more interactive than we are used to. Actors, in character, would often address the audience directly, and the audience might respond out loud to that direct address as well as to slapstick action, rousing speeches, witty repartee, and stage violence. A play that did not sufficiently reward the audience's attention might be met with guffaws, verbal abuse, or missiles of bad fruit.

Didn't these interchanges with the actors disrupt the play for the audience? In extreme cases they surely did, and actors then as now would complain about poor audiences. At the same time, Shakespeare's theater could absorb more of such behavior than ours.

There are schools of playwrights in our time who, partly to distinguish the live theater from the movie experience, strive to make plays more interactive with their audiences. But in general in the modern realistic theater we require a play environment to have minimal distractions.

Because we have higher demands for realism in our plays, external noise threatens to break the illusion for us. One beep from a cell phone in the theater disrupts our focus. Also, because we are generally so over-stimulated by the voices all around us—all those salesmen, politicians, preachers, news reporters, talk show hosts, disk jockeys, and podcasters who yak at us non-stop on radio, TV, loudspeakers, computers, cell phones, etc.—it is harder for us to devote our full attention to, thereby to lose ourselves in, the speech of *anyone*.

Shakespeare's audience, lacking radio, TV, movies, and internet, was much more captivated by theatrical speech, for which the demands of realism were less stringent and which was the more precious for being rare. Therefore, in general, they were probably less easily distracted.

To sum up, the state of the theater in Shakespeare's time was technologically primitive by our standards. But thanks in large part to Shakespeare himself, it was the furthest thing from primitive in the quality of experience it provided its audiences. And it wasn't long after he had arrived in London from Stratford-upon-Avon that Shakespeare had become the Elizabethan theater's most popular playwright.

---

[1]   Quoted in Schoenbaum, *Compact Documentary Life*, p. 139.

[2]   Check out http://www.shakespearesglobe.com/ for more about Shakespeare's Globe theatre and the modern reconstruction of it on the Bankside in London.

[3]   F.E. Halliday, *A Shakespeare Companion: 1564–1964* (Baltimore, MD: Penguin Books, 1964), pp. 19–20.

[4]   Halliday, pp. 69, 389.

[5]   Halliday, p. 69.

[6]   Halliday, p. 330.

[7]   Halliday, p. 255, 330, and cf. Jennifer Waghorn, "Playing Shakespeare's Music" at https://www.shakespeare.org.uk/explore-shakespeare/shakespedia/playing-shakespeares-music/.

[8]   Halliday, p. 126.

[9]   Halliday, p. 395.

4

Did People Really Talk Like That?
—Shakespeare's Language

Did people in Shakespeare's time talk the way his characters do? Yes and no.

They didn't need the footnotes we do because for them Shakespeare's language was not four hundred years old. Words that seem unusual to us were usual to them: *meed* meaning "reward," *pard* meaning "leopard," *saw* meaning "maxim," *zounds* meaning "I swear by his (i.e., Christ's) wounds." Some words have changed their meanings since Shakespeare's time: *still* meant "always," *jealous* meant "suspicious," *stomach* meant "appetite."

On the other hand, Shakespeare invented a lot of words that his own audience had never heard before. They got the meaning, as we do, from the context. Examples include *consanguineous* (*Twelfth Night*, II.iii.77), *fathomless* (*Troilus and Cressida*, II.ii.30), and *retirement* (*1 Henry IV,* V.iv.6, *Henry V*, I.i.58). Like these, most of the words Shakespeare invented we still use today.

But the biggest difference between the stage speech and street speech in Shakespeare's day was that the people in his audience did not usually speak in poetry.

WHAT IS POETRY FOR?

The best definition of poetry that I can come up with is this: poetry says with words what cannot be said in words.

Poetry is a medium of getting across an experience of meaning in a way that normal language cannot do. It does so by expressing thought not only through the literal meanings of words but (as we said under Sound and Sense in Chapter 1) through the complex interrelation of the meanings, associations, and sounds of words—in short, through the use of rhetorical devices, also called figures of speech, like metaphor and simile, rhythm and rhyme, antithesis and repetition, and many more. (I'll define these and other terms later in the chapter.) These devices are not foreign to our daily speech. We often use them unconsciously. "Where can I catch the bus to San Diego?" is a five beat line containing varied rhythm (see Meter and Rhythm), a visual image (*catch*—see Metaphor), repetition of initial consonants (*can/catch*—see Alliteration), repetition of vowel sounds (*can/catch/San*—see Assonance), and internal rhyme (*can/San*—see Rhyme). The difference is that the poet uses figures of speech like these elaborately and with intention. Through the complex combination of such rhetorical devices, poetry extends and deepens our responses to the meanings of sentences.

Here's an example of how one might express in normal speech an idea from one of Shakespeare's sonnets:

> The more we trust a friend who seems to merit our trust, the more we are disappointed if he or she later betrays us.

This is a clear and familiar idea, and we can all understand it. But unless we are particularly vulnerable to the idea at a given moment, it doesn't move us much. We say "true" and let it go. But watch what happens when Shakespeare expresses the idea in the verse couplet concluding Sonnet 94:

> For sweetest things turn sourest by their deeds;
> Lilies that fester smell far worse than weeds.

What's the difference? The second passage creates an entirely different kind of experience in us. We respond to the first version with understanding but minimal personal engagement or excitement (see Empathy in Chapter 15). But in the second version, the words convey more than information. Reading and hearing them, especially after reading the first twelve lines of the sonnet, becomes an intense personal *experience*. In our response we empathically smell the sweetness of that lily turned to the foul smell of rot. The change of feelings we have when someone betrays our affection or trust has been *incarnated*, that is, given a body, in our mental and emotional experience by evoking in words the physical experience of rotting flowers. (See the discussion of Sonnet 94 in Part 2.) We not only *think* the idea; for a moment we live it.

Shakespeare, like all poets, uses the tools of poetry to achieve this heightened personal experience of whatever his subject happens to be.

IS IT VERSE OR PROSE?

All speeches in Shakespeare are either verse or prose. *Verse* means the lines have a given metrical length and tightly or loosely fit a particular metrical form, whether or not they rhyme, the way the words of a song fit the rhythm of its music (see Meter and Rhythm below.) *Prose* is what we would call normal non-metrical speech or writing in paragraph form. This paragraph is written in prose, whereas the next three lines are written in verse:

> This above all: to thine own self be true,
> And it must follow as the night the day
> Thou canst not then be false to any man.   (*Hamlet*, I.iii.78–80)

Until recent times, the conventional way of indicating verse in printing was to set each line of verse as a separate line of print, beginning with a capital letter, and this is true for the works of Shakespeare. Here is the beginning of Hamlet's famous verse soliloquy:

> To be, or not to be, that is the question:
> Whether 'tis nobler in the mind to suffer
> The slings and arrows of outrageous fortune,
> Or to take arms against a sea of troubles,
> And by opposing, end them. . . .   (*Hamlet*, III.i.55–59)

By contrast, prose is printed in standard paragraph form. Here is the beginning of Hamlet's prose speech to the players:

> Speak the speech, I pray you, as I pronounced it to you, trippingly on the tongue; but if you mouth it as many of our players do, I had as lief the town-crier spoke my lines. Nor do not saw the air too much with your hand, thus, but use all gently; for in the very torrent, tempest, and, as I may say, whirlwind of your passion, you must acquire and beget a temperance that may give it smoothness.
> (*Hamlet*, III.ii.1–8)

Whether characters are speaking in verse or prose makes a difference in Shakespeare's plays, and therefore the shift from a scene or passage in verse to one in prose, or vice versa, is also significant. In general, verse is used for scenes of greater seriousness, for speakers of higher rank, for formal public speeches, for weighty soliloquies, for romantic exchanges of love, and so on. Prose is generally used for scenes that are more comic, for speakers of lower rank, for informal or intimate exchanges, for lighter soliloquies, for common joking, and so on.

But these are not hard and fast rules. There are highly serious moments in prose and lighter scenes in verse. Hamlet's profound "The readiness is all" (*Hamlet*, V.ii.222) is in prose. Benvolio's "Supper is done, and we shall come too late" (*Romeo and Juliet*, I.iv.105) is in verse.

The only firm rule is that when Shakespeare switches from prose to verse, or verse to prose, we are intended to notice the contrast with what went before and the relative direction of the change. A shift from prose to verse will usually move us up the scale of seriousness, weight, formality, rank, poetic intensity. A shift from verse to prose usually means a relaxation toward informality, familiarity, comedy, lower rank, and common speech. So while Shakespeare is not a slave to stylistic formulas, he builds upon his audience's expectations about what kinds of things get said in verse and what kinds in prose. (Then, as always, he also pushes against the limits of those expectations.)

That said, even Shakespeare's prose, whether weighty or light, is highly poetical. Notice the use of effective poetical metaphors in Hamlet's serious prose speech to the players quoted above: "trippingly," "mouth it," "town-crier," "saw the air," "whirlwind," "smoothness"—all these phrases intensify our response to the point Hamlet is making. Notice also that no matter how realistically Shakespeare imitates the common prose talk of his day, he also gives it a heightened meaning and intensity. Here's a middle-aged shepherd complaining about teenagers:

> I would there were no age between ten and three-and-twenty, or that youth would sleep out the rest; for there is nothing in the between but getting wenches with child, wronging the ancientry, stealing, fighting— (*The Winter's Tale*, III.iii.59–63)

It would take pages to point out all the poetic elements in this bit of common speech, which includes hyperbole (= exaggeration), a preposition used as a noun ("the between"), repetition ("getting, wronging, stealing, fighting"), an adjective turned into a noun ("ancientry"), repetition of vowel sounds ("age/ancientry," "three/sleep/between/ancientry/stealing"), and so on. The point is that even when writing simple prose, Shakespeare cannot put pen to paper except poetically.

RHETORICAL DEVICES

"Rhetorical devices," "figures of speech," "schemes," "tropes"—these phrases refer to techniques or patterns of language that modify, enhance, or intensify the meanings of words and sentences. Rhetorical terms have been discussed, debated about, promoted, demoted, and redefined by theorists of language and literature from the ancient Greeks to modern times. As suggested in Chapter 2, Shakespeare had studied all the forms of rhetorical device inherited from the ancient, medieval, and Renaissance grammarians, logicians, and rhetoricians, and from the poets who used them. By the time he began writing, he had mastered them all. Then he devoted his working life to engaging them in the service of a poetic language more vivid, fluid, and imaginative than they had ever served before.

We are not to think of Shakespeare's obviously rhetorical patterning of language, verbal artifice, and wordplay as merely decoration. It is the very medium of thought and feeling, especially intense feeling. As Shakespeare matured, his use of figures of speech became more and more subtle, rhetoric and meaning more absorbed into one another. But from the Renaissance viewpoint, even in the highly figured speech of earlier plays—like *A Midsummer Night's Dream*, *Richard II*, and *Romeo and Juliet*—the use of formal rhetorical devices does not obscure the speaker's passion but rather expresses it.

We will not delve too deeply into the study of rhetorical terms. But in order to appreciate Shakespeare's poetic accomplishment, we will need to identify a few of the major ones. Others will be identified as needed in the discussions of particular passages.

For convenience, we'll distinguish the devices rooted in meaning (like metaphor and simile), those rooted in sound (like meter, rhythm, and rhyme), and those rooted in structure or arrangement (like antithesis and repetition), always remembering that one of the signs of a great poet is his ability to unite meaning, sound, and structure into a single indivisible experience.

Rhetorical Devices Rooted in Meaning—Imagery

In Shakespeare the most important rhetorical device rooted in the meanings of words is *imagery*, words that call images of things into the mind in order to convey meaning. We use imagery all the time. When someone responds to a request by saying "no," there is no use of imagery. But if instead a person were to say "over my dead body" or "when hell freezes over" or "in your dreams" or "don't hold your breath," he or she is using imagery. Depending on which image is chosen, we get a somewhat different empathic response (see Empathy in Chapter 15). "Don't hold your breath" is not nearly so drastic a denial as "over my dead body"—if one is alive one can decide to start breathing again.

What Is a Metaphor For?

The fundamental tool for producing imagery is the *metaphor*.

A metaphor uses a word denoting something, usually physical, to evoke a strong empathic response to something usually not in itself physical. Every metaphor is a word or phrase denoting a thing that carries a meaning. Literature professors call the meaning carried the *tenor* and the thing that carries it the *vehicle*. For example, in "Don't hold your breath" the image of a person holding his breath is the vehicle, carrying the meaning, and the tenor or meaning is "a short time." Its negation by the word "Don't" stresses the opposite idea. So "Don't hold your breath" carries the meaning "not soon" or "never."

Let's take a more complex example: Hamlet's phrase "sea of troubles" in the "To be or not to be" soliloquy quoted above. "Troubles" is an abstract idea naming anything that might cause discomfort or suffering. Watching the play, we know what particular troubles Hamlet is suffering from. But in this speech he is generalizing about all men. So how does Shakespeare get us to feel the weight of all those potential troubles?

He uses an image from an entirely different realm of our experience, not emotional pain but physical sensation. The "sea" is big, powerful, uncontrollable, strange, and potentially deadly. When we hear "sea of troubles" we know—we *feel*—exactly what Hamlet means: troubles so many and various and uncontrollable that to suffer from them feels like being overwhelmed by the sea, which is far greater than we are and could easily finish us. Shakespeare was probably also implying in the word "sea" the specific nautical sense of a huge wave that washes over a ship. The effect of both senses is similar.

But there is more to the image. Shakespeare has given us what's called a mixed metaphor. Hamlet says "to take arms against a sea of troubles." Normally we don't think of taking arms (in Shakespeare's time, wielding a sword or bow and arrows or maybe a pistol) against the sea or a huge wave of the sea. Can one defeat water with a sword or a gun? Why has Shakespeare joined these inappropriate images? Because while a sword is useless against the sea, one can perhaps defeat one's troubles with a sword. Or can one? It depends on the troubles. And what would it say about someone that he chose to face the sea with a sword despite the futility of doing so? The metaphor embodies in itself the whole dilemma in Hamlet's mind at this point in the play: the idea of man's smallness, helplessness, and frustration in the face of his troubles, the desire to respond to them nobly, and the awareness that any response may be both heroic and futile.

An effective metaphor incarnates meaning in our experience, making it real to us.

Simile

A second tool, the *simile* (pronounced Sĭ-mĭ-lē), works in the same way. A simile is a metaphor that makes the relation between the tenor, the meaning, and the vehicle, what carries the meaning, obvious by using the comparison words *like* or *as*. When Romeo says

> But soft, what light through yonder window breaks?
> It is the east, and Juliet is the sun.   (II.ii.1–2)

he is speaking in metaphors: the light in the window *is* the light of the sunrise in the east; Juliet *is* the sun. When he says

> thou art
> As glorious to this night, being o'er my head,
> As is a winged messenger of heaven   (II.ii.26–28)

he is speaking in a simile: you are (not exactly an angel but) as glorious *as* an angel. Whether the poet uses metaphor or simile, the effect is to get us to experience the meaning of one thing under the image of another. To Romeo, Juliet is bright, light-giving, exalted, angelic, standing literally above him, and perhaps unattainable. And we know how he feels about her because we ourselves have looked up, seen the sun, imagined angels, yearned for unattainable brightness, and perhaps been in love and felt this way about our own beloved.

Rhetorical Devices Rooted in Sound

We all empathize not only into what we see but also into what we hear.[1] Painters appeal to our sight, composers to our hearing. In a broad way, dramatic poets have the advantage (and the challenge) of appealing to both—we see characters on the stage doing things, and at the same time we hear them saying words.

As illustrated under Sound and Sense in Chapter 1, whether or not it is part of a dramatic performance on stage, poetry combines three vehicles of meaning into a single experience. That is, when we hear or read a poem, a) we see the images that the words or sentences form in our mind's eye, b) we understand the abstract concepts that the words denote, and c) we hear the sounds of the words and of their arrangement. In the work of great poets, this fusion of pathways into our empathic experience is complete. Image, idea, and sound become a single experience of meaning.

Let us look now specifically at the sound elements in Shakespeare's poetry. The three most fundamental ways of manipulating sounds in English poetry are onomatopoeia, pacing, and repetition.

Onomatopoeia

The first fundamental way of conveying meaning through sound is in some ways the simplest and most obvious figure of speech: *onomatopoeia*. This word (from the Greek *onoma*, name, and *poiein*, to make) names the quality of a word or phrase whose sound, when we say it, is the same as the sound of what it names. The words *buzz* and *hiss* are good examples. Shakespeare can be very inventive with this figure of speech. For example, in the first line of Sonnet 12, "When I do count the clock that tells the time," the regular rhythm and repetition of the hard *c* and *t* sounds make the line itself sound like the ticking of a clock. Shakespeare can make this simple figure of speech carry profound meaning, as when, in the great temptation scene, he has Lady Macbeth sounding like the serpent she has alluded to in her hunger for "solely sovereign sway and masterdom" (*Macbeth*, I.v.70; see Sound and Sense in Chapter 1).

Pacing

The second fundamental method of making sound meaningful is by pacing. By this I mean here, not the overall pace of a speech or a scene, but the arrangement of stresses in any single line of verse. That arrangement can be subdivided into meter and rhythm. As actor and dramaturge Dakin Matthews points out, meter is the imposition of an artificial beat upon the natural rhythms of normal speech.[2] Or we may see it the other way round and say that rhythm is the variations that natural speech plays upon an expected meter.

Meter

By contrast with ancient Greek and Latin verse, which was *quantitative* (i.e., measured by the longer or shorter length of time it took to pronounce a syllable's vowel), English verse is *accentual*, that is, founded on the difference in our speech between stressed and unstressed syllables. *Stress* refers to the greater power with which we drive air through our vocal cords when we say a stressed syllable. In the word "smoky," for example, English speakers place a heavier weight or stress on the first syllable than on the second: *SMOK-y*. In the word "computer" the heavier stress is on the middle syllable (*com-PUT-er*). The other syllables are called unstressed. (In practice there are varying degrees of stress, heavy and light, but here we will focus only on the major distinction.)

I've indicated the stressed syllables above by putting them into capital letters, but in discussions of poetry it is more common to indicate stressed syllables by placing a small acute accent mark or slash above them (*smóky*). Where both stressed and unstressed syllables are marked, an unstressed syllable is indicated by a *breve* (the lower half of a little circle) above the letter (*cŏmpútĕr*).

In English, then, meter refers to the expected arrangement of stressed and unstressed syllables in a line of verse that could be indicated by a drumbeat. Remember Polonius's line quoted above?

Thou canst not then be false to any man.

If we wanted to speak the meter of this line without using words, we could indicate it this way:

ta-TUM ta-TUM ta-TUM ta-TUM ta-TUM

ta symbolizing the unstressed syllables and *TUM* symbolizing the stressed. If we used the traditional way of marking the stressed syllables in a poem, it would look like this:

Thŏu cánst nŏt thén bĕ fálse tŏ ánў mán.

This process of discerning the stressed and unstressed syllables in a line of verse is called scanning or scansion.

What Is Iambic Pentameter?
Once we have scanned a line and discerned the metrical pattern, we can name it. Its name will be a combination of two parts. The first part

is the name of the *foot*, that is, the particular combination of stressed and unstressed syllables forming a metrical unit. The principal metrical *feet* in English poetry are these:

iamb	(˘ ´	= *ta-TUM*)
trochee	(´ ˘	= *TUM-ta*)
spondee	(´ ´	= *TUM-TUM*)
dactyl	(´ ˘ ˘	= *TUM-ta-ta*)
anapest	(˘ ˘ ´	= *ta-ta-TUM*)

Other feet used in English include the amphibrach (˘ ´ ˘ = *ta-TUM-ta*), the amphimacer (´ ˘ ´ = *TUM-ta-TUM*), and the pyrrhic (˘ ˘ = *ta-ta*), which can appear only as a variation within other meters but obviously cannot form its own poetic meter.

The second part of the name of a meter is the number of feet in the line. In the case of Polonius's line—

Thŏu cánst nŏt thén bĕ fálse tŏ ánў mán

—the line has five iambic feet.

Hence the meter of Polonius's line is called iambic pentameter: *iambic* because the particular metrical foot, made of an unstressed syllable followed by a stressed syllable (˘ ´), is called an iamb (from the Greek word *iambos*, meaning a metrical foot with one short-vowel syllable followed by one long-vowel syllable); and *pentameter* (from the Greek *penta*, meaning "five," and *metron*, meaning "measure") because there are five iambs in each line. So *iambic pentameter* simply means lines of verse that fit the expected meter of five iambs per line—

ta-TUM ta-TUM ta-TUM ta-TUM ta-TUM

—no matter what particular rhythmic variations the poet has introduced into a given line.

Sometimes Shakespeare will split a line of verse among two or more characters. When this happens, in the printed version the start of each speaker's speech after the first will be indented. In the following quotation from *Julius Caesar* (I.iii.41), the three printed lines form one iambic pentameter line:

Cassius:	Who's there?	
Casca:	A Roman.	
Cassius:		Casca, by your voice.

The vast majority of verse lines in Shakespeare's plays and poems are in iambic pentameter. But Shakespeare also uses other meters for particular effects. Here is an example of iambic tetrameter (four feet per line, from *tetra*, meaning "four" in Greek):

> As you from crimes would pardon'd be,
> Let your indulgence set me free.
>
> (*Tempest*, Epilogue ll. 19–20)

Some examples of other meters in Shakespeare are trochaic tetrameter:

> More nor less to others paying
> Than by self-offenses weighing
>
> (*Measure for Measure*, III.ii.265–66)

amphibrachic dimeter (two feet per line):

> Have more than thou showest,
> Speak less than thou knowest.   (*King Lear*, I.iv.118–19)

iambic trimeter (three feet per line):

> That lord that counsell'd thee
> To give away thy land   (*King Lear*, I.iv.140–41)

and trochaic tetrameter catalectic (from the Greek *katalektikos*, meaning "cut off," here referring to the expected final unstressed syllable), as in "The Phoenix and the Turtle" (see Chapter 12):

> So they loved as love in twain
> Had the essence but in one   (ll. 25–26)

What Are Masculine and Feminine Endings?

Within Shakespeare's standard iambic pentameter, lines can properly end in two ways: with a stressed syllable or with an additional unstressed syllable. The first is called a *masculine ending* and the second a *feminine ending*. Here are two consecutive lines from *King Lear*:

> Allow not nature more than nature needs,
> Man's life is cheap as beast's. Thou art a lady
>
> (II.iv.266–67)

The first line has a masculine ending, that is, it ends on the stressed syllable of a final iamb. The second line has a feminine ending, the *–dy* of "lady" forming an extra unstressed syllable at the end of a line of five iambs. Here are two more examples from *Twelfth Night*:

> Masculine: If music be the food of love, play on   (I.i.1)
> Feminine: She loves me sure, the cunning of her passion
>
> (II.ii.22)

What Is Blank Verse?

Blank verse is the name given to lines of iambic pentameter that do not rhyme.[3] The vast majority of the verse lines in Shakespeare's plays are in blank verse.

RHYTHM

By contrast with meter, the ordered structure of stresses in the general model or template of a line of verse, *rhythm* refers to the variations played upon the meter by the way the particular words and their arrangement in a particular line would be uttered in natural speech. We could say that if the meter is the drumbeat of expected stresses, then the rhythm is the melody of actual stresses. Let's take some examples. Here's a silly parody spoken by Bottom the Weaver in *A Midsummer Night's Dream* (I.ii.31-38):

> The raging rocks
> And shivering shocks
> Shall break the locks
>   Of prison gates;
> And Phibbus' car
> Shall shine from far,
> And make and mar
>   The foolish Fates.

This poem is in iambic dimeter (two iambic feet per line: *ta-TUM ta-TUM*). If we scan the lines, the poem will look like this:

Thĕ rágĭng rócks
Ănd shívĕrĭng shócks
Shăll bréak thĕ lócks
    Ŏf prísŏn gátes;
Ănd Phíbbŭs' cár
Shăll shíne frŏm fár,
Ănd máke ănd már
    Thĕ foólĭsh Fátes.

You'll see that every line except the second is perfectly regular. That is, the rhythm and meter are the same. Only in the second line is there a possible variation if we pronounce the one additional unstressed syllable. But even that line may be intended to be regular if we take the e in "shivering" to be elided to "shiv'ring." Now let's scan the lines of Sonnet 94 quoted above, marking the stressed and unstressed syllables as we would say them aloud:

Fŏr swéetĕst thíngs tŭrn soúrĕst bý thĕir déeds;
Lílĭes thăt féstĕr sméll fár wórse thăn wéeds.

The first line is largely a regular iambic line with five stresses in normal iambic position (or we might read it as four heavy stresses and one light stress on "by"). The second line, however, considerably alters the expectation, adjusts the template, modifies the model. There is a stress on the first syllable ("Líl-"), which makes the first foot a trochee (´ ˘ = *TUM-ta*). That is followed by an iamb ("thăt fést-"). The stress on the first syllable of the line followed by two unstressed syllables together ("-lĭes thăt") throws a heavier than usual stress onto the fourth syllable of the line ("fést-"). So instead of "*ta-TUM ta-TUM*" we get "*TUM-ta ta-TUM*," ("Lílĭes thăt fést-"). Then where the meter would cause us to expect an unstressed syllable on "far," we actually put a rhythmic stress on the word, which makes three stresses in a row. These, together with the final stress on "weeds," which is also the final rhyme word of the couplet, make a line of unusually emphatic stresses, the emphasis arising, in part, from this audible departure from the expectations set up in us by the regular rhythm of the previous line. In nonsense syllables, the rhythm of these lines would look like this:

ta-TUM ta-TUM ta-TUM ta-TUM ta-TUM
TUM-ta ta-TUM ta-TUM TUM-TUM ta-TUM

Again, *meter* means the expected pattern of stresses of the line; *rhythm* means the actual arrangement of stresses in a line, whether it fits the meter exactly or not. Here, the meter is iambic pentameter, and it appears almost exactly in the rhythm of the first line. In the second line, the rhythm plays intentionally and significantly against the meter.

If the actual rhythm of verse fits reasonably into its expected meter, we say that the line *scans*. If not, it fails to scan. Here are two versions of a two-line poem in anapestic tetrameter, four anapests (ˇ ˇ ´ = *ta-ta-TUM*) per line. Which of them scans and which fails to scan?

> Then a pounding of hoofbeats was felt in the earth
> When the horses, stampeding, appeared on the ridge.

> Then a pounding of hoofbeats was felt in the earth
> When the horses, stampeding, appeared on the horizon.

In the second version, where the meter demands a stressed word of one syllable (like "ridge") at the end of the second line, we get instead a three-syllable word ("horizon") that, because of its two excess unstressed syllables, simply doesn't fit the meter. We say the line does not scan.

Scanning a line for the meter is essential in knowing how Shakespeare means a line to be said. For example, the meter of a line will determine whether or not we must pronounce the *-ed* of a past tense verb or participle as an unstressed syllable. In the following line of Horatio from *Hamlet* (I.ii.203)—

> By their oppressed and fear-surprised eyes

—we pronounce "oppressed" as "oppress'd" and "-surprised" as "-surprisèd" thus:

> By their oppress'd and fear-surprisèd eyes.

With any other pronunciation of those syllables the line would not scan, that is, the rhythm of the line would fail to fit the meter. Here is another line from *Hamlet* (III.i.70) in which scanning the line tells us how to say it:

The oppressor's wrong, the proud man's contumely

We would have way too many syllables if we gave full weight to "The" and gave "contumely" four syllables with the stress on the second syllable, as in modern speech (*con-TOOM-uh-lee*). Shakespeare means us to elide the "The" with "oppressor's" and to make "contumely" three syllables with the main stress on the first syllable and another lesser stress on the last, thus:

Th' oppréssor's wróng, the próud man's cóntum'lý (*CON-toom-LEE*)

(Technically, here the –ly syllable takes not a full stress but a secondary stress, which would be represented by ỳ.)

Repetition of Sounds

The third fundamental method of making sound meaningful is repetition, which refers to any pattern of repeated sounds within a line or passage of verse. Under repetition of sounds we will distinguish between rhyme, alliteration, assonance, and consonance.

Rhyme

Rhyme is the name we give to identical-sounding vowel-consonant combinations at the ends of successive words or phrases: go/slow, attest/ depressed, oration/predation, upper story/lavatory are all rhyming pairs. Usually rhyme appears at the ends of lines. End rhymes may appear in rhyming couplets (lines rhyming two by two). For example,

Full thirty times hath Phoebus' cart gone round
Neptune's salt wash and Tellus' orbèd ground
And thirty dozen moons with borrowed sheen
About the world have times twelve thirties been,
Since love our hearts and Hymen did our hands
Unite commutual in most sacred bands.

(*Hamlet*, III.ii.155–60)

End rhymes may also appear in any number of possible arrangements of alternating rhymes. Here are two examples:

> The woosel cock so black of hue,
>   With orange-tawny bill,
> The throstle with his note so true,
>   The wren with little quill—
>   (*Midsummer Night's Dream*, III.i.125–28)

> No more dams I'll make for fish,
>   Nor fetch in firing
>   At requiring,
> Nor scrape trenchering, nor wash dish.
>   'Ban, 'Ban, Ca-Caliban
>   Has a new master, get a new man.   (*Tempest*, II.ii.180–85)

Sometimes the poet uses rhymes within lines rather than at their ends. This is called *internal rhyme*. For example *double* and *trouble* in

> Double, double, toil and trouble   (*Macbeth*, IV.i.10 etc.)

or *yesterday* and *way* in

> And all our yesterdays have lighted fools
> The way to dusty death.   (*Macbeth*, V.v.22–23)

The *rhyme scheme* of a poem is indicated by giving a letter of the alphabet to each distinct rhyme sound. So the rhyme scheme of Bottom's poem quoted above,

> The raging rocks
> And shivering shocks
> Shall break the locks
>   Of prison gates;
> And Phibbus' car
> Shall shine from far,
> And make and mar
>   The foolish Fates.

would be indicated thus: a, a, a, b; c, c, c, b. (For the normal rhyme scheme of a Shakespearean sonnet, see Chapter 11.)

ALLITERATION

Alliteration refers to the repetition of initial sounds of words, that is, sounds at the beginnings of two or more words in a line or passage of verse. Bottom's lines above are filled with alliteration. The *r* sound in "raging rocks," the *sh* sound in "shivering shocks/Shall" and again in "Shall shine," the *m* sound in "make and mar," and the *f* sound in "foolish Fates" are all examples of alliteration.

ASSONANCE

Assonance refers to the repetition of vowel sounds within words (as opposed to the beginnings of words). In Bottom's lines, "raging," "break," "gates," "make," and "Fates" are all assonant words, repeating the long *a* sound. The repeated short *i* sound makes "Prison," "shivering," and "Phibbus'" assonant. (The assonance makes funnier the fact that Bottom is mispronouncing Apollo's name as "Phibbus" instead of "Phoebus.")

CONSONANCE

Consonance refers to the repetition of consonant sounds within words, again as opposed to at the beginnings of words. In Bottom's lines, the *n* sound in "prison" and in "shine" is an example of consonance.

If we look again at the couplet from Sonnet 94—

> For sweetest things turn sourest by their deeds;
> Lilies that fester smell far worse than weeds.

—we will find a very rich complexity of sound repetitions: alliteration (For/fester/far, sweetest/sourest/smell, things/their/than, worse/weeds), assonance (sweet-/deeds/weeds, -est/-est/their/fester/smell, things/Lil-, sour-/worse), and consonance (For/turn/sour-/their/-ter/far/worse, sweet-/worse/weeds, -est/-est/fest-, etc.). (For the overall effect of this complexity, see the discussion of Sonnet 94 in Part 2.)

Sounds Woven Together

One of Shakespeare's great gifts is the ear for weaving all of these kinds of repetitions of sound together in complex ways in order to achieve the effects he wants. Here is a final example of Shakespeare's complex use of sound, taken from the Ghost's speech in *Hamlet* (I.v. 9–13), written in the period of Shakespeare's maturity:

> I am thy father's spirit,
> Doom'd for a certain term to walk the night,
> And for the day confin'd to fast in fires,
> Till the foul crimes done in my days of nature
> Are burnt and purg'd away.

Notice the alliteration on *f* (*f*ather's, *f*or, *f*ast, *f*ires, *f*oul) and *d* (*D*oom'd, *d*ay, *d*one, *d*ays); the consonance together with alliteration on *s* (father'*s*, *s*pirit, *c*ertain, fa*s*t, fire*s*, crime*s*, day*s*), on *f* (con*f*in'd), on *t* (spiri*t*, cer*t*ain, *t*erm, nigh*t*, fas*t*, burn*t*) and on *d* (confin'*d*, purg'*d*); the assonance on *i* (*I*, n*i*ght, conf*i*n'd, f*i*res) and on *a* (d*a*y, d*a*ys, n*a*ture, aw*a*y). The repetition of the combinations *er* and *ur* unites assonance and consonance (c*er*tain, t*er*m, nat*ur*e, b*ur*nt, p*ur*g'd). The letters *d* and *m* tie the word "Doom'd" to other words, but the vowel *oo* is unique in the passage, as if all the other sounds are included in it. Three end-stopped lines (ll. 9–11) lead to the enjambment in lines 12–13 (see End-stopped Lines and Enjambment below). In the word "Doom'd" at the beginning of the sentence, the hardness of the *d*'s and the force of the long vowel *oo* contrast with the long-drawn-out fading of the long *a* sound in the word "away" at the end of the sentence.

More could be said about this remarkable sentence, but the essential point about Shakespeare's use of sound is this: Thanks to his subtle art, we do not experience these figures of speech as mere ornamentation. They are one with the meaning of the words in conveying the intensity of thought and emotion we experience in hearing the sentence.

Rhetorical Devices Rooted in Structure
Antithesis

If the key to Shakespeare's imagery is metaphor, the key to his drama is *antithesis*, meaning the use of contrary ideas (large/small, hot/cold, virtuous/sinful). We will discuss the antitheses of character against character, good against evil, knowledge against ignorance, reality against illusion, and so on in other chapters. Here we focus on the antithesis of image against image. In each of the vast majority of Shakespeare's individual lines, as well as in his whole speeches, the meaning is built up out of antitheses, which give dramatic force to the movement of ideas.

The theme of Hamlet's "To be or not to be" soliloquy is founded on the antithesis expressed in its first six words. The rest of the speech is a set of antitheses contrasting bearing the trials of this life with putting an end to them, leading to the contrast between the known sufferings of this life and the unknown potential sufferings in the hereafter.

But let's take a speech that does not seem to be specifically about contrasting ideas. Here's a fairly un-dramatic passage from *Hamlet* (I.ii.50–56). The present King of Denmark has asked Laertes, the son of the King's minister Polonius, what he wishes to do, and Laertes responds that he wants to return to France.

> King: What wouldst thou have, Laertes?
> Laertes: My dread lord,
> Your leave and favor to return to France,
> From whence though willingly I came to Denmark
> To show my duty in your coronation,
> Yet now I must confess, that duty done,
> My thoughts and wishes bend again toward France,
> And bow them to your gracious leave and pardon.

Here are some of the specific antitheses that give interest and tension to the passage: return to France/came to Denmark; came to Denmark/bend toward France; show my duty/that duty done; willingly I came/thoughts and wishes bend again; my thoughts and wishes/your leave and pardon; etc. In addition, the whole passage moves in imagination from France to Denmark and back again to France. And it also moves from Laertes' will to the King's will, back to Laertes' will, and again to the King's will ("What wouldst thou have . . . Your leave and favor . . . My thoughts and wishes . . . your gracious leave and pardon"). There is no dramatic conflict in the speech or in the relationship, and yet the interest of the speech depends on these contrasting elements.

In the couplet of Sonnet 94, quoted above, we can see a good example of Shakespeare's use of antithesis combined with sound to convey drama:

> For sweetest things turn sourest by their deeds;
> Lilies that fester smell far worse than weeds.

Notice the antitheses of sweetest/sourest, Lilies/weeds, Lilies/fester, sweet/fester, sweet/smell worse. The effect of the antithesis between "sweetest" and "sourest" is made more pointed because of the alliteration of *s* sounds, consonance of *w* sounds, and both assonance and consonance of *–est* sounds. Then the long *e* of "sweetest" is repeated in "Lilies" and the *–est* sounds in "fester." The result of this melding of antithesis and sound is a striking image (actually, an experience) of what it feels like to be betrayed by a friend.

Repetition of Syntax

Another figure rooted in structure is repetition of syntax or phrasing. Such repetition can express extreme intensity, as in the verse litany of murders perpetrated by the evil king in *Richard III*:

> Queen Margaret: I had an Edward, till a Richard kill'd him;
> I had a Harry, till a Richard kill'd him;
> Thou hadst an Edward, till a Richard kill'd him;
> Thou hadst a Richard, till a Richard kill'd him.
> Duchess of York: I had a Richard too, and thou didst kill him;
> I had a Rutland too, thou holp'st to kill him.
> Queen Margaret: Thou hadst a Clarence too, and Richard kill'd him.
> (*Richard III*, IV.iv.40–46)

The repetition of words, syntax, and images in addition to sounds in Ophelia's verse speech of sorrow over the supposedly mad Hamlet is also poignant:

> O, woe is me
> T' have seen what I have seen, see what I see!
> (*Hamlet*, III.i.160-61)

Benedick's comical prose speech in *Much Ado about Nothing* combines repetition with antithesis:

> I have known when there was no music with him but the drum and the fife, and now had he rather hear the tabor and the pipe; I have known when he would have walked ten mile afoot to see a good armor, and now will he lie ten nights awake carving the fashion of a new doublet. (II.iii.12–18)

This repetition of contrasts between Claudio's behavior before he fell in love and his behavior now builds toward the climax in which Benedick asks about himself, "May I be so converted?" (l. 22), implying both the desired contrast and the feared similarity of himself to Claudio.

Shakespeare pokes fun at excessive repetition of structural elements for rhetorical purposes in a speech of Polonius in *Hamlet*. The Queen has asked him to use "more matter with less art" (meaning more substance with fewer figures of speech):

> Madam, I swear I use no art at all.
> That he is mad, 'tis true; 'tis true 'tis pity;
> And pity 'tis 'tis true—a foolish figure [of speech],
> But farewell it, for I will use no art. (II.ii.96–99)

Chiasmus

Another figure rooted in structure is *Chiasmus*, from the Greek letter Chi (X), a figure of speech in which a word or phrase is followed by a mirror image of itself in a structure that can be illustrated as *a-b-b-a*. (Sometimes it is called Antimetabole.) Polonius uses it above in the order of his key words: mad-true-pity/pity-true-mad. Later Hamlet will say, "To punish me with this, and this with me" (III.iv.174) (me-this/this-me). One of the greatest uses of chiasmus in all of Shakespeare is the moment in *Richard II* (IV.i.201) in which the crown is passed from Richard's hand to that of his successor, Henry Bullingbrook, who is deposing him and will become King Henry IV. Bullingbrook asks Richard, "Are you contented to resign the crown?" Richard's response is "Ay, no, no, ay." This is heard by the audience not only as meaning "yes, no, no, yes" but also as meaning "I know no I" and "I know no ay." The point between the "ay, no" and the "no, ay" is the turning point of the play, in which the kingship passes from one man to another. It is also the point in the play in which the falling star of Richard crosses the path of the rising star of Bullingbrook. Thus, in a sense, the entire play is built metaphorically in the form of a historical chiasmus, the fall of one king and the rise of the other, and the verbal chiasmus ("Ay, no, no, ay") is the X that marks the spot of the historical turning point.

End-Stopped Lines and Enjambment

An *end-stopped line* is one in which the end of the line corresponds to the end of a grammatical unit or phrase. An *enjambed line* is one in which the syntax or meaning continues or wraps around onto the next line. (Think of a door jamb, which connects the door to the wall; one line is being connected to the next line with no pause.) In Sonnet 29 (beginning "When in disgrace with Fortune and men's eyes") all the lines until line 11 are end-stopped. This is in keeping with the speaker's dreary mood. Each line is a depressed instance of his misery: "I all alone beweep my outcast state"—breath, sigh—"And trouble deaf heaven with my bootless cries"—breath, sigh—"And look upon myself and curse my fate"—breath, sigh—and so on. Then, after he has thought about his beloved, his mood and tone are entirely changed. He's so happy that he is ready to sing, and he does so in the enjambed line:

> . . . and then my state,
> Like to the lark at break of day arising
> From sullen earth, sings hymns at heaven's gate . . .

Notice that after the word "arising" there is no punctuation to indicate a pause, a breath or a sigh, but rather the phrase keeps right on going into the next line, just as the European skylark rises into the heavens at dawn to sing, and just as the speaker's mood is now uplifted in joy. It is a classic use of end-stopped vs. enjambed lines to embody a contrast in meaning and tone.

Shifting from end-stopped lines to enjambed lines is one of the ways that Shakespeare punctuates the difference between the rhymed couplets of the King of France and those of King Lear (discussed under Sound and Sense in Chapter 1):

France: Gods, gods! 'tis strange that from their cold'st neglect
            My love should kindle to inflam'd respect.
            Thy dow'rless daughter, King, thrown to my chance,
            Is queen of us, of ours, and our fair France.
            Not all the dukes of wat'rish Burgundy
            Can buy this unpriz'd precious maid of me.
            Bid them farewell, Cordelia, though unkind,
            Thou losest here, a better where to find.

King Lear: Thou hast her, France, let her be thine, for we
           Have no such daughter, nor shall ever see
           That face of hers again. [*To Cordelia*] Therefore be gone,
           Without our grace, our love, our benison.

                                        (*King Lear*, I.i.254–65)

The lines of France, whose mind is well ordered, are for the most part end-stopped. Those of Lear, whose mind is in chaos, are enjambed. Here, as everywhere, the figure of speech exists to embody and convey meaning.

VARIATION IN SPEECH

There is another rhetorical device that is essential to appreciating Shakespeare's poetry, namely variation. As C.S. Lewis points out in his excellent essay on variation in Shakespeare,[4] there are two ways one can set about describing something in words. One way is construction: You start with one part of your subject and add descriptive elements in a logical progression until the reader or audience has the whole picture. For example, "My girlfriend is wonderful: She's five-foot-four, has blond hair and very fair skin, blue sparkling eyes and a great smile; she plays tennis like a pro, gets A's in math, and never forgets where her car keys are; she can be very funny, and she knows how to take a joke."

The other way of describing something Lewis calls *variation*: You try to capture the whole in one image, then in another, then another, in a series of attempts at conveying the essence of the thing or the idea instead of treating one element at a time. Here is Romeo describing *his* girlfriend:

O, she doth teach the torches to burn bright! . . .
Beauty too rich for use, for earth too dear!
So shows a snowy dove trooping with crows,
As yonder lady o'er her fellows shows.
(*Romeo and Juliet*, I.v.44–49)

And later "It is the east, and Juliet is the sun" (II.ii.3). This method of variation is by far Shakespeare's most common method.

Let's look at Prince Hal's soliloquy (*1 Henry IV*, I.ii.195–217) in which he is informing us that his "riot and dishonor," hanging around with the thieves and drunkards of London, is not really self-indulgence but rather wise political calculation. The prince is alone on stage, sharing his thoughts with us, beginning with an address to his low-life companions, though they have left the stage, and ending with a formal rhymed couplet. Here is the speech:

I know you all, and will a while uphold
The unyok'd humor of your idleness,
Yet herein will I imitate the sun,

Who doth permit the base contagious clouds
To smother up his beauty from the world,
That when he please again to be himself,
Being wanted, he may be more wond'red at
By breaking through the foul and ugly mists
Of vapors that did seem to strangle him.
If all the year were playing holidays,
To sport would be as tedious as to work;
But when they seldom come, they wish'd for come,
And nothing pleaseth but rare accidents.
So when this loose behavior I throw off
And pay the debt I never promisèd,
By how much better than my word I am,
By so much shall I falsify men's hopes,
And like bright metal on a sullen ground,
My reformation, glitt'ring o'er my fault,
Shall show more goodly and attract more eyes
Than that which hath no foil to set it off.
I'll so offend, to make offense a skill,
Redeeming time when men think least I will.

Now what do these twenty-three lines of the Prince's thought amount to? One single idea—that people will be so relieved at the contrast between his present (supposed) dishonorable behavior and his future (apparent) reformation that he will win their approval. But this one idea is expressed in about fourteen ways:

I know you all, and will a while uphold
The unyok'd humor of your idleness,
> 1. I will temporarily support you fellows in idleness (frivolity, self-indulgence).

Yet herein will I imitate the sun,
Who doth permit the base contagious clouds
To smother up his beauty from the world,
That when he please again to be himself,
Being wanted, he may be more wond'red at

By breaking through the foul and ugly mists
Of vapors that did seem to strangle him.

> 2. I will imitate the sun, which is the more welcome after a period of overcast.

If all the year were playing holidays,
To sport would be as tedious as to work;

> 3. I am now unwanted like tedious work-days, but later I'll be desired like a rare holiday.

But when they seldom come, they wish'd for come,

> 4. I will be like what comes seldom and is therefore wished for.

And nothing pleaseth but rare accidents.

> 5. I will be like a rare event, which pleases more than a common event.

So when this loose behavior I throw off

> 6. Eventually I will throw off this (apparently) immoral behavior.

And pay the debt I never promised,

> 7. I will pleasingly surprise by paying a debt I never promised to pay.

By how much better than my word I am,

> 8. I'll be even better than what I seem to promise.

By so much shall I falsify men's hopes,

> 9. I'll lead people to expect less of me than I'll finally deliver.

And like bright metal on a sullen ground,

> 10. I'll be like gold or silver seen against a dull background.

My reformation, glitt'ring o'er my fault,

> 11. My (apparent) reformation will shine the brighter against the dull background of my faults.

Shall show more goodly and attract more eyes
Than that which hath no foil to set it off.

> 12. My later character (like a jewel set against a foil background) will win more approval than if I had not set it off against my present (apparently bad) behavior.

I'll so offend, to make offense a skill,

> 13. My bad behavior is not real but planned.

Redeeming time when men think least I will.

> 14. This investment of time in apparent dishonor will pay off later, much to everyone's surprise.

You see why Lewis calls this method "variation." It is like variations on a theme in music. The same idea is conveyed in a lot of different ways, and all of them vivid, apt, appropriate—in short, poetically effective.

But why doesn't this become boring repetition? Because, as Lewis also points out, Shakespeare makes his characters, even as they engage in this repetition, sound as if they are really thinking or really speaking. This is because in life we almost never compose our thoughts perfectly the first time, once and for all, in trying to say the thing we mean. In reality, we go at it several times, in various different ways, until the person we are speaking to gathers what we mean.

This method of variation allows Shakespeare to make his characters do two things at once: They speak in rich and elaborate poetic metaphors that plumb the depths of an idea in vivid language, and, at the same time, they sound as if they are real people really speaking, trying to express what is difficult to say, going at it again and again till they get it right.

Lewis writes,

> The problem which Shakespeare solved, perhaps unconsciously, is a very difficult one. If the character speaks as living men speak, how are we to have in his language the revealing splendours of imagination? for real passion is not articulate. He must give his poetic metaphors the air of being thrown off accidentally as he gropes for expression in the very heat of dialogue. He must have a slight stammer in his thought, and his best things must not come at the first attempt. For on those rare occasions when real life finds the inevitable phrase, that is how it arises. The man fumbles and returns again and again to his theme, and hardly knows which of his words has really hit the mark. . . . Without sacrificing the splendour, he has kept the lower and more factual reality as well; it is the very marriage of the mimetic [imitative of nature] and the creative, and it can hardly be done except by variation.[5]

This is the magical accomplishment of Shakespeare's method of variation: the union of realistic human speech and rich poetic imagery into a single experience of meaning.

DID SHAKESPEARE'S AUDIENCE GET IT ALL?

We have Shakespeare's own word for it that they did not. Check out the prologue to *Romeo and Juliet*, Act I, where the Chorus says,

if you with patient ears attend,
What here shall miss, our toil shall strive to mend.   (ll. 13–14)

In other words, the speaker of the prologue says to the audience, whatever you miss in this prologue, you'll catch later if you pay attention. So Shakespeare himself knew that some audience members were bound to miss some things.

But the question is more complicated. When we study Shakespeare's language in all the ways discussed above (and others), we may wonder whether Shakespeare's audience could possibly have been aware of this complexity and richness and variety. Were they sitting or standing in the Globe Theatre registering these elements that we observe when we are looking closely at the text of a play? Again, the answer is both no and yes.

They certainly are not counting the stresses of iambic pentameter lines when Romeo is observing Juliet on her balcony, nor are they thinking "Aha—chiasmus!" when Richard II is about to surrender the English crown. How many of us, when watching a movie, are measuring the cinematographer's camera angles or noting his lighting system? We can certainly become conscious of these things when we study a movie in detail, and that study may well enrich our appreciation of the movie as a work of art. But when we are watching it for entertainment, those elements disappear into the whole experience. The same was true for Shakespeare's audience.

Nonetheless, they were conscious of the clarity, the fitness, and the authenticity of the play they were hearing. They would surely have felt uncomfortable if lines failed to scan or a young man in love spoke in language appropriate to an old nurse or a noble duke started speaking in comical malapropisms. In other words, they got it all, as we "get" the meaning and quality of a movie even if we are not film critics or experts in the art of cinematography.

They got it because Shakespeare's art was all of a piece. Every element of language contributed to the total meaning and effect of the play. His audience could feel the quality of the whole in every part, and so can we if we ready ourselves to receive the experience as it was intended to be received.

---

[1]   We sympathize *with* (the Greek prefix *syn-* or *sym-* meaning "with") but empathize *into* (the Greek prefix *en-* or *em-* meaning "in" or "into"). For more on empathy, see Chapter 15.

[2]   Dakin Matthews, "Sheltering with Shakespeare" podcast, episode 16, "Rhythm and Meter," accessed 10/9/20 at https://www.youtube.com/watch?v=zE7jaX-yUY4&feature=youtu.be.

[3]   Dakin Matthews argues that "blank" indicates a form of verse available, because unlimited by rhyme, for any variety of stress determined by the meaning with which the poet wants to fill it, like a "blank slate."

[4]   C.S. Lewis, "Variation in Shakespeare and Others" in *Selected Literary Essays*, ed. Walter Hooper (Cambridge: Cambridge University Press, 1969, paperback reprint 1980), pp. 74–87.

[5]   Lewis, pp. 74–83.

5

Foiled Again?—Shakespeare's Characters

PARTICULAR AND GENERAL

As we saw in Chapter 1 (under Universal Realism), one of the elements of Shakespeare's greatness is his ability to make characters both believable as real people and at the same time universally significant. And in Chapter 4 (under Variation in Speech), we saw how Shakespeare's use of the technique C. S. Lewis called variation achieved a similar unity of poetic splendor and realistic speech. Here let's remember that every character in Shakespeare is meant to be taken both as believably real and at the same time as representative of a kind of person or attitude, a part of the self, or a universal principle that is meaningful to any human being.

The degree of realism of a character will partly depend on the context, what kind of play it is—comedy, history, tragedy, satire, or romance. For example, the characters in a history play will generally be more realistic, more literally believable, than those in a late romance. We are meant to believe literally that Richard II was a real man, a king of England who actually lived and was deposed by Henry IV.

When it comes to Prospero's magic in *The Tempest*, we must suspend our disbelief a little more. We must believe that Prospero is what a virtuous magician would be like if there were such a man. And, at the extreme, we are not meant to believe that Ariel and Caliban ever did or could literally exist, but within the confines of the play we certainly must and do believe in the particular reality of this aery spirit and this earthy monster. We are persuaded that if there were such an island as Prospero's containing creatures like Ariel and Caliban, they would speak and act as Ariel and Caliban do. Each character is to be taken seriously as really existing for the purposes of the kind of play it is.

In all cases, however, the characters are meant to be taken as both psychologically convincing particular people and representative of more general concepts. In different ways, Richard II and Prospero both embody the universal problem of the relation between human power and moral responsibility. Ariel is both himself and a representation of the part of the human spirit that longs for freedom from physical confinement. Caliban is both himself and an embodiment of the human being's lower natural passions and of their potential for depravity and for redemption. The character Falstaff never actually existed in history, but whenever he is on the stage in the *Henry IV* plays, we certainly believe in the absolute, particular reality of this fat, witty, hilarious, indomitable man, and we cannot imagine the world ever existing without him. At the same time, we recognize him as the world's greatest fictional embodiment of dishonorable self-indulgence.

GOOD AND EVIL
The Mixed

Shakespeare was an astute enough student of human character to know that most people are neither all good nor all bad but mixed, and the majority of his characters reflect this truth. As Feste the Clown says in *Twelfth Night*, "virtue that transgresses is but patch'd with sin, and sin that amends is but patch'd with virtue" (I.v.48–49). The character of Hamlet is filled with admirable qualities, but he nonetheless succumbs to a terrible temptation. His flaw, its consequences, and its purging make up the central drama of the play. In a lighter vein, the same is true of Katherine in *The Taming of the Shrew*. Apart from her obvious beauty, she has many wonderful qualities that are obscured by her shrewishness until they are liberated when her bad attitude is altered by Petruchio's commitment to ensuring her happiness. In *The Tempest*, even the monster Caliban, son of the devil and a witch, would-be rapist, murderer, and usurper, has in him the possibility to be healed of his evil will and to "seek for grace."

Neither is the mixture of qualities in a character always a matter of his or her changing from one sort of person to another, though that does happen. Sometimes the particular mixture of qualities in a character is constant. In *Antony and Cleopatra*, Antony is a noble Roman drawn to abandon his soldierly calling by the attractions and the wiles of the great seductress Cleopatra. The play is filled with his wavering from Egyptian thoughts of love to Roman thoughts of duty and back again, even until the last moments before his death. And all through the same play Cleopatra is by turns witty, sarcastic, petulant, girlish, violent, sweet, plotting, lying, humble, queenly, traitorous, faithful, self-abasing, self-exalting, and more. That changeability is the only constant in her character until her final alteration—death—puts an end to it, though not to our memory of it. King Lear is a remarkable combination of petulant self-will and magnificent kingliness. The potential of Beatrice and Benedick to love one another is slowly revealed through their witty battle of mutual insults.

Because Shakespeare was so great a portrayer of the subtleties of human character, we are tempted to take it for granted that every one of his characters is equally morally complex. This, however, turns out to be a mistake.

The Good

A very important, and too often denied, fact for modern readers and audiences to know about Shakespeare's characters is that Shakespeare meant some of his characters to be really and truly and simply good, and that his audience found such goodness believable. For several reasons we have a harder time believing that they are good.

First of all, as suggested above, many Shakespearean characters exhibit mental and moral complexity, so that we are tempted to assume that all do. But there are two additional major reasons why it is hard for us to believe in the simple goodness of his good characters.

The first reason is universal: All of us know that we ourselves are not really and truly good (or at least not thoroughly good yet). Depending on your own spiritual belief, you will probably agree that most or all human beings are imperfect or flawed or limited or laboring under illusions or fallible, whether because we are incompletely evolved, or because we are (in biblical terms) fallen, or because of a corrupting society, as Rousseau preached, or for some other reason. Each of us knows that not all our motives are pure, unselfish, kind, and virtuous. This was as true of Shakespeare's audience as it is of us, and Shakespeare knew it very well.

As a result of this inner knowledge, every one of us has reason to doubt that anyone else's motives are totally pure and good. Insofar as we judge them by our awareness of our own mixed motives, we tend to doubt the reality of any character presented to us as exemplifying pure goodness. This is especially the case when an author strives to make his character realistic, believable as a real person, as Shakespeare does.

The second reason for our doubt of the goodness of even apparently good characters in drama or fiction is our own modern ideas about psychology. The tremendous influence of Freudian ideas upon our thinking in the last hundred or so years has caused us to assume that every apparently good motive has its roots in the unsavory swamps of the unconscious. The ego may pretend to virtue, but we have been persuaded that the selfish id is the real source of our choices.

Add to the above reasons the pleasure we all take in seeing through others' pretenses, in spotting rationalizations, in not being fooled. And add as well the proliferation in the news and social media of dirt about people once thought to be above suspicion. The result is an age that finds it almost impossible to believe that any character on the stage is really good. As my own great teacher, Mary Holmes, said, in our age we find it impossible to believe that anyone or anything is or can be innocent. We are always, therefore, second-guessing the good character, always reading into the author's intentions an underlying irony or moral critique or psychological wrinkle, however approving we may be of the characters' external behavior and words.

With most modern authors, who are equally influenced by these disillusioning forces of our age, we are usually not wrong to be so skeptical. The authors write their plays and movies expecting us to be so. In Shakespeare's time, however, things were different. Not that Shakespeare could not portray mixed or ulterior or unconscious motives, false pretenses, or rationalization. He could indeed, as in the hypocrisy of Richard in *Richard III*, or of Worcester in *Henry IV, Part 1*, or of Goneril, Regan, and Edmund in *King Lear*, or in the self-realization of Gertrude in *Hamlet*, or of Enobarbus in *Antony and Cleopatra*. But at the same time, Shakespeare and his audience believed that true and thorough goodness was possible.

They held this belief not only because, like each of us, they probably all knew at least one person whom they would call good, even though they saw that person from the outside. They believed people could be truly good also because the Christian religious tradition they shared taught them that there had been, and were still, saints in the world, though many might be unknown as such, and that Jesus, representing the perfection of God as incarnated in a man, had set an example of a good life which in theory it was possible to follow.

So for Shakespeare and his audience, the picture of a person saying or doing the right thing for the right reason at the right time was not necessarily assumed to be a falsification of reality or a hoax. Such a portrayal was exciting and pleasing because it confirmed the reality of the audience's belief in the possibility of human virtue, even in trying circumstances.

As a result, we make a serious mistake if we are always striving to find unsavory motives, self-delusions, and psychological complexes in Shakespeare's good characters. For example, when King Lear, wanting to evoke flattery, asks his daughter Cordelia the loaded question "What can you say to draw / A third more opulent than your sisters?" (*King Lear*, I.i.85–86), we lose the meaning of the moment if, when she answers "Nothing," we allow ourselves to think she is being coy or proud or superior or any other unsavory thing. The dramatic significance lies in her speaking the simple truth, her only firm foundation in the face of the hypocrisy around her, and her only hope of breaking through her father's destructive self-delusion. She is being simply honest and good, though she correctly fears that doing so will get her into trouble, and the good character Kent confirms our judgment of the rightness of her response (l. 183).

Another example: When the surprisingly wise jailer in *Cymbeline* says, "I would we were all of one mind, and one mind good" (V.iv.203–204), it is tempting for modern audiences not to take him seriously. Who really can believe someone who actually says such a thing? But in fact he is expressing an honest wish, though, as he says, he would lose his income if it came true. When we allow ourselves to believe him, we discover that his simple words articulate the very wish that the play has produced in the audience and that the play's ending rewards.

Of course there are many characters in Shakespeare who present themselves as good but really are not so. But Shakespeare makes sure we recognize them as such. King Lear thinks he's doing the right thing, but Shakespeare gives us plenty of evidence to make us realize he isn't. Iago seems to Othello to be totally honest when we know, from his soliloquies, that he is totally the opposite. But though such characters are meant to be fooling the other characters in the play and perhaps fooling themselves, they are not meant to be fooling the audience. The audience is clearly let in on the false appearance.

Where Shakespeare makes a good character speak words of goodness, do acts of goodness, and be recognized as good by other good characters, we are simply to believe that the character is good. Good does not mean shallow or uncomplicated or dull. And that's part of Shakespeare's amazing accomplishment in inventing good characters. He makes them both good and believable, a very satisfying theatrical accomplishment, if only we will let ourselves trust that Shakespeare means them to be good when there is no specific evidence that tells us we are to think otherwise.

So a rule of thumb is this: If you want to get the meaning Shakespeare means the play to have, you must believe that a character really means what he or she says, so long as Shakespeare gives you no explicit reason to think otherwise. Where Shakespeare wants to complicate a character's psychology with hidden agendas or ulterior motives or rationalization, he will make the complication explicit and clear. As Hamlet says about actors in a play, "The players cannot keep counsel [meaning keep a secret], they'll tell all" (III.ii.141–42). They exist to do so.

The Bad

Evil characters are far easier for us to believe in because we know from the inside what it's like to be bad, at least a little. Shakespeare's evil characters can be as thoroughly evil as any in literature—Richard III, Macbeth, Iago, Goneril. But even though that is so, we can recognize bits of ourselves in them, a recognition that gives authenticity to the extremity of their evil desires and deeds. Have we ever wanted to be captain of the team or CEO of the company even though we know another player or a colleague is more competent? That choice is called envy. Have we ever pretended to like someone we were planning to dump, or publicly agreed with opinions that in private we deplore? That's called hypocrisy. Have we ever been tempted to disrespect our parents because we know better than they, or complained about an inheritance smaller than we expected from a dead relative? That's called ingratitude. Since most of us have been tempted by such thoughts, we have known, if only for a moment, what it is like to be Richard III, Macbeth, Iago, or Goneril. When we see or read the plays they appear in, we know that their temptations and the potential to make evil choices are in us too.

The Humorous

In addition to the moral qualities in a character—good, bad, or mixed—there are other qualities that are determined not by choice but by nature. In Act II, Scene ii, of *Hamlet*, the prince mentions the actors— he calls them "players"—who perform the roles of the various stock characters that make up a typical play of the period (ll. 319–25). Along with the king, the adventurous knight, the lover, the clown, and the lady (always played by a boy), he mentions "the humorous man." By this he does not mean a comedian or a funny-man. He means the type of character who suffers from the excess of one of the four humors of medieval and Renaissance physiology (blood, phlegm, black bile, and yellow bile—see The Humors in Chapter 7). These interior substances are partly fluid and partly spirit, sort of like, say, our image of adrenalin. A good balance in the proportions of these humors results in a well-balanced character, orderly in himself and in his general relations with the world. But when one or another of the humors is excessive, the result is that one aspect of the character's personality and behavior becomes to a degree exaggerated. In extreme cases of an excess humor, the character may reach the point of being anti-social and even self-destructive. Jaques in *As You Like It* is an example of a humorous character suffering from an excess of black bile called melancholia (from *melan*, meaning black, and *cholē*, meaning bile), producing the dark and depressed attitude toward things called melancholy. Sir John Falstaff in *Henry IV, Part 1*, is an example (among many other things) of a man exhibiting excess blood, which produces a sanguine personality (from *sanguis*, meaning blood), that is, jolly and red-faced and fat, like Santa Claus. In the same play, Hotspur exemplifies the man possessed by excess yellow bile (called *choler*), who is therefore choleric, short-fused, flying into intemperate rages. Shakespeare always makes more of the humorous character than a mere stock figure, but in many of his plays the type is easily recognizable. Other examples of humorous characters are Don John in *Much Ado about Nothing* and Parolles in *All's Well That Ends Well*. At the very end of *Twelfth Night*, the morally healed Orsino says about Malvolio, who has run off in a vengeful rage, "Pursue him, and entreat him to a peace" (V.i.380). In *Hamlet*, close in date to *Twelfth Night*, the prince in the speech mentioned above promises that "the humorous man shall end his part in peace." This echo—"entreat him to a peace" and "shall end his part in peace"—provides rather explicit testimony that Malvolio is to be thought of as the elaboration of a stock humorous character.

Character Clues

Shakespeare's characters are depicted for us not only by the words they say and the things they do. Our image of them is significantly built up by all that is said about them by other characters. To take only one example, in *King Lear* Kent's words about Cordelia confirm our impression that she is good:

> The gods to their dear shelter take thee, maid,
> That justly think'st and hast most rightly said!   (I.i.182–83)

The play confirms that Kent's words, too, are to be trusted because he himself is good, as we know not only from his own words and actions but also from what others say about him: "ah, that good Kent" (III.iv.163), "o thou good Kent" (IV.vii.1), "he's a good fellow" (V.iii.285). Awareness of this element in dramatic characterization is invaluable for discerning meaning in Shakespeare's plays. It is an especially important principle for actors in Shakespeare's plays, who will find a lot of help in learning how to play a particular role not only from the character's own words but from all that is said about the character by the others.[1]

Characters Change

We should not assume that a character who begins bad must end up good, or that a good character must inevitably go bad. But neither should we assume that the qualities of a character are always fixed and can never change. Shakespeare and his audience believed that the thinking and behavior of human beings could be altered: by the free will, by the influence of divine grace and revelation, by the force of circumstances, by the arguments of others, by love or hate or change of fortune or sudden inexplicable "affections," and by the near approach of death. Will Katherine's shrewishness be corrected? Will Orsino ever get over his sentimental attachment to Olivia? Will Lear learn his lesson? Will Edmund repent in time. Will Falstaff? The human potential to change is part of what keeps us on the edge of our seats in a Shakespeare play.

FOILS

Most people who have studied even one play by Shakespeare have been taught the word *foil*. English teachers are always pointing out that this character is a foil for that one. They aren't wrong. But Shakespeare uses foils in a more complex way than many realize.

What Is a Foil?

The word comes from the Latin *folium*, meaning "leaf," and came to be applied to metal that is beaten till it is flat and thin, like a tree leaf or a leaf of paper (as in aluminum foil). Such metal foil (usually gold or silver) was used as background in the settings of jewels to contrast with the gemstone or to brighten it by reflecting light back through it, especially if the gem was of paste rather than precious stone. Because of this function of metal foil in setting off a jewel by contrast, the word came to be used as a metaphor for anything that sets off something else by contrasting with it. So the word passes into theatrical usage to mean any character whose characteristics bring another character into sharper focus. As Hamlet says, punning on another meaning of foil (a blunted fencing sword),

I'll be your foil, Laertes. In mine ignorance
Your skill shall like a star i' th' darkest night
Stick fiery off indeed.   (V.ii.255–57)

Hamlet's supposed lack of skill in fencing with foils will make Laertes' mastery shine the brighter by contrast, just as the dark background of the night sky allows the stars to shine brightly to our eyes.

So a theatrical foil character is one whose qualities, actions, words, or other characteristics bring out and clarify those of another character by contrast. In *Hamlet*, Laertes' way of seeking revenge for the death of his father makes us the more conscious of Hamlet's way of seeking revenge for the death of his. (Laertes' passion is channeled by the King, Hamlet's by the Ghost and by his own reason.) In *Henry IV, Part 1*, Hotspur's pursuit of honor through battle is a foil for Falstaff's rejection of the very principle of honor. The father-approved affection of Paris for Juliet emphasizes by contrast the feud-forbidden passion of Romeo. So Laertes is said to be a foil for Hamlet, Falstaff and Hotspur are foils for one another, and Paris is a foil for Romeo.

The Shakespearean Complication

But, being the master he was, Shakespeare transforms this relatively obvious dramatic device into an instrument of great poetic power. What he generally does, more and more thoroughly and subtly as he matures, is not merely to give us a foil character for a main character but to multiply foils, making them abound in every direction. Falstaff and Hotspur are foils not only for one another but for the Prince, whose truer and deeper honor shines out against their two backgrounds. Though the Prince seems to be dishonorable in his friendship with the self-indulgent Falstaff and by contrast with the heroically pugnacious Hotspur, in reality Prince Hal's dishonor is only a disguise. Like Hotspur he also fights and wins, but his true honor is shown in his doing so, unlike Hotspur, only for virtuous and noble reasons rather than for mere personal glory. In *Romeo and Juliet* Paris is a foil not only for Romeo but also for Mercutio and for Benvolio, who are themselves both foils for Romeo and for one another. Old Capulet and Old Montague are foils for one another, but they are also foils for all four of the youthful boys. Juliet's nurse is a foil for her, for her mother, and for Friar Lawrence. The Friar is also a foil for the Prince, both trying in different ways to make peace between the feuding families. And the Prince, too, is a foil for Romeo as well as for Old Capulet and Old Montague. (This list is not complete!)

In *Hamlet*, not only Laertes but Horatio, Fortinbras, and (in the player's speech) Pyrrhus are foils for the Prince. Old Norway is a foil for Hamlet's father and for Claudius. The Priest and Gravedigger are foils for one another, and for Laertes. Ophelia's real madness is a foil for Hamlet's pretended madness, and Ophelia's innocence for Gertrude's guilt. In *King Lear*, Gloucester is an obvious foil for Lear. So is the Fool. But in addition, Lear's daughters are foils for one another, Gloucester's two sons for one another, and the two sons are foils for the three daughters. Kent and Edgar's disguises are foils for one another, and Oswald's corruption is a foil for Kent's virtue.

One could go on and on in this vein. In short, Shakespeare's art of composition with characters is such that every character within a play is in some ways similar to and in other ways contrasting with every other character. The foil effect works in a myriad ways to sharpen every kind of similarity and difference among the characters.

Doesn't this multiplication of foil contrasts produce theatrical and interpretive chaos? No, and the reason it doesn't is unity, as you may see in the next chapter.

---

[1] I first learned to apply this principle to the teaching of acting from my mentor in Shakespearean theatrical dramaturgy, Diana Maddox.

6

Why the Play's the Thing—Unity in Variety

UNITY AND MEANING

As I suggested in Chapter 4, poetry says with words what cannot be said in words. We may say also that plays say with words, characters, movement, story, sets, costumes, and sound effects what cannot be said any other way. That is, the medium of plays is complex, but all its various elements must be harmonized into a single experience if the play is going to be meaningful. If those elements are not harmonized, the play fails to satisfy us.

In a faulty play there may be a character who does not fit the context, or, in other words, breaks decorum (see Chapter 7), like a stand-up comic at a funeral or a country bumpkin on the Supreme Court. Or perhaps the through-line of the play—the developing main movement of story or idea—breaks off in the middle or changes direction or comes to no satisfactory conclusion. Let's say a teenager runs away from home in the first act but in the second act is back home with never any mention made of the escape or its effects. A play may have anachronisms, like a cell phone in a play about Julius Caesar or an oxcart in a play set in twenty-first-century Los Angeles. All such breaks, unless they can somehow be resolved in a greater unity by the end of the story, limit our appreciation of a play.

Here's an example. In the parts of *Two Noble Kinsmen* written by Shakespeare, the noble cousins, Palamon and Arcite, are paragons of chivalry and loyalty to their beloved Emilia. But at one point in the middle of the play, in a section written by Shakespeare's collaborator Fletcher, the two characters have a locker-room chat about the girls they had made love to in earlier years. Their talk would be just fine for two *other* young men talking about girls, but it does not fit at all with what *these* virtuous young men say and do in the rest of the play, or with what is said about them. This conversation is totally out of character. It is an example of Fletcher's breaking the play's unity of tone and character as well as decorum in order to have some uncouth fun.

To be satisfying, a play must combine all its various parts into a single meaningful reality. Unless the play is shallow, that reality is not something that can be expressed in any fewer words than those of the whole play. This is not because the meaning in a good play is unclear. The good play makes it crystal clear. But its clarity comes to us through the experience of the play as a whole. We know it when it's there and we miss it when it's not, but the meaning itself is beyond simplification.

For this reason, though it can be useful for comparison, it can be misleading to take Shakespeare's plots, characters, and language out of their context. Be very careful when people quote "Shakespeare" to you without being aware of the context. People who get a kick out of quoting "The first thing we do, let's kill all the lawyers" (2 *Henry VI* IV.ii.76–77) usually don't realize that the lines in context express the folly and danger of mob rule. When at the end of *Macbeth* the title character says that life "is a tale / Told by an idiot, full of sound and fury, / Signifying nothing" (V.v.26–28), the line is a sign of the despair of the character, not of the author.

SHAKESPEARE AND THE HOLOGRAM

As all roads once led to Rome, in the world of any Shakespeare play, every road—every word, image, speech, action, character, scene, plot element, and theme—leads to the heart of the play's meaning. Each part contributes to the whole picture and contains the whole picture in little, as in a hologram.

Have you had the experience of seeing a hologram? It's a three-dimensional (3-D) image made using laser light. When laser light, which is coherent (a principle in physics too complex to explain here), is beamed at an object and reflected back to a photographic plate along several different paths, the result is a 3-D picture. Let's say you've made a hologram of a room in your home. When you look at it, everything seems to be in 3-D space, not flat as in a normal photograph. The desk chair really feels as if it is in front of the desk, the curtains as if they really are behind the couch; everything comes forward or recedes as it does in reality. You feel you could step into the picture.

But here's more mystery: If you cut the 3-D hologram image in half, each half contains the whole picture. Cut the hologram of a room in half, and each half will still show your whole 3-D room; cut those halves in half again, and each quarter will show the whole room. The only difference is that the size of the image will be smaller. Because of the coherent nature of laser light, the image is so imprinted on the photographic plate that every part records the whole.

The hologram may serve as a metaphor for any play by Shakespeare. All the parts imply the whole. Shakespeare's imagination is such that each of his plays provides an experience of a single, unified meaning with deep implications for the personal, social, political, moral, and spiritual life of man. At the same time, that whole meaning is there in every part of the play, only smaller. Because Shakespeare's vision, too, is coherent, like laser light, he is able to make the play's meaning clear and at the same time full of entertaining variety. Thus in a Shakespeare play, as in any great work of art, all roads lead to the meaning.

ALL ROADS LEAD TO THE MEANING OF A PLAY

Let's look at some examples of unity within variety.

Word

Particular words or phrases may be repeated in various places in a single play to build up a composite meaning. Or they may change their meaning depending on who is saying them and under what circumstances.

Take the word *water* in *Macbeth*. When Macbeth has killed the good king, he comes in with bloody hands and says,

> Will all great Neptune's ocean wash this blood
> Clean from my hand? No; this my hand will rather
> The multitudinous seas incarnadine
> Making the green one red.   (II.ii.57–60)

He has not used the word *water* itself, but his phrases assert that all the water in the world cannot clean his hands of blood. A few lines later, Lady Macbeth says, of her own bloody hands, "A little water clears us of this deed" (II.ii.64). Is she right? We know water can wash off the physical blood. Can water clear them of guilt? Macbeth next sees blood itself as a river:

> I am in blood
> Stepp'd in so far that, should I wade no more,
> Returning were as tedious as go o'er.   (III.iv.135–37)

Toward the end, when Lady Macbeth comes in sleepwalking, her hell is to be washing her hands forever and never succeeding in washing the imaginary blood away:

Doctor:	Look how she rubs her hands.
Gentlewoman:	It is an accustom'd action with her, to seem thus washing her hands. I have known her continue in this a quarter of an hour.
Lady M.:	Yet here's a spot. . . . What, will these hands ne'er be clean? . . .Wash your hands. (V.i.26–62)

All this washing, in physical water and imaginary water, cannot rid her of her guilt. The implication is that the only water that might serve is the holy water of repentance. But she is far from repenting.

There is a wonderful pun in the title of the play *Twelfth Night, or What You Will*. The subtitle is partly a theatrical joke, a cliché phrase, as in the titles of *Much Ado about Nothing, All's Well That Ends Well,* and *As You Like It*. But the word *will* in *What You Will*, also hints at the subject of the play. *Will* in Shakespeare's time meant not only one's ability to choose (free will), but also willfulness, and also sexual desire. The play shows us a world of people locked into their own willful ideas about love until a pair of twins from outside their world break in to it and turn things upside down. It is Providence's way of correcting the proud human will: mix things up in order to straighten them out as the people never could do for themselves.

Follow the word *nothing* in *King Lear*, and you will find that five repetitions of the word begin the dramatic conflict of the play:

Lear:	. . . what can you say to draw
	A third more opulent than your sisters'? Speak.
Cordelia:	Nothing, my lord.
Lear:	Nothing?
Cordelia:	Nothing.
Lear:	Nothing will come of nothing, speak again
	(I.i.85–90)

Thereafter, the word appears over and over in many significant variations on the theme. When asked later in the same scene whether he will change his mind about disinheriting his good daughter and instead give something for her dowry, Lear replies, "Nothing. I have sworn. I am firm"

(I.i.245). When in the next scene Gloucester asks his bastard son,

Gloucester:	What paper were you reading?
Edmund:	Nothing, my lord.
Gloucester:	No? What needed then that terrible dispatch of it into your pocket? The quality of nothing hath not such need to hide itself. Let's see. Come, if it be nothing, I shall not need spectacles.

(I.ii.30–35)

Lear has the following exchange with his fool, beginning with the conclusion of a song:

Fool:	. . . And thou shalt have more Than two tens to a score [a score = twenty].
Kent:	This is nothing, Fool.
Fool:	Then 'tis like the breath of an unfee'd lawyer, you gave me nothing for't. Can you make no use of nothing, nuncle?
Lear:	Why, no, boy, nothing can be made out of nothing.

(I.iv.126–133)

The fool soon adds,

thou hast par'd thy wit o' both sides, and left nothing i' th' middle.
. . . I am better than thou art now, I am a Fool, thou art nothing.

(I.iv.187–194)

When the Earl of Kent, in disguise as a lowly serving man, is put in the stocks, he observes, "Nothing almost sees miracles / But misery" (II.ii.165–66). And when Edgar, to save his life, takes on the disguise of a mad beggar, he says, "Edgar I nothing am" (II.iii.21). Seeing that mad beggar, Lear thinks the fellow has been brought to his plight by daughters like Lear's own:

Couldst thou save nothing? Wouldst thou give 'em all? . . .
Death, traitor! nothing could have subdu'd nature
To such a lowness but his unkind daughters.   (III.iv.64–71)

Edgar observes to the air, "The wretch that thou has blown unto the worst / Owes nothing to thy blasts" (IV.i.8–9). And when he is beginning to take on his own voice again, "In nothing am I chang'd / But in my garments" (IV.vi.9–10). Finally, when Edgar is facing his villainous brother, he says, "thou art in nothing less / Than I have here proclaim'd thee" (V.iii.94–95).

What do all these "nothings" add up to? Something very profound indeed, but not something that can be properly said apart from the words of the whole play. It is true that measuring by arithmetic, more than two tens to a score (twenty) is zero, since two tens equal twenty. But measuring by the spirit, by the moral implications, "nothing" is a gift when having "all" blinds men to what is valuable. In order to save Lear from himself, from his worship of his own ego, reality (or we might say nature, or the gods, or Providence) has reduced him to nothing (no kingdom, no possessions, no knights, no place to sleep, and finally no rationality). But this reduction through suffering redeems him. Kent has said, "Nothing almost sees miracles but misery": Lear's misery, his becoming nothing, prepares him to see the miracle of the continued goodness in his youngest daughter, Cordelia. It also prepares us to see the miracle of his restored love.

Image

As we saw with the idea of water in *Macbeth*, not only words may be repeated and developed through a play to unfold its meaning. Images, too, may be repeated and developed.

In *The Merchant of Venice*, those suitors who wish to marry the wealthy Portia must guess in which of three caskets her picture lies. If they pick the wrong one, they must swear never to marry. Each casket has a motto upon it: On the gold casket, "Who chooseth me shall gain what many men desire"; on the silver, "Who chooseth me shall get as much as he deserves"; and on the lead, "Who chooseth me must give and hazard all he hath" (II.vii.5,7,9). Guess which casket holds the picture of the lady. The play is filled with images of gold and silver and money and acquisition and wealth. Some seek to gain it. Some seek to give it away. Where does true reward lie? The caskets tell the answer.

Follow the images of black and white through *Othello* and you will see how Shakespeare uses their contrast to unify the play. The stereotype of the time had white representing good and black evil. (In medieval and Renaissance paintings, the devil was painted black.) Othello is, in Shakespeare's speech, a blackamoor, meaning a dark-skinned African.

Desdemona is white. The difference in their complexions is the ground of this use of images in the play. But difference of race is not the play's point, nor is the play implying that Othello is bad because he is black or Desdemona good because she is white. The deepest evil in the play is that of Iago, who is also white. Othello stands for man, and the question of the play is whether man will choose to side with good or with evil, whether he will love or hate, forgive or kill. In other words, will Othello give up his pride for his wife or his wife for his pride.

Shakespeare and his audience believed that all men are sinners, that is, to some degree black on the inside. Othello is, like all of us, tainted with the devil's color. Nonetheless, like all of us he has a choice: Desdemona (who means faith and love) or Iago (who means jealousy and betrayal). What will he do? Will he keep his soul pure despite his fallen human nature? Or will he rather choose to corrupt his soul by killing her?

Note that in Shakespeare's day, when the actors would have been Caucasian, the actor playing Othello would have added to the words some heavy makeup to make the character's race visible. In our modern, diverse society many theatres engage in color-blind casting, and our power to suspend disbelief (see Chapter 15) makes the race of the actor irrelevant in most cases. In this case, however, the colors of the skins of Othello and Desdemona play a crucial role in the imagery of the play. Casting a white actor as Othello or a black one as Desdemona would significantly obscure the overall effect of the play.

Speech

Like words and images, figures of speech, too, contribute to a play's unity.

Romeo and Juliet is a play filled with oxymorons (from the Greek *oxys*, sharp, and *moros*, foolish). An oxymoron, in Shakespeare's time also called a *paradox*, is a phrase that is pointedly foolish because it intentionally contradicts itself (like "hot ice" or "cold fire"). Romeo has one whole speech filled with oxymorons and Juliet another. Here are some of Romeo's oxymorons:

> Why then, O brawling love! O loving hate!
> O any thing, of nothing first create!
> O heavy lightness, serious vanity,
> Misshapen chaos of well-seeming forms,
> Feather of lead, bright smoke, cold fire, sick health,

> Still-waking sleep, that is not what it is!
> This love feel I, that feel no love in this.   (I.i.176–82)

Here are some of Juliet's:

> O serpent heart, hid with a flow'ring face!
> Did ever dragon keep so fair a cave?
> Beautiful tyrant! fiend angelical!
> Dove-feather'd raven! wolvish ravening lamb!
> Despisèd substance of divinest show!
> Just opposite to what thou justly seem'st,
> A damnèd saint, an honorable villain!   (III.ii.73–79)

But Shakespeare is up to more than just playing with this rhetorical device. He has taken the rhetorical device of the oxymoron as a unifying principle for the play as a whole, not only for its phrases but for its characters and plot. *Romeo and Juliet* is a tragedy of opposites: lovers from families that hate, youth in conflict with age, marriage and killing on one day, hope and despair, fate and defiance of fate, healing and poison, rash haste and agonizing delay. What hate divides, love joins; what love initiates, death ends. The whole play is built on the joining of opposites. One almost cannot speak of this play except in oxymorons.

Action

Action too, like words, images, and figures of speech, can contribute to unity.

Consider *Richard II*. Just as the form of *Romeo and Juliet* is built upon the oxymoron, so *Richard II* is built upon the rhetorical device called *chiasmus* (a mirror-image or *a-b-b-a* structure—see Chapter 4). Henry rises as Richard falls. Merit comes to power as Right declines. As the play proceeds, we feel the focused, strong-minded, kingly qualities of Henry as he grows, step by step, into a strong and capable king. At the same time, we see the weak, self-indulgent, sentimental qualities of the rightful but incompetent King Richard as his abuses of the kingship bring him closer and closer to being deposed. In the middle of the play, the two movements cross when the kings both have their hands on the crown as one is handing it over to the other. The chiasmus of speech ("Ay, no, no, ay"—IV.i.201) illuminates this chiasmus of action, the crossing of the paths of the falling king and the rising king. Then, at the very end of the play, Henry begins to suffer the troubles that come from his having deposed the rightful king. At the same time, Richard, in prison and about to be killed, is moved to a burst of uncharacteristic nobility—another chiasmic reversal.

What is the meaning of these contrasting events? The variety of movements—up from banishment to kingship, down from kingship to prison and death—are a representation of the up and down movement of English history toward a single truth: England can be well only if her king has *both* right and merit. There is no stability in a rightful king without merit (like Richard II) and none in a meritorious king without clear right (like Henry IV). Henry's son, Prince Hal, knows this and will strive to unite them both in himself for the good of the commonwealth when he becomes King Henry V. His effort is recorded in the following three plays of the tetralogy (*1* and *2 Henry IV* and *Henry V*).

Scene

The small, seemingly non-dramatic scenes in Shakespeare are no less contributory to the plays' unity of theme than the big ones. The Old Man and Ross in *Macbeth*, who list the forms of chaos seen in the natural world on the night of Duncan's murder, reinforce our comprehension of the significance of Macbeth's crime (II.iv.1–20). The little mini-scene at the beginning of Act II, Scene ii, of *Hamlet*, comprising Hamlet's speech to the players, is central to the philosophical meaning of the play. In *Richard II*, the condition of England is reflected in a small scene in which a gardener compares the King's garden that he keeps to the kingdom of England:

> Bullingbrook [i.e., Henry IV]
> Hath seized the wasteful King. O, what pity is it
> That he [i.e., Richard II] had not so trimmed and dressed his land
> As we this garden! We at time of year
> Do wound the bark, the skin of our fruit-trees,
> Lest being over-proud in sap and blood,
> With too much riches it confound itself;
> Had he done so to great and growing men,
> They might have lived to bear and he to taste
> Their fruits of duty. Superfluous branches
> We lop away, that bearing boughs may live;
> Had he done so, himself had borne the crown,
> Which waste of idle hours hath quite thrown down. (III.iv.54–66)

In *Henry IV, Part 1,* the state of the local inn discussed by the two carriers in Act II, Scene i, serves a similar function. "This house is turned upside down since Robin ostler died" (ll. 10-11). (An *ostler* or *hostler* was the caretaker of the horses and mules of travelers stopping at an inn.) The traveler here implies that England is turned upside down since the time of King Richard II (or perhaps of King Edward III). It always pays to attend to the little scenes.

Character

Of course characters, too, contribute to a play's unity.

The use of foils in *Hamlet* and *Henry IV, Part 1,* was discussed in Chapter 5. Now we can better understand what that complex use of foils accomplishes. The similarities between different characters sharpen our awareness of their differences, and their differences sharpen our awareness of the thematic unity of the play. There could hardly be two more different characters than the fat, self-indulgent, cowardly Sir John Falstaff and the intense, battle-hungry, brave Hotspur. Yet both talk a lot about honor, and, in opposite ways, both miss the bull's-eye of honor.

Falstaff misses it because he doesn't care for honor at all. He'd like to be *thought* honorable, but not by risking anything to earn the "good name." "I would to God thou and I knew where a commodity of good names were to be bought" (I.ii.82–83), he says—*bought* not *earned*. He wants to save his skin whatever the cost to his reputation. Hotspur says he wants honor, but it is glorious reputation that he really wants, reputation to be gained by winning in battle against no matter what opponent. Moved by the idea of victory for its own sake, he fails to see the dishonor in causing a civil war in the kingdom. Prince Hal, who appears to everyone but the audience to be dishonorable, turns out to be the representative of true honor in the play. He shows us that honor lies neither in other people's impressions nor in winning battles. It lies in right action based upon right thought. It lies even in getting a bad reputation when such a sacrifice serves the good of the commonwealth. It is all the characters together that lead us to this underlying truth about honor. That is the unity within this remarkable variety.

Similarly, in *Hamlet* the characters Hamlet, Laertes, Fortinbras, Horatio, Claudius, the Gravedigger, and others shed light on the question of revenge, of how to do the right thing when doing the wrong thing might lead to hell. In *King Lear* all the characters in the play support the two main characters, Lear and Gloucester, in contributing to the theme of the purgatorial potential in human suffering.

Plot

The most obvious element of a play that contributes to its unity is the main story it is telling—the plot. But Shakespeare adds subplots for variety, not to divide or weaken, but to enhance and deepen the play's unity.

What the scholars call a *subplot* is a story secondary to the main one. It unfolds among different characters in a different situation. A subplot is used not simply to vary our attention and to build suspense for the main plot, though it does do these things. The real point of a good subplot is to reinforce the meaning of the whole. The meaning of the play comes through the *relation* between the subplot and the main plot. In this art, as in many others, Shakespeare is supreme.

One of the greatest examples is in *King Lear*. In the main plot a king has three daughters, two of whom are evil and do their best to destroy their father, and one of whom is good, though the king does not realize it until he has disowned her and suffered profoundly. In the subplot, an earl has two sons, the elder legitimate and loving, the younger a bastard and a villain. The subplot is so well developed that it could easily make a whole play by itself. Early in both plots the evil children overthrow their fathers, warring against the order of nature and society. This happens in large part because of the moral and spiritual blindness of the fathers.

The contrasts between the two plots emphasize their parallel structure. The good children are the youngest daughter and the older son, the evil are the older daughters and the younger son. The king bestows his kingdom on the evil daughters, not realizing they will try to ruin him. The earl bestows his earldom on the evil younger son, not realizing that the younger son has tricked him into believing his elder son is a villain. Both fathers are self-deluded. During the course of the play both learn their errors. The earl's moral blindness is punished and purged by his being physically blinded. The king's irrational egotism is punished and purged by his going mad.

Why tell the story twice? Isn't one version of it enough? But it is just here that Shakespeare's genius comes to fullness. Because the most important relation between the stories is not that they are similar tales. In being similar, they become two versions of *one* tale. The earl, Gloucester, has committed the specific sin of adultery. He is later physically blinded. When he wants to die, he tries to jump off a cliff. His evil son is literally a bastard who worships nature and wants to gain the earl's (and the legitimate brother's) land through breaking the laws of nature and of nations. The good son disguises himself as a mad beggar to escape his brother's trap. Thus, in the earl's tale, the conflicts are explicit, external, visible, political, and practical.

By contrast, in the king's tale, the conflicts are implicit, internal, invisible, emotional, spiritual. The king's sin is not legally adultery. But when he disowns the good daughter and trusts the evil ones, he commits a kind of moral adultery. We recognize that all the more because Shakespeare has located the literal adultery elsewhere, bringing it to mind even as he gets it out of the way, so that we can go more deeply into what moral adultery means. The loss of physical sight in the earl prepares us to comprehend the deeper loss of rational understanding in the king. Where the earl tries to commit suicide by jumping off an imaginary physical cliff, the king imagines he is in hell and the vision of his good daughter is of a "soul in bliss." While the earl's good son, to disguise himself, sinks to the lowest level of humanity, a mad beggar, and then labors to help his father, the king's good daughter loses first an army and then her life in the effort to help her father. Pretend madness in the earl plot becomes real madness in the king plot. Where the earl is physically blinded and thereby comes to recognition of the external truth, the king is intellectually blinded—i.e., he goes mad—and thereby comes to insight about the internal truth. And so on.

What is accomplished by all this external/internal parallelism? By using the double plot, Shakespeare enables us to enter more deeply into the invisible realms of the soul than we could if the plot were single. Having understood the significant relation between father and children in the more obvious subplot, we are awakened to the less easily visible spiritual mysteries of such relations in the main plot.

One can point to parallel plots in almost every Shakespeare play, whether early in his career (two sets of twin brothers in *The Comedy of Errors*; three couples in *The Taming of the Shrew*) or late (four couples in *The Winter's Tale*; three sets of castaways in *The Tempest*). And always, in the midst of this variety, the interwoven plots draw us to the central meaning of the play, together making a deeply unified whole.

Setting

In Chapter 4 we looked at antithesis in language, in Chapter 5 at antithesis of character with the use of foils, and in the previous section at antithesis in parallel plots. All these kinds of antithesis point us toward unity of meaning. To the same end of unity Shakespeare also uses antithesis of settings. The word *settings* refers to the imagined places in which the various scenes of a play take place. In play after play—comedy, tragedy, history, and romance—the playwright often moves the story from an initial social setting, a city or town or court, out into a natural or rural setting, and then back again.

In the medieval and Renaissance imagination, the city was an image of the ideal social life of man. At its best it exhibited man's highest form of development: materially productive, socially harmonious, artistically fruitful, spiritually coherent, reflecting man's highest gifts of language, reason, art, and the capacity to worship. The good order of the churches, palaces, houses, workshops, markets, waterworks, and defenses of the ideal city reflected the revealed aspect of the order of creation.

By contrast, the forest of the medieval and Renaissance imagination was an image of extra-human and pre-human nature. The darkness and mystery of woods and wilderness were associated not only with what we would call nature—wolves and bears and the threatening elements—but also with the supernatural—the hidden aspect of the order of creation. In the eyes of the church, the dark of the forest was associated with evil spirits, and in the eyes of the common people with the magic and charms of fairies, ogres, and witches.

Both these images—city and forest—reflected not only art and nature in general but also the interior make-up of the individual person. From Plato's time on, the well-run city was an image of the government of the aspiring, rational, artful, just, and worshipful mind over the passions of the heart and the pre-conscious natural forces of the body. The forest, in northern Europe, or wilderness, in southern, was an image of the dark recesses of our human nature—our predispositions and impulses, our hidden fears and desires, and our dreams.

For Shakespeare, when the town or city or court goes wrong, it is often a journey to the country or forest or wilderness that heals, just as when people fall into sickness they may be restored by surrender to the hidden forces of healing deep within their natures, or through the application by the physician of what Friar Lawrence calls "the powerful grace that lies / In plants, herbs, stones, and their true qualities" (*Romeo and Juliet*, II.iii.15–16). Hence, very often Shakespeare depicts movement from one kind of setting to another, from town, city, or court to wood, forest, heath, or sometimes just a different kind of town. This movement almost always involves a journey out of an imperfect social setting, into the wilderness of nature and imagination, and back to the society, whose rational order has been regenerated by its contact with the underlying forces of nature, or the supernatural, or both.

The idea that the health of the city depends on its being in touch with ancient and mysterious natural and supernatural forces can already be seen in *The Eumenides* of the Greek playwright Aeschylus. For Shakespeare, these changes of setting in a sense reverse the story of the Fall of Man (see Christianity in Chapter 7). The characters begin in a social world of faulty or corrupt order, escape its depravities into a healing Edenic world, and then return healed to re-establish a redeemed social order.

Examples of this movement abound in Shakespeare:

In the comedy *A Midsummer Night's Dream* the four lovers, suffering from the artificial love imposed by the social order of Athens, escape into the forest, governed by nature and pervaded by fairy magic, and return to the welcoming city in their right pairs. In *The Merchant of Venice*, we move from the selfishly mercantile world of Venice to the love-governed rural Belmont ("beautiful mountain"), then back to Venice to see it put it into order, and then again to Belmont to celebrate the triumph of love. In the Forest of Arden in *As You Like It* all the escapees from the corrupt court are tested and properly coupled, until the court (in the person of the usurping Duke), pursuing them, itself is healed there.

The antithesis of setting is as useful in tragedy as in comedy. The murder of Julius Caesar in Rome is expiated outside the city on the fields of battle. Hamlet must go on a sea voyage to find his true calling at home. Lear must go out onto the heath in a storm and into madness so that his reason and his will may be healed. Macbeth seeks power at court by succumbing to the poisonous temptations met on the heath, representations of the wilderness in his own mind, and Birnam Wood itself seems to go on a healing march toward Dunsinane Castle to cure Scotland of that poison. In *Antony and Cleopatra*, the order of Rome is explicitly and repeatedly contrasted with the indulgences of Egypt.

In the histories, too, the same contrast may be observed. Though uncorrupted, Prince Hal must seem to descend into the corrupt ale houses of London and must win a crucial battle in the open fields in order to secure his place as king back at the court.

The romances bring this technique to its fullest richness. In *The Winter's Tale* the wintry court of injustice of the jealous Leontes in Sicilia is contrasted with the summery pastoral delights of Bohemia. The entire play of *The Tempest* takes place on the deserted island governed by Prospero's magic, its context the past corruption and future restoration of order in Naples and Milan.

Theme

Finally, unity is achieved in Shakespeare's plays through theme. There are often more than one or two themes developed in a play, but the themes are always related by an underlying unity.

Macbeth's motive for murdering the good king is "Vaulting ambition" (I.vii.27). The theme of the unnaturalness of that selfish ambition is conveyed in Macbeth's soliloquies. That same theme is reflected in the natural world itself when a little mousing owl attacks a great falcon. It is reflected in the words of the drunken porter, who imagines that letting people into Macbeth's castle is like letting the damned—selfishly sinful souls—into hell. It is reflected by contrast in the self-sacrificing courage of Macduff and Malcolm and Siward, even of Young Siward, whom we see in only one scene. What it means to kill the good king Duncan is a mirror image of what it means to kill the innocent children of Macduff. The anguish of the guilty conscience expressed in Lady Macbeth's madness is a version of the anguish of the guilty conscience in Macbeth's last soliloquies. The witches, the stormy night, the comments of the Old Man, the holiness of the English king, the "dagger of the mind" that Macbeth sees, and the apparent moving of Birnam Wood—every detail of the play reinforces the central drama of a man who has chosen to war against the natural order of the universe. "For mine own good all causes shall give way," says Macbeth (III.iv.134–35), and that sentence, too, is a hologram of the whole play, which shows us what happens, both inside and outside of him, when a man betrays all good to serve only himself.

In *Measure for Measure*, when the Duke of Vienna makes Angelo his deputy to rule in his absence, he says,

> Mortality and mercy in Vienna
> Live in thy tongue and heart.   (I.i.44–45)

That is, you have the power both to punish and to forgive. Capital punishment lies in the power of the ruler's speech; pardon lies in the promptings of his heart. The Duke continues,

> Your scope is as mine own,
> So to enforce or qualify the laws
> As to your soul seems good.   (I.i.64–66)

Enforce in justice, or qualify in mercy. In a soliloquy, the Duke adds,

He who the sword of heaven will bear
Should be as holy as severe. (III.ii.261–62)

That is, as merciful as he is just. The theme then runs all the way through the play. Isabella represents the principle of mercy but must act with severe justice. The Duke represents the principle of justice but teaches the whole city about mercy. He is dressed alternately as a duke and as a Franciscan Friar, representing that the same man wears the mantles of both principles, justice and mercy. The play becomes a representation of the tempering of justice with mercy that is required in every ruler in the macrocosm of the state and every person in the microcosm of his own life. In the end, the play itself becomes a dramatic representation of the marriage of the seemingly irreconcilable virtues of justice and mercy.

UNITY JOINS US

The ultimate unity of each play is that to which it gives birth in our own imagination—the imagination of the audience or the reader. Not that we invent it. Shakespeare so arranges our experience of his plays that we will see the unity, no matter how many particular lines we may get or miss in any one performance or reading. And whatever our avenues of entry into a play may be, shared or personal, whether we first grasp the play through words or sets or characters or story or all of them together, by the end of the play, we will have come, with all the rest of the audience, to the same unity of meaning that the play has striven to incarnate in our experience.

The epilogue to *The Tempest* is one of the greatest illustrations in Shakespeare's writing of this audience experience of unity. And it gives a typically rich Shakespearean sense to the term *meta-* as applied to our awareness of the meaning of a play. At the surface level, that of the plot of the play, the character Prospero is requesting the audience's permission to depart from the imaginary island to imaginary Naples—the play's setting for its version of "happily ever after." At another, somewhat more "meta," level, the epilogue, spoken by the actor who has played Prospero, is a conventional request for applause from the audience at the play's end. (Similar gestures are made by Puck at the end of *A Midsummer Night's Dream*, by the chorus at the end of *Henry V*, by the boy actor who played Rosalind in *As You Like It*, by Feste in his song at the end of *Twelfth Night*, and by Gower at the end of *Pericles*.) The actor is asking permission to leave the stage, and the play is over only when the audience claps to give that permission. Scholars debate whether there is a third "meta" level, the level at which Shakespeare himself, the playwright, is uttering his own farewell to the stage, from which he is about to retire to Stratford. (My own view is that indeed this third level is present here.)

But there is yet one more "meta" level to the Epilogue. What are the character Prospero, the actor playing Prospero, and the playwright asking the audience to do? Here is his speech:

> Now my charms are all o'erthrown
> And what strength I have's mine own,
> Which is most faint. Now 'tis true,
> I must be here confined by you,
> Or sent to Naples. Let me not,
> Since I have my dukedom got,
> And pardoned the deceiver, dwell
> In this bare island by your spell,
> But release me from my bands
> With the help of your good hands.
> Gentle breath of yours my sails
> Must fill, or else my project fails,
> Which was to please. Now I want
> Spirits to enforce, art to enchant,
> And my ending is despair,
> Unless I be relieved by prayer,
> Which pierces so, that it assaults
> Mercy itself, and frees all faults.
> As you from crimes would pardoned be,
> Let your indulgence set me free.   (Epi. 1–20)

Let us imagine that we are in the audience at the Globe or the Blackfriars when this play was performed. What do we do after these final words of the play? We clap our hands, as requested. And what does our clapping mean? For Prospero, who has pardoned his enemies and freed his servant Ariel, has asked us to set *him* free; and the actor, in the same words, has asked us to set *him* free to go home for supper; and the author in the same words has asked us to set *him* free too, after his career of pleasing us with magical plays. Each is praying for us to judge his play mercifully by clapping. And we are asked to do so on what grounds? We are asked to pardon the character, the actor, and the author for their respective theatrical crimes on the grounds that we too wish to be pardoned for our own perhaps moral crimes, to free them from their faults with our forgiveness. When we do clap, our gesture therefore now becomes four things.

1. the sign of the ritual ending of the play and the fading of the insubstantial pageant and its fictional world;
2. the sign of our approval of the accomplishments of the character Prospero, the actor of Prospero, and the playwright and our forgiveness of their theatrical "crimes";
3. the sign of our own wish to be forgiven for our crimes or sins; and
4. the sign of our approval of and participation in the doctrine of forgiveness expressed in the final lines, a doctrine quite familiar to Shakespeare's audience in a slightly different set of words: "Forgive us our debts, as we also forgive our debtors," words which may be found in the Gospel of Matthew (6:12) in the Geneva edition of 1599 that was probably the one Shakespeare read.

The entire play has been a story of sin and forgiveness, of virtue overcoming vice not only with magical power over the physical world but with spiritual power over the temptation to revenge. Prospero has said,

> Though with their high wrongs I am struck to th' quick
> Yet, with my nobler reason, 'gainst my fury
> Do I take part. The rarer action is
> In virtue than in vengeance. They being penitent,
> The sole drift of my purpose doth extend
> Not a frown further.   (V.i.25–30)

Now he asks us to thank the players and the play, to release him, to release the actor playing him, to release the author, and to release all our penitent debtors from the bands of debt, and to express our own willing participation in the doctrine of forgiveness that the play has brought to life—all through bringing that doctrine to life here and now in our own clapping.

Here, in one bit of theatrical genius, an imaginary world, the literal world, the moral world, the Christian faith, and the individual soul of each audience member are united in a single gesture, the ritual gesture of clapping. The epilogue turns that simple gesture into a communion, a common participation in the doctrine of the relation of repentance and forgiveness to salvation, which the play illustrates and its author believed to be the deepest truth of life.

7
Why All the Footnotes?
—Shakespeare's Mental Furniture

There are three basic reasons that we need footnotes in editions of Shakespeare's works: 1. He uses words we don't know; 2. He uses words we think we know but in a different sense; and 3. He writes within a Renaissance worldview that is in many ways very different from ours. This does not mean that what he writes is not deeply meaningful to us, to people in all times and places. But just as we need to know what his words signify if we are to perceive those meanings, so we need to grasp the differences between his audience's worldview and our own.

Let's start with words Shakespeare uses that we don't know.

WORDS WE DON'T KNOW

Because the language has changed in the four hundred years since Shakespeare lived, we need footnotes to clarify words with which we are no longer familiar. When we read Hamlet's phrase "hoist with his own petar" (III.iv.207), we recognize the need for a footnote. That footnote would explain that *hoist* is a past participle of the old verb *hoise*, meaning to blow up into the air, destroy, and *petar* is an older form of *petard*, an explosive device for breaching walls or knocking out gates, so that the phrase means "blown up with his own bomb."

WORDS WE THINK WE KNOW

We also need footnotes—though we may not at first recognize that we do—to explain the words that Shakespeare used in one sense that we use in another. To us *still* means continuing up to and through the present: "Are you still studying Latin?" "Do you still like chocolate?" But Shakespeare uses the same word to mean "always": "The world is still deceived with ornament" (*Merchant of Venice*, III.ii.74), meaning the world is always deceived by outward shows. Similarly for Shakespeare *suggestion* most commonly means "temptation." *Ghostly* can mean "spiritual," as in "ghostly father," meaning priest. *Happy* can mean "fortunate." *Addition* can often mean "description, list of characteristics, the qualities of one's reputation" (from what is added to a person's name in order to distinguish him or her). Because we may often assume that our modern sense of a word fits the context, we often overlook the actual meaning that Shakespeare intends. For this reason, reading any Shakespeare play a second time with all the footnotes can yield a richer experience than just reading the play through without the notes.

But much more than the specific senses of words stands between us and our appreciation of what Shakespeare means. His world view and ours differ in many crucial respects, and grasping those differences is essential to our experiencing the deepest meanings in Shakespeare's works. I'm going to try to illustrate what I mean with a little fantasy called "Shakespeare and Electricity."

SHAKESPEARE AND ELECTRICITY

Imagine that Shakespeare is suddenly conveyed by a time machine to the present. Sitting in a bar, which he would call a tavern or an alehouse, he overhears two men in conversation. One says, "My supervisor blew a fuse today when his website froze." The other says, "You think that's bad? My girlfriend just pulled the plug on our relationship."

What does Shakespeare think they mean? From the Latin he would know that a supervisor is someone who looks over something. But "blow a fuse"? He would guess that *fuse* was from Latin, but he would have no idea that "to blow a fuse" is a metaphor for losing one's temper. (If you've grown up only with circuit breakers, perhaps even you may need a footnote to define the word *fuse* as used by the man in the bar.) "When his website froze" might bring to Shakespeare's mind the image of winter cold freezing a spidery place or, metaphorically, a place where the over-looker had laid a trap. In other words, he'd have it all wrong. He would feel that the phrase made no sense and want a footnote, which he would call a gloss.

So far the need for a footnote for the sake of Shakespeare's under-standing is obvious. But let's now look further. Let's assume he could guess the meaning of *girlfriend* and *relationship*. But what about "pulled the plug"? Shakespeare didn't use the word *plug*, which came to English, late in Shakespeare's life, from the Dutch for what he would have called a bung, the wooden stopper in the opening (or "bung hole") of a barrel. If, indeed, he had heard the word, Shakespeare might at first suppose that the girlfriend had pulled out the stopper of a beer barrel to celebrate with endless drink. But then, seeing the man's unhappiness, he would imagine the man's metaphor to mean that the couple's affection was slowly draining away, like beer from a barrel—glug, glug, glug—not instantaneously vanished as we would think, imagining the electric plug of a lamp, TV, or computer suddenly jerked out of the wall socket. Here, Shakespeare would think he knew what the man meant. Not realizing his image was off the mark, he would not look for a footnote.

What would you have to do to explain to Shakespeare what these men at the bar really did mean? You might say, "You have to think of lights and computers and stuff. You know, electricity." "Elec-*what*?" says Shakespeare. "The power that comes out of the wall socket to run things." "Power from the wall? Are you talking about spirits?" Whew, this is going to be harder than you thought, and not because Shakespeare is stupid. You realize you've got to start from the beginning. You will have to explain our ideas about lightning, describe Ben Franklin with the key on his kite, mention the inventor Thomas Alva Edison, generators, batteries, the Hoover Dam, power lines on telephone poles, and insulated copper-wire. (You can tell him about radio waves and smartphones in a graduate seminar later.)

After a few hours of explanation, Shakespeare will say one of two things: a) "I think I'm beginning to get what they meant by 'blew a fuse' and 'pulled the plug'"; or b) "you must be out of your mind."

And so it is with us trying to understand Shakespeare. We share a language with him and *do* understand the vast majority of his words. But unless we become familiar with the ideas he took for granted, as we take electricity for granted, we will come away from reading and hearing his words with many misconceptions about what he meant. Moreover, the better we know a word, the more likely we are to be misled. Just as we need no footnotes on electricity to explain what "pulled the plug" means, so Shakespeare's audience needed no footnotes to know what the "music of the spheres" meant. But without an introduction to electricity, Shakespeare will hear "web" and "plug" and think of spiders and beer barrels, and without a similar introduction, we hear "music of the spheres" and think of wind-chimes or some musical instrument made of metal balls.

In this chapter you will find brief explanations of a few of the fundamental shared ideas that Shakespeare and his audience took for granted, as we take electricity for granted. Being aware of these ideas will prepare you to understand Shakespeare in his own terms. This does not mean that Shakespeare's work is any less universal. He may not have known about electricity, and we may not think of the sky as crystalline spheres, but like him we can experience the wonder of the starry heavens on a clear night, and like us he knew all about relationships and how they sometimes end.

What Shakespeare is really talking about—body and soul, nature and society, good and evil, success and failure, this world and the next, and so on—are as relevant to us as to audiences of his own time. But our access to what he is saying about those subjects depends on understanding not only the words but also the concepts through which they are expressed. So let's look at the worldview that is the context for all of Shakespeare's thinking.

THE MEDIEVAL SYNTHESIS

In his useful book called *The Discarded Image: An Introduction to Medieval and Renaissance Literature*, the great literary historian and popular writer C.S. Lewis discusses the medieval vision of the world that stands behind Shakespeare's Renaissance vision. He points out how systematic were the minds of medieval thinkers, devoted to unifying all knowledge and belief in works like the summation of theological knowledge (*Summa Theologica*) by Saint Thomas Aquinas and Dante's *Divine Comedy*, which strives to combine into one epic poem about a man's journey to hell, purgatory, and heaven all that was known and believed about earth, the heavens, past and future history, life and death, virtue and sin, redemption and damnation, classicism and Christianity, human psychology, science, language, and literature.

Lewis sets beside these two kinds of work a third, which he calls "the medieval synthesis itself, the whole organization of their theology, science, and history into a single, complex harmonious mental Model of the Universe." This model was "capable of giving . . . satisfaction to the mind . . . vast in scale, but limited and intelligible. . . . Its contents, however rich and various, are in harmony . . . everything links up with everything else . . . in a hierarchical ladder." By "everything" Lewis means all that was known, especially from books, including "Judaic, Pagan, Platonic, Aristotelian, Stoical, Primitive Christian, [and] Patristic" books, or "(by a different classification) chronicles, epic poems, sermons, visions, philosophical treatises, satires." All these traditions and works along with all their contradictions the medieval mind strove to interrelate, arrange, and harmonize in the great "Model of the Universe."[1]

This Medieval Model of the Universe "was not totally and confidently abandoned till the end of the seventeenth century," says Lewis, and it stands behind Shakespeare as the foundation for all the unwavering universal principles that underlie his plays and as background for all the philosophical, moral, theological, social, and political questioning, doubts, and conflicts of his time. The more we are familiar with that Model of the Universe that strove to synthesize all faith and knowledge, the more complete will be our appreciation of Shakespeare's works.

The following are some of the elements that characterize the medieval-Renaissance synthesis inherited by Shakespeare.

HIERARCHY
Universal Hierarchy

The first thing to understand about that medieval Model of the Universe, and therefore about Shakespeare's ideas of the nature of things, is that the whole universe was hierarchical, meaning that everything was in a vertical order, from highest to lowest, in relation to everything else. We tend to think of all men as created equal, as the American Declaration of Independence states, meaning not identical but having equal rights under the rule of law. We believe, often without thinking about it, that a person's rank in society should be determined by his or her individual merits, not by the rank of one's parents, or by religion or race or place of birth. And thanks to Darwin, we also tend to think of all natural beings as equally competing for food and habitat. In our imaginations, the place of a plant or animal in the world depends on physical conditions and adaptations, not on a fixed, God-given plan. To some degree, we may also apply that idea to society, imagining all men, at least in the "state of nature," to be, in the words of Hobbes, in a "war of all against all."

In Shakespeare's time, the picture of the world was different. For the most part, the Renaissance world, including Shakespeare and his audience, believed, with some modifications, in the medieval system of thought. According to those inherited ideas, minerals, plants, animals, human beings, the planets, and the angels were all arranged by God in an order of rank that could not be broken. That vast hierarchy was sometimes called "The Great Chain of Being."

Every created being had its place in the hierarchy as though it were a link in a chain extending from the throne of God down to the lowest elements of brute matter. (The idea grew from concepts in Plato and Aristotle as developed by the Neoplatonists.)[2] To try to change that order was to go against both the will of God and, importantly, one's own nature. Angels like Lucifer and human beings like Macbeth who did try to step above their places in the order suffered for it. Thus Hobbes's war of all against all was possible, but only when free will choices were attempting to break apart that great orderly chain of the hierarchical creation.

The great hierarchy of the universe was recreated within each realm (meaning "kingdom") of our world as well. This idea is not totally foreign to us because we retain vestiges of that system of thought. We still use the term *kingdom* in our scientific classification of living things. And if I ask you (non-scientifically) who is the king of the beasts, you will not hesitate to say the lion. Many still know that the king of the birds is the eagle. King of the fish? The dolphin—because of his magnanimous treatment of men in myth and in the reports of seamen, though some said it was the whale, because of his size. King of the plants? The oak tree. Of the minerals? Gold.

Hierarchical Responsibility

This doctrine of hierarchy was not merely a doctrine of power that gave the higher the right to beat up on the lower. That a king ruled by divine right and could not, under most circumstances, be rightly overthrown did not mean that he could do whatever he wanted. He was obligated to fulfill his function in the hierarchy with justice and mercy, just those qualities with which God ruled the whole universe. And not only the king, but every person at any point in the hierarchy was responsible *to* those above and responsible *for* those below. This principle is concisely exemplified by a sentence in the *Rule for Monasteries* of St. Benedict (Chapter 63: On the Order of the Community): "The juniors . . . should honor their seniors, and the seniors love their juniors."[3]

A knight had to obey and be loyal to his lord, his lord to the king, and the king to God. But at the same time, the king was responsible for taking the best possible care of all those within his realm, making sure not only that his lords were obedient and loyal but also that they in turn looked after their own knights and other dependents too. A good man was defined, in part, by loyalty and obedience to his rightful masters, trustworthiness toward his friends and equals, and just and merciful treatment of his subordinates.

Since all levels of the hierarchy corresponded symbolically to all others, a prince was not only a fallible human being but a representative of rightful authority. He was obeyed not only because he had power but also because everyone recognized that his position was, in the state, akin to that of God in the universe. The aristocrat in his mansion, the father in his family, the lion in the jungle, the eagle in the sky, and the oak in the forest were all honored as kings—the hierarchy in each microcosm reflecting the macrocosm.

The church formed a parallel hierarchy in which clerics represented the government of God over the soul and its eternal condition. Thus a Franciscan friar was seen both as an individual person and as an authoritative voice of the Christian doctrines of free will, love (including the love of one's enemies), and humility, for which no knowledge can substitute. Those doctrines may be summed up as follows: Just as powerful herbs and swords can be turned to good or bad use, so every human being has a free will that can be turned to good or to evil. And just as no herb or sword controls its own destiny, so even the human free will is partly subject to forces greater than itself.

The Angels

According to the very influential work of a Christian Neoplatonist called Dionysius the Areopagite,[4] the hierarchies of angels were arranged under God in three orders of nine ranks: The highest order (devoted to the contemplation of God) included Seraphim, Cherubim, and Thrones; the intermediate order (charged with translating divine potential into created actuality) consisted of Dominations (sometimes called Dominions), Virtues, and Powers; and the third order (charged with action in the created world) was made up of Principalities, Archangels, and Angels. The last were in charge of communicating with human beings.

The Cosmos

The physical cosmos itself was also hierarchical. The hierarchies of the stars, arranged in the order of the zodiac, comprised the constellations, the stars, and the planets, including the sun and the moon. The other planets had names corresponding to the Roman gods: Mercury, Venus, Mars, Saturn, and Jupiter. Light—of the sun (called the "eye of heaven" in Shakespeare's Sonnet 18), the moon, and the stars—was an image of the intellectual light of God. All of these "stars" were imagined to be fixed upon concentric crystalline spheres that revolved, turned by the will of God, in circular (= perfect) motion and produced magnificent harmonies ("the music of the spheres"). Except in moments of special grace, that music was inaudible beneath the lowest sphere, that of the moon, which divided the perfect and unchangeable realm of the heavens from the changeable and fallen world of earth. The sphere of the moon itself partook of both natures, partly changeable (seen in the waxing and waning of the moon each month) and partly unchangeable (seen in the regularity of the moon's changes). On earth, all was subject to change (called "mutability," from the Latin *mutare*, to change, from which we also get our words *mutation* and *mutant*).

Each sphere was thought of as receiving God's grace from above and mediating its descent to everything below, including the realm of man (from emperors and kings to beggars and slaves), the realm of animals (from lions to beetles), the realm of plants (from the oak to the grass in the fields), and the realm of brute matter (from gold to plain dirt).

As C.S. Lewis points out, when we moderns look up at the night sky, we feel we are looking out from a tiny safe place of accidental life into an infinite emptiness dotted with distant light-generating hydrogen fusion reactions, which earlier men called stars, arranged by chance and the laws of nature. And we feel that those fusion reactions could not care less about us. But from ancient times through Shakespeare's day, when people looked at the sky, they felt they were looking in—from a specially created though fallen outskirt, through a harmoniously elaborate dance of created intelligences (invisible except for their light, intentionally arranged in perfect order and beauty), toward the center, the cause and end of all being—the mind of God. If that center did not appear to the human eye as bright as they believed it to be in reality, if they could not actually hear the music of those spheres, this was only because of man's fallen nature. Man's own sinfulness was what obstructed the direct perception of the heavenly realities.

Fortune

In this general understanding of the world as hierarchical there was some mobility both upward and downward. However, such movement happened not solely by man's free choice but also governed by the will of God and the turning wheel of Fortune.

The ancient Roman goddess Fortuna was re-imagined in the Middle Ages as having God's permission to be in charge of the distribution of worldly goods and power, which all knew to be changeable. She was pictured sitting blindfolded on a throne that rested upon the globe of the world and turning a big spinning wheel or wagon wheel. Pictured at the top of the wheel was a little king on his own throne, and at the bottom a beggar in misery. On one side of the wheel was a person climbing upward as the wheel turned, on the other side a person falling downward. So a king might fall to the position of a beggar, and a beggar might rise to the position of king, as Fortune turned her wheel. But because the wheel kept turning, the new king might easily fall again to being a beggar. For this reason, in Shakespeare's plays Fortune was often called a strumpet or a whore because she would not be faithful to any man for long. Some medieval cathedrals depicted this wheel on their western fronts, its spokes being of stone and the spaces between them being windows of glass. That same architectural structure, when seen from inside the church, was a great rose, symbol of the Virgin Mary, to whom the medieval cathedrals were dedicated. So though from outside the world seemed governed by the strumpet Fortune, from inside the same world was revealed to be living under God's grace as represented in the always merciful Virgin Mary.

The Elements

If we have studied any chemistry, we may think of the physical world as being composed of about—as of today—118 elements. Based on the ancient teaching of Empedocles, followed by Plato and Aristotle, the Middle Ages and Renaissance thought of the world as being composed of various combinations of *four* elements: fire, air, water, and earth. And these four, too, had their hierarchical relation. The highest was fire, whose property was to rise upward, attracted to its proper sphere, the sphere of fire imagined to be just beneath the sphere of the moon. Next came air, in a sphere surrounding our globe, then water, and then earth, whose property was to sink downward attracted to its proper sphere, *the* earth.

In addition, based on the teaching of Aristotle, the four elements were characterized by two pairs of opposite qualities: Hot and Cold, Dry and Moist. Fire was thought of as hot and dry; air as hot and moist; water as cold and moist; and earth as cold and dry. You will find these four elements referred to again and again in Shakespeare's writing. For example, King Lear, raging in the storm, calls on each element in turn: fire in "sulph'rous and thought-executing fires," air in "blow winds," water in "cataracts . . . spout till you have drench'd," and earth in "the thick rotundity of the world" (*King Lear*, III.ii.1–9).

The Human Order

The great order of the universe is called the macrocosm (from Greek *macro*, meaning "great, large," and *cosmos*, meaning "order." A *cosmetic* is something that puts the face in order.) Within that macrocosm, there were any number of microcosms (from Greek *micro*, meaning "small"). The state was a microcosm in relation to the universe but a macrocosm in relation to the microcosm of the household or the individual person. Each microcosm was a reflection or mini-version of the macrocosm.

Within the human cosmos, at the top were the emperor (especially in ancient times when the Roman emperor ruled the known world) and then the kings of particular nations. Below the king were the aristocratic hierarchies: dukes and duchesses, earls and their ladies, counts and countesses, barons and their ladies, knights and their ladies. Then came the middle classes: gentlemen and gentlewomen. And finally the lower classes: yeomen, craftsmen, servants, peasants, and beggars. Slaves and mad beggars were at the very bottom of the human hierarchy, a fact that bears remembering when we see Edgar disguising himself in *King Lear*.

What are the implications of this concept of hierarchical order for the government of society?

Monarchy vs. Democracy

Because of the Enlightenment and Romantic ideas to which we are heir, we take for granted that democracy is the best (or least worst) form of government. As Winston Churchill said, "democracy is the worst form of government except for all those others that have been tried." We take for granted, too, the natural equality of all men and the belief that being treated equally by the government is a natural right. These are great advancements in human civilization. But in the eighteenth century, these ideas were relatively new.

In Shakespeare's time, by contrast, the only proper government was monarchical. This idea is clearly related to the hierarchical image of reality. The king, ruling in the microcosm of the state by God's will and answerable only to God, reflected the absolute rule of God in the macrocosm. Not all monarchs were good, of course, but if they were bad, the fault lay in them, not in the form of government. Just as we believe that when our democratically elected leaders lie, cheat, steal, or tyrannize, the fault lies not with our form of government but with individual people.

Unfolding within this prevailing Renaissance idea about monarchy, Shakespeare's plays are filled with discussions of who is a good ruler and who a bad one, who is a rightful ruler and who a wrongful, when may a king be overthrown and when not, and so on. As noted in the section called Good and Evil in Chapter 5, for Shakespeare a good ruler could be really and truly good, even if he were an absolute monarch. Since the order of the universe was hierarchical, the government of any human institution could not be in harmony with the rest of reality if there were not one capable person in charge. A state in which the monarch ruled with strength and wisdom, tempering justice with mercy, was for Shakespeare and most of his audience the best possible form of government, and the only legitimate form.

Conversely, Shakespeare's plays depict democratic rule as synonymous with mob rule. Every gathering of "the people" was subject to being swayed by the demagoguery of one individual who could speak well, and the mob was portrayed as the worst possible instrument for determining the rightness of any course of action. The mob could be swayed as easily to bad behavior as to good. (The American Founders were aware of this danger as well, and strove to protect against it with a representative form of government, checks and balances, the Electoral College, etc.)

When we read *Julius Caesar*, we tend to sympathize with the conspirators, who want to overthrow the man who would supplant the Roman Senate and become a dictator. But Shakespeare means us to see that the motives of the conspirators are either selfish or, as in Brutus, tragically flawed. For while Caesar is a fallible mortal, being a weaker swimmer than Cassius, having one bad ear, and suffering from the falling sickness (i.e., epilepsy), yet at the same time he is in Shakespeare's conception the greatest leader of men of his age and the man destined to consolidate the Roman Empire.

For Shakespeare's world, the killing of Caesar was the worst historical event to have happened in human history apart from the Crucifixion. Shakespeare presents it as being analogous to the Crucifixion in its immediate consequences: darkness in the daytime, eclipse, comet, earthquake, screaming ghosts, lions whelping in the streets, etc. To overthrow Caesar, the secular emperor of the known world, no matter what his weaknesses as a particular man, was akin to attempting the overthrow of God. (Dante had imagined the souls of Brutus and Cassius along with Judas Iscariot in the mouths of Satan in the lowest level of hell, that of the traitors to their rightful rulers.)

It is crucial to understand this attitude toward kingship in order to make Shakespearean sense not only of *Julius Caesar* but also of *Romeo and Juliet, Hamlet, King Lear, Measure for Measure*, the *Henry IV* plays, *A Midsummer Night's Dream*, and in fact every Shakespeare play in which any sort of ruler appears.

The Two Bodies of the King

Shakespeare founds his concept of monarchy partly on the Renaissance idea of the two bodies of the king. In all Shakespeare's plays the king is thought of as both a natural man and the embodiment of the body politic. The body of the natural man refers to the individual person who is the king. He has a character, a personality, a set of physical characteristics, the abilities and weaknesses that might accompany any particular human being. The other body of the king implies the concept that the king is not only a natural man but also an embodiment of the state. As Tudor legal scholar Edmund Plowden wrote,

> the King has in him two Bodies, *viz.* a Body natural, and a Body politic. His Body natural (if it be considered in itself) is a Body mortal, subject to all Infirmities that come by Nature or Accident .... But his Body politic is a Body that cannot be seen or handled, consisting of Policy and Government, and constituted for the Direction of the People, and the Management of the public-weal [= welfare], and this Body is utterly void of ... natural Defects ... which the Body natural is subject to, and for this Cause, what the King does in his Body politic, cannot be invalidated or frustrated by any Disability in his natural Body."[5]

This is why the kings in *Hamlet* are called "Denmark" and "Norway," meaning the king of Denmark, who represents Denmark itself, and the king of Norway, who embodies Norway as a whole. This is also why the king speaks in the royal plural. In *Hamlet* Claudius uses the phrases "our dear brother's death / ... it us befitted ... our hearts ... our whole kingdom / ... we ... think / ... remembrance of ourselves" (I.ii.1–7). "We are amaz'd" says King Richard II (*Richard II*, III.iii.72). When the king speaks as king rather than only as a particular person, he speaks as both himself and the voice of the state. And to attack a king is to attack not only the man who happens to be occupying the throne but the throne and the state themselves.

The Family

The hierarchy was not limited to public life but prevailed in the microcosm of private life as well—the family. A man's home was his castle. That meant that in his own home a man was analogous to a knight or lord in his castle and had the right to defend it from attack. Within that home, he ruled with full authority. Wives were expected to obey their husbands and children their parents. But again, this did not mean that the man of the house was justified in behaving in any way he wanted toward his wife and children. Just as they were obligated to serve and obey him, so was he obligated to care for, protect, and instruct them. Any man who used his God-ordained right to rule as an excuse for the cruel oppression of his wife and children would have been considered a brute who had compromised his right to their obedience.

Of course in practice, then as now, there was distance between reality and the ideal. In Shakespeare's time some men mistreated their wives just as they do now. Then, in addition to breaking the universal rules of justice and kindness, such men were breaking the rule of their responsibility in the hierarchy. Now such men, in addition to breaking the universal rules, break the rule of equality. Thus it is important to realize that in Shakespeare's time the hierarchical right to govern in one's family gave no justification for cruelty or injustice to spouse or children, any more than today such misbehavior is justified by the democratic right to equal treatment under the law or the right to life, liberty, and the pursuit of happiness. The universal values of justice and kindness have not changed.

We should also note that some wives disobeyed their husbands, and whether or not they were justified depended on why. The hierarchy did not demand that they obey a violent drunken brute giving sinful orders. But neither did it justify willful disobedience to reasonable commands meant for their ultimate good.

The Individual

In the modern Western world, we think of a human being as a free individual, who, unless oppressed by wrongful authority, may live however and wherever he or she likes, identifying with whatever group he or she chooses. So much do we take this idea for granted that we too often forget that this freedom for the individual is a new thing in the world, won at great cost. In the medieval and Renaissance world, by contrast, the individual was not an absolute. People were defined (and thought of themselves) in terms of their physical place, social rank, professional class, guild, gender, city, and nation.

Today, in answer to the question "who are you?" (unless you have become a victim of the obliteration of the individual by so-called "identity politics"), you will say your name. Your name would be enough to identify you as you. If you added details, it would only be for particular purposes

(I'm a season-ticket holder; I'm a taxidermist; I was born in Vermont; etc.). In earlier times, by contrast, in answer to "who are you?" you would have to say something like this: "I am Romeo of the Montagues, a Christian gentleman of Verona, of whose Prince I am a loyal subject."

This complex nature of individual identity stands behind the conversation between Romeo and Juliet about Romeo's name.

Juliet: Art thou not Romeo, and a Montague?
Romeo: Neither, fair maid, if either thee dislike.

It also stands behind the power of the word "banishment." To be banished is not only to be forced to move from here to there (packing, change-of-address card to the yet-to-be-invented post office, etc.). It is to be threatened with the loss of one's very identity. If I am banished from Verona—no city, no prince, no rank, no family, no place—then I am reduced to being almost a non-person. In this light note Richard's meditations on who he is once he is no longer king (*Richard II*, IV.i) and "Edgar I nothing am" (in *King Lear*, II.iii.21).

Soul and Body

Even within the microcosm of the individual person there was a hierarchy, which could be either in harmony with the elements, the state, the world, and the heavens, or not. In a well-ordered person the highest authority was the soul, sometimes identified with the mind, sometimes with right reason. Beneath the soul or mind or reason were the emotions or passions, often called *affections*. Then came the physical needs and desires and the physical body itself. A well-ordered human being was one in whom, as Plato had taught, the virtuous mind governed the body and its desires through the rightly trained emotions or affections. By contrast, a failed human being—internally chaotic and therefore inevitably both unhappy and morally bad—was one in whom the higher faculties weakly submitted to the government of the lower, in whom emotions tyrannized over the mind, or the physical desires of the body tyrannized over both.

Each of the aspects of the self was imagined to be located in an organ called its *seat* (from the idea of the throne, and thence the building, where an official, like a king or a judge, sits): reason in the brain, emotions in the heart, lower desires in other organs. The seat of sexual desire, for example, was thought of as being in the liver. Hysteria happened when vapors or spirits called humors arose, against the hierarchical arrangement, out of their proper seat in the womb (*hysteria* comes from the Greek word for womb, *hystera*).

Sometimes these three functions were thought of, again based on Plato, as three souls, or three aspects of soul: the intelligible soul, responsible for intellect and self-consciousness; the sensible soul, responsible for basic awareness, feelings, emotions, and sensations; and the vegetable soul, responsible for physical growth and biological processes. Plants were thought to have vegetable souls only; animals (from the Latin *anima*, meaning soul) to have both vegetable and sensible souls; human beings to have vegetable, sensible, and intelligible souls; and angels to have only intelligible souls, hence they were called pure intelligences.

The Humors

The hierarchy of elements extended into the human body. Each person was characterized by the particular relation, or *complexion*, of the four interior elements, called humors, each combining two of the fundamental natural qualities—blood (hot and moist), phlegm (cold and moist), yellow bile or choler (hot and dry), and black bile (cold and dry). These four humors governed not only skin tone but the whole complex of qualities that made up the body and personality together. Excess blood caused one to be of the *sanguine* type (from Latin *sanguis*, meaning "blood")—red faced and cheerful, like Santa Claus or Sir John Falstaff. Excess phlegm caused one to be *phlegmatic*—dull spirited and lazy, like a couch potato, or gloomy or sullen. Excess yellow bile (*choler*, from the Greek *chole*, bile or gall) made one *choleric*—quickly upset or stirred to anger, like the otherwise cowardly Sir Andrew Aguecheek in *Twelfth Night* or like the brave Hotspur in *Henry IV, Part 1*. And excess black bile (from the Greek *melan*, meaning black) made one *melancholic*— sad or depressed, like Don John in *Much Ado about Nothing* or Jaques in *As You Like It*.

A person in whom these four humors were properly mixed was said to be in *temper* (from *tempus*, the Latin word for time—to be temperate comes from the idea of adjusting to the need of the time). One's *temperament* was one's particular characteristic proportion of the humors, and to be momentarily out of balance was to lose one's *temper*. This way of accounting for human moods will seem less foreign if you consider how we now believe ourselves to be affected by "humors" like adrenaline, endorphins, serotonin, and the other hormones.

The Five Wits

What we call the five senses the Renaissance called the five external senses or wits: sight, hearing, touch, taste, and smell. There were also understood to be five internal wits or capacities of the mind variously named and defined, including the *common sense* or *common wit*, which combines the impressions of the senses and includes the awareness of sensing; *memory*, which retains impressions; *imagination*, which brings impressions to awareness or invents them; *fantasy*, which separates and unites impressions or "play[s] with mental images"; and *estimation*, which evaluates impressions and is aware of "the practical . . . significance of things," enabling "a cow to pick out her own calf" or "an animal to fly from its natural enemy."[6]

CORRESPONDENCE

Related to the idea of universal hierarchy in Shakespeare's time was the doctrine of *correspondence*. According to this concept, every link of the Great Chain of Being was analogous to every other link, every realm to every other realm, each microcosm to the macrocosm. As God is the master of the universe, so the rightful king is master of the state, the man of any family is master of his household, reason is master of the human faculties, the lion is king of the beasts, and so on. The harmony of the spheres is reflected in the harmony of the elements in creation, in the well-run state and household, in the harmonious ordering of the humors and of reason and will, emotion and passion, need and desire in a well-tempered character.

Conversely, when the angels rebelled, hell came into being. Eclipses in the heavens portended trouble for men. The resulting war among the elements brought chaos in the form of storms, earthquakes, lightning descending to earth contrary to its nature, just as disorder in the commonwealth brought civil war among men. Lucifer rebelling against God behaved like a nobleman rebelling against his king, a child supplanting his father, the desires of the blood overwhelming reason, a horse disobeying its human master (as in *Macbeth*, II.iv.14–18), or a sparrow trying to attack an eagle (cf., *Macbeth*, I.ii.35 and II.iv.12–18).

This governing idea of correspondence, expressed through the technique of variation (described under Variation in Speech in Chapter 4), made the whole universe into a treasure trove of living metaphors and poetic imagery to be mined by Shakespeare's fertile imagination.

To take only one of thousands of examples of Shakespeare's use of the doctrine of correspondence, let's look at Friar Lawrence's speech about natural herbs in *Romeo and Juliet*:

> I must up-fill this osier cage of ours
> With baleful weeds and precious-juicèd flowers.
> The earth that's nature's mother is her tomb;
> What is her burying grave, that is her womb;
> And from her womb children of divers kind
> We sucking on her natural bosom find:
> Many for many virtues excellent,
> None but for some, and yet all different.
> O, mickle [= much] is the powerful grace that lies
> In plants, herbs, stones, and their true qualities;
> For nought so vile that on the earth doth live
> But to the earth some special good doth give;
> Nor aught so good but, strain'd from that fair use,
> Revolts from true birth, stumbling on abuse.
> Virtue itself turns vice, being misapplied,
> And vice sometime by action dignified.
> Within the infant rind of this weak flower
> Poison hath residence and medicine power;
> For this, being smelt, with that part cheers each part,
> Being tasted, stays all senses with the heart.
> Two such opposèd kings encamp them still [= always]
> In man as well as herbs, grace and rude will;
> And where the worser is predominant,
> Full soon the canker death eats up that plant.   (II.iii.7–30)

After giving the general structure of things, Friar Lawrence likens the qualities in plants to those in human beings. As the gifts in plants are medicine if well used and poison if misapplied, so the gifts of any person are good and healing when guided by virtue and destructive when guided by vice. The speech is in rhymed couplets to give a sense of quiet, orderly meditation to the friar's thoughts. The order of balanced pairs of lines in the verse recreates the order of balanced opposites in the natural and human worlds: baleful/precious, weed/flower, etc. (see Antithesis in Chapter 4). In these antitheses, the idea of correspondence is implicit.

Now let's also consider the specific images. The earth is like mother, tomb, and womb; plants are like children, infants, people; their qualities are like forms of grace, residents, and human virtues, and their right use is like human dignity; their wrong use is like poison, revolt, stumbling, vice, rude will, a worser opposèd king, a bad astrological influence (implied by the word "predominant"), a canker worm, and death. All of these images, whether stated or implied, speak to the correspondence of realms—the realm of nature (implied in the images of weed, flower, plant, herbs, stones), the realm of the human body and soul (in images like stumbling, senses, heart, virtue, vice, life, death), the realm of society and the state (in the images true birth, revolt, opposèd kings, worser king), the realm of the heavens (in the image of predominance, which implies the influence of stars and constellations), and the realm of the divine order (implied in the word "grace").

The use of this kind of correspondence among all realms is a staple of Shakespeare's metaphorical language, and being aware of it helps us to perceive the full weight of his images.

AUTHORITY

First let's be clear about what we mean by the word "authority." Being heirs of the Enlightenment, we believe in human reason and individual liberty. Being heirs of Romanticism, we believe in individualism and progress. As a result, we tend to think of authority as oppressive by definition. We think of the past as inferior to the present and even more inferior to the future. Unless we stop to think about it, liberty to many of us means the freedom to do whatever we want short of hurting others, unhindered by tradition, religion, God, government, teachers, parents, and the past.

As a result of this pre-existing tendency, we delight, for example, in such bumper stickers as "Question Authority." We don't seem to notice the authority that the bumper sticker itself is claiming. Should we question *its* authority? By what authority should we question authority? Suddenly we are faced with the problem of *which* authority we should question.

If we are honest, these questions will lead us to examine our fundamental principles. Is questioning authority the most basic of our beliefs? Are some authorities more authoritative than others? By which principles of judgment are we to judge an authority?

What Shakespeare meant by the word "authority" was significantly different. Whereas we tend to judge authorities in the light of our own desires and goals, Shakespeare and his audience, along with most traditional cultures, East and West, tended to judge their desires and goals in the light of past authorities. Though Shakespeare knew that, being human, traditional authorities must themselves have been fallible, he nevertheless also believed that they were truly authoritative. He believed more or less that Aristotle and St. Paul and Dionysius the Areopagite and Plutarch and Holinshed knew what they were talking about. This is a huge difference from us, and it is crucial in understanding not only references to Aristotle or dramatizations of Plutarch and Holinshed but also the motivations of characters and the meanings of plays.

His belief in the authority of past masters does not mean that Shakespeare did not have a problem with authority. But his problem with it was different from ours. Our problem is to decide whether something said or done in the past has value for us and to know on what grounds we judge it. By contrast, Shakespeare's problem was how to make the self-evident authority of the best authorities of the past into vivid, moving, and significant experience in the present.

To a great extent Shakespeare inherited the authority of the medieval synthesis discussed above, whose unification of the Christian and classical visions of man and his place in Creation not only formed the background of Shakespeare's worldview but provided the poet with a wealth of images and stories.

Christianity

Because of the religious conflicts in England in Shakespeare's time, it was dangerous for any writer to take an open and clear stand on any matter that might become a subject of religious controversy. Shakespeare was a child less than fifty years after Martin Luther's Ninety-five Theses inaugurated the Protestant Reformation. There was no separation of church and state in Shakespeare's England. Both Protestants under Catholic monarchs and Catholics under Protestant monarchs were in danger of persecution. All books and plays were subject to censorship.

As a result, Shakespeare had to make a point of avoiding explicitly sectarian arguments in his plays. He could poke fun at Malvolio for his stuffed-shirt ways, but he had to stop short of directly accusing him of Puritanism. He could show the ghost of Hamlet's father, in the setting of a foreign country, come from "purgatorial fires," but he couldn't be too explicit about where he stood on the Catholic doctrine of purgatory.

As for Shakespeare's own personal beliefs about the various religious controversies of his time, we do not know precisely what they were. However, the obstacles that prevented many from expressing opinions and beliefs in that time, so far from hampering Shakespeare, in fact seem to have had the opposite effect on him. They drove him to articulate in his plays a version of Christianity that *any* Christian believer could embrace. We will probably never know exactly what Shakespeare believed in his heart about the differences in particular doctrines that divided one Christian sect from another. But no poet apart from Dante has ever portrayed the universal, humane spirit at the center of the Christian religion so clearly or so movingly.

There is not room here to outline the entire Christian view of the universe, but several basics that reappear over and over in Shakespeare are worth keeping in mind: God created the universe and man. God gave man free will, the capacity to make free moral choices however constraining the circumstances of nature, society, fortune, and individual psychology. Man, seduced by the serpent, a rebel angel in disguise, fell from grace through his own pride, and falls again daily to the temptations in the world and within his own heart. At man's fall the human soul was weakened, the body was subjected to corruption and eventual death, and the world was cut off from the company of heaven and the music of the spheres. Mankind became subject to mutability, corruption, and mortality. Every human being, whatever his or her circumstances, has the opportunity to be redeemed from corruption, sin, and death through faith in the redeeming grace of God made available to man through the Incarnation and Crucifixion of Christ. (For Catholics that faith was exercised under the authority of the Church and its sacraments, for Protestants under the sole authority of Holy Scripture.) In the meantime, in this life every human person is being tested and will be judged by God, either at the moment of death or at the Last Judgment, for his or her free will choices.

As we saw in Chapter 5, Shakespeare's characters reflect that people may be good (with their virtue rewarded in the next life if not in this), or bad (with their evil punished, eventually, in this life *and* in the next), or mixed, in which case change of heart and penitence are called for to clear the way for redemption.

All these principles, for Shakespeare, are not merely articles of a faith that may be taken seriously here but ignored there. They are built in to the structure of reality and hold true in little ways and in great. Shakespeare set *King Lear* in a pre-Christian world to demonstrate precisely that.

Compare how Kate (in *The Taming of the Shrew*) rebels against rightful authority and how Macbeth does. According to Shakespeare's inherited view of the nature of things, Kate cannot live happily ever after with

Petruchio unless she is converted from pride and rebelliousness to humility and obedience, whereupon she discovers that reality, in the person of her husband, means everything for her good. Macbeth, who refuses to repent for his utterly self-serving rebellion, is hunted down by a coalition of all of reality, including his own nature, and finally expunged from the world he has polluted with his evil will. These plays are not, for Shakespeare, merely illustrations of abstract principles. They are not merely moral lessons. They are representations of the way things really are. And this remains true for all his plays from the first to the last.

Hamlet may struggle to work out just what is going to happen to him in death, but there is no doubt in his mind that God exists and judges all souls. These are unquestioned givens in Hamlet's meditations. Of the four protagonists (who are also sinners) in Shakespeare's four greatest tragedies—*Hamlet*, *Othello*, *King Lear*, and *Macbeth*—we are explicitly meant to believe that two are saved and at least one is damned. Hamlet's "readiness" (V.ii.222) and "Heaven make thee free of it" (V.ii.332), followed by Horatio's "flights of angels sing thee to thy rest" (V.ii.360), and Lear's "forget, and forgive" (IV.vii.83) and "It is a chance that does redeem all sorrows / That ever I have felt" (V.iii.267–68), followed by "Look there, look there!" (V.iii.312), enforce our sense that the spiritual progress of these men has been from benightedness to insight, from self-will to redemption. Macbeth is clearly damned as he explicitly chooses to be. And Othello, choosing to throw away his soul in a final act of pride, will certainly be damned unless he is granted by our imaginations an exceptional divine mercy not expressible within the confines of the play.

Renaissance Classicism and Humanism

By Shakespeare's time, the Renaissance rediscovery of much of the art of antiquity had inspired new attention to the power of human reason in understanding the nature of man and society. Church doctrine, though for the most part not repudiated by the early humanists, underwent re-examination in the light of human reason and classical literature. Much canon law (the law of the church) was replaced by civil law (the law of the city or state). The arts of drama, poetry, music, painting, and architecture flourished. The value of educational preparation for the priesthood gave way to classical learning directed to secular careers. Figures associated with this resurgence of human-centered classical learning include the poets Petrarch and Boccaccio and the Neoplatonists Ficino and Pico della Mirandola. It can be argued that the Protestant Reformation, the

Catholic Counter-Reformation, the Enlightenment, and secular science all grew out of this movement.

Upon Shakespeare the influence of Renaissance Humanism came largely through the influence of the great Christian Humanist scholar Erasmus of Rotterdam and of his friend Sir Thomas More, who succeeded Cardinal Wolsey as Lord High Chancellor of England under Henry VIII. (More was one of the first to educate his daughters as well as his son in the classical languages and literature.) The commitment of Erasmus and More to the training of capable youth in the language and literature of the ancients fostered the foundation of many grammar schools of the kind that Shakespeare probably attended in Stratford (see Did Shakespeare Go to School? in Chapter 2).

As a result of this resurgence of classical learning, in addition to the basic teachings of Christianity, Shakespeare inherited a huge body of knowledge and belief from the classical world: that is, from ancient Greece and Rome and the philosophical and literary traditions to which they gave birth. Just as the Romans traced their mythical origins through Aeneas back to Troy, so Britain traced its mythical origins through Brutus (a different one from the conspirator against Julius Caesar) back to Rome. Greek and Roman history provided not only stories that Shakespeare might dramatize but examples of the lives of important and great men and women, whose experience might shed light on the circumstances and attitudes of his own time and ours.

It would be hard to find a Shakespeare play that lacks a reference to something in Ovid's *Metamorphoses*, for example, and Shakespeare based whole plays on Plutarch's *Lives*. As we saw in Chapter 2, Shakespeare's education consisted in learning (by our standards) a huge amount of Latin literature and history. He and his audience were perhaps more familiar with the names of Hercules and Hector and Achilles and Caesar and Brutus and Mark Antony and Cleopatra than with the Richards and Edwards and Henrys of English history.

In addition, the classical world was the source of the long and elaborate literary tradition which Shakespeare inherited, including stories (from Greek and Roman epics, drama, romance, and history), genres (epic, lyric, oratorical, meditative, and dramatic), theories of education, including the Trivium (grammar, logic, and rhetoric) and the Quadrivium (Arithmetic, Geometry, Music, and Astronomy), and philosophy (Socrates, Plato, Aristotle, Marcus Aurelius, and Boethius, to name only a few).

DISINTEGRATING FORCES

At the same time that Shakespeare was inheriting the great medieval synthesis as the ground of his thought, there were forces in motion that tended to the disintegration of that great synthesis. These forces had been set in motion by the resurgence of the study of ancient languages and art, the emphasis on human reason, and the reassessment of Christian doctrine, all of which characterized Renaissance Classicism and Humanism. Specifically, the fifteenth and sixteenth centuries produced calls for religious reform, radical skepticism, and a passion for the science of the physical world.

Protestant Reformation and Religious Wars

The reassessment of religious doctrines and the reaction to the corruption of elements among the clergy of the Catholic Church were among the forces that led to the Protestant Reformation, whose central figures were Martin Luther and John Calvin. Luther's *Ninety-five Theses*, a list of arguments submitted for debate, and probably nailed to the door of All Saints' Church in Wittenberg, Germany, in 1517, is considered to mark the beginning of the Reformation.

The reform movements, passionately embraced by many, particularly in Northern Europe, focused on certain theological differences with Catholic dogma. Protestants believed that salvation comes only through faith (*sola fide*) and not also through good works (i.e., the sacraments of the Church). Protestants believed that only scripture (*sola scriptura*) and not the Church was the source of true doctrine. Other controversies involved the existence and nature of Purgatory, whether men could benefit spiritually from the merits of the saints, the Church's authorization of the sale of spiritual indulgences, and the actual and perceived corruption of the Catholic clergy and in particular of the Roman Curia (the upper echelons of the Church hierarchy).

The Reformation movement, intertwined with political divisions in Europe, led to a long series of religious wars—Roman Catholics against Huguenots (Calvinists) in France, Belgian and Netherland Protestants against Catholic Spain—culminating in the devastating all-out Thirty Years' War (1618–1648), which resulted in eight million dead. The Peace of Westphalia (1648) effectively ended the European wars between Protestants and Catholics by establishing several principles that became staples of later European and world political history: sovereign states, peaceful coexistence, balance of power, and *cuius regio, eius religio* (the ruler's religion determines the religion of those he rules).

In England, the conflict between the Protestant movement and the Catholic Church took the form of persecutions—of Catholics, then of Protestants, then again of Catholics—by the successive monarchs and their courts and parliaments.

Henry VIII was the first to break with Rome over his desire to divorce his wife and marry Anne Boleyn. He called Parliament into the series of sessions later called "The Reformation Parliament" (1529–1536), which outlawed various relations to the Church of Rome. In 1534, by the *Act of Supremacy*, he made himself the head of the Church of England. (For refusing to accept that act, Sir Thomas More died a martyr and later was recognized as a saint by the Catholic Church.) By 1536 nearly four hundred lesser monasteries had been suppressed and Henry's *Ten Articles of Faith* were published. In 1539 over six hundred of the greater monasteries were suppressed and their property given to the king's favorites or sold. Under Henry's short-lived son, Edward VI, the Catholic mass was abolished and in 1549 use of the Protestant "First Prayer Book" was made compulsory.

When Mary Tudor became queen (1553–1558), she took many steps to restore the position of Catholics and the Church. She married the Catholic Philip II of Spain, reconciled with Rome, and in 1555 repealed the Act of Supremacy, thereby restoring the English church's loyalty to the Pope. She also had many illustrious Protestant leaders burnt at the stake.

Then Elizabeth I became queen and, with the Parliament of 1559, reestablished Protestantism in England. By the *Second Act of Supremacy* Elizabeth became not "supreme head" (because Christ is called the "head of the church") but "Supreme Governor of the Church of England." Use of the Prayer Book of 1552 was required, as was regular church attendance. Under Elizabeth the Puritan movement grew, and by the "Act to Retain the Queen's Majesty's Subjects in Their Obedience" of 1581 Parliament made it an act of high treason to be converted to Catholicism.

Upon the death of Elizabeth in 1603, King James VI of Scotland became King James I of England, thereby uniting the two kingdoms and succeeding Elizabeth as the Supreme Governor of the Church of England. Because he rejected the various demands of the Puritans in the Hampton Court Conference (1604), and because of what they felt to be religious intolerance, the "Pilgrim Fathers" under John Bradford set sail in 1620 for the New World, landing near what was later to become Boston and founding the New Plymouth colony.

During Shakespeare's life (which overlapped with the reigns of Elizabeth and James) all public discussion, including fictional discussion, of religious matters took place in the context of this succession of alternating rules and persecutions. It was always dangerous to espouse, or even seem to espouse, a theological or religious position not approved by the monarch and Parliament. Hence Shakespeare took care to avoid articulating unauthorized religious claims in his plays, or to put them, when necessary, into the mouths of villains or foreigners or both.

Machiavelli

In this context of religious and political conflicts, radical skepticism about religion in the light of practical politics came to be most influentially represented by Niccolo Machiavelli. In his work *The Prince* he advised his prince—meaning the advice to apply to any prince—on how to maintain power and control over the state in the name of stability and the achievement of political goals. The work treats religious observance, faith, and morality as tools of the ruler rather than as absolute goods. As a result, to many Machiavelli seemed to overturn the ultimate authority of God and the moral law in favor of practical success. Where morality served the practical purposes of the prince, it ought to be practiced. Where compromise of moral or religious principles might serve the prince's political purposes, compromise and immorality were called for. As a result of this inversion of the hierarchy of values, Machiavelli became a watchword of English Renaissance drama, a representation of all that was proud, self-serving, immoral, and undermining of the moral tradition and of the political tradition that held the prince to be responsible to God above all.

The clearest example of this perhaps somewhat unjust representation of Machiavelli comes in the prologue to Christopher Marlowe's play *The Jew of Malta*, in which Machiavel says, "I count religion but a childish toy, / And hold there is no sin but ignorance" and "Might [i.e., not God] first made kings, and laws were then most sure / When like the Draco's they were writ in blood." (Draco was an ancient lawgiver of Athenian tradition who made death the penalty for most offenses. The idea that he wrote his laws in blood rather than ink comes via Plutarch.) In Marlowe's play, Machiavel appears as the sponsor of the evil Barabas, whom, ironically, he wishes us to "grace . . . as he deserves." Barabas ends up boiled in the cauldron he had prepared for others, the just punishment for his Machiavellian crimes.

There are three references to Machiavelli in Shakespeare: The English in *Henry VI, Part 1*, before condemning Joan De Pucelle (Joan of Arc) to death, hear her claim three different men, one of whom is the

French Duke of Alanson, to be the father of her supposed unborn child. Thereupon the Duke of York says of his enemy Frenchman, "Alanson, that notorious Machevile?" (V.iv.74). In *Henry VI, Part 3*, the evil Richard, Duke of Gloucester, later to become Richard III, says,

> I can add colors to the chameleon,
> Change shapes with Proteus for advantages,
> And set the murtherous Machevil to school.
> Can I do this and cannot get a crown?
> Tut [= tsk], were it farther off, I'll pluck it down.   (III.ii.191–95)

Through intrigue and murder, he succeeds, though temporarily. To "set to school" means that Richard could teach Machiavelli a thing or two about using evil means to pursue one's own self-interest. Finally, in *The Merry Wives of Windsor*, the Host of the Garter Inn, in an effort to make peace between Sir Hugh Evans, the Welsh parson, and Doctor Caius, the French physician, who are intending to have a duel, rhetorically asks, "Am I politic [= cynically plotting]? Am I subtle [= crafty]? Am I a Machivel [= an intriguer]?" (III.i.101). The implied answer is no.

However moral or immoral the historical Machiavelli may have been, his book seemed to compromise the generally shared values of the age. Possibly under the influence of a book called *Anti-Machiavel: A Discourse upon the Means of Well Governing* (1576), by Innocent Gentillet, a French Huguenot, the English playwrights took the image of Machiavelli to represent the enemy of religion, morality, justice, and righteousness in embodying moral relativism in the service of self-interest and political advantage. The characters who espouse his views almost invariably end up suffering just punishment, and their plans, after varying amounts of destruction, come to nothing.

The New Science

The Reformation movement's renunciation of the absolute authority of the Church and the Machiavellian renunciation of the absolute authority of traditional morality were joined by the new worship of human reason in the area of comprehending and mastering the physical world. The central representative of the aspirations of the new science was Sir Francis Bacon, who served Queen Elizabeth I as her attorney and King James I as Attorney General and then Lord Chancellor.

Bacon was influential as a legal theorist, and his work is said to have influenced the Napoleonic Code and the English law reforms of the nineteenth century. It is to Bacon that we owe the report that the Earl of Essex, just before his failed attempt to overthrow the Queen in 1601, sent his co-conspirator Gelli Merrick to hire Shakespeare's company to do a performance of *Richard II*, about the deposing of a king. Merrick had to pay extra for that performance because, as the company said, it was an old play that "they should have loss in playing . . . because few would come to it." The report appears in Bacon's *Declaration of the Practises and Treasons . . . by Robert late Earle of Essex*. But Bacon's greatest importance was as the author of the *Novum Organum Scientiarum* (1620), his updating of Aristotle's *Organon* on deductive logic. Bacon's new method favored inductive reasoning and experimentation, which became, in practice, the foundation of the modern scientific method. The *Novum Organum* was published after Shakespeare's death, but Bacon had already published *The Advancement of Learning* in 1605. Both these and other works articulate a major force contributing to the disintegration of the medieval synthesis discussed above.

In *The Abolition of Man*, C.S. Lewis points out that Bacon's enterprise was the same as that of the magician: to make man, rather than God, the master of the physical world. Lewis writes,

> For the wise men of old the cardinal problem had been how to conform the soul to reality, and the solution had been knowledge, self-discipline, and virtue. For magic and applied science alike [by contrast] the problem is how to subdue reality to the wishes of men. [To achieve this goal, both the magician and the scientist] are ready to do things hitherto regarded as disgusting and impious—such as digging up and mutilating the dead.[7]

In Christopher Marlowe's *Doctor Faustus*, the protagonist, seeking magical "power" and "omnipotence," sells his soul to the devil in order to become, as he says, "a mighty god."[8] Francis Bacon "rejects magic because it does not work, but his goal is that of the magician,"[9] finding ways to make the physical world do man's bidding.

There is plenty of evidence that Shakespeare valued practical knowledge in the service of people. Friar Lawrence's knowledge of the power of herbs and flowers to harm and heal, quoted above, is an example. Nonetheless, Shakespeare rejects Bacon's valuing of the practical benefits of knowledge above virtue. He is of the older school, as one sees in his portrayal of the art of medicine. What Shakespeare stresses in his good doctors is knowledge in the service of healing and healing in the context of virtuous piety and humility. Examples include the doctor in *King Lear*, English and Scottish Doctors in *Macbeth*, Cerimon in *Pericles*, and Cornelius in *Cymbeline*.

Aware of the disintegrators, Shakespeare throughout his career dramatized the perennial authenticity of the older integrated picture of the world.

DECORUM

Imagine a Superman or Spiderman or Batman movie in which the hero dies after the intermission and there is no sequel. Imagine an automobile commercial on TV that showed the advertised car dusty in normal city traffic instead of squeaky clean on the open highways of Utah. Imagine a TV show featuring a soccer mom without an SUV, or a construction worker having quiche for lunch, or a corporate executive who values virtue more than the bottom line. Hard to do except as a joke? This is because, often without realizing it, we have very specific expectations of our popular entertainments. And when a movie or TV show inadvertently goes too far against those expectations, it loses its audience. (The intentional breaking of our expectations is another matter—see Chapter 15.)

All ages have such expectations of art. But the content of those expectations changes with time and place. In Shakespeare's time and place, such expectations were elaborate and explicit. People spoke and wrote about what was fitting or unfitting for any particular kind of entertainment.

This principle, the "doctrine of appropriateness" as Professor Madeleine Doran describes it,[10] the Renaissance called *decorum*, which, for Shakespeare and his audience, was a fundamental value in every realm of human life. In his *Art of English Poesy* the Elizabethan writer George Puttenham (pronounced "Putnam") writes,

> . . . there is a decency to be observed in every man's action and behavior as well as in his speech and writing. . . . And this decency of man's behavior as well as of his speech must also be deemed by discretion, in which regard the thing that may well become one man to do may not become another, and which is seemly to be done in this place is not so seemly in that, and at such a time decent, but another time undecent, and in such a case and for such a purpose, and to this and that end . . . .[11]

Professor Doran adds,

> Speech and behavior must be appropriate to the person, the place, the time, the circumstance, the end or purpose. . . . The lore of decorum was abundant [in Shakespeare's time] in such forms as the four (or seven) ages of man, the four humours or temperaments, the differences in the sexes, the trades, the social classes, the characteristics of different nationalities and so on.

As we've seen, we too engage in generalizing expectations, which we might call stereotyping. But, writes Professor Doran,

> the renaissance distinctions were more detailed and formalized than with us and were brought home more sharply in the visible signs of color, dress, insignia, and ceremony both public and private. Every renaissance man must have absorbed these things as a commonplace background to his own judgments about people. And everything he learned in school or read in critical theory—if he concerned himself with that—would have confirmed the habit of identifying class [meaning classification, of whatever kind] by signs.[12]

On the subject of the ages of man, Jaques in *As You Like It* gives a set speech famously beginning "All the world's a stage" (II.vii.139ff.). Shakespeare lends his particular magic to the details of the speech by the melancholy Jaques, but the concept was a standard one: Each person's attitude and behavior corresponded more or less to his or her age. That the stage was a mirror of the world was also a commonplace. Shakespeare's own theater was called the Globe, and its motto was *Totus mundus agit histrionem*, meaning "the whole world [i.e., everyone] plays the actor." The world was a macrocosm of the stage, and the stage was a microcosm of the world.

Tied to this idea was the expectation that the characters and situations played on the stage must be representative of what is generally true. To Shakespeare's audience, if a character were not representative of a type, it could be neither significant nor believable. Quirky particularity was either a sign of an underlying type in disguise (to be revealed later) or unbelievable. Only the universal was really true. In practice this meant decorum. What people took for convincing portraits on stage had to fit, or at least acknowledge, their expectations. As Hamlet says to the players, "let your own discretion be your tutor. Suit the action to the word, the word to the action" (*Hamlet*, III.ii.17–18).

Of course Shakespeare is not simply a maker of type characters. The trick was to bring the type alive, to give it particular authenticity, freshness, vitality. And so he did. But we don't have much trouble seeing the individuality and vitality of Shakespeare's characters. What is more difficult for us is to see how much those characters also adhere to Renaissance types that we no longer have in mind.

Look at Portia's satirical list of the qualities of her suitors in *The Merchant of Venice* (I.ii). The Neapolitan cares only about horses; the County Palatine is melancholic; the Frenchman is all changeable surface and no substance; the Scotsman is choleric; the German is a drunk. Among the others Portia makes fun of an Englishman, challenging the audience to laugh at themselves:

> He hath neither Latin, French, nor Italian.... He is a proper man's picture, but alas, who can converse with a dumb show? How oddly he is suited! I think he bought his doublet in Italy, his round hose in France, his bonnet in Germany, and his behavior every where.   (I.ii.69–76)

This would not be so funny if it didn't fit what the audience knew to be true of the typical Englishman abroad.

When Hamlet says, "Frailty, thy name is woman!" (I.ii.146) he is not being guilty of misogyny. Rather, he always thought his mother was of the virtuous-woman type, the kind of woman who will die rather than compromise her own chastity or any other virtue. Examples of that type include Isabel in *Measure for Measure*, Helena in *All's Well That Ends Well*, Cordelia in *King Lear*, and most of the heroines of the late romances—strong, faithful, determined women whose commitment to virtuous love no male argument can derail. Now Hamlet is forced to recognize, with pain, that Gertrude, his mother, is of the frail-woman type, whose receptive nature cannot stand up against intense masculine persuasion. Other members of that category are Lady Anne in *Richard III*, Cressida in *Troilus and Cressida*, and Hamlet's beloved Ophelia, who is not unchaste, but who tragically succumbs to the arguments of her brother and the commands of her father in turning away from Hamlet. Even women who do not collapse under pressure are aware of the danger of doing so. Viola observes,

How easy is it for the proper-false
In women's waxen hearts to set their forms!
Alas, our frailty is the cause, not we,
For such as we are made of, such we be.
(*Twelfth Night*, II.ii.29–32)

And Isabel says,

Women? Help heaven! . . .
                Nay, call us ten times frail
For we are soft as our complexions are,
And credulous to false prints.
(*Measure for Measure*, II.iv.127-30)

This identification of women with softness is a shared commonplace of the age. For a female character to assert otherwise would be to discredit herself, as Lady Macbeth does when she asks the evil spirits to "unsex" her, meaning to remove her feminine softness and compassion and to make her hard, cruel, and remorseless (*Macbeth*, I.v.40ff.).

Yet another type of woman is the quick-witted, inventive, way-ahead-of-men-in-getting-it type. Examples are Portia in *The Merchant of Venice*, Beatrice in *Much Ado about Nothing*, Viola in *Twelfth Night*, Rosalind in *As You Like It*, Paulina in *The Winter's Tale*, and, in a very particular sense, Cleopatra in *Antony and Cleopatra*.

Among men, there is the prudish or detached type, who pretends that his blood is cold and women cannot tempt him (like Benedick in *Much Ado about Nothing* or Malvolio in *Twelfth Night* or Angelo in *Measure for Measure*) and who is always riding for a fall. There is the calculating villain (Richard III, Shylock in *Merchant of Venice*, Don John in *Much Ado about Nothing*, Iago in *Othello*, Edmund in *King Lear*, Antonio in *The Tempest*); there is the servile courtly fop (Osric in *Hamlet*, Oswald in *King Lear*); and there is the melancholic (Don John in *Much Ado about Nothing*, Jaques in *As You Like It*).

When Hamlet hears that the troupe of actors has arrived in Elsinore, he says he will welcome them as follows:

He that plays the king shall be welcome—his Majesty shall have tribute on me, the adventurous knight shall use his foil and target, the lover shall not sigh gratis, the humorous man shall end his part in peace, the clown shall make those laugh whose lungs are tickle o' th' sere, and the lady shall say her mind freely, or the blank verse shall halt for't.   (*Hamlet*, II.ii.319-25)

Hamlet gives us a standard list of the types of characters that an audience in the country could expect to be portrayed by a small traveling troupe: king, knight, lover, humorous man (like Shylock, Don John, Malvolio, Jaques, and Angelo), clown (meaning untutored country fellow), and lady (played by a boy, of course). The larger companies in the city, like Shakespeare's, would have a wider variety of types to choose from, but the categories of expectation remain. All these are common types that Shakespeare incarnates into particular characters, who are, to his audience, believable both for their unique vitality and for their representation of their type.

Not only characters had to fit decorum in age and type. Speech itself had to have decorum. For Shakespeare's audience, the speech of a dramatic character was believable only if it was the kind of speech that the audience expected to be spoken by a person with the character's age, rank, gender, wealth, profession, nation, friends, and so on. People of higher status in society don't make verbal blunders like those of the low-born Dogberry in *Much Ado about Nothing* or Elbow in *Measure for Measure*. Older men, like Polonius in *Hamlet*, give pithy advice in old, wise sayings; they don't, like young men in love, write extravagant rhymed verse in praise of their beloveds as Orlando does in *As You Like It*. As Corin, a shepherd, says to Touchstone, a court fool:

> Those that are good manners at the court are as ridiculous in the country as the behavior of the country is most mockable at the court. You told me you salute not at the court but you kiss your hands; that courtesy would be uncleanly if courtiers were shepherds.
> (*As You Like It*, III.ii.45–51)

The same is true for language. Throughout his work, Shakespeare draws particularities of individual speech out of characters who are also speaking consistently with their type, or whose *not* doing so is for a good dramaturgical reason. If a country bumpkin spoke in blank verse or the royal plural, it would be a sure sign that he was either pretentious or mad. Dogberry in *Much Ado about Nothing* comically uses words too big for him. And in *Henry IV, Part 1*, when Prince Hal wants to disguise his nobility in the cloak of a commoner, he makes an effort to learn from the drawers (meaning the tavern waiters) that "They call drinking deep, dyeing scarlet" and strives to become "so good a proficient . . . that I can drink with any tinker in his own language during my life." He then makes a wonderful joke that again depends on reversing decorum: He says to Poins, "thou hast lost much honor that thou wert not with me in this action," using the words "honor" and "action" (meaning military exploit), usually applied to the nobility, ironically about his winning the approval of the commoners by drinking with them (*1 Henry IV*, II.iv.15–21). Compare this with his real mission, which is to win the loyalty of the nobility, and you see how Shakespeare can use decorum, and its reversal, to help convey his meaning.

The main thing for us to realize is this: For Shakespeare and his audience, decorum in characters and language was not a form of confinement but a path toward truth. Just as the lines and net of a tennis court confine the players only to make the game meaningful, or the sonnet, by limiting the poet to a given form, liberates his imagination (see Chapter 11), so character type and style of speech in the Renaissance were vehicles of meaning, which could be either static and predictable or scintillating with vitality, depending on the gifts of the poet.

For Shakespeare, decorum was like language itself. We don't, like Humpty Dumpty, demand that words mean whatever we want them to mean. Only because their meaning is given can we use them to convey our feeling, thought, and experience. For Shakespeare, the same was true of decorum. Only by adhering to it could he bring his characters and situations alive. The better we understand this, the richer and deeper will be our experience of the meaning of his works.

REALISM OR MORALITY PLAYS?

We tend to think of a play as being either of the realistic kind, or of the morality-play kind, either specific and particular—a slice of life—or general and moralizing in a way that applies to all. But when we apply this either/or to Shakespeare, we are bound to be missing something. For example, is *Hamlet* a realistic drama about a particular man with specific characteristics, one we might know if we lived in the Renaissance? Or is it a morality play generally applicable to all men? The answer is both. The principle at work here is discussed in Chapter 1 under Universal Realism. Here we need only add that Shakespeare was the heir to a tradition extending back to the medieval morality plays (like *Everyman*, about a man who is told he will die) and forward to our own time (for example *Star Wars* or the Harry Potter novels and movies).

A morality play is a play that embodies a moral lesson or insight applicable to everyone. In the early years of the tradition, the names signified the abstract idea being represented. Hence Everyman is greeted by Death who tells him he has to go on a journey to God to be judged. Everyman wants moral support from people like Kin and Cousin and Friendship and Good (meaning worldly goods) and Beauty and Strength. They all refuse to go with him. Knowledge (meaning of Christian doctrine) goes most of the way with him. But at the last, only the character named Good Deeds accompanies him to death and judgment. The characters are named by the abstractions they represent. In our time the demands of realism require that we name our hero not "Hero" but "Luke Skywalker" or "Harry Potter." Luke doesn't know his father. Harry wears glasses. They have to be utterly specific and realistic in order for us to believe in them while we read the book or watch the movie. And yet the stories are morality tales trying to be as universally significant as possible.

Shakespeare lived in an age and was master of an art that allowed him to make his plays at one and the same time—in the same words, characters, settings, and plots—*both* specific, realistic, and believable *and* universally significant. To quote from "The Annotated *Hamlet*," that play "is about a man who, like every man, is given a paradoxical assignment: to do the right thing in response to a complex situation not of his own making."[13] Hamlet is unique. There is no one in the world or in fiction who is like him. Yet at the same time, Hamlet is everyman. It helps to know that in *Twelfth Night* Malvolio's name means "bad will"; that in *The Tempest* the name of Prospero is a Latin synonym for the Greek word "Faustus," so that Shakespeare's good magician is an intentional answer and opposite to Marlowe's Doctor Faustus.[14] In *Henry VI, Part 3,* Shakespeare has the following stage direction: "Enter a Son that hath kill'd his father, at one door, . . . Enter a Father that hath kill'd his son, at another door" (II.v.54,78). Both characters speak personally and eloquently. At the same time both inescapably and intentionally represent the terrible effects of civil war.

"FOREGROUND IS BACKGROUND"

How are we to keep all of this background in our minds as we read or watch a play by Shakespeare? The answer is, we don't need to. Fortunately for us, Shakespeare himself provides us—even without footnotes—a great percentage of the above elements of background that we need in order fully to appreciate his plays and poetry. The American poet and scholar J.V. Cunningham said about Shakespeare's plays that in them "foreground is background." All we need to do is to pay attention to all the words of a play. For example, "If you want to know what Shakespeare's audience believed about ghosts," said Cunningham, "read everything said about ghosts in *Hamlet* and believe it."[15] In other words, Shakespeare tells us what we need to know to understand Shakespeare.

This is because Renaissance writers, like their medieval forebears, enjoyed putting into words everything that mattered to them. They tirelessly found meaning in saying, again and again, what they knew and believed and what their readers and audiences knew and believed and wanted to be reminded of (see Why Art? in Chapter 15). Living in a time before newspapers, radio, TV, movies, computers, and smart phones, in a time when printing was a young technology and there were no public libraries, people felt very strongly that words of knowledge and traditional wisdom were both powerful and valuable. As a result, writers felt free to say what people already had heard because they knew the people wanted to hear it again, especially when it was said in interesting, fresh, lively ways. That knowledge provided a context of meaning so audiences and readers knew where they were.

Let's take Cunningham's example of the ghost in *Hamlet*. What can we know of the beliefs of Shakespeare's audience about ghosts based on what is said about the ghost in the play? If we pay attention to Act I, Scenes i, ii, iv, and v, Act II, Scene ii, and Act III, Scene iv, we will learn the following: Ghosts appear at or after midnight. They may or may not be merely a fantasy of the mind. They can be called "thing," "sight," "apparition," "illusion." They may look like someone who has died. Their appearance may fill even rational men (like Horatio) with fear and wonder, causing them to tremble and look pale. Rational men might not believe in them until they see them with their own eyes. Ghosts may appear for various reasons: to be helped by the living and thereby eased from some torment, to give warning about future events, to reveal where buried treasure lies, or to report an otherwise hidden crime. They may come, or represent someone as coming, from heaven or purgatory or hell and have good or evil intentions. They may depart when the cock crows and morning comes. They may not dare to appear during the holy season of Christmas. They may be spoken with and may or may not respond. They may be devils in disguise, change shapes, drive men mad, lead them to despair and suicide. Or they may be honest messengers of divine providence revealing otherwise hidden facts and delivering divine assignments. They may appear to one person while at the same time being invisible to another.

The fact that the Ghost in *Hamlet* does not reveal his purposes to the watch or even to Horatio is significant. His message is meant for Hamlet only, and we, like the guards, are meant to be wondering what is going on until the Ghost at last speaks to Hamlet. And then we understand exactly what the Ghost's apparent mission is—because he tells us explicitly. (His honesty is confirmed later when Hamlet proves his words to have been true.) The mission of the Ghost is to call the prince to right thought and right action. His challenge to Hamlet is complex: how can Hamlet enact revenge without tainting his mind? But that is precisely the human problem Shakespeare means to dramatize in the play.

If we pay careful attention when reading Shakespeare, we will see that he gives us everything we need to know about the characters and situations in his plays, whether foreground or background, and we will consequently respond accordingly. It is when we ignore large chunks of what the characters are saying that we become confused and begin asking irrelevant questions that the play was not crafted to answer and are tempted to supply answers that distract us from the essential meanings of the play—meanings that, for all the differences between Shakespeare's worldview and ours, we may find both moving and profoundly valuable.

---

[1] C.S. Lewis, *The Discarded Image: An Introduction to Medieval and Renaissance Literature* (Cambridge: Cambridge University Press, 1964, rpt. 1988), pp. 10–13.

[2] For the source of the idea in Plato's *Timaeus* and its extension in Aristotle's *De Anima* and *Metaphysics*, see Arthur O. Lovejoy, *The Great Chain of Being: A Study of the History of an Idea*, William James Lectures at Harvard University, 1933 (Cambridge, MA: Harvard University Press, 1936, 1964), Ch. 2. The most valuable modern discussion of the Renaissance ideas of hierarchy and correspondence, and a source for much that follows here, is E.M.W. Tillyard, *The Elizabethan World Picture* (New York: Vintage, 1959).

[3] *St. Benedict's Rule for Monasteries*, tr. Leonard J. Doyle (Collegeville, MN: The Liturgical Press, St. John's Abbey, 1948), p. 88.

[4] Actually not St. Dionysius the Areopagite of the first century but a later thinker who adopted the persona of the saint and is now called by scholars Pseudo-Dionysius the Areopagite.

[5] Edmund Plowden, *The Commentaries: Or Reports of Edmund Plowden . . .: Containing Divers Cases upon Matters of Law . . . [1548–1579]: to which are Added, The Quaeries of Mr. Plowden* (London: S. Brooke, 1816) at https://archive.org/details/commentariesorr00plowgoog.

[6] Quotations here are from C.S. Lewis, *The Discarded Image*, pp. 162–63. Dramaturge Dakin Matthews catalogues the five internal wits somewhat differently: common sense (which receives and combines sense impressions into an image), cognitive sense (which

receives an imprint of the image), memory (which retains the image), fantasy/imagination (which reproduces the image), and estimation (which evaluates the image)—Dakin Matthews, *Sheltering with Shakespeare*: Psychology II, at https://www.youtube.com/watch?v=CXQHU4LGi6w. Differences in the ways of categorizing the functions of the sensible soul—that is of those faculties human beings share with animals—arise from the complex history of the treatment of the subject. The ideas derive from Aristotle and descend to Shakespeare through, among others, Martianus Capella, Augustine, Boethius, Avicenna, Averroes, Albertus Magnus, Thomas Aquinas, Geoffrey Chaucer, and Stephen Hawes.

[7]   C.S. Lewis, *The Abolition of Man or Reflections on Education with Special Reference to the Teaching of English in the Upper Forms of Schools* (New York: Simon & Schuster / Touchstone, 1996), pp. 83–84.

[8]   Christopher Marlowe, *The Tragical History of the Life and Death of Doctor Faustus*, in Brooke and Paradise, eds., *English Drama 1580–1642* (Boston: D.C. Heath, 1933), ll. 52, 60.

[9]   C.S. Lewis, *The Abolition of Man*, p. 84. Cf., Sir Francis Bacon, *Filium Labyrinthi*, 1 ("The magicians perform nothing that is permanent and profitable"), at https://archive.org/stream/worksfrancisbaco06bacoiala#page/416/mode/2up.

[10]   Madeleine Doran, *Endeavors of Art: A Study of Form in Elizabethan Drama* (Madison: University of Wisconsin Press, 1964), p. 217.

[11]   George Puttenham, *Art of English Poesy*, III.xxiv (quoted in Doran, p. 217).

[12]   Doran, p. 217–218.

[13]   Gideon Rappaport, "The Annotated *Hamlet*" (yet to be published), p. iv.

[14]   A parallel pointed out to me by the Jungian analyst James Kirsch.

[15]   J.V. Cunningham, in a graduate seminar on *Hamlet* at Brandeis University, 1974.

8

Whose Interpretation Is Right?
—Principles of Interpreting Shakespeare

PRINCIPLE 1: "The players cannot keep counsel; they'll tell all."

Teachers of acting often say that Shakespeare's drama has no subtext, only text. This is a distinct contrast to modern drama. Subtext means an implied dramatic meaning different from the literal meaning of the words. It usually involves irony of some kind, or an emotion that the character, given the circumstances, may be feeling without directly expressing it words (as in Chekhov or Pinter). It may be present when social convention (as in Ibsen) or the threat of censorship (as in plays written under Communist regimes) prevents the expression of a character's actual thought.

The playing of subtext arose from an acting technique called "The Method" developed in the United States by The Actor's Studio based on the work of the Russian director Konstantin Stanislavski. "The Method" is useful, sometimes essential, in the performance of the works of modern playwrights and film-makers. Here is an example of how the acting of a modern script might require the development of subtext. The passage is from the New York Film Academy's student resources page:

INT[ERIOR] LIVING ROOM
A man enters the room. A woman is sitting on the couch.

MAN
How are you?

WOMAN
I'm fine.

There are 1,000 different ways to play this scene and they all hinge on the choice of subtext. Is the Woman really fine? Does the Man really care?[1]

By contrast, for the most part characters in Shakespeare's plays say explicitly in their words what they mean. There are often layers of meaning, but generally there are not underlying, unstated thoughts different from what is said. Characters make explicit what is happening in the plot and what is going on in their minds. If they are clear in their aims or fears, they tell us. If they are undergoing inner conflict, or doubts, or uncertainties, they tell us that as well. Hence we need not speculate about what a character intends, for the character will tell us. And when one character happens to be attempting to deceive another, he or she will tell us so explicitly either before or after, perhaps in asides or soliloquies. Richard III, Iago in *Othello*, Edmund in *King Lear* are obvious examples. We do not need to guess that the mad beggar who appears on the stage in *King Lear* is really Edgar in disguise. He has told us already that he is about to disguise himself. Kent does the same. Hamlet tells us that he is going to play at madness, and often reminds us amidst his doing so that he is only acting. In short, Shakespeare's style of drama is to tell the audience what they need to know rather than leaving them to guess for themselves or leaving it to the actor to imply it merely by tone or gesture. The tones and gestures are governed inescapably by the spoken lines.

This is the meaning of Hamlet's ironic assertion to Ophelia that "The players cannot keep counsel, they'll tell all" (*Hamlet*, III.ii.141–42). They are there to do just that. It is not the business of an actor to keep secrets from the audience or to leave them guessing once the play is over. In Shakespeare's theater the players say what the characters mean or the author and the actor have not done their jobs.

This is why directors of Shakespeare will tell their actors to play the text, not the subtext. At least understand clearly exactly what the words are saying before trying to shade them with tones and gestures. So Principle 1 in the effort to come to a valid interpretation of any Shakespearean speech or scene or character or play is to pay close attention to the meaning of the words. The words almost always say explicitly what the character means.

PRINCIPLE 2: Know Shakespeare's Context

That the players will "tell all" implies that knowing the meaning of the words and lines in the context of Shakespeare's own time and place is crucial. Comprehending what the players say and the characters mean depends upon knowing as much as possible about the elements of the background world view discussed in Chapter 7.

For example, when Othello finally confronts the villain Iago, who has seduced him into murdering Desdemona, he says, "I look down toward his feet; but that's a fable" (V.ii.286). What Shakespeare's audience knew, and what we might need a footnote to tell us, is that the devil was believed to appear with cloven hooves instead of feet. Othello is thinking of Iago as a literal devil, though for that idea, and the notion that the devil could not be killed but only shamed, we need no footnote, for his next line is "If that thou be'st a devil, I cannot kill thee" (see "Foreground Is Background" in Chapter 7).

Othello's final gesture is an even more important example from the same scene of how correct interpretation depends on knowing the Renaissance background. A modern audience might find Othello's suicide heroic and admirable: he is executing the murderer of his wife, i.e., himself. But in Shakespeare's time, as Hamlet explicitly says, the Everlasting has "fix'd / His canon 'gainst self-slaughter" (*Hamlet*, I.ii.131–32). In committing suicide rather than going to his knees in repentance, Othello is assuring his own damnation. This understanding of his action is prepared for by the earlier words of Gratiano about Desdemona's father Brabantio:

> Did he live now,
> This sight would make him do a desperate turn,
> Yea, curse his better angel from his side,
> And fall to reprobance.   (*Othello*, V.ii.206–209)

"Desperate turn" implies suicide, the consequence of despair, and "reprobance" here means damnation. In Gratiano's speech, we see yet another example of J.V. Cunningham's principle "Foreground is background" (see Chapter 7). Gratiano articulates the spiritual context of Othello's final act. But unless we know what was believed about the eternal consequences of suicide, we may misunderstand both Gratiano's speech and the full horror of Othello's last choice for Shakespeare's audience.

So Principle 2 in arriving at valid interpretations of Shakespeare is to know the background and context as well as possible.

PRINCIPLE 3: Know the Critic's Underlying Assumptions

As C.S. Lewis argues in *The Discarded Image* (see Chapter 7), the greatest change in modern history is not from medieval times to the Renaissance and Reformation, but rather from the medieval, Renaissance, and Reformation periods to the modern period. There have been many great advances in civilization since the height of the Middle Ages. Two of the most valuable have been the modern scientific method, which has lifted millions out of disease and poverty, and the establishment of limited governments that secure individual liberty and the rule of law. At the same time, many important figures in the modern intellectual history of the West, whatever you may think about their ideas, have contributed to the disintegration of that great medieval synthesis of the classical and Judeo-Christian views of the world that held sway through the seventeenth century and into the eighteenth and that stands behind Shakespeare's work.

What follows is a brief list of the main historical figures whose ideas have crept between us and the accurate appreciation of Shakespeare's art. It is offered as a caution against assuming their post-Shakespearean premises in trying to understand reality as Shakespeare saw it.

Plato had seen the human being as made up of three functions—mind, heart, and body, or intellect, emotion, and physical need and desire. The medieval Christian believed that God breathed a divine soul into the human being to unify those functions into one person, and that the world was created by God and was good and that man was created with free will and, though fallen through sin, could choose between good and evil. These beliefs were fused in the medieval synthesis that Shakespeare and his audience inherited (see Chapter 7). They were increasingly rejected after Shakespeare's time by, among others, the following:

René Descartes (1596–1650) split the human being into two: a merely physical body—nothing but a machine—and a mind, with no meaningful relation between them imaginable.

Thomas Hobbes (1588–1679) saw human life in the state of nature as "solitary, nasty, poor, brutish, and short," and believed that all men, in the absence of an overarching political force, were inescapably in a war with all other men for power.

Jean-Jacques Rousseau (1712–1778) thought that the only source of good was nature itself and that all the forms of society—government, law, church, school, property, trade, the arts—were corruptions of the natural goodness of men. Authority was located not in God, rational thought, language, society, or tradition, but in nature, the body, and those emotions schooled only by nature.

Charles Darwin (1809–1882) imagined the human being to be the product of a merely material natural process driven by no divine purpose but only by itself. In his vision moral standards and spiritual values are merely accidents of nature having no ultimate authority.

Karl Marx (1818–1883) applied the concept of unconscious natural evolution to human history, which is then seen as an inexorable movement from the oppression of the poor by the rich toward a universal egalitarian utopia. Men, values, arts, and spiritual aspirations are mere products of economic necessity, and virtue lies only in the promotion of the utopian future, which (illogically) is at the same time supposed to be inevitable.

Friedrich Nietzsche (1844–1900), warrior against hypocrisy, in one of his aspects announces the decay of religion and the death of God and returns to the "heroic" value system he sees in ancient epics according to which not virtue but only strength matters. There is no right—only might.

Sigmund Freud (1856–1939) finds Hobbes's war now fought within the human mind itself. Unconscious desire (the id) battles guilt driven by fear (the superego) for control of the conscious self (the ego). No final peaceful resolution is possible short of the nothingness of death.

Jean-Paul Sartre (1905–1980) asserts that there is no God, no meaning of life, no nature of man, therefore no right and no wrong. To this moral nihilism Sartre adds that the only sin is hypocrisy, not noticing the illogic of disapproving of hypocrisy after denying the existence of all values, including truth.

Postmodernism: The latest stage of the destruction of the medieval synthesis comes with the invasion of the British and American study of humanities by the theoretical approaches—semiotics, structuralism, post-structuralism, deconstruction, post-modernism, neo-Marxism, critical theory—brought to bear on art and literature by theorists like linguist **Ferdinand de Saussure** (1857–1913), Freudian psychoanalyst **Jacques-Marie-Emile Lacan** (1901–1981), Marxist social and literary critic **Michel Foucault** (1926–1984), and Marxist semiotic deconstructionist **Jacques Derrida** (1930–2004), and their many followers, about whom critic Camille Paglia writes, "Never have so many been so wrong about so much."[2] Clinical psychologist Jordan Peterson adds, "It is almost impossible to over-estimate the nihilistic and destructive nature of this philosophy."[3]

These modern ideas, some of which we may ourselves hold consciously or unconsciously, can obscure for us the meaning of the lines that Shakespeare wrote. Interpretations based on them have turned heroes (like Henry V, his brother Prince John in *Henry IV, Part 2*, and Duke Vincentio in *Measure for Measure*) into villains, the humble (like Cordelia in *King Lear* and Desdemona in *Othello*) into egotists or milksops, the virtuous (like Portia in *Merchant of Venice* and Helena in *All's Well That Ends Well*) into hypocrites, the chaste (like Isabel in *Measure for Measure*) into frigid prudes, and the innocent (like Hermione and Polixenes in *The Winter's Tale*) into suspects. Hence, Principle 3 in making valid interpretations of Shakespeare's plays is to beware of the underlying assumptions the interpreter is making. If he or she is assuming the truth of post-Shakespearean ideas and bringing them to bear on the interpretation of Shakespeare's plays, it is likely that the results will be at least misleading, if not totally destructive of our experience of the plays. Superimposing our specifically modern preoccupations upon the plays of Shakespeare can easily rob us of the experience of meanings that Shakespeare meant us to have, meanings relevant and valuable not only for his own time but for us and for all time.

WHOSE MIRROR IS IT ANYWAY?—Directors' Innovations

In Act III, Scene ii, of *Hamlet*, at lines 21–23, the prince asserts to the troupe of actors come to perform at Elsinore that the purpose of the art of playing, meaning theatrical drama, is to "hold the mirror up to nature—to show virtue her feature, scorn [meaning what is worthy of scorn] her own image." In short, art is meant to reflect reality as accurately as possible.

In all times, directors must adjust productions of Shakespeare to be faithful to that purpose. And because times change, in order to make Shakespeare's meanings accessible to their own time, place, and audiences, directors often find it necessary to cut lines from Shakespeare's plays, alter the times and places in which they are set, restyle costumes, redistribute characters' lines or change their genders, introduce subtexts through director's notes or sound, lighting, and video cues. In the hands of good directors who are knowledgeable about and loyal to Shakespeare's meanings, such alterations may successfully represent Shakespearean intentions and themes. I have seen a production of *Coriolanus* that was excellent, though it was set not in the context of ancient Rome but in the context of modern American warfare; in it Menenius was portrayed as a Southern Senator. The director had used the alterations to serve, not to substitute for, Shakespeare's thematic intentions in the play. There have been excellent productions of *Twelfth Night* set in the 1920s and of *Hamlet* performed in modern dress.

Too often, however, the pursuit of modern relevance causes such manipulations to confuse, mask, or radically alter the actual themes and meanings of the plays. When that happens, a knowledgeable audience comes away feeling robbed. They were promised Shakespeare and were given, instead, a TV soap opera or a propaganda vehicle. Here are a few famous examples:

Orson Welles' 1937 Mercury Theatre production of Shakespeare's *Julius Caesar* was lauded for making the play come alive by giving Caesar's Rome the overtones of fascist Italy and Nazi Germany. Caesar was dressed like Mussolini. Instead of the wild mob, it was the fascist secret police who murdered Cinna the poet. (The topical horror of the scene stopped the show.) However, the production obscured Shakespeare's intention to show the assassination of Caesar as a world-historical disaster rather than a triumph of the people's legitimate revolution against a tyrant. Instead of portraying Caesar's assassins as the victims of tragic pride and envy, it turned them into heroes of resistance mercilessly hunted by the next generation of fascist demagogues. Thus the production created the impression that Shakespeare's play was meant to promote not legitimate monarchy but resistance to fascism. It may have been explosively powerful theatre, but it wasn't Shakespeare.

In 1948 Lawrence Olivier, the most effective and compelling Shakespearean actor of his age, directed and starred in a film version of *Hamlet*. His interpretation of the play is focused on two clichés of modern thought, the protagonist's supposed unconscious Oedipus complex—a reading influenced by the writing of Freudian psychoanalyst Ernest Jones (1879–1958)—and an excess of self-conscious thought characteristic of and mistrusted by the modern mind. Gertrude's bed becomes a central physical focus of the drama, and in the voiceover introducing the play, Olivier intones, "This is a play about a man who could not make up his mind." Both of these ideas are not only extraneous to the meanings and themes Shakespeare's language actually develops in the play—which is in fact about the hero's moral and spiritual fall and subsequent regeneration—but obstruct any possibility of the audience's perceiving those meanings and themes. The play's depiction of moral and spiritual responsibility in the context of divine revelation is buried under an extra-Shakespearean layer of popular ideas that the modern age inherits from Rousseau: the worship of emotion and the mistrust of rational thought. (If you want to see Olivier the Shakespearean at his best, see films of the productions of *Henry V* [1944] and *Richard III* [1955], which he directed and starred in, and of *King Lear* [1983], directed for TV by Michael Elliott, in which Olivier played the King.)

Peter Brook's film version of *King Lear* (1971) was made under the influence of Polish critic Jan Kott (1914–2001), who interpreted Shakespeare as prefiguring the nightmare of twentieth-century history (to which Kott's own support of Stalin made a minor contribution) and the Theater of the Absurd. The film makes Shakespeare's play relentlessly bleak, militating against the play's actual subject—a profound reinforcement, in a fictional pre-Christian world, of the Christian idea that the possibility of redemption through purgatorial suffering is built in to the structure of Creation. Among other betrayals, Brook gives some of the villain Edmund's lines to the virtuous Edgar, and vice versa, thereby making the play imply that there is no significant difference between good and evil or good men and bad—the farthest thing from the actual intention of Shakespeare's words.

Another example of the way in which a director may, for the sake of topical relevance, make choices that obscure Shakespearean meanings is the depicting of strong male friendships as homoerotic. Antonio in *The Merchant of Venice*, for example, is not an unrequited gay lover but an example of the ancient ideal of selfless and self-sacrificial male friendship. Directors who in their interpretations force an erotic cliché of popular entertainment onto that relationship rob us of a valuable (and rare) image of true friendship (see "Was Shakespeare Gay or Not?" in Chapter 11).

Hamlet's exhortation "to hold as 'twere the mirror up to nature" (*Hamlet*, III.ii.21) was meant to encourage the players to make the play as authentic and transparent a portrayal as possible of what it really means to be a human being living in the world. Instead, like those in charge of the productions described above, some directors choose to set up a mirror between the audience and the play, a mirror that reflects back to the audience only the superficial and commonplace notions that the audience members bring with them into the theater. The practical effect of such productions is to obscure—often intentionally—anything in Shakespeare's vision of reality that might challenge the audience to greater spiritual depths. Such productions may be theatrically powerful. But a sensible person, on leaving the theater after these kinds of productions, might well say, "If that's what you want the play to mean, why don't you leave Shakespeare alone and write your own damn play!"

[1] At https://www.nyfa.edu/student-resources/the-importance-of-subtext-for-actors/.
[2] Camille Paglia, "Junk Bonds and Corporate Raiders: Academe in the Hour of the Wolf," in *Sex, Art, and American Culture* (New York: Vintage Books, 1992), pp. 214–215.
[3] Jordan Peterson, *12 Rules for Life: An Antidote to Chaos* (Random House Canada, 2018), p. 311.

9

Is This What Shakespeare Actually Wrote?
—Shakespeare's Texts

MANUSCRIPTS

We have not a single play in Shakespeare's own handwriting. The only examples of his handwriting that we do have are a few signatures on business documents and his will and a few pages thought to be in Shakespeare's hand in the manuscript of a play called *Sir Thomas More* (a manuscript much revised that exhibits the handwriting of as many as six people). The plays and poems of Shakespeare that have come down to us exist in early printed versions based upon either Shakespeare's own manuscripts (now lost) or upon copies of them handwritten by someone else (called *scribal copies*).

Over the last several centuries, and particularly in the twentieth century, a tremendous amount of scholarly work has been done to establish the nature of the manuscript copies used for the early printed editions and the degree of fidelity the typesetters demonstrated in transferring the manuscript words into print. Scholars have studied the technical operation and finances of Renaissance printing houses, legal documents of the period, even the particular characteristics of individual typesetters. They have pored over Elizabethan and Jacobean handwriting, paper, parchment, and ink. They have analyzed the Stationer's Register, in which the government required that every book printed in the period be listed. In recent years, they have used the computer to count particular words, unique spellings, allusions, images, and concepts. They have examined every nook and cranny of the age in search of potential evidence—bibliographical, legal, chemical, psychological, social, and intellectual—in order to establish, with as much certainty as possible, exactly what Shakespeare actually wrote.

Every modern edition is the fruit of this vast scholarly effort along with some (unfortunately necessary) guesswork, called *conjecture*. The conjecture is necessary because here and there in Shakespeare we come across a missing word, or phrase, or line, or a phrase so obscure that, despite all our scholarship, we simply don't know what Shakespeare meant. Did Shakespeare slip? Did the copyist? Did the typesetter? Has the language so changed that we've lost the meaning of a word or phrase? Some combination of any of these? In some cases we just don't know. Such a passage is called a *crux* (pl. *cruxes* or *cruces*, from the Latin for "cross" or "torture").

For example, in the beginning of the great soliloquy in Act I, Scene ii, of *Hamlet*, does our hero say "O that this too too sallied flesh would melt," or "Oh that this too too solid flesh would melt"? Or, as some editors suggest, "O that this too too sullied flesh would melt"? Probably we can never know the answer. Nonetheless, as tortured as some of us may be by a Shakespearean crux, we must be profoundly grateful that the vast majority of Shakespeare's words have been faithfully preserved in print.

EARLY PRINTED EDITIONS

The early printed editions of Shakespeare's works were of two kinds, called *quarto* and *folio*, based upon their size. The quarto was made from a standard sheet of printer's paper with four blocks of print on each side (hence "quarto"). It was folded twice before being bound into a book, making four leaves and eight pages. The folio was printed with two blocks of print per side and was folded once, making two leaves and four pages. About twenty of Shakespeare's plays were printed in quarto editions during his lifetime, and all the plays now ascribed to Shakespeare except *Pericles* and the Shakespearean sections of *Two Noble Kinsmen* and *Sir Thomas More* were published in the First Folio of 1623, about seven years after Shakespeare's death.

The Good Quartos

When a play was successful in performance on Shakespeare's stage, his company might find it financially beneficial to have it printed in a single edition. The company would provide a printer with the theater promptbook copy, Shakespeare's manuscript (called *foul papers*), or a rewritten copy (called a *fair copy*), from which the printer would set the type for the printed version. These quartos are called "good" because the versions of the plays used by the printer are authoritative. That is, they're as close as we can get to what Shakespeare actually wrote.

The Bad Quartos

Because it was profitable to publish plays, especially if they were by

Shakespeare, sometimes his plays were pirated, just as today someone might pirate a musical album or video and sell it. In the case of Shakespeare's plays, the pirates were often actors, not necessarily leading actors, who got together to reconstruct the play from memory, write it down, and then have it printed and sold under Shakespeare's name. Generally actors have good memories for their own lines, though few are word perfect. But when actors are trying to remember lines not their own, or lines from scenes during which they were backstage changing costumes, their memories get a little fuzzy. As a result, some of the speeches in these pirated editions are very close to the originals as we have them in the good quartos or First Folio, but many, often most, of the speeches are very far from the originals—sometimes hilariously far.

Here's an example from Hamlet's "To be or not to be" soliloquy (III.i.55–87):

In the good quarto (1604):

To be, or not to be, that is the question,
Whether tis nobler in the minde to suffer
The slings and arrows of outrageous fortune,
Or to take Armes against a sea of troubles,
And by opposing, end them, to die to sleepe
No more, and by a sleepe, to say we end
The hart-ake, and the thousand naturall shocks
That flesh is heire to; tis a consumatien
Deuoutly to be wisht to die to sleepe,
To sleepe, perchance to dreame, I there's the rub,
For in that sleepe of death what dreames may come
When we haue shuffled off this mortall coyle
Must giue vs pause, there's the respect
That makes calamitie of so long life:
For who would beare the whips and scornes of
                                        [time,
Th'oppressors wrong, the proude mans contumely,
The pangs of despiz'd loue, the lawes delay,
The insolence of office, and the spurnes
That patient merrit of th'vnworthy takes,
When he himselfe might his quietas make
With a bare bodkin; who would fardels beare,

To grunt and sweat vnder a wearie life,
But that the dread of something after death,
The vndiscover'd country, from whose borne
No trauiler returnes, puzzels the will,
And makes vs rather beare those ills we haue,
Then flie to others that we know not of.
Thus conscience dooes make cowards,
And thus the natiue hiew of resolution
Is sickled ore with the pale cast of thought,
And enterprises of great pitch and moment,
With this regard theyr currents turne awry,
And loose the name of action.

In the bad quarto (1603):

To be, or not to be, I there's the point,
To Die, to sleepe, is that all? I all:
No, to sleepe, to dreame, I mary there it goes,
For in that dreame of death, when wee awake,
And borne before an euerlasting Iudge,
From whence no passenger euer retur'nd,
The vndiscouered country, at whose sight
The happy smile, and the accursed damn'd.
But for this, the ioyfull hope of this,
Whol'd beare the scornes and flattery of the world,
Scorned by the right rich, the rich curssed of the
                                    [poore?
The widow being oppressed, the orphan wrong'd,
The taste of hunger, or a tirants raigne,
And thousand more calamities besides,
To grunt and sweate under this weary life,
When that he may his full Quietus make,
With a bare bodkin, who would this indure,
But for a hope of something after death?
Which pusles the braine, and doth confound the
                                    [sense,
Which makes vs rather beare those euilles we haue,
Than flie to others that we know not of.
I that, O this conscience makes cowards of vs all.

The poet and scholar J.V. Cunningham had the wonderful theory that as the actor (who obviously had not played Hamlet) was trying to remember the lines of this speech, he knew he had got them wrong. According to this theory, when he said "No, 'To sleep, to dream'—Ay, marry, there it goes!" he meant, "No, that's not how it goes. It goes 'To sleep, to dream.' Now I've got it!" ("Marry" was a mild oath derived from "by the Virgin Mary.") According to this theory, the person copying down what the actor was saying kept writing, not distinguishing between the character's lines ("To sleep, to dream") and the actor's words to himself about trying to remember them ("I [= ay] mary there it goes").

In any case, such quarto editions are called "bad" because they are not based on Shakespeare's written word but on often faulty reconstructions from memory. They remain useful for comparison when textual problems in the good quartos and folio arise. For example, the Bad Quarto of *Hamlet* confirms that the Folio is probably correct in adding the phrase "of us all" to line 82 in the speech above, where the Good Quarto has "Thus conscience does make cowards." And the bad quartos give at least some sense of what the actor *thought* the words should be and the speech should mean. But we are very fortunate that, except perhaps in the case of *Pericles* (see Chapter 13), we do not have to depend on them for most of what Shakespeare wrote.

The First Folio

In 1623, about seven years after Shakespeare's death, his friends, John Heminge and Henry Condell, who were members of Shakespeare's acting company, got together the best texts of Shakespeare's plays that they could find. They gathered thirty-six plays and had them printed in a folio edition by William Jaggard. It was called "Mr. William Shakespeare's Comedies, Histories, & Tragedies. Published according to the True Original Copies." This was the first collected edition of the works of William Shakespeare. It is called the First Folio (F1 for short).

The First Folio edition contains the only early texts we have of eighteen of Shakespeare's plays, and the best texts we have of seven others. For this reason, every Shakespeare lover in the world owes a huge debt of gratitude to Heminge and Condell and the printer William Jaggard.

LATER EDITIONS

The First Folio was followed by three folio editions (F2 in 1632, F3 in 1663, and F4 in 1685), each printed from the previous one. Each made some corrections and compounded some errors. During the eighteenth century several brilliant editors produced valuable collected editions with their editorial emendations and notes, including Nicholas Rowe (1709), the poet Alexander Pope (1725), Lewis Theobald (pronounced Tíbbald) (1733), Sir Thomas Hanmer (1744), William Warburton (1747), the great Dr. Samuel Johnson (1765), Edward Capell (1768), George Steevens (1773), and Edmond Malone (1790). In the nineteenth century there were advances in scholarship, focus on aesthetic criticism fostered by the poet Samuel Taylor Coleridge and the essayist William Hazlitt, and several important editions, including the *New Variorum* edition by H.H. Furness, which attempted to list all the variants in the early texts and all the previous editors' suggested emendations.

MODERN EDITIONS

All modern editions of Shakespeare are based primarily on the early good quarto and First Folio editions. Where they find confusions or cruxes editors will adopt some emendations of previous editors and reject others, some making emendations of their own. The goal is to produce a text as close as possible to what Shakespeare actually wrote.

Most editors will choose either a good quarto or the First Folio version as the version to start from (*copy text*) and then will combine (*conflate*) the best readings from quarto, folio, and inspired emendation into a single version. "Best" does not mean the one the editor likes the most but the one the editor believes likeliest to be what Shakespeare intended. Some editors prefer to cut away all later emendations and stick as close as possible to the original printed editions. Where both good quarto and First Folio versions exist, some will print both, side-by-side, for ease of comparison.

It is now possible for any reader to examine the original editions in excellent photographically reproduced (*facsimile*) editions of the quartos[1] and the First Folio.[2] The facsimile editions will show that the crux from *Hamlet* given above appears as "sallied" (meaning "under attack") in both the bad quarto (Q1) and the good quarto (Q2) of the play and as "solid" in the First Folio (F1). If you were editing the play, you would have to decide which you thought Shakespeare actually wrote: "sallied" or "solid" or perhaps "sullied" (meaning "dirtied") as some editors have thought. How would you defend your choice? In the theater, all three spellings would have sounded nearly the same. Did Shakespeare intend the audience to hear only one of these meanings? or two of them at once? or all three?

Of course ultimately it is no one word but the entire play in which the playwright's meaning lies (see Chapter 6). But it is worth remembering the hard work the editors of Shakespeare have done to solve textual problems in order that we may appreciate each play as a whole.

---

[1]   Michael J.B. Allen and Kenneth Muir, *Shakespeare's Plays in Quarto* (Berkeley: University of California Press, 1981).

[2]   Charlton Hinman, *The Norton Facsimile: The First Folio of Shakespeare* (New York: Paul Hamlyn, 1968).

10

What Kind of Thing Is It?—Categories of Plays

TRAGICAL-COMICAL-HISTORICAL-PASTORAL

In Act II, Scene ii, of *Hamlet*, Polonius announces the arrival at Elsinore of a troupe of traveling actors: "The best actors in the world, either for tragedy, comedy, history, pastoral, pastoral-comical, histori-cal-pastoral, tragical-historical, tragical-comical-historical-pastoral" (II. 396–99). The sentence is itself comical because in trying to make his list exhaustive, Polonius ends with a combination that, whether or not there is any play that it might describe, sounds absurd. But his sentence is also revealing.

The initial categories are those that Shakespeare and his fellow playwrights held to be authoritative. They inherited that classification of types of drama—tragedy, comedy, history, pastoral, and satire—from the ancient world, especially Aristotle's *Poetics* and Horace's *Ars Poetica* ("The Art of Poetry"), chiefly through the fourth-century Latin grammarians Donatus, Evanthius, and Diomedes. But, as the above sentence of Polonius illustrates, while the Elizabethan playwrights took those ancient categories seriously, Polonius's hyphenated categories, which describe well some actual plays of Shakespeare's age, hint at the freedom with which the Elizabethan playwrights modified the inherited categories, adjusting or merging them in their attempts to make meaningful dramatic entertainments for their audiences.

The categories of Shakespeare's plays are tragedies, comedies, histories, romances (sometimes called tragi-comedies), and a satire.

WHAT MAKES TRAGEDIES TRAGIC?

The classical category of tragedy referred to a play with the following three characteristics:

- The characters were high-ranking figures, kings and queens, princely heroes, rulers and potentates.
- The story focused on serious and important, often world-class, events.

- The trajectory of the story was from happiness to misery, order to chaos, power to loss—i.e., a tragedy had an unhappy ending.

The Renaissance added one more element to these three characteristics:

- The tragedy ended with the violent death onstage of one or more characters.

Within this definition of tragedy, there were some subcategories.

Kinds of Tragedy

A *De Casibus* tragedy (from the Latin *casus*, meaning fall or downfall, misfortune, destruction) tells the story of the fall of a great prince from power to powerlessness, from mastery to loss and death, from the top to the bottom of Fortune's wheel (see Fortune in Chapter 7). Examples in Shakespeare include *Richard III*, *Richard II*, *King Lear*, and *Coriolanus*.

An **Italianate** or **Intrigue** tragedy tells the story of intrigues or secret crimes, whether of noble persons or others. Of this type the **Revenge** tragedy forms a subset. The greatest Shakespearean example of an intrigue/revenge tragedy is *Hamlet*. Other plays have elements of the intrigue tragedy woven into them, like *Othello*, *King Lear*, and *Cymbeline* (though the last is not a tragedy but a romance or tragi-comedy—see below).

A **Domestic** tragedy is usually, though not always, focused on private citizens engaged in private misdeeds, i.e., crimes that involve a family rather than a whole city or a nation. *Othello* has often been called a domestic tragedy, though it also exhibits elements of the *de casibus* and intrigue forms. Another example of this type is *Arden of Feversham*, which is sometimes falsely ascribed to Shakespeare (see Chapter 14).

Classical vs. Christian Tragedy

The differences between classical tragedy and Elizabethan tragedy were not only a matter of category. There is also the difference in theme and tone arising from differences in the conception of reality. The context of classical tragedies, like those of the Greeks Aeschylus (*The Oresteian Trilogy* etc.), Sophocles (*Oedipus Rex* etc.), and Euripides (*The Bacchae* etc.) and the Roman Seneca (*Hercules Furens* etc.), was the mythic stories of the Greek and Roman gods and the shadowy afterlife of Hades. By contrast, the background of Renaissance tragedies, apart from those written in specific imitation of the classical style, was Christianity. Hence the single greatest difference between the two conceptions of tragedy was this: In classical tragedy generally the fate of the protagonist tends to be inevitable, whatever choices he or she makes. In Christian tragedy the ultimate outcome tends to depend on the protagonist's free will choices. Another important difference is between the conceptions of the afterlife, between the classical images of Hades and Elysium and the Christian images of Hell, Purgatory, and Heaven.

The classical tradition gives us the sense that tragedy is about there being no viable options for the protagonist, no good way out. Orestes in Aeschylus's *Libation Bearers* is faced with the horror of either killing his mother to avenge his father (whom she killed) and facing the wrath of the Furies, or of not killing her and facing the wrath of Apollo. In Sophocles' *Oedipus Rex* (Greek, *Oedipus Tyrannos*), which Aristotle took to be the best example of tragic drama, the character, fate, and choices of Oedipus all lead in only one possible direction. In fact they have already led there even before the play begins. There is no escape for him from the vice grip of the fate that is contained in the will of the gods, his own character, the choices he makes, and the extraordinarily unfortunate circumstances of his life—as if prophecy and outcome, fate and free will, past and future were all one inescapable thing. The tragedy lies in there being absolutely no right answer, no escape from doing (= having done) the most intolerable things that could be done—parricide and incest.[1]

By contrast, in Shakespearean tragedy, the trajectory ending in death is always a function of the relation between one's choices and the divine order of things, which includes man's responsibility for the choices of his free will. Except in those tragedies that Shakespeare sets in the ancient world and in the context of the Greek or Roman gods, the context behind a tragedy is not the shadow world of Hades but God's judgment of souls and the prospect of heaven or hell. And even in Shakespeare's Roman plays (see below) there are implications of a better way of looking at reality that was unknown to an ancient Brutus or Timon or Coriolanus but, as Shakespeare believed, was known to his own audience because it had been revealed by the life of Christ.

As was pointed out in Chapter 7 (under Christianity), of Shakespeare's four greatest tragic protagonists, two are ultimately saved (Hamlet and King Lear) and two damned (Othello and Macbeth). In *King Lear*, Shakespeare explicitly sets out to demonstrate the truth of the Christian idea of the structure of reality by setting the play in a pre-Christian world. For despite all the evil and brutality in the play, *King Lear* dramatizes a proud will purified by purgatorial suffering and thereby readied for heaven. The implication is that all men, whether they know it or not, live in a world the truth of whose structure has been revealed in the Christian message.

Does this mean that Shakespeare's Christian tragedies in which the protagonists are saved are actually comedies, heaven taking the place of a happy ending? No, for, as Renaissance scholar Morton Bloomfield once said, "the joy of the next world in Christian tragedy is different from the joy of the happy ending in this world in comedy."[2] Nonetheless for Shakespeare there is always the spiritual dimension that prevents the horror of death, even of violent death—the essence of the Elizabethans' definition of tragedy—from being final. There may be a worse horror, namely hell, or a redeeming transfiguration in heaven. In any case, the ultimate context of Shakespearean tragedy is the unseen realm of divine judgment and the eternal life of the soul.

The Roman Plays

The category "Roman Plays" is not a formal category, but it is possible to group under this heading the tragedies that Shakespeare set in Ancient Rome or (in one case) Ancient Greece: *Titus Andronicus*, *Julius Caesar*, *Antony and Cleopatra*, *Coriolanus*, and *Timon of Athens*. These plays, very different from one another, are set in the context of the classical rather than the Christian world. To appreciate them properly the reader must understand something of the moral, ethical, and social norms of the ancient world that Shakespeare knew well from his reading. But the reader must also be able to observe how Shakespeare's own Christian consciousness chose to treat them. To take only one example, the assassination of Caesar by Brutus and the other conspirators in *Julius Caesar* can be seen as a tragedy of character. The mantle of the good intentions of the supposedly virtuous Brutus cannot save him from the consequences of his own pride, and it is a kind of tyranny over history to assassinate the ruler of the known world for fear of *his* tyranny. But one can also see in the play, performed for a Christian audience, the great disaster attendant upon man's attempt to overrule the hierarchy established and willed by the one God, of whom the characters in the play knew little but in whom the members of the audience believed.

Comic Relief or Comic Intensification?

One feature of almost any Shakespearean tragedy is the inclusion of moments that seem to have been brought in from comedy—witty word-play or slapstick byplay engaged in by characters, often of lower classes, that set off the seriousness of the tragedy by contrast. Often critics will call this phenomenon "comic relief," as if the audience could not take too much tragedy without a break. There is some truth to this idea of the need for emotional relief from the intensity of tragic scenes. But it would be a mistake to read the comic scenes in *Romeo and Juliet* or *Hamlet* or *Macbeth* as injected for emotional relief alone. The same scene that relieves us also sets us up for the increase of emotional intensity that is bound to follow. More importantly, always in Shakespeare such scenes are thematically integral to the play. They exist as foil scenes to intensify the awareness of the themes being developed in the main plot of the tragedy.

In *Richard II*, Act III, Scene iv, is not particularly comical, but the Gardener's discussion of the need to "trim" and "dress" a garden is given as an explicit analogy to Richard's failure to "trim" and "dress" the "other Eden" and "blessed plot" that is England. In Act II, Scene i, of *Henry IV, Part I*, the Carriers' low-life complaints about the flea-infested inn and its haven for thieves provide commentary on the condition of the kingdom. Such thematic parallels, whether or not explicit, are everywhere in Shakespeare. In *Romeo and Juliet*, the battles among the servants are comical versions of the life-and-death battles between the Montagues and the Capulets. The comical gravedigger in *Hamlet* (V.i) introduces a foolish version of the serious and profound argument between Laertes and the Doctor of Divinity about the fate of Ophelia's soul and also the classical-Christian theme of *memento mori* ("remember that you will die"), a reminder of mortality. And the comical drunken Porter in *Macbeth* enacts a highly significant fantasy of welcoming to hell various sinners who are guilty of the same kinds of crimes as Macbeth.

ARE THE COMEDIES FUNNY?

Often they are, but that is not necessarily why they are categorized as comedies. According to the grammarians, where tragedy treated of princes and potentates, comedy treats of non-aristocrats, gentlemen and ladies of middle rank, men and women of lower rank, private rather than public citizens. The events in a comedy are not world-shaking but local and limited in scope to families and communities rather than to cities and states. And perhaps most consistently, the trajectory of comic plots is from chaos to order, unhappiness to happiness, dysfunction to harmony. One could argue that—funny or serious—a comedy is defined by having a happy ending.

As in tragedy, Shakespeare can be seen to be pushing the limits of the expectations for comedy as well. It's true that his comedies have happy endings, but in all but two of them there is a serious threat of death. Some of the main characters in his comedies are of high rank, and sometimes the comic resolution does involve the whole city. And the characteristics of what we might call romance—fantastic recognitions and reunions, divine or otherwise mystical interventions, the fulfilment of desire in the sacrament of marriage—are not present in classical comedy (like the plays of the Romans Plautus and Terence). In fact, Shakespeare's comedies inherit elements of their forms from many different source. As Madeleine Doran writes, "The lines of [comedy's] heritage—from medieval farce and juggling turn, from comic episode and realistic scene in mystery and morality [plays], from chivalric romance and saint's legend, from Roman comedy, from Italian comedy both learned and popular, from Greek romance and Italian novel, from pastoral eclogue and pastoral romance— are complexly interwoven to issue in many new patterns."[3]

Doran's observation reinforces our recognition that the age of Shakespeare, largely led and inspired by the imaginative craft of Shakespeare himself, both rested upon and refashioned all literary and dramatic categories in pursuit of the authentic and effective fulfillment of the goal articulated by Hamlet: "to hold as 'twere the mirror up to nature" (*Hamlet*, III.ii.22).

ARE THE HISTORIES TRUE?

In Shakespeare's time any play that told a story might be called a history, but the editors of the First Folio specifically classified as "Histories" Shakespeare's ten English history plays. All of them grow out of the chronicle play form, in which a slice of history is told without any necessarily tragic or moral agenda. Some of Shakespeare's histories are essentially chronicles, like the three *Henry VI* plays and *King John*. Some, like *Henry V* and *Henry VIII*, can also be described as pageants (see below). And some, like *Richard II* and *Richard III*, are histories that are also tragedies, specifically called so on their title pages. As with tragedy and comedy, here too the fluidity of the dramatic forms of the age made it possible for Shakespeare to treat those forms as malleable clay depending partly on what the particular story seemed to require and partly on the topical issues of Shakespeare's own time.

Shakespeare's English history plays are largely built on the writings of two sixteenth-century English historians, Edward Hall (c. 1498–1547) and Raphael Holinshed (c. 1529–1580). It is illuminating to study the ways in which Shakespeare accurately preserved facts, orders of events, and characters he found in the chronicles and the ways in which he modified and altered them to serve his dramatic and thematic purposes. Once again, Elizabethan reverence for authority and freedom of artistic invention went hand-in-hand, harmonized by Shakespeare's remarkable imagination.

Eight of the ten English histories that Shakespeare wrote (leaving aside *King John* and *Henry VIII*) form two tetralogies (from the Greek *tetra*, meaning "four"). That is, two sets of four plays each that trace English history from what Shakespeare, in keeping with established Tudor opinion, saw as the tragic deposing of the rightful but bad king Richard II. The series brings the audience through the Wars of the Roses to the final defeat of the scourge Richard III and the establishment of the House of Tudor by Henry VII. The Wars of the Roses were called so because each of the major warring houses had a rose as its symbol: white for the house of York and red for the house of Lancaster. The plays were wildly successful by Elizabethan standards, not least because the question of a successor to the long reigning Elizabeth I, Henry VII's granddaughter, was a live issue, and the threat of a new round of civil wars was much feared.

To avoid confusion, keep in mind that the order of composition is not the order of historical events. The tetralogy that Shakespeare wrote first, early in his career, depicted events later in English history than the tetralogy he wrote later, at the height of his powers. The historical order of kings in the two tetralogies was

> Richard II
> Henry IV
> Henry V
> Henry VI
> Edward IV
> Edward V
> Richard III
> Henry VII.

The order in which the plays were written was as follows.

The tetralogy written first (about a later time):

> *Henry VI, Part 1*
> *Henry VI, Part 2*
> *Henry VI, Part 3*
> *Richard III*

The tetralogy written later (about an earlier time):

> *Richard II*
> *Henry IV, Part 1*

Henry IV, Part 2
Henry V.

Pageants

One particular kind of history play is called a pageant. The word *pageant* is rooted in the Latin *pagina* (page, leaf of a book), from the Latin *pango, pangere* (to fix or fasten, later to write or compose). *Pageant* has two early meanings in English: 1) a "scene displayed on a stage," specifically "one scene or act of a medieval mystery play," and 2) a "stage on which a scene is exhibited or acted," especially "the movable structure or 'carriage,' consisting of stage and stage machinery . . . used in the open-air performances of the mystery plays."[4]

The mystery plays were dramatized stories from the Bible, usually performed in what are called "cycles," groups of relatively short plays on related subjects. Each guild of craftsmen would be responsible for performing a particular story connected with its craft, as the building of Noah's ark by the carpenters' guild, the angels' appearance to the shepherds (to announce Christ's birth) by the shepherds' guild, etc. The performances took place in public places, often inn yards, where the audiences remained where they were and the performers for each play acted on a platform built upon a wagon, which would be drawn into the yard for the performance of that play and then drawn out again. The scene itself and the wagon-platform on which it was performed each came to be known as a pageant.

In the time of Shakespeare, the term *pageant* was used for shows of various degrees of elaboration: tableaux, allegorical mini-dramas, full-scale poetic productions with allegorical figures, nymphs, faeries, fire-works, water-works, etc. Some such pageants were performed for the monarch on the occasion of a "progress"—the slow midsummer processions of the entire court to visit the country houses of the nobility—and others were written and produced in London for special public occasions. "Some of the ablest poets and dramatists were employed in devising these City pageants: Peele, Munday, Dekker, Jonson and Middleton."[5] Such productions were generally one-time showy entertainments.

As applied to plays of Shakespeare, the term *pageant*, though it derives from the older usage implying a series of related scenes more than a coherent and unified drama, refers to an original hybrid of Shakespeare's own. As we have seen, Shakespeare often engages in (and is probably responsible for) such hybrids, which are later accepted by others as formal categories under the persuasive influence of his own instances of them. In any case, Shakespeare could not help bringing his powerful unifying imagination even to such works as he would think of as pageants. The result is illustrated by the two plays of Shakespeare (and one probably by Shakespeare) that we might call pageants, so long as we remember that they are much more than mere successions of set-pieces or chronicle scenes: They are *Edward III, Henry V*, and *Henry VIII. Edward III* is discussed in Chapter 13. *Henry V* gives us Shakespeare's great vision of a triumphant hero-king, the brilliant though short-lived unifier of the principles of right and merit that were split apart in the person and the consequent deposing of *Richard II. Henry VIII* is an earnest evocation in terms of history of the theme of hope for the harmonious reconciliation of opposing parties and the atonement for evil within the soul, themes characteristic of the four late Shakespeare plays called "romances" (see below) written just before it.

ARE THE ROMANCES ROMANTIC?

Four late plays by Shakespeare come under the category of Romance. They are sometimes also called Tragi-comedies or Late Comedies or Late Romances. These are the last plays Shakespeare wrote before retiring to Stratford, namely *Pericles, Cymbeline, The Winter's Tale*, and *The Tempest*. To these we may add *The Two Noble Kinsmen*, on which Shakespeare collaborated with John Fletcher (see Chapter 13) in the same year as *Henry VIII* was written (1613). In fact, based on their structure, these four late plays—*Pericles, Cymbeline, The Winter's Tale*, and *The Tempest*—may properly be categorized as comedies, which in terms of their underlying forms, are not so very different from Shakespeare's earlier comedies. The variety of category names for these plays indicate attempts to account for their unusual tone and atmosphere. They are all somehow magical, mystical, healing, in ways that subtly differ from Shakespeare's earlier work. (They may be thought of as aesthetically analogous to the last quartets of Beethoven, or the last paintings of Rembrandt.)

What we call "romantic love" plays a part in each of these plays, but that's not why they are called *romances*. The term *romance* is applied because of the magical, unlooked-for, surprise redemptions that these four last plays depict, though many of Shakespeare's earlier comedies have similar sorts of surprise reunions and unlooked-for happy endings. The term *romance* comes from the name for medieval tales based on legend, chivalric love, adventure, or the supernatural and for narratives set in remote times and places with imaginary characters engaged in adventures sometimes involving the mysterious.

The term *Tragi-comedy* is applied to these plays because not just the threat of death (as in all but two of Shakespeare's earlier comedies) but actual deaths happen in them.

The use of various terms for these four plays suggests that we must be careful about forcing Shakespeare's work too strictly into meeting our expectations of the pre-existing categories of drama. He was aware of those forms and depended on them, but he also and often pushed against their boundaries to powerful effect.

Are the Romances Believable?

Of course not, but then neither are many of the earlier comedies and many parts of the tragedies. But we suspend our disbelief in apparent impossibilities (see Willing Suspension of Disbelief in Chapter 15) in order to be able to appreciate the deeper and otherwise invisible meanings that they are meant to convey, just as we believe while watching a Superman movie that Superman can fly or while watching *Star Wars* that there is life on other planets or while watching *Harry Potter* that magic spells work. What is *made* believable in these plays is the healing spiritual truth of the nature of man's life in the world, of which these plays give us irresistible and uplifting experience.

WHAT IS A SATIRE?

Most editors do not recognize satire as a distinct category in Shakespeare's toolbox of dramatic forms, but they should. There are many satiric elements in all Shakespeare's plays, but one play, namely *Troilus and Cressida*, can be properly thought of only as a satire and cannot fit comfortably into any other category, though many critics have labored to categorize it otherwise, seeing in it elements of comedy, tragedy, and chronicle. The word *satire* is derived from the Latin *satura* (meaning full) in the phrase *lanx satura* (meaning a full dish, a dish filled with all kinds of fruit or food). The term was then applied to a "discursive composition in verse treating of a variety of subjects"[6] and was later identified, by confusion, with the Greek word *satyr* (meaning a minor divinity, half-man and half-goat) because of the comical ancient Greek satyr plays, which took their name from the satyr characters that formed their choruses. The combination word came to describe a play or other composition in which the follies of men are ridiculed, sometimes comically, sometimes savagely.

As it did so often, Shakespeare's imagination here again transforms a conventional form into a great and previously unknown phenomenon. His one satire, which is not a tragedy (though there is violent death on stage) and not a comedy (because there is no happy ending) and not a history (though it does tell part of the ancient history of Troy), holds up for ridicule not one or a few men guilty of common human foibles, but an entire age of the world. Shakespeare is depicting what it looks like for a whole civilization to collapse through its own moral and spiritual blindness, which the play fiercely ridicules so that we might recognize our own potential for such folly and thereby avoid bringing a similar disaster upon ourselves.

A NON-CATEGORY—PROBLEM PLAYS

For four of Shakespeare's plays the late nineteenth century coined, and the twentieth century enshrined, the category of "Problem Play," though its definition and the list of plays to be included in it have always been matters of debate. Most commonly the term was used to refer to plays that the critics felt to be problematic in structure or content—that is, not that the play depicted a character with a problem to be solved but that the play itself was an insoluble problem for critics, though most did not want to go so far as to call the plays failures. The four plays first put into this category by F.S. Boas are *Measure for Measure*, *All's Well That Ends Well*, *Troilus and Cressida*, and *Hamlet*.[7]

As readers will see in Part 2 in the discussions of individual plays, this category is an invention of critics who do not understand, or refuse to adopt, the premises of Shakespeare's drama. The critics experience problems with these plays because they are asking them the wrong questions, questions irrelevant in the world of Shakespeare's dramatic art. By doing so, such critics are distracted from what Shakespeare has actually given us in these plays. It is as if one were to reject the premises of an argument and then become surprised and even offended that its conclusions make no sense, or as if one were to criticize a child for enjoying a swing in the park on the grounds that the child could get a lot farther on a skateboard.

In fact, so far from being problems in their execution, *Measure for Measure*, "an ordinary Christian story," as the poet Philip Thompson called it,[8] is one of Shakespeare's greatest and most coherent plays. *All's Well That Ends Well*, too, though its language is challengingly dense, tells a perfectly standard Shakespearean story. *Troilus and Cressida*, as argued above, makes perfectly coherent sense if seen as a satire about a collapsing civilization. The "problem" of it arises only from trying to shoehorn it into another category of drama. And *Hamlet* is only a "problem" for those who cannot accept what Shakespeare and his audience believed and assumed (and what the play explicitly tells us) about God, death, judgment, heaven and hell, and providence.

Rather than adopting this false category, the reader is invited to recognize that Shakespeare's greatness transcends the limited horizons of a great number of modern critics. Unlike theirs, Shakespeare's imagination was quite at home in both respecting the box and thinking outside it. That is because when Shakespeare went outside the box, he was not going out into an irrational universe of emotional and existential chaos. For all the doubts and questioning of his age, and for all the playful experimentation of his extravagant imagination, the universe of reality for Shakespeare remained morally and spiritually intact.

---

[1]   Aeschylus and Sophocles offer their audiences another dimension to human life besides the grip of fate. In the Oresteian trilogy the ancient cycle of violent revenge ends with the establishment of the justice of the city of Athens by its patron Athena, the goddess of wisdom. And in *Oedipus at Colonus* Sophocles shows the gods to be up to something besides the entrapment of the human protagonist. What they are up to is an unfathomable mystery, but it is something beyond man's enchainment in fate. But these are rare hints of a spiritual dimension in a tradition in which for the most part death is the end—and the only end—of the tragic story. Unlike in Christian stories, if anything of most classical tragic heroes lives on, it is only in the story itself.

[2]   Morton Bloomfield, in a lecture series entitled "Medieval and Renaissance Tragedy and Notions of Tragedy" delivered at Brandeis University, Spring, 1978.

[3]   Madeleine Doran, *Endeavors of Art: A Study of Form in Elizabethan Drama* (Madison: University of Wisconsin Press, 1964), p. 148.

[4]   OED pageant *sb.*

[5]   F.E. Halliday, *A Shakespeare Companion 1564–1964* (Baltimore: Penguin, 1964), p. 350.

[6]   OED satire *sb.*

[7]   F. S. Boas, *Shakespeare and His Predecessors* (London: John Murray, Third Impression 1910), pp. 384–408, at https://archive.org/details/shakespearehispr00boasuoft/page/n5.

[8]   Quoted from Notes on Shakespeare in Gideon Rappaport, ed., *Dusk and Dawn: Poems and Prose of Philip Thompson* (San Diego: One Mind Good Press, 2005), p. 224.

11

What Is a Sonnet For?

FIRST OF ALL, WHAT IS A POEM?

The best way I have found to answer this question is that a poem says with words what can't be said in words. Or, more prosaically, a poem unites the sense, sounds, and rhythms of words and sentences into an experience of meaning that could not be conveyed otherwise. As in each of us the body and soul form a single complex being, so in a poem—or at least in a good poem—the form and content become a single significant vehicle of meaning that can be found in no other particular combination. We know a poem is great if it evokes an empathic experience that is inexplicably and significantly moving, or, as Prof. Mary Holmes, my greatest teacher, used to put it, it raises the hair on the back of your neck (see Chapter 15.)

NOW WHAT IS A SONNET?
History

A sonnet, until modern times almost always a love poem, is a fourteen-line poetic form that was invented in the thirteenth century, increased in popularity through the Renaissance, and has lasted into the modern world. It descends from a Sicilian peasant form of poem called the *strambotto*, an eight-line poem rhyming a b a b, a b a b (i.e., all *a* lines rhyme with one another, and all *b* lines rhyme with one another). The sonnet itself was invented c. 1230 by an attorney named Giacomo da Lentino, called *il Notaio* (The Notary), active in the court of the King of Sicily (later Holy Roman Emperor) Frederick II (1188–1240). Da Lentino added six lines to the *strambotto* form, making the new form called the sonnet (from the Italian *sonetto* meaning "little song").[1]

From Sicily the form traveled to Tuscany. There it joined the courtly love poetry of medieval France in influencing the group of poets writing in the *dolce stil nuovo* (sweet new style) inspired by Guido Guinizelli (c. 1230–1276) and including Dante Alighieri (1265–1321) and his friend

Guido Cavalcanti (c. 1255–1300). Dante became the first poet to compose a sonnet sequence, *La Vita Nuova* (The New Life), love poems to the woman who would later become the figure of Beatrice in the *Divine Comedy*. Petrarch (1304–1374) wrote a sonnet sequence to his beloved Laura, and later Michelangelo Buonarroti (1475–1564, the year of Shakespeare's birth) too wrote sonnets.

From Italy the sonnet form came to England, where it was popularized by Sir Thomas Wyatt (1503–1542) and others. The two great sonnet sequences in English preceding Shakespeare's were *Astrophel and Stella*, by Sir Philip Sidney (1554–1586), and the *Amoretti*, by Edmund Spenser (1552–1599). Shakespeare's sonnets were most probably written in the 1590s but were printed together only in 1609. (Two of them, Sonnets 138 and 144, appeared in 1599 in *The Passionate Pilgrim*, a collection in which various poems, most by other poets, were attributed to Shakespeare—see Chapter 14.) There is hardly a critic who would not agree that Shakespeare's sonnet sequence contains the greatest sonnets ever written.

Structure

There are two styles of sonnet in English, both using the iambic pentameter meter but distinguished by their rhyme schemes:

The *Italian* or *Petrarchan sonnet* is structured as an *octave* (an eight-line unit) made of two *quatrains* (four-line units) and a *sestet* (a six-line unit). The rhyme scheme of the octave is always *abba, abba*. The sestet may have any of a number of rhyme schemes: *cde, cde* or *cd, cd, cd* or *cde, edc*, and so on. Despite its name, this form never entirely fell out of use in English.

The *English* or *Shakespearean sonnet* is made of three quatrains and a *couplet* (a rhyming two-line unit). The rhyme scheme of the typical Shakespeare sonnet is *abab, cdcd, efef, gg*.

Some may wonder how so highly structured a short form can have become the vehicle of such great and profound poetry. Don't the rules of sonnet structure limit the inventiveness of the poet? The answer is just the opposite. Robert Frost, when asked about free verse (poetry without meter or rhyme), said, "I'd just as soon play tennis with the net down."[2] It's a profound comment. Think how you might answer someone who asks "What fun is it to play tennis when you have to avoid the net yet still keep the ball inside the lines?" You would say that without the net and the lines tennis does not exist. There could be no game, no great shot, no winner or loser, no Roger Federer or Serena Williams, unless the conventional limits of the game were agreed upon.

The same is true for the sonnet. Because the poet has to "stay within the lines," that is, keep to the iambic five-foot meter (see What Is Iambic Pentameter? in Chapter 4) and the rhyme scheme of fourteen lines, there is a kind of aesthetic pressure, the poet's idea pushing against the limits of the form. When the limits hold, the idea can be profoundly and movingly conveyed and the poet can achieve (to appropriate a line from Christopher Marlowe's *Jew of Malta*) "Infinite riches in a little room."[3]

One of the sources of the Shakespearean sonnet's force is the universal nature of pattern-making by the human mind. When we experience a single item or instance of a phenomenon, we do not perceive a pattern. Why is this thing or instance being shown us? When we are given a second item or instance, we begin to see a relation between them, though we may not be sure what relation we are meant to be seeing. But once there is a third item or instance, suddenly we perceive the pattern that unites them. And then we are ready to perceive the point being made about that pattern. In Sonnet 73, for example, the first quatrain images a season, the second a day, and the third a fire, all to illustrate the effect of the ending of life. The three quatrains in succession imply a shortening of time before the ending (of the season, of the day, of the fire, and of the sonnet). This shortening of time is the pattern that sets us up for the powerful reversal in the couplet:

> This thou perceiv'st, which makes thy love more strong,
> To love that well, which thou must leave ere long.

(This three-part pattern is also the basis of the familiar kind of joke that might begin "A priest, a minister, and a rabbi walk into a bar . . . ".) Perhaps this is a reason that in every culture in the world the number three is powerful, magical, or sacred. In any case, this is generally how a Shakespearean sonnet works (though there are exceptions). One can think of its structure as "one, two, three, POW."

SHAKESPEARE'S SONNETS

"The solid facts about the Sonnets that can be called undisputed are few," writes Anthony Hecht in his introduction to the New Cambridge Shakespeare edition.[4] What we know is that the first edition, in quarto, was printed by Thomas Thorpe in 1609. Probably most of the sonnets were written in the 1590s at the height of the popularity of the sonnet-sequence form. The rest is speculation, and it has been voluminous.

Some have speculated that the First Quarto edition was unauthorized by Shakespeare, pirated and printed by Thorpe to cash in on Shakespeare's name. Many have speculated about the identity of "Mr. W.H." to whom the volume is dedicated. Many have speculated about the identities of the "dark lady" and the "rival poet." Various proposals have been made for rearranging the order of the sonnets, though none has won general agreement. Some have questioned the author's sexuality, since the poems to the young man are romantic, though only the sonnets to the "dark lady" are explicitly sexual (see Was Shakespeare Gay or Not? below). Those interested in pursuing these questions may consult the Suggestions for Further Reading in Appendix 1.

Apart from all the speculation, Shakespeare's sonnets may be read in two ways: Any particular sonnet read closely will yield greater riches of experience the more one studies in it Shakespeare's phenomenal gift for incarnating meaning in poetic form. The sonnet sequence may also be read all the way through at one sitting, and there is nothing else in our literature to equal that experience of the variety and profundity in the phenomenon of human love.

DID SHAKESPEARE REALLY MEAN IT?

Some critics argue that Shakespeare's sequence of sonnets is a collection of poems constructed entirely artificially, all form and no personal content. In other words, the poet is inventing a "speaker" of the poem who only happens to share his name ("Will") and is engaging in a purely imaginary exercise with no involvement of the poet's real feelings for any actual person. Others argue that the sonnets are unfiltered literal recreations of Shakespeare's personal feelings about the man and the woman to whom almost all the poems are addressed. Then there are those critics who, more wisely, recognize that both are partly true: The poems could not exist if they were not inspired by specific feelings really experienced by the historical Shakespeare about actual people he knew. At the same time, the poems are extremely complex artful compositions some of whose effects depend on the readers' appreciating not only the emotions they bring to life but the inventive, witty, highly self-conscious construction of the forms themselves.

HOW LONG DID IT TAKE SHAKESPEARE TO WRITE A SONNET?

No one knows. Some might have been written in a moment. Perhaps some took weeks or months—probably not years—to perfect. We know that generally Shakespeare worked fairly quickly. But more importantly, he had the knack. Shakespeare was a man of great gifts of talent, memory, invention, and so on exhibited throughout a career that involved thinking in iambic pentameters. It is difficult to imagine that he would have had to struggle much to compose a sonnet once the idea for it came to his mind. Some of the sonnets are greater than others, of course, but all of them exhibit Shakespeare's extraordinary talent for uniting the meanings and music of words in ways that, as Emily Dickinson might say, take the top of your head off.[5]

TO WHOM DID SHAKESPEARE WRITE THE SONNETS?

Sonnets 1–126 (the last of which is rare in being irregular—a twelve-line poem of rhymed couplets) are written to or about a young man, probably an aristocrat and patron, whom Shakespeare loved in a relationship that was passionate but almost certainly not sexual. (See the next section for a discussion of what this means.) We do not know for certain who the historical person was, and there are many candidates. The likeliest is Henry Wriothesley (probably pronounced Risley), 3rd Earl of Southampton (1573–1624), to whom Shakespeare had dedicated his two long poems, *Venus and Adonis* (1593) and *The Rape of Lucrece* (1594). But nothing we might learn about the historical person to whom these sonnets were written could add to or subtract from the greatness of the poems.

This part of the sequence begins with poems urging the young man to marry in order that his good qualities and physical beauty should be reproduced. Then the series goes through every variety and nuance of love—affection, devotion, attachment, jealousy, recrimination, self-immolation, and renunciation—that a man might feel for a handsome and beloved younger man who is his patron and to whom he has dedicated his early work. (Remember that such a list of emotions can offer nothing of the real experience of the sonnets themselves. If it could, the poems would not have needed to be written.)

Sonnets 127–152 are written to or about the so-called "dark lady," a woman with whom the speaker/poet has a love relationship that is explicitly sexual. She is called "dark" because she has dark hair, dark eyes, and possibly a brown or olive complexion, contrasting with the ideal image of feminine beauty of the age, which was blond hair, blue eyes, and fair skin. The poems to the dark lady express a variety of emotions—admiration, passion, lust, jealousy, and disgust. At one point, the poet suspects that the beloved young man and the dark lady are themselves having an affair, evoking his jealousy of both. There are also sonnets indicating jealousy over the young man's patronage of a rival poet.

Was Shakespeare Gay or Not?

Was Shakespeare romantically attracted to the young man? Yes. Was he sexually attracted to the young man? Almost certainly not. The proof of the former is in almost every poem to the beloved friend, including Sonnet 20. But that poem also offers proof of the latter. In Sonnet 20 Shakespeare plays with the idea that the young man is beautiful enough to be a woman but remains sexually unavailable to him by virtue of his male genitalia. How can this be? Was he attracted to the man or wasn't he?

In our age, so thoroughly suffused with Freudian ideas that we believe every strong emotion must be rooted in sex, we find it almost impossible to imagine that a romantic attraction can be anything but sexual. Hence many men of our time are averse to any but the most superficial kinds of male bonding for fear of the potential sexual implications of strong emotions of attachment to someone of the same sex. But Shakespeare inherited a long tradition of passionate and self-sacrificial friendship from the classical world and the Bible. That tradition held male friendship to be superior to erotic love between man and woman. It is present in the myth of Damon and Pythias, in Homer's Achilles and Patroclus, in the arguments of Aristotle and Cicero on friendship, in the biblical David and Jonathan (1 Samuel 18:1, 2 Samuel 1:26), and in the Gospel of John 15:13, and, sustained by Neoplatonic teachings, it continues down through Malory's *Morte d'Arthur* to Montaigne and John Lyly in Shakespeare's own time. It is that tradition that stands behind the male friendships in Shakespeare's plays and behind the passionate friendship in the sonnets.

As usual Shakespeare not merely follows a tradition but expands on it. Calling upon the tradition of idealized male friends, Shakespeare expresses in the sonnets the most powerful emotions of love without ever intending them to be expressed sexually. He can even play with the idea of sexual attraction, fearlessly and wittily, because it is clear that he considers it out of the question to act on it. By contrast, when it comes to his relationship with the dark lady, the poems are far from promoting an ideal of pure friendship. On the contrary, the relationship is clearly sexual and the poems are explicitly so, even luridly genital and sometimes (in elaborate puns) obscene. Except in Sonnet 20, where he rejects the notion, no such explicitly sexual images or language attend his devotion to the male beloved.

Here is an exercise to help the modern person realize the possibility of a non-sexual romantic love. Can you remember a time when you were about six or seven or eight years old and you had a best friend of the same sex? Did you love being together? Did you want to sleep over at one another's house? Did you walk your friend to his or her home only to be walked back to yours so as not to be separated? Were you so attached that parting was pain and reunion was joy? If you can answer yes to any of these questions, suppose I now ask "Was this relationship sexual?" You will probably answer, "Eeuuuwww no!" In your childhood, you would not even think of such a friendship as having a sexual source or aim. Yet it is perfectly reasonable to call such attachments romantic, devoted, and passionate.

Shakespeare knew the experience of such a relationship later in life. And he also knew the difference between that kind of passionate, romantic friendship—the total absorption in the being of another person—that could and would never be expressed sexually and an erotic relation of any kind. You can bring whatever Freudian suspicion you wish to this question, and if you wish you can categorize Shakespeare's feelings as repressed or gay or bisexual or confused or gender fluid. The reality is that, as with the friendships portrayed in the plays (like Antonio and Bassanio in *The Merchant of Venice,* Antonio and Sebastian in *Twelfth Night,* Hamlet and Horatio in *Hamlet,* and Palamon and Arcite in *The Two Noble Kinsmen*), any such superimposition of our categories on the sonnets will obscure rather than reveal their meanings. Study Sonnet 20 carefully and you will discover the distinction that Shakespeare himself makes. That will safely guide your reading of the other sonnets.

Selected sonnets are discussed in detail in Part 2.

---

[1]   His doing so is ascribed to various possible causes: an unexplained inspiration, a play on the number of notaries in Frederick's court, a response to Plato's theory of numbers in the *Timaeus* and its discussion of Pythagoras's Golden Section (also called the Golden Mean and the Divine Proportion), a response to the number series articulated in the *Liber Abbaci* (1202) by Leonardo Pisano Fibonacci (1170–1250), with whom Frederick corresponded, or a combination of all of these. The "Golden Section" is a proportion in which a whole is divided such that the ratio of the smaller to the larger part is the same as the relation of the larger part to the whole. In logic this proportion can be expressed as b : a :: a: (a + b); in algebra as (a + b) ÷ a = a ÷ b; in arithmetic as an irrational number designated Phi (φ) and expressed as

$$1 + \frac{\sqrt{5}}{2}$$

which works out to approximately 1.62 to 1; in geometry as a rectangle (called a golden rectangle) that, placed next to a square whose side is equal to the longer side of the rectangle, forms with it a larger golden rectangle. That is, the ratio of the smaller rectangle to the square is the same as the ratio of the square plus the smaller rectangle to the larger rectangle. This proportion has been known since Pythagoras and Euclid. The Fibonacci series is a series in which each number is the sum of the two preceding numbers: one plus zero, one plus one, two plus one, three plus two, etc. (1,1,2,3,5,8,13,21, etc.). Building up a series of squares the length of whose sides correspond to numbers in the Fibonacci series produces a series of golden rectangles. A spiral drawn to be tangent to the edges of those squares, called the Fibonacci spiral, reproduces the spiral growth of many things in nature: the leaves on plants, the branches of trees, the flower of the artichoke and the chamomile, the scales of pine cones and the pineapple. Many see it as well in the shell of the chambered nautilus, in the spirals of galaxies, in every spiral growth in nature. And since throughout Western history people have found that the golden section produces the forms most pleasing to the eye (in architecture and painting) and to the ear (in music), there remains great power in the Platonic and Neoplatonic ideas of a congruence between the created natural universe and the most pleasing products of human art. Some think the source of the proportion is the human face itself (the distance from the hairline to the bottom of the chin, divided at the eyes, forming the Golden ratio φ). There are literalists who, blind to the aesthetic and metaphysical implications of the Fibonacci spiral and the Golden Section, are determined to debunk their significance. They gloat on finding that the spiral of the chambered nautilus is not exactly congruent with the Fibonacci spiral. But while it is true that the Golden Section and the Fibonacci Series do not *explain* anything in nature, the skeptics would themselves be hard pressed to explain why the proportions of the ancient Greek temples, for example, have been found so pleasing to the eye of human beings of every age and culture.

2   Robert Frost quoted in *Newsweek*, January 30, 1956, p. 56, at http://www.writing.upenn.edu/~afilreis/88v/frost-tennis.html.

3   Christopher Marlowe, *The Jew of Malta* (1589), I.i.37, which rewords a phrase from John Heywood, *The Foure PP* (c. 1530), l. 591,"Here lyeth muche rychesse in lytell space."

4   Anthony Hecht, Introduction to G. Blakemore Evans, ed., *The Sonnets* (Cambridge: Cambridge University Press, 1996, repr. 1998), p. 15.

5   She put it like this: "If I feel physically as if the top of my head were taken off, I know *that* is poetry." From *The Letters of Emily Dickinson*, ed. Thomas H. Johnson and Theodora Ward (Cambridge, Mass.: The Belknap Press of Harvard University Press, 1958), L342a, quoted at https://www.emilydickinsonmuseum.org/later_years.

12

Did Shakespeare Write More than Plays and Sonnets?—The Poems

Yes. He wrote other poems.

VENUS AND ADONIS

Venus and Adonis, a narrative poem written in 1592–93 and first printed in 1593, became the most popular of Shakespeare's works during his lifetime. It appeared in about ten editions by 1602 and six more soon after Shakespeare's death. Why was it so popular? Because then as now, sex sells, and the poem is an exercise in a form of erotic poetry based on Greek and Roman mythology that was very popular among young aristocrats and therefore was often produced by poets who wanted the patronage of those aristocrats. Christopher Marlowe wrote one called *Hero and Leander* that became similarly popular. (Some critics believe that Shakespeare had seen Marlowe's poem in manuscript and was influenced by it, others that Marlowe's poem was influenced by Shakespeare's.)

Venus and Adonis is written in stanzas of six iambic pentameter lines forming a quatrain and a couplet (*a,b,a,b,c,c*), a stanza used previously by Thomas Lodge in "Scilla's Metamorphosis" (1589). The source for the Shakespeare's story is Ovid's *Metamorphoses* Book 10, with elements from Books 3 (Salmacis and Hermaphroditus) and 4 (Echo and Narcissus). The poem was dedicated to the Earl of Southampton, to whom the Sonnets may also have been dedicated.

The poem tells the story of the irresistible erotic love of Venus for the beautiful boy Adonis, who was interested in hunting wild animals but not in love, even the love of the goddess of love and beauty. (For a change the goddess is tormented by the mortal rather than the other way around.) The poem is an elaborate series of suggestive descriptions of the approach-avoidance of the two, along with speeches on the value of reproduction and the attractions of love and on the dangers of love and the attractions of hunting. The ending turns tragic when Adonis, abandoning the goddess, is killed by the boar he is hunting. It is not safe to refuse a goddess in love.

THE RAPE OF LUCRECE

The Rape of Lucrece (1594), another narrative poem, is also, like *Venus and Adonis*, dedicated to the Earl of Southampton, to whom in the dedication to the earlier poem Shakespeare had promised a "graver labor," a promise this poem no doubt fulfilled. Its dedication is more personal and its subject is more serious. It was also popular, appearing in six editions before Shakespeare's death.

The verse is *rhyme royal*, that is stanzas of seven iambic pentameter lines each with the interlocking rhyme scheme *a,b,a,b,b,c,c*. It is the form of stanza Chaucer used in *Troilus and Criseyde* (c. 1385) and the one "recommended in the critical treatises for tragic matters, complaints, and testaments."[1] It is also used in "A Lover's Complaint" (see below), and indeed this work is an elaboration of the complaint style of poem into a complete tragic tale. It begins, like many tragic narratives, by plunging us *in medias res* (into the middle of things), i.e., into the middle of the story, and it climaxes with suicide.

In the story, the evil Tarquin, inflamed by lust for the virtuous and married Lucrece, threatens her not only with death, if she will not yield to him, but with the dishonor of putting her dead body into the arms of a slave that he will kill for the purpose, thereby destroying her reputation for virtue. She pleads unsuccessfully and is raped. When her husband returns, she tells the whole story and then kills herself.

The plot comes from Livy's *History of Rome* (I.56–60) and from Ovid's *Fasti* (II.711–852) and is retold in Chaucer's *Legend of Good Women* (c. 1387), Painter's *Palace of Pleasure* (1566–67), a Bandello *novella*, and Belleforest's translation of Bandello in *Histoires Tragiques*, all of which Shakespeare probably knew.[2]

At lines 1366–1568 Shakespeare includes a digression into the matter of Troy—that is, the subject of the war between the Greeks and the Trojans over Helen (to which he will return in *Troilus and Cressida*) and the grief of Hecuba, Queen of Troy (to which he will return in *Hamlet* at II.ii). There is also a strong parallel between ll. 162–68 and Macbeth's evocation of the image of Tarquin in *Macbeth* II.i.49–56.[3] In general, in *The Rape of Lucrece* we can see Shakespeare at work developing the dramatic scenes, imagery, dialogue, and language that will later serve him well in the tragedies written at the peak of his career.

"THE PHOENIX AND THE TURTLE"

Of all the works of Shakespeare, the short poem called "The Phoenix and the Turtle" is the most mystical. There is nothing else like it in Shakespeare, though the epilogue to *The Tempest* aims at a similar unification of levels of meaning. It is a love poem, in the form of an allegory, about a love that transcends the body and the world and the lifespans of the lovers.

According to myth there was only one phoenix alive at any time, and it was said to be beautiful. (Shakespeare often identifies rarity with excellence and beauty—see Sonnet 130.) The Phoenix lived a long time (some say 500 years) and then died on a funeral pyre, out of whose ashes the new phoenix would arise to new life. The turtle (from the Latin *turtur*, turtledove, not from the French *tortue*, tortoise, which is derived from Tartarus) symbolized fidelity and constancy in love. Following in the tradition of making allegorical poems about birds, Shakespeare unites these two seemingly incompatible beings, marrying them to one another in a union of beauty and fidelity in which division is abolished, and celebrating them in a dirge or requiem, their death having removed Truth and Beauty from the world.

The poem is made of thirteen stanzas of four lines each in trochaic tetrameter catalectic, plus five stanzas of three lines each in trochaic trimeter catalectic. (*Catalectic* means that the unstressed syllable of the last troche of the line is cut off—see Chapter 4.) An introductory voice invites various birds to join in the ceremony of mourning the dead, excluding the screech owl (which foretells death) and all birds of prey except the eagle, king of the birds. Together they sing the "anthem," which praises the union of the phoenix and the turtle in a series of paradoxical statements that under normal conditions would make no sense. The Anthem ends by quoting Reason, who composes the last section of the poem called the "Threnos" (the Greek form of the word *threnody*, funeral song), which mourns the deaths of the two birds who were one, now at rest in eternity, at which we are invited to "sigh a prayer."

"A LOVER'S COMPLAINT"

At the end of the first edition of Shakespeare's Sonnets (1609) appears a poem, explicitly ascribed to Shakespeare, called "A Lover's Complaint." It is an example of the complaint style of poem mentioned above, a literary form, popular among the Elizabethans, in which a young woman laments her downfall, here resulting from seduction by a false lover. As in *The Rape of Lucrece*, which may be read as another example of the complaint poem, the verse form is rhyme royal (seven lines of iambic pentameter verse rhyming *a,b,a,b,b,c,c*). The style of the complaint poems, including this one, is highly rhetorical. Other Elizabethan examples of the form include two that were similarly attached to a sonnet sequence, "The Complaint of Rosamund" by Samuel Daniel (1592) and "The Complaint of Elstred" by Thomas Lodge (1593).

As Robert Giroux writes, "The poem is a joke, a fact mentioned by none of its critics."[4] Giroux is right, but he gets the tone of the joke wrong, claiming that at the end of the tale of her betrayal by the handsome seducer, "she realizes that she wants it to happen again."[5] Giroux's misreading is based on taking the five *that*'s in the last stanza for subordinate conjunctions rather than for the demonstrative adjectives they are. The woman cries,

> "O, that infected moisture of his eye,
> O, that false fire which in his cheek so glowed,
> O, that forc'd thunder from his heart did fly,
> O, that sad breath his spungy lungs bestowed,
> O, all that borrowed motion seeming owed,
> Would yet again betray the fore-betray'd,
> And new pervert a reconcilèd maid!"   (ll. 323–329)

("Reconcilèd" means repentant.) She is not saying "O that he would seduce me again" (I wish he would) but "O those qualities of his would seduce me again" (that is, if he were to try, I would not be able to resist). In any case, the joke, which Giroux says "could be called black humour,"[6] lies in the reversal of the reader's expectations. We expect the betrayed maiden's anguish to be final, but at the end she reiterates the impossibility of resisting seduction by such a handsome and persuasive young man and would fall again if given the opportunity.

Shakespeare's authorship of "A Lover's Complaint" and the date of composition have been significantly disputed. Brian Vickers[7] argues that the poem is by an imitator of Spenser and Shakespeare named John Davies of Hereford (not to be confused with the Renaissance poet Sir John Davies), a writing master and author of various philosophical and theological prose works who (as we saw in Chapter 2) called Shakespeare "good Will," "generous . . . in mind and mood," a sower of honesty, worthy to be companion to a king. Vickers' arguments are highly technical, but the main thematic argument is that Shakespeare generally sympathizes with the wronged maiden and condemns the betraying lover whereas here it is illicit eros and feminine surrender rather than virtue and chastity that have the last word. In equally technical studies MacDonald P. Jackson claims that there are flaws in Vickers' arguments and supports the attribution to Shakespeare.[8] If the poem was meant to be tongue-in-cheek and not intended for publication, argues Jackson, it could easily be by Shakespeare, who could perfectly well play at imitating the style of Spenser, as he plays at imitating Gower in *Pericles*, and would do it much more easily than a writing master like John Davies of Hereford.

There is no factual evidence that this poem is not by Shakespeare, and significant stylistic elements point to Shakespeare as the author: The lady and the man are not specifically identified, as they are in other poems of the period, but are generalized, one could say universalized, figures. There is a dense economy of antitheses. The wit of the reversal of expectations has much in common with that in Shakespeare's Sonnets 129 and 130. And despite the formal structure of a lament poem, there is a powerful evocation of the attractiveness of the youth and beauty of the young man that seems to echo the sonnets. If the poem is by Shakespeare and intended, as many such poems were, to be a kind of coda to the Sonnets, it can be seen as both wittily ironic flattery and at the same time subtle critique of Shakespeare's handsome and beloved patron. The young man's charms are so compelling that they can seduce not only innocence but also experience, demonstrating the power and irresistibility of love. The poem thereby becomes a fitting envoi to the sonnets in which Shakespeare has evoked all the facets of love and its sway over the heart of man.

---

1   Hallett Smith, Introduction to *The Rape of Lucrece* in G. Glakemore Evans, ed., *The Riverside Shakespeare*, Second Edition (Boston: Houghton Mifflin, 1997), p. 1814.
2   F.E. Halliday, *A Shakespeare Companion* (Baltimore: Penguin, 1964), p. 402.
3   Smith, p. 1815.
4   Robert Giroux, *The Book Known as Q: A Consideration of Shakepeare's Sonnets* (New York: Atheneum, 1982), p. 210.
5   Giroux, p. 211.
6   Giroux, p. 211.
7   Brian Vickers, "Did Shakespeare write *A Lover's Complaint*?" at https://journals.openedition.org/shakespeare/1026#ftn1.
8   For the technical argument, see MacDonald P. Jackson, "A Lover's Complaint and the Claremont Shakespeare Clinic" in *Early Modern Literary Studies* at https://extra.shu.ac.uk/emls/journal/index.php/emls/article/viewFile/67/22. For the broader argument see MacDonald P. Jackson, *Determining the Shakespeare Canon:* Arden of Faversham *and* A Lover's Complaint (Oxford: Oxford University Press, 2014).

13

Did Shakespeare Collaborate?

Of course we know that Shakespeare collaborated with his company in acting plays on the stage. But did he collaborate in authorship?

There are a few plays and poems called Shakespeare's in which scholars have discerned one or more authorial hands that are not his. For two, *The Two Noble Kinsmen* and *Sir Thomas More*, we have good external evidence of collaboration. For a very few others the only evidence is internal, that is, the style of the writing itself. The arguments for and against Shakespeare's sole authorship of these plays have waxed and waned over the years. This much we can say for sure: Anyone who believes that Shakespeare was just another good playwright like the others of the age need only read a play known to be by Shakespeare and one known to be by anyone else. The reader's actual experience will be all the evidence needed to see the difference. Any reader may then bring that experience to bear on trying to discern where the seams lie when it comes to the few plays or poems in which Shakespeare may not have had the only hand. Of course critics and scholars have brought their much greater experience and sometimes elaborate computer techniques to bear on the question, sometimes (but not always) helpfully. Where they all agree, we can be fairly confident of their conclusions. Where they don't, we are left to ourselves to divide up the assignment of specific passages between Shakespeare and his collaborator(s).

This chapter briefly addresses the works thought to be collaborations.

EDWARD III (Shakespeare's work with significant collaboration possible but not certain)

Edward III was printed in 1596 but had probably been performed earlier, for the title page reads "The Reign of King Edward the Third as it hath been sundry times played about the City of London." The mystery arises because no author is listed. Critics are more or less in agreement that four scenes are by Shakespeare, the three so-called Countess scenes

(I.ii, II.i, and II.ii) and IV.iv. This conclusion is fairly obvious because of the apparent connection of various parts of these scenes to Shakespeare's *Rape of Lucrece*, *Measure for Measure*, and *Henry V*, and because of the appearance at II.i.451 of line 14 of Shakespeare's Sonnet 94 ("Lilies that fester smell far worse than weeds"). The use of dramatic antithesis, the preoccupation with conflicting loyalties, and other elements point to Shakespeare's imagination at work. His use and treatment of them, however, though they are signatures of Shakespeare's art and of no one else's writing at the time, suggest a young Shakespeare just learning the craft, perhaps even younger than he was when writing the *Henry VI* plays. The end-stopped lines and more obvious metaphors of the other scenes of the play may indicate either that the whole play is a reworking by Shakespeare of an earlier play or that a collaborator was involved. But though the lines are somewhat less inspired and the metaphors less complex, nonetheless some antitheses and some themes nudge us toward the possibility that Shakespeare did write the entire play, but did so as an aspiring playwright not yet the master that he was to become, even by the time of the *Henry VI* plays and *Richard III*.

The conquest of France by Edward III and several of his sons serves as the background to Shakespeare's two later tetralogies. It is perfectly conceivable that Shakespeare set himself to write a play about that king and conquest before setting out to write the plays about the civil wars among Edward's descendants that lasted until Henry VII, grandfather of Elizabeth I, ended the conflict and established the Tudor dynasty. If *Edward III*, a pageant similar in structure to *Henry VIII*, is that play, it is interesting to note that Shakespeare both begins and ends his career with pageants that bracket his two history tetralogies. In *Edward III* one can see the young Shakespeare already using the techniques that would later become, though far more subtly, his most pervasive techniques for constructing dramas: verbal and dramatic antithesis, reversal of expectations, omens coming true, virtue and self-interest at loggerheads, character foils, and a whole library of classical and biblical allusions, to say nothing of the combination of familiarity and inventiveness in his use of metaphor.

Why then was the play not more popular, and why did Heminge and Condell not include it in their First Folio edition? The answer may be, and many have believed, that it was excluded because the editors thought the play not (or not wholly) by Shakespeare, though there is no hard evidence for this conjecture. My own impression is that the play is by a young Shakespeare learning his trade. That impression is shared by Giorgio Melchiori, editor of the New Cambridge edition (1998). He argues that the play fell out of favor because its negative portrayal of David the Second, King of Scotland, evoked a public protest. In addition, by the time Heminge and Condell were preparing Shakespeare's collected works for publication (1623), King James VI of Scotland had been King James I of England for twenty years, and the anti-Scottish passages in the play might have endangered the entire publication.[1]

It is to the credit of the editors of several modern editions (Riverside, Arden, and Oxford) that *Edward III* is now included among the Shakespearean canon and therefore available so that readers may decide the question for themselves.

PERICLES (Shakespeare's work with significant collaboration possible but not certain)

The situation of the text of *Pericles* is extremely obscure, so that it is difficult to come to a final conclusion about who else besides Shakespeare may be behind the play we have.

The only early text of the play is Quarto 1 (1609), a "bad quarto," meaning a text reconstructed from memory by actors who had performed in one or more live productions of the play (see Chapter 9). The play was not included in the First Folio for reasons we do not know. Some argue that it might have been because the editors knew the play not to be entirely Shakespeare's. But again there is no hard evidence for such a conjecture. Heminge and Condell may have excluded it because their edition purported to be printed "according to the true original copies," and they found the "bad quarto" of *Pericles* to be unacceptably corrupt.

In any case, most readers perceive that Acts I and II of *Pericles* are different in tone and style from Acts III, IV, and V, and that Shakespeare is certainly responsible for the later acts. The differences in the two parts of the play have caused some scholars to speculate that the manuscript behind the bad quarto, retrieved and reconstructed by memory, was "reported" by two different people, one better than the other. This theory has been generally rejected in favor of the theory of dual authorship. But, as Hallett Smith writes,

> It is difficult to believe that a play so disparate in its parts could have been the result of a planned collaboration in which Shakespeare was one of the partners, particularly if we take

Henry VIII and *The Two Noble Kinsmen* to be examples of what such collaboration actually produced. A much likelier hypothesis is that Shakespeare revised a play by another hand.[2]

But if so, whose? And what did he do to it? Could Shakespeare's collaborator have been "a brothel-keeper called George Wilkins," as Jonathan Bate, co-editor of the *RSC Shakespeare: Complete Works*, believes?[3]

Perhaps Shakespeare picked up an old play, or a new play imitating the old plays, as was the fashion, left the first two acts more or less intact, and thoroughly revised the last three. If so, whose "old play" or "new play" was he revising? Various scholars have proposed various names, but none has been agreed upon. Or perhaps Shakespeare intentionally recreated in Acts I and II the newly popular old-fashioned style in imitation of the poetry of Geoffrey Chaucer's contemporary John Gower (c. 1330–1408)—whose *Confessio Amantis*, Book VIII, provides one of two main sources for the story—and then shifted into his own late style in Acts III through V, so that the whole play is his after all.

If only we had a "good" original text of the play, we might be able to answer some of these questions. But between us and whatever Shakespeare did write stands the faulty memorial reconstruction of a live play. We seem therefore to be permanently left with guesswork and scholarly frustration.

Nonetheless, whatever readers feel about the problem of the authorship of the first two acts, by the time the play ends, Shakespeare has made of *Pericles* a great and moving drama. It is a profound study of loss and recovery, of destiny and virtue, of patience and divine intervention, of good triumphing—only at the very last—over misfortune and evil. As such, it serves well as the first of Shakespeare's four last romances, each suffused with spiritual insight and mystical poetry (see Chapter 10). Let no one ignore this play because not all the words may be Shakespeare's. It is a tribute to Shakespeare's greatness that even through the vehicle of a bad memorial reconstruction, his poetic genius can so compel our imaginations and illuminate our minds and hearts.

HENRY VIII (Shakespeare's work with possible but not significant collaboration)

Henry VIII was written in early 1613, probably to celebrate the wedding of the Princess Elizabeth, daughter of King James I, to Prince Frederick, the Elector Palatine, leader of the German Protestant union. That wedding was on February 14. We know the play was being performed at the Globe on June 29 because eyewitnesses, who called it a "new play," report that the firing of canons called for in the stage direction at I.iv.49—"chambers discharg'd"—caused the Globe Theatre to burn to the ground on that day. Hence we conclude that Shakespeare wrote *Henry VIII* after his retirement from the theatre, to which he was probably alluding in the epilogue of *The Tempest* (1611–12).

Henry VIII is a history, based mostly on Raphael Holinshed's *Chronicles* (Vol. III, 1587) and bits from John Foxe's *Acts and Monuments* (1597). But it is not a drama like the *Henry IV* plays. Rather it is a pageant, in structure more like *Edward III* and *Henry V* (see Chapter 10). Because it was written late in Shakespeare's career, because it aims more at pageantry than at drama, and because therefore it lacks the soaring poetry of Shakespeare's finest art, many have felt the play not to be very good. In truth it is good at what it aims to do, but bringing the wrong expectations to it makes it seem to be rather work-a-day Shakespeare.

Until the nineteenth century, the authorship of the play was not questioned. It was included in the First Folio (1623), in which the editors, Heminge and Condell, Shakespeare's friends and fellow "sharers" in the theater, were committed to reproducing the "true original copies" of Shakespeare's plays. The authenticity of Shakespeare's authorship is reinforced by the fact that those editors of the First Folio are known to have excluded other plays for which we have external evidence of Shakespeare's collaboration with John Fletcher (1579–1625), i.e., *Two Noble Kinsmen* and *Cardenio* (see Chapter 14).

However, in 1850, in an article in *Gentleman's Magazine*, J. Spedding argued that about half the play was written by Fletcher.[4] Spedding's arguments were based on internal evidence alone (i.e., style, diction, sentence structure, etc.), there being no external factual evidence of collaboration. Many have followed Spedding in believing in this collaboration with Fletcher, though they differ about which passages should be ascribed to him. Many have argued equally persuasively against the collaboration. Cyrus Hoy, taking a middle path, argued that Fletcher was responsible for parts of the play but fewer than Spedding had claimed. He believed that Fletcher did "nothing more than touch up a Shakespearean passage, or insert a passage of his own in a Shakespearean context," and that Fletcher is "assuredly there" but not so much as has been claimed.[5]

The arguments for Fletcher's hand in the play are largely fueled by critics' conviction that the play is not so good as Shakespeare would have made it were he working alone. The arguments against it are fueled by the conviction that the play exhibits, given its purposes, a thoroughly Shakespearean tone and quality. My own conclusion is that, though small bits of the play may be written or "touched up" by Fletcher, the over-all impression of the play is of a single mind at work—and that mind Shakespeare's. Though the play does not achieve the depths of the great earlier histories, it nonetheless exhibits the same spirit as that seen in Shakespeare's most recently preceding plays (i.e., *Pericles, Cymbeline, The Winter's Tale,* and *The Tempest*). Here, as there, virtue, grace, forgiveness, religious humility, and the hope for joy overcome evil pride and social disharmony and result in triumphant celebration. Of this spirit Fletcher would have been incapable, as we can see from the works he wrote on his own. No true appreciation of this play depends on attempting to surmise the relatively insignificant role, if any, that Fletcher played in writing it. For better or for worse, *Henry VIII* is most likely Shakespeare's.

THE TWO NOBLE KINSMEN (Shakespeare's work with significant collaboration almost certain)

   The Riverside Shakespeare properly categorizes *The Two Noble Kinsmen* among the Romances, with which it fits in date and atmosphere. Its story is a retelling of The Knight's Tale, the longest in Chaucer's *Canterbury Tales,* which Chaucer had taken from an even longer story in Boccaccio. In the play the drawn-out conflict between the two noble cousins, who are both in love with the same girl, in the end cannot be resolved by human beings. The resolution is achieved not even by the great hero-duke Theseus, but only by the ineffable gods, in this case Mars, Venus, and Diana. Addressing the gods in the concluding scene, Theseus says,

> O you heavenly charmers,
> What things you make of us! For what we lack
> We laugh, for what we have are sorry, still
> Are children in some kind. Let us be thankful
> For that which is, and with you leave dispute
> That are above our question.   (V.iv.131–36)

("[L]eave dispute" means leave off or cease disputation; in "That are above our question" the word *That* refers to the gods; and "above our question" means beyond the power of human reasoning.) Both the style and the sentiment here are characteristic of Shakespeare's last plays. But

The Two Noble Kinsmen is the only play in the generally accepted canon of Shakespeare's works for which we have external as well as internal evidence of divided authorship.[6]

The external evidence for collaboration includes both the title page of the first quarto (1634) and the entry in the Stationers' Register for April 8, 1634, which list William Shakespeare and John Fletcher as the authors.[7] The internal evidence for collaboration with Fletcher lies in the differences in the two characteristic styles of the play: parts of the play sound like Shakespeare, parts like other plays we know to be by Fletcher. Scholars are fairly confident in being able to divide the play into the scenes that are by Shakespeare (I.i–II.i, III.i, V.i.34–173, V.iii and iv) and those that are by Fletcher (Prologue, II.ii–vi, III.ii–V.i.33, V.ii, Epilogue), with a few short scenes remaining questionable. The weightier scenes depicting the main characters at the beginning and end of the play and their meeting in the middle are by Shakespeare; much of the rest, including the subplot, is by Fletcher.

Distinction in the two styles can be seen in an example of interlocking speeches. In a Fletcher passage Palamon responds, "'Tis too true, Arcite" (II.ii.46). In a Shakespeare passage Arcite says, "Dear cousin Palamon," and Palamon responds "Cozener [= cheater] Arcite" (III.i.43–44). Note how Fletcher shifts the speaker with a distancing rote phrase while Shakespeare shifts the speaker with an earnest phrase and a punning response that increases the emotional stakes.

Distinctions in content, too, can be discerned. In Fletcher's subplot a doctor advises the honest wooer of the Jailer's daughter, not yet married to her, to go to bed with her in order to cure her of the madness caused by unrequited love. The good doctor's cavalier attitude to woman's chastity is characteristic of Fletcher's work but far from the devotion to chastity of Shakespeare's good characters in all his plays from the early *Much Ado about Nothing* to the late *Tempest*.[8]

The likely date of *The Two Noble Kinsmen* is 1613, the same year as *Henry VIII*, though unlike *Henry VIII*, a performance of which burnt down the Globe Theatre that year, the title page of *The Two Noble Kinsmen* indicates that it was performed at the private Blackfriars Theatre. But like *Henry VIII* it was written after Shakespeare's farewell to the public stage (if we may take the Epilogue of *The Tempest*, 1611, to indicate that retirement). Whether Shakespeare had finally settled in Stratford at this point or remained in London or continued to travel back and forth between the two is not known. And we have no evidence of how or why the collaboration with Fletcher was formed. Was Shakespeare grooming Fletcher to take his place?[9] Was Fletcher sent by the company to Stratford to beg Shakespeare to write another play (or maybe both *The Two Noble Kinsmen* and *Henry VIII*)? Did Shakespeare and Fletcher divvy up the scenes of a projected play, major dramatic scenes vs. the rest? Was Shakespeare asked to fill out a play Fletcher had begun writing? Did Shakespeare begin writing *The Two Noble Kinsmen* and then tire and send the partial manuscript to Fletcher to be completed? Without evidence, we are free to speculate. What is sure is that Shakespeare's voice, style, and imagination are clearly at work in some parts of the play and missing from others that bear the stamp of Fletcher's style.

SIR THOMAS MORE (Shakespeare's work with significant collaboration certain)

In the British Library there is a manuscript of a play called *Sir Thomas More*. It was apparently never printed until the editor Alexander Dyce (1798–1869) published it for the Shakespeare Society in 1844, and we have no evidence that it was ever acted in its day. What we do know is that the manuscript is written in the handwritings of six different people, one theatrical scribe (Hand C) and five playwrights whose names we know— Henry Chettle (Hand A), probably Thomas Heywood (Hand B), Thomas Dekker (Hand E), and Anthony Munday (Hand S). Except for the passage written in Hand D, the play "never rises above more or less competent mediocrity." No one but scholars would be interested in the manuscript if it were not for one thing: Hand D is most probably that of William Shakespeare.[10]

Scholars base the attribution of the Hand D passages to Shakespeare on comparisons of the handwriting with the very few other examples of Shakespeare's hand that we have, on comparison of spelling and punctuation to passages in the Quartos and Folios thought to be closest to Shakespeare's manuscripts, and on Shakespeare's characteristic vocabulary, meter, and "what R.W. Chambers calls 'the expression of ideas.'"

> [*Sir Thomas More*] belongs to a group of chronicle histories or semi-historical dramas on well-known English figures. . . . The life of More, his rise from Sheriff of London to Lord Chancellor of England with his fall and execution, affords the loose plot line of the play.

The source for the play is Holinshed's *Chronicles* (1587 ed.), which gives a

quite detailed account . . . of the so-called Ill May Day riot of 1517
. . . , in which, historically, More . . . tried and failed to control and
win over the rioters.

It is that event that is depicted in the passage of the manuscript written in
Hand D. However, in that passage, unlike in Holinshed, More succeeds
in quelling the mob of commoners. He does so with a fine speech that has
much in common with others Shakespeare wrote, among them those of
Ulysses in *Troilus and Cressida* (I.iii.75ff.) and Menenius in *Coriolanus* (I.i).

The Ill May Day riot was an uprising against foreign workers, bankers,
and merchants from the continent who were perceived to be an economic
and perhaps a social threat to native Englishmen. Based on the similarity
of those riots in More's London to events taking place in Shakespeare's
London, we can surmise that *Sir Thomas More* was written during 1592–93,

years in which the London merchants and shopkeepers had
surreptitiously circulated various libels against 'strangers' then
living and conducting business in London (e.g., French, Flemish,
Dutch, and Lombards), who . . . were viewed as posing a serious
threat to the native English business ventures. Apparently, they
even incited their apprentices and journeymen to violence . . . .

It is no doubt because of the danger of an uprising by the commoners
that Sir Edmund Tilney, the master of the Revels, and therefore the gov-
ernment censor,

called for very substantial deletions and revisions [in *Sir Thomas
More*], as evidenced particularly by a note at the beginning of the
[manuscript]: "Leave out the insurrection wholly and the cause
thereof and begin with Sir Thomas More at the mayor's session
with a report afterwards of his good service done being Sheriff of
London upon a mutiny against the Lombards—only by a short
report and not otherwise—at your own perils."

"At your own perils" meant at the risk of displeasing the Crown and
incurring punishment. It was politically and practically dangerous to
depict an insurrection from the past in a London on the brink of possible
insurrection in the present. Perhaps because of this injunction from Sir
Edmund Tilney, or perhaps to forestall it, Shakespeare was called in

to revise the insurrection scene, contradicting the historical source, by giving Sir Thomas More a powerful speech that turned the tide and quelled the fictional mob. However, the play as we have it, even with Shakespeare's contribution, does not adhere to Sir Edmund's injunctions, for the "insurrection . . . and the cause thereof" that were to be "wholly" left out still appear. It is therefore highly likely that the political climate is what prevented the play from being produced or printed before the nineteenth century.

One can see his uncommon imagination at work in the two additions to the manuscript of *Sir Thomas More* ascribed to Shakespeare (Additions II and III). In one addition Shakespeare has More offer an argument in favor of keeping to the order and hierarchy of society. In the other addition he has More give voice to a meditation on the temptations of power. Both are worth reading.

---

[1] Giorgio Melchiori, ed. *The New Cambridge Shakespeare: King Edward III* (Cambridge: Cambridge University Press, 1998), pp. 12–13.

[2] Hallett Smith, Introduction to *Pericles, Prince of Tyre* in G. Blakemore Evans, ed., *The Riverside Shakespeare*, Second Ed. (Boston: Houghton Mifflin, 1997), p. 1527.

[3] Jonathan Bate, " Is there a lost Shakespeare in your attic?" in *The Telegraph*, April 21, 2007, at https://www.telegraph.co.uk/culture/books/3664626/Is-there-a-lost-Shakespeare-in-your-attic.html.

[4] J. Spedding, "Who Wrote Shakespeare's *Henry VIII*?" *Gentleman's Magazine*, clxxviii (August–October 1850), pp. 115–24 and 381–82, quoted and ref. in R.A. Foakes, ed., *King Henry VIII* The Arden Edition, (Cambridge: Methuen and Harvard University Press, Third Ed, 1957, Repr. 1966), pp. xvii.

[5] Cyrus Hoy, "The Shares of Fletcher and his Collaborators in the Beaumont and Fletcher Canon (vii)," *Studies in Bibliography*, xv (1962), p. 79, quoted and ref. in R.A. Foakes, ed. *King Henry VIII*, pp. xxvii–xxviii.

[6] Hallett Smith, Introduction to *The Two Noble Kinsmen* in *The Riverside Shakespeare*, p. 1689.

[7] According to Jonathan Bate, co-editor of the *RSC Shakespeare: Complete Works*, Shakespeare "was grooming [Fletcher] to take over as the in-house dramatist for his acting company, the King's Men," see Note 3.

[8] In "A Lover's Complaint," which I take to be by Shakespeare, the maiden's final self-defense of her breach of chastity is also uncharacteristic of Shakespeare's plays. However, the Doctor's recommendation of extramarital sex in *The Two Noble Kinsmen* is unmitigated by the wit that underlies the ending of the poem (see Chapter 12).

[9] See Note 7.

[10] The source of most of the information in this section on *Sir Thomas More* and of the quotations is G. Blakemore Evans, Introduction to *Sir Thomas More*: The Additions Ascribed to Shakespeare, in *The Riverside Shakespeare*, pp. 1775–79.

14

Hypothetical, Spurious, and False Shakespeare

HYPOTHETICAL WORKS

There are two plays for which we have no texts at all. If they ever did exist, they were probably written by Shakespeare. I'll call them "hypothetical works."

Love's Labour's Won (Shakespeare's hypothetical work with no evidence of collaboration)

Among the comedies ascribed to Shakespeare in *Palladis Tamia: Wit's Treasury* (1598) by Francis Meres, a compendium of sayings that included an assessment of English writers from Chaucer to Meres' own time, is a play called *Love's Labour's Won*. Scholars thought that title must have been applied to a play that we know under another name, say *The Taming of the Shrew*, until "in 1953 a London bookseller discovered a list of the books that the stationer Christopher Hunt had in stock in August 1603, and these include" both *The Taming of the Shrew* and *Love's Labour's Won*.[1] It is possible that the play was "one that was later included in the Folio but had been published by 1603 under another title, possibly *All's Well that Ends Well*,"[2] but it is also possible that the play is simply lost to us. Jonathan Bate, co-editor of the *RSC Shakespeare: Complete Works*, conjectures that it is a "genuinely lost play" written after *Love's Labour's Lost*, whose conclusion, he believes, "positively invites a sequel."[3]

Cardenio (Shakespeare's hypothetical work with collaboration probable)

In 1613, about the time that Shakespeare was collaborating with John Fletcher on *The Two Noble Kinsmen* and probably on *Henry VIII*, John Heminge, Shakespeare's fellow shareholder in their acting company, The King's Men, and later co-publisher of the First Folio, was paid for two performances of a play called in the records *Cardenno* or *Cardenna*, one played at the royal court and one at Greenwich for the ambassador of the Duke of Savoy. No author is mentioned. Forty years later, in 1653, one Humphrey Moseley, a collector of play manuscripts, registered a play called *"The History of Cardennio*, by Mr. Fletcher & Shakespeare." Moseley was known on other occasions to have claimed Shakespeare's authorship falsely in order to sell books, but the timing of the two productions in 1613 makes it possible that this play was one of several that Shakespeare, perhaps after his retirement, worked on with Fletcher. This is all we know about the play, of which no version has been found.

There was a play, produced in 1727 and published the next year, called *Double Falsehood*, which Lewis Theobald, the astute third editor of Shakespeare's complete works, claimed he had revised and adapted from a play by Shakespeare. But no manuscript of his source play has been found and Theobald did not include it in his edition of Shakespeare's plays.

The original source of the lost play *Cardenio* and of *Double Falsehood* was the story of Cardenio in the first part of Cervantes' *Don Quixote* (1605), which had appeared in an English translation by Thomas Shelton in 1612.[4] Don Quixote and Sancho Panza find Cardenio living like an animal in romantic agony in the wilderness because, in love with Lucinda, he has been betrayed by his friend Fernando, who has himself fallen for Lucinda. After plot complications involving the Don and Sancho and Fernando's first love, Dorotea, the story ends happily, the right man with his right mate. It is tantalizing to imagine the drama that Shakespeare would have made of the story. But unless one day a copy of *Cardenio* is found, we have got only our own imaginations in place of the play.

SPURIOUS INTERPOLATION
The Hecate Passages in *Macbeth*

Scholarship has detected some degree of revision in the manuscript source for the First Folio printing of *Macbeth*, our only early text of the play. The play is shorter than the other great tragedies, and some see what G. Blakemore Evans calls "raggedness" in I.ii and the implication of a perhaps missing scene at I.vii.46–54.[5] If cuts were indeed made for a performance at court, or for one in the country, they were made judiciously, and, as Frank Kermode writes, guesswork is pointless, for "we shall hardly discover the nature of what is lost."[6] But we have lost little, if anything, even if there were cuts—I imagine that Shakespeare intended the play to be precisely as short and intense as we find it—for the play as we have it holds together with almost perfect coherence. That is, it is all perfectly coherent except at three points: The Hecate passages—i.e., all of Act III, Scene v, and Act IV, Scene i, lines 39–43 and 125–32, with their respective stage directions about songs to be inserted.

It is obvious that these passages are not by Shakespeare. The rhymes in these speeches are pedestrian and the tone is inappropriate. The Hecate speech at III.v.2–33, in predicting what is to come later in the play and ending in a platitude, reveals its inferiority to the subtlety and depth of those omens in the play that are clearly the work of Shakespeare himself. As Kermode writes,

> These passages are usually attributed to Thomas Middleton because the interpolated songs called for in the stage directions at III.v.33 and IV.i.43 are certainly his, but it has recently been argued that Middleton's Hecate in his play *The Witch*, where the songs appear, bears no resemblance to the Hecate of *Macbeth*, and that some other, still anonymous, author must have the credit or blame for the material by which Middleton's songs are foisted into Shakespeare's play.[7]

"Foisted" is the right word, for these passages—speeches and songs—are nothing but a distraction from the drama. Students of *Macbeth*, apart from those interested in such textual questions for their own sake, will lose nothing, and will avoid distracting incoherence, by entirely ignoring these three passages.

FALSE ATTRIBUTIONS

Because Shakespeare was such a success in his time and so widely recognized as a uniquely great poet, works ascribed to him were likely to sell. As a result, less than scrupulous editors and publishers who wished to be assured of lucrative sales would claim Shakespeare or "W.S." to be the author of various poems and plays that were not in fact his. There is almost a library of works making such claims. Many of these have been recognized to be by other poets of the age whom we know. The authors of many others remain unidentified. However, several such works have been taken up by scholars who claim Shakespeare to be the author after all. The four most notorious of them are the following:

The Passionate Pilgrim: Five poems by Shakespeare—probably pirated

The Passionate Pilgrim would be of little concern for us if the publisher,

William Jaggard, had not claimed on the title page that all the booklet's twenty love poems were by Shakespeare. Jaggard is known to have published others' work under Shakespeare's name as a money-making scheme, and that is very likely what happened here. Only five of the poems in the collection are by Shakespeare, and all five already existed in earlier texts, so that Jaggard's version of them has almost no textual authority.

The five poems by Shakespeare are, in Jaggard's numbering, (1) a mangled version of Sonnet 138; (2) a slightly less mangled version of Sonnet 144; and three poems from Shakespeare's play *Love's Labour's Lost*, printed in 1598, a year before *The Passionate Pilgrim*, namely (3) a version of the sonnet spoken by Longaville (IV.iii.58–71), (5) a version of the sonnet written by Berowne and read by Nathaniel (IV.ii.105–118), and (16) an eighteen-line version of the twenty-line poem in tetrameter couplets read by Dumaine (IV.iii.99–118).

The remaining, non-Shakespearean, poems in *The Passionate Pilgrim* are by four known poets—Richard Barnfield, Bartholomew Griffin, Christopher Marlowe, and Sir Walter Raleigh—and by some number of unknown ones.

> The first four stanzas of [(19)] are a very inferior version of Christopher Marlowe's great pastoral lyric "The Passionate Shepherd to His Love," which had not been printed before but was to appear in its full text, properly attributed to Marlowe, in *England's Helicon* (1600); it is there followed by "The Nymph's Reply to the Shepherd," attributed since the seventeenth century to Sir Walter Raleigh, from which the final stanza of [(19)] is taken.

The other poems, of no very remarkable quality, are of unknown authorship.[8]

Arden of Feversham

Some readers, notably the poet Swinburne, have thought the domestic tragedy called *Arden of Feversham* to be by Shakespeare. But Shakespeare's name does not appear on any of the first three editions (1592, 1599, and 1633) and becomes associated with it only in the edition printed by Edward Jacob in 1770. In recent times, MacDonald P. Jackson argues for Shakespeare's authorship of at least some scenes.[9] Others ascribe the play to Thomas Kyd, author of *The Spanish Tragedy* (1588–89). The play is well crafted and the so-called "argument" scene (III.v) shows dramatic flair, but its end-stopped lines and uninspired imagery lack Shakespeare's poetic touch. Barring further substantive evidence, it seems rash to ascribe the play to Shakespeare. The play is available online so that readers may decide for themselves.[10]

"Shall I Die"

In 1985 Gary Taylor, co-editor of *The Oxford Shakespeare*, claimed that this poem of nine 10-line stanzas should be attributed to Shakespeare.[11] The poem is found in two early manuscript collections by different authors (1637 and 1639), only one of which ascribes the poem to Shakespeare. Most scholars reject the attribution, including Donald Foster,[12] who first ascribed *A Funeral Elegy* to Shakespeare and then retracted his claim. It is improbable and seems to most readers impossible that this pedestrian and unimaginative poem could be by the poet of the sonnets and the plays we know to be Shakespeare's.

A Funeral Elegy

In 1989, Donald W. Foster published a book called *Elegy by W.S.: A Study in Attribution*. In it he argued that a published 578-line poem, written in memory of the speaker's murdered friend, ascribed on the title page to W.S., and published in 1612, was written by Shakespeare. The argument was based on an elaborate computerized study. Many scholars were persuaded by that argument and many were not. Eventually Gilles D. Monsarrat published a refutation of Foster's claim, attributing the poem instead to John Ford.[13] His claim has prevailed with most scholars, including Foster himself, who published a recantation of his argument for Shakespeare's authorship of the poem.[14]

---

[1]   F.E. Halliday, *A Shakespeare Companion 1564–1964* (Baltimore: Penguin Books, 1964), p. 289.
[2]   Ibid.
[3]   Jonathan Bate, "Is there a lost Shakespeare in your attic?" in *The Telegraph*, April 21, 2007, accessed 8/13/18 at https://www.telegraph.co.uk/culture/books/3664626/Is-there-a-lost-Shakespeare-in-your-attic.html.
[4]   The source of most of the information in the section on *Cardenio* is Halliday, pp. 83–84, 491–92.
[5]   G. Blakemore Evans, Note on the Text of *Macbeth*, in *The Riverside Shakespeare*, Second Ed., (Boston: Houghton Mifflin, 1997), pp. 1387–88. See also Frank Kermode, Introduction to *Macbeth* in the same edition, pp. 1355–56.
[6]   Kermode, p. 1355.
[7]   Kermode, p. 1356.

[8]   Hallett Smith, Introduction to *The Passionate Pilgrim* in *The Riverside Shakespeare*, p. 1881.

[9]   MacDonald P. Jackson, *Determining the Shakespeare Canon*: Arden of Faversham *and* A Lover's Complaint (Oxford: Oxford University Press, 2014). See also MacDonald P. Jackson, "Shakespeare and the Quarrel Scene in Arden of Faversham," *Shakespeare Quarterly*, Vol. 57, No. 3 (Autumn, 2006), pp. 249–93.

[10]   *Arden of Feversham*, ed. Ronald Bayne (London: J.M. Dent, 1897) at http://www.gutenberg.org/files/43440/43440-0.txt.

[11]   Gary Taylor, "Shakespeare's New Poem: A Scholar's Clues and Conclusions," *New York Times*, December 15, 1985, at https://www.nytimes.com/1985/12/15/books/shakespeare-s-new-poem-a-scholar-s-clues-and-conclusions.html.

[12]   Donald Foster, Letter to the *New York Times*, January 19, 1986, at https://www.nytimes.com/1986/01/19/books/l-a-new-shakespeare-poem-238486.html.

[13]   G.D. Monsarrat, "A Funeral Elegy: Ford, W.S., and Shakespeare" in *The Review of English Studies* New Series, Vol. 53, No. 210 (May, 2002), pp. 186-203, at https://www.jstor.org/stable/3070371?seq=1#page_scan_tab_contents.

[14]   William S. Niederkorn, "A Scholar Recants on His 'Shakespeare' Discovery," *New York Times*, August 21, 2002, at https://www.nytimes.com/2002/06/20/arts/a-scholar-recants-on-his-shakespeare-discovery.html.

15

The Nature of Art

Deepening one's understanding of what art is in general must help to deepen one's appreciation of Shakespeare's art specifically. Hence I offer this chapter on the nature of art. Its relevance will soon become clear. The main ideas are those of the late Mary Holmes, painter, professor of art history, cultural historian, and my greatest teacher. The words in boldface type are quotations or paraphrases from her lectures, writings, and conversations.[1]

WHY ART?

Human life is paradoxical. We are thinking, self-aware beings living in physical bodies in the physical world. This joint being, consciousness tied to physicality, causes us no end of mystification. It yields rich complexity of experience, but also, inevitably, frustration. We are amazed that our bodies can do a whole range of remarkable things, from breathing and reproduction to decathlons and playing the violin. And at the same time we are frustrated that our bodies can't or won't do what our minds imagine they might, like flying or never sleeping or having a tea party at the bottom of the sea.

Because we have imaginations that take our thoughts beyond our bodies' limits, we are always striving to get our bodies to catch up, to give physical reality to images in our minds. We cook dinner not only to have something to eat but because we can imagine the pleasure and satisfaction of eating, and perhaps sharing, a tasty meal; we practice lay-ups because we can imagine making the perfect shot or winning the championship or maybe impressing a girl or a scout; we learn to drive because we can imagine getting to work or to the beach in a car; we sit more or less still in classrooms because we can picture our parents reading our report cards or the life that learning might bring us or the pleasure in having our conceptions expanded or relief in having our questions answered. Anyone who has been in love knows what it means to strive to realize a mental image.

Because our bodily experience is so powerfully present to us, and because our minds can imagine all sorts of things that we can never experience in our bodies, we find it hard to believe in the reality of anything that is only a concept in the mind. If it is not also present to our physical senses, how can we be sure that it is any more than a fantasy? **This is why seeing is believing.** Whether it's an abstract idea (like winning the game) or a memory (like your first birthday party) or a future hope (like becoming President) or an ideal image (like your future wife or husband) or a divine being (like an angel or God himself), unless we can physically sense it, we can't quite believe in it.

At the same time, we all know that our senses can be fooled. That lake on the desert road ahead turns out to be a mirage; that heavy ceramic bowl turns out to be light plastic; and so on. But here too, the senses, along with reason, are called upon to confirm or deny our mental pictures. I can know about optical illusions, but only stepping physically into that lake proves to me beyond a doubt that it was a mirage: I didn't get wet. Only my hands lifting that plastic bowl confirm that my eyes misled me into thinking it was heavy ceramic. Except in the most abstract of human enterprises (like logic or mathematics), only seeing (i.e., experiencing with the senses) is believing.

But this condition is a frustrating predicament if the concept is not easily perceivable by the senses. And such is the case with the vast majority of our concepts. The past cannot be retrieved, the distant cannot be embraced, the hoped-for future cannot be grasped in the present, the ideal can rarely if ever be realized in the world of space and time, and the invisible is invisible.

Because only seeing is believing, people make art to confront this predicament. The work of art brings into the realm of our physical experience what would otherwise be an unbelievable concept. You make a word picture about winning the game, a snapshot of your first birthday party, a journal entry about the desire to be President, a novel about the perfect, or perfectly awful, wife or husband, a poem about your distant beloved, a painting of angels, a psalm about God—all in order to make the idea accessible to sensible experience. **We will not live without images** that make real to our senses that which we imagine or hope or desire or believe. We want to see it. Therefore, as Mary Holmes says, **the purpose of art is to make the invisible visible.**

Because all human beings need the invisible to be made visible, since only seeing is believing, human beings simply will not live with-

out art. For this reason, at all times and in all places, wherever there have been human beings, there has been art.

WHAT IS ART?

After a lifetime of teaching and thinking about art, Mary Holmes concluded that **the only trustworthy definition of art is "anything made by a human being."** If a human being didn't make it, if it was made by nature or divine creation or accident, it's not art. If a human being made it, then it's art. These statements at first seem uselessly general, but really they convey a deep truth. Anything made by a human being is art because **anything made by the human hand exhibits the choices of the person doing the making.**

You can test the truth of this definition of art by imagining the following: You are walking along the beach with a friend who picks up a beautiful shell to show you. You notice the shape and the intricacy and the color and the texture and so on. You see its beauty and are moved by it. Now suppose the friend says, "You know, that shell I just pretended to find on the sand? It's actually man-made." Let's say by Tiffany and Co. in the nineteenth century.

What just happened to your inner feelings? They did a sudden flip-flop. Knowing that the shell was made by a human being, you now see and feel and judge it in a completely different way. Your wonder at nature's handiwork becomes a different kind of wonder—now it's wonder at the handiwork of the human artist.

Everything we know to be made by human beings evokes from us that second kind of feeling, interest, and judgment. And that is why anything people have made we call art.

But though everything made by a human being is art, that doesn't mean that everything made by a human being is _good_ art. It means that everything made by a human being is an attempt to make an idea—an image in the mind—accessible to our physical experience in the body, through seeing (a painting or a photograph), hearing (a piece of music or a school bell), touching (a Jacuzzi or the Rosary beads), tasting (a fine wine or a tiny plastic spoonful of the new flavor at the ice cream stand), or smelling (a perfume or a garlic-basil pesto).

Not only great paintings or plays or cathedrals but the chair you're sitting in and the clothes you're wearing and the dishes you eat from—all are chosen by human beings to be made as they are and to look the way they do, whether for practical use or for aesthetic effect or for both. And each man-made thing reveals in its form the choices—both practical and aesthetic—that went into making it.

Those choices may be good ones or not, and so the work may be anything from a complete success to a total failure, great or hideous or anything in between.

This is why it is silly for people to use the word *art* **as a form of praise:** "That painting my niece made was a real work of art!" Well yes, it's art, all right, because she's a human being and she made it. But is it any *good?*

HOW DOES ART WORK?

Just as we ourselves are paradoxes (minds mysteriously tied to bodies), so art works on us through four basic sets of paradoxes.

Paradox 1: Empathy and Psychic Distance
Empathy
The basic foundation of all art is empathy, meaning "feeling into." Our empathic response is that capacity we all have to *feel into* **what we are looking at, to intuit meaning in form. We are always exercising this capacity,** whenever we are seeing or hearing or tasting or touching or smelling anything. When we see something, we are also **feeling what it feels like to feel the way it feels.**[2]

Let's say you see someone walking along and suddenly crack his shin on the corner of a bench. What happens to you? You feel it! Not in your body. You're not going to have the other person's bruise on your shin. But you feel it in your mind's version of your body. Your inner life experiences a mental version of that pain, and you experience something very like what the other person is feeling. You might even wince. That's empathy. It's not just the idea of his pain or the understanding of it, which you also have. It's the direct immediate experience of it inside yourself that precedes any idea about it or reaction to it.

Another example: **You're sitting in the theater** and at a certain point you feel that a silence on stage has gone on a little too long. **You realize that one of the actors has forgotten his or her lines.** With each passing second the silence gets heavier and heavier. **How are you feeling? Uncomfortable, anxious, starting to squirm? Why? You're not the one on stage being totally embarrassed. You're sitting in the dark among hundreds of other people, none of them looking at or thinking about you. And yet you feel the actor's agony as if it were your own, and you can't wait for it to end. That is empathy.**

When you see a smile or a frown, a limping person or a scampering cat, in fact **anything with a visible physical shape, moving or still, you empathize into it, knowing,** in your own mental version of your body, **what that shape or movement or gesture means, because you know what it would mean if your own body were in that shape or were making that gesture.** The same is true for hearing: the resolution of a piece of music on the final tonic chord means one thing, a fingernail on a blackboard another, and you know the difference in meaning just by hearing them, even just by reading the words that describe them! A tap on your shoulder can mean friendliness or threat, and you can usually tell which it is by the feel of the thing. **Empathy is the power to experience and recognize meaning in form, and we are empathizing all the time.**

One day every year Mary Holmes would come into the lecture hall and make two drawings on the blackboard. Look at these two versions of them:

Suppose you came into the lecture hall or classroom and saw these two lines on the blackboard. **And suppose I told you that the line on the right represents chaos, disorder, confusion, anxiety, and frustration, and that the line on the left represents simplicity, elegance, smoothness, easiness, and calm. You would say that I was crazy (or lying). And you'd be right. How do you know? Your empathic response to the lines tells you so, even if you have not seen them being drawn. Because all form has meaning to us simply by virtue of the physical things we are.** Even if we can't put into words what the lines mean, even if we come from entirely different cultures or different periods of history, the line on the left means the same thing to all of us, as does the line on the right, simply because we have bodies that are shaped in certain ways and experience the world as they do. Despite the varieties of our physical and cultural experiences, the basic human empathic response is universal, which is why we can appreciate works of art made by people from far away and long ago—an ancient Chinese vase, say, or an Egyptian pyramid, or the Parthenon.

Not only visible images have meaning and evoke our empathy. Let's say you are in my lecture hall and I ask you to close your eyes, and then I say the word *butterfly*. You and every English-speaker in the room will have an empathic response very different from the one you'll have—keep your eyes closed—when I then say the word *hippo*. (This also works for the words printed on the page you are reading.) That difference in the way we feel in response to the words and their images in our minds is evidence of our empathy. We know what it feels like to feel like a butterfly, though we've never had wings, and what it feels like to feel like a hippopotamus, though we'll never weigh three thousand pounds. And because of that, we associate the feelings we get from the words with the feelings we get from the things they signify.

So our empathic response to a word is a combination of the feeling evoked in us by the image the word calls up in our minds *and* the feeling evoked by the shape and sound and spelling and image of the word itself, which, once we have learned a language, we associate with the thing the word signifies.

All art depends upon these empathic responses to images, sounds, and words. If we are not empathizing into the meaning of the forms in a work of art, we feel nothing. We don't "get it" and we're not moved. Being moved depends upon empathizing into what is moving us. When you are watching Shakespeare's Othello smothering his innocent wife Desdemona, you are feeling both what it feels like to have your hands on that pillow on that face and what it feels like to be suffocated under that pillow. You empathize with Othello and with Desdemona; you also empathize with the pillow—all at the same time. (You just empathized into the word "suffocated" too!) And the horror of the dramatic moment depends on your doing so.

Psychic Distance

Now, you don't like being suffocated or want to be murdering your wife or to be murdered. So if you are empathizing into the way Othello is feeling doing the murder and the way Desdemona is feeling being murdered, why don't you jump up at this point in the play and shout "Stop! Your wife is innocent!"? If you are empathizing into the characters while watching *Star Wars*, what keeps you from drawing your light saber and rushing to help defend Luke Skywalker from attack?

The answer is the other half of Paradox 1: Psychic (or Aesthetic) Distance. It is the awareness, even while you're thoroughly empathizing into the scene, that it's only a play or a movie. You know that if you do shout out at Othello, the actors in the play will stop what they're doing and everyone in the theater will be looking at you. The play will be interrupted and ruined. If you draw your own light saber, first you'll realize that you don't *have* a light saber because there's no such thing. And then you'll be thrown out of the movie theater for disrupting the show. The illusory world of the play or movie will be destroyed, and you and everyone else will come crashing back to reality.

Very naïve people, including young children, do such things, but you don't, and the reason is that you have psychic distance. Even while you are empathizing, you have the awareness that what you're seeing is art and not life.

Thus, all art depends just as much on psychic distance as on empathy. If we did not have that distance, we would not be able to value any quality in a work of art. We wouldn't know it was art, something made by human beings. (Remember that sea shell?) We would treat it as if it were life and would behave very differently in relation to it.

Imagine that you are staying in a hotel room with thin walls and that in the next room you hear a man and woman arguing and then hear what sounds like the man killing the gasping woman. Your impulse would be to break in on them or call the police to stop the violence. And so you should. But how embarrassed would you be if you did break in to the room, or the police did, and then found that the man and woman were actors rehearsing the last scene from *Othello*? that the murder you thought you were hearing was a play rehearsal? Have you ever bumped into a department store dummy and started to apologize, only to discover that it wasn't a real person? In both cases you were empathizing into a work of art as if it were life. Your psychic distance was missing, and when it came flooding back, *you* felt like the dummy.

In order to make sure that we don't react to a work of art as if it were life, every work of art must establish psychic distance in its audience. The work of art must do something to make sure that we know it is art and not life. And it does so by making boundaries. Painters put frames around their paintings (so we don't try to walk into them); music has rhythm (so we notice that it is a different thing from the sounds of the everyday world); statues are painted, made bigger or smaller than life, and placed on pedestals. All these things tell us to expect to experience not life but a work of art.

What happens when you ask a question of the guard in a wax museum and then discover that he too is made of wax? The artist has intentionally removed your psychic distance for a joke. But there's no joke until your psychic distance returns and you realize your initial error.

Plays especially, which have the greatest danger of being taken for life (because they are made of live people actually moving around and talking), use many means to establish psychic distance. You pay to get in, you get a program that tells you which fictional people the real people will be portraying, you sit still in rows in the dark while the actors, often wearing unusual costumes, move around in the light on a stage either higher or lower than you, and so on. All these conditions make sure you know that what you're watching is art, not life, so that you will remain silent and not destroy the play.

The coexistence of these two paradoxical forms of human perception—empathy and psychic distance—is essential to the appreciation of art. And you can see why by imagining what would happen if someone had all empathy and no psychic distance. Let's say someone watching *Star Wars* or *Harry Potter* empathizes totally with Luke Skywalker or with Harry Potter and loses all psychic distance. When he comes out of the theater, he thinks he *is* Luke Skywalker or Harry Potter and spends the rest of his day, or his life, wielding an imaginary light saber and believing he is living on some distant planet or wielding his magic wand and believing he is casting spells. We would call him mad, and rightly so. **He would be treating art—the movie—as if it were life. He would have all the empathy the moviemaker could ask for, but not nearly enough psychic distance.**

And the opposite is also a form of madness. Suppose you're visiting your friend's house, sitting in the living room and watching TV, and your friend's parents come in having a fight, and your friend's father takes a pillow and, like Othello, starts to suffocate your friend's mother. What would it mean if, instead of screaming or calling the police, you sat watching the scene, saying to yourself, "Wow, this is exciting! I wonder how it's going to turn out"? **You would be treating life as if it were art. It would mean that you had an excess of psychic distance and not nearly enough empathy.**

Empathy and psychic distance are not exercised separately in time. They are both working at the same time in harmony with one another. At the very same moment that we are horrified by Othello's act of murder, we are aware that we must not say a word but must just keep watching and listening. And the meaning of the experience, which depends on both capacities in us, comes through our exercising them, unconsciously, together.

Willing Suspension of Disbelief

Related to this paradox is what has been called the "willing suspension of disbelief"—that is, the agreement every member of the theater audience makes to treat the characters and events on stage as real. Empathy does not depend on this suspension of our skepticism. We are empathizing with the characters whether we choose to believe in their reality or not. But the willing suspension of disbelief in their non-existence—in other words, choosing to pretend they are real for the time being—allows our capacity for empathy to work deeply and consistently.

Here's what I mean: If, sitting in the theater, you keep telling yourself that the person playing Othello is an actor and the suffocating of the actress playing Desdemona is not happening in reality, you will still be empathizing, but you won't let yourself care very much. You won't be getting the full force of the empathic experience. You are holding on to your psychic distance too much. If, on the other hand, you let yourself believe in the reality of the action (always knowing, at the same time, that it is a work of art), then the events receive your fully committed attention. Your engagement will be much greater and the experience will have far more meaning.

The willing suspension of disbelief allows us the joy of escape into the story, and that brings us to the next paradox.

Paradox 2: Escape and Return

Escape

You have probably heard people say that escapism or escapist art is bad. If you believe them, you probably feel a little guilty every time you escape into art (movies, TV, books, music, dance, video games). But the truth is that **escape is essential to art**, and also essential to life. The people who say escapism is bad would be right if they said that art is bad, and bad for you, when escape is its *only* goal. **But any work of art that does not succeed in causing us to escape from ourselves is a failure—and also a bore**. Not just weak or self-indulgent people but **all human beings crave and need to lose ourselves in art**.

What does it mean to lose ourselves in a work of art? Let's say you go to a good movie in the late afternoon. When the movie is over and you come out of the theater, it's dark. Are you surprised? Why? Because during the movie you were completely unaware of the passage of time. Did you think the laws of physics had been suspended? Of course not. You were not thinking about the laws of physics or the passage of time at all. **You were simply lost in the movie.** You were not aware of sitting in a chair or of having a dentist's appointment tomorrow or of wearing new shoes. **In fact, you were not even aware even of being yourself, of being anything. If you were aware of those things, it's a sure sign that the movie was a failure. It failed to take you out of yourself, which is something we demand of any work of art.**

The work of art must carry us utterly away. If it doesn't, we call it boring, and it *is* boring. No one would pay to go into a movie theater to sit and watch a blank screen for two hours. If you did not see something up on that screen to make you forget yourself, and pretty quickly too, you would demand your money back. On the other hand, at the end of the best movies or concerts or plays or roller-coaster rides or contemplation of the best paintings or eating of a deliciously well-cooked meal, **we say, "I really lost myself. I was carried away. I lost the sense of time. I didn't know where I was."**

Why do we crave to lose ourselves? And why is causing us to escape from ourselves essential to a good work of art? The answer is that every one of us feels bound in by the severe limits within which we live, and we need relief. It's that familiar frustration of being expandable minds tied to limited physical selves.

Suppose the temperature went up only a few hundred degrees. We would die. If it went down only a hundred degrees, we'd die. We can travel for many miles on the earth's surface without much danger, but if we went up just a few miles (without a space suit), we'd die. If we went under water for an hour or so or stepped off a sixteen-story building or offered someone else the use of our heart for a few minutes, we would die. **None of us will ever be shorter than two feet tall again, or taller than ten feet.** We won't fly by flapping our arms or know what it is like to be born as a kitten or a puppy. We can't live in the past or in the future, nor can we stop the present from turning the future into the past at a faster and faster rate. We'll probably never know what it's like to be 200 years old.

One of the most severe limitations we live under is that none of us will ever be someone else. Whatever we do, however we grow and change, it will be our own familiar self doing it. And the most severe limitation of all is that we will die.

Now all the animals live under the same limitations, but they don't make art for escape. Why not? Because they don't have the same sort of consciousness or imagination we do. They don't seem to suffer from these limitations because (so far as we can tell) they aren't aware of them as limitations or of what it might mean not to have them.

But we can and do imagine being taller or shorter or more beautiful or uglier or flying or living under water or being someone else or living for a thousand years. **And the contrast between that mental capacity to imagine being more (or better or perfect or worse or just different) and the inescapable knowledge of what we really are, and will never *not* be, is agonizing—if we cannot sometimes escape from it**.

But the good news is that we *can* escape from it. And we do escape from it again and again. Some people escape in destructive ways like excessive drinking, compulsive gambling, promiscuous sex, mind-altering drugs, avoidable physical danger, or wanton violence. Most of us escape in better ways **like meaningful work, love, and worship. All of us escape daily in sleep. And we all also escape in art**.

Again, as with empathy and psychic distance, escape in art can be dangerous. When the movie's over, even if we don't think we're Luke Skywalker or Harry Potter, we may decide that living in the movie is better than being ourselves, and so we may fill our rooms with *Star Wars* or *Harry Potter* posters and listen to the sound track twenty times a day and watch the movie over and over and wear *Star Wars* clothes and speak *Star Wars* language and worship "the force" or dress like Harry Potter and carry a wand and make up incantations. This is escapism made into an end in itself, and it too is the enemy of art.

The real value of the movie is lost in this attempt to make into reality the escape that the movie originally provided. In the meantime, reality itself has been fruitlessly and often dangerously abandoned.

Return

Most of us, however, not only escape through art but also return to ourselves. This is the other half of the paradox. **The value of the escape is known and appreciated only when we return to awareness of ourselves and recognize what has happened to us, where we have been.** We can appreciate having enjoyed the movie only when we return to consciousness of ourselves having watched it. So long as we are still in it, its meaning escapes *us*.

Escape from and return to ourselves make up the second paradoxical pair on which art depends.

Paradox 3: I and We

Imagine you are walking along with a friend. Your friend is talking about something, looking down at where his or her feet are going. In the meantime you look up and see a magnificent sunset. What do you do? Do you keep walking along, silently listening to your friend and enjoying the sunset alone? No. You say, "Wow! Look!" and point toward the western sky.

Why? You are enjoying the sunset quite well, are moved by it, perhaps deeply. Why interrupt your experience and your friend's conversation to say "Look!" The answer is that even though each of us is an individual, forever compelled to experience as ourselves and as no one else what we do experience, at the same time we crave to share our experiences, especially our most intense and meaningful experiences, with others.

What does your friend say when looking up and seeing the sunset you've pointed out? He or she says something like, "Yeah, wow! Look!" He or she wants to share it with you as well and is grateful that you have pointed it out.

The sunset is not only being appreciated but also being shared. Each of you is having an interior, individual experience; at the same time, both of you are sharing that experience. And the experience is only fully satisfying when it is not just personally moving but also shared. This is part of what it means to say that we are social beings. Human beings want to share what moves them.

Just as we need to have visible representations of ideas and beliefs and desires, we have a need to share those ideas and beliefs and desires with others, and art is a way of doing so. Making a work of art, any kind of art, is a way of saying to others, "Wow! Look!" In other words, "this moved me; I expect it will move you too; let's share it."

"Here's a picture of my girlfriend" or "boyfriend," you might say, meaning "Look at the captivating beauty and exciting personality and delightful spirit I see in her or him." Or you might say, "You'll never believe what just happened to me on the way here. Listen to this!" and a story follows. Or "That was a cool movie. Remember the part where . . . ." We crave to share, and whether the medium is a story, a snapshot, a string quartet, a cartoon, or a play by Shakespeare, the goal is the same: "Wow! Look!"

One could say that *Othello* is, in one sense, an elaborate and quite successful way Shakespeare has found to say "Wow! Here's what jealous pride is and does and looks like and feels like and leads to. Look!" This book too, being a work of art, exists to share something: It is my way of saying to you about Shakespeare, "Wow! Look!"

Now when a work of art succeeds at getting a great many people over a long period of time to look, and to feel rewarded for looking, that work of art becomes what we call a "classic." A classic is not a boring old work that older people use for torturing younger ones or sophisticated people for feeling superior to the unsophisticated, though unfortunately some people do use classics that way. A classic (in this sense of the word) is really any work of any kind of art that almost everyone capable of "getting it" responds to the way your friend responded to your pointing out the sunset. "Yeah. Wow! Thanks for showing me." In other words, a classic satisfyingly binds together a great number of people, a great number of unique, individual experiences, in a shared reality, reflecting the paradox of our being both individual and social beings.

Paradox 4: Integrity and Change

Having empathized into a work of art while retaining psychic distance (Paradox 1), having escaped from ourselves into a work of art and then returned from the experience (Paradox 2), having been individually moved and also shared the work of art (Paradox 3), what do we do? We may forget it if the work was forgettable. Or we may want to forget it but not be able to. Sometimes it stays with us and keeps replaying itself in our minds in bits and pieces. Sometimes it forces us into doing more than remembering it. Maybe we want to see or read or hear it again. Maybe we find ourselves thinking about it, analyzing what it means, trying to record or copy or recreate it.

We may even become aware that we ourselves have been changed by the experience. Maybe it has moved us so much that we will never again look at—fill in the blank—the same way.

Are we still ourselves? Of course. Are we changed? Often, maybe in huge and noticeable ways. (I see *Star Wars* and spend the next fifteen years of my life preparing to be an astronaut; I see *Julius Caesar* and decide to learn Latin and become a historian of Rome.) Or maybe we are changed in small, not noticeable ways. The next time I eat breakfast out I order apple juice instead of orange juice because, whether I remember it or not, the movie's hero—or villain—did so. (This is why the art of advertising works.)

We may even wish to judge a work of art on the basis of how it has changed us. Are we better or worse because of our experience of the work? Are we smarter, wiser, deeper, subtler, more insightful, more loving, more generous, more aware, more kind, more courageous after going to this movie or seeing this picture or hearing this symphony or watching this dance or reciting this poem? Or are we stupider, more foolish, shallower, duller, more obtuse, more self-absorbed, foggy, selfish, nasty, violent, or fearful? Do we know more about life, human nature, ourselves? or less? Is the world we live in clearer or cloudier? more lovable or more repulsive? more pregnant with meaning or emptier?

In any case, two paradoxical things have happened. **We have returned to being our same old limited selves.** The integrity of what makes us who we are has not changed. We have the same name and personality and essential characteristics, and we feel ourselves to be ourselves. **And at the same time, we have been affected by our experience, changed in some way, small or great.**

If we are self-analytical types, we might spend some time thinking about what the experience of the work of art has done to us. If not, not. In either case, our experience has altered us, subtly or dramatically. We may realize only years later, when we remember a particular work of art vividly, that before we saw it we thought or felt one way, and after, another. Or we may never think of ourselves as changing at all. But whatever our degree of self-awareness, we are both the same and different, unchanged from the limited particular person we were before and also altered to whatever extent.

THE POWER OF ART

Because of this capacity of art to change us, in small or great ways, you must never let anyone say, "why are you getting so worked up? It's only a work of art," as if art had no power. **Art has terrible power, for good and for ill**, and a very few examples will suffice to prove it. Marx's *Communist Manifesto* and Hitler's speeches, the first news reports about Sputnik and the filmed images of the collapse of the World Trade Center, the microscope and Gutenberg's printing press and the automobile—all are works of art, as are Plato's dialogues, St. Augustine's *Confessions*, The Declaration of Independence, the Constitution, the American flag, every TV commercial, and the Apple logo.

Some works of art are good, some neutral, some misleading, some truly evil. But all exist to move human beings in some way, and to the extent that they succeed, they have power. **To say "it's only a work of art," implying that there's no need to worry because art can't hurt you, is one of the greatest mistakes anyone can make.**

THE GOAL OF ART

Of all the elements that go into our experience of works of art, the most significant, in a sense the fruit of all the rest, is this: **Art gives us the experience of meaning.**

All human beings crave meaning. For the sake of meaning we will sacrifice anything of lesser value to us, not only time and money and work and attention, but in extreme situations, our health, our happiness, even our lives. Meaning is the one thing we will not live without. We seek meaning in our work, in love, and in worship. Some of us seek meaning in our looks, our grades, our sports teams, our astrological signs, our family histories, our children. **All of us seek it in our own and others' behavior, our experiences, and our suffering.** [3]

And we all seek meaning in art. We go to plays and concerts and movies, we go to museums and to the skating rink, watch the Olympics on TV, we download music and tell jokes and play tennis and read and sometimes write poems, all in part to find meaning.

Now let's say you spend Tuesday afternoon playing a computer game and Thursday evening watching Shakespeare's *Othello*. On Tuesday you'll be experiencing empathy and psychic distance and the same on Thursday. On Tuesday you'll be carried away from yourself while you're playing the game and return when it's over, just as on Thursday you'll be carried away from yourself by the play and return when it's over. On Tuesday someone (whether the friend you're playing against or the voice of the game) might say, "Wow! Look (at how you just smashed the enemy)!" and on Thursday, Shakespeare might say, "Wow! Look (at this great man destroyed by jealousy)!" And on Tuesday evening after your game you'll be yourself, and on Friday morning after the play you'll still be yourself, and at the same time, the game will have changed you in some ways and so will the play.

In other words, all four paradoxes of art are present in both kinds of experience, the popular art and the classic. This is just to say that the computer game and the play are both forms of art.

Can we say that one form is more meaningful than the other? If you expect me to tell you that the play is more meaningful than the game, you'll be surprised. There's no such guarantee. Let's say you have never seen a Shakespeare play before and don't get the language and haven't yet read this book. And let's say you know computer games pretty well, and this one is especially challenging, and you're really good at it, and you're right on the point of beating the highest score of any player you know. Which experience is going to mean more to you?

In addition to its fulfillment of the four paradoxes we discussed above, the meaning of the computer game lies, in part, in the thrill of triumph, the sense of accomplishment, perhaps a new understanding of what's possible in hand-eye coordination, perhaps a pleasurable symbolic experience of good conquering evil. The play might be a big bore, except maybe for the moment that poor Desdemona is being suffocated, but that thrill will hardly be worth the two and a half hours of talk that led up to it.

But now let's imagine that you have read this book and have been to a few Shakespeare plays and are familiar with the language and concepts of Shakespeare's drama. Then what might seeing a production of *Othello* provide you? Insight into the nature of jealousy, maybe your own jealousy, discovery that guilt can be proven but innocence can't, awareness of how the temptation of a negative picture works on the mind, articulation of what it feels like to be hurt by the one you love and betrayed by someone you trusted, experience of the danger of loving in pride, of life's tragic potential, and so on.

If you now compare the meaning of the computer game to the meaning of the play, can you make a value distinction? Which will mean more to you?

Let's say you still feel the answer is "the computer game! No contest." Fine. Once you are out of school, nobody (with the possible exception of a spouse) makes you sit through a Shakespeare play if you don't want to.

But when people say things like "*Othello* is a great work of art," what they mean is that the meaning it has conveyed to people who appreciate it is of great value, of deep, lasting, true, uplifting, and universal significance. If such things are rarely said about a computer game, it's because conveying that kind of meaning was never the game's goal. In any case, the purpose of this book is not to convince you to like Shakespeare instead of computer games or any other popular art form. It is simply to help you appreciate your own experience of Shakespeare as well as you can.

A by-product of that appreciation will be that you will also become a better and more authoritative judge of the quality of Shakespeare's work, and of the quality of theatrical and cinematic productions of his work. Then if you want to compare Shakespeare's meaning to that of the computer game, go ahead. The judgment of the kinds of meaning each provides will be up to you.

JUDGMENTS OF ART

Here it is important to say something about judgment itself. **All of us engage in judgment all of the time.** This brand of ice cream tastes better than that; yesterday's sunset was dull, but today's is stunning; that tennis serve was too high; and so on. **And when we experience any work of art, one of our pleasures is to exercise our judgment upon it.** That role was well performed; that pitch was a strike; that film was technically impressive but shallow; and so on.

Because this is so, you must not be fooled by people who say, "Who are you to judge? Who's to say?" Such statements merely put an end to the discussion by pretending that judgment itself is bad. But did you ever notice that the person making that statement is engaging in judgment too? Implicit in the statement "who's to say?" is the judgment "no one is to say; it is wrong to say." Well, on what grounds is it wrong? That too is a judgment. People who say "who's to judge?" are putting an end to the discussion without ever examining their own assumption (their own judgment) that making judgments is bad. It is a way of avoiding responsibility for one's choices.

The truth is that we make judgments all the time, and it is our human nature to do so. The real question is whether our judgments are good ones or not, are well-founded on knowledge and experience and insight and wisdom or not. The honest challenge is not "who are you to judge?" but "have I done all I can to become the best judge I can be" of whatever the question is.

Another thing most people don't realize when they are making judgments (including the judgment "making judgments is bad") is that the judgments we make are reflections of who we are. In making any judgment we are revealing the extent of our capacity to judge. This is why **the work of art that we judge also judges us. Every judgment you make about the quality or value of a work of art is a revelation of you, just as much as of the work of art.**

Here's what this means: Let's say I see a great painting by Rembrandt and my response is "That painting is boring and dull." Well, I'm telling a partial truth. To me it *is* boring and dull. I'm not lying about my experience of it. But at the same time, in finding such a painting boring and dull, I am revealing my own incapacity to appreciate the greatness of that painting. Likewise, if I say that a shallow or sentimental or self-indulgent work of art is great and profound, I am revealing to all those who can see the work's flaws my own shallowness or sentimentality or self-indulgence.

In other words, works of art exhibit real qualities that those who know how to appreciate them can discern, and every judgment we make about a work of art reveals our own capacity, or lack of capacity, to judge well. If we call a trivial work great, or a great classic trivial, we are showing our own judgment to be flawed, just as if we consistently mistake a ball for a strike or box wine for Chateau Lafitte Rothschild.

This is *not* because the majority rules in such things. It is purely and simply because being human, sharing in human nature, we participate in reality together. And reality is characterized by certain objective universal values that govern all of us, that govern therefore every act of discernment of quality, or lack of it, in a work of art. This is not a popular idea at the present time, when we are so often told that preference is purely a matter of opinion and that all opinions are equal. But a few minutes' thought will convince you that you don't believe this and certainly don't act upon it even if you think you believe it.

Of course certain judgments of taste are matters of opinion. If I say, "I like vanilla," you will not say, "No you're wrong; I like chocolate." But if someone says, "Here, try this freshly ground habañero chili pepper, its taste is so delicate and soothing," you will say, "You're either lying or crazy." The effect of eating a habañero pepper is simply not a matter of opinion. One may like or not like that it makes the eyes water and the mouth and throat burn fiercely, but there is a reality to the relation between the pepper and our taste buds, and the words "delicate" and "soothing" do not describe it.[4]

Likewise, there are realities described by words like *beautiful, clear, honest, subtle, strong,* and *profound* and by words like *ugly, confused, false, obvious, weak,* and *shallow,* and we can recognize the differences, the more so the better we are trained to recognize them. To learn about a work of art or a kind of work of art is to make oneself a better and better judge, so that the judgments we make about it not only are more accurate, but also reveal an increasing capacity in us to judge it well.

Some people are better at discerning colors than others, but we will not agree that a red car is green just because a person who is color blind thinks it is. Similarly, some people are better than others at judging the quality of a wine, the turnout of a ballet dancer's leg, the strategy of a football play. If we said to such people, "who are you to judge?" they would laugh at us, and rightly. If we want to tell a great wine from a mediocre one, a prima ballerina from a capable member of the corps, an inspired coach from an incompetent one, we must learn about the arts of wine-tasting, ballet, and football. We must train our judgments in order to become competent judges. And we do that by judging and then comparing our judgments with those of others, especially others who are better judges than we are.

Now, what can we say about the people who love a computer game (or a soap opera or kindergarten finger paintings) and are bored by *Othello*? We will not say they are lying about their experience. We will not deny them the right to prefer the computer game or the soap opera or the kindergarten art to Shakespeare. We will not assert that those arts are meaningless. And we will not force them to watch *Othello* if they do not want to.

But we will say that in not appreciating *Othello*, they are missing out on something valuable. They have not (or not *yet*) been able to see how much *Othello* has to offer, which of course says nothing about how good they are as people. It only says that this particular avenue of meaning is (we hope temporarily) closed to them. In the same way, what a person who has no capacity to judge computer games is missing out on will be known only to the good judge of computer games.

The purpose of this book is to help you develop the capacity to appreciate the truly and universally meaningful in Shakespeare, to give you the ability to judge for yourself the value of Shakespeare's plays. Once you've become a capable judge, the rest is between you and Shakespeare. (Chances are he will not let you down.)

WHAT DOES THE WORK OF ART MEAN?—TALKING ABOUT ART

There is an apocryphal story about the great composer Beethoven. After he had played a sonata in a salon performance, a woman came up to him and said, "Herr Beethoven, that sonata was very beautiful and moving. But tell me, please, what does it *mean*?" Beethoven replied, "Madam, this is what it means: . . . " And he sat down and played it again.

The point of the story is that the meaning of a work of music cannot be expressed in words. If Beethoven could have conveyed its meaning in words, he would have been a writer or a poet, not a composer. There is art, and there is talking about art. Talking about a work of art can help you to appreciate that work, but **there is absolutely no substitute for experiencing the work of art itself**.

No matter how well your friend describes a movie he or she has seen, it is never the same as seeing it for yourself. A symphony has to be heard, a tennis match has to be watched or played, a painting has to be seen if it is going to have any real meaning to you. Talking about the background of a work of art before seeing it can help deepen your experience, and so can talking about the work itself after you've seen it. But there is no substitute for the seeing. However eloquent the scholar, critic, reviewer, or friend may be, nothing he or she says can substitute for your own experience of the work of art itself.

As I said in Chapters 4 and 11, the best definition of poetry I know is this: Poetry says with words what cannot be said in words. That is, a poet forms words into a poem in order to convey the experience of meaning that cannot be conveyed in any other way. If the meaning could be expressed in some other form, the poet would not have to go to all the trouble of making the poem. The same is true of every work of art. It is only what it is and must be experienced as what it is. Its meaning is *in* it. If its meaning could be conveyed in any other way, it would not need to exist.

The purpose of talking or writing about works of art, then, is not to substitute a different experience for the experience of the work of art. It is to prepare you to experience the work of art itself more thoroughly and deeply, and to enhance your appreciation of that experience afterwards through thinking about it yourself and sharing it with others.

This is important because we have been talking a lot about Shakespeare's works. But you must never take anything you have read in this book as a substitute for reading the plays and poems on your own. In fact, even reading them is not enough: The poems need not only to be read but to be read aloud and heard in the ears; the plays need not only to be read but, whenever possible, also to be seen and heard, preferably, of course, in good productions. This book exists to enhance your experience of Shakespeare's art, but it is no substitute for the experience itself.

WHAT MAKES A WORK OF ART GREAT?

As I said in Chapter 1, how an artist like Shakespeare becomes great is a mystery. But we can somewhat describe the difference between a great work of art and one that isn't great. At a minimum the work of art must evoke our empathic response, establish psychic distance, carry us away, allow us to return to ourselves, and succeed in making the connection implied by "Wow! Look!" Otherwise we call the thing a bore. But when we think about what the experience of the work of art has *meant* to us, when we *judge* it, what have we got? Are we better or worse off? Are we grateful or complaining? Have we been delighted, uplifted, illuminated, deepened, chastened, moved? Or have we been made tired, confused, depleted, frustrated, resentful? Do we return having experienced something true (even if through fantasy) or something false (even if through realism)? something healing or something harming? something we remember with love, reverence, delight, respect, or awe, or something we remember with disapproval, disgust, or unsatisfied hunger? In short, what meaning have we found in our experience of the work of art?

What makes a work of art great is its ability to return us to ourselves having had a rich, illuminating, bettering, deepening, and meaningful experience, one which impels us to say to someone we care about, "Wow! Look!"

---

[1]   The full text of Mary Holmes' Descriptive Notes to Art 5a is at www.Maryholmesart5a. com. You can read more about Mary Holmes in Addi Somekh and Charlie Eckert, *Mary Holmes: Paintings and Ideas* (Los Altos, CA: Very Press, 2002), at www.maryholmesbook.com, and at www.maryholmes.org.

[2]   Mary Holmes' ideas on empathy are partly influenced by those of Theodor Lipps and Vernon Lee [Violet Paget] though she differs from them in important respects.

[3]   Read more about the basic human need for meaning in Victor Frankl, *Man's Search for Meaning* (New York: Washington Square Press, 1963).

[4]   The most important book to read on the subject of objective values is C.S. Lewis, *The Abolition of Man* (New York: HarperCollins, 2001).

Part 2:
Plays and Sonnets

Comedies

214

The Taming of the Shrew

If we are to appreciate and be entertained by *The Taming of the Shrew* as Shakespeare intended, it is necessary to remember that the world as Shakespeare and his audience conceived it was hierarchical (see Part 1, Chapter 7) and that the hierarchy reached into every area of life, including family relations between husbands and wives. Wives were obliged and expected to obey their husbands in their just and reasonable instructions, and husbands were obliged and expected to care for their wives. That is the ideal and the norm that stands behind the justification for the "taming" of Katherine in this play.

In our time, of course, while we can understand the psychological self-destructiveness of Katherine's behavior, we find it very difficult to approve of Petruchio's cure. We live in a society whose ideals and expectations tend toward the egalitarian. While many communities maintain the "man of the house" or "the pants in the family" expectations for men, many other communities and most of our media entertainments suggest that men and women are obliged and expected to be equal in the marriage relationship, neither one compelling the submission of his or her marriage partner.

At root, the relation between men and women in society and in nature constitutes a profound mystery, one in whose midst we all find ourselves, no matter who or what or when we are. There are various ways in which reasonable people can think about this mystery and about the best possible relation between spouses. Even the book of Genesis in the Bible presents two distinct versions of the creation of man: In one, man and woman are created together, implying an existential equality (1:27), and in the other, woman is created out of the side (or rib) of man, implying an existential hierarchy (1:20–23). From our own experience, too, we may conclude that, apart from individual differences, in general men are better than women at some things and women better than men at other things, and that therefore in matters involving the former, wives ought to comply with their husbands, and in matters involving the latter, husbands ought to comply with their wives. This would presumably involve both a kind of equality and at the same time a variable kind of hierarchy. This being the case, we may have something to learn about our own psychology from Shakespeare's depiction of the healing of a problematic relationship between a man and a woman, even if the external social conditions of that relationship are no longer acceptable to us.

Unfortunately, to appreciate the meaning of this play we must also overcome a pre-existing prejudice of such large influence that doing so may not be possible. The reason is the influence of leftism on modern feminism and of modern feminism on our imaginations.

It would be difficult to find many communities in the Western democracies that did not approve of the modern achievement of equal rights for women under the law: the right to vote, to own property, to sue for divorce. And hardly anyone would object these days that where women and men do the same work for the same hours they should be paid the same wage. But having helped to achieve these goals of our egalitarian society, the feminist movement then came under the influence of Marxist thought, and in particular the so-called Frankfurt school of Neo-Marxism. Marx's idea had been that all of history was the record of the oppression of poor by rich, or workers by owners of property. The Frankfurt school converted the idea of history into a record of the oppression of everyone else by straight white males. The supposed oppression of women by men has come to be known by the term *patriarchy*, used always in this context as a pejorative. And this idea—that history is largely a record of the oppression of women by men—has been so promulgated by the educational institutions and the entertainment and news media of our time, that it has become almost impossible for anyone reading or seeing *The Taming of the Shrew* to see Petruchio as anything but an instance of the oppressive, millennia-old patriarchy. (See Jordan Peterson's *12 Rules for Life: An Antidote to Chaos* for some salutary correction of this image of history.[1])

As a result of this cultural influence, modern performances of this play often undermine the text. Petruchio is depicted coming onto the stage in III.ii cracking a whip. And Katherine is shown at the end giving a nudge-and-wink to the audience, as if her great final speech were merely the political posturing of a woman who—far from obedient—is going to govern her man through secret wiles instead of openly defying him. Well, men have been known to whip women, and women have been known to govern men through secret wiles—Shakespeare has depicted a few of them. The problem is that there is absolutely no evidence in the play for such behavior in Petruchio and Katherine or for an ironic ending. And injecting these attitudes into modern productions undermines the play's healing theme and joyful conclusion.

So let us see whether we can get at what Shakespeare means us to comprehend and enjoy about this play. Doing so does not mean that we will be promoting Petruchio's methods in the real world. The play is a comedy and a kind of joke, though it reveals something very true about human relations and human happiness. It need not be taken as a prescription for action.

In fact, Petruchio's actions are a witty humanization of the story in an old ballad that stands behind the plot. In *A Merry Jest of a Shrewd and Curst Wife Lapped in Morel's Skin for Her Good Behavior*, a husband beats his would-be domineering wife with a birch rod, then kills an old plough horse (named Morel), flays it, salts its skin, and wraps his wife in it until she submits. Shakespeare knew that ballad, and knew it for a joke. In adapting its idea of taming for the stage, he utterly transposed the meaning of the story.

Katherine is young, beautiful, and rich. But she has fallen into the habit of outraging her father, her younger sister, and her suitors by her choleric temper (see The Humors in Part 1, Chapter 7). She flies into rages to get her way. She is furious that her younger sister, Bianca, has suitors and she does not. This envy and rage cause her to drive away all potential suitors and thereby confirm her in her misery.

Petruchio hears of Katherine and for very good reasons decides to marry her. His father and hers have known one another well, and she is young, rich, and beautiful. In other words, given the world of comedy that they inhabit, they are a perfect match. But how is Petruchio to turn Katherine away from her shrewishness toward being an appropriate wife for him? He will woo her "with some spirit":

> Say that she rail, why then I'll tell her plain
> She sings as sweetly as a nightingale.
> Say that she frown, I'll say she looks as clear
> As morning roses newly washed with dew.   (II.i.169–73)

And later, creating havoc around her in his own home, he tells us

> Ay, and amid this hurly I intend
> That all is done in reverend care of her . . .
> This is a way to kill a wife with kindness,
> And thus I'll curb her mad and headstrong humor. (IV.i.203–209)

He will cure her by creating around her the very havoc that she has been creating around herself. But instead of claiming to do so to satisfy his own will, as she is serving her own will in creating conflict, Petruchio will claim to be doing it for her sake. And in fact, it *is* for her sake, because only by having her "humor" curbed can she come to know peace and happiness in herself and consequently with a husband.

The word "kindness" in Petruchio's speech quoted above is weighted. Petruchio is obviously acting toward Kate extremely unkindly on the surface—preventing her from eating and sleeping. But in the long run his intention is indeed kind, meaning both compassionate and natural, for he is making possible their harmonious marriage.

Of course when Katherine finally shows that she is submitting to Petruchio by calling the sun the moon and an old man a young girl (IV.v), she knows, and Petruchio knows, and we know, that she is not really thinking that the sun is the moon. The whole episode is comically symbolic of the submission of the will to a rightful authority in the name of peace and quiet and harmony and normality. Out of that submission arises the great voice of wisdom in Katherine's final monologue (V.ii.136ff.). It is directed at the other wives, who, despite their pretense of obedience, are in fact as willful as she has been but without the energy and fire to reveal it, precisely the energy and fire that Petruchio loves in Katherine once it is brought into the service of the good—both his and hers:

> Fie, fie, unknit that threat'ning unkind brow
> And dart not scornful glances from those eyes,
> To wound thy lord, thy king, thy governor.   (V.ii.136–38)

Then we see an explicit example of the principle of correspondence visible throughout Shakespeare's works and discussed in Chapter 7 of Part 1. According to that principle every microcosm is analogous to the macrocosm and to other microcosms. Katherine says,

> Such duty as the subject owes the prince,
> Even such a woman oweth to her husband.   (V.ii.155–56)

The family is a kind of city or state, and the husband in the well-run city or state of the home must be obeyed if there is to be peace and harmony, if there is to be even eating and sleeping. This is Katherine's argument at the end, enforced by the simple fact that men are stronger than women. This means that a husband can enforce his will by sheer power if necessary. But that is not the whole story, despite what the anti-patriarchal polemicists would claim. The husband also is, according to Katherine,

> one that cares for thee,
> And for thy maintenance; commits his body
> To painful labor, both by sea and land;
> To watch the night in storms, the day in cold,
> Whilst thou li'st warm at home, secure and safe;
> And craves no other tribute at thy hands
> But love, fair looks, and true obedience—
> Too little payment for so great a debt.   (V.ii.147–54)

In other words there is a kind of reciprocity here despite the hierarchical relationship. The hierarchy of things as imagined by Shakespeare and his audience had love moving both upward and downward—care and obedience in one direction and care and maintenance in the other.

The conclusion of the speech is Katherine's offering to place her hand below her husband's foot in symbolic submission of her will to his. What Shakespeare then does is *not* to have Petruchio step on her hand and say "Now that's the way I like it—power to the patriarchy!" No. Petruchio's response to Kate's symbolic offer of true submission is "Why, there's a wench! Come on, and kiss me, Kate" (V.ii.180). In other words, in place of the gesture of dominance, husband stepping on wife's hand, Petruchio embraces her in a kiss, the incarnation and dramatization of their harmony, communion, even equality as lovers, and therefore of joy.

Shakespeare has begun his play with an *induction* (a leading in), which we would call an *introduction* (a leading into). His induction is not just a speech but two dramatic scenes based on another comical old story: A lord tricks a drunken beggar by bringing him asleep into his palace, where the beggar wakes up to find himself surrounded by wealth and servants who treat him like a prince. When Shakespeare's beggar, named Christopher Sly, wakes up to be treated as a lord, actors appear in his supposed mansion to perform a play for his entertainment, and the play they perform is "The Taming of the Shrew." So Shakespeare has given us the main play within the context of a small frame-play. Why did he choose to include the frame story?

One answer is practical. The initial situation of Christopher Sly is familiar to Shakespeare's audience, a sort of "local color." The frame story easily engages the empathy of the audience, providing an effective transition to the story within the story.

Another answer is thematic. The question of the play is to what degree people's behavior may be altered by an alteration in the way they are treated. Just as Sly begins to think of himself as a lord when he wakes up to find he is being treated as one, so Katherine learns to think of herself as virtuous, patient, obedient, rational, and loving when all the chaos for which she has been responsible is reflected back at her under the guise of care and protection and kindness for her. The taming of Kate is a deeper transformation than that of Sly, and it is undertaken for far more serious reasons. But both stories illustrate the truth that our image of ourselves depends in large part on the role we are expected to play in the world. Sly's transformation is a joke and a fake; Kate's is serious and real though comical.

But Shakespeare cuts short the frame-play after Act I, Scene i, and *The Taming of the Shrew* ends with no further mention of Christopher Sly. Why is that? There is another play, similar to *The Taming of the Shrew*, performed about five years earlier and published at about the same time as this play. It was called *The Taming of a Shrew*. Scholars debate whether it is a source for *the Shrew*, or a bad quarto (i.e., memorial reconstruction) of it, or a version of an earlier play that was the source for both. The subplot of *a Shrew* somewhat differs from that of *the Shrew*, and most of the characters' names are different. It is far inferior to Shakespeare's *the Shrew*, whatever its origin. However, apart from its interest to textual scholars, it is interesting in that in it, unlike in *the Shrew*, the Christopher Sly frame story is completed at the end. There Sly falls asleep drunk in his supposed palace, and the lord who brought him in to trick him now has him returned to the street where he was found. When Sly awakes, he believes he has had "the best dream / That ever I had in my life" and then goes home to tame his wife as he has learned to do from the play performed for him in the supposed dream. Why does Shakespeare choose not to complete the frame story about Christopher Sly?

The last scene of Shakespeare's frame story, which is interposed at the end of I.i, gives us a hint. (In this scene, the page boy is disguised as Sly's supposed wife):

First Servant:	My lord, you nod [= doze], you do not mind the play.
Sly:	Yes, by Saint Anne, do I. A good matter, surely; comes there any more of it?
Page:	My lord, 'tis but begun.
Sly:	'Tis a very excellent piece of work, madam lady; would 'twere done! (I.i.249–54)

Sly clearly is bored by the first scene of "The Taming of the Shrew," which is being performed for his entertainment, and he cannot wait for it to be over though it has just begun. This is a subtle indication that, no matter how convincingly he might be treated as a lord, he is not a lord in fact. The proof is that he cannot appreciate the quality or significance of the play that we, who are more sophisticated, are finding perfectly fit for *our* entertainment. The leopard will not change his spots, and Sly will remain the poor beggar in himself no matter how much those around him pretend that he is a lord, and no matter how much he comes to believe it himself. By contrast, the joke played on Katherine in "The Taming of the Shrew" play that Sly is watching, instead of making her think she is something she is not, in fact causes her to discover who she really is. And that discovery is so much more important than the waking of Sly from his supposed dream that we can imagine Shakespeare deciding to abandon the relatively shallow frame story for the sake of retaining the full force of the conclusion of the more profound story.

In short, *The Taming of the Shrew* is not about fooling someone into believing she is what she isn't, but about cajoling someone into realizing and embracing what she at her best truly is.

KEY LINES:

1. II.i.22 s.d.: In striking her sister Bianca, Kate gives an important sign of her unregenerate spirit. Her shrewishness is expressed not merely in words but in violent deeds. It cries out for taming.

2. III.ii.117–20: Petruchio says, "To me she's married, not unto my clothes. / Could I repair what she will wear in me, / As I can change these poor accoutrements, / 'Twere well for Kate, and better for myself." *Wear* means wear out, as clothing is worn out. But Kate will be wearing out two kinds of things in Petruchio: a) his practical support and gifts of kindness, and b) his character as a caring and loving husband. If he can keep renewing his practical gifts to her, and if he can keep renewing

his character as a patient and loving husband no matter how much Kate abuses it, the fruits will be good for *both* of them.

3.   IV.i.180–209: Petruchio's servant Peter says, "He kills her in her own humor." Her own humor is choler (see The Humors in Part 1, Chapter 7), that is, the predisposition to excessive and violent rages. Petruchio is using his own apparent choler to subdue Katherine's real choler. But this line is connected with Petruchio's next speech, in which he says "This is a way to kill a wife with kindness" (IV.i.208)—not the usual meaning of that phrase. He is killing in her the choler that would make a happy life with her—and for her—impossible. "And thus I'll curb her mad and headstrong humor" (IV.i.209), he says. Once again, the goal is not power but peace and harmony.

SPECIFIC NOTES TO HELP IN YOUR READING:

1.   A *shrew* is a small nocturnal long-nosed mole-like insectivore that was believed to be venomous and therefore malicious and dangerous. The term came to be used of a vexatious, scolding, brawling woman. Shakespeare's word *shrewd* is an adjective from *shrew*. (We would say *shrewish*.)

2.   The name Petruchio is so spelled by Shakespeare in order to be pronounced as the Italian name Petruccio—Pe-TROO-cho. Those performers who persist in pronouncing it "Petrukio" to show off their knowledge of Italian, in which the *ch* is pronounced like a *k*, fail to realize that Shakespeare was a step ahead of them. He knew his English actors would pronounce the Italian spelling with a *k* sound in error and wanted them to get it right. So he spelled it and expected us to pronounce it with the *ch* as in English.

3.   Induction.i.67–68: The Lord says about the plan to trick Christopher Sly, that "It will be pastime passing [= surpassingly] excellent, / If it be husbanded with modesty." Note the use of the words *husbanded* and *modesty*, which prefigure the theme of the main drama. *To husband* means to take care of, govern well, preserve. *Modesty* means moderation, freedom from excess, self-control. We will, unlike Christopher Sly, enjoy the play we are about to see, and Petruchio will *husband* Kate with what appears at first to be madness but is finally revealed to be a deeper and truer *modesty*, and one which he teaches to Kate.

4.   I.i.31–33: Tranio says, "Let's be no Stoics nor no stocks, I pray, / Or so devote to Aristotle's checks / As Ovid be an outcast quite abjur'd." A *stock* is a piece of wood, hence someone insensible. Aristotle, the author

of the Nicomachean Ethics, stands for morality; Ovid, the author of *Ars Amatoria* (the Art of Love), stands for love.

5. III.ii.228–39: When Petruchio is about to carry Kate off from the wedding, he says, "Nay, look not big, nor stamp, nor stare, nor fret." He is speaking *about* what Kate is doing, which is trying to have her own way. But he is speaking *to* the gathered wedding guests, pretending that they are threatening Kate and his right to possess her. He fancifully proclaims that he is protecting her from *them* in order to teach her what he would do if ever she were threatened in fact. "Fear not, sweet wench; they shall not touch thee, Kate." In short, he is enacting a drama of his commitment to be her protector though she is the only real threat to their happy marriage.

6. IV.v.76: "jealous" here means suspicious.

7. V.ii.109: "aweful" here means commanding respect and obedience.

---

[1] "It looks to me like the so-called oppression of the patriarchy was instead an imperfect collective attempt by men and women, stretching over millennia, to free each other from privation, disease and drudgery." Jordan Peterson, *12 Rules for Life: An Antidote to Chaos* (Random House Canada, 2018), p. 304.

A Midsummer Night's Dream

Shakespeare's comedy *A Midsummer Night's Dream*, one of his most lyrical, delves sweetly but profoundly into the mystery of human love. Do we love by choice or by necessity? Do we love this person and not that because of conscious preference? unconscious predisposition? nature? fate? hormones? sixth sense? social expectation? magic? divine dispensation? more than one of these? all of them? The play does not exactly answer these questions. But it meaningfully and joyfully reconciles us to the irreducible mystery of love. It does so by uniting two settings, six plots, and four worlds into one dream-like tale, told in highly rhetorical verse.

The two settings are court and forest. The story moves from the court of ancient Athens into the forest, and back again to court (see Settings in Chapter 6 of Part 1).

The six plots are those of 1) the four lovers, 2) the marriage of Theseus and Hyppolita, 3) the brawl between the fairy king and queen, 4) the story of the Indian boy who is the object of their contention, 5) the rehearsals and performance of the "mechanicals" play, and 6) the Pyramus and Thisbe story forming that play-within-the-play.

The four worlds are 1) the world of ancient Greek mythology, 2) the fairy lore of the English countryside, 3) the idealized English royal court dressed up as the ancient court of Athens, and 4) the everyday lives of the artisan class of Shakespeare's London disguised as Athenian "mechanicals."

Through the elaborate use of rhetorical figures, Shakespeare achieves a beautiful and touching lyricism. It is counterintuitive to us that highly formalized rhetoric should be used to express the thoughts and feelings of love. Heirs of Romanticism, we believe that all true feeling must come straight from the heart in the most natural language possible and that rhetorical devices equal insincerity. But Shakespeare and his audience would have found our most natural speech to be unimaginative and shallow. Even though the last line of Sonnet 1 in *Astrophel and Stella* by

Philip Sidney (1554–1586) reads "said my Muse to me 'look in thy heart, and write,'" that line itself appears in a poem of elaborate rhetorical development. For the Elizabethan audience, elaborate figures of speech were the only medium sufficiently rich and complex to express the realities of love. Madeleine Doran writes,

> The [rhetorical] patterns are used to strike the note of love. . . . . [The emotions of love] sweep them into the [rhetorical] schemes . . . . The young people display . . . obvious artifice, and this artifice they pursue, not because they do not have feelings but because they have.[1]

Here's an incomplete list of rhetorical devices used in the play: anadiplosis, anaphora, antanaclasis, antimetabole (or chiasmus), antistrophe, aphorismus, asteismus, asyndeton, conceit, epanalepsis, epizeuxis, hypallage, isocolon, oxymoron, paronomasia, ploce, polyptoton, prosopopoeia, stichomythia, syllepsis, zeugma.

The title of the play alludes to the ways in which the English celebrated the eve of Midsummer, the summer solstice and feast of St. John the Baptist (June 25). The Puritan Phillip Stubbs complained that on such occasions, as on May Day and Whitsun, "all the young men and maids, old men and wives, run gadding over night to the woods, groves, hills, and mountains, where they spend all the night in pleasant pastimes; and in the morning they return . . . ."[2] (He accused them of worshipping Satan in doing so, but Shakespeare does not subscribe to Stubbs's puritanism.) The fairy Puck ends the play by suggesting that if we did not enjoy the experience of the play, we should consider it no more than a dream. But there are also dreams, or pseudo-realities, within the play: The lovers awaken transformed from their Midsummer Eve sleep in the woods. Both Bottom and Titania, the Fairy Queen, awaken from slumber imagining their actual experiences to have been dreams. As so often in Shakespeare's plays, here too, reality and illusion are set against one another. But in *A Midsummer Night's Dream* the levels of reality merge with the various senses in which we think of dreams—meaningful revelations, wish fulfillment fantasies, artful illusions, and fluff. And in all cases the theme is love—true, genuine, and natural love on the one hand, and on the other, love that is artificial, illusory, and monstrous.

In the frame story of the play, love is the power that causes opponents to come into harmony. The famously rational and just ruler Theseus, who has defeated the Amazon Queen Hippolyta in battle, is now to marry her in joy on the occasion of the new moon. But within that frame story, disruptions to love initially multiply. Egeus has decided that his daughter Hermia must marry Demetrius, though she loves the equally respectable Lysander. Seconding Egeus, Theseus offers Hermia two alternatives: perpetual virginity in a convent devoted to the service of the chaste goddess Diana, or death. Hermia's bosom friend Helena loves Demetrius, who swore his love to her but shifted his attentions upon seeing Hermia. In the meantime nature itself is disrupted because the Fairy King, Oberon, and the Fairy Queen, Titania, are in mutually jealous conflict over possession of an Indian boy. And love is comically threatened with disruption by the comically inappropriate choice of the tragic love story of Pyramus and Thisbe (based on the tale in Ovid's *Metamorphoses*) to be performed by the workmen of Athens in celebration of the royal wedding. Love is both the source and the victim of all these conflicts, and Shakespeare has Lysander call upon all previous tales and histories, read or heard, to assert aphoristically, "The course of true love never did run smooth" (I.i.134).

Bottom complains that "reason and love keep little company together nowadays. The more the pity that some honest neighbors will not make them friends" (III.i.143–46). However, being a comedy, the play does make reason and love friends, for it ends in reconciliations, healing, and happy marriage. But how? How is this harmony achieved? By what means are all these rough courses of love smoothed?

Shakespeare does not take the obvious route of ascribing the resolutions either merely to nature or merely to the magic of the fairies. Nature within is as likely to lead astray as to guide aright. And magic wielding fairies, like Puck, are as often mischief-makers as harmonizers. Oberon and Titania, though intimate with and tied to nature, are themselves also in unnatural conflict because of competing loves.

The real vehicle of healing is the proper use by the wise Oberon of two plants, which represent neither nature alone nor magic alone but rather a mysterious union of divine and natural powers. The pansy flower, called "love-in-idleness," has the power to cause one to fall in love with whatever one sees when one's eyes have been anointed by its juice. But this is not just a natural power within the plant. This power is in it because Cupid's "fiery shaft[,] / Quenched in the chaste beams of the wat'ry moon," has landed on it (II.i.161–62). In other words, Oberon has seen what even Puck could not, that the flower's virtue has its source in the invasion of the natural by divine qualities. The formerly white flower, having received "love's wound" and turned purple (II.i.167), now can "make man or woman madly dote / Upon the next live creature that it sees" (II.i.171–72). And Oberon knows, too, that the arrow that landed upon the flower was not only fiery with erotic power but also drenched in the moonbeams of the goddess of chastity. It is that arrow—itself a paradoxical union of seemingly divine contraries—which gives to the flower its capacity to evoke irresistible love, whether for the appropriate object (as in Demetrius) or for the inappropriate one (as in Lysander and Titania). Similarly, that effect can be reversed by another herb. Oberon hints (at II.i.184) that this other herb can remove the charm of the love-in-idleness flower. But later he reveals that this second herb is an antidote not to love but to error:

> Then crush this herb into Lysander's eye,
> Whose liquor hath this virtuous property,
> To take from thence all error with his might
> And make his eyeballs roll with wonted [= appropriate] sight.
> (III.ii.366–69)

This is why this second herb is not used on Demetrius. The juice of the pansy flower caused him to return to his true love of Helena; the juice of this second herb caused Lysander to return to his true love of Hermia. Either may be used for disruption or for healing, and it is Oberon's gift to know the powers of both and to will their proper use in the name of reconciliation, harmony, "wonted sight," and "natural taste."

When the lovers have awakened from their various real or apparent dreams to find the conflicts resolved, Demetrius says that, having,

> as in health, come to my natural taste,
> Now I do wish it, love it, long for it,
> And will for evermore be true to it. (IV.i.174–76)

That is, harmony is achieved with the union of natural feeling, conscious desire, and free will choice. This union is the cure to the earlier rejection of true love and results in the appropriate pairing of the right lovers. The union of feeling, desire, and choice also resolves the conflicts between Theseus and Hippolyta and between Oberon and Titania.

In the case of Theseus and Hippolyta, reconciliation is expressed not only by the union of conqueror and conquered, but by the union of masculine and feminine attitudes as expressed in their contrasting points of view at the beginning of Act V. Hippolyta notes the strangeness of the report that the lovers give of their adventures in the forest. The rational Theseus accepts the strangeness of the tales but not their truth. He says,

> I never may believe
> These antique fables nor these fairy toys.
> Lovers and madmen have such seething brains,
> Such shaping fantasies, that apprehend
> More than cool reason ever comprehends. (V.i.2–6)

He groups together lunatic, lover, and poet as producers of "airy nothing" (V.i.16). He cannot believe in the validity of the lovers' report about what we, the audience, have seen with our own eyes. Reason seems to be demoting love. By contrast, Hippolyta asserts that their experience is something more than fantasy and "grows to something of great constancy; / But howsoever, strange and admirable" (V.i.26–27). She accepts the adventure as being real and full of wonder, even though it is inexplicable. Love seems to be demoting reason.

In this good-natured conflict of interpretation, Theseus represents masculine reason, logic, and skepticism and Hippolyta feminine insight, intuition, and acceptance. And the point is not only that Hippolyta's insight corrects the limited vision of Theseus. In a similar and balancing way, Theseus will later correct Hippolyta by his magnanimous attitude toward the mechanicals' performance (V.i.89–105). The point is that their love and wedding unite their two points of view in a joyful harmony, reason and love made friends.

In an equally pleasing parallel, the reconciliation of the royal fairies results in a restoration of the natural succession of the seasons in their proper places. Oberon, waking Titania to the harmony of music, says

> Now thou and I are new in amity
> And will tomorrow midnight solemnly
> Dance in Duke Theseus' house triumphantly
> And bless it to all fair prosperity.
> There shall the pairs of faithful lovers be
> Wedded, with Theseus, all in jollity. (IV.i.87–92)

Marriage for all, here celebrated in six lines sharing a single rhyme, symbolizes joyful harmony for all.

The play concludes by making the tragedy of Pyramus and Thisbe into a vehicle of celebratory hilarity. Shakespeare transforms the tragic tale into farce and through it into high comedy with the implied contrast between the naïveté of the performers and the sophistication of their audience, not only their courtly onstage audience but the audience for whom Shakespeare wrote. (Most likely that was a gathering of aristocrats, possibly including Queen Elizabeth, in a manor house to celebrate an actual wedding. Eventually it was also the public theatre audience, for whom we know the play was later performed.) As Harold Brooks writes, "the artisans' anxiety is part of a major joke: their fear of creating too much dramatic illusion, when it is obvious they will create far too little."[3] All art depends on the paradoxical simultaneous experiences of empathy and psychic or aesthetic distance. We must lose ourselves in believing that the characters we are seeing onstage are real, and at the same time we must remain aware that what we are seeing is art, not life (see Chapter 15 of Part 1). The mechanicals are fearful of their audience's excess empathy—they fear that the lion will frighten the ladies, costing the players their lives—and labor to create as much psychic distance as possible. At the same time, they lack any faith in the power of words to evoke empathy, so that they feel they must use actors to portray the moon and the wall, since, unlike the actual theater audience, they cannot imagine believing in them based on words alone. The naïveté of these mechanicals aspiring to acting, mediated by the light-hearted critical commentary of the onstage aristocratic audience, causes Shakespeare's own audience to revel in their own sophistication in the midst of their hilarity.

Thematically, however, there is more to the farce than the self-approval of the audience. The story being told by the mechanicals is a tragedy of a sort that *might* have happened to Hermia and Lysander. Pyramus and Thisbe, too, disobeyed their fathers and ran off to be married against the parental will, and they died for it. So did Romeo and Juliet (about whom Shakespeare wrote in the same year). Here the tragic tale is turned into farce in order to reinforce the relief and the joy of the happy ending for all the lovers in the play: the reconciliation of the young lovers to one another and to the older governing generation.

As Theseus and the court point out the naïve follies of the performers, they are also enacting a magnanimity that weighs the players' good will far above their lack of skill. When Hippolyta says, "[Philostrate] says they can do nothing in this kind," i.e., they are not any good at performing a play, Theseus replies,

The kinder we, to give them thanks for nothing.
Our sport shall be to take what they mistake:
And what poor duty cannot do, noble respect
Takes it in might, not merit. . . .   (V.i.88–92)

The phrase "Takes it in might, not merit" means measures the gift not by actual merit but in respect to the capacity of the giver (cf., Mark 12:41–44, Luke 21:1–4, and the proverbial "take the will for the deed").[4] By some this passage is thought to be a bit of flattery to Queen Elizabeth, who might actually have been in the audience and who prided herself on appreciating the good will of her subjects. But thematically Theseus is reinforcing the power of love, including the good will of the mechanicals, who wish to please their prince with their performance, however inept it is.

Puck has observed, "Lord, what fools these mortals be!" (III.ii.115). Because he is right, all of us are in need of the magnanimity of love that Theseus shows to the mechanicals. Once the play has revealed this to us and its plot has brought into harmony all the forces that have impelled and disrupted love, it remains only for Oberon to order his fairies to bless "every several chamber . . . with sweet peace" and safe rest (V.i.417–20).

No analysis of this play can possibly convey its delights better than the poetry of the play itself. And no play of Shakespeare's until *The Tempest* so perfectly merits all that we mean by the word magical.

---

[1] Madeleine Doran, *Shakespeare's Dramatic Language* (1976), p. 11, quoted in Harold Brooks, ed., *A Midsummer Night's Dream*, Arden Edition (New York: Methuen, 1983), pp. lii–liii.

[2] Frederick J. Furnivall, ed., *Phillip Stubbs's Anatomy of the Abuses in England in Shakespeare's Youth: A.D. 1583*, Part II (London: The New Shakespeare Society, 1877–79), p. 149, at https://archive.org/details/phillipstubbessa00stubuoft/page/148.

[3] Brooks, p. xxxv.

[4] Cf., "Rather weigh the will of the speaker than the worth of the words," Pettie *A Petite Palace of Pettie His Pleasure* I.135 quoted in Morris Palmer Tilley, *A Dictionary of the Proverbs in England in the Sixteenth and Seventeenth Centuries* (Ann Arbor: University of Michigan Press, 1950), W393, at https://babel.hathitrust.org/cgi/pt?id=mdp.39015016495585&view=1up&seq=8.

The Merchant of Venice

The dramatic conflict of *The Merchant of Venice* raises profound and universal human questions that its ending resolves joyfully. But the play is also one of Shakespeare's most challenging to modern readers and audiences. There are two major difficulties. One is the tendency to treat Shakespeare's play like a modern slice-of-life drama instead of a Renaissance comedy. This results in our posing irrelevant questions that the play does not and cannot answer. The other is that the dramatic conflict in the play is built upon a cultural tradition that the modern Western world at its best has rightly repudiated, namely the 2000-year history of Christian anti-Semitism. Let us begin with what the play is really about and then turn to the difficulties.

The Merchant of Venice as Shakespeare intended it to be seen provides a brilliant and moving conflict between true and false valuation. The drama unfolds as a conflict between the opposed wills of the virtuous Antonio, the merchant, and the villainous Shylock.

Antonio values quality rather than quantity. In the name of quality he is willing to sacrifice any quantity, including quantity of life. His language is that of gift, affection, concern for others, and self-sacrifice. He is an exemplary Christian not merely in preaching the doctrine of love but in embodying it.

By contrast, Shylock misvalues everything, in keeping with Shakespeare's received and affirmed ideas about the spiritual blindness of the Jews in refusing to embrace the Christian redemption through Christ (see below). Shylock values quantity rather than quality. His language is that of possession, material advantage, concern for himself, and justice in the form of the letter of the law. To him a daughter lost is exactly like ducats lost. A Jew is like other men in having eyes and ears, being able to be poisoned, having a right to revenge. Shylock makes no mention of the higher human gifts: reason and the capacity to love.

The two friends, Antonio and Bassanio, embody the same values in their respective arenas, and their friendship represents the marriage of true minds of Shakespeare's Sonnet 116. Antonio stands for self-sacrifice in the world of Venice, which is characterized by commerce, fortune, action, law courts, and the acquisition of wealth. Bassanio stands for self-sacrifice in the world of Belmont, which is characterized by love, matrimony, music, casket tests, and the enjoyment of wealth. In Belmont, Bassanio is willing to "give and hazard all he hath" for Portia. In Venice, Antonio is willing to do the same for Bassanio.

Everyone in the play is called to discern true value in situations where it may be disguised. In the law court, true value lies not in the mere letter of the law but in justice seasoned with mercy. (Compare with *Measure for Measure*.) In the winning of the lady, Portia, true value lies not in outward show (the gold casket), nor in presumed deserving (the silver casket), but in willing self-sacrifice (the lead casket). In the household of Shylock true value lies in escape—away from possessiveness, materialism, and soulless obligations and toward Christian love and joy, represented by marriage and by music, against which Shylock shuts his house's ears (i.e., its windows).

Launcelot desires to leave Shylock's service against his conscience. In this his impulse is right, his reason wrong, for his supposed "conscience" is a golden casket containing a devil, and his supposed "fiend" is a leaden casket containing his true conscience. His actual choice reveals the truth about Bassanio's liberality: Bassanio is not a spendthrift, as Shylock claims, but a bestower of gifts. Shylock lives in a miserly fashion, seeking to acquire more than he needs and grudging expenses, including the food of his servants. By contrast, Bassanio generously spends money on liveries for his servants and on entertainment for his friends, taking joy in the sharing of his substance, as Antonio takes joy in giving to Bassanio what he needs and as Portia takes joy in giving to both.

Portia expresses the need for the seasoning of justice: "earthly power doth then show likest God's / When mercy seasons justice," and without its seasoning, "none of us / Should see salvation" (IV.i.196-200). In every character and arena the ability to season judgment is challenged. The betrayal of one's father by escape is wrong unless, as in Jessica, it is seasoned with the true motive of fidelity to higher values. Bassanio's desire for Portia is seasoned with wisdom, no mere fancy bred in the eyes where it must soon die (III.ii.63–69). In the giving of the rings, oaths and symbols are seasoned with understanding and forgiveness. Oaths and bonds must be adhered to or justice would collapse, but superior to them are the values of forgiveness, mercy, and faithful love—the bonds of the heart. Having been put in good order, mercantile Venice is left behind for the delights of Belmont, intimating that, analogously, the practical world of time and space will ultimately be left behind in heaven. In Belmont the mock quarrels over the ring season love with mirth and point to the generous love that underlies them.

The whole play is of a piece, a variety of dances to a single theme, ending in one of the loveliest scenes of harmony in all Shakespeare's works.

MISGUIDED QUESTIONS

If we see the play thus, as Shakespeare crafted it to be seen, we will find that many questions addressed to the play by critics are misguided—the result of treating the play as a modern realistic psychological drama instead of a Renaissance moral one. Seeing the play in Shakespeare's own terms, we find that such questions disappear like images in a funhouse mirror when we go out into the sunlight.

ANTONIO

Why is Antonio sad (meaning serious, solemn, gloomy) at the very start? Is he feeling unrequited gay love for Bassanio, as some directors insist? Is he worried about his ships, contrary to his claim? Is he secretly feeling guilty about hating Jews?

Shakespeare shows us Antonio trying to understand why he is sad and failing to do so (I.i). Antonio's "I know not why I am so sad" is emphasized by being the first line of the play. His speeches are not intended to make us guess at a cause that he himself cannot discover. If there were such a cause, how would we know what it was unless Shakespeare conveyed it to us explicitly? There is no time in the theater, as there is in the study, to invent it for ourselves. And Shakespeare is not one for keeping secrets from his audience. As Hamlet says, "The players cannot keep counsel, they'll tell all" (*Hamlet*, III.ii.141-42). Shakespeare tells us what he wants us to know, and more than once. What he wants us to know in this case is simply that Antonio is sad without knowing why.

It turns out that what actually makes Antonio unaccountably sad is a true premonition of disaster—a common Shakespearean technique of foreshadowing. Compare, for example, Clarence's dream of drowning (*Richard III*, I.iv), Hamlet's "how ill all's here about my heart" (*Hamlet*, V.ii.212–13), and Desdemona's "Willow" song in *Othello* (IV.iii), all of which forebode something that neither the character nor the audience knows until it happens. Here Antonio is feeling as premonition what he is soon to feel as reality—the threat of death. Shakespeare means us to know about his gloom without knowing why it is there until the plot gets around to showing us why it is.

BASSANIO

Isn't the supposedly ideal lover Bassanio selfish and mercenary? He seems to be willing to put his friend at mortal risk for the sake of material and matrimonial gain and to give away his wife's ring against his oath. But these questions ignore the text.

Bassanio has said, "You shall not seal to such a bond for me; / I'd rather dwell in my necessity" (I.iii.154–55), and Shakespeare punctuates the assertion with the rhymed couplet. Bassanio agrees to Antonio's bond with Shylock only because of Antonio's persuasion. Bassanio is the embodiment of virtue in the young lover, a Jason seeking the golden fleece that is Portia (cf., I.i.172, III.ii.241). In Venice Bassanio is a generous entertainer and master, not a miserly valuer of quantities like Shylock. At the same time he is conscious of his debts and wishes to pay them off. His debts themselves are not the issue, for no one makes an issue of them. His desire to repay Antonio's love *is* the issue, as he says (I.i.127–34). His request of Antonio, to furnish him with the means to win in one journey a fair and virtuous wife and the wealth to pay his debts, is indeed thrift (= a way of thriving—l. 175). And his mind correctly foretells good fortune (ll.175–76) as Antonio's sadness correctly foreshadows loss. Bassanio does call himself "something too prodigal" (l. 129), but that is modesty. We know so because Antonio says that Bassanio always stands "Within the eye of honor" (ll. 136-37). Bassanio's wise words in the casket scene (III.ii.73–107) are an expression of the true lover's insight, as the words of Morocco express the blindness of pride and those of Arragon the blindness of folly. Portia is right to love Bassanio, and her father's casket test is vindicated in Bassanio's victory. Bassanio is also an exemplary friend to Antonio, whose predicament is not Bassanio's fault but the result of bad fortune coupled with Shylock's implacable will. In the trial scene, Bassanio says he would give up all to save Antonio (IV.i.282-87), the true friend's answer to his friend's own willingness to be sacrificed.

When Bassanio gives the supposed Balthazar (really Portia) Portia's ring (IV.i.453), he is not betraying Portia in any moral or spiritual way. Rather, he seasons his actions to the time and situation. His giving up the outward symbol of their love is called for by the circumstances, which, after all, Portia has set up precisely to see what Bassanio really values and to have fun. Bassanio gives the ring when Antonio asks him to do so. And Portia would have him do so, for she knows he is faithful in wanting to keep the ring and also in wanting to give it up for his friend's sake. If it looks to an outsider as if he has betrayed his love, one who has insight and the capacity to value things rightly will know better. And of course, as we know and he does not yet, giving the ring to "Balthazar" is really giving it to Portia and so is the best way to keep it.

JESSICA

How can Jessica be justified in betraying and robbing her own father and abandoning her heritage? She answers this question herself:

> Alack, what heinous sin is it in me
> To be ashamed to be my father's child!
> But though I am a daughter to his blood,
> I am not to his manners. O Lorenzo,
> If thou keep promise, I shall end this strife,
> Become a Christian and thy loving wife.   (II.iii.16-21)

Her fear of "heinous sin" is the appropriate hesitation any daughter should feel in being ashamed to be her father's child. It is parallel to Launcelot's fear of obeying the fiend by changing masters. But Shylock being what he is, it is no sin to leave him and become a Christian. Notice that there is no talk of Jessica's betraying her faith or her people, which there would be if Shakespeare cared to make apostasy an issue. The issue is leaving a house that is hell for a life of love and a path to heaven, which is what becoming a Christian means to the Elizabethan audience. The singing and dancing and masques that Shylock wants to shut out are symbols of joy, which Jessica rightly prefers to the miserliness and isolation she knows at home.

Jessica's "heinous sin," like Portia's saying she is an "unlessoned girl" (III.ii.159) or has a bad voice (V.i.113), like Bassanio's saying "I was a braggart" (III.ii.258), like Antonio's saying he is made a "want-wit" by sadness (I.i.6), like Launcelot's thinking he is following the fiend rather than his conscience in leaving Shylock's service for Bassanio's (II.ii)—all these are versions of figures of speech (*antiphrasis* and *meiosis*) used in humble self-deprecation by the characters and intended by the author to imply rhetorically their self-evident opposites. Portia is far from "unlessoned," and no one but she says she has a bad voice or indeed any defects at all. Bassanio has been honest and no braggart. Antonio is no want-wit. The voice that tells Launcelot to leave Shylock is that of true conscience. Jessica, as Lorenzo says of her, is not guilty of any sin; she is, as he calls her, "wise, fair, and true" (II.vi.56). And their banter about false lovers (V.i.1–22), just like the banter about the rings, is love play. Lorenzo and Jessica, like Portia and Bassanio or Nerissa and Gratiano, jestingly accuse one another of infidelity and slander precisely because none of them is guilty of any such thing. Their jesting bespeaks and punctuates the happiness in their fidelity that unfaithful lovers could never enjoy. Jessica's actions are justified by events as well, for her fidelity to Lorenzo has brought her father more mercy than would have come to him if she had not stolen from his house. In regard to Shylock, Lorenzo has said,

> If e'er the Jew her father come to heaven
> It will be for his gentle daughter's sake.   (II.iv.33-34)

This prediction comes true in part, for Antonio has Lorenzo and Jessica in mind at the trial's end when he stipulates that Shylock leave half his wealth to them and become a Christian.

Jessica's taking on a disguise in order to escape Shylock's domain is not sin but symbol. Portia's picture is encased in the lead casket as love is encased in the will to "give and hazard all." Portia is dressed in the robes of a doctor of laws as mercy in the robes of justice. (Again compare to the Duke in *Measure for Measure*.) Antonio's right is hidden in Shylock's bond as blood in the flesh and the spirit of the law in the letter. The soul is dressed in the body. And like all these disguises, the loving Jessica is disguised as the daughter of the Jew. But since, as she says, she is "daughter to his blood" but "not to his manners" (II.iii.18-19), to disguise herself in order to escape Shylock is not to falsify herself but to become her true self. As Bassanio is characterized as a Jason who finds his golden fleece in the leaden casket, so Lorenzo is another Jason who finds his golden fleece in an equally unlikely place, the house of a Jew. Jessica, as his torch bearer, lights their way to joy.

PORTIA

Even the marvelous Portia is abused by critics of her supposed flaws. Isn't she racist in her comments on Morocco's complexion? Isn't she weak in choosing to obey her dead father's instruction instead of just marrying Bassanio, whom she loves, as a liberated woman would? Doesn't she cheat by playing a song for Bassanio that she did not play for the other suitors? In the trial scene of Act IV doesn't she entrap Shylock by suggesting that even if he is not merciful he will win the case? Isn't her quibble about the blood just legalistic self-serving? Why does she force Bassanio to break his oath about the ring and then tease him about it? All these objections to Portia are a function of expecting the play to be a modern, "politically correct" soap opera instead of what it is. Seen from the Elizabethan perspective, such objections dissolve into irrelevance.

The Elizabethan attitude toward dark-skinned people, like Christian anti-Semitism, is another of history's tragedies. But Shakespeare's purpose in Portia's characterization of Morocco is not to give vent to racial prejudice. Here, as in *Othello*, the relation between skin color and character is developed for specific dramatic purposes. According to Renaissance belief, black is the color of the devil (cf., *Love's Labour's Lost*, IV.iii.250 and *All's Well That Ends Well*, IV.v.42–43), and Portia's two comments about Morocco's color—though Morocco is a "tawny Moor" not a "blackamoor" like Othello—use the word "complexion." That word signified not merely the hue of one's skin but the complex of elements and humors in a person and therefore the nature of the character (see The Humors in Part 1, Chapter 7). Before Portia sees Morocco, she says, "If he have the condition of a saint, and the complexion of a devil, I had rather he should shrive me than wive me" (I.ii.129-31), expressing both her aesthetic preference and her recognition that the outward shows may be least themselves. But she says she will marry him if he chooses right. Once he has chosen wrong, she hopes that all of his "complexion" choose so—that is, that all of not only his skin color but his moral makeup. We do not blame her because we have seen Morocco's shortcomings for ourselves. It turns out that the fun Portia makes of her suitors is the fun that ought to be made of them, for all but Bassanio, including the Englishman (presumably a white Anglo-Saxon), are in one way or another proud, foolish, or cowardly.

The terms of the casket test include the provision that any suitor swear never to marry if he should choose wrongly. Most of the suitors leave unwilling to accept those terms and so exhibit their unworthiness. The casket test proves itself not only by winning for Portia the man whom she loves and ought to love and who truly loves her, but also by preserving Portia and at least two other potential wives from marrying fools (II. ix.11–13). Even from the grave, Portia's wise father shows mercy to other men's daughters as well as to his own, in distinct contrast with Shylock, for whom the relation between death, daughters, and caskets is "Would she were hears'd at my foot, and the ducats in her coffin!" (III.i.89-90). In acquiescing to the will of a dead father, Portia, like Bassanio, gives and hazards all, and in doing so wins both what she desires (cf., the gold casket) and what she deserves (cf., the silver casket).

The song sung while Bassanio is choosing among the caskets is not a form of cheating. It cannot help anyone who has not the wit to see its point. And if Shakespeare meant us to see it as cheating, someone somewhere would have said so.

In the courtroom scene (IV.i) Portia's legal judgment is unexceptionable, and her speech on mercy (ll. 184–202) is sublime. She concludes the speech with a statement that has been read as a trap for Shylock:

> I have spoke thus much
> To mitigate the justice of thy plea,
> Which if thou follow, this strict court of Venice
> Must needs give sentence 'gainst the merchant there. (ll. 202-205)

These words are meant not to tempt Shylock to ignore mercy but to put Shylock's choice dramatically before him and us: justice or mercy, the letter of the law or its spirit. Portia offers him the chance to be merciful several more times before she nails him with the flesh-blood distinction, derived from an old folk tale. The point of that distinction is not that the Christians are as petty as Shylock. It is that implacable justice and nothing but justice will in the end hurt the accuser even more than the accused. The golden rule—do unto others as you would have them do unto you—is shown to be essential to everyone's life.

Portia's ring test is delightful fun, but it is also a comic version of the serious testing of Shylock in the court scene and of Bassanio in Belmont. Will the person being tested trust to the outward show: the glittering casket, the letter of the bond, the possession of the ring? Or will he rather trust to the greater reality of which these are external disguises? Shylock fails his test; Bassanio passes both the casket test and the ring test, and Portia knows it.

Shylock, remembered in the harmony of Act V as a man in whom there is no music and who is "fit for treasons, stratagems. and spoils" (V.i.85), is consistently guilty of blindness to true value, just as on medieval cathedrals the personified synagogue was pictured blindfolded in the presence of the personified church. His speech is repetitive and mechanical (I.iii.1–15, II.v.1–18, III.iii.1–17, IV.i.42–62, etc.). To him the murderous hatred of a fellow human being is indistinguishable from another man's hatred of a rat, a gaping pig, a cat, a bagpipe (IV.i.52–62). He trusts to the letter of the law, which means to his own will. Barring a redemption unimaginable to him, he is appointed to loneliness and destruction.

Portia, by contrast, treats the ring as no more valuable than it should be treated and loves Bassanio the more for his having given it away for good reason. There is no exclusion in love. Loving a wife and loving a friend are equally valid and valuable. In well-tuned minds one love is not jealous of another, especially when mere caskets and rings are at issue. Jessica could be happy loving both Shylock and Lorenzo if only Shylock would let her. And Portia wants Bassanio to love Antonio truly, for it means that he can also love her truly. This is the unity of love, which in Shylock's arithmetic is unimaginable. Giving the ring in thanks to the "Doctor of Laws" for saving Antonio's life, Bassanio is being true to Portia, who is the Doctor of Laws not only by virtue of her disguise but by virtue of her actual "doctoring" in the courtroom of Venice. She is also, symbolically, a doctor of the law of love, which supersedes the law of contracts and bonds as the New Testament was believed to have superseded the Old. The physical ring makes a circuit—from Portia to Bassanio, from Bassanio via Antonio (who requests that it be given) and Gratiano (who carries it) to the supposed Balthazar, from Balthazar to Portia (a short trip), and again from Portia to Bassanio. But the circuit that the ring makes in being given and given again is a far greater ring than the physical ring itself. In giving up the mere golden ring, Bassanio and then Portia complete the ring of love.

Portia gives Antonio life, with the court judgment, and living, with the letter about his safely harbored ships (V.i.286). Thus the play ends with the true dispensation of the wealth that has served as the medium of exchange throughout. For Shylock that material wealth has been all, measurable against love and life itself, until it is weighed against his own life. For the others it is the means of enjoying both life and love precisely because it is valued only with "respect" (V.i.99), that is, willingly hazarded for that which is more valuable. In Venice, Shylock closes up his house's ears against the entry of music from the world (II.v.34–36), just as he has been enclosed in his own selfish will. In Belmont, the music of Portia's house spreads out into the world (V.i.97–98), as Portia herself goes out to Venice to redeem Antonio from Shylock and Shylock from himself. Shylock's house is a hell, Portia's is a heaven, and the play that shows us so ends in heavenly harmony.

SHYLOCK

The second of the major difficulties with this play is the anti-Jewish doctrines and stereotypes that Shakespeare and his audience had inherited and that Shakespeare made use of for dramatic purposes.

The impulse behind Shakespeare's characterization of the Jew was not racial or ethnic prejudice. To see this we need only notice that the moment the spiritual orientation of Shylock's Jewish daughter Jessica is recognized, she is embraced by the Christians. Nor was the anti-Semitism of Shakespeare's time an active persecution spurred by fringe-group propaganda and conspiracy theories arising from a supposedly alien presence. There were almost no Jews in England between 1290, when they were expelled, and the mid-seventeenth century, when they were invited back.

There certainly were conspiracy theories about the Jews, but they arose in England not as a response to the presence of actual Jews. They arose from two millennia of Christian religious myth rooted in the reaction of the early Christian theologians to Judaism's rejection of the divinity of Christ. From ancient times Christians had justified their persecution of the Jews by claiming to be God's instruments in punishing them for denying Christ. As noted above, during the Middle Ages, the synagogue was personified in cathedral sculpture as a blindfolded woman, signifying that the Jews were a people benighted by God for having rejected Christian salvation. Because of this theological tradition, Jews were imagined to be guilty of every vice that Christian doctrine had repudiated: greed, lust, pride, violence, faithlessness, and revenge. Through the Middle Ages and into Shakespeare's time, Jews were portrayed on the stage as just such archetypal villains, usually with red wigs and leering, malicious faces.

Shakespeare inherited this tradition, and he was a Christian. But he was also the greatest poetic and dramatic genius in history. When he wrote dramas about inherited beliefs and live moral issues, he did not do it with cardboard characters. He brought his characters to life. Under his hands the stereotype of the Jew became a realistic, eloquent, and convincing human being. That character, Shylock, has all the traditional characteristics of spiritual blindness that Christians ascribed to Jews: he is selfish, materialistic, greedy, usurious, possessive, and revengeful. But brought to life by Shakespeare's art, he also feels pain, disappointment, and sorrow, and he justifies his villainy with reasons—lots of them.

Shakespeare's audience, as Shakespeare well knew, would have seen through Shylock's fallacious reasons. They would have felt the power of Shylock's feelings but at the same time recognized his reasons as what we now call rationalization. They would have seen clearly that murder was not justice and that a Jew's having eyes, hands, and feelings like a Christian could not justify revenge. Not even the elopement of a daughter could justify murder, no matter how believable Shakespeare made Shylock's grief. And Shylock's forced conversion at the end, which is shocking to us, or should be, would have been seen by the Renaissance audience as a gift of mercy to Shylock, a last-minute redemption from hell, bestowed by a forgiving Antonio and a beneficent Duke.

The difficulty for us is that halfway between Shakespeare's time and ours, in the late eighteenth and early nineteenth centuries, the Western world changed. The Enlightenment and Romanticism happened and the American and French revolutions happened. They profoundly changed our most basic ideas about what we ought to value. Newly defined values developed: equality, democracy, freedom for the individual from the perceived or real oppressions of tradition, religion, and class and from stereotypes of all kinds. These are *our* received ideas, as fundamental to our thinking as Christianity and its traditional concept of the Jews were fundamental to Shakespeare's.

So in the early nineteenth century, Shylock began to be portrayed differently. He was reconceived to gain our sympathy. His protest against being vilified came to seem more justified and his desire for revenge less evil. Soon *The Merchant of Venice* was transformed from a play about love and self-sacrifice triumphing over selfish greed into a play about a poor wronged victim rising up against unjust persecution. The altered world view of directors and actors forced Shylock's words to mean to audiences what Shakespeare never intended.

The play's Christians were also transformed. Where Shakespeare's audience saw in Antonio the virtue of self-sacrificial love, now audiences were compelled to see hypocrisy and racism. Where audiences used to find profundity in Portia's plea for Shylock to be merciful and genius in her solution of the justice problem, now they found a cheap trick in the former and oppression in the latter.

But this modern attitude didn't sit right because the words of the play didn't actually support it. In the early twentieth century, some directors began to feel that modern interpretations had come too far from Shakespeare's intentions, and there was a backlash. But instead of going back to Shakespeare's humanized stereotypical Jew, they went even further back, to the medieval stage villains of Shakespeare's youth. There was the old cardboard Jew, in the red wig and malicious smile, cackling and being hissed off the stage. This portrayal had the virtue of restoring the Christians to their rightful admirable positions in the play. The trouble was that Shylock's words couldn't be contained in such a shallow rendering. They kept bringing the cardboard villain back to life.

Then the Holocaust happened, in which the German Nazi regime and its abettors murdered 6,000,000 Jews because they were Jews, the most monstrous offspring of the 2000-year tradition of Christian persecution of the Jews. After that, directors could not imagine portraying Shylock except as the poor wronged victim of oppression.

As a result of this complex history of Christian anti-Semitism, in our time we struggle with how to approach this great play, especially with how it can be produced on the stage. There seem to be four possibilities, all of them problematic:

1. We can try to remain as authentically Shakespearean as possible. This means making the Christians good and Shylock a convincing and realistic villain, hoping that even a modern audience can embrace the play's values of love, forgiveness, and self-sacrifice despite the discredited tradition of anti-Semitism behind the drama. But such productions also run the risk of perpetuating Shakespeare's inherited stereotype.

2. We can adapt the play to modern sensibilities, making Shylock the hero and de-legitimizing the Christians, forcing the play to be not about greed and revenge and legalism but about racism and hypocrisy. But to do so we must ruin the play's profound treatment of justice and mercy, of reductive materialism and loving self-sacrifice, entirely obscuring what Shakespeare meant the play to be.

3. We can try to eat our cake and have it too by combining elements of both interpretations and letting the audience decide what to think. This choice results in a production that projects moral confusion and leaves us bewildered instead of uplifted.

4. We can refuse to produce the play at all on the grounds that doing it right misleads audiences about the Jews and doing it wrong misleads audiences about the play. This means shelving one of the world's great plays for fear of how people will respond to it.

Perhaps there is no right way to produce this play in our time. But those who do mount theatrical or cinematic productions of the play should keep several things in mind: First, the play is a comedy, which meant in Shakespeare's time that the ending is a happy one in which nobody dies. Second, *The Merchant of Venice* as Shakespeare conceived it is not mainly about Shylock, any more than *Much Ado about Nothing* is mainly about Don John, or *As You Like It* mainly about Duke Frederick, or *Twelfth Night* mainly about Malvolio. Like the casket test, like the shipwrecks, Shylock is an obstruction in the unfolding story of the meaning of love. Third, in Shakespeare's terms, the ending is happy not only because Shylock's evil intentions are thwarted and Antonio's life saved, but because even the villain is saved from the consequences of his own villainy. (If he had taken his pound of flesh, he would have been guilty of murder; if he had not become a Christian, he might have been damned.) Fourth and most important, the deepest values that Shakespeare was trying to bring to life in *The Merchant of Venice* are values that in reality good Christians and good Jews—in fact all people of good will— share. They are that justice must be tempered with mercy, that loving sacrifice must be rated above greedy acquisition, that as we look for divine mercy for ourselves, so we must temper with mercy our justice to others, and that we all ought to do unto others as we would have them do unto us, a principle which the New Testament imports from the Old.

Still, the conflict remains. The play is a comedy of the triumph of a good we should all value over an evil we should all reject. But that triumph is dramatized through the use of a stereotype arising from one of history's most deplorable tragedies: the Christian theological justification of the persecution of the Jews. Whenever we look at *The Merchant of Venice*, no matter how the play is directed, that unavoidable fact hits us squarely in the eye.

KEY LINES:

1. I.iii.42–52: "I hate him for he is a Christian; . . . Cursed be my tribe / If I forgive him!" To the Elizabethan audience these words introduce Shylock as beyond doubt a villain. That he calls down a curse on the Jews if he shows forgiveness for Antonio's lending money "gratis" (in keeping with Christianity's forbidding of usury) recalls to the audience the curse they believe is already upon the Jews for not accepting the Christian doctrine of forgiveness and vicarious redemption through Christ.

2. I.iii.102: "O, what a goodly outside falsehood hath!" Compare Antonio's comment on Shylock with the caskets and what is hidden in them in II.vii, II.ix, and III.ii.

3. III.i.53–73: Shylock tries to justify his intention to take a pound of Antonio's flesh by arguing Jews have "eyes, hands, organs, dimensions" (etc.) just as Christians do. The argument is seen by modern readers

as equivalent to our principles of justice and equality. That is not Shakespeare's intention, however, and the flaws in Shylock's argument demonstrate as much. The first is that in equating Jew and Christian he appeals only to the lowest common elements in human nature: the physical body and the passions. About the mind and spirit of men and their capacity to reason and to love he says nothing. The second is that he concludes his oration with a justification of revenge. To the Elizabethan audience such a conclusion completely undermines the argument. Even in the complex case of *Hamlet*, the desire for personal revenge in a Shakespeare character is *always* a sign of error if not of outright villainy. The appeal to similarities in order to justify murderous revenge entirely discredits the appeal.

4. III.ii.73ff.: "So may the outward shows be least themselves — / The world is still [= always] deceived with ornament. . . ." Bassanio's internal reasoning about the caskets articulates the theme of the contrast between false appearance and true reality, and his speech applies it to various areas of life, including the law court that will be the setting of the climactic trial scene (IV.i).

5. III.iv.11–18: Portia recognizes the true nature of the friendship between Antonio and Bassanio when she observes that

> in companions
> That do converse and waste the time together,
> Whose souls do bear an egall [= equal] yoke of love,
> There must be needs a like proportion
> Of lineaments, of manners, and of spirit;
> Which makes me think that this Antonio,
> Being the bosom lover of my lord,
> Must needs be like my lord.

6. IV.i.184ff.:

> The quality of mercy is not strained / . . .
> Though justice be thy plea, consider this:
> That in the course of justice none of us
> Should see salvation. We do pray for mercy,
> And that same prayer doth teach us all to render
> The deeds of mercy.

Portia's plea pointedly articulates the theme of justice and mercy, both essential values, neither sufficient in itself without the right seasoning of the other. She makes explicit this idea of "seasoning," in the sense of tempering or moderating, in her use of the word "seasoned" at V.i.107 (see Key Line 9 below).

7. IV.i.368–94: "*Duke*: That thou shalt see the difference of our spirit, / I pardon thee thy life before thou ask it. . . . *Shylock*: I am content." The Duke's mercy is allied to Antonio's. Antonio agrees to let Shylock keep half his wealth on condition that he become a Christian and that upon his death he leave his fortune to his daughter, both of which stipulations would be seen by the Elizabethan audience as manifest examples of mercy and kindness. The Duke allows Shylock to keep his mortal life, and Antonio compels Shylock to find eternal life. Shylock's next-to-last speech, though forced, is the sign of his will's acquiescence in saving his own soul.

8. V.i.58–65: Lorenzo observes to Jessica,

> Look how the floor of heaven
> Is thick inlaid with patens of bright gold.
> There's not the smallest orb which thou behold'st
> But in his motion like an angel sings,
> Still [= perpetually] quiring to the young-ey'd cherubins;
> Such harmony is in immortal souls,
> But whilst this muddy vesture of decay
> Doth grossly close it in, we cannot hear it.

Enclosed in flesh we cannot see the soul it encloses or hear the harmonious music of the spheres (see Part 1, Chapter 7). But we may know the soul and the heavenly music are there and may value both above what we see and hear in the "outward show" of the fallen and sin-riddled world. Lorenzo's speech makes explicit the philosophical grounds of all proper valuation.

9. V.i.99–108: "Nothing is good, I see, without respect; . . . / How many things by season season'd are / To their right praise and true perfection!" Portia here utters the point of the play: Valuing each thing with "respect," seasoning (in the sense of tempering or moderating) our judgments, we become capable of right praise and are ourselves seasoned to "true perfection."

SPECIFIC NOTES TO HELP IN YOUR READING:

1. I.iii.142: "This is kind I offer." Kind is both kindness and natural dealings, the treatment one would offer to his own kind (i.e., his own family, his own species). Shylock claims to be offering the ducats at no interest instead of engaging in his usual usury, to which Antonio is opposed because it is unnatural to make "barren metal" (l. 134) breed. (Antonio's attitude is in keeping with traditional Christian doctrine's opposition to usury, which in Shakespeare's time was under severe pressure from the developing mercantile world of London.) Shylock's "kindness" will reveal itself to be radical *un*kindness when Shylock decides to enforce his bond.

2. V.i.307: The last line of the play refers to "Nerissa's ring." The joke is lost unless one is aware of the sexual innuendo: Gratiano is vowing to keep safe not only Nerissa's golden ring but also her sexual fidelity.

Much Ado about Nothing

Like "What You Will," the subtitle of *Twelfth Night*, the title of *Much Ado about Nothing* is a pun as well as the sort of cliché phrase Shakespeare liked to use for the titles of his middle-period comedies, e.g., *As You Like It*, *All's Well That Ends Well*, and *Measure for Measure*. If he were living now, Shakespeare might title a play *What Goes Around Comes Around* or *Is It What It Is?* The pun in the title of *Much Ado about Nothing* lies in the fact that the Renaissance pronunciation of the word "nothing" was very close, perhaps identical, to the pronunciation of the word "noting," and *to note* meant, among other senses, a) to observe closely, pay attention to, notice; b) to point at or indicate by pointing; c) to accuse, stigmatize, denounce, brand with disgrace. Hence, without giving away the plot, the title of the play implies that it will depict much ado about observing, about people pointing at one another, and about accusations. The public accusation and humiliation of Hero in IV.i is an extreme instance of *noting* in sense c. So the pun in the title hints that the denunciation arising from observation that is erroneous (nothing) will lead to a comic rather than a tragic ending. In short, the worst of the noting comes to nothing.

The play involves four interwoven plot lines: the love story of Claudio and Hero; the story of the love underlying the verbal battle between Beatrice and Benedick; the story of the envious serpent-spoiler in the garden of Messina, Don John and his cronies; and the saving of the day by the well-meaning Watch in spite of the hilarious incompetence of the constable Dogberry.

Though the title suggests that it will come to nothing, the threat of death becomes intense in this play. It is mild at the beginning of the play when we hear that "But few of any sort, and none of name" (I.i.7) have died in the military action just ended. But when, in public at the wedding, Claudio denounces Hero, that is "notes" her in sense c of the word, she faints, and though she does not die, she might well have died from such a shock, as Friar Francis says when suggesting that they all pretend that she has died in fact. The charge of Beatrice to Benedick to "kill Claudio" (IV.i.289) hits us with a fierce intensity. Benedick is persuaded to do so. Admirably he chooses to do so not by stealth, as would Don John, but by formal challenge to a duel. The challenge is serious. When Benedick says to Claudio, "You are a villain. I jest not" (V.i.145–46), they are what we would call fighting words; the implication is that a duel to the death will result. All these threats of death being finally disarmed, the happy ending of the play is a significant redemption from disaster.

In order for us to enjoy that redemption, and the joy of Hero's dramatic though not literal resurrection, we must believe in Claudio's sincere love of Hero and in his sincere repentance. In addition to all the obvious passages, Claudio's love for Hero is shown dramatically in the very passage where he is denouncing her for her supposed betrayal of him, as for example,

> You seem to me as Dian in her orb,
> As chaste as is the bud ere it be blown [= blossomed].
>
> (IV.i.57–58)

It is precisely the chaste, maidenly loveliness he sees in her that makes her supposed betrayal so painful to him, and makes forceful his rejection of her and his commitment never to love again:

> For thee I'll lock up all the gates of love,
> And on my eyelids shall conjecture hang,
> To turn all beauty into thoughts of harm,
> And never shall it [i.e., beauty] more be gracious.   (IV.i.105–108)

That is, never again shall beauty seem to me a good thing.

Later, after what he has done to her, we can believe in her continued love for him and in his ability to live with himself only if we are thoroughly persuaded that he is converted from the furious avenger of his own honor into the loving husband that Hero deserves. Shakespeare succeeds in persuading us of that conversion in several ways:

First, when they initially hear Borachio's description of how they were fooled about Hero, Don Pedro says, "Runs not this speech like iron through your blood?" and Claudio responds, "I have drunk poison whiles he utter'd it" (V.i.245–46). They are shocked and horrified.

Second, immediately after he has drunk this poison of self-knowledge, Claudio says, "Sweet Hero, now thy image doth appear / In the rare semblance that I loved it first" (V.i.251–52), thereby fulfilling the prophecy of Friar Francis, who had predicted that

> When [Claudio] shall hear she died upon his words,
> Th' idea of her life shall sweetly creep
> Into his study of imagination,
> And every lovely organ of her life
> Shall come apparell'd in more precious habit,
> More moving, delicate, and full of life,
> Into the eye and prospect of his soul,
> Than when she liv'd indeed.   (IV.i.223–30)

Third, Claudio's transformation is confirmed in Act V, Scene iii, in which Claudio places an epitaph on the supposed tomb of Hero. Though the scene is a short one, its verse is solemn, and we are meant to understand that Claudio is deeply moved and utterly serious about his vow to do "this rite" of mourning "yearly" in memory of Hero. Productions that gloss over the scene or leave it out do a disservice to their audiences and to the play. Of course we know that Hero is not dead in fact, but Claudio must believe that she is and be thoroughly sorry for his part in her death before he can merit the rewards of her resurrection. As Leonato later says, "She died, my lord, but whiles her slander lived" (V.iv.66). But the death of the slander has to happen not only in the external world of facts but in the heart of Claudio, and in V.iii the slander in his heart is exorcised by repentance. Friar Francis had predicted this too:

> what we have we prize not to the worth
> Whiles we enjoy it, but being lack'd and lost,
> Why, then we rack the value; then we find
> The virtue that possession would not show us
> Whiles it was ours. So will it fare with Claudio   (IV.i.218–22)

And so indeed it does.[1]

These transformations—the death of the slander, the repentance of Claudio, and the escape from all the threats of death—have been effected by the good will of the Watch, though not by their comical ineptitude. They are foils for the expert and not at all comical bad will of Don John and his acolytes. That the Watch overhear, capture, and "note" the malefactors Conrad and Borachio resolves the conflict of the main plot, restores the reputation and life of Hero, the life of Claudio, and the friendship of Claudio and Benedick, and foils (in both senses) the evil plot of Don John.

In the meantime, Benedick and Beatrice have been engaged in an ongoing misreading of one another. That misreading is parallel to the pointed misreading of Hero by Claudio under the influence of the villains. And both are comically symbolized by the intentional and inadvertent misreadings of the maskers in II.i. But Benedick hints at the underlying attraction between him and Beatrice that their verbal sparring disguises, even from themselves. Benedick has said to Claudio about Beatrice, "There's her [i.e., Hero's] cousin, and [= if] she were not possess'd with a fury, exceeds [Hero] as much in beauty as the first of May doth the last of December" (I.i.190–92). That is, Beatrice, if she were not possessed with a fury, is far more beautiful than your heartthrob Hero.

There is a parallel passage from Beatrice: When Don Pedro says to her that she has "lost the heart of Signor Benedick," she replies,

> Indeed, my lord, he lent it me awhile, and I gave him use [= interest, usury] for it, a double heart for his single one. Marry, once before he won it of me with false dice; therefore your grace may well say I have lost it." (II.i.278–82)

These two sentences seem to be a duplication of the idea using two different metaphors, one of which Shakespeare perhaps intended to delete. In any case, they both suggest that at some earlier point Beatrice had been attracted to Benedick but believed she had found that he had only pretended to love her. He "lent" rather than gave her his heart, or he won her heart with "false dice." In both metaphors she is expressing that she had once fallen for Benedick but failed to find reciprocity in him.

The reason for that failure is not to be ascribed to infidelity in Benedick. It is only that Beatrice has got ahead of Benedick in her feelings. At that earlier time, Benedick, like Claudio, was headed for the wars and was not thinking about love. Claudio has said to Don Pedro,

> When you went onward on this ended action [= war campaign],
> I look'd upon her with a soldier's eye,
> That lik'd, but had a rougher task in hand
> Than to drive liking to the name of love.
> But now [that] I am return'd, and that war-thoughts
> Have left their places vacant, in their rooms

Come thronging soft and delicate desires,
All prompting me how fair young Hero is,
Saying I lik'd her ere I went to wars.   (I.i.297–305)

We may assume a similar experience behind the hints at a previous connection between Beatrice and Benedick. But parallel to Beatrice's misperception that Benedick's affection for her was "false dice," Benedick's misperception about Beatrice is that, being a woman, she is inevitably destined to make her husband a cuckold (i.e., a man whose wife has betrayed him in sexual intercourse with another man). When Benedick says "In faith, hath not the world one man but he will [i.e., who will not] wear his cap with suspicion?" (I.i.197–99), he is expressing his motive for "being a professed tyrant" (I.i.168-69) to women and one determined never to marry, namely fear of betrayal. The traditional symbol of a cuckold is that on his forehead grow horns visible to everyone but himself.[2] That is, all but he know that his wife has been unfaithful, and the dishonor in that, depending on the man, may be unbearable (as in *Othello*). To wear a cap with suspicion means to wonder whether one has the cuckold's horns on his head.

Thus the genuine mutual affection of Beatrice and Benedick hides under the cover of a mutual mistrust of one another that takes the form of their war of wits, fueled by the hypothetical betrayal of their expectations. But since Benedick is truly attracted by Beatrice, and since Beatrice would never commit adultery, these betrayals are only apparent, like the supposed betrayal of Claudio by Hero. And it is because love underlies the "merry war" (I.i.62) between Beatrice and Benedick that the "love-gods" (II.i.386)—Don Pedro, Leonato, Claudio, and Hero—can work Cupid's magic upon them, revealing rather than transforming the couple's feelings.

At the end, when both love stories are about to be consummated in a double wedding, Benedick defends himself against the jibes of Claudio and Don Pedro about his transformation from confirmed bachelor to married man:

In brief, since I do purpose to marry, I will think nothing to any purpose that the world can say against it, and therefore never flout at me for what I have said against it; for man is a giddy thing, and this is my conclusion.   (V.iv.104–109)

That "man is a giddy thing" is his light expression of a deep truth of the play. All men are fallible, and therefore prone to misunderstanding others and themselves. Therefore, essential to life's happiness is the capacity to change one's mind—to repent of one's misreadings, to acknowledge the primacy of love over the false noting of oneself and others, to replace the bad will evoked by error with repentance and forgiveness rooted in good will. Benedick then invites all to the celebration of that happiness by commanding the music and dancing that ends the play. All but Don John, that is, with a brief line about whose capture Shakespeare confirms the justice as well as the happiness of the ending. But the punishment of the villain is postponed. Dancing, wedding, and joy take precedence.

KEY LINES:

1. I.i.162ff.: Claudio asks, "Benedick, didst thou note the daughter of Signor Leonato?" The word play on *noting* begins here. Claudio asks whether Benedick paid attention to Hero. Benedick replies, "I noted her not, but I looked on her" (l. 164), meaning I didn't point at her or accuse her of anything, but I did notice her. More wordplay on *note* takes place at I.i.256 ("notable") and at II.iii.54–57, beginning with the sense of a musical note and ending with "Note notes, forsooth, and nothing," i.e., sing and stop talking. Again "noting" and "nothing," pronounced the same, make a pun. It reappears at III.iii.117–119, where Borachio says, "Thou knowest that the fashion of a doublet, or a hat, or a cloak, is nothing to a man," implying several senses: is of no significance by comparison with a man, is of no significance to a (real) man, is that by which a man is noted (= recognized), is that by which a man achieves note (= fame or honored position), is that by which a man may be stigmatized. The sentence leads to a discussion of the superficiality and giddiness of fashion (cf., Key Line 3 below), and thence to the confession that Borachio has wooed Margaret under the name (= fashion of address) of Hero, the crux of the ado at the wedding the next day, when Claudio notes (= defames) Hero in public. Friar Francis returns the word to its proper place after the debacle when he asserts that "By noting [= closely observing] of the lady" (IV.i.158), he is absolutely certain that Hero is "guiltless here / Under some biting error" (IV.i.169–70). The friar is exemplary both in his observation and in his conclusion.

2. I.iii.13–39: Don John explicitly voices the sin of envy, like Oliver and Duke Frederick in *As You Like It* and like the more terrifying Iago in *Othello*. Conrad has said that Don John, forgiven by Don Pedro for his earlier rebellion, could take root in his brother's grace only "by the fair

weather that you make yourself" (ll. 23–24). But Don John prefers his weather foul: "I cannot hide what I am . . . I had rather be a canker in a hedge than a rose in his grace . . . I am a plain-dealing villain . . . If I had my mouth I would bite . . . I make all use of [my discontent], for I use it only." His attitude spreads discontent to others, who, unlike him, are redeemed from it ultimately by the opposite of envy, namely good will.

3. V.iv.108: Benedick says at the end, "for man is a giddy thing" (i.e., changeable, inconstant, fickle, swirled around by variable forces). One may be giddy with drink, like Borachio; with envy, like Don John; with vengeance, like Claudio at IV.i.31ff. and like Beatrice at IV.i.289; with indignation, like Leonato at IV.i.120ff. and V.i.53ff.; with folly like Dogberry and his Watch; and of course with love and the joy of love. Giddiness is fallibility, making us subject to taking "nothings" seriously for a time. Its only antidote is a good will, the kind that causes marriage to redeem the giddiness of lovers and the kind that causes patience, humility, and forgiveness to redeem the misprisions of the social fabric. Only Don John is unworthy of the happy ending, for it is only a resolutely bad will that stands in the way of joy.

SPECIFIC NOTES TO HELP IN YOUR READING (MUCH ADO ABOUT NOTING?):

1. The name Borachio comes from the Spanish *borracho*, drunk, and *borrachón*, drunkard, and Borachio's behavior enacts a common problem: "What is in the heart of the sober man is in the tongue of the drunkard."[3]

2. I.i.26: "A kind overflow of kindness" refers to the tears of Claudio's uncle on hearing good news of his nephew. (We never hear of this uncle again, probably because Shakespeare changed his mind about making him a character in the plot.) "Kind" here means both natural, the response appropriate to such news of one's kin, and kindhearted.

3. I.i.151: "he is no hypocrite," probably a reference to Matthew 15:7–8, denouncing those whose heart and lips are at odds.

4. I.i.271–72: "if Cupid have not spent all his quiver in Venice, thou wilt quake for this shortly": Benedick has been proclaiming that he will never marry. Don Pedro says that if Cupid has not used up all his love arrows in Venice, famous for prostitution, Benedick will "quake" in three senses, all with a play on *quiver* in the sense of tremble: a) quake with fear in punishment for his defiance of Cupid, b) quake with love, for Cupid will teach him his lesson, and c) quake in sexual intercourse.

5. I.i.318: "Look what will serve is fit: 'tis once, thou lovest, / And I

will fit thee with the remedy." "Look what" means whatever; "'tis once" means to say it all at once or in a word. The line means "whatever will serve the purpose will do; only say you love and I will help you out."

6.   I.ii.7: In "As the event stamps them" "event" means outcome. The news will be good if the outcome is good. But in keeping with the play's theme of false noting, Antonio here ironically gets things wrong—not the principle, but the facts. Don Pedro will woo Hero not for himself, as Antonio assumes, but for Claudio.

7.   II.i.40: A "berrord" or "bearherd" or "bearward" is one who wards (= is in charge of or keeps) bears, and who often as well kept and trained apes.

8.   II.i.41: "lead apes into hell": proverbial for the fate of women who die as virgins.

9.   II.i.47–48: "So deliver I up my apes, and away to Saint Peter. For the heavens, he shows me where the bachelors sit, . . .": This punctuation in Q and F is erroneous and makes little sense. The punctuation should be "So deliver I up my apes, and away to Saint Peter for the heavens. He shows me where the bachelors sit, . . ." The phrase "for the heavens" means simply in the direction of the heavens, as opposed to the direction of hell, with which the passage began. Cf., "to make for the opposite shore" (see OED under "for" *prep.* and *conj.* 12.). Here the word "bachelors" means the unmarried of both sexes (cf., Mark 12:25).

10.   II.i.60: "mettle": *mettle* and *metal* made a common pun.

11.   II.i.72: "dance out the answer": "answer" means not only response but, in the context of music, the repetition of a musical phrase by another instrument.

12.   II.i.96–99: "My visor is Philemon's roof . . . speak love": "Philemon's roof" and "thatch'd" are references to the story (in Ovid's *Metamorphoses* 8, also referred to in *As You Like It* at III.iii.11) of Jupiter in disguise visiting the thatched cottage of the peasants Baucis and Philemon. When Hero objects that Don Pedro's mask is not "thatched" with a beard and therefore that his metaphor is not fitting, he responds by driving their exchange into rhymed verse, though the Q and F texts, and therefore some modern editions, unfortunately print it as prose:

> My visor is Philemon's roof
> Within the house is Jove.
> Why then your visor should be thatch'd.
> Speak low if you speak love.

13. II.i.139–42: "None but libertines . . . beat him": That is, only libertines—those who turn against propriety and toward self-indulgence—delight in Benedick. They are the ones whom he pleases and who laugh, and it is the true men who are angered by him and beat him.

14. II.i.344: "not ever sad then": here "ever" means always. "She is never sad but when she sleeps, and not [even always] sad then . . ."

15. II.iii.42: "We'll fit the kid fox with a pennyworth": "kid fox" is often emended to "hid fox," which would be fittingly ironic because the three plotters are about to outfox Benedick, who believes he is outfoxing them by spying on them to hear their conversation. However, "kid fox" makes sense as well. A kid is a victim, so that Benedick, who thinks he is the fox here, is really the kid being led to slaughter (i.e., love). He believes he is the wise one in resisting love, but we will capture and sacrifice him to love. A "pennyworth" is also ironic, implying "more than he bargained for."

16. II.iii.60–61: "Well, a horn for my money, when all's done." Benedick is saying that in the final analysis I prefer a horn, implying martial music, to the lute, implying love music. But we are also meant to hear irony in his expressing a preference for his greatest fear about love, namely cuckold's horns. And we are not wrong to detect here and at the end of the play ("tipped with horn" at V.iv.123–24) a third and explicitly sexual sense of the word *horn* (from which we get our word *horny*).

17. II.iii.110–11: "What effects, my lord? She will sit you—you heard my daughter tell you how." The dash (which may or may not appear in modern editions but should be there) is the sign of the failure of Leonato's invention. He can think of nothing to say to illustrate the effects of passion. So he tosses the ball to the others. (The "you" in "sit you" is in the ethical dative case, not the objective case.) He finally picks the ball up again at ll. 130ff.

18. III.i.71–72: "*Ursula*: Sure, sure, such carping is not commendable. / *Hero*: No, not to be so odd, and from all fashions, / As Beatrice is, cannot be commendable": Either Hero awkwardly duplicates the point for added emphasis on "cannot," leaving out the pronoun and making the subject do double duty, or there is a punctuation error in Q and F. In other words, either "No [it is] not [commendable] to be so odd and from all fashions as Beatrice is, [it] cannot be commendable," or else we must emend in some such way as this:

Ursula:	Sure, sure, such carping is not commendable.
Hero:	No, not. To be so odd and from all fashions
	As Beatrice is cannot be commendable.

19. III.ii.93: "If there be any impediment": cf., "If either of you know any inward impediment" (IV.i.12–13). The phrase is from the marriage service in the Book of Common Prayer of 1559 ("if any man do allege and declare any impediment, why they may not be coupled together in matrimony by God's law, or the laws of this realm . . . "). Shakespeare alludes to the phrase in Sonnet 116.1–2: "Let me not to the marriage of true minds / Admit impediments."

20. III.iv.30: "Is not marriage honorable in a beggar?" i.e., *even* in a beggar.

21. III.iv.56: "For the letter that begins them all, H." The line plays on the old pronunciation of the word *ache*, namely *aitch*, a pun on the letter H. Beatrice claims to be "ill," "sick," and "stuffed," suffering from a cold and the ache it causes. Margaret, who is in on the tricking of Beatrice into believing Benedick is in love with her, needles her with hints of Beatrice's being in love and only "stuffed" because of weeping over Benedick. She recommends for a remedy *carduus benedictus* (holy thistle) in a series of puns on Benedick.

22. IV.i.234–35: in "doubt not but success / will fashion the event"— "success" means what follows (succeeds) and "event" means outcome, result, what will happen "eventually."

23. IV.ii.12–13: When Dogberry asks Conrad's name, he says "Yours, sirrah?" using the phrase appropriate to inferiors and servants. Conrad responds "I am a gentleman, sir," meaning, it is inappropriate to address me with the phrase *sirrah*.

24. V.i.308–309: Dogberry says about Conrad, "They say he wears a key in his ear and lock hanging by it." Dogberry thus erroneously interprets the First Watchman's saying "I know him, 'a wears a lock" (III. iii.170), meaning a love-lock of hair. This is one of the many errors that turns Dogberry into the comical ne plus ultra of verbal false noting, of which the nearly tragic example of moral false noting is Claudio, who has said "Yet sinn'd I not / But in mistaking" (V.i.274–75).

25. V.iv.74, 77: "Why, no, no more than reason" and "Troth, no, no more than reason": Both Beatrice and Benedick, echoing her, claim they love rationally but without passion or desire or longing—i.e., unstruck by Cupid's arrow. Their own sonnets to one another refute the claim.

1   Compare the Friar's assertion with Shakespeare's Sonnet 73 and with the lyrics of Joni Mitchell's song "Big Yellow Taxi": "Don't it always seem to go that you don't know what you've got till it's gone" (1970).

2   When one youngster makes "bunny ears" behind the head of another in a photograph, he is enacting an ancient joke of which he usually does not know the significance. The gesture means "Unbeknownst to him I am sleeping with this man's wife."

3   Quoted by Tilley from Erasmus, *Adagia* (267 E): "*Quod in corde sobrii, id in lingua ebrii.*" Lyly paraphrases it in *Euphues, The Anatomy of Wit* (p. 279). See Morris Palmer Tilley, *A Dictionary of the Proverbs in England in the Sixteenth and Seventeenth Centuries* (Ann Arbor: The University of Michigan Press, 1950), H333, p. 302

As You Like It

The setting of *As You Like It* is a dukedom somewhere in France not too far from the Forest of Arden, an imaginary composite of a) the real Forest of Arden in central England, in whose outskirts Shakespeare's birthplace, Stratford-upon-Avon, was located; b) the real Ardennes forest in northern France; and c) the imaginary Forest of Ardennes in Thomas Lodge's prose romance *Rosalynde*, which is a source for Shakespeare's play.

At the beginning of the play, the dukedom is in moral breakdown, corrupted by the sin of envy. As Dorothy Sayers explains in her introduction to Dante's *Purgatorio*, envy is the second of the deadly sins identified by the Christian tradition as the seven roots from which spring all other sins. The fundamental meaning of the word *envy* (from the Latin *invidia*, to look or see into) is "love of one's own good perverted to the wish to deprive other men of theirs."[1] The early scenes of *As You Like It* depict Duke Frederick as having overthrown his older brother, the rightful Duke Senior, in order to rule in his place. He is also on the point of banishing Rosalind, Duke Senior's daughter, because her virtues seem to him to throw his own daughter's virtues into shadow. At the same time, Orlando's older brother Oliver, who has sent their middle brother away and kept Orlando from getting a proper education, now is trying to have Orlando killed. As Oliver says at the end of Act I, Scene i, he hates Orlando for his virtues:

> I hope I shall see an end of him; for my soul, yet I know not why, hates nothing more than he. Yet he's gentle, never schooled and yet learned, full of noble device, of all sorts enchantingly beloved; and indeed so much in the heart of the world, and especially of my own people, who best know him, that I am altogether mispris'd.
>
> (I.i.164–71)

This is a classic articulation of the sin of envy. Like Duke Frederick, Oliver feels that his own good depends upon causing his good brother's harm.

By contrast with this corrupt world of envy at court, in the Forest of Arden the ousted Duke Senior is living with his loyal followers in virtue and simplicity, embracing their exile and finding "these woods / More free from peril than the envious court" (II.i.3–4). Here they feel "[but] the penalty of Adam" (see Specific Note 2 below)—i.e., mortality itself, including the difficulties of wind and weather and the necessity of laboring in order to eat (including having to hunt and kill deer). But they do not feel the threat from the human vices of high society. For what is there to be envied in one who lives in the lap of nature, with no palace, no land, and no possessions?

These two worlds represent respectively man sinfully at war with his own nature and man virtuously embracing and making the best of his nature. The migration of people early in the play from the court to the forest and the intention to return to the court at the end of the play depict both the individual's and the society's journey from sin through self-knowledge to peace (see Setting in Chapter 6 of Part 1). And that self-knowledge comes with embracing one's true nature, which is a mystery of the transforming and healing power of love.

In the forest, Oliver is converted by Orlando's risking his life to save him. At the edge of the forest, Frederick is converted by an "old religious man" (V.iv.160). As a result of these transformations, Duke Senior recovers his dukedom and Orlando his patrimony and more. This healing, with its consequent reordering of society, happens not at court but only away from it, in Arden. For it is only in the forest that love is permitted to triumph despite the "penalty of Adam."

But in the idyllic natural world of the forest, love triumphs in more ways than moral regeneration. Rosalind, Celia, and Orlando, who all seek asylum there from the envy-corrupted court, are not themselves in need of correction. But they are in need of a restoration of faith in the forms and relations of love, by which they have been deeply betrayed. In Arden their faith in the selflessness of lover, brother, and ruler is restored, and a desirable future once again opens up for them.

Rosalind takes the opportunity of her disguise as a boy to test the sincerity of Orlando's love by challenging that love in the person of the supposed "Rosalind" that Rosalind-as-Ganymede pretends to be. Does Orlando really love her, or is he going to turn out like the as yet unregenerate Frederick or Oliver? Is he characterized by virtue and constancy or subject to corruption like his brother and her uncle? Would he be discouraged by a real-world wife's human fallibilities or remain faithful to his word? To accomplish his trial, Rosalind pretends to have cured another man of his love, and then sets about inventing as trying an image of Orlando's ideal Rosalind as she can. As the imaginary other lover's pretend beloved, she says that she used to

> grieve, be effeminate, changeable, longing and liking, proud, fantastical, apish, shallow, inconstant, full of tears, full of smiles; for every passion something and for no passion truly anything . . . would now like him, now loathe him; then entertain him, then forswear him; now weep for him, then spit at him . . . .
>
> (III.ii.410–17)

And so, she says, she cured that poor lover of love. Later, speaking of how she (as Ganymede's fictional Rosalind) would inevitably behave in marriage:

> I will be more jealous of thee than a Barbary cock-pigeon over his hen, more clamorous than a parrot against rain, more new-fangled than an ape, more giddy in my desires than a monkey. I will weep for nothing, like Diana in the fountain, and I will do that when you are dispos'd to be merry. I will laugh like a hyen, and that when thou art inclin'd to sleep.
>
> (IV.i.149–56)

(The word *hyen* is an older form of hyena.) And when Orlando asks "But will my Rosalind do so?" she swears, "By my life, she will do as I do" (IV.i.158)—meaning to Orlando "yes" and to us "no."

We know that Rosalind is not doing justice to the image of herself. The real Rosalind will not behave in the inconstant manner she claims for the imaginary Rosalind. We know this because we know her to have a virtuous, loyal, and patient character, despite the giddiness of her confession to Celia of her love for Orlando. The point of the wild changeability of the imaginary Rosalind is to see how Orlando will respond under the inevitable variation of moods that must occur in a real marriage. Orlando passes these tests of his character without disappointing Rosalind, though she pretends that his tardiness has disappointed the imaginary Rosalind.

However, the final proof of Orlando's character is no test that Rosalind devises, but one devised by Providence. It is Orlando's choice to risk his own life to save his hitherto evil brother from the hungry lioness. When

Rosalind hears this about him (IV.iii.98ff.), there is no more question of her concern for his becoming a Frederick or an Oliver. He is heart whole. Her attempt to cure him of love, which he denies the possibility of her doing, ends when his evident virtue cures her of doubt.

In addition to the brotherly love Orlando has shown and the spiritual love to which Frederick is converted, the four couples marrying at the end represent four degrees of the erotic relation, and their weddings incarnate their respective potentials for harmony. These four meanings of marriage are punctuated and solemnized by the miraculous appearance of the god of marriage, Hymen. The words of Hymen (V.iv.131–36) are recast about fifty lines later in the words of the cynical Jaques (V.iv.188–92). Both summations clarify the way that love works in the world differently for those differently gifted to receive it. Hymen's prediction is that "No cross shall part" Orlando and Rosalind, and Jaques' bequest to Orlando is "a love that your true faith doth merit." Their love has all along been deeply rooted in virtue, and in their marriage eros and virtue are harmoniously wedded. Oliver and Celia are "heart in heart." Their love is a sudden revelation, and their wedding embodies the virtue of true submission to that true revelation, predicated on Oliver's restoration through repentance. Phebe must accord to Silvius, and she does so, saying "now thou art mine, / Thy faith my fancy to thee doth combine" (V.iv.149–50)—that is, she is now attracted to him and no longer to the illusory Ganymede and commits to being faithful to him. Jaques predicts for Silvius "a long and well-deservèd bed" (V.iv.190). Their wedding and their marriage bed are a single image of the triumph of nature over wayward fancy. As for the somewhat cynical and lustful Touchstone and his rather dim but virtuous Audrey, Hymen predicts that they are "sure together / As the winter to foul weather" (V.iv.135–36), and Jaques predicts "wrangling" (V.iv.191). For those who can rise no higher than marrying only for sexual gratification or merely stupidly, the harmonious uniting of bodies will be attended by a predestined interdependent marital discord.

The road to all these harmonies is paved with wit—the endlessly inventive wit of Rosalind and of her author.

KEY LINES:

1. II.iv.54–56: Touchstone says, "We that are true lovers run into strange capers; but as all is mortal in nature, so is all nature in love mortal in folly." To which Rosalind responds, "Thou speak'st wiser than thou art ware of," in order to make us aware of the deeper implication of his

words. Touchstone's term *mortal* has two senses, subject to death, and subject to error (being a mere mortal). He means that just as every natural living thing is destined to die, so every person who by nature falls in love is fallible and therefore destined to commit follies in relation to love. The deeper wisdom that Rosalind finds in his words is that in a nature in love, folly itself is mortal and dies. Those who by nature fall in love are redeemed from their folly by love. In other words, the same true love that makes us commit follies in its name heals our natures of their mortal fallibility.

2. II.vii.166–67: The set-piece speech of Jaques on the seven ages of man (II.vii.139–66) is a brilliant evocation of the lifespan of a human being from the dark viewpoint of the melancholic. Man starts in "mewling and puking," whines his way to school, loves the superficial in his mistress, fights for no principle but the "bubble reputation," makes a comfortable show of himself when he should be serving justice, wastes away unaware of the evanescence of material things, and ends "Sans [= without] teeth, sans eyes, sans taste, sans every thing." So says the melancholy Jaques. But not Shakespeare, for he has Orlando just then appear carrying his old servant, Adam, in his arms. We know this because in the very next line Duke Senior says, "Set down your venerable burthen." Thus our eyes are treated to an immediate and perceptible refutation of Jaques' dark vision in a reverse Pietà, in which instead of the dead young man in his mother's arms we see the still living old man in the young man's arms. And we are to conclude that even the fading old man is *not* "sans every thing" so long as there is love, here in the form of the virtue of devoted loyalty. The old man Adam is of course a namesake of the Adam of the Garden of Eden and embodies a reference to that in our natures which is in need of regeneration and redemption, which appear here embodied in the Christ-like kindness of Orlando to his own servant, which rewards the earlier self-sacrifice in Adam's loyalty to Orlando.

SPECIFIC NOTES TO HELP IN YOUR READING:

1. I.iii.36–38: Rosalind and Celia are engaged in playing with words and logic. Celia says, "Why should I not? [hate Orlando]. Doth he not deserve well [to be hated]?" She is asking, since her father hates Orlando, whether he does not well deserve to be hated by her too. Of course she does not really mean that she ought to hate Orlando. She is trying by her ironical assertion to discredit the logic of her own argument. Rosalind's response, "Let me love him for that . . . ," intentionally changes the

meaning of the word "well" in Celia's phrase "deserve well" in two ways: a) from an adverb to an object, from meaning "very much deserve" to "deserve all good things," and b) from "deserve well [to be hated]" to "deserve well [to be loved]."

2.   II.i.5: "Here we feel but the penalty of Adam": The F text here, and the Riverside edition following it, reads "Here we feel not the penalty of Adam." It can be argued that F's "not" makes sense: we experience but don't care so much about the penalty of Adam's original sin, namely change of seasons, labor, and mortality, because we experience no additional human sin of envy. However, Theobald's emendation of "not" to "but" makes simpler and better sense: "here feel we *only* the penalty of Adam," namely the curse of work and of not being in the Garden of Eden, but not the additional torments of the flattering, the envious, and the otherwise depraved among men in society back at court. Having to decide between these two readings is a good example of the agonizing trials of a modern editor.

3.   II.iv.1: Rosalind says not "O Jupiter, how merry are my spirits" (as in F) but (as Theobald and Warburton emend) "O Jupiter, how weary are my spirits." Unlike the emendation in the previous note, this one poses no agony for the modern editor because it is clearly justified by Touchstone's reply in the next line: "I care not for my spirits, if my legs were not weary." Rosalind has called on Jupiter because the name she has taken for the boy she is pretending to be, Ganymede, was the name of the beautiful lad whom, in the myth, Jupiter had carried up to heaven to be his cup-bearer.

---

[1]   Dorothy Sayers, Introduction to *The Comedy of Dante Alighieri the Florentine: Cantica II: Purgatory*, tr. Dorothy Sayers (London/New York: Penguin Books, 1955), p. 67.

Twelfth Night, or What You Will

Deep down everyone knows the difference between authenticity and fakeness, though we can sometimes be fooled. And everyone who is not the victim of a corrupt soul or a corrupt culture prefers authenticity. In matters of emotion, authenticity is represented by the word *sentiment* and fakeness by the word *sentimentality*. What is the difference?

Sentiment is the emotion or feeling we have in response to an actual experience—of a thought, an event, a person, a work of art. By contrast, sentimentality is the cultivation of an emotion or a feeling for the sake of the feeling itself. What you feel when the vet tells you that your dog has a terminal disease is sentiment—grief and sorrow (if you love your dog), or perhaps relief (if you don't). What you engage in when you intentionally seek out the image of a dying pet in order to have a good cry is sentimentality. An authentic work of art, say Tolstoy's *Anna Karenina*, evokes sentiment because what it says matters. A typical pornographic film is pure sentimentality: what it says doesn't matter at all; it exists only to arouse the viewer sexually. Meeting someone attractive, falling in love, and being refused may evoke the sentiment of melancholy. Fantasizing about an unattainable ideal beloved in order to wallow in melancholy on purpose—that is sentimentality.

Twelfth Night tells the story of an entire society corrupted and immobilized by sentimentality. Nearly all its inhabitants are stuck in the cultivation of various fantasies of love in order to wallow in their own feelings. Orsino, young, rich, and eligible, enjoys lying around listening to music that makes him miserably hungry for love because his fantasy Olivia won't marry him. Olivia, young, rich, beautiful, and eligible, locks herself away from all men to spend her youth in sorrowing for her dead brother. Sir Toby Belch devotes his life to partying, avoiding any real relationship, trying to make every day of the year into Twelfth Night—nothing but revels. Malvolio is consumed by a fantasy image of rising above his proper station in life to boss people around after marrying his boss, a Twelfth Night fool wanting to be king. Sir Andrew Aguecheek foolishly wastes his money in pursuit of the fantasy of marrying Olivia. No one in Illyria is in touch with reality except Maria, Olivia's waiting gentlewoman, and the official court fool, Feste, who satirizes the real fools in wit and song. But neither the wit of Maria nor the commentary of Feste can cure the society of its disease of sentimentality.

What does cure it is an invasion from outside. Three people from over the sea, who have lost everything and survived real suffering, providentially enter the scene seeking refuge and a way to live. Their authenticity is so irresistible that the sentimentalists who meet them are compelled out of their fantasy lives into real love.

For safety, Viola, whose name is a near anagram of Olivia, disguises herself as a boy. But there is a big difference between outward disguise adopted out of necessity and the inward inauthenticity of sentimentality. The relationship that develops between Viola and Orsino is a sharing of hearts and minds. As a result, Orsino comes to recognize that his true love is the inner Viola—not the outward pseudo-boy Cesario and not the outward beauties of Olivia, whose inner life he has never taken the trouble to know. Olivia likewise falls for the inward Viola disguised in the outward form of a boy, and, luckily for her, Viola's character and that of her brother Sebastian, whose dress she copies, are equally virtuous and authentic, so that fantasy yields to reality and happiness results.

The title of the play is significant. "Twelfth Night" refers to the twelfth night after Christmas, the feast of Epiphany (meaning manifestation), celebrating the revealing of the Christ child to the Magi (related to our word *magic*). The Magi were Persian wise men or astrologers, who, according to Matthew 2:2, came to Jerusalem and asked "where is he that is born King of the Jews? for we have seen his star in the east, and are come to worship him." The manifestation of the Christ child to them symbolizes the revelation of God to the world in the form of the incarnation. The holiday was celebrated in England during Shakespeare's time with feasting, wassail (drinking hot mulled cider), and topsy-turvy antics and pranks, including treating the local fool as a king for the day.

The title of the play, intended figuratively, thus implies that everything is upside down in Illyria until the manifestation of the truth of reality in Act V. That comes in the form of the revelations that the boy Cesario is really the girl Viola and that Sebastian is alive and present. These revelations resolve the mistakings of the plot and correct the confusion of hearts.

The subtitle of the play, *What You Will*, is also significant. For Shakespeare the word *will* had at least seven senses: 1) The primary meaning is the free will of man, our choice-making power, which was considered God's greatest gift to human beings and one quality by which we are distinguished from the animals. 2) From that sense of the word comes the form of the future tense of verbs. "I will call home" literally means "I wish—intend, choose—to call home." 3) Also from the primary sense comes the sense willfulness—that human impulse that sets our will against nature, reality, and God's will, namely our self-indulgent desires and compulsions. 4) That sense, narrowed, led to the sense sexual desire or erotic compulsion. 5) And that sense led to *will* as a euphemism for the human genitalia, both male and female (cf., Sonnet 135). 6) The word also means, as for us, the document called a "last will and testament." 7) Finally, in several of his sonnets Shakespeare makes these various senses into puns on his own name Will(iam). In the subtitle of *Twelfth Night*, it is senses 1–4 that are implied, and the play itself adds sense 6. In the play, "What you will" can mean what you use your free will to choose, whether for good or ill, what you choose or intend to do in the future, what your willfulness seeks despite the impediments of morality or reality, your erotic or sexual desire, and your intentions about what you leave behind you at death.

The combination of the title and subtitle works at two levels. At one level the subtitle is a cliché title for a comedy, like the phrases "as you like it" or "all's well that ends well" or "much ado about nothing." The author is saying "Call this play either 'Twelfth Night' or whatever else you want to call it." At the deeper level, the title and subtitle together give us a choice—between "Twelfth Night," i.e., the manifestation of the divine, and "What You Will," i.e., our selfish, self-directed, sentimental choices—in other words, between reality and our own fruitlessly fanciful willfulness. The plot of the play in fact leads the characters from what they erroneously desire toward what reality intends for them for their own good, from "what you will" to "Twelfth Night."

The phrase "what you will" pops up during the play as well: Malvolio's name means "bad will," and he embodies the most extreme example of self-will in the play short of Orsino's threat to kill Viola/Cesario in V.i. Olivia utters the exact form of the subtitle when she says "If it be a suit from the Count, I am sick, or not at home; what you will, to dismiss it" (I.v.108–109). Malvolio says, "He'll speak with you, will you or no" (I.v.153–54). Olivia says to Viola/Cesario, "Your will?" (I.v.168–69).

Viola says to Orsino, "Our shows are more than will" (II.iv.117). Malvolio asserts his will eight times in resolving to win the lady, from "I will be proud" to "I will do everything that thou wilt have me" (II.v.161–79). Antonio claims, in a good sense, his "willing love" (III.iii.11). And many of the normal uses of the future tense in the play should be construed as expressing not merely futurity or intention but commitment of the force of the free will.

The plot of the play slowly brings to a good resolution this contest between the revelation and celebration of love implied in the phrase "Twelfth Night" and the willful sentimentality implied in the phrase "What You Will" as one character after another is forced to confront reality in the form of the invaders Viola, Sebastian, and Antonio. Orsino's sentimental love of being in love is driven out by his real and actual love of his disguised companion, Viola. Olivia's sentimental pretense of love for her brother is driven out by her real and actual love of a real Viola disguised as an imaginary Caesario, and comes to fruition in the person of the imaginary boy's real and actual brother, Sebastian. Sir Toby's self-indulgent partying is converted to the real celebration of marriage to Maria when his imaginary opponent gives him a real and actual knock on the head. Malvolio's sentimental fantasy of marrying Olivia and governing his betters is cured by the revelation that the supposed letter from Olivia, too, was a fantasy and by his consequent treatment as a real madman. It is left to us to imagine whether Sir Andrew's own knock on the head and rebuff by his parasitical drinking companion can awaken him from his own foolish fantasy.

As in the epiphany that the Twelfth Night holiday celebrates, so in the play named for it, the banishment of the fruitless fantasy of self-will is accomplished through the unimaginable invasion of the healing reality of love.

KEY LINES:

1. Feste to Olivia at I.v.47–52: "Anything that's mended is but patched; virtue that transgresses is but patched with sin, and sin that amends is but patched with virtue. . . . As there is no true cuckold but calamity, so beauty's a flower."

This speech articulates a central theme of the play. The first part asserts that human beings are not perfect. Since Adam and Eve were exiled from the Garden of Eden, men are born in sin and any pretense they have to perfection is illusory. For the most part, their errors are not thoroughly evil but are merely blots on their general virtue. Likewise, their virtues do not make them perfect, as only Jesus was believed to be, but patch up what inevitable original sin and latterly chosen sin have marred. People who cannot accept their patchedness will suffer consequences. Olivia believes she can mourn for her brother for seven years without paying a price. But the price will be the loss of her youth and beauty and therefore her hope for a happy life, the real threat being not only time and aging but the kind of self-delusion that will make her unavailable and unacceptable to a loving husband.

The second part of Feste's speech applies the general principle to Olivia's condition, and full weight must be given to the word "true." "There is no *true* cuckold but calamity" means that the only one whom it would be appropriate and valid to make into a cuckold (i.e., to betray by loving another man) is calamity itself. The only one Olivia would make a cuckold of by loving a man who is not her dead brother is calamity. She ought not to be faithful to her foolishly prolonged sorrow but should make a cuckold of the calamity of her brother's death by being willing to entertain an appropriate suit of love. "Beauty's a flower" means simply that one's desirability will not last forever. It is a mistake to pretend that youth, beauty, and eligibility should be sacrificed to excessive mourning. The idea is repeated in Feste's song "What is love? 'Tis not hereafter . . ." (II.iii.47–52).

In short, face facts and get over your sentimentality if you ever want to be happy. Viola affirms the principle at I.v.188–89 and 241–43: "what is yours to bestow is not yours to reserve" and "Lady, you are the cruell'st she alive / If you will lead these graces to the grave, / And leave the world no copy." You have been given youth, beauty, and wealth to use (in bestowing them upon a loving husband and in reproduction), not to keep fruitlessly to yourself. (Cf., the Parable of the Talents, Matthew 25:14–30, and Shakespeare's Sonnets 1–17.)

2. Olivia, Viola, and Sebastian all three speak to themselves (and the audience) words of acceptance at I.v.310–11, II.ii.40–41, and IV.i.60–65 respectively:

The two girls, Olivia and Viola, recognizing that things beyond their control are happening to them, surrender control to the higher powers, which they call respectively Fate and Time and which we may call Providence or the Will of God. Olivia, under the compulsion of a real attraction to Viola/Cesario, is moved out of her sentimental mourning to welcome the reality of love: "Fate, show thy force: ourselves we do not owe

[= own]; / What is decreed must be; and be this so"—i.e., let this be so, may it be so. She turns her will toward the confirmation of her attraction by wishing her love for Cesario (and hypothetically his for her) to flourish. This decision will be rewarded because fate has decreed that she will be loved in return by the actual male version of Cesario, namely Sebastian.

Viola is caught loving Orsino who loves Olivia who loves Viola as Cesario. This is the knot that she cannot herself untangle, and she knows it. "O time, thou must untangle this, not I; / It is too hard a knot for me t'untie." But whereas Olivia's surrender to Fate was a transformation of her sentimental willfulness in the face of true sentiment, Viola's surrender to time reveals no change in her character but an instance of her consistent hope and humility, for early in the play, in circumstances where her brother, like Olivia's, may be lost, she says, "Mine own escape unfoldeth to my hope . . . The like of him" (I.ii.19–21), and "What else may hap, to time I will commit" (I.ii.60). Love and hope cause the wills of both girls rightly to make a cuckold of calamity.

Sebastian, who arrives at Illyria with nothing but the friendship of Antonio, finds himself unaccountably loved by Olivia, who is ready to bestow on him not only her lovely self but her substantial estate. To this unexpected good fortune he too submits: "If it be thus to dream, still let me sleep!" When Olivia asks him to be ruled by her, his reply is "Madam, I will." He welcomes the gifts of fortune, now changed from disastrous to positive, as Olivia does her new fate and as Viola does the working of time.

3. Sir Toby Belch to Malvolio at II.iii.114–16: "Art any more than a steward? Dost thou think because thou art virtuous there shall be no more cakes and ale?"

Sir Toby's denunciation of Malvolio resonates through the play in ways he does not himself intend. We are all no more than stewards of what is given us, as Olivia may, in Viola's words quoted earlier, bestow her youth and beauty and wealth but not reserve them (I.v.188–89). Orsino ought to be a better steward of Illyria rather than wallowing in love melancholy. Sir Toby himself ought to quit wasting his life and Maria's happiness in partying every night. There will be cakes and ale despite Malvolio's pseudo-virtue. But the line works both ways. There will also be bumps on the head (V.i.176, 196) despite Sir Toby's cakes and ale. And there will be the passage of time, but also the possibility of the invasion of real love, despite Olivia's and Orsino's respective self-indulgences.

4. V.i.376–77: "And thus the whirligig of time brings in his revenges."

Feste means that there is justice in the universe. Compare "pleasure will be paid, one time or other" (II.iv.70–71), meaning self-indulgent pleasures will be paid for by suffering of some kind under the ultimate equity of justice. "Revenges" of time are to be distinguished from human vengeance, which is forbidden. Feste has noted that Malvolio has had his comeuppance. Malvolio, the humorous man (see The Humors in Chapter 7 of Part 1) storms off saying, "I'll be reveng'd on the whole pack of you" (V.i.378). But that threat does not end the play, for Orsino gives us hope for Malvolio by saying two lines later, "Pursue him, and entreat him to a peace" (V.i.380). Orsino needs Malvolio to report on the captain, but he is also showing a degree of magnanimity appropriate to him now that he too has been brought to peace by time and love. We are invited to hope that Malvolio's will will come around and permit him to benefit from the same whirligig of time that has punished him. (Orsino's phrase is echoed by, or echoes, the words of the magnanimous prince in *Hamlet* at II.ii.322–23, written at about the same time, "the humorous man shall end his part in peace.")

5.   V.i.389–408: Feste's final song sums up the lessons of the various characters in the play. "A foolish thing was but a toy" when one was young, but when one grows up "to man's estate," there is no room for "knaves and thieves." "By swaggering could I never thrive" in matters of love. Orsino, Olivia, Malvolio, and Sir Andrew Aguecheek have all demonstrated as much. As for Sir Toby, "With tosspots still had drunken heads" means that the head of a literal drunk is itself "still" (= always) metaphorically drunk, that is foolish, self-indulgent, and hence self-destructive. "The rain it raineth every day" implies that through the operation of justice by the whirligig of time, men are healed of their follies, by painful experience if necessary. The rain, which falls upon the sentimental as the discipline of disappointment, is in fact the rain of grace, always descending, always available, to which the proper response is humility and gratitude. And that is what the feast of the Epiphany celebrates.

SPECIFIC NOTES TO HELP IN YOUR READING:

1.   I.i.2: "Give me excess of it": In a Shakespeare play anyone looking for excess of anything is asking for correction.

2.   I.i.10–11: Some editions, following F, print as two sentences what should be one: "notwithstanding thy capacity, / Receiveth as the sea. Nought enters there . . ." The editor Rowe first showed that the punctuation

should be "notwithstanding thy capacity / Receiveth as the sea, nought enters there . . .". That is, although the capacity of love to receive and be fed (as by music) is as great as that of the sea, nevertheless nothing enters there, however valuable, that is not soon reduced in value by comparison with love itself—or rather with what Orsino takes for love.

3. I.i.14: Orsino is confusing the "spirit of love" in line 9 with "fancy"—our word *fantasy*—in line 14, another clue that his character is laboring in confusion and needs correcting. His supposedly inexhaustible "fancy," which he mistakes for the "spirit of love," finds that excess of music, as he predicted, leads to surfeit. Only the true spirit of love will convert him from this unlimited indulgence of the fanciful desires that "like fell and cruel hounds, / . . . pursue me" (ll. 21–22) into real and fruitful loving.

4. I.ii.15: Arion is pronounced uh-RYE-ŏn. "Arion, a Greek poet and musician, on a voyage from Sicily to Greece charmed dolphins with his singing and playing on the lyre. When he leaped overboard to escape murder by the sailors, he was saved by a dolphin on whose back he rode to shore" (Riverside). He is not to be confused with the mythical Orion, the great hunter of classical mythology, who became a constellation in the heavens.

5. I.iv.38–40: Orsino says, "Prosper well in this, / And thou shalt live as freely as thy lord, / To call his fortunes thine," meaning *if* you prosper in this, your reward will be to name your price. In the lines we may hear a foreshadowing of Viola's future as his wife. The irony is that he is asking Viola, his true future wife, to achieve that status by winning Olivia to be his wife, a paradox only "Time" can "untangle" (cf., II.ii.40).

6. I.v.5–6: Feste says, "He that is well hang'd in this world needs to fear no colors." This is a pun. To fear no colors means literally not to fear the military flags of an enemy army and figuratively not to fear anything. The pun is on "collars," i.e., a) the noose, and b) any controlling device, like a collar on a dog. Parallel versions of the commonplace are "the end of life cancels all bands [= bonds]" (*1 Henry IV*, III.ii.157) and "he that dies pays all debts" (*Tempest*, III.ii.131).

7. I.v.15: "talents": a reference to the Parable of the Talents (Matthew 25:14–30).

8. I.v.246–47: "labell'd to my will." The sense of the word *will* here is "last will and testament," and Olivia's irony recalls Feste's warning (see Key Line 1), for there is no way for the elements of her beauty to be left to others when she dies.

9. II.i.47–48: Antonio says, "I do adore thee so / that danger shall seem sport, and I will go." Shakespeare, like his age and every age until the time of Freud, believed in the possibility of true friendship between males that was devoted, passionate, and loving but not erotic or sexual (see Was Shakespeare Gay or Not? in Part 1, Chapter 11). Antonio here is the opposite of Orsino, who believes he loves Olivia because of her physical beauty. Antonio's devotion to the noble and virtuous Sebastian drives him into danger and makes him willing to sacrifice his own safety for Sebastian's. At III.iv.312–14 Antonio says, "If this young gentleman / Have done offense, I take the fault on me; / If you offend him, I for him defy you." It is the apparent betrayal of this willing self-sacrifice that torments him when Sebastian, really Viola/Cesario, seems to deny knowing him.

10. II.iii.82–83: Sir Andrew Aguecheek says, "He does it with a better grace, but I do it more natural." Theologically, it is grace that redeems nature. As a noun, the word "natural" meant a fool. Thus Sir Andrew is unwittingly confessing to being a fool, from which condition he does not yet recognize any need to be redeemed. Whether he will recognize it after Sir Toby denounces him as "an ass-head and a coxcomb and a knave, a thin-fac'd knave, a gull" (V.i.206–207) Shakespeare leaves it to us to imagine.

11. II.iv.73–78: After he performs his melancholy love song to please the sentimental Orsino, Feste says,

Now the melancholy god protect thee, and the tailor make thy doublet of changeable taffeta, for thy mind is a very opal. I would have men of such constancy put to sea, that their business might be every thing and their intent every where, for that's it that always makes a good voyage of nothing.

Feste is subtly accusing Orsino of being inconstant and frivolous. "Changeable taffeta" is thin silk "woven of threads of different colors, so that its color shifts with movement" (Riverside). "Opal" is a gem with iridescent colors, hence also changeable. "Such constancy" means constancy like yours, i.e., inconstancy. "Makes a good voyage of nothing" implies a) makes a voyage in pursuit of mere fantasy into something of use (meant ironically); b) makes a voyage come to nothing, arriving nowhere (since the intent is to go everywhere) and bringing back no fruits; and c) makes such a voyage good in that it is worthy of noting, i.e., from it a lesson is to be learned (*nothing* was pronounced like "noting" as in *Much Ado about Nothing*).

12. II.iv.85–86: Orsino says, "But 'tis that miracle and queen of gems / That nature pranks [= adorns, decorates] her in [that] attracts my soul." It is Olivia's physical body that attracts the fancy of Orsino. Hence the superficiality and inconstancy that Feste sees in him is confirmed. By contrast, it will be not Viola's outward form but her character that will in fact cause Orsino to love her.

As with Antonio's love of Sebastian, so here directors who seek to appeal to their audiences with "gender-bending" interpretations in which Orsino almost but not quite kisses Viola/Cesario, or (less often) Viola/Cesario almost kisses Olivia, distract us from the point of those relationships. There is no support for such gestures in the text. Orsino is not moved by Cesario's feminine charms to kiss him. He mistakenly believes that those charms will be a useful tool for winning for him the love of Olivia, whom he loves only for her body. The point is that his relationship with Viola/Cesario is developing in the realms of mind and heart, not body. Viola is of course attracted to Orsino, but sexually that is a one-way attraction until Orsino can see Viola in her "woman's weeds [= clothing]" (V.i.273).

13. II.v.60: "or play with my—some rich jewel": Malvolio was about to say "play with my chain," i.e., the metal chain worn around his neck as the indication of his office as steward of Olivia's estate. He stops himself, realizing that in his fantasy he will no longer be a steward, and shifts his image to "some rich jewel." There should be a dash after "play with my" in the text.

14. II.v.108: Fabian says, "A fustian riddle!" Fustian is a kind of rough cloth made of cotton and flax. As an adjective it means high-flown, bombastic, pretentious and also fake, made-up, nonsensical. We are not, like Malvolio, to treat the four letters M.O.A.I. as a code Shakespeare is using to convey a message to us. To do so is to become Malvolio ourselves. The message is just what Fabian says it is, a pretentious nonsense riddle in which it will be our pleasure to watch Malvolio try to find the meaning he wants. Maria has taken some of the letters of Malvolio's name to lead him on, and in his bloated vision of himself, he reaches just the conclusion she intends him to reach.

15. III.ii.14–15: "I will prove it legitimate, sir, upon the oaths of judgment and reason." Fabian is engaging in some sleight of hand to hoodwink Sir Andrew. Based on Jeremiah 4:2, "And thou shalt swear,

The Lord liveth, in truth, in judgment, and in righteousness," St. Thomas Aquinas articulates the conditions under which an oath is valid: judgment or discretion, truth, and justice. Fabian is leaving out truth because he is persuading Sir Andrew to believe a falsehood. And he is being ironical because Sir Andrew, being a fool, is blind to reason and judgment. In fact, Fabian is engaging in argumentation ("I will prove it legitimate") rather than taking an oath.

16.   IV.ii.2: Feste takes on the disguise and persona of "Sir Topas the curate" in the attempt of Maria, Sir Toby, and Fabian to punish Malvolio by pretending that Malvolio has gone mad. The name Sir Topas probably comes either from Chaucer's *Canterbury Tales* or from John Lyly's *Endymion*, or both. In *The Canterbury Tales*, the character Chaucer begins a verse tale of a knight named Sir Thopas who is in love with an elf-queen and is determined to kill the giant protecting her. The tale is interrupted by the Host, who is bored with its old-fashioned rhyming style. The story is almost certainly meant to be a parody of certain kinds of romances, and Shakespeare's point may be that Feste is likewise about to give a satirical performance made up of clichés, pseudo-scholarship, and madcap. It will also, like the tale of Sir Thopas, be aborted. In *Endymion*, Sir Tophas is a braggart soldier fond of tautological rhetoric. There may also be a play on the gemstone topaz, which was believed to cure insanity.

17.   V.i.18–23: After Feste has argued that he is the better for his foes, who "tell me plainly I am an ass" and the worse for his friends, who "praise me, and make an ass of me" and by whom "I am abus'd," he ends by saying, "so that conclusions to be as kisses, if your four negatives make your two affirmatives, why then the worse for my friends and the better for my foes." Feste is engaging in chop logic to make a true point: flattery harms but criticism helps. Where the kisses come in is not entirely clear. Sir Philip Sidney had played on grammar and kisses in Sonnet 63 of *Astrophel and Stella*: When Stella says "no no," Astrophel takes her to mean yes because who can contradict the rules of grammar by which two negatives make an affirmative? In any case the playful logic of Feste's argument is in the service of the moral point: One is made an ass of by being flattered; one who is told the truth is the better for it. ("Abus'd" in line 20 means fooled, tricked, or lied to.)

18.   V.i.164–67: Orsino asks, "what wilt thou be / When time hath sow'd a grizzle on thy case? / Or will not else thy craft so quickly grow, / That thine own trip shall be thine overthrow?" Orsino is predicting awful things for the Cesario he believes has betrayed him. Compare with his

prediction about Olivia at I.i.34–38 ("How will she love . . . one self king!").

19.   V.i.200–201: Sir Toby says of the doctor, "Then he's a rogue, and a passy-measures pavin." Feste is trying to teach Sir Toby his lesson by saying that the doctor Toby needs is drunk and unavailable, as Toby has been until now, and that Dick surgeon's eyes had "set," like the sun, i.e., closed, already by eight in the morning, presumably because, like Toby earlier, he had been drinking all night. In Toby's insult "passy-measures" may refer to the Italian *passamezzo*, a dance tune whose sections are "eight bars each (hence suggested to Sir Toby by Feste's 'set at eight'). The pavin or pavan(e) was a slow and stately dance" (Riverside). Sir Toby is condemning the doctor for being so slow to come to his aid.

20.   V.i.374–77: Feste says, "But do you remember? 'Madam, why laugh you at such a barren rascal? And you smile not, he's gagg'd.'" He is quoting to Malvolio Malvolio's own verbal attack against him at I.v.83–88.

Measure for Measure

Measure for Measure is one of Shakespeare's greatest plays. Unfortunately it is also one of his most often mistreated by critics. The good characters have been attacked as "problematic" and "disturbing" and the themes have been obscured by the failure to read the play as a Renaissance rather than a modern drama. So let us try to be clear about what Shakespeare is actually accomplishing in this great and serious comedy. Seen properly, it is as deep, uplifting, and healing as anything Shakespeare had previously written.

Anyone who has raised children, run a business, joined an organization, taught school, or lived in any way among people knows that one of the greatest challenges of leadership is to govern with both justice and mercy. The reason is that these two great principles of the moral life are paradoxical opposites. Justice is the principle by which we hold all human beings, who are endowed with free will, to the unalterable standards of human behavior. To choose to break one of these absolute standards is to open oneself up to retribution and correction, by which justice restores the condition of harmony in the soul and in society. However, since all human beings are fallible and endlessly prone to error, there is an equal and opposite principle that offers the human maker of mistakes and committer of sins a path away from despair, namely the principle of mercy. For as Portia says in *The Merchant of Venice*, "in the course of justice, none of us / Should see salvation. We do pray for mercy, / And that same prayer doth teach us all to render / The deeds of mercy" (*Merchant of Venice*, IV.i.199–202).

There is a difficulty, however. Perfect justice and perfect mercy are mutually exclusive. A parent cannot both punish his child for stealing *and* look the other way. A ruler cannot both justly put a thief in jail *and* mercifully let him off the hook. Neither can we pick only one of these principles and safely ignore the other. A parent who justly punishes his child for every infraction whatever the circumstances will rear either a fearful wet noodle or a rebel against all rules. A parent who mercifully gives his child a pass no matter what nastiness has been committed will rear an anti-social egotist. Likewise, if a leader rules only by justice, none of us would be found free of error and punishments would be constant. But if the leader rules only by mercy, the lack of fear of just punishment invites the multiplication of crimes and society topples. This is what Escalus means by "Pardon is still [= always] the nurse of second woe" (II.i.284). Hence the paradoxical condition and question of every ruler: how can one rule with *both* justice *and* mercy?

Over thousands of years Judeo-Christian civilization, acknowledging the paradox, has established a principle for resolving it: Justice must be tempered with mercy. Or, in Portia's words, "earthly power doth then show likest God's / When mercy seasons justice" (*Merchant of Venice*, IV.i.196–97). Tempering, seasoning, modification of justice with mercy, the right measure of each—it's a great solution.

But a difficulty remains: How does one rule *in this particular case*? When is this specific offender to be put into jail, and when is he to be let off with a warning? Does it depend on the severity of the crime? the specifics of the crime? the offender's attitude? mitigating circumstances? All of these considerations enter into the deliberations of a judge loyal to both justice and mercy. No judge but God could ever achieve perfection in the challenge to temper justice with mercy. Judges too are fallible. But that proper tempering must be every judge's goal. And the degree to which that goal is achieved depends on the wisdom and the character of the judge.

The challenge is particularly acute when it comes to erotic matters because eros is one of the most powerful forces at work in human beings—all human beings. And though it involves us in the most private and intimate of interactions, its universality makes it also one of the most potentially positive *and* negative forces subject to choice and error in the life of a community and of a state. Hence a state must have laws governing erotic activity. And, like the parent, the state and society may stray too far to one side or the other, toward justice or toward mercy. One state may busy itself too much with sitting in judgment on the most intimate details of bedroom behavior. Another may permit such license that bigamy, adultery, rape, incest, and sexual trafficking go unpunished.

But even in a state characterized by a well-balanced legal system, when the justice of reasonable laws runs up against the overwhelming power of erotic desire, to which every man and woman may become subject at one time or another, even a wise judge is especially challenged. Women must be protected from predatory men, and the city must be protected from the corruptions of prostitution and venereal disease. That requires justice. At the same time, like all men, the judge himself is subject to erotic desire and therefore ought to be disposed toward mercy about the sexual behavior of others.

How is a judge to temper justice with mercy in governing a city rife with sexual misbehavior? This is the subject of *Measure for Measure*. In dramatizing it, Shakespeare universalizes the principle underlying the behavior of the wise judge and shows us what it might look like when, in the words of Psalm 85:10, "Mercy and truth have met; righteousness and peace have kissed."

Duke Vincentio is beloved. He has ruled with mercy for many years. The result of his mercy is that Vienna is teeming with corruption, particularly sexual corruption: brothels, venereal diseases, irresponsible fathers of children born out-of-wedlock, and sexual harassment by the powerful. Sound familiar? Under Vincentio's leadership Vienna has drifted too far to the mercy side, and as the play opens he has decided to see the city corrected.

In order to accomplish this goal, he puts Angelo in charge and announces that he himself is leaving town. Why does he choose Angelo? Angelo, whose name implies messenger of God, has a reputation for virtue, in particular for absolute sexual self-control. As the Duke's deputy he will begin enforcing the old laws again and rein in the city's self-indulgent corruptions, represented in the witty depravities of Lucio, whose name in Latin means visible light, implying (in a pun that works in English for those who know the meaning of the Latin) *morally* light, as opposed to serious. Angelo begins by arresting Claudio for getting his fiancée, Juliet, pregnant before they are married. The law decrees that the punishment is death. And Angelo is determined to make an example of Claudio for the rest of Vienna. (Compare this decision with Escalus's initially merciful treatment of Pompey at II.i.244–51, where he lets him off with a warning.)

But why, ask the critics, doesn't the Duke just get strict himself instead of having Angelo do the dirty work for him? He himself tells us why:

> Sith [= since] 'twas my fault to give the people scope,
> 'Twould be my tyranny to strike and gall them
> For what I bid them do; for we bid this be done

When evil deeds have their permissive pass
And not the punishment.   (I.iii.35–39)

If we permit evil to go unpunished, it is as if we are promoting the evil. That being so, it would be cruel to let the people misbehave without punishment and then suddenly begin enforcing the laws. The Duke then says a few lines later that Angelo will "strike home" in the Duke's name, "And yet my nature never in the fight / To do in slander" (I.iii.42–43). This is a crucial point often misunderstood. It is not for his own sake that the Duke wants to keep the people from disliking him. It is for the sake of the city and the people that he must protect his image from being abused. We later see Lucio engaging in just such abuse of the Duke, in his case totally groundless slander, and risking severe punishment for it. It is for the good of the whole that the Duke chooses to let the famously upright Angelo do the punishing in his name. If anything goes wrong, the Duke will be there, in disguise, to fix it. And he will do so without losing the respect and obedience of the people, without which, as Shakespeare and his audience believed, cities and states fall into chaos and everyone suffers. In *King John, Richard II, Julius Caesar, King Lear,* and other plays, Shakespeare illustrates this consequence of the loss of faith in one's prince.

The Duke has another reason for putting Angelo in charge. He wants to test him. In this he is re-enacting several parables in the New Testament in which a lord gives orders, leaves, and returns later to judge how his orders have been followed. As the Duke knows, but we find out only later, despite Angelo's reputation for virtue, he has in fact been guilty of breach of promise toward his own fiancée, Mariana. He called off the wedding because her dowry was lost at sea but pretended it was because she was unchaste. She wasn't. So, as the Duke says to Friar Thomas, "hence shall we see, / If power change purpose, what our seemers be" (I.iii.53–54). That is, we will see whether Angelo's new power over others will reveal fallibility in himself. And then the Duke puts on the disguise of a Franciscan friar and sticks around to watch what happens.

It is a profound intentional irony of the play that Angelo and Claudio are precise foils for one another. Claudio jumps into bed with Juliet before their marriage is solemnized. Angelo abandons Mariana before their marriage is solemnized. Claudio is possessed by lust, Angelo by greed. Both betray the union of man and woman, of body and soul, of lower and higher, that is the essence of sacramental marriage—Claudio by too soon embracing his beloved and Angelo by failing to embrace his and abandoning her instead. Both come under the threat of death for their sins, and both find mercy in the justice of the Duke.

Angelo and Claudio are not the only ones tested in the play. Isabel is preparing to become a nun. The Vienna of Lucio and Mistress Overdone has become inhospitable for a virtuous maid, and she wishes to join the Sisters of St. Claire, known to be the most restrictive of the orders of nuns, specifically because she desires "a more strict restraint" (I.iv.4). When Lucio, the emissary of the world of self-indulgence, comes to ask her to plead with Angelo for her brother's life, she is at first humbly diffident, doubting her own power to help: "Alas, what poor ability's in me / To do him good!" (I.iv.75–76). But in response to Lucio's persuasion she agrees to do what she can. And as Claudio has told us, Isabel is good at reasoning, discourse, and persuasion (I.ii.184–86). The test comes when, overcome by lust for Isabel, lust that has been ignited by the very fact of her virtue, Angelo offers to free her brother if she will permit Angelo to possess her sexually.

Some have found Isabel hard-hearted in refusing to do so. What's a little act of sex when your brother's life is at stake? But for the virtuous Isabel, there is no such thing as "a little act of sex." For her, sexual intercourse is either sacramentally justified by marriage, or it is mortal sin. She first reacts to her brother's sexual sin with Juliet by saying "O, let him marry her" (I.iv.49). That would redeem Claudio's haste in going to bed with his fiancée before the wedding. But were Isabel to surrender her body to Angelo willingly, she would be burdening her soul with what she believes to be a damnable sin. This is what she means when she says, "Better it were a brother died at once, / Than that a sister, by redeeming him, / Should die for ever [= be damned]" (II.iv.106–108) and "More than our brother is our chastity" (II.iv.185). She is not either a prude or an emotionally frigid victim of sex-panic, as she is accused of being by critics of various stripes. Such critics take for psychological dysfunction what is in fact her virtue. Isabel's resistance to illicit sexuality is a sign of her goodness, not of any flaw that needs correcting. She is concerned about the condition and therefore the eternal fate of her own immortal soul and of her brother's.

When Isabel tells her brother of Angelo's offer, Claudio's first response is quick and noble, as she expects it to be: "Thou shalt not do it" (III.i.102). (We know it is quick because his words complete the pentameter line she has begun.) But then, succumbing to the fear of hell and damnation

(III.i.117–31), Claudio joins Angelo in asking Isabel to give in to Angelo so that Claudio's life may be prolonged. This Isabel experiences as a violent attack not just on her body but on her soul. First Angelo and now her own brother ask her to risk damnation for their own benefits: for Angelo, the satisfaction of lust; for Claudio, a life of selfishness. In response to this attack, Isabel is rightly outraged and condemns her brother for his weakness and his injustice to her.

As they turn out, events totally justify Isabel's decision. The deal would not in fact have won Claudio's life. Angelo, thinking he has slept with Isabel, sends word that Claudio should be killed immediately, lest Claudio seek revenge later for being given life at the cost of his sister's chastity. As the poet Philip Thompson writes, "doesn't anyone notice that by afflicting [Claudio] with justice, Isabella makes him a just man? When the play's action is concluded, ask Claudio if he resents his sister's passion for purity."[1]

The end of the play is one of the most moving scenes in all Shakespeare's work. Isabel, who has argued so eloquently for mercy in Act II, now appears calling for "justice, justice, justice, justice!" (V.i.25). Yet before the end of the scene, once Angelo is caught, penitent, and harmless, she kneels to beg mercy for him, her worst enemy. Far from being cold-hearted or prudish as some critics have accused her of being, she has in fact responded to every situation confronting her with the particular virtue called for: justice, kindness, self-sacrifice, righteous indignation, patience, mercy, and forgiveness.

The Duke too has embodied all the virtues of a both righteous and merciful leader, and his alternating costumes represent his successful effort to temper justice with mercy. He is dressed as the embodiment of love and mercy when wearing the robe of a Franciscan friar, and also as the embodiment of justice itself when he reappears in his ducal attire. As he has told us himself, "He who the sword of heaven will bear / Should be as holy as severe" (III.ii.261–62). The sword of heaven is the power of the ruler, the deputy of God, to dispense justice, even to the point of executing a criminal. That severity must be tempered with holiness—i.e., mercy, behavior comporting with the Christian ideal of loving even one's enemies.

In this tempering of justice with mercy Angelo has failed. Early on, Angelo has said, "When I that censure him do so offend, / Let mine own judgment pattern out my death" (II.i.29–30). Once he is caught, he remains true to that merciless principle, even when it is applied to himself: "let my trial be mine own confession. / Immediate sentence, then, and sequent death / Is all the grace I beg" (V.i.372–74) and "I crave death more willingly than mercy; / 'Tis my deserving, and I do entreat it" (V.i.476–77).

By contrast, the action of the play's final scene exhibits the Duke's great triumph in tempering justice with mercy. He first sees to it that Angelo confesses, marries Mariana, and recognizes the justice in his impending execution. Similarly, he pronounces upon Lucio the verdicts of marriage to correct his fornication and whipping and hanging to punish his slandering of his prince. But once Isabel passes the test of her capacity to have mercy on her justly condemned enemy, the Duke tempers his own justice with mercy toward Angelo. Then he shows mercy even to his own slanderer, Lucio. Thus the double values of justice and mercy are achieved: The corruption of Vienna is corrected and its villains are redeemed without loss of life. This wisdom of the Duke's tempering is confirmed by heaven, which has provided the death by "cruel fever" of the "most notorious pirate" Ragozine (IV.iii.70–71), whose head is sent to Angelo in place of Claudio's, so that even Barnardine, who is "unfit to live, or die" (IV.iii.64), is mercifully spared, also to be acquitted of all his earthly faults by the Duke (V.i.483).

But why does the Duke allow Isabel to believe that her brother is dead when we know he is not? Isn't this cruel? We must remember that the Duke is not an equal misbehaving toward an equal. He is the rightful ruler and Isabel his subject, and he tells us the reason, if only we will believe it:

> But I will keep her ignorant of her good,
> To make her heavenly comforts of despair,
> When it is least expected. (IV.iii.109–11)

That is, to turn her despair into unexpected joy. It is by virtue of this decision of the Duke that the final scene becomes not only an enactment of justice tempered with mercy in the worldly realm but a prefiguring of the harmony of heaven, in which justice and mercy and their tempering are one.

That the Duke is a representative of the divine government of the world is made explicit in the words of Angelo:

> O my dread lord,
> I should be guiltier than my guiltiness,

To think I can be undiscernible,
When I perceive your Grace, like pow'r divine,
Hath look'd upon my passes [= trespasses].   (V.i.366–70)

In the testing of Isabel, as in the testing of Angelo, the Duke is not arrogantly playing at being God. He is enacting a parable. His testing of his subjects is an image of God's testing of all men. Challenged to beg for mercy for her enemy Angelo, even though she believes he has killed her brother, Isabel enacts a triumph of Christian love and proves the excellence of her character. The reward for that act of mercy is immediate. The living Claudio is produced, thanks to the foresight of the Duke and the loyalty of the Provost, and Isabel experiences on earth a reunion of precisely the kind that she believes awaits all saved souls in heaven and a resurrection of precisely the kind that she believes awaits all saved souls at the end of earthly time.

Thus this realistic drama of human beings who might well have lived in such a time and place as Shakespeare makes of Vienna becomes also a parable of the right relation between love and sex, between justice and mercy, between state and individual human being. It provides an image of how, under a just and merciful ruler, virtue—the tempering of justice with mercy—may be rewarded on earth as it is in heaven. Remembering the concepts of hierarchy and correspondence discussed in Chapter 7 of Part 1, we will see in the Duke here not only a just and merciful man and ruler but the embodiment in parable of the relation of God to his world.

The play ends with a proposal of marriage, which must be understood to be accepted by Isabel's moved silence. There have been directors who cause Isabel to storm off in a huff, as some just as wrongly cause Katherina do at the end of *The Taming of the Shrew*, because she feels abused, imposing a misleading modern agenda upon Shakespeare's play. But such a gesture destroys the entire thematic point of the drama. The Vienna from whose corruption Isabel was in retreat has been corrected thanks to the Duke's wisdom and action. Justice and mercy are united within Isabel and within the Duke. And now the two best human beings in Vienna will be united to one another. Instead of becoming in a Catholic sense a bride of Christ by becoming a nun, Isabel becomes the bride of God's deputy on earth, fulfilling both her spiritual and her mortal callings in a sacramental marriage that figures the union of the redeemed soul with God. In fact, as Philip Thompson has noted, the Duke and Isabel are of one mind[2]—both committed with their whole selves to virtue: to justice when it is called for, to mercy when it is called for, and to their ultimate harmony under the government of the world by God and under the government of the city by God's virtuous deputy on earth. Their marriage is the embodied wedding of justice and mercy.

KEY LINES:

1. I.i.19, 44, 65: "terror . . . love," "Mortality and mercy," "enforce or qualify": The Duke in all three of these lines is alluding to the same idea, three versions of one antithesis, namely justice and mercy, the theme of the play. The parallelism of "Mortality and mercy in Vienna / Live in thy tongue and heart" (ll. 44–45) is that the power to execute a man (justice) lies in the tongue of the ruler, who can speak the words "off with his head," and the power to mitigate that punishment or qualify the law requiring it arises from his heart's capacity to experience mercy.

2. II.i.50ff.: The humor in the Elbow scenes depends, among other things, upon recognizing Elbow's malapropisms. Though he is a good man, he has a shaky grasp of English vocabulary and often unintentionally substitutes a word meaning the opposite of what he intends: "benefactors" for "malefactors" (l. 50), "detest" for "protest" (l. 69), "cardinally" for "carnally" (l. 80), etc. (The figures of speech are acyrologia and cacozelia.) Though his outward presentation is flawed, he is inwardly virtuous, as his behavior demonstrates. In this he is a foil for Angelo, whose outward behavior is supposedly spotless while his inward thoughts are corrupt.

3. II.ii.41–47: Isabel, unfamiliar with the world of men, having asked for mercy once for her brother, is about to accept Angelo's first argument rejecting her plea and to depart: "O just, but severe law! / I had a brother then. Heaven keep your honor." As at first (I.iv), again here it is Lucio who encourages her to keep the argument going ("Give not o'er so. To him again" etc.) until Angelo begins to waver, though not in mercy, but because of lust. That Isabel needs the prodding of Lucio is evidence of the simplicity and purity of her faith and of her humility. That Lucio should be the one doing the prodding fits with his being a representative of the principle of self-indulgent sexual depravity. He is energized to work for her success, as he says earlier to Claudio, "as well for the encouragement of the like [i.e., his own sexual indulgence] . . . as for the enjoying of thy life" (I.ii.187–89). Isabel, Angelo, and Lucio in this scene can be understood as a representation of the psychomachia or inner moral warfare about to take place within Angelo. Isabel represents virtue, Lucio the temptation

to depravity. Angelo, who believes he is akin to Isabel, is so only on the outside. Inside, as he is about to find out about himself, he is a far more dangerous version of Lucio.

4. II.ii.73–75: "Why, all the souls that were were forfeit once, / And He that might the vantage best have took / Found out the remedy": Isabel is referring to original sin in all men and the sacrifice of Christ as God's remedy for it. That is, in strict justice all men would be condemned by God for Adam's fall and the manifold sins following it if it were not that in mercy God provided Christ as the vehicle of man's redemption. As Philip Thompson writes, "*Measure for Measure* is an ordinary Christian story."[3]

5. II.ii.179–80: "O cunning enemy that, to catch a saint, / With saints dost bait thy hook!" The enemy Angelo means is the devil, who, to catch him, is tempting him not with the body of Isabel but with her virtue. He calls her a saint, as Lucio did, and it is her saintliness that tempts him to lust. A few lines earlier he asks himself, "Dost thou desire her foully for those things / That make her good?" (ll. 173–74), and the answer is yes. But where Isabel in humility denied Lucio's implication of her saintliness ("You do blaspheme the good in mocking me"—I. iv.38), Angelo is significantly claiming sainthood for himself. This piles the sin of pride on top of his sin of lust. That pride is reiterated two scenes later (II.iv.9–10) when he says he takes pride in his own gravity (i.e., his moral seriousness and spiritual weightiness, or the appearance of them), a line revealing that it is not morality itself but his reputation for it that Angelo values.

6. III.i.5–41: "Be absolute for death . . . ." The Duke's long speech to Claudio on the pains and evils that beset a human life are more in character for a classically educated stoic than for the Franciscan friar that the Duke is pretending to be. But the purpose of the speech is to buck Claudio up with a dose of stoicism, training him in the contempt of worldly life by which, according to the argument, death is made the less to be feared. It was Claudio's worldliness that tempted him to bed with Juliet before their marriage. To this weakness of character, the Duke applies the power of reason. And it seems to work upon Claudio (ll. 41–43) until Isabel informs him that there would be a way, though an immoral one, to preserve his life. It is that ray of perverse hope that plunges Claudio into terror of death with visions of damnation (III.i.117–31). By that fear he becomes temporarily blind to the doctrine that Isabel entirely embraces, the doctrine that salvation, not damnation, awaits those who repent and die in faith.

7.   IV.i.70–72: The Duke assures Mariana that to deceive and lie with Angelo in Isabel's place "is no sin" since "He is your husband on a pre-contract." The irony is that he is fostering exactly the same act for which Claudio and Juliet stand condemned. But the parallel is crafted intentionally to suggest that sin and virtue lie not in the act itself but in the soul's free will. Claudio, inwardly committed to Juliet, rushed to consummate their marriage before the outward wedding. Angelo, outwardly committed to Mariana, rushed to escape from consummating their marriage before the wedding. Though they are apparently opposite in practice, both choices are in reality equally sinful forms of self-indulgence. Claudio's sin was lust for his beloved and a weak lack of restraint; Angelo's sin was lust for lucre and a weak lack of fidelity. To pay his debt, Claudio must be separated from Juliet, at least for a time. To pay his debt, Angelo must be joined with Mariana, who still loves him. The Duke's plan is additionally justified in its effect on Angelo. Going to bed with Mariana thinking that she was Isabel did in fact satisfy Angelo's desire, and that satisfaction later proves to him that his lust for Isabel was an illusion.

8.   V.i.411: "Like doth quite like, and Measure still for Measure." The line gives the title to the play. It is a reference to Matthew 7:2, and the context of this verse in the Gospel sums up the theme of the play:

> 1 Judge not, that ye be not judged. 2 For with what judgment ye judge, ye shall be judged, and with what measure ye mete, it shall be measured to you again. 3 And why seest thou the mote, that is in thy brother's eye, and perceivest not the beam that is in thine own eye? 4 Or how sayest thou to thy brother, Suffer me to cast out the mote out of thine eye, and behold, a beam is in thine own eye? 5 Hypocrite, first cast out that beam out of thine own eye, and then shalt thou see clearly to cast out the mote out of thy brother's eye.
>
> (Matthew 7:1–5, Geneva Bible)

In the light of this passage, consider, for example, Escalus's attempt to get Angelo to see himself in Claudio: "Let but your honor know . . . / Whether you had not sometime in your life / Err'd in this point which now you censure him" (II.i.8–16). And Isabel's: "If he had been as you, and you as he" (II.ii.64) and "How would you be / If He, which is the top of judgment, should / But judge you as you are?" (II.ii.75–77). Of course "measure for measure" is not the final word. In the last scene of the play the Duke, like Isabel, finds "an apt remission in myself" (V.i.498) and in the end tempers all his just measures with mercy.

SPECIFIC NOTES TO HELP IN YOUR READING:

1. I.i.7–9: "Then no more remains / But that, to your sufficiency, as your worth is able, / And let them work." This sentence as we have it in F, the only early text of the play, presents an insoluble crux. The lines makes no sense, and we conclude that there is at least one line missing from the text, possibly more than one, either after "sufficiency" or after "able." Probably the missing passage was dropped by the typesetter. It is futile to try to make sense of the lines as they are, though some editors have tried to imagine the missing words. As is common in such cases, nothing the editors have come up with satisfies us as being Shakespearean.

2. I.ii.32, 33, 34: "piled" means layered, having a nap to the cloth, with a pun on "pilled," meaning pealed, here stripped of hair or bald. Baldness was one of the effects of the treatment for syphilis.

3. I.ii.34-35: "Do I speak feelingly now?" i.e., have I touched you in a sore spot? The next line puns with the implication that he is speaking with pain because of a syphilitic sore in the mouth. This leads to "I will . . . learn to begin thy health; but . . . forget to drink after thee" (I.ii.37–39), meaning if there is only one cup between us, I will toast your health and drink from the cup before you drink from it, but not after you do, lest I become infected with your venereal disease.

4. I.ii.90: "groping for trouts in a peculiar river." The sexual innuendo needs no note, but it helps to know not only that the word *fish* was slang for a woman, but that the word *peculiar* means privately owned, hence forbidden, illegal to be fished.

5. I.ii.91–92: "is there a maid with child by him? . . . No; but there's a woman with maid by him." A maid, meaning virgin, cannot be with child, meaning pregnant, because being pregnant she is no longer a virgin. But a woman, no longer a maid, is with maid, meaning pregnant, by him, with a pun, picking up the fishing image of the earlier lines, on the word *maid*, which also means a young fish.

6. I.ii.168 and I.iii.21: Another crux. At I.ii.168 Claudio observes that "nineteen zodiacs [= years] have gone round" since the "enrolled penalties" of the law have been enforced. At I.iii.21 the Duke says that he has let the strict laws of Vienna slide "for this fourteen years." Which is it—nineteen or fourteen years? It is possible that Claudio is exaggerating and the Duke being precise about the number of years. More likely,

Shakespeare (or the typesetter) slipped up. But though we will never know which number Shakespeare really intended, we also know that it doesn't matter. The point is that it has been a long time that mercy has prevailed in Vienna in matters of sexual misbehavior.

7. II.i.5–6: F has "Let us be keen, and rather cut a little, / Then fall, and bruise to death." The word *fall* is probably a typesetter's error. Some editors have tried to preserve it by interpretation, but perfect sense is made by emending to *dull*, which completes the antithesis with "keen" in the previous line (keen and cut a little rather than dull and bruise to death).

8. II.iv.121–23: "*Angelo*: We are all frail. *Isabel*: Else let my brother die, / If not a fedary, but only he, / Owe and succeed thy weakness." Angelo voices the commonplace "We are all frail," meaning fallen, fallible. Isabel replies that if that were not so, then let my brother die, if there is no other person equally guilty of this sin ("fedary" = confederate in the sin), i.e., if my brother were the only one to own and inherit ("owe and succeed")— both verbs in the subjunctive—the weakness you speak of ("thy") from Adam's original sin. In her use of "thy" there is an additional implication, unintended by her but caught by us, that it is indeed Angelo's sin too.

9. IV.iii.100: "By cold gradation and weal-balanc'd form." Most editors emend "weal" to "well." "Cold" implies calm reason as opposed to passion, and "gradation" careful steps rather than headlong rushing. If the word intended is indeed *weal*, the Duke means the balancing of personal desires with the requirements of state. In any case, the whole phrase implies the measured application of justice and alludes to the title of the play.

10. V.i.524: "Slandering a prince deserves it." This assertion of the Duke is to be taken seriously. Unlike in modern America, where the First Amendment to the U.S. Constitution secures the right to freedom of speech, in Shakespeare's hierarchical world, slandering a prince is a significant and heavily punishable offense. The Duke has in fact been merciful to Lucio, forgiving his slanders and remitting his other "forfeits" (i.e., punishments) (ll. 519–20). But Lucio will nevertheless be made to marry the woman he has gotten with child for the sake of the woman, the child, and the commonwealth.

---

[1] From "Notes on Shakespeare" in Philip Thompson, *Dusk and Dawn: Poems and Prose of Philip Thompson*, ed. Gideon Rappaport (San Diego: One Mind Good Press, 2005), pp. 223–24.

[2] In personal conversation. Cf., previous reference, pp. 224–26.

[3] Philip Thompson, *Dusk and Dawn*, p. 224.

Tragedies

Romeo and Juliet

The rhetorical device called the oxymoron, which unites opposites in a paradoxical phrase, gives *Romeo and Juliet* its essential structure. The play holds in exquisite tension two of the most extreme and paradoxical opposites of human experience—love and death. In the self-immolating love of the lovers is contained not only erotic passion for, and total commitment to, another human being, but also all hope for a future of fruitfulness and peace. Within the death-dealing feud of the families is contained not only one of the most poignant losses that death can deal, the early demise of promising youth, but also the roots of disharmony, strife, and warfare. The relation between these two principles—love and death—is not merely one of juxtaposition. In the context of the family feud, the love of the lovers arises out of the hatred that is a kind of death-in-life and death-in-society. And the lovers' self-sacrificial deaths expiate the death-dealing hate of the feud and resolve it into love when the fathers make peace at the end. The play thus becomes a powerful early example of Shakespeare's ingenious imaginative capacity to bring paradoxical opposites into the unified experience of a single and moving drama.

Already at this early stage of his career—the play was probably written in about 1595–96—Shakespeare gives us perhaps the most compelling empathic experience of the power, beauty, and magic of young love in all our literature. And in the same play he gives us an equally compelling experience of grief at one of the most hideous and unbearable losses that death can deliver, the death of the beautiful and promising young. Detached from the vociferous grief of Capulet, Lady Capulet, and the Nurse in IV.v because we know that Juliet is not really dead, we suffer all the more grief ourselves when we see the two lovers really dead in V.iii. That their deaths are presented as both avoidable and at the same time inevitable heightens the agony and is another instance of the tragic union of opposites.

Despite the presence of Friar Lawrence, the play does not provide us much consolation in the Christian afterlife that increasingly suffuses Shakespeare's later dramas. The lovers are never thought of as damned for their suicides. The deaths of the lovers are horrible to us not because of the despair in their souls that leads to damnation, as in the characters Richard III, Othello, and Macbeth, but because of the horror of their mere loss to one another and to us. If there is any significant Christian implication in the play, it lies in the fact that their deaths become expiations of the family feud, as if the lovers' mutual love were itself the sacrifice of love on the altar of death. That they rise again in statues of gold is but pitiful consolation. The play is a tragedy that mitigates nothing of the promise of young love and nothing of the pain at its loss.

This representation of the agonizing paradox of love and death is what I mean by saying that the oxymoron is the essential structure of the play. But there are also passages which make specific rhetorical use of that figure of speech. In the first scene Romeo, a Montague, suffering from the rejection of his love by Rosaline, a Capulet, sees evidence of the street brawl between the followers of the two feuding families. He says,

> Why then, O brawling love! O loving hate!
> O any thing, of nothing first create!
> O heavy lightness, serious vanity,
> Misshapen chaos of well-seeming forms,
> Feather of lead, bright smoke, cold fire, sick health,
> Still-waking sleep, that is not what it is!
> This love feel I, that feel no love in this. (I.i.176–82)

Similarly, when Juliet first hears that her new husband, a Montague, has killed her cousin Tybalt, like her a Capulet, she cries,

> Beautiful tyrant! fiend angelical!
> Dove-feather'd raven! wolvish ravening lamb!
> Despisèd substance of divinest show!
> Just opposite to what thou justly seem'st,
> A damnèd saint, an honorable villain! (III.ii.75–79)

These oxymorons arise from the very substance of the drama, as love has arisen amidst and despite the feud of the two houses.

Related to the oxymoron are the antitheses in Friar Lawrence's meditation on the "powerful grace that lies / In plants, herbs, stones, and their true qualities" (II.iii.15–16). His speech, expressed in rhymed couplets, is built of opposites: morn/night, clouds/light, "baleful weeds and precious-juiced flowers" (line 8), womb/tomb, vileness/good, virtue/ vice, poison/medicine. The speech is a good example of the technique of variation, the same idea repeated in a variety of ways, which was discussed in Chapter 4 of Part 1. It also illustrates the poetical use of metaphorical correspondence discussed in Chapter 7 of Part 1, treating the twofold nature of plants and flowers as analogous to the twofold nature of man:

> Two such opposèd kings encamp them still [= always]
> In man as well as herbs, grace and rude will;
> And where the worser is predominant,
> Full soon the canker death eats up that plant.   (II.iii.27–30)

Just as "Within the infant rind of this weak flower / Poison hath residence and medicine power" (ll. 23–24), so man is the arena of a *psychomachia*, an interior spiritual war, between the gifts given and virtues taught by God and the lower willfulness that leads to sin, of which death, both in Adam and in everyman, was believed to be the consequence. (See the essay on *Othello* for further discussion of *psychomachia*, and cf., "quintessence of dust" in *Hamlet*, II.ii.308.)

Romeo and Juliet is filled with many other pointed antitheses. There are contrasts between youth and age, intense feeling and outward formality, individual passion and social convention, meeting and separation, union and interruption, kissing and dying, day and night, sun and moon, stars and star-crossing, dawns and endings (five of them), passion and reason, sacrifice and reconciliation, comedy and tragedy. The foils to Romeo's and Juliet's idealism are the satirical cynicism of Mercutio and the practical cynicism of the Nurse. The magnetic passion of love that draws Romeo and Juliet together is mirrored by the magnetic passion of conflict that draws Mercutio and Tybalt to their fateful encounter. Friar Lawrence, who advises Romeo to move "wisely and slow" (II.iii.94), later bolts from the tomb in a fright (V.iii.159). Romeo goes from using a fateful blade on Tybalt to using poison on himself, Juliet from swallowing fateful (pseudo-) poison for Romeo's sake to using a blade on herself. Reversals abound: Romeo's love is Rosalind then Juliet; fights break out and the Prince stops them; Tybalt flies into a rage that Capulet suppresses; Capulet arranges a wedding, suddenly changes its date, then flies into a rage at Juliet; Benvolio and then Romeo try to make peace, and Tybalt, Mercutio, and Romeo turn to violence; in an alchemical transformation the dead lovers are turned to gold in the final reconciliation of the families, and the feuding city is turned to peace. And of course prose alternates with verse, as well as blank verse with rhymed.

To the rhetorical figures of oxymoron and antithesis is joined a manifold use of Shakespeare's storehouse of rhetorical art. The play is written in the period in which Shakespeare was energetically discovering, among other things, the power of rhetorical figures to convey intense meaning and experience. (Other plays in this period include *Richard III, A Midsummer Night's Dream* and *Richard II*, all plays exhibiting extensive and consciously elaborated figurative rhetoric.) In *Romeo and Juliet* notice the prose stichomythia at I.i.44–62 and at II.iv.52–87 and the verse stichomythia between Romeo and Benvolio at I.i.160–72 and between Juliet and Paris at IV.i.18–36. Other figures of speech that form the poetic substance of this play include, among others, the following daunting list: anaphora, antanaclasis, antimetabole, antistasis, aphorismus, aporia, apostrophe, asteismus, asyndeton, diacope, epitheton, epizeuxis, hypozeuxis, litotes, meiosis, paronomasia, pleonasmus, ploce, polyptoton, polysyndeton, threnos, tmesis, and zeugma.

There is one more rhetorical device that is essential to the play's effect. That is the sonnet. Traditionally a vehicle of love, the form here rhetorically intensifies the love-tragedy. The prologues to Acts I and II take the form of sonnets, and the play ends in a curtal sonnet.

More crucially, the first words spoken between Romeo and Juliet take the form of a sonnet (I.v.93–106). He takes her hand in his and says the first quatrain:

> Romeo: If I profane with my unworthiest hand
> This holy shrine, the gentle sin is this,
> My lips, two blushing pilgrims, ready stand
> To smooth that rough touch with a tender kiss.

Juliet then responds with the second quatrain:

> Juliet: Good pilgrim, you do wrong your hand too much,
> Which mannerly devotion shows in this:
> For saints have hands that pilgrims' hands do touch,
> And palm to palm is holy palmers' kiss.

Palmers are pilgrims, originally those who had made pilgrimage to Jerusalem, of which the symbol that they carried was the palm branch. When they met one another, their form of greeting was to touch the palms of their hands. The third quatrain is divided between the two lovers:

> Romeo: Have not saints lips, and holy palmers too?
> Juliet: Ay, pilgrim, lips that they must use in prayer.
> Romeo: O then, dear saint, let lips do what hands do,
>   They pray—grant thou, lest faith turn to despair.

This is Romeo's request to move from holding her hand to kissing her lips. Then, moving toward becoming one, the couple shares the couplet and its rhyme:

> Juliet: Saints do not move, though grant for prayers' sake.
> Romeo: Then move not while my prayer's effect I take.

Romeo then kisses Juliet, though many editors erroneously put the stage direction for the kiss a line below. It must come here as the climax of the sonnet leading to it. And so the lovers meet in a mutual love expressed in a mutual sonnet. It is one of the sweetest touches of the play.

But the play is an oxymoron. The placement of the kiss at the end of the sonnet is followed and confirmed by the beginning of another sonnet, uttered in pursuit of a second kiss. Again its first quatrain is shared by the couple:

> Romeo: Thus from my lips, by thine, my sin is purg'd.
> Juliet: Then have my lips the sin that they have took.
> Romeo: Sin from my lips? O trespass sweetly urg'd!
>   Give me my sin again.

After these three feet of the line, Romeo impetuously kisses Juliet again, and she responds with the quatrain's last two feet:

> Juliet: You kiss by th' book.   (I.v.107–110)

That is, he kisses both methodically and by rhetorical conceit.

But this second sonnet is interrupted after its first quatrain. The sonnet form, signifying love, and complete in their first meeting, is now broken off. By what? And what does its interruption signify? The Nurse says, "Madam, your mother craves a word with you" (I.v.111), and her prose injection into the verse of the sonnet leads immediately to Romeo's rhyming couplet of recognition, "Is she a Capulet? / O dear account! my life is my foe's debt" (I.v.117–18). The second sonnet is cut short by the fact of the feud, by hate, by the threat of death.

The passage is thus to be read both literally and symbolically. The first sonnet is both an instance and a symbol of the wooing of the lovers, first kiss a symbol of their wedding, second kiss a symbol of its consummation, and the abrupt interruption of the second sonnet a symbol of the early death of their marriage because of the very fact that interrupts their second sonnet, namely that Romeo is a Montague and Juliet a Capulet. The symbolic second kiss then prefigures the tragic last kiss, when Romeo will say, "Thus with a kiss I die" (V.iii.120). The passage stands as a representation in little of the structure of the whole play: In the context of the death-dealing feud, the lovers meet, love, marry, consummate their marriage, and die young, their marriage and their lives cut short like the prefiguring second sonnet.[1]

The use of the sonnet form reappears at the end of the play, at Act V, Scene iii, Lines 296–310, when we get that form broken up into internal rhyme, rhymed couplets, and unrhymed lines, in a series divided between the two patriarchs:

> Capulet: O brother Montague, give me thy hand.
> This is my daughter's jointure, for no more
> Can I demand.
> Montague: But I can give thee more,
> For I will raise her statue in pure gold,
> That while Verona by that name is known,
> There shall no figure at such rate be set
> As that of true and faithful Juliet.
> Capulet: As rich shall Romeo's by his lady's lie
> Poor sacrifices of our enmity!

In Capulet's speech we have an internal rhyme (*hand / demand*), then Montague exactly rhymes with Capulet (*more / more*) and ends with the rhyme (*set / Juliet*), then Capulet adds an eye rhyme (*lie / enmity*). Finally the Prince concludes the play with a curtal sonnet, the last quatrain and couplet of a partial sonnet about the woeful death of the lovers, as if he is completing the interrupted sonnet of the lovers' first meeting.

A glooming peace this morning with it brings,
The sun, for sorrow, will not show his head.
Go hence to have more talk of these sad things;
Some shall be pardon'd, and some punishèd:
For never was a story of more woe
Than this of Juliet and her Romeo.

As in *A Midsummer Night's Dream* the rhetorical figures incarnate the play's lyricism, so in *Romeo and Juliet* they become forms by which the magical power of love and the horrible power of its enemy death reach deeply into our experience.

KEY LINES:

1. Mercutio's wild and much beloved Queen Mab speech (I.iv.53–95) engages in extreme elaboration to illustrate the thin, inconstant substance of dreams, "the children of an idle brain, / Begot of nothing but vain fantasy" (I.iv.97–98). The point of the speech is to disparage and debunk the premonitions of Romeo (I.iv.50, 106–111):

I dreamt a dream to-night . . . my mind misgives
Some consequence yet hanging in the stars
Shall bitterly begin his fearful date
With this night's revels, and expire the term
Of a despisèd life clos'd in my breast
By some vile forfeit of untimely death.

But despite Mercutio's belittling, the premonition comes true, as does Juliet's at III.v.54–56:

O God, I have an ill-divining soul!
Methinks I see thee now, thou art so low,
As one dead in the bottom of a tomb.

Mercutio's debunking is in keeping with his role throughout: with a reductive wit to set off by contrast the earnest, idealistic depth of passion in Romeo and Juliet. His satirical choler is a foil as well to Tybalt's earnest choler. The undermining of seriousness by Mercutio, the man of humors, operates even when he is mortally wounded himself: "a scratch, a scratch . . . Ask for me to-morrow and you shall find me a grave man" (III.i.93–98).

Here the pun on "grave" serves to punctuate the rhetorical figure called meiosis, belittling with a demeaning word or phrase.

SPECIFIC NOTES TO HELP IN YOUR READING:

1. I.Prol.11: "but" here means "except for." The rage between the two families could not be removed by anything *but* their children's end.

2. II.ii.33: in "wherefore art thou Romeo," "wherefore" means "why": Why are you Romeo, implying, why must you be a Montague?

3. II.iv.37: "Without his roe, like a dried herring." This is a complex and ribald pun. *Roe* is the milt or sperm fluid of a male fish. Dried herring would have had its roe removed as a delicacy (cf., shad roe and Falstaff's phrase "shotten herring" in *I Henry IV*, II.iv.130). Mercutio presumes that Romeo is creeping home depleted, either because he has slept with Rosaline and is depleted of semen or, more likely, because his spirits (a synonym for semen, as in Sonnet 129.1) are depressed because of *not* being able to sleep with her. But Mercutio is also punning on Romeo's name: Romeo is creeping home in woe saying "me-o" (= O me) as if without the first syllable of his name (*Ro*), which is also the first syllable of Rosaline's name.

4. V.iii.295 "brace of kinsmen": A brace means a pair; the Prince is referring to Mercutio and Paris, who are both relatives of his.

---

[1] This meaning of the interrupted sonnet was first presented in Gideon Rappaport, "Another Sonnet in 'Romeo and Juliet'," *Notes and Queries*, 25:2 [223], April 1978, p. 124.

Julius Caesar

To appreciate Shakespeare's tragedy of *Julius Caesar* it is essential to be aware of the difference between Shakespeare's conception of monarchal government and our own.

We have been trained to think of monarchs as synonymous with tyrants, and "tyrant" is what Cassius and other conspirators call Caesar in the play (e.g., I.iii.103). When Caesar is killed in Act III, Scene i, the assassin Cinna shouts "Liberty! Freedom! Tyranny is dead!" (l.78) and Brutus shouts "Peace, freedom, and liberty!" (l. 110). These cries tempt us to think of the American Revolution and the Declaration of Independence, liberty and equality. But in Shakespeare's hierarchical conception of the world (see Chapter 7 of Part 1), the overthrow of a rightful monarch meant not peace, freedom, and liberty but civil war and chaos. Was, then, Caesar a rightful monarch?

The historical Julius Caesar, whom Shakespeare knew from Plutarch's *Lives* in Thomas North's translation, was the man responsible for Rome's pivot from republic to empire. Though he never officially ruled as monarch, he is considered the founder of the Roman Empire, responsible for the shift in power from senate to emperor consolidated by his heir, Octavius, who became Caesar Augustus. Shakespeare had to remain true to the historical facts of Caesar's life and death, which were known to all educated members of his audience.

However, embedded in the cultural inheritance of Shakespeare's time were two different attitudes toward the same historical facts. Some in Shakespeare's audience admired Caesar and disapproved of the conspiracy against him as treachery; some disapproved of Caesar and admired the conspirators as liberators. The pro-Caesar attitude was founded on the traditional medieval picture of the world, which was hierarchical and monarchist. It focused on Caesar's historical role rather than on his particular human qualities. It is best represented by the complex treatment of Caesar in the *Inferno* of Dante. Dorothy Sayers writes,

Dante's attitude to Julius Caesar is ambivalent. *Personally*, as a pagan, Julius is in Limbo (Canto IV.123). *Politically*, his rise to power involved the making of civil war, and Curio, who advised him to cross the Rubicon, is in the Eighth Circle of hell (Canto XXVIII.97–102 and note). But, although Julius was never actually Emperor, he was the founder of the Roman Empire, and *by his function*, therefore, he images that institution which, in Dante's view . . . was divinely appointed to govern the world. Thus Brutus and Cassius, by their breach of sworn allegiance to Caesar, were Traitors to the Empire, i.e. to World-order. Consequently, just as Judas [Iscariot] figures treason against God, so Brutus and Cassius figure treason against Man-in-Society; or we may say that we have here the images of treason against the Divine and the Secular government of the world.[1]

Like Dante, Shakespeare thought of Julius Caesar as the embodiment of the Roman Empire, which had been prepared by God to serve as the secular order governing most of the known world, subduing the space in which Christianity and its Church could spread the word of universal salvation. As head of the empire, the emperor was ordained by God to rule in the worldly realm as Christ ruled in the spiritual. To assassinate Caesar, then, no matter how noble-sounding the motives, was treachery, the results of which would be mob rule and civil war until the emperor's seat was occupied again. As Sayers points out, the assassins were held to be world-historical traitors, parallel in the secular realm to Judas Iscariot, the betrayer of Christ.

The contrary view, which was humanist, focused on Caesar's human qualities, and particularly his faults, especially his ambition. It was shared by Renaissance writers like Marlow and Jonson,[2] who were influenced by Cicero and in some cases by Lucan's *Pharsalia*. Montaigne notes Caesar's somewhat lesser cruelty than that of others in punishing captive enemies[3] and lists Caesar's various amorous conquests by way of criticizing his insatiable lust.[4] Others describe Caesar's physical defects. In this view Caesar's ambition threatened a new tyranny over the ancient order of the Roman Republic. His defeat of Pompey, the Senate's representative, in a civil war called forth the heroic conspirators to risk their lives to defend the Republic against the potential tyrant.

As he so often does, Shakespeare in his *Julius Caesar* is able to have it both ways—up to a point. The play imports a good deal from the humanist characterization of Caesar as fallible and of the conspirators as brave. At the same time, the play holds firmly to the hierarchical view that the assassination of Caesar was a great calamity. One way Shakespeare manages to include both attitudes is by distinguishing between the man Caesar and the Spirit of Caesar.

The man Caesar is a tragic character in the play. From the humanist tradition Shakespeare imports Caesar's various human frailties. As we hear from Cassius, though Caesar is brave, he once nearly drowned in a river until Cassius saved him (I.ii.111–15); he shook with ague (I.ii.119–28); he is deaf in one ear (I.ii.213); he has the falling sickness (i.e., epilepsy—I.ii.254); he is subject to flattery (II.ii.70–107); he is temporarily subject to the apparent superstitions of his wife (II.ii.75–82); though he has good reason, by virtue of his military conquests, to be proud, his pride is extreme and intemperate (II.ii.44–45, III.i.60–70 and 74). (In *As You Like It*, V.ii.31–32, Rosalind calls Caesar's "I came, I saw, and overcame" a "thrasonical brag," the adjective coming from the braggart soldier Thraso in Terence's *Eunuchus*.) In *Julius Caesar*, Caesar dies because he will not heed the omens or stoop to moderating the senators' impression of his inflated image of himself, and, as the Book of Proverbs has it, "Pride goeth before destruction, and an high mind [KJV: haughty spirit] before the fall" (16:18 Geneva Bible).

At the same time, Shakespeare stresses that Caesar's greatness lies not in his mortal body but in his spirit—what Sayers has called his historical function as founder of the Empire. Brutus expresses the wish that the conspirators "could come by Caesar's spirit, / And not dismember Caesar!" (II.i.169–70). Brutus's error lies precisely in his opposition to the spirit of Caesar, to the very principle of Empire. Brutus thinks that by dismembering Caesar's body he can obstruct Caesar's spirit. But the divine will as expressed in history dictated that Caesar's spirit could not be killed by the killing of his body. As proof, we see Caesar's ghost appearing to Brutus (IV.iii.275–86) and later Brutus reporting that

> The ghost of Caesar hath appear'd to me
> Two several times by night; at Sardis once,
> And this last night, here in Philippi fields. (V.v.17–19)

Brutus realizes that, despite the killing of Caesar's body, the spirit of Caesar could not be assassinated:

O Julius Caesar, thou art mighty yet!
Thy spirit walks abroad, and turns our swords
In our own proper entrails.   (V.iii.94–96)

Antony has correctly predicted that Caesar's spirit will be "ranging for revenge" and will

                with a monarch's voice
Cry "Havoc!" and let slip the dogs of war,
That this foul deed shall smell above the earth . . . . (III.i.270–75)

As with the English kings of the history plays, Shakespeare founds his concept of the Roman Emperor on the medieval and Renaissance idea of the two bodies of the king. The king is thought of as both the natural man and the embodiment of the body politic (see Chapter 7 in Part 1). In Caesar's case, the body politic is Rome, which, if not under the living Julius, then under his spirit abiding in Octavius, will fulfill its function in history not as a republic but as an empire. *That* is the Caesar—the embodiment of Rome itself—that cannot be assassinated.

Caesar's function as founder of the Empire also accounts for all the portents that attend his death, in this play and in Horatio's recounting of them in *Hamlet* (I.i.113–120), written shortly after. The earthquakes, lightning and thunder, ghosts and lion in the streets, men all in fire, Calpurnia's dream of Caesar's statue spouting blood—all foreshadow the disaster to Rome and its people and the chaos that will follow the assassination. These evils of chaos and civil war that in fact do follow end only with the rise of Octavius, upon whom the mantle of the spirit of Caesar comes to rest. Thus the assassination of the man Caesar does not kill the principle of empire but only delays its fulfilment, and Shakespeare's characterizations of Brutus and Cassius confirm the characterization of the murder of Caesar as far more a crime than a noble act of heroism.

Caesar is the pivotal figure of the play, but the greater tragedy is that of Brutus, for which that of Cassius is a foil. For the high-minded motives of Brutus and the ugly envy of Cassius spring also from the pride that goeth before destruction. It is these faults that blind them to the reality that is the spirit of Caesar.

In Cassius especially, as in all the other conspirators but Brutus, it is not idealism but envy that is at work. Cassius cannot bear to serve a mere mortal like himself. Trying to seduce Brutus to his faction, Cassius says,

I had as lief not be as live to be
In awe of such a thing as I myself. . . .
                 And this man
Is now become a god, and Cassius is
A wretched creature, and must bend his body
If Caesar carelessly but nod on him. . . .
           Ye gods, it doth amaze me
A man of such a feeble temper should
So get the start of the majestic world
And bear the palm alone.   (I.ii.95–131)

The ironic effect of Cassius's envy of Caesar, built on the observation of Caesar's mortality, is that by his revolt Cassius immortalizes Caesar as emperor and himself as traitor.

The greater tragedy of Brutus lies in the fact that he succumbs to pride not out of worldly self-aggrandizement but both in spite and because of his nobility. That Brutus is noble is amply reinforced. In analyzing his own motives, Brutus says,

I know no personal cause to spurn at him,
But for the general.   (II.i.11–12)

Let's be sacrificers, but not butchers, Caius. . . .
Let's kill him boldly, but not wrathfully. . . .
                 This shall make
Our purposes necessary, and not envious;
Which so appearing to the common eyes,
We shall be call'd purgers, not murderers.   (II.i.166–80)

Shakespeare, though of course not Brutus, perhaps ironically intends the word "purgers" to hint at the word "perjurors" in the ears of the audience. In any case, Mark Antony's eulogy confirms Brutus's nobility:

This was the noblest Roman of them all:
All the conspirators, save only he,
Did that they did in envy of great Caesar;
He, only in a general honest thought
And common good to all, made one of them.   (V.v.68–72)

("Made one of them" means joined them, counted as one of their number.) But trusting to his own nobility, Brutus assumes in himself the authority to commit an obvious present crime in order to prevent a hypothetical future evil. Afraid that Caesar will later turn tyrant, Brutus turns tyrant to Caesar. In a sense Brutus becomes a de facto moral emperor in deciding to execute the would-be political emperor. Where Caesar ignores the Soothsayer, who can see into the future, Brutus presumes that he himself can see into the future when he cannot. His motives, it is true, were the general welfare rather than personal animus or gain. But the conviction that his principled Roman nobility gave him the right or duty to betray his friend and to murder the greatest man of the age, leaving Rome subject to no authority but that of the mob—was a monumental error, of the kind against which Messala later cries out:

> O hateful error, melancholy's child,
> Why dost thou show to the apt thoughts of men
> The things that are not? O error, soon conceiv'd,
> Thou never com'st unto a happy birth,
> But kill'st the mother that engend'red thee!   (V.iii.67–71)

The error of Brutus is to trust to his own noble judgment in performing an act of supreme treachery. He uses his idealistic opinion of himself to justify overruling every practical suggestion of the less honorable but more savvy Cassius. It is that same idealistic opinion of his noble self that Brutus then uses to justify his decision to overrule Caesar's greatness and his destiny—that is, reality—by killing Caesar "in the shell" (II.i.34). The error is confirmed when a few lines later Shakespeare shows us Brutus in rebellion against himself, the inner chaos prefiguring the outer:

> Between the acting of a dreadful thing
> And the first motion . . . the state of a man,
> Like to a little kingdom, suffers then
> The nature of an insurrection.   (II.i.63–69)

This inner chaos, like the secrecy of the conspirators, like the metaphysical portents, reinforces the essential error in the enterprise. (A few years later, Shakespeare will again portray this relation of inner chaos to outer in the tragedies *Othello* and *Macbeth*.) That Brutus experiences the wrongness of insurrection within himself ought to have warned him away from the conspiracy. But Brutus proves to be as great a believer in his own infallibility as Caesar is in his.

The rebellion within Brutus is extended to his noble wife Portia, whose own father, Cato of Utica, fought Caesar with Pompey and chose to commit suicide rather than to live under tyranny when Caesar won. Portia observes correctly about Brutus that "You have some sick offense within your mind" (II.i.268), and she wants him to share it with her. Proclaiming her own great Roman virtue of "constancy" (II.i.299), meaning courage and firmness of mind, she prevails: Brutus promises to share the secret of the conspiracy with her. By the time we next see her (II.iv) she knows that secret. And knowing it, she, too, is now divided within herself. She cannot focus on her instructions to the servant Lucius (ll. 1–12); she hears the non-existent "noise" of "bustling rumors, like a fray" (ll. 16–18); aside she tries to reinforce her fortitude for fear of blabbing:

> O constancy, be strong upon my side,
> Set a huge mountain 'tween my heart and tongue!
> I have a man's mind, but a woman's might.　　　　　(II.iv.6–9)

A few lines later she fears she has inadvertently given the plot away to Lucius and tries to correct it with "Brutus hath a suit / That Caesar will not grant" (ll. 42–43), and then says "I grow faint" (l. 43). Finally she participates in the conspiratorial hypocrisy by telling Lucius to "Say I am merry" (l. 45). In short, her inner life, because she is now a sharer in the plot, becomes chaotic, like that of Brutus, about whom she speaks more truly than she means in saying to Lucius that Brutus "went sickly forth" to the Capitol (l. 14). Portia being Brutus's other half, her inner conflict—depicted as a kind of sickness—is parallel to his, and her end in suicide (IV.iii.155–56) prefigures his.

Though Marc Antony is temporarily on the right side of history in this play, he and his errors, too, are instruments of the invisible divine disposition of historical events. His actions are essential to the triumph of the spirit of Caesar, but like those of the conspirators, his character is compromised. Brutus imagines that Antony "can do no more than Caesar's arm / When Caesar's head is off" (II.i.182–83). This is another error of judgment. Cassius is more astute:

> We shall find of him [i.e., Antony]
> A shrewd contriver; and you know, his means,

If he improve them, may well stretch so far
As to annoy us all. (II.i.157–60)

Antony's shrewdness is then demonstrated by his pose of humility to the
assassins in III.i and his effective speeches in III.ii. But though Antony's
performance to the crowd furthers the project of Caesar's revenge,
Shakespeare's audience would be highly unlikely to approve of such
exhortation of mobs to mutiny and violence. Antony is thus a vehicle
not only of Caesar's revenge but of the punishment of Rome for the
conspiracy. Antony's later conflict with the heir apparent, Octavius, about
the disposition of their battle forces foreshadows what we know will be
Antony's own tragic fate: self-immolation in the love of Cleopatra and a
war against Octavius, by whom he will ultimately be defeated.

Octavius, both here and in the later play *Antony and Cleopatra*, is not
a particularly sympathetic character. He is cool, serious, practical, and
determined. But it is not his function as a character to be beloved. (He
is no Christian prince like Prince Hal in the second history tetralogy.)
Rather, in Octavius we find the greatness of Caesar reanimated without
the boasting. Brutus and Cassius quarrel with one another (IV.iii); Marc
Antony almost quarrels with Octavius (IV.i and V.i). But Octavius shows
himself to be above that kind of fray, his higher function evident in
his saturnine character. His key line, when Antony asks "Why do you
cross me in this exigent?" is "I do not cross you; but I will do so" (V.i.20).
Crossing Mark Antony is beneath Octavius. He will do as he pleases,
using the help of Mark Antony but having minimal concern for his
opinions. His self-confidence, like Caesar's but without the boasting, is a
revelation of his destined function: as Augustus Caesar he will make of
Rome the empire for which Julius Caesar prepared the way.

KEY LINES:
1. II.i.28–34: Brutus says,

> And since the quarrel
> Will bear no color for the thing he is,
> Fashion it thus: that what he is, augmented,
> Would run to these and these extremities;
> And therefore think him as a serpent's egg,
> Which, hatch'd, would as his kind grow mischievous,
> And kill him in the shell.

"Color" means excuse, justification, pretext (a figurative use from the sense "battle flag"). The whole speech is expressed in hypotheticals: being crowned "*might* change his nature" (line 13), "he *may* do danger" (line 17), "So Caesar *may*" (line 27). Brutus is acknowledging that nothing Caesar is or has yet done justifies the assassination; he "fashions" his thinking to justify killing the real Caesar as a preventive measure based on the conjectures of his own imagination.

    2.   III.i.77: "*Et tu, Brute?*—Then fall Caesar!" The Latin means "Also you, Brutus?" Caesar dies of his multiple stab wounds only when he recognizes that the "noblest Roman of them all" (V.v.68) has turned against him.

SPECIFIC NOTES TO HELP IN YOUR READING:

    1.   II.i.261: "Is Brutus sick? and is it physical . . . ." The word *physical* here means healthful.

---

[1] From notes on the major images in Canto XXXIV in Dorothy Sayers, tr., *The Comedy of Dante Alighieri the Florentine, Cantica I, Hell* (London: Penguin, 1949), p. 289.

[2] See William Blisset, "Caesar and Satan," *Journal of the History of Ideas* Vol. 18, No. 2 (Apr., 1957), pp. 221-232, at https://www.jstor.org/stable/2707625?seq=1#page_scan_tab_contents.

[3] Montaigne, *Essays* II:11, Of Cruelty.

[4] Montaigne, *Essays* II:33, The Story of Spurina.

Hamlet

"There is less to be said about *Hamlet* than has been said," quipped American poet and scholar J.V. Cunningham.[1] The reason he is right is that so much said and written about the play has been wrong. It is not about a man who "could not make up his mind," as the voiceover introduction to Olivier's film (1948) asserted. It is not about a man with an Oedipal complex, as the Freudian biographer Ernest Jones would have it. It is not about a twentieth-century existentialist who thinks too much, or about a madman, or about someone too passionate, or too rational, or incapable of deciding whether to be a scholar or a soldier, or suicidal. The character Hamlet is not meant to be too mysterious to be comprehended nor the play *Hamlet* too multifaceted to have a clear meaning. Only someone laboring under the weight of these wrong ideas could think the play a dramatic failure, as T.S. Eliot thought it was.

Hamlet is the dramatized story of an intelligent man, both rational and passionate, in a particular time and place, whose free will is caught between the moral law and the pressures of the morally corrupt world. Because of a bad habit of mind, the man goes wrong, and his error leads to tragedy. However, thanks to providential circumstances, his will is corrected before it is too late—that is, before he dies. The trajectory of his moral growth is so deeply portrayed that it becomes universally representative, relevant to any human being in any time and place. The form of drama in which this trajectory is conveyed is the "revenge tragedy," a popular form of Renaissance entertainment. Specifically, a ghost gives Hamlet the task of avenging his father's death. He is also told to do it without "tainting" his mind. This turns the task into a profound moral dilemma which can only be resolved by an equally profound moral breakthrough.

Vengeance is always a problem for man. In the European aristocratic tradition a nobleman is obligated to exact vengeance upon the murderer of his kin. In the biblical tradition, one can enact that vengeance only as an instrument of divine justice, for "Vengeance and recompense are mine"

(Deuteronomy 32:35) and "Vengeance is mine, I will repay, saith the Lord" (Romans 12:19). *Hamlet*, the greatest of all plays in the tradition of revenge tragedy, is a response to and a commentary on the very popular revenge play called *The Spanish Tragedy* by Thomas Kyd. That play was itself built on the model of the plays of the ancient Roman tragedian Seneca. In Kyd's play, as in Seneca, the context of the drama is the afterlife as imagined by the ancient classical world. The dead cross the river Styx and go to Hades to be judged by Minos and Rhadamanthus, and it is Pluto and Proserpine who send a ghost back to earth to invite the living relative of the murdered man to avenge the man's death. In this way the moral problem of revenge in a Christian context is avoided. The aristocratic ethos prevails.

In *Hamlet* Shakespeare takes upon himself a much greater challenge: to examine the problem of revenge, including aristocratic revenge, in the context of the afterlife in which Shakespeare and his Christian audience actually believed. In the universe pictured by Christianity, when a person dies, his or her soul faces the judgment of God, and the consequences will certainly be either heaven or hell. In that context, the problem of revenge becomes an instance of the universal problem: how is man to do the right thing in a morally complex situation whose backdrop is the divine judgment?

Hence, the first question for the character Hamlet is whether the Ghost is an emissary from God or a temptation from the devil. The first half of the play is devoted to Hamlet's attempt to find the answer to that question. To find it Hamlet does two things: He pretends to be mad (and will continue to do so even when he knows the Ghost has told the truth), and he mounts a play-within-the-play to detect the guilt—if any—of Claudius.

Pretending to be mad is also part of the revenge-play tradition and is central to *The Spanish Tragedy*. The avenger needs to investigate the possibly guilty parties while not giving away that he knows from a ghost that there has been a murder. Hamlet, too, pretends to be mad. He is never mad in fact, though Shakespeare has him playing at madness in several different moods and in two forms. Sometimes Hamlet is in a calm mood and pretending to be mad: "Excellent well, you are a fishmonger [etc.]" (II.ii.174–420). Sometimes he is furious, always for good cause, and also pretending to be mad: "Get thee to a nunn'ry [etc.]" (III.i.102–149) and "'Swounds, show me what thou't do. / Woo't weep, woo't fight [etc.]" (V.i.254–83).

Hamlet's performance of madness is complicated also by his pretending to two different forms of madness: the madness a man may be driven to by thwarted ambition, and the madness he may be driven to by thwarted love, both classic forms of stage madness. The former is evoked by the "ambition" talk of Rosencrantz and Guildenstern (II.ii.252) and is exemplified by Hamlet's saying "I am most dreadfully attended" (II.ii.269). The latter, thwarted love madness, is evoked by Ophelia's rejection of his love tokens and is exemplified in Ophelia's description of him at II.i.74ff.:

> Lord Hamlet, with his doublet all unbrac'd,
> No hat upon his head, his stockings fouled,
> Ungart'red, and down-gyvèd to his ankle,
> Pale as his shirt, his knees knocking each other,
> And with a look so piteous in purport
> As if he had been loosèd out of hell
> To speak of horrors . . .

(In the third line above "down-gyvèd" is pronounced with a soft *g*.) This description gives a classic picture of the man dejected by disappointment in love. As Hamlet intended, Polonius is taken in by that pretense: "Mad for thy love?"(II.i.82) and "The origin and commencement of his grief / Sprung from neglected love" (III.i.177–78).

But whatever his mood and whatever the form of madness he is pretending to, Hamlet tells us early, late, and often that his madness, which he calls an "antic disposition," is only "put on" (I.v.172), i.e., playacted. He interrupts his madness act to tell us that he is aware of how others are trying to deceive him ("[*Aside.*] Nay then I have an eye of you!"—II.ii.290). Later he tells his mother that he is mad only "in craft" (III.iv.187–88). There is real madness depicted in the play, but it is the madness of Ophelia in IV.v. Hamlet is never actually mad.

The second method of Hamlet's investigation, in addition to pretending to be mad, is to mount a play. The purpose of the play that Hamlet orders to be performed, and for which he writes a few lines (though we never know which), is to determine whether the Ghost has spoken the truth about Claudius. Though on first hearing the Ghost's words Hamlet wanted to sweep to his revenge (I.v.31), on second thought he realizes that "The spirit that I have seen / May be a devil . . . [that] / Abuses me to damn me" (II.ii.598–603). The "To be or not to be" speech (III.i.55ff.) articulates that the fear of judgment after death, and the consequent possibility of hell, prevent people in general from rushing to do things (like taking revenge) that might satisfy their desire but could cause them to be damned as a consequence. The two soliloquies ("O, what a rogue and peasant slave am I!" at II.ii.550ff. and "To be, or not to be, that is the question" at III.i.55ff.) both address the same question, the former personally and emotionally, the latter generally and rationally. (The word *question* in the first line of the latter soliloquy, from the Latin *quaestio*, means a topic to be discussed by considering both a hypothesis and its refutation, as was done by divinity students in the medieval and Renaissance universities like Wittenberg, where Hamlet and Horatio have been at school.) The two soliloquies lead to the same conclusion, the first particular, the second general: Hamlet chooses to refrain from killing Claudius until he is sure it is the right thing to do lest he be damned for doing it. This is not indecision, as many modern critics would have us believe. It is rational wisdom.

The "Murder of Gonzago" play, which Hamlet jestingly calls "The Mousetrap" (III.ii.237), proves to the satisfaction of both Hamlet and his rational friend Horatio that the King is in fact guilty. This brings Hamlet to the climax and turning point of the play, the remarkable double-soliloquy scene, Act III, Scene iii. The soliloquy of Claudius first confirms for the audience that Claudius is indeed guilty of murdering his brother, as the Ghost had said. Hamlet, who cannot of course hear that soliloquy as the audience can, then chooses to postpone the killing. Why? Out of indecision? Out of compassion for a man at prayer? Out of cowardice? Not for any of these hypothetical motives that critics have posited. Hamlet's own soliloquy reveals explicitly the actual reason for his choice, and the reason is an evil one. It constitutes Hamlet's fall and the cause of the tragedy.

Knowing now that Claudius is guilty, Hamlet assumes that the kneeling Claudius is repenting. Hamlet chooses *not* to execute Claudius when the soul of a repentant Claudius might go to heaven. He decides to wait in order to kill Claudius when Claudius is doing something evil so that his soul must perforce be damned. In other words, to satisfy his personal desire for revenge, Hamlet is playing God.

Hamlet's potential for making this tragic error was prepared for earlier in the play. In I.ii Hamlet complains about the haste of the marriage of his mother to his hated uncle. About the wedding day Hamlet says, "Would I had met my dearest foe in heaven / Or ever I had seen that day, Horatio!" (I.ii.182–83). That is, to Hamlet the next-to-worst thing of all would be to see his worst enemy saved instead of damned. The worst thing of all would be to see his mother marry his uncle. This attitude toward one's enemy would have been seen by Shakespeare's Christian audience as a moral flaw, not yet a sin, but a sinful habit of mind. They would have recognized it as understandable, but wrong. Why? Because a good Christian would *want* to see his enemy in heaven. It would mean that the enemy had repented before dying, and Christ commanded his followers to love their enemies and to "forgive us our debts, as we also forgive our debtors" (Matthew 6:12). At I.iv.23ff. Hamlet has meditated on the idea that a single flaw in a man's character may result in his damnation, no matter how great his other virtues. The fear is a real one, and Hamlet will himself illustrate it by "tak[ing] corruption" from this "particular fault" (I.iv.35–36), the desire never to see his enemy in heaven. It is the "dram of evil" (I.iv.36) in Hamlet's character that leads to his fall in III.iii when he decides to wait to kill the King in order to be sure the King will go to hell when killed. Between Hamlet's Ghost-communicated mission and its execution has stepped Hamlet's personal desire for "ultimate revenge."[2]

Would it be right for Hamlet to kill the King in III.iii, when Claudius seems to be praying, considering that everything goes wrong because Hamlet does not do it? It would be right. Hamlet is in fact the rightful king of Denmark, since his uncle, were it known, would be disqualified for having stolen the crown by murdering Hamlet's father. (In the play, as in history, Denmark is an elective monarchy. That is, the monarch does not automatically inherit the throne but is chosen from among members of the royal family by aristocratic electors.) It is presumably Hamlet's obligation, knowing Claudius to be guilty, to kill him, for Hamlet is in fact the only rightful executor of justice in Denmark. It seems that Providence has set up this moment of Claudius's vulnerability, after the play-within-the-play that has publicly demonstrated his guilt, precisely so that Hamlet could easily execute him. Also, Hamlet's task of avenging his father's murder has been conveyed to him by a Ghost, who is now known to be honest, i.e., sent from heaven, not from hell. However, the Ghost had added a stipulation: "Howsomever thou pursues this act, / Taint not thy mind" (I.v.84–85). That is, take revenge without tainting your mind with evil or sin. Thus the play raises this question: How is it possible to take revenge, which belongs to God, without tainting one's mind with sin? To see the sense in the play's answer, let us ask the question like this: Is the avenger killing the villain out of personal vengeance or as the instrument of the divine justice, of the vengeance that "is mine, sayeth the Lord"?

The answer is that Hamlet might have acted as divine instrument in either of two ways: as a result of passion or as a result of reason. It is Hamlet's nature that he flies into passions and then becomes reasonable again. This is a pattern revealed in Hamlet's soliloquies as well as in dialogue. He is in a passion in the soliloquy at I.ii.129ff.: "O that this too too sallied flesh would melt"; but concludes with rational self-control: "But break, my heart, for I must hold my tongue" (I.ii.159). He is a passion after the Ghost speaks to him in I.v: "O most pernicious woman! / O villain, villain, smiling, damnèd villain!" (I.v.105–106); but he is calmly rational by the end of the scene: "Rest, rest, perturbed spirit! [meaning the Ghost] . . . The Time is out of joint—O cursed spite, / That ever I was born to set it right!" (I.v.182–89). In the soliloquy at II.ii.550ff. he flies into a passionate rage: "Bloody, bawdy villain! / Remorseless, treacherous, lecherous, kindless villain!" (II.ii.580–81); but he turns himself around with "Why, what an ass am I!" (II.ii.582) and concludes with calm reason: "The play's the thing / Wherein I'll catch the conscience of the king" (II.ii.604–605). This pattern of passion replaced by reason remains characteristic of Hamlet's personality throughout. It still applies in V.i when he rages at Laertes—"Woo't weep, woo't fight, woo't fast, woo't tear thyself?" (V.i.275)—and then becomes calm and rational again:

> Nay, an thou'lt mouth,
> I'll rant as well as thou. . . . Hear you, sir,
> What is the reason that you use me thus?
> I lov'd you ever. (V.i.283–84, 288–90)

Thus, had Hamlet's calm but false reasoning not obstructed his natural passion, he might have killed the King in III.iii: "Now might I do it pat, now 'a is a-praying;/ And now I'll do it—and so 'a goes to heaven / And so am I revenged" (III.iii.73–75). That is, his passionate nature might have been the very instrument that the divine revenge chose to use to punish Claudius. What prevented heaven's using Hamlet's passion as its instrument at that moment was Hamlet's free will, which obstructed that course with false reason, in the form of his decision to wait until he were sure Claudius would be damned when Hamlet did kill him.

Alternatively to a passionate outburst, Hamlet might have correctly reasoned himself into killing Claudius. Had he been concerned with justice in Denmark rather than with his own personal desire for revenge, he might with perfect justice have executed the murderer of the previous king. It was, after all, his task given by the Ghost and by his position as the rightful king of Denmark. But instead of using his reason correctly, he uses reason to justify the perverse intention not merely to kill the King but to be certain he would be damned. This is an instance of just what Hamlet accuses his mother of doing in the next scene when he says that her "reason panders will" (III.iv.88). That is, the higher human function of reason has served as a pimp for the lower human will. We would call it rationalization, the mind justifying what it knows to be wrong in order to satisfy some desire.

Hamlet fails on both counts—passion and reason. He fails because his mind is tainted by the desire to be certain that Claudius be not merely killed but damned. This is an evil desire, a sin of pride, no service to God or to Denmark but a worship of one's own fallible self

The climax and turning point of the whole play is a two-letter word, to which Shakespeare gives an entire line of verse:

> And am I then revenged
> To take him in the purging of his soul
> When he is fit and seasoned for his passage?
> No.   (III.iii.84–87)

Hamlet's fall lies in that one word "No." With that word he substitutes for his mission his own personal desire. His personal desire for revenge takes the place of his mission as rightful avenger that was given him by God through the Ghost. Having heard the Ghost describe as "most horrible" (I.v.80) the fact of being sent unshriven to purgatory, Hamlet now wills Claudius to be sent unshriven to hell.

Hamlet's error is punctuated by the dramatic irony of the scene. After Hamlet's departure, Claudius tells us that he is not in fact penitent after all. "My crown, mine own ambition, and my queen" (III.iii.55) were desires too strong to permit him to repent, so that, he concludes, "My words fly up, my thoughts remain below. / Words without thought never to heaven go" (III.iii.97–98). So if Hamlet had killed Claudius just now, Claudius would likely have been damned, though not by Hamlet's will but only by God's.

Because of Hamlet's choice to damn rather than merely to kill Claudius everything goes wrong. In the next scene (III.iv), having failed to kill Claudius at the perfect moment for it to be done, Hamlet kills Polonius by mistake. Having pretended to see through the kneeling gesture of Claudius into his presumably repenting but in fact impenitent soul, Hamlet now fails to see a man's external identity through a mere physical arras (a hanging tapestry). He falsely assumes that it is the King, not Polonius, behind the arras ("I took thee for thy better"—III. iv.32) and flies into the kind of passion that might have caused him to kill Claudius in the previous scene. These two errors, the physical error in this scene resulting from the moral error in the previous scene, are disastrous for Denmark. In light of the doctrine of the two bodies of the king discussed in Chapter 7 of Part 1, we may observe that Hamlet, given the guilt of Claudius, *is* Denmark, and therefore, as Laertes says, "on his choice depends / The safety and health of this whole state" (I.iii.20–21). Thus the results of Hamlet's one-syllable word "No" in III.iii are, apart from the eventual death of Claudius, that Ophelia goes mad and dies; that Laertes plots with Claudius against Hamlet and dies; that Gertrude mistakenly drinks the poison meant by Claudius for Hamlet and dies; that Rosencrantz and Guildenstern die; and of course that Hamlet, murdered by the avenger Laertes, dies. Thus the whole tragedy springs from Hamlet's one-word fall.

However—by the time of all these disastrous consequences in the physical world of the court, an entirely different transformation has taken place within the soul of Hamlet. In the soliloquy at IV.iv.32ff. ("How all occasions do inform against me"), Hamlet appears at his lowest and most confused. That soliloquy is the source of the notions that Hamlet is a coward or thinks too much or cannot "make up his mind" because critics mistakenly generalize from these words to the whole play:

> Now whether it be
> Bestial oblivion, or some craven scruple
> Of thinking too precisely on th' event [= outcome]—
> A thought which quarter'd hath but one part wisdom
> And ever three parts coward—I do not know
> Why yet I live to say, "This thing's to do," . . .
> O, from this time forth,
> My thoughts be bloody, or be nothing worth!　　　　(IV.iv.39–66)

But the truth is that we, the audience, *do* know why Hamlet has not done "this thing," meaning killing Claudius. We have seen why he chose *not* to do it at the perfect moment for him to do it. And in fact he *did* act to do it—as he thought—in III.iv. Only it was the wrong man behind the arras. Hamlet's conclusion that his thoughts must be either bloody or worthless are unworthy of him at his best. The whole speech conveys that Hamlet is laboring in error, incapable of figuring out what he should do because he has not yet realized his error at the climactic moment of III.iii.

Then, a transformation happens. There is a deep transformation of Hamlet's attitude, and two kinds of experience work to cause it. The first experience, which is revealed in V.i, actually happens later in time. It is the combination of Hamlet's general pondering of man's mortality and his discovery of the death of Ophelia. The contemplation in the graveyard in V.i moves from the abstract deaths of lawyers and landowners, of Alexander the Great and Julius Caesar, to the death of someone Hamlet knew long ago, namely Yorick, to the shocking present death of Hamlet's beloved Ophelia. The contemplation of the skull is a classic image of *memento mori*, Latin for "remember that you die." (Almost any saint or monk shown in his study in a medieval or Renaissance painting was likely to be depicted with a skull before him, on his desk or a nearby shelf, intended to be a reminder of his mortality.) Then that general truth of human mortality, arising from his contemplation of the skull of Yorick, is brought home to Hamlet by the funeral procession for Ophelia. The fruit of this scene is what every instance of *memento mori* intends to inspire, namely humility.

The second kind of experience is all the providential events of the sea voyage taken together, which have already happened by V.i but are not made entirely known to the audience until the private conversation between Hamlet and Horatio in V.ii. Those events include:

1. On his way to England (to be killed, as only the audience knows), Hamlet happens not to be able to sleep.
2. Hamlet feels an impulse to steal and read the letter of Claudius to the King of England, in which he discovers he is to be executed by the English king.
3. Hamlet happens to have learned in his youth how to write in formal court handwriting.
4. Hamlet happens to have his father's royal signet ring with him.
5. After Hamlet has rewritten the letter, which now says that the *bearers* are to be put to death, and has secretly replaced it, Hamlet's ship happens to be attacked by pirates.
6. Hamlet jumps aboard the pirate ship to fight them (proving he is no coward).
7. The ships happen to drift apart with only Hamlet on board the pirate ship.
8. The pirates happen to be merciful to him in return for his putting

in a good word for them to Claudius, and they take him back to Denmark.

We know that Shakespeare means us to think of all these events as providential because Hamlet says so. In recounting the events to Horatio, Hamlet says, "Why, even in that [his having had the signet ring with him] was heaven ordinant" (V.ii.48). Hamlet understands there is a higher will than his that has arranged these events of his life. He expresses this recognition to Horatio thus:

> Rashly—
> And prais'd be rashness for it—let us know
> Our indiscretion sometime serves us well
> When our deep plots to pall, and that should learn [= teach] us
> There's a divinity that shapes our ends,
> Rough-hew them how we will—   (V.ii.7–11)

(Notice the double sense of "ends" here: goals and deaths.) Then he goes on to describe what he did rashly—that is, on impulse—namely getting up from his cabin, stealing the letter, rewriting it, etc. Hamlet's philosophical parenthetical reveals that his attitude is utterly changed from what it was in III.iii. There he was getting in heaven's way in trying to shape the end of Claudius toward damnation. Now he is humbled before the will of heaven. The lines resolve poetically the always paradoxical relation of man's free will to God's will. (Sometimes this paradox is expressed as free will vs. predestination or free will vs. fate.) Shakespeare has Hamlet use a simple metaphor to express the essence of this profound paradox. It is the metaphor of rough-hewing a rock or a block of wood and then shaping it. What actually appears in a sculpture is the result of both rough-hewing and shaping. What actually happens in life is the result of the rough-hewing of our lives by our human will and the ultimate fine shaping of them by the divine will. Hamlet's moral breakthrough is confirmed by the rational Horatio: "That is most certain" (V.ii.11).

At the end of the play Hamlet still can fly into a passion for cause. We see this not only with Laertes in V.I, but even with Horatio. When, in a moment of uncharacteristic passion, Horatio himself tries to drink of the leftover poison, Hamlet is roused to stop him: "As th' art a man, / Give me the cup. Let go! By heaven, I'll ha't [= have it]!" (V.ii.342–43). Thus, we find that the transformation in Hamlet is not a change of personality. He is still and always a man who can fly into a passion when there is cause for it, and then grow reasonable. But he is changed in the relation of his will to reality.

When Hamlet has a dark (and, as it turns out, true) premonition about the coming fencing match (V.ii.212–16) and Horatio offers to postpone the match, Hamlet says no, because "We defy augury" (V.ii.219). *Augury* means foretelling, and the word *defy* here is used as it is when we say that something "defies description." That is, we human beings cannot be augured about. No one knows the future. Our deaths are a function of the "special providence" that governs even the fall of a sparrow (V.ii.219–22), a reference to Jesus' words in Matthew 10:29: "Are not two sparrows sold for a farthing, and one of them shall not fall on the ground without your Father?" Hamlet's conclusion, "Let be," means two things at once: one meaning is superficial and practical—"let's stop talking because people are coming"; the other meaning is a profound expression of Hamlet's corrected will— "let happen whatever heaven wills to happen." These short prose speeches are the sign of a complete moral transformation in Hamlet from the willful attempt to play God in an effort to cause the damnation of Claudius in III. iii to a thorough surrender to the divine will.

The complex structure of the play includes a series of foils for Hamlet's moral trajectory. The foil story of Fortinbras comes early: He sets off willfully to retake land his father lost, is recalled by his uncle-king (a good but weak foil for the strong but evil Claudius), repents ("receives rebuke"—II.ii.69), and then sets off to Poland under proper commission. His reward for surrendering his own will to the higher will of his king is that on his return from victory all of Denmark falls into his lap. The foil journey of Laertes comes late: Out of a desire for revenge he puts himself into the service of the murderous Claudius and only with his impending death repents and asks for and offers forgiveness (V.ii.329-31). Horatio's similar journey is even later: Rational and balanced throughout, even he is tempted to sin by the power of his passion of grief when he claims to be "more an antique Roman than a Dane" (V.ii.341) and tries to commit suicide. Recalled from that rash act by Hamlet, he then fulfills his true function, to tell Hamlet's story (V.ii.349). Even Osric is a foil for Hamlet, for when Hamlet asks him to put on his hat (V.ii.92), inappropriate in the presence of the prince, Osric is caught between duty to the custom, which exists to honor the prince, and duty to the prince himself. It is an exact though comical equivalent to Hamlet's being asked to avenge his father's murder without tainting his mind. Like Hamlet in III.iii, Osric makes the wrong choice, deciding to serve his own picture of reality instead of the prince's picture. Osric has falsely presumed that Hamlet is mad, just as, in III.iii, Hamlet falsely presumed Claudius was repenting.

The philosophical heart of the play, which prepares us to comprehend the healing transformation in the soul of Hamlet, is Hamlet's own speeches to the Players at III.ii.1ff. The performance of a play on a stage is akin to living a life. Shakespeare's theatre was called "The Globe." Hence, in addition to being very good advice to all actors from the experienced actor-playwright Shakespeare, Hamlet's speech may be read for its universal implications. Do not overdo your part (ll. 1–14, 24–25). Do not underperform either (l. 16). Do not be tardy in performing it (l. 25). Don't add lines that aren't yours to say (ll. 38–45). "Suit the action to the word, the word to the action" (l. 17–18). We may wish to hear that instruction as an echo of the Gospel of John 1:1, where "Word"— a translation of the Greek *logos*, which gives us *logic* and all *–ologies*—refers to God and his laws of life bestowed on man for man's own ultimate good. As the actors must suit their actions to the playwright's words, Hamlet, and every one of us, must suit our actions to the Word, the Logos, the logic of divinity.

In III.iii Hamlet fails every one of his earlier strictures to the players: He overdoes his part, playing God, not God's avenger. He is tardy in performing his role. He writes lines not set down for him by the divine playwright—deciding not merely to kill the villain but to make sure of his damnation. He fails in readiness. But by the end of the play, Hamlet has learned his lesson and has let his rough-hewing become the instrument of the divine shaping. Hamlet's last words to the players are "Go make you ready." Later, once he himself has been made morally ready, enlightened by the humbling events of the sea voyage and the *memento mori* of V.i, Hamlet says to Horatio, "the readiness is all" (V.ii.222).

The truth of Hamlet's words is sealed and the evidence of his having been cured of his evil will is confirmed as he is dying in the last scene. Like a good Christian he is able to forgive his own (now penitent) murderer: "Exchange forgiveness with me," says Laertes (V.ii.329); "Mine and my father's death come not upon thee, / Nor thine on me!" Hamlet replies, "Heaven make thee free of it!" (V.ii.332).

KEY LINES:

1. Imperatives: The play is filled with an unusual number of imperatives—tasks given by one character to another. In many of them there is a stipulation about how the task is to be done. The central example

initiates the entire plot of the play. It is the Ghost's to Hamlet: "Revenge [my] foul and most unnatural murder / . . . But . . . /Taint not thy mind" (I.v.25, 84–85). All other imperatives in the play are foils for this one. Among many others, Claudius to Cornelius and Voltemand:

> [W]e here dispatch
> You, good Cornelius, and you, Voltemand,
> For bearers of this greeting to old Norway,
> Giving to you no further personal power
> To business with the King, more than the scope
> Of these delated articles allow.   (I.ii.33–38)

That is, do it, do it a certain way, and do not overdo it. The same is explicit in Hamlet's speeches to the Players (III.ii.1ff.). Polonius gives the famous golden mean lecture to Laertes (I.iii.58ff.), tells Ophelia to drop Hamlet (I.iii.131–35), instructs Reynaldo (II.i.1ff.). Tasks are given by Old Norway to Fortinbras; by Claudius to Gertrude, to Rosencrantz and Guildenstern, to Laertes; by Hamlet to Horatio, to Gertrude, to Osric. The second line of the play is an imperative ("answer me. Stand and unfold yourself"—I.i.2), and so is the last line of the play ("Go bid the soldiers shoot"—V.ii.403). The point is that all the imperatives in the play recreate Hamlet's position in little, the position of every human being. You are given a task to do, are expected to do it appropriately without overdoing it, and will be judged by whether, when, and how it is accomplished. What the trajectory of Hamlet's inner life shows us is that providence gives us more than one chance to get it right.

2. Hamlet says about the deaths of Rosencrantz and Guildenstern, "They are not near my conscience" (V.ii.58). Some critics have thought that Hamlet ought to feel more guilt over the deaths of his two schoolfellows. In accusing him of a cavalier lack of compassion they overlook four crucial points: 1. Hamlet, being the rightful king, has the right and the duty to care for the well-being of Denmark, which involves the responsibility for executing traitors, including those loyal to the state's actual enemy, namely Claudius. 2. Unlike with Claudius in III.iii, Hamlet is not attempting to assign the souls of Rosencrantz and Guildenstern to heaven or to hell. He is merely preventing them from seeing to Hamlet's death, that is, the unjust murder of their rightful king. Though their lives will be ended by his forged order, their souls will be subject to God's judgment, not to Hamlet's. 3. Hamlet has every reason to believe that his two supposed

friends, who serve Claudius and have lied to him, are in on the plot to kill him. He has said earlier that he will trust them as he will "adders fanged" (III.iv.203). 4. When Hamlet is writing the commission that will lead to the deaths of Rosencrantz and Guildenstern, he believes that he, too, along with them, will soon be appearing before England's king. He has no idea that there will be a pirate ship or that he will be separated from the Danish ship on its way to England. The deaths of Rosencrantz and Guildenstern are not near Hamlet's conscience—here the word *conscience* means "the awareness of having done wrong"[3]—because they arise only from Hamlet's attempt to save his own life, that is, the life of Denmark's rightful king.

SPECIFIC NOTES TO HELP IN YOUR READING:
1. Ophelia's madness can be understood by seeing the situation from her viewpoint: She loves Hamlet, who appears to love her. Her brother goes to Paris. Her father tells her to drop her lover. She obeys, and her doing so drives her lover mad (as her father tells her to think). After exhibiting his madness, seeming to accuse her of infidelity, and instructing her to go to a nunnery, her lover kills her father in a fit of madness. All this is too much for her to bear and drives her mad. Hers is a real form of the disappointed-in-love madness that Hamlet was merely playacting in II.i.
2. Is Ophelia guilty of committing suicide? The question is debated comically by the two gravediggers (V.i.1ff.) and seriously by Laertes and the Doctor of Divinity (V.i.235–42). The truth is that they are debating two positions on a question to which the answer cannot be known by human beings. To know the spiritual state of another's soul is not within the human purview, and every pretense of knowing it results in error. Whether Ophelia's free will chose her own death or whether her free will was so impaired by madness that it had no part in her death cannot be known this side of the afterlife. The gravedigger comically and the Doctor of Divinity seriously are both pretentious in arguing that Ophelia should not be buried in consecrated ground because she took her own life. They cannot know what was the actual choice of her free will. Similarly, Laertes is pretentious in asserting that the Doctor of Divinity will be damned and Ophelia become a "minist'ring angel" (V.i.241). (Incidentally, Laertes' line is in large part responsible for the erroneous modern idea that the souls of the saved become angels in the afterlife. Laertes is being hyperbolical and metaphorical; he is not asserting a

theological heresy.) These two debates throw light back on Hamlet's error in III.iii when he assumed that he could know and determine the eternal fate of the soul of Claudius.

3.   V.ii.165–67: Osric says, "The King, sir, hath laid, sir, that in a dozen passes between yourself and [Laertes], he shall not exceed you three hits. He hath laid on twelve for nine." The key to understanding this fencing match lies in understanding that a "pass" means not a "bout" but a specific attack, which at this time was made as one fencer ran past his opponent, putting his "point in line" and creating a "right of way" that required a "parry" (block) and potentially a "riposte" (counter-attack). The "pass" may result in a "touch" (hit) scored by either fencer or in no hit at all. By contrast, a "bout" is some agreed upon number of passes. Thus, the King has bet that 1) In any one bout of twelve passes, Laertes will not score above three hits more than Hamlet scores, and 2) that for every twelve hits scored by Laertes in any number of bouts Hamlet will score at least nine hits.

---

[1]   J.V. Cunningham, in a graduate course on *Hamlet* at Brandeis University, Spring 1975.
[2]   The phrase is from Philip Thompson, "Notes on Shakespeare: *Hamlet*" in *Dusk and Dawn: Poems and Prose of Philip Thompson*, ed. Gideon Rappaport (San Diego: One Mind Good Press, 2005), p. 222.
[3]   See C. S. Lewis, *Studies in Words*, Second Edition (Cambridge: Cambridge University Press, 1967, reprinted 1988), Ch. 8.

Othello

Othello is often classified as a domestic tragedy because its tragic events take place largely within a private household. It can also be classified as a *de casibus* tragedy since it depicts the fall of a great man from greatness (see Kinds of Tragedy in Chapter 10 of Part 1). Beyond these classifications, the play is to be understood poetically as well as literally. In fact, *Othello* is a realistic allegory of the fall of man. The character Othello is a particular man with a tragic flaw. He is also Man, an everyman, who suffers from the besetting sin of pride and falls to destruction because of his choices, like Adam in the Garden of Eden. The snake in this version of the story is Iago, who uses a serpentine and devilish pseudo-logic to seduce Othello into tragic error. However, the final choice that results in perdition is Othello's own.

"Realistic allegory" sounds like an oxymoron, and in a sense it is, expressing in one phrase the unity of paradoxical opposites that Shakespeare achieves in the drama of the play. The allegorical implications of *Othello* take nothing away from the empathic power of its realistic drama. Shakespeare's ability to unite these two apparently disparate modes of drama—realistic particulars and universal significance—into a single experience of meaning is perhaps the greatest glory of his art.[1] But since the tendency of our time is to focus on particulars at the expense of universals, we may right the imbalance by stressing the more universal implications that this drama would have held for Shakespeare's audience.

Those who have been exposed to Disney's Donald Duck may remember cartoons in which Donald had a decision to make. In them an angel-Donald and a devil-Donald appeared beside him out of his own head and proceeded to tempt him to do the right and the wrong things respectively.[2] This allegorical representation of a conflict between good and evil within the mind has a long history beginning with an early-fifth-century poem by Prudentius called *Psychomachia*, meaning "soul-battle," in which representations of human virtues battle representations

of human vices. Shakespeare has inherited this tradition of depicting a soul in inner conflict. However, in *Othello*, true to his style of "universal realism," Shakespeare embeds his allegorical *psychomachia* in a realistic drama, giving to the opposing forces at war within the mind of Othello "A local habitation and a name," as Theseus calls it in *A Midsummer Night's Dream* (V.i.17).

Desdemona's name comes from the Greek for "unfortunate," or, by another possible derivation, "twice-blessed." She is both a real person of virtuous character and an angelic spirit who draws Othello's free will toward the Christian virtues of humility, patience, and forgiveness. Iago is named for Saint James (or Santiago) the Greater, the Moor-slaying patron saint of Renaissance England's enemy, namely Catholic Spain. He is both a real person of evil character and the incarnation of a demonic force—a devil. He tempts Othello into doubt, jealousy, betrayal, and murder. The story of this play is the fall of Othello not only from happiness to misery and death but from grace to damnation.

Desdemona is a modest, obedient, and faithful wife. But she is also an embodiment of the angelic principle of grace, Othello's most precious companion in both senses. As we will see, Cassio calls her "The divine Desdemona" (II.i.73). In the play's last scene Gratiano (whose name comes from the Italian for "grace" and "pardon"), when he finds that Othello has killed Desdemona, says that if her father were alive to see this sight, it would cause him to "curse his better angel from his side, / And fall to reprobance [= damnation]" (V.ii.208–209). Cursing his better angel from his side is exactly what Othello has done in killing his innocent wife under the influence of his worser angel, Iago. (For further evidence of Desdemona's angelic role, see Key Line 1.)

According to traditional Christian doctrine, the seven deadly sins are the roots of all other sins. The second of the deadly sins is envy, for which, in addition to the first sin of pride, it was believed that Lucifer was cast out of heaven into hell. One form that envy may take is jealousy. As Iago poisons Othello's mind with jealousy, Shakespeare compels us to think of Iago himself not only as an evil man with a grudge but as a devil of jealousy. He does so partly by giving us a variety of motives for Iago's hatred of Othello without allowing us to settle on any one of them. Coleridge called Iago a "motiveless malignity" because with every appearance he offers a different reason for his choice to ruin Othello. But each of those pretexts represents a form of envy. In addition, many lines contribute to the impression of Iago's demonic metaphysical existence. At the end of I.iii, Iago says of his plan to destroy Othello, "Hell and night / Must bring this monstrous birth to the world's light" (I.iii.403–404). And when Iago's crimes are known in Act V, Othello says, "I look down toward his feet; but that's a fable. / If that thou be'st a devil, I cannot kill thee" (V.ii.286–87), whereupon he stabs Iago but fails to kill him. The devil was traditionally figured as having the cloven hooves of a goat instead of feet, and human beings cannot "kill" the devil but only shame him through their own choice for good over evil. Iago, then, is both a 28-year-old Venetian human villain and an incarnation of the devil of jealousy. (For further evidence of Iago's demonic role see Key Line 2.)

Desdemona is herself and also an angel; Iago is himself and also a devil. Othello, then, is himself and also Man. He is a particular man tricked by evil servant into jealousy about his innocent wife, but he is also a representation, like Donald Duck in the cartoons, of every man's inner life as a battlefield between humility and pride, trust and suspicion, fidelity and betrayal, good and evil, Desdemona and Iago. But in the contest for Othello's soul—unlike in the Donald Duck cartoons—the stakes could not be higher.

To shed light on this war within Othello between the spirits of Desdemona (patient humility) and Iago (envy), Shakespeare establishes a symbolic parallel in the outer world. He makes Cyprus the locus of the war between the Christian Venetians and the Muslim Turks, who since medieval times were thought of as the infidel enemies of Christian Europe. At I.iii.8 we hear that the Turkish fleet is threatening Venice-held

Cyprus. At l. 14 the Duke and Senators are told that the Turks are heading instead for Rhodes. About this news the First Senator wisely observes, "This cannot be / By no assay of reason; 'tis a pageant / To keep us in false gaze" (ll. 17–19). Considering their general nature and motives, the Turks must be engaging in a ruse and are no doubt headed in fact for Cyprus. The Duke agrees, and then further news confirms their conclusion: the Turks are indeed headed for Cyprus after all (ll. 38–39). Thereupon Othello enters and is put into service as general to lead the Venetian fleet against the enemy Turks. This conflict over the island of Cyprus becomes a metaphor for Othello's inner conflict. By his pretense of honesty, Iago plays the role of the deceitful Turks, intentionally misleading the deliberations of the senate within Othello's mind. Iago's real intention is to destroy Othello through the unjustified attack on the Cyprus that is Desdemona.

Pride is the first and most fundamental of the seven deadly sins. Envy, the second sin, can grab hold only of a will already corrupted by pride. Pride in his image of himself is Othello's besetting sin. It is because of it that the villain of envy, Iago, can work upon him so effectively. In I.ii, Othello boasts, while recognizing that it is not proper to do so, that

> I fetch my life and being
> From men of royal siege, and my demerits
> May speak unbonneted to as proud a fortune
> As this that I have reached. (I.ii.21–24)

And a few lines later he says,

> My parts, my title, and my perfect soul
> Shall manifest me rightly. (I.ii.31–32)

The assertion that anyone has a "perfect soul" would fall on the ears of the Christians in Shakespeare's audience as unchristian arrogance. They believed that all men are sinners and hence ought to be humble. Perfection of soul belonged to Christ alone, and only through penitence and faith in Christ could a man be redeemed from sin and damnation. This hint of self-worship in Othello is the "dram of evil" in his character that will be fanned into fatally sinful action by Iago and destroy "all the noble substance" of Othello (cf., *Hamlet*, I.iv.36–37).

Othello has been a fighter all his life, "little bless'd with the soft phrase of peace" (I.iii.82); "And little of this great world can I speak / More than pertains to feats of broils and battle" (I.iii.86–87). In psychological terms, it is that battle mentality that he brings, with Iago's subtle guidance, into the realm of marriage, where it proves disastrous. In spiritual terms, Othello, originally a pagan, has nominally become a Christian (cf., II.iii.170–72, 343–44), but his soul has not absorbed the essence of the Christian message to the point of humbling his pride. He is used to confessing "the vices of my blood" (I.iii.123), but apparently recognizes no vices of his mind. For this reason he is susceptible to the wiles of Iago. (For further evidence of Othello's pride, see Key Line 3.)

Act II, Scene i, gives a dramatic and poetic metaphor of Othello's condition. Surprisingly, the defeat of the Turks at sea is accomplished not by a sea battle guided by the hero Othello but by a providential storm. That it is providential is implied by the Second Gentleman's description, in which earthly water threatens heavenly fires: "I never did like molestation view / On the enchafèd flood" (II.i.16–17). Like the main characters, this storm at sea is itself and also a metaphor for the trials that man, represented by Othello, faces in the world. By contrast, angels and devils are not subject to testing by worldly challenges, having long since made their choices for and against God. Thus, both the angel Desdemona and the devil Iago supernaturally pass from Venice to Cyprus without incident or delay despite the storm. As Cassio puts it,

> Tempests themselves, high seas, and howling winds,
> The gutter'd rocks and congregated sands,
> Traitors ensteep'd to enclog the guiltless keel,
> As having sense of beauty, do omit
> Their mortal natures, letting go safely by
> The divine Desdemona.   (II.i.68–73)

By contrast, Cassio has prayed about Othello,

>   O, let the heavens
> Give him defense against the elements,
> For I have lost him on a dangerous sea.   (II.i.44–46)

Cassio adds that Othello has some things going for him: "His bark is stoutly timber'd, and his pilot / Of very expert and approv'd allowance" (ll. 48–49). The strong ship in the physical realm represents in the moral realm Othello's gifts of strength, courage, and heroism, and also the fact of his conversion from paganism to Christianity. The skilled pilot is Othello's free will, given by God to be equal to whatever task he may face.

The heaven-sent defeat of the Turks and his difficult but successful passage ought to humble Othello. But his self-glorifying habit of mind remains. Happy to find Desdemona safely at Cyprus ahead of him, Othello figures his reunion with her under the metaphor of Judgment Day:

> If after every tempest come such calms,
> May the winds blow till they have wakened death! (II.i.185–86)

And then,

> If it were now to die,
> 'Twere now to be most happy; for I fear
> My soul hath her content so absolute
> That not another comfort like to this
> Succeeds in unknown fate. (II.i.189–93)

Othello can conceive no greater fulfillment than reunion with his wife in the physical world. He implies that now that he personally has arrived at ultimate happiness, it would be fine for the world to end. This is a dangerously self-important attitude for a Christian, and Desdemona corrects him:

> The heavens forbid
> But that our loves and comforts should increase
> Even as our days do grow! (II.i.193–95)

From birth a virtuous Christian who hopes for heaven, Desdemona recognizes the danger of Othello's vainglory in assuming they have already arrived at the destination of ultimate love and comfort. Meanwhile Iago hears this exchange, and observes, "O, you are well tun'd now! / But I'll set down the pegs [= the tuning pegs of a stringed instrument] that make this music" (II.i.199–200).

The center of the play is Iago's subtle untuning of that marital music: the long, complex, seemingly rational cultivation of jealousy in the mind of Othello in III.iii under the pretense of honesty. During it, Othello will come to trust Iago's reputation for honesty more than he trusts the fidelity of his own wife. Iago's words work at appealing to and injuring Othello's characteristically proud self-image by inventing an imaginary infidelity in Desdemona. From there Iago leads Othello through one false premise, innuendo, illogical deduction, and lie after another to the fatal conclusion. He begins with "Hah? I like not that" (III.iii.35), moves on to implications about Cassio, then to appealing to Othello's pride by setting a very high value on reputation, then to cautioning against jealousy.

Since Othello is failing to see through the hypocrisies of Iago, there is terrible irony in his boasting of a discernment founded on a logical fallacy:

> No! to be once in doubt
> Is once to be resolv'd. . . .
> I'll see before I doubt; when I doubt, prove;
> And on the proof, there is no more but this—
> Away at once with love or jealousy! (III.iii.179–92)

In this fallacy we may discover the genius of our modern judicial system's assertion that an indicted person is to be presumed innocent until proven guilty. Why? Because innocence cannot be proven. Only guilt can be proven. It can be shown by evidence that one has been present and has done an evil deed—witnesses, fingerprints, video, DNA. But absence of witnesses, fingerprints, video, or DNA cannot prove that one was *not* there and did *not* do it. That is why our juries are instructed to find defendants either proven to be guilty or not proven to be guilty; they cannot be expected to find them proven to be innocent. Thus when Othello asserts that if once he doubts Desdemona, he will prove her either guilty or innocent, and then abandon either love or suspicion, he is falling into a trap. First of all, to suspect one's wife of infidelity is already to have betrayed her. Second, there can be no "ocular proof" (l. 360) that she did *not* sleep with Cassio. By this fallacy Othello has opened the door to Iago's further assault upon his trust in his wife.

Once Othello suspects that Desdemona may be unfaithful, all that is needed for the apparent proof of her guilt in the mind of Othello is the imagery provided by Iago's words and a little handkerchief, for, as Iago says, "Trifles light as air / Are to the jealous confirmations strong / As proofs of holy writ" (III.iii.322–24). ("Proofs of holy writ" were still, in Shakespeare's time, thought to be authoritative—see Authority in Chapter

7 of Part 1.) Iago's performance does the trick within the space of one long scene (III.iii). When Othello, as a formula of thanks for Iago's professed love to him, says "I am bound to thee forever" (III.iii.213), we are chilled to the bone at the foreboding metaphysical implication of this verbal betrothal to the demon. The seduction scene then concludes with hell's version of their wedding. Kneeling, Othello vows "revenge" (III.iii.459) on the innocent Desdemona and Cassio. Kneeling with him, Iago then vows to put all "his wit, hands, heart, / To wrong'd Othello's service!" (III.iii.466–67). What we know that Othello does not is that Othello is wronged not by Desdemona and Cassio but by Iago himself, and the service he will do Othello is to destroy him. Allegorically, Othello has divorced his soul from Desdemona's and wedded it to the devil of jealousy. The consummation of that wedding will lie in vengeful murder disguised (as Iago is disguised) as justice. "The justice" of strangling his wife in her bed "pleases," says Othello (IV.i.207–209).

In the beginning of V.ii, the last scene of the play, Othello enters imagining that he is the embodiment of Justice itself. His first speech is calm and slow, suggesting his certainty about the rightness of the murder he is about to commit. He imagines that he is killing not Desdemona but her guilt, her sin, her betrayal—"the cause" (V.ii.1). He makes it an obligation to kill her "else she'll betray more men" (V.ii.6). Then he says, "O balmy breath, that dost almost persuade / Justice to break her sword!" (V.ii.16–17). Worse, he imagines he is acting like God: "This sorrow's heavenly, / It strikes where it doth love" (V.ii.21–22). There is sadness in him, but no Christian humility and no self-doubt. And it is not long before Desdemona's plea for mercy makes Othello "call what I intend to do / A murder, which I thought a sacrifice" (V.ii.64–65).

After Othello has done the deed, his language explodes into disjointed chaos (the dashes in modern editions indicating shifts in the person being spoken to, here Emilia and then himself):

> Yes.—'Tis Emilia.—By and by.—She's dead.
> 'Tis like she [= Emilia] comes to speak of Cassio's death;
> The noise was high. Hah, no more moving?
> Still as the grave. Shall she [= Emilia] come in? Were't good?
> I think she [= Desdemona] stirs again. No. What's best to do?
> If she come in, she'll sure speak to my wife.
> My wife, my wife! what wife? I have no wife.
> O insupportable! O heavy hour!

Methinks it should be now a huge eclipse
Of sun and moon, and that th' affrighted globe
Did yawn at alteration.   (V.ii.91–101)

Othello's calm certainty is gone, his mind now flitting from one thing to another. Earlier he has said about Desdemona,

Perdition catch my soul
But I do love thee [= if I do not love thee]! and when I love thee not,
Chaos is come again.   (III.iii.90–92)

Here now, after he has killed Desdemona, is that foreshadowed chaos—not of the world, but of Othello's mind, expressed in Shakespeare's subtle but powerful alteration in the quality of the verse. However, despite the anguish, there is still no self-reproach. Hence perdition will indeed catch his soul. Othello imagines that the death of Desdemona should bring on the same eclipse and earthquake that attended the death of Christ (cf., Matthew 27:45, 51, etc.). As in II.i his greeting of Desdemona was riddled with vainglory, so after killing her Othello expresses self-glorification in the universal significance of his deed, which he still believes to have been just. But now his imagery also foreshadows the death of Christ—of mercy, forgiveness, humility—in his own soul.

Before that happens, redemption is still possible. For Othello now faces the most crucial choice of his life. With the evidence that Emilia offers, Othello realizes his error in presuming Desdemona guilty and punishing her with death. The question now is, will he admit to his own fallibility? Will he, in guilt and repentance, humble himself before the state and God? Will he bear his error with real patience (contrasting with the patience recommended in the fruitless platitudes of the Duke at I.iii.202–209). Desdemona still might guide him rightly. She had spoken words of hope even for the guilty: "God me such uses send, / Not to pick bad from bad, but by bad mend" (IV.iii.104–105). And with her last breath Desdemona has forgiven Othello—"Commend me to my kind lord. O, farewell!" (V.ii.125). Given this hope, will Othello repent and seek forgiveness and thereby redemption?

Othello's answer is no. And now there is no question of any external influence by Iago. Despite having heard Desdemona's word of forgiveness, Othello belies his wife even now:

> when we shall meet at compt,
> This look of thine will hurl my soul from heaven,
> And fiends will snatch at it.   (V.ii.273–75)

("Compt" means accounting, judgment, and the Last Judgment.) He has never really understood Desdemona's goodness, and he cannot imagine it even now. He negates it as completely as Iago negates all virtues he confronts. Toward his own soul Othello has now become an Iago. He takes God's judgment into his own hands. He calls upon the devils to "Whip me . . . / Blow me about in winds! Roast me in Sulphur! / Wash me in steep-down gulfs of liquid fire!" (V.ii.277–80), traditional images of the punishments of the damned. He refuses to imagine the forgiveness that repentance would evoke even from Desdemona, who has proven her willingness to forgive him, let alone from God, who *always* forgives the penitent. That refusal dramatizes the spiritual condition of despair, the final act of Othello's human pride. As Philip Thompson writes, Othello's state of mind is

> one of complete satisfaction with the blamelessness of his intentions and with his manner of ending the whole "unfortunate" business. He should have gone down on his knees, accused himself, watered the earth with tears of repentance, and surrendered to the state to undergo an acceptable public death. Instead he produces a soaring self-eulogy in the course of which he admits only "perplexity" [V.ii.346] and a love too strong for wisdom [V.ii.344] (the latter states the opposite of the truth).[3]

Othello says that he was "one that lov'd not wisely but too well" (V.ii.344). That he has loved "not wisely" is true; that he has loved "too well" is self-delusion. Had he loved Desdemona more than his own self-image, Iago-Jealousy could never have found a way into his mind.

Othello's ending is far from the heroic death some have seen in it. The fatal error of Othello's final gesture is confirmed when Lodovico says "O bloody period! [= conclusion of the speech and of the life]" and Gratiano says "All that is spoke is marred" (V.ii.357). Othello brags of having killed a Turk who was beating a Venetian and then turns his knife upon himself in imitation of how he had punished that Turk (V.ii.352–56). But in punishing himself, *he* has become the Turk, killing the Venetian that is his own eternal soul.

KEY LINES:

1. Further evidence of Desdemona's role as good angel: "What e'er you be, I am obedient" (III.iii.89); "If any such there be, heaven pardon him!" (IV.ii.135); "his unkindness may defeat my life, / But never taint my love" (IV.ii.160–61); "Beshrew me, if I would do such a wrong / For the whole world" (IV.iii.78–79); "A guiltless death I die" (V.ii.122); "O, the more angel she, / And you the blacker devil!" (V.ii.130–31); "O, she was heavenly true!" (V.ii.135).

2. Further evidence of Iago's role as devil: Saying "Heaven is my judge, not I for love and duty, / But seeming so, for my peculiar end" (I.i.59–60), Iago echoes the sentiment of Lucifer in rebelling against God. He confirms as much with "I am not what I am" (I.i.65), an inversion of God's proclamation of his own name to Moses, "I am that I am" (Exodus 3:14). Throughout the play Iago devalues all value, as when he defines love as merely a "lust of the blood and a permission of the will" (I.iii.332–35). When his calumny against women causes Desdemona to call him "slanderer," he responds, "Nay, it is true, or else I am a Turk" (II.i.113–14). He is a slanderer, his conclusion is not true, and morally speaking he is what Shakespeare means by a Turk, i.e., an infidel. In II.iii he proclaims hell's "Divinity," meaning teaching or theology:

> Divinity of hell!
> When devils will the blackest sins put on,
> They do suggest [= tempt] at first with heavenly shows,
> As I do now. (II.iii.350–53)

In the middle of the seduction scene, Iago sneaks in an honest confession that "oft my jealousy / Shapes faults that are not" (III.iii.147–48), though of course Othello is not meant to take it seriously. Ironically, Othello curses Iago in a way that, unlike Othello, we know to be apt:

> If thou dost slander her and torture me,
> Never pray more; abandon all remorse;
> On horror's head horrors accumulate;
> Do deeds to make heaven weep, all earth amaz'd;
> For nothing canst thou to damnation add
> Greater than that. (III.iii.368–73)

In III.iv, Emilia says about jealous souls,

They are not ever jealous for the cause,
But jealous for [= because] they're jealous. It is a monster
Begot upon itself, born on itself.   (III.iv.160–62)

And in the same scene Cassio says about Bianca's jealousy, "Throw your vile guesses in the devil's teeth, / From whence you have them" (III. iv.184–85). When Othello hints at thinking Desdemona dishonest, Emilia says, "If any wretch have put this in your head, / Let heaven requite it with the serpent's curse!" (IV.ii.15–16), referring to the biblical curse upon the serpent in Genesis 3:14–15. Later she says, "I will be hang'd if some eternal villain . . . / Have not devis'd this slander" (IV.ii.130–33). At V.i. Iago expresses a classic instance of envy, saying of Cassio "He hath a daily beauty in his life / That makes me ugly" (V.i.19–20). At V.ii.292 he is a "damned slave," at l. 301 a "demi-devil," at l. 316 a "damned villain." Finally, at the end Lodovico seeks to punish Iago with some "cunning cruelty / That can torment him much and hold him long" (V.ii.333–34), an image that approximates the definition of hell.

3.   Further evidence of Othello's pride: Othello says that if ever sexual desire blinds his intellect, then let "all indign [= disgraceful, undeserving] and base adversities / Make head [= raise an army] against my estimation [= reputation]!" (I.iii.273–74), in other words, "if ever my mind becomes clouded by sexual desire, let all disgraceful adversities make war against my reputation." It is only in his reputation, not his soul, that Othello can imagine being injured. His agony at Desdemona's supposed betrayal is substantially about his self-image, his reputation: "My name, that was as fresh / As Dian's visage, is now begrimed and black / As mine own face" (III.iii.386–88).[4] "Cuckold me!" he shouts at IV.i.200. In the next scene, in the name of the wound to his pride he rejects the virtue of patience:

> Had it pleas'd heaven
> To try me with affliction, had they rain'd
> All kind of sores and shames on my bare head, . . .
> I should have found in some place of my soul
> A drop of patience; but, alas, to make me
> The fixed figure for the time of scorn
> To point his slow unmoving finger at!
> Yet could I bear that too, well, very well;
> But there, where I have garner'd up my heart,

> ... to be discarded thence!
> .... Turn thy complexion there,
> Patience, thou young and rose-lipp'd cherubin—
> Ay, here look grim as hell! (IV.ii.47–64)

After bragging that he could patiently bear any affliction, he renounces patience just when he is called to embrace it. Once again, he has learned the concept of humble patience but not absorbed it into his will, which remains locked in pride.

SPECIFIC NOTES TO HELP IN YOUR READING:

1. Othello's race: There is an antithesis of images in the play in the use of the colors white and black. White is the color of Desdemona and the Venetians, and Othello is what was called a "blackamoor," that is a dark-skinned African. It is important to be clear about the role that the color of Othello's skin plays in the play. Just as Shakespeare had inherited the doctrinal anti-Semitism that suffused the history of Christian Europe, as discussed in the chapter on *The Merchant of Venice*, so he inherited the medieval idea that black was the color of the devil. (In women the ideal of beauty was to be fair-skinned rather than tan or brown or olive, a distinction that gives point to Shakespeare's "dark lady" sonnets.) In *The Merchant of Venice* Shakespeare had humanized an old stereotype character and given him a choice to make between the good that was open to him and the evil that would confirm the justice of his being vilified. And so it is in *Othello*. Shakespeare turns the stereotype of the uncivilized black African into a nobleman, a heroic general, a defender of civilization against the also stereotypically infidel Turks. As with Shylock, Shakespeare gives Othello a moral choice to make. The Duke says to Brabantio,

> If virtue no delighted beauty lack,
> Your son-in-law is far more fair than black. (I.iii.289–90)

The Duke's point is not to make a racist slur but to turn Brabantio from thinking about Othello's color to thinking about Othello's character (as Martin Luther King, Jr., exhorted us all to do about one another in his great "I have a dream" speech).[5] And Othello's great choice, entirely apart from the color of his skin, is between pride and penitence. Had Othello repented for killing Desdemona and gone to his knees before

God's judgment, he might have hoped for redemption. But in taking the judgment of his soul upon himself, as he took the judgment of Desdemona upon himself, he makes the evil choice. In short, Shakespeare gives us in Othello not a man condemned to be seen as evil because of his color but a responsible moral being who must make the same spiritual choices and be held to the same universal standards as everyone else. It is only the villains Iago and Roderigo who call Othello by epithets that we would consider racist slurs. By the others he is admired until his own actions reveal him to have chosen the path of evil.

2.   A note on the text of *Othello*: The text of *Othello* presents extreme difficulties because while both Q1 and F have some authority, they differ in many significant respects, and neither their relation to one another nor their relation to their manuscript sources is clearly discernable. Most modern editions involve some conflation of readings from both early texts based on varying principles of choice. Those interested in further study of the textual problems with *Othello* should begin with the note on the text in any reputable edition of the play. There they will find references to longer scholarly studies.

3.   II.i.182: When Othello arrives safely on shore, he greets Desdemona as "O my fair warrior!" Literally he means that she has sailed into a war zone to be with him. At the same time we understand metaphorically that Desdemona is in the role of a Christian Venice warring against the infidel Turk (Iago) for the Cyprus that is Othello's soul.

4.   IV.i.1: Philip Thompson has suggested a possible emendation of the text: "Othello's first speech should be stretched to include the 'What' that begins Iago's second line:

Iago: Will you think so?
Othello: Think so, Iago. What?
Iago: To kiss in private?[6]

5.   V.i.35–36: Othello says, "Forth of my heart those charms, thine eyes, are blotted; / Thy bed, lust-stain'd, shall with lust's blood be spotted." The clotted (no pun intended) arrangement of sounds and pauses in this couplet force it to be spoken extremely slowly and deliberately. The awkwardness indicates Othello's clotted mind, which at the beginning of V.ii is overlaid with the pseudo-ceremony of his soliloquy before the murder, expressed in calm, smooth, ordered speech (V.ii.1–34); after the murder his mind explodes into chaos and is expressed in chaotic speech (V.ii.91–105).

6. V.ii.346–48: Othello says, ". . . of one whose hand, / Like the base [Judean / Indian], threw a pearl away / Richer than all his tribe." F has "Iudean" and Q1 has "*Indian*." The word "Iudean" could easily become "Indean" by the typesetter's turning upside-down of the letter *u*. The word "Indian" could easily become "Iudian" in the same way. How the two respective typesetters got to the two spellings we have is unknown, and we are left to judge for ourselves which of the two readings seems superior. My own argument would be for "Iudean" as a reference to Judas Iscariot, who betrayed Jesus as Othello has betrayed Desdemona and who by his suicide threw away the possibility of heaven (cf., the "pearl of great price" in Matthew 13:45–46). (It could also refer, less aptly, to Herod the Great, who had his beloved wife Mariamne killed.) This reading of the image is in keeping with the Christian imagery that runs through the play. The reference to a random Indian ignorant of the value of a random jewel, while possible, seems significantly less plausible.

---

[1]   In a modern expression of the idea, Thomas Mann writes, "we wander in the footsteps of others, and all of life is a pouring of the present into mythic forms," in Thomas Mann, *Joseph and His Brothers*, tr. John E. Woods (New York: Alfred A. Knopf, Everyman's Library, 2005), p. 669. See Universal Realism in Part 1, Chapter 1, and Endnote 2 there.

[2]   See "Donald's Better Self" at https://en.wikipedia.org/wiki/Donald%27s_Better_Self and "Donald's Decision" at https://en.wikipedia.org/wiki/Donald%27s_Decision.

[3]   In "Notes on Shakespeare" in Philip Thompson, *Dusk and Dawn: Poems and Prose of Philip Thompson*, ed. Gideon Rappaport (San Diego: One Mind Good Press, 2005), p. 220.

[4]   At III.iii.386 Q2 has "Her" in place of F's "My." I believe "My" to be the better reading, but even if he means Desdemona's name rather than his own, it is reputation that focuses his attention. See Specific Note 2, "A note on the Text of *Othello*."

[5]   Martin Luther King, Jr., "I Have a Dream," speech delivered August 28, 1963, at the Lincoln Memorial in Washington DC: "I have a dream that my four little children will one day live in a nation where they will not be judged by the color of their skin but by the content of their character."

[6]   Thompson, p. 220.

King Lear

Being incarnate in bodies, living in space and time, human beings find it nearly impossible to believe what we cannot directly experience. Hence we say that "seeing is believing." One way of seeing in order to believe is through art. As Professor Mary Holmes has said, "art exists to make the invisible visible" (see Part 1, Chapter 15).

Like all faithful Christians, Shakespeare believed the universe—reality itself—to be a mystery of love. That belief is inevitably tested in every believer by the fact of suffering: If God is good and loves his creation, how can he permit his creations to suffer? The answer to that question lies too deep to be expressed in a sentence, and perhaps too deep for human comprehension. Yet those who believe that God created the universe and saw that "it was very good" (Genesis 1:31) must also believe that there is meaning in suffering. In *King Lear*, perhaps his greatest play, Shakespeare has given us a supreme work of dramatic and poetic art in which the otherwise invisible meaning of suffering in a universe structured by God to be good is revealed to us, not as a proposition but as an experience.

Because Shakespeare has made suffering so vivid in *King Lear*, some modern readers have seen the play as a depiction of the ultimate bleakness of human life, as if Shakespeare were an existentialist 350 years before his time. The opposite is the case. The arc of the suffering of the characters of Lear and Gloucester exhibits a profound downward movement to anguish as a result of the failure of love. It then exhibits a healing movement upward toward redemption through the restoration of human love. The play succeeds at making visible the belief that human love is an incarnation of God's love and that suffering as a vehicle of purgation is ultimately a divine gift.

One of the ways Shakespeare allows us to experience this Christian view of life is by setting the play in a pre-Christian pagan world. Because the characters do not know the doctrine of the redemption of man through Christ, have not heard the good news that "If we love one another, God dwelleth in us, and his love is perfect in us" (1 John 4:12), the play is the more persuasive. For it depicts purgatorial redemption as built in to the very structure of reality even in a time and place in which that doctrine is yet unknown.

As Shakespeare and most of his audience believed, "Pride goeth before destruction, and an high mind before the fall" (Proverbs 16:18). *King Lear* begins with the King's proud self-indulgence. He wants to retire before his time, to enjoy the pleasures and honor of kingship without continuing to execute its duties. In order to do so, he intends to divide the kingdom into three, an idea that Shakespeare's audience, after a hundred years of civil wars, would believe to be abhorrent folly. Sentimentally and foolishly Lear hopes by this division "that future strife / May be prevented now" (I.i.44–45). Once preferring the good Albany to the evil Cornwall (I.i.1–3), Lear now decides to base this division of the kingdom not on the recipients' virtue but on a contest of flattery, which he, in his delusion, supposes to be a contest of love. He tries to drag his daughters and the court into sharing his delusion by asking, "Which of you shall we say doth love us most . . . ?" (I.i.51). Pleased with the flattery of the two elder daughters, he then curses the youngest daughter and the loyal Earl of Kent for speaking the truth.

Lacking the fear and direction of the king who has dispossessed himself of authority and power, the two evil daughters begin to persecute their father for their own advantage. The first half of the play, then, depicts the downward slide of Lear and his kingdom into the civil strife that must prevail in a world in which rightful authority is lost and self-aggrandizement rules in its place. Purgation and restoration of order, in the minds of Lear and Gloucester and in the commonwealth, are the business of the second half of the play.

Shakespeare has built the drama of this play out of a complex and subtle relation of two plots, both of which tell the same story at different levels (see the discussion of Plot in Chapter 6 of Part 1). The Gloucester plot gives a more outward, politically and psychologically familiar version of the story. This parallel plot of Gloucester allows Shakespeare to deepen our comprehension of the greater spiritual implications of the main plot of Lear.

Gloucester shares the moral blindness of Lear: Both fail to distinguish among the respective characters of their children. In the case of Gloucester there is an obvious cause of self-delusion: He has committed adultery and begotten his younger son out of wedlock. Yet, Gloucester says, the elder, legitimate, and virtuous son is "no dearer in my account" (I.i.20–21) than the younger, illegitimate, and vicious son. This is a willfully self-serving denial of the obvious hierarchical differences between the two sons. Laboring under this error of insight, Gloucester allows Edmund to trick him into turning against Edgar, who is driven away, as Cordelia and Kent have been driven away by Lear. The downward slide of England is then echoed in both families: As Gloucester pretends there is no difference between Edgar and Edmund, so Lear treats Albany and Cornwall, Cordelia and her two sisters, as equals. Lear's family, Gloucester's family, and England itself become divided against themselves, and as Shakespeare's audience knew well, "Every kingdom divided against itself, shall be brought to naught, and every city or house divided against itself shall not stand" (Matthew 12:25).

Both Kent and Edgar, under the threat of death, disguise themselves by a highly significant lowering of their status. Kent pretends to be a plain-speaking servant, Edgar a nearly naked mad beggar, the lowest level in the human hierarchy to which a man can sink. Gloucester does not choose to lower himself, but is forced. At his lowest he is physically blinded, and the moment he is so, he sees clearly that he has been deluded, that Edgar, his true son, has been betrayed by the evil Edmund. Lear is similarly driven down the scale of creation against his will. His own lowest point is reached when he is driven mad by the insupportable conflict between his willful delusion and the facts of reality.

Lear's exchange with Kent, who is sitting in the stocks in II.iv, exemplifies the conflict:

Lear:	What's he that hath so much thy place mistook To set thee here [i.e., in the stocks]?
Kent:	It is both he and she, Your son and daughter.
Lear:	No.
Kent:	Yes.
Lear:	No, I say.
Kent:	I say yea.
Lear:	No, no, they would not.
Kent:	Yes, they have.
Lear:	By Jupiter, I swear no.
Kent:	By Juno, I swear ay. (II.iv.12–22)

The essence of Lear's pride is that the family, the nation, the world, the elements, even the gods must behave according to his will. When they fail to do so, he flies into raging and cursing. But raging and cursing and willfulness do not work against the facts of reality—not against the evil of the two daughters, not against the war among the elements that is the great storm, not against the will of the gods. Since Lear's will does not give way to these realities, reality must break his will—and it does. As Gloucester must be blinded before he can see who is good and who evil, Lear must go mad before he can understand what it means to love and to be loved. (In the 1983 TV production of the play, directed by Michael Elliott, Lear, played by Laurence Olivier, and Gloucester, played by Leo McKern, sit together on the heath. Gloucester's head, slightly lower, is encircled by a bloody bandage over his eyes, and Lear's head, slightly higher, is encircled by a crown of weeds. The parallel blindings, Gloucester's physical and Lear's mental, are thus astutely made visible.[1])

In addition to the pagan setting and the double plot, Shakespeare invents a unique character to illustrate what is happening in the mind of Lear. On the surface, the Fool is an example of the court jester or the "allow'd fool" (*Twelfth Night* I.v.94) that any ruler might keep in the household to be sure that someone, at least, is telling him or her the truth without flattery. But this fool has an additional function. He appears when Cordelia has been banished and he disappears before Lear's reunion with her. So in one sense he is the persisting voice of her truth. At a deeper level yet, the Fool is an incarnation of the wisdom of Lear himself—separated from Lear's mind into an external character as a kind of representation of Lear's having willfully separated himself from his own wisdom. The Fool remains external so long as Lear's will and his wisdom are at war, and he is charged with voicing the truth that Lear refuses to face but must know deep in his soul. Once Lear's willful mind is broken into shards and through madness his awareness begins to be healed with truth, the Fool disappears, as if reintegrated into the mind of Lear, who, when he wakes in the presence of Cordelia, is slowly revealed in his new condition of humility and love. In short, the Fool is, ironically, the voice of wisdom in the mind of a wise man fallen into folly.

In Act I, Scene ii, the villain Edmund expresses his worship of nature, which he uses to justify his increasing villainy (I.ii.1–22). In the end, however, the wheel of his fortune "comes full circle" (V.iii.175) (see the discussion of Fortune in Chapter 7 of Part 1). And then, at the last possible moment, Edmund chooses to do some good "Despite of mine own nature" (V.iii.244–45). This kind of spiritual turning at the point of death is fairly common in Shakespearean drama. Using his free will to do some good for a change, Edmund may have hope of redemption. The parallel children by contrast, the two evil daughters of the King, die murdering and self-murdered, unredeemed and destined for hell.

But how can the end of this play be said to be about healing when the innocent Cordelia dies along with the guilty? The question is answered by recognizing that such a death, though tragic, is not the end of the story either for Shakespeare's characters or for his audience. For them the context of life is neither the pagan shadow world of Hades nor modern existentialist annihilation but the same divine will that governs reality through all time whether pre-Christians know it or not. That reality does not guarantee justice in this life, but for those whose will is turned toward the good it does guarantee redemption from suffering in the next. For all men it guarantees ultimate meaning, even in suffering and death.

Lear's final words express the essence of the most fundamental paradox of human life: we live and then we die. What does it mean to have lived if at the end of life we die? But the play does not leave us in modern existential nihilism or agnostic ignorance. Because the soul of Lear has been healed by love, his mission is complete and he leaves the world of time, space, and body in a state of pure love of his daughter Cordelia, the sacrificial victim, who, like Desdemona in *Othello*, goes stainless to heaven.

Lear's final words have been thought to be evidence that Shakespeare, at least in his "tragic" middle period, held a bleak view of human life. Lear dies deluded, yet again, into thinking Cordelia is alive when we know she is dead. But this reading misses the point. Once again the key lies in the Gloucester plot. Edgar reports that he had revealed himself to Gloucester in his role as guide and as savior from despair (V.iii.191–92). Then he adds

> But his flaw'd heart
> (Alack, too weak the conflict to support!)
> 'Twixt two extremes of passion, joy and grief,
> Burst smilingly. (V.iii.197–200)

Gloucester has died between the two extremes of passion: joy at the reunion with his now newly beloved Edgar, and grief at his own error in having wronged him and at the suffering that resulted. This sentence is a precise gloss also on the death of Lear. In anguish at Cordelia's death,

he cries, "Thou'lt come no more, / Never, never, never, never, never"
(V.iii.308–309). This is the voice of his deepest grief, at his own having
wronged Cordelia, and at her loss to him in death. Next he says, "Pray
you undo this button." What is this button? At the literal level, it is a
button on his shirt. He is having trouble breathing. Like Gloucester's
(V.iii.197–200) and Kent's (V.iii.217–18), Lear's heart is breaking. But it is
also metaphorically the mysterious button that ties the soul to the body.
Lear is asking for his soul's deliverance.

Before he is released, however, he has a final vision: "Do you see this?
Look on her! Look her lips. / Look there, look there!" (V.iii.311–12). At the
literal level, he believes he sees Cordelia's lips moving, meaning she is
not dead after all but is still alive. We know that at this level he is in error.
She really is dead. But *is* he deluded? If the Christian and Platonic view
of reality is true, as Shakespeare believed, even though it is unknown
within the pagan setting of the play, Cordelia's soul is not dead but lives.
Lear has said earlier, hoping to see the feather stir at her lips,

> If it be so [i.e., that she is alive],
> It is a chance which does redeem all sorrows
> That ever I have felt.   (V.iii.266–68)

So purged and healed by love is Lear's soul now that he can assert that, if
Cordelia lived, his joy in her would outweigh all his long arc of suffering.
His pride has been abolished, and what is left is the potential for joy in the
love of Cordelia. He then actually comes to experience that joy at his last
moment. Informed by that earlier assertion, we hear in his final words that
he has moved from the grief of those *never*'s to pure joy at what can only
strike Shakespeare's audience as Lear's experience, even before he is quite
dead, of something like redemption, or resurrection, or the next life. (How
poor are our words by comparison with the experience that Shakespeare
provides us!) At the literal level, Lear believes he sees her lips moving. At
the metaphorical level, he sees Cordelia alive. Only then does he give up
the ghost, and there can be no doubt that Shakespeare meant us to see his
redeemed spirit united to the spirit of his innocent daughter in whatever
spiritual realm may be meant by the word *heaven*.

In *King Lear*, his greatest play, Shakespeare conveys to the audience
the experience of the purification of one person's flawed love for another
and the divine gift of the purgation of man's pride, both purification and
purgation accomplished through suffering. Thanks to the combination

of Shakespeare's deep insight about the human condition and his gift for poetic dramatization, this play is able to incarnate in our experience the invisible reality of God's love for man.

KEY LINES:

1. Following the word *nothing* through the play reveals a profound dimension to its arc of fall and regeneration. The word dramatically initiates the action when Cordelia says only "Nothing" (I.i.87) in refusing to compete with her sisters' flattery. Lear challenges her with "nothing will come of nothing" (I.i.90), alluding to the principle that God created the world *ex nihilo*, out of nothing, but human beings cannot make anything without starting with some raw material already created by God. Lear repeats that Cordelia will have nothing from him (I.i.200, 245). In the next scene Edmund uses exactly Cordelia's phrase in a calculated lie (I.ii.31), and Gloucester says, "Come, if it be nothing, I shall not need spectacles" (I.ii.34–35), foreshadowing the relation between "nothing" and Gloucester's metaphorical and later physical blindness. The key to all the uses of the word lies in the Fool's question, "Can you make no use of nothing, nuncle?" (I.iv.130–31). By the end of the play we will understand that God makes use of "nothing," not only by creating *ex nihilo*, but by making "nothing" of a man's pride in order to make "something" out of the man himself. The Fool implies that a wise man recognizes that in the eyes of God he is and has "nothing," whereas Lear will have to be made nothing of before he learns it. Unlike Lear, who refuses to bend his will to reality, Edgar chooses to lower himself in order to save himself: "Edgar I nothing am" (II.iii.21). Other significant instances include the Fool's "thou hast par'd thy wit o' both sides and left nothing i' th' middle" (I.iv.187–88), Kent's "Nothing almost sees miracles / But misery" (II.ii.165–66), Lear's "Couldst thou save nothing?" (III.iv.64) and "nothing could have subdu'd nature / To such a lowness but his unkind daughters" (III.iv.70–71), and Edgar's "In nothing am I chang'd / But in my garments" (IV.vi.9–10). Metaphorically, in having become nothing, Edgar is changed from rejected to beloved son with the change he has helped to foster in his father. As Gloucester himself observes, often "our mere defects / Prove our commodities" (IV.i.20–21), that is, our utter deprivation (= having "nothing") is sometimes to our benefit. Gloucester's sight is made into nothing so that he can have insight, and trying and failing to nothing himself by jumping from a cliff that is in fact nothing, he is healed by the love of his true son. Lear has asked, "Who is it that can tell me who I am?"

to which the Fool responds, "Lear's shadow" (I.iv.230–31), that is, the nothing where light would fall were Lear not obstructing it. Along with his mind, Lear's willfulness is turned to nothing so there may be room in it for the something that is love.

2.   At II.iv.302–304 Regan says, "to willful men. / The injuries that they themselves procure / Must be their schoolmasters." This is a major theme of the play, though it is spoken by a villain who fails to heed her own words. Regan speaks out of selfish rebellion and not in hope of Lear's regeneration, but the platitude is true, and the play dramatizes it.

3.   The words of Gloucester's despair, "As flies to wanton boys are we to th' gods, / They kill us for their sport" (IV.i.36–37), are not to be taken as final as they have been by some readers. Gloucester's despairing thoughts are healed by the "miracle" orchestrated by Edgar (IV.vi.55) and by Edgar's telling Gloucester of their "pilgrimage" (V.iii.197).

4.   Oswald perfectly expresses his own corruptly inverted loyalty in criticizing Albany: "What most he should dislike seems pleasant to him; / What like, offensive" (IV.ii.10–11). The words are true of himself and their opposite is true of Albany, who says later in the scene, "Wisdom and goodness to the vile seem vile, / Filths savor but themselves" (IV.ii.38–39).

5.   The parallel process of rebirth from self-regard to caring for others in both Gloucester and Lear is clear in the comparison of these two passages:

Lear: Poor naked wretches, wheresoe'er you are,
               That bide the pelting of this pitiless storm,
               How shall your houseless heads and unfed sides,
               Your loop'd and window'd raggedness, defend you
               From seasons such as these? O, I have ta'en
               Too little care of this! Take physic [= medicine], pomp,
               Expose thyself to feel what wretches feel,
               That thou mayst shake the superflux to them,
               And show the heavens more just.   (III.iv.28–36)

Gloucester: heavens, deal so still!
               Let the superfluous and lust-dieted man,
               That slaves your ordinance, that will not see
               Because he does not feel, feel your pow'r quickly;
               So distribution should undo excess,
               And each man have enough.   (IV.i.66–71)

("Superfluous" means over-indulged, having too much, and "slaves your ordinance" means enslaves your rules to his own willfulness.) These parallel sentences are not prescriptions for some communistic social program but indications of the birth of charity in the souls of two previously self-regarding men.

6.   At the beginning of the play, Cordelia has said, "what I well intend, / I'll do't before I speak" (I.i.225–26), setting it against "To speak and purpose not" (I.i.225). In Act IV, when Cordelia asks King Lear, just waking from his period of madness, for his benediction, Lear tries to kneel to Cordelia (IV.vii.58) and then says, "Pray you now forget, and forgive" (IV.vii.83). Later, Lear says, "When thou dost ask me blessing, I'll kneel down / And ask of thee forgiveness" (V.iii.10–11). Thus Lear's period of suffering has burnt away all blustering speech and willfullness in him. He has already done in Act IV what in Act V he says he *will* do, fulfilling the virtuous principle articulated by Cordelia in the beginning, doing the good deed before ever speaking of doing it.

SPECIFIC NOTES TO HELP IN YOUR READING:

1.   III.ii.27–34: The Fool's poem is about putting the lower in place of the higher. Housing a "codpiece" (the pouch that in Renaissance breeches holds the male genitals, metaphorical for the penis) before housing one's head (i.e., fornicating before marrying and establishing a household) leads to head and genital lice and beggary. In beggary, the beggar, whose body feeds many lice, must depend on many other people rather than on one helpmeet. Similarly, being led by one's toe rather than one's heart, that is, one's physical desires rather than love, dooms one to misery at the material losses that are inevitable.

2.   III.ii.81–94: The obscurity of the Fool's prophecy as printed in F (the speech is not in Q) can be resolved by moving up the lines "Then shall the realm of Albion / Come to great confusion" to follow "No heretics burn'd, but wenches' suitors." The first four lines of the prophecy, which describe a society in corruption, are summed up by the concluding phrase "great confusion," everything the opposite of what it should naturally be. The rest of the speech describes a society in harmony and concludes with "Then comes the time . . . / That going shall be us'd with feet," i.e., that people will walk using their feet, meaning society will operate in a natural rather than an unnatural way.

3.   The smiles ascribed by the Gentleman to Cordelia at IV.iii.16–24 are smiles not of happiness but of patience, which is striving against

the tears of sorrow. The theme of the speech is not the antithesis happy/ sad but rather "Patience and sorrow strove / Who should express her goodliest," that is, sunshine/smiles/patience contrast with rain/tears/ sorrow.

---

[1] Michael Elliott, director, *King Lear* (Granada Television, UK 1983, USA 1984; Kultur DVD), 1:52:35.

Macbeth

Motivated by ambition, Macbeth and Lady Macbeth represent the masculine and feminine versions of the human choice to go against one's own nature and the moral law. In Shakespeare the word *ambition* implies not merely the aim to improve oneself or one's circumstances. It is a negative term implying a desire to step above one's rightful place in the hierarchies of the state and of the world (see Chapter 7 of Part 1). Hence the Macbeths' ambition itself is unnatural and immoral and, if not checked, will lead inevitably to unnatural and immoral acts. In *Hamlet* Claudius confesses his motive for killing the king to be "my crown, mine own ambition, and my queen," none of which rightfully belongs to him. It is the same with Macbeth and his wife. Their bad motive—"Vaulting ambition" (I.vii.27)—is to step above their proper place, to be monarchs in the place of the rightful king (Duncan) and his rightful heir (Malcolm). Their evil motive is then pursued with evil means, namely the killing of the King. That act constitutes a violent attack not only on the man and on the state of Scotland, which he embodies (see The Two Bodies of the King in Chapter 7 of Part 1) but on the order of human society and the order of the universe that it reflects, as Macbeth himself recognizes:

> He's here in double trust:
> First, as I am his kinsman, and his subject,
> Strong both against the deed; then, as his host,
> Who should against his murderer shut the door,
> Not bear the knife myself. (I.vii.12–16)

In addition, Duncan has been a good king. Hence killing Duncan goes against human nature, universal hierarchy, moral law, societal stability, and personal conscience.

Lady Macbeth's version of "Vaulting ambition," expressed as her desire for "solely sovereign sway and masterdom" (I.v.70), impels her to call for her feminine compassion to be turned not merely to masculine strength but to cruelty:

> Come, you spirits
> That tend on mortal thoughts, unsex me here,
> And fill me from the crown to the toe topful
> Of direst cruelty! . . .
> Stop up th' access and passage to remorse . . .   (I.v.40–44)

These masculine and feminine versions of the same choice are not caused by the prophecies of the Weird Sisters, who have the power to tempt but not to destroy, as we see in the matter of the unfortunate sailor (see Key Line 1). The Witches' prophecies to Macbeth form a temptation to which Macbeth and Lady Macbeth *might* have responded with patience and humility, as we know from the response of Banquo to the prophecy about *him*. Banquo first recognizes the appearance of the Weird Sisters as a possible temptation of the devil:

> . . . oftentimes, to win us to our harm,
> The instruments of darkness tell us truths,
> Win us with honest trifles, to betray 's [= us]
> In deepest consequence.   (I.iii.123–26)

Then he explicitly renounces the use of evil means to achieve the desirable end:

> Macbeth: If you shall cleave to my consent, when 'tis,
>   It shall make honor for you.
> Banquo: So I lose none
>   In seeking to augment it, but still [= always] keep
>   My bosom franchis'd and allegiance clear,
>   I shall be counsell'd.   (II.i.25–29)

Despite Banquo's example, Macbeth and his wife, tempted by the Witches' promise of kingship, make the evil choice in Act I and act on it at the start of Act II. The rest of the play depicts the consequences of that choice and that action. The consequences include horror among all who witness the discovery of the murder; escape to safety by the King's rightful heirs (II.iii.135ff.); inversions in the order of the natural universe, including owl screams and cricket cries (II.ii.15), storm (II.iii.54–63), darkness at noon (II.iv.5–10) as at the death of Jesus (Mark 15:33, etc.), an attack on a falcon by a small mousing owl (II.iv.12–13), and the disobedience of the king's horses and their attempt to devour one another (II.iv.14–18). To these are added the additional murders committed by Macbeth in order to secure his position and Ross's later description of the chaos and suffering of all of Scotland (IV.iii.164–76).

These chaotic consequences are accompanied by two other movements, one external and one internal. In the outer world, in response to the disorder, all the forces of good gather and rise up to expel Macbeth and his wife from the kingdom and from the natural and human worlds. The good Macduff, having convinced the rightful heir of his loyalty, joins him in mounting a counter-attack against the tyrant. The blessed King Edward the Confessor of England sends an army to support them. The trees of Birnam Wood offer disguising branches. Decent men, previously afraid to do so, leave Macbeth to fight on the side of the right. The sword arm of Macduff acts for all these forces when he finally defeats and kills Macbeth.

While this external reversal is developing, there is also a decay taking place within the souls of Macbeth and Lady Macbeth, a decay made visible to us through their words and actions and the words of others. As the tide turns, we are given a vivid image of Macbeth's condition:

> Now does he feel his title
> Hang loose about him, like a giant's robe
> Upon a dwarfish thief. (V.ii.20–22)

This speech subtly recalls both the damned thief and the damned tailor in the Porter's imaginary hell (see Key Line 7 below). The ambition of Macbeth and his wife drives them to betray truth, duty, virtue, justice, and order, and by means of equivocation, hypocrisy, murder, theft, and cruelty they achieve an illusory external success. But it is at the cost of their souls. Though salvation was certainly open to them, as Shakespeare and his audience believed, it could come only with true repentance. However, both Macbeth and Lady Macbeth repeatedly and resolutely choose not to repent but rather to confirm themselves in sin.

Though she has cynically said "A little water clears us of this deed" (II.ii.64), Lady Macbeth is condemned by her own guilt to relive the night of the murder and its horror over and over, no amount of imaginary water, let alone real water, clearing her of anything, until she kills herself in despair (V.ix.36–37). Macbeth, even in the face of defeat, decides it is better to kill others than to kill himself:

> Why should I play the Roman fool, and die
> On mine own sword? Whiles I see lives the gashes
> Do better upon them. (V.viii.1–3)

("Lives" here is the noun, not the verb.) Having chosen to murder Duncan, Macbeth has thereby murdered his own capacity for peaceful sleep (II. ii.32–40). In the great and terrifying "Tomorrow" speech (V.v.19–28), Macbeth reveals himself to be in complete despair, not only of life, but of all its possible meaning—the fitting and inevitable end of a man who has warred against every value that gives meaning to life, the "honor, love, obedience, troops of friends" he despairs of earlier (V.iii.25).

Macbeth's conclusion that "Life's . . . a tale / Told by an idiot, full of sound and fury, / Signifying nothing" (V.v.26–28) not only depicts the utter despair that inevitably leads to damnation in the afterlife. It reveals that Macbeth, like his lady, is already in hell even before he dies. His soul is now nothing but the awareness of the eternal agony of meaninglessness. Lady Macbeth's sleepwalking nightmare and Macbeth's despair together present Shakespeare's most explicit evocation of the meaning of damnation: Hell is not merely a place to which one is sent for punishment but, as in Dante's earlier *Divine Comedy* and Milton's later *Paradise Lost*, the eternal condition of the self-damning soul.

Finally, the play illustrates the structure of reality. The difference between evil and good is not arbitrary. It is built in to the nature of the universe and the nature of man. That structure makes it impossible to enjoy any promised good that is pursued with evil. The play thus illustrates the implication of the question in the Gospel of Mark: "For what shall it profit a man, though he should win the whole world, if he lose his soul?" (Mark 8:36, Geneva Bible). Macbeth has said, "For mine own good / All causes shall give way" (III.iv.134–35). Acting on that principle, he discovers that what he thought his own good could not be enjoyed when divorced from the good of the whole. Seeking his own good alone in fact turns his good to evil, and then to nothingness. By evil means he gets what he thought he wanted and finds that, like the Witches' prophecies, it is not what it promised to be. Not because kingship itself is nothing, but because, betraying all value, Macbeth has made a nothingness of himself.

KEY LINES:

1. At I.iii.4–25 the First Witch describes a sailor whom she intends to torment. Importantly she concludes her verse with

> Though his bark cannot be lost,
> Yet it shall be tempest-toss'd. (I.iii.24–25)

That is, she does not have the power to destroy the sailor; she has only the power to raise a tempest that will toss him about. The implication is that the Witches cannot determine life and death. That determination is God's alone. They can test and tempt men but not destroy them. The power to ruin a human soul lies only in the soul's own free will. This line has crucial implications for the play: Macbeth and Lady Macbeth cannot be damned by the intentions or prophecies of the evil supernatural powers but only by their own free-will choices to ally themselves with those powers. The evil Witches turn out to be external representations of the soul's own capacity to be tempted to choose evil.

2. At I.iii.149–50 Macbeth begins his career of lying by saying "my dull brain was wrought / With things forgotten" when in fact—as we know from his soliloquy—he was thinking about the hypothetical future rather than the past. This lie begins the descent that ends in despair, death, and damnation—or rather damnation and death, since, like Friar Alberigo and Branca d'Oria in the ninth circle of hell in Dante's *Inferno*, Macbeth is already damned even before he dies.

3. Macbeth's soliloquy at I.vii.1–28 lists all the reasons for not killing Duncan and the inevitable reaction of horror that will come from doing so. He recognizes the evil of his intention and confesses his motive to be nothing but ambition (see Specific Note 4 below).

4. The Thane of Cawdor is a crucial foil for Macbeth. First there is the powerful foreshadowing rhyme:

> Go pronounce his present death
> And with his former title greet Macbeth. (I.ii.64–65)

Then in I.iv we discover how Cawdor died:

> . . . very frankly he confessed his treasons,
> Implored your highness' pardon, and set forth
> A deep repentance. (I.iv.5–7)

As soon as we are told this, Duncan says,

> There's no art
> To find the mind's construction in the face.
> He was a gentleman on whom I built
> An absolute trust. (I.iv.11–14)

At which precise moment, ironically, Macbeth enters. Now Macbeth is the Thane of Cawdor. On him, too, Duncan will build an absolute trust, again misreading the mind behind the face, and Macbeth will prove an even more significant traitor than the former Cawdor. It is left to Duncan's son Malcolm to discover the "art / To find the mind's construction in the face," and we will see him applying that art in testing Macduff at IV.iii.1–137 (see Specific Note 10 below). At the end Macbeth will resolutely persist in his battle against the good and, in contrast to the former Cawdor, will die unrepentant and in despair.

5. Both Lady Macbeth and Macbeth call upon nature to keep their murder secret:

> Macbeth: Stars, hide your fires,
> Let not light see my black and deep desires (I.iv.50–51)

> Lady Macbeth: Come, thick night,
> And pall thee in the dunnest smoke of hell,
> That my keen knife see not the wound it makes,
> Nor heaven peep through the blanket of the dark
> To cry "Hold, hold." (I.v.50–54)

> Macbeth: Thou sure and firm-set earth,
> Hear not my steps, which way they walk, for fear
> The very stones prate of my whereabout,
> And take the present horror from the time,
> Which now suits with it. (II.i.56–60)

Macbeth's line "take the present horror from the time, / Which now suits with it" means simply that he wants nothing to prevent this horrible murder from happening at this most opportune moment for it to happen. Macbeth and Lady Macbeth are two versions of one evil mind, asking the natural world to go against itself and to serve them in what they well know are unnatural and selfish aims. It is significant that both of them get exactly what they ask for—the night of the murder is dark and stormy and nothing gives Macbeth away before the deed is done. But though they get what they thought they wanted, they soon find out that they have killed all the good that it can do them by having killed the good in themselves. Compare this to the prophecies of the Witches and to Macbeth's demands of the Ghost of Banquo in the banquet scene, discussed in Key Line 9 below.

6. Macbeth's resolution in setting off to kill Duncan is expressed in slow and calm rhyming: "Hear it not, Duncan, for it is a knell / That summons thee to heaven or to hell" (II.i.63–64). But once the murder is done, the language of the dialogue between Macbeth and his wife is violently disjointed and chaotic:

> Macbeth: I have done the deed. Didst thou not hear a noise?
> Lady Macbeth: I heard the owl scream and the crickets cry.
> Did not you speak?
> Macbeth: When?
> Lady Macbeth: Now.
> Macbeth: As I descended?
> Lady Macbeth: Ay.
> Macbeth: Hark! Who lies i' th' second chamber?
> Lady Macbeth: Donalbain.
> Macbeth: This is a sorry sight. (II.ii.14–18)

The "sight" is of Macbeth's own bloody hands. The act of killing the King has exploded the illusion of a safe and tranquil usurpation with happy results, the "trammel[ed] up . . . consequence" and "success" that Macbeth imagined at I.vii.1–4, and now chaos governs both in Macbeth's mind and in the world. (Compare this alteration from calm to chaotic rhetoric with the similar alteration in Othello's speech in V.ii of *Othello*.)

7. Though the Porter's speech (II.iii.1–21) offers what some like to call "comic relief"—relaxation of emotional tension and preparation for greater emotional intensity—it also provides significant thematic intensification. The knocking at the gate that began in the previous scene (II.ii.54) continues. Coming in to answer that knocking, the Porter pretends to be busy welcoming imaginary souls into an imaginary hell, giving us three examples:

a) The Porter's imaginary farmer, having invested everything in the hope that a bad crop year would drive up prices to his profit, finds that a bumper crop has ruined his expectations. He had hoped to gain from the suffering of others; their benefit and his loss drive him to suicide and damnation.

b) An equivocator is a man who, arrested for heretical beliefs and treasonous plots, swears to an apparent loyalty in ambiguous language that he intends to mean one thing to the authorities and another to God. The Porter's imaginary equivocator has fooled the authorities, but he could not fool God. This theme of equivocation is developed through the play. All the Witches' prophecies are equivocal, seeming to mean something attractive but turning out to mean something ironically quite different. Macbeth himself has prophesied his own fate by saying "damn'd [be] all those that trust them" (IV.i.139). Too late he begins "To doubt th' equivocation of the fiend / That lies like truth" (V.v.42–43), and too late comes his resolution:

> And be these juggling fiends no more believ'd,
> That palter with us in a double sense,
> That keep the word of promise to our ear,
> And break it to our hope. (V.viii.19–22)

c) A tailor in Shakespeare's day would be given money to buy fabric with which to make the clothes he sells. The Porter's imaginary tailor has been caught skimping on the fabric in making the clothes so he can profit from the stolen portions. English hose were loose so that without discovery one could use less fabric than was paid for. French hose were tight-fitting so that the habitual theft of the English tailor in making them would be easily discovered.

The Porter ends his list with "What are you?" to imply, perhaps looking at the audience, "for what sins am I welcoming *you* to hell?"

Each of the crimes mentioned by the Porter applies metaphorically to Macbeth. Like the farmer, he has founded his own self-aggrandizement on the sufferings of others. Like the equivocator he has pretended to loyalty while in fact being a traitor. And like the tailor, he is a thief, stealing the kingdom from its rightful owner. For this reason, the last line of the speech, "I pray you remember the porter" (II.iii.20–21), bears a triple significance: The Porter is putting out his hand for a tip from Macduff; he is pointedly warning the audience members about the fate in store for any sinners among them who remain unrepentant; and he is instructing us to keep the thematic significance of his three damned souls in mind as the story of Macbeth unfolds.

8. Macbeth, who has envied Duncan for his kingship and killed him to take his place, then expresses no less envy of Duncan for his peace in death. Macbeth muses,

> Better be with the dead,
> Whom we, to gain our peace, have sent to peace,
> Than on the torture of the mind to lie
> In restless ecstasy. Duncan is in his grave;
> After life's fitful fever he sleeps well.
> Treason has done his worst; nor steel, nor poison,
> Malice domestic, foreign levy, nothing,
> Can touch him further. (III.ii.19–26)

("Ecstasy" here means frenzy, agitated madness.) This suggests that envy is the condition of soul Macbeth has chosen. The envy of the demonic Iago of *Othello* is here incarnated in one who has reached the top of the human hierarchy. But being a sin in the will, envy cannot be assuaged by any external gains, even of kingship, any more than mere physical water without penitence can clear the conscience of Lady Macbeth.

9. In III.iv, the banquet scene, it is noteworthy that once again Macbeth gets exactly what he calls for. The Ghost of Banquo takes literally what Macbeth says hypocritically. When Macbeth pretends to flatter the murdered Banquo publicly by saying "our country's honor" would be "roofed" [i.e., present under the roof of this house] if only Banquo were present (ll.39–40), Banquo's ghost appears. When Macbeth says "Would he were here" (l. 90), the Ghost appears again. When Macbeth cries "Hence!" (ll. 105–106), the Ghost departs. This ironical obedience of the Ghost to Macbeth's commands dramatizes the hypocritical divorce between Macbeth's words and his will, while illustrating most terrifyingly that though reality gives Macbeth everything he wants (as in Key Line 5 above), it turns out not to be what he imagined his "black and deep desires" (I.iv.51) would yield. Again, it is the nature of reality that success achieved through evil cannot be enjoyed.

SPECIFIC NOTES TO HELP IN YOUR READING:

1. In Macbeth's soliloquy at I.iii.134–42, several words need clarification. In the phrase "that suggestion / Whose horrid image doth unfix my hair," "suggestion" means temptation. The image of his being king, initially presented by the Weird Sisters, in Macbeth's mind becomes the temptation to kill Duncan in order to make the prediction come true. The "horrid image" is the image of killing the King, which throws Macbeth's body into terrified chaos—hair standing on end, heart knocking at ribs—"Against the use [= normal condition] of nature." To this extent Macbeth is simply human, horrified by what would—and ought to—horrify anyone. "Present fears / Are less than horrible imaginings" means that the killing of Duncan, which is at this point only "fantastical," i.e., merely imaginary, not yet realized, frightens him more than the actual dangers of the battlefield from which he has just come. The normal functioning of his body "Is smother'd" under the "surmise" that is his image of killing the King. And "nothing is but what is not" means nothing is real to him except what is not real yet. In short, the killing of the King that he imagines doing is more real and more terrifying to him than any killing in war (for the sake of the King) that he has actually done.

2. For a detailed discussion of Lady Macbeth's speech at I.v.60–70, see Example 1 under Sound and Sense in Chapter 1 of Part 1, which points out the composite experience Shakespeare gives us of the image of the serpent, the idea of Satan, the ambitious desire for "solely sovereign sway and masterdom," and the sound of hissing.

3. At I.vii.7, in the phrase "we'd jump the life to come," the word "jump" means risk. Macbeth says that he would be willing to risk eternal damnation if he could be sure that "here, upon this bank and shoal of time," meaning on this side of death, he could avoid the bad consequences of the evil act he is contemplating.

4. I.vii.25–28 presents a challenging condensation of metaphors. Macbeth concludes his soliloquy thus:

> I have no spur
> To prick the sides of my intent, but only
> Vaulting ambition, which o'er leaps itself,
> And falls on th' other—

A rider wears spurs on his boots with which to prick the sides of a horse to make it leap a stream or barrier. Here the horse is Macbeth's intention (to become king by killing the King) and the spur is his ambition. "Vaulting ambition" might mean that Macbeth has an ambition to vault (from his present position into the kingship), or it might mean that his ambition itself is vaulting (overreaching). Or it might mean both at once. The ambition then "o'erleaps itself, / And falls on th' other—." Many editors gloss this as the image of either a rider who leaps too forcefully onto the saddle and falls on the other side of the horse or a horse that leaps too soon, too high, or too far and falls on the other side of the barrier. The image of the spur in line 25 gives weight to the latter image. But the word *side*, which some editors insert, making "And falls on th' other side" does not appear in the text. What can "fall on th' other" mean without that word *side*, which is a pure editorial conjecture? The answer lies in another meaning of the phrase *to fall on*, namely to attack. In this sense, the ambition o'erleaps *itself* (that is, goes beyond its proper limit, as in Shakespeare it is the essence of *ambition* to do) and literally falls on, in the sense of "attacks," the *other* (i.e., Duncan). But to this literal sense should be added the metaphysical idea that by "falling on" the King, in the sense of attacking and killing him, Macbeth will also fall from the pinnacle of fortune, his own kingship, into defeat and death, and from the pinnacle of grace into sin, and thence into hell. The image of *falling on the other* thus unites the physical attack on the King, the collapse of the ambition itself, and the fall into damnation, embodying in a single phrase the union of free will choice, physical action, and spiritual consequence.

5.   At I.vii.60, Lady Macbeth says, "But screw your courage to the sticking place . . ." The word *But* here means "only" or "just." The words "screw" and "sticking place" are metaphors alluding to the crossbow, some models of which were cocked with a screw mechanism like a windlass. The sticking place is the point on the shaft of the crossbow at which the string or band, when screwed to its limit, was hooked to the trigger. The metaphor gains force from the fact that at various times during the Middle Ages the use of the crossbow was banned by the church and by some kings, and from the fact that, though less efficient than a longbowman (two shots per minute for the crossbow vs. twenty shots per minute for the longbow), a crossbowman required far less training and was therefore afforded far less honor, though it took courage to man a crossbow during battle because of the time required to reload it. Hence, Lady Macbeth is using the image of a fierce weapon in the hands of a lower ranking and possibly dishonorable soldier whose courage is essential to wielding that instrument of death.

6. At III.i.67–69 Macbeth repines that he has "mine eternal jewel / given to the common enemy of man / To make them kings—the seeds of Banquo kings." The "common enemy of man" refers to Satan, and "mine eternal jewel" means his own immortal soul.

7. The Third Murderer in III.iii is sometimes said to be Macbeth himself, but there is no textual evidence for this supposition. There is also no explicit indication that he is the devil. However, because of the significance of the number three in this play (three witches, three early prophecies, three later prophecies, three entrants into the Porter's imaginary hell, and so on), we may suppose that the addition of a Third Murderer gives the murderers a supernatural dimension. The Third Murderer is the one who asks "Who did strike out the light?" and "There's but one down; the son is fled," recalling the limitation on the forces of darkness implied by the First Witch at I.iii.24–25 (see Key Line 1). Compare this mysterious third murderer to Macbeth's calling out to Seyton at V.iii.19–20, discussed below in Specific Note 12.

8. All of III.v, IV.i.39–43, and IV.i.125–32, along with the songs included there in some editions, are spurious. They are not written by Shakespeare, and their inclusion distracts from the integrity of the play. Except by textual scholars, they should be ignored (see Chapter 14 of Part 1).

9. At III.vi.1–20 Lennox must be understood to be criticizing Macbeth with veiled but bitter sarcasm. In Macbeth's Scotland speaking directly can be fatal.

10. In IV.iii it must be understood that Malcolm's self-accusations are fabrications to test the loyalty of Macduff. As dramaturge Dakin Matthews astutely observes, Malcolm accuses himself in increasing degrees of evil: first of lust, i.e., a sin of the body or of the vegetable soul (ll. 60–65), then of avarice, i.e., a sin of the heart or of the sensible soul (ll. 78–84), and lastly of malice, i.e. the sin of the mind or of the intelligible soul, the sin of Satan (ll. 91–100).[1] If Macduff were to support the claim to the throne of one as evil as Malcolm makes himself out to be, it would signify that Macduff did not care about Scotland but only about tricking Malcolm into returning to be killed as Macbeth would desire. When Macduff rejects such a king as Malcolm paints himself to be (IV.iii.102–114), Malcolm realizes that Macduff's loyalty is genuine. Malcolm has learned from painful experience the "art / To find the mind's construction in the face" (I.iv.11–12) that his father had once innocently but fatally claimed not to exist (see Key Line 4 above).

11. At IV.iii.146–59 Malcolm reports that the touch of Edward the Confessor, the English king, cures the disease called "the king's evil." That disease is now called scrofula. The healing touch was a heavenly gift supposedly passed down to every succeeding king of England, including James I, who was king when this play was written. The report emphasizes that the King is "full of grace" (l. 159), which implies that his military support of Malcolm's claim to the throne of Scotland has the blessing of heaven.

12. At V.iii.19–20, Macbeth calls out for a follower named "Seyton." The pronunciation guides tell us the name is probably to be pronounced *SEE-tun*. But it is likely that in Renaissance English the diphthong *ey* and the long *a* were nearly indistinguishable. In any case, Shakespeare must have intended the audience to hear the name "Seyton" as very close to, if not identical with, "Satan." The implication is that the character and his name exist to cause us to hear Macbeth calling for the attendance and assistance, not of God, but of the devil. (See also Specific Note 7 above).

13. At V.vii.10 Young Siward says to Macbeth "Thou liest," claiming not to find Macbeth's name "fearful" though he finds it "hateful." Young Siward's bravery is confirmed at V.ix.12–13 when Siward asks about his dead son, "Had he his hurts before?" That is, were his wounds on the front or on the back of his body? Ross answers "Ay, on the front," meaning Young Siward died bravely, facing Macbeth, not running away.

---

[1] Dakin Matthews in Podcast #26 "The World, the Flesh, and the Devil" in his series "Sheltering with Shakespeare," at https://www.youtube.com/watch?v=lgd3KiOE8nM&feature=youtu.be.

Antony and Cleopatra

Antony and Cleopatra is the last and most mature of Shakespeare's three plays named for pairs of lovers. The conflict in the early romantic tragedy *Romeo and Juliet* is between love and death, youthful impetuosity meeting a "star-crossed" fate in the form of a feud between families. In the satire *Troilus and Cressida* both love and death are trivialized by the corruption of heroic ideals. In *Antony and Cleopatra* Shakespeare expands the tragedy of love and death to the world-historical stage in a supreme example of the incarnational style (see Universal Realism in Chapter 1 of Part 1)—that capacity to dramatize realistic particulars and universal generalities in one set of words, characters, and actions, and thereby in one single experience of meaning.

The conflict between universal opposites dramatized in *Antony and Cleopatra* may be characterized in any number of ways: as West vs. East, mind vs. nature, reason vs. passion, duty vs. self-indulgence, conquest vs. suicide, and order vs. chaos. But the drama is played out in a pageant of the lives of real historical figures. Shakespeare's Octavius Caesar is the particular figure we know from history even as he embodies, in himself and in his career, the first of each of the pairs of abstractions listed above: Rome and the rational mind and duty and the order of the West, which grow in effective power until Octavius, consolidating the conquests of Julius Caesar, subdues the known world to his government. Similarly, Cleopatra is the seductress we know from history, even as she embodies the second of the pairs of abstractions—Egypt and the passion and self-indulgence and mystical impracticality of the East, which are governed by feeling and mere nature and are represented by the life-giving Nile River and its death-dealing serpents. Antony is the historical Antony brought to life, even as he embodies the conflict between these two opposite worlds and worldviews, between which he vacillates.

Octavius conquers the practical world of fact, but he cannot govern the extreme passion that draws Antony to Cleopatra. That world-dividing passion, culminating in the suicides of the lovers, conquers the human imagination mythically—their names title the play—but it cannot survive in the world in the face of Caesar's practicality. The tragedy lies in the irreconcilable conflict between the two worlds—Rome/reason/duty and Egypt/passion/self-indulgence—embodied in the lives of the characters. Under Shakespeare's masterful hand, we experience as a single thing the conflict between Caesar's historic destiny and the particular world-conquering passion of Antony and Cleopatra. To this conflict Shakespeare gives a "local habitation and a name" (as Theseus calls it in *A Midsummer Night's Dream*, V.i.17), thereby making it both universally significant and thoroughly and believably personal.

The only early text of *Antony and Cleopatra* is in the First Folio. The plot is based mainly on the life of Marcus Antonius in Thomas North's English translation (1579) of Jacques Amyot's French translation (1559) of Plutarch's *Parallel Lives of the Greeks and Romans*. The play was written in about 1606–7, probably after *Macbeth* and before *Coriolanus*. The language of the play is rich and intense and mostly clear; there are few significant cruxes.

The first half of the play scintillates with wit and cleverness, not least in the inventiveness of Cleopatra in winding her toils around the heartstrings of Antony, who finds that "every thing becomes" her—"to chide, to laugh, / To Weep" (I.i.49–50). She begs him to tell her how much he loves her (I.i.14); she sarcastically tells him to obey the commands to leave her that she imagines coming from Antony's wife Fulvia and his co-triumvir Caesar (I.i.20–32); she calls him a liar while wanting his words to be true (I.i.40, I.iii.39); she refuses to "look upon him" (I.ii.87); to Charmian she says,

> See where he is, who's with him, what he does.
> I did not send you. If you find him sad,
> Say I am dancing; if in mirth, report
> That I am sudden sick. (I.iii.2–5)

When he appears a few lines later, she pretends to be dying (I.iii.13–17); then she pretends to chase him away (I.iii.33); then "Cut my lace, Charmian" [to relieve her bursting heart], followed immediately by "let it be; I am quickly ill, and well, / So [= so long as] Antony loves" (I.iii.71–73). When Antony threatens really to lose his temper with her, she says, "forgive me, / Since my becomings kill me when they do not / Eye well to you"

(I.iii.95–97). When Charmian says that Cleopatra would do better to "cross him in nothing," Cleopatra replies, "Thou teachest like a fool: the way to lose him" (I.iii.9–10). These wildly inventive vacillations in Cleopatra take on tragic proportions when she causes her fleet to turn tail and flee the sea battle (III.x) and later when, to avoid his wrath, she sends word to Antony that she is dead (IV.xiii–xiv).

Another fount of wit is the plain-speaking Enobarbus. About the death of Antony's troublesome wife, Fulvia, he says, "the tears live in an onion that should water this sorrow" (I.ii.169–70). He engages in sallies of wit with Antony in an attempt both to affirm the "wonderful piece [= masterpiece] of work" (I.ii.153–54) that is Cleopatra and through satire to cause Antony to get some distance from her. About Cleopatra's likely response to news that Antony must leave her, he says,

> Cleopatra, catching but the least noise of this, dies instantly; I have seen her die twenty times upon far poorer moment. I do think there is mettle in death, which commits some loving act upon her, she hath such celerity in dying.   (I.ii.140–44)

To this Antony responds with a phrase that takes on mythic significance: "She is cunning past man's thought" (I.ii.145), whereupon Enobarbus ironically confirms her cunning by pretending to deny it:

> Alack, sir, no, her passions are made of nothing but the finest part of pure love. We cannot call her winds and waters sighs and tears; they are greater storms and tempests than almanacs can report. This cannot be cunning in her; if it be, she makes a show'r of rain as well as Jove.   (I.ii.146–51)

Yet for all his satire, Cleopatra continues to cultivate her "celerity in dying" through the play until she dies indeed. And for all his awareness of her cunning, Antony cannot avoid being ruined by loving her.

The inventive language seen in the wit of the early acts rises into language of mythic grandeur as the lovers approach their deaths and Caesar his triumph: A soldier, about strange music heard "Under the earth":

> 'Tis the god Hercules, whom Antony loved,
> Now leaves him.   (IV.iii.16–17)

Antony about himself:

> Unarm, Eros. The long day's task is done,
> And we must sleep.   (IV.xiv.35–36)

>   I, that with my sword
> Quarter'd the world, and o'er green Neptune's back
> With ships made cities, condemn myself to lack
> The courage of a woman—less noble mind
> Than she which by her death our Caesar tells,
> "I am conqueror of myself."   (IV.xiv.57–62)

Caesar about Antony:

>   I must perforce
> Have shown to thee such a declining day,
> Or look on thine; we could not stall together
> In the whole world. But yet let me lament . . .
> That thou, my brother, my competitor
> In top of all design, my mate in empire,
> Friend and companion in the front of war,
> The arm of mine own body, and the heart
> Where mine his thoughts did kindle—that our stars,
> Unreconcilable, should divide
> Our equalness to this.   (V.i.37–48)

Cleopatra about Antony:

>   the odds is gone,
> And there is nothing left remarkable
> Beneath the visiting moon.   (IV.xv.66–68)

> His face was as the heav'ns, and therein stuck
> A sun and moon, which kept their course, and lighted
> The little O, th'earth. . . .
> His legs bestrid the ocean: his rear'd arm
> Crested the world, . . . For his bounty,
> There was no winter in't; . . . His delights
> Were dolphin-like, they show'd his back above

The element they liv'd in. In his livery
Walk'd crowns and crownets; realms and islands were
As plates dropp'd from his pocket.   (V.ii.79–92)

Cleopatra about herself:

> what's brave, what's noble,
> Let's do't after the high Roman fashion,
> And make death proud to take us.   (IV.xv.86–88)

> My resolution's plac'd. I have nothing
> Of woman in me; now from head to foot
> I am marble-constant; now the fleeting moon
> No planet is of mine.   (V.ii.238–41)

> Give me my robe, put on my crown, I have
> Immortal longings in me.   (V.ii.280–81)

All of this heightened language, calling upon the vast geography of the universe to exalt the lovers and their conqueror, raises the famous story itself to the level of universal myth. It is precisely the opposite movement from that of *Troilus and Cressida*, in which all the famous heroism is disintegrated amidst worldly decay. Here all worldliness—conquest of war and passion of love—is raised by the language to the extremest pitch of world-historical importance.

The mythologizing language is counterbalanced by the character of Enobarbus, who is entirely Shakespeare's invention. Plutarch gives us the name of Enobarbus but not his character. In the role of Enobarbus Shakespeare puts the world-historical story into perspective.

The first thing to say about Enobarbus is that he is a plain speaker, a type on the Elizabethan stage like the character that Kent in *King Lear* pretends to be when he goes into disguise. Enobarbus speaks truth as he sees it. Pompey says of Enobarbus, "Enjoy thy plainness, / It nothing ill becomes thee" (II.vi.78–79). He can speak in exalted language too, especially in his justly famous description of Cleopatra (II.ii.191–239), but he also serves as a counterweight to the exaggerated glorifications of both Antony and Cleopatra. That is until he condemns himself for betraying them (IV.vi.29–38).

Because of his plain speaking, to others and more importantly to himself, Enobarbus serves as a trustworthy commentator. He is obviously moved by Cleopatra's charms, as an observer though not a lover, but he also can see her manipulations and (from the Roman viewpoint) her follies. He is a perfect servant for Antony because he both has Roman values *and* can see why Antony won't leave Cleopatra despite her abuses of him in his efforts to remain a Roman. The double reverse of Enobarbus at the end—leaving Antony and then repenting for having done so—is in a sense the reflection, in the mirror of his loyalty, of Antony's own wavering between Roman thoughts and the Serpent of Old Nile. Enobarbus has blamed Antony for the disaster at sea because he "would make his will [i.e., sexual passion for Cleopatra] / Lord of his reason" (III.xiii.3–4) and follow "the itch of his affection" which "nick'd his captainship" (III.xiii.7–8). (*Nicked* is a term from the dice game called *hazard* and means "cut into" or "got the better of.") Because of the conflict within Antony between Rome and Egypt, the loyal Enobarbus is at war with himself:

> Mine honesty and I begin to square [= face off against one another].
> The loyalty well held to fools does make
> Our faith mere folly; yet he that can endure
> To follow with allegiance a fall'n lord
> Does conquer him that did his master conquer,
> And earns a place i' th' story. (III.xiii.41–46)

Despite his Roman loyalty, a few lines later, hearing Cleopatra temporize with Caesar's messenger, Enobarbus says, aside as if to Antony,

> Sir, sir, thou art so leaky
> That we must leave thee to thy sinking, for
> Thy dearest quit thee. (III.xiii.63–65)

By the end of the scene, seeing Antony fantasizing about valorously winning a losing battle, Enobarbus observes about Antony,

> Now he'll outstare the lightning: to be furious
> Is to be frighted out of fear, and in that mood
> The dove will peck the estridge; and I see still [= always]
> A diminution in our captain's brain
> Restores his heart. When valor preys on reason,

It eats the sword it fights with. I will seek
Some way to leave him.   (III.xiii.194–200)

(An "estridge" is a kind of hawk.) Those eight monosyllables—"I will seek / Some way to leave him"—are fiercely telling. Enobarbus does abandon Antony, but when a soldier tells Enobarbus that "Antony / Hath after thee sent all thy treasure, with / His bounty overplus" (IV.vi.19–21), Enobarbus cannot bear his own betrayal of Antony's nobility.

I am alone the villain of the earth,
And feel I am so most. O Antony,
Thou mine of bounty, how wouldst thou have paid
My better service, when my turpitude
Thou dost so crown with gold! This blows my heart.
If swift thought break it not, a swifter mean
Shall outstrike thought, but thought will do't, I feel.
                                                          (IV.vi.29–35)

("Blows" here means swells to bursting.) He is right. Conflicted thought itself does it. He dies, without having to kill himself, crying, "O Antony!" (IV.ix.23). Thus, the conflict between Rome and Egypt, Caesar and Cleopatra, mind and heart, is incarnated not only in Antony but also in Enobarbus.

As a former colleague of mine has said, the death of Enobarbus is utterly un-Roman. Simply, he dies of a broken heart. But there is a marvelous Shakespearean reason for it. He dies of a combination of shame and love, that is, of having shamed his love of Antony's nobility. It is one more example of how the this-worldliness in the play is suffused by an almost transcendently metaphysical commitment to passion, the heart, love, as if the universe were trying to give birth to a revelation of the super-reality and pre-eminent value of love above all else and could not (yet) quite do so. Not only Enobarbus but Iras, too, dies of no physical wound but simply of a broken heart. Eros dies of love because he would rather die than see Antony die. Charmian does the same in relation to Cleopatra. Everybody is literally dying of love. Except Caesar. But Caesar must not, because it is his destiny—though he esteems the lovers and their deaths—to unite and pacify the Roman Empire, whose own destiny, as Shakespeare and his audience believed, was to become the seat of the world religion arising from the birth, in a manger in Roman Judaea, of a greater and redeeming doctrine of love.

The play is not explicitly Christian. But it seems to be Shakespeare's effort to make the greatest lovers of the ancient historical world into a pageant of the furthest that natural man can imagine going in giving up the world for love. Cleopatra is in love with Antony but even more in love with his and others' love for her. As the poet Philip Thompson writes:

> The irresistible magic of Shakespeare's Cleopatra lies in her self-centered but universal erotic vision, in her "poetic" imagination that makes erotic myth of all experience and with its fullness suspends all disbelief regarding its divine source of inspiration.

> Think on me
> That am with Phoebus' amorous pinches black
> And wrinkled deep in time.   [I.v.27–29]

> A wrinkled, sun-browned body worthy of some aging, perpetually beach-bound modern vacationer is here transformed into the coat of arms of Eros himself (painted by his deputy Apollo). She has her own vision of "the love that moves the sun and the other stars" [the last line of Dante's *Divine Comedy*]: it is desire for her.[1]

Antony is divided and rushes back and forth between Rome and Egypt, between duty to Rome and love for Cleopatra. Enobarbus sees both and at first thinks this radical love is madness. Then he feels it is better to succumb to that madness than to betray it for Caesar. Then he betrays it, and then repents for betraying it. Caesar himself must defeat Antony because, to establish and embody Rome, he must resist the disorderly valuing of passion of those who betray him, the dissolving of order in the waters of the Nile. But even in his conquest Caesar says, "yet let me lament" (V.i.40) the passionate Antony whom the fates have decreed he must defeat.

"The god Hercules," that is, the spirit of triumph in battle, "whom Antony lov'd," mystically "leaves him" before Antony's last battles (IV.iii.16–17). But the language of Antony's death, like that of the deaths of Cleopatra, Enobarbus, Iras, and Charmian, and even the pronouncement of Caesar upon them, proclaim the longing for a world in which love is realer than death. Shakespeare's audience believed that they knew what the ancient Romans did not: how that longing could be fulfilled. The play powerfully presents an image of how such a fulfillment might look—though in a pagan way misread—in the lives and deaths of lovers, including Enobarbus, who had not the benefit of revelation but only their own transcendence-hungry passion to lead them. Caesar, speaking about the *Pax Romana* to come, must have been heard by Shakespeare's audience to be speaking unwittingly of the birth of Christianity:

> The time of universal peace is near.
> Prove this a prosp'rous day, the three-nooked world
> Shall bear the olive freely. (IV.vi.4–6)

"Three-nooked" refers to the three realms—namely Asia, Africa, and Europe—into which, after the great flood, God had parceled the world to the three sons of Noah—Shem, Ham, and Japheth (Genesis 9:19 and 10:1–32). All three "nooks" come under the rule of Rome, and the olive they bear symbolizes peace.

However much or little Shakespeare expected to call to the mind of his audience the Christianity that would resolve the paradoxes between reason and passion, or East and West, the story itself unites those paradoxical opposites in our experience of the play. In the concluding lines of the play Caesar echoes Enobarbus (III.xiii.46) in referring to the story itself, in which he has not only *a* place, like Enobarbus, but the pre-eminent place:

> No grave upon the earth shall clip in it
> A pair so famous. High events as these
> Strike those that make them; and their story is
> No less in pity than his glory which
> Brought them to be lamented. (V.ii.359–63)

That is, the story of these lovers is as full of pity for them as of glory for their conqueror (namely Octavius himself). Here Caesar sums up the contrasting forces that the story has united—not only Rome and Egypt, West and East, reason and passion, but here, in its ending, glory and pity. In doing so, he goes as far as Shakespeare believed the Roman imagination could go in uniting the world-historical opposites. At war in the world, they are united in the story. But Shakespeare has gone further than his character in the uniting of apparently paradoxical opposites: By his own pre-eminent art, he has united the general to the particular, incarnating universal meaning in the particulars of the story and its characters. Only the story to be told at Jerusalem, as Shakespeare believed and as this play hints, could unite such opposites in ultimate reality, and that story was to be crafted by the only hands greater than Shakespeare's at the art of incarnation.

KEY LINES:

1. Compare how messengers with bad news are treated by the rational Romans and by the passionate Cleopatra: Antony says, "Who tells me true, though in his tale lie death, / I hear him as [= as if] he flatter'd" (I.ii.98–99). Caesar responds to a message of bad news, "I should have known no less" (I.iv.40). Pompey says, "I could have given less matter [= less significant news] / A better ear" (II.i.31–32). By contrast, when Cleopatra hears news she does not like, she says to the messenger, "The most infectious pestilence upon thee!" (II.v.61) and then, the stage direction tells us, "*Strikes him down*" (II.v.61 s.d.). She adds, "Though it be honest, it is never good / To bring bad news" (II.v.85–86), and then she dismisses the messenger with no tip but only his own bad news for reward (II.v.103–106). In this difference in the treatment of messengers we see the difference between the virtue of Rome and the passion of Egypt.

2. The whole conflict of the play is pictured in little in several lines from Act II. Maecenas says, "Now Antony / Must leave [Cleopatra] utterly" (II.ii.232–33). Enobarbus replies, "Never, he will not: / Age cannot wither her, nor custom stale / Her infinite variety" (II.ii.233–35). Maecenas says, "If beauty, wisdom, modesty, can settle / The heart of Antony, Octavia is / A blessed lottery to him" (II.ii.240–42). The contrast between Cleopatra and Octavia is here explicit, Egyptian seductiveness vs. Roman virtue. Octavia, Caesar's sister, is the bait to lure Antony back to Rome and to peace with Octavius. But in the next scene, Antony asks the Soothsayer "whose fortunes shall rise higher, / Caesar's or mine?" (II.iii.16–17). The Soothsayer says, after two and a half empty feet for effect, "Caesar's" (II.iii.18). Then he explains:

> Thy daemon, that thy spirit which keeps thee, is
> Noble, courageous, high unmatchable,
> Where Caesar's is not; but near him, thy angel
> Becomes a fear, as being o'erpow'r'd: therefore
> Make space enough between you . . . thy spirit
> Is all afraid to govern thee near him;
> But he away, 'tis noble. (II.iii.20–31)

Antony himself confirms the Soothsayer's words: "He hath spoken true. The very dice obey him [meaning Caesar], / And in our sports my better cunning faints / Under his chance [meaning luck]" (II.iii.34–36). Antony concludes, "I will to Egypt; / And though I make this marriage [to Octavia] for my peace, / I' th' East my pleasure lies" (II.iii.39–41). Cleopatra, being the queen of Egypt, is often called "Egypt"—by Antony (III.xi.51,56, IV.xv.18,41), by Iras (IV.xv.70), by Caesar (V.ii.115)—in keeping with the Elizabethan notion of the two bodies of the king (see Chapter 7 in Part 1). Here, when he says "I will to Egypt," Antony means both the land of Egypt and its queen. In the world of this play, Rome and Egypt are irreconcilable. From Shakespeare's point of view, the historical world had to wait for a higher power to incarnate the ultimate reconciliation between mind and heart.

3. There is a brief but telling antithesis in the speech of Menas at II.vi.118–19: "I think the policy of that purpose made more in the marriage than the love of the parties." The antithesis is between policy (i.e., politics, plotting) and love. Here again, in little, is the great antithesis of the play: reason vs. emotion, politics vs. love, Rome vs. Egypt.

4. In a series growing more urgent, Antony calls for and addresses his servant Eros: "What, Eros, Eros!" (IV.xii.30); "Unarm, Eros" (IV.xiv.35); "Come, Eros, Eros!" (IV.xiv.54); "Eros" (IV.xiv.71); "Now, Eros" (IV.xiv.93). Having lost the sea battle, and later hearing that Cleopatra is dead (though she is not yet), Antony cries out for his servant Eros and soon thereafter commands Eros to kill him. Eros kills himself instead. In all this addressing of the servant, Shakespeare must mean us to hear Antony crying out—in equal parts of desire and anguish—as if to erotic love itself.

5. Note Shakespeare's daring irony in Cleopatra's expressing the fear that, if she is captured alive,

> The quick comedians
> Extemporally will stage us, and present
> Our Alexandrian revels: Antony
> Shall be brought drunken forth, and I shall see
> Some squeaking Cleopatra boy my greatness
> I' th' posture of a whore. . . .
> Nay, that's certain. (V.ii.216–22)

We have seen Antony drunk on liquor (II.vii, and cf., I.iv.4–5, II.ii.177–78, II.v.21, IV.ii.21) as well as on love, and the actor playing Cleopatra in

372 | Tragedies Antony and Cleopatra

Shakespeare's theatre is indeed a boy. It is "certain" because we have just seen it, confirming that Cleopatra's prophecy reaches far beyond Rome, even though she was not taken there alive. Yet so compelling is the force of the story, the characters, and the poetry, that the witty meta-theatrical self-consciousness can only enhance, not interrupt, the drama.

SPECIFIC NOTES TO HELP IN YOUR READING:

1. In the first speech of the play, Philo, Antony's friend and fellow Roman, expresses disapproval of Antony's "dotage" on Cleopatra. Note how Shakespeare uses the rhetorical devices of alliteration and consonance to incarnate in our audible experience the essential conflict of the play. Specifically listen to how the plosive sounds of *b, t, p,* and *d* are contrasted with sibilant *ps, st, sf,* and soft *l* sounds to embody the conflict between Rome and Egypt, the Roman *b* repeatedly driving to the Egyptian *l* and *s* in the very words "burst," "buckles," and "breast" and the Roman *t* and *p* dissolving in the *sf* and *l* of "strumpet's fool." All of this rhetorical point is summed up in the last three words, "Behold and see":

> his captain's heart,
> Which in the scuffles of great fights hath **burst**
> The **buckles** on his **breast**, reneges all temper,
> And is **become** the **bellows** and the fan
> To cool a **gypsy's lust**. . . .
> Take but good note, and you shall see in him
> The **triple pillar** of the world transform'd
> Into a **strumpet's fool**. Behold and see.   (I.i.6–13)

This conflict between plosives and sibilants in the very beginning of the play sets up symbolically and onomatopoetically the thematic conflict of the play. (Note the Roman "trumpet" absorbed within Nile-like *s*'s of "strumpet's.") Here, in sounds, the Rome that is in Antony is melting not in the Tiber, as Antony imagines a few moments later (I.i.33), but in the Nile that is Cleopatra.

2. Notice the shifts between verse and prose in I.ii. Antony speaks in verse when contemplating the death of his wife, Fulvia (ll. 122–30). When Enobarbus enters to engage in banter about how their leaving Egypt will kill the women (i.e., Cleopatra), he and Antony speak in prose (ll. 131–75). Enobarbus concludes the prose passage with the sexual innuendo about Cleopatra's "business" depending on Antony's "abode" (ll. 173–75). Then Antony, saying "No more light [= frivolous] answers," returns to verse (ll.

176–96). The shifts in tone are thus conveyed not only in the sense of the words but in the shifts between verse and prose, an example of decorum in speech discussed in Chapter 7 of Part 1.

3.   Cleopatra's "Ha, ha!" at I.v.3 indicates not laughter but sighing or yawning.

4.   At II.ii.44 "the word of war" means the watchword of the war, the person in whose name it was pursued, as also in "his name / That magical word of war" at III.i.30–31.

5.   At II.ii.48–51 Antony asks,

> Did he not rather
> Discredit my authority with yours,
> And make the wars alike against my stomach,
> Having alike your cause?

This apparently cryptic question may be paraphrased thus: "Did he [my brother] not rather bring my authority into discredit along with yours, and make wars against my desire as against yours, I having the same cause [i.e., the same purposes or aim or matter in hand or grounds for objection] as you?" In short, didn't my brother act just as much against me as against you?

6.   At II.ii.52-54 Antony says, "If you'll patch a quarrel, / As matter whole you have to make it with, / It must not be with this." The antithesis is between "patch" and "matter whole": patching up (= concocting) a quarrel out of bits and pieces vs. having a substantial and complete justification for the quarrel. The lines may be paraphrased thus: "If you are going to invent a quarrel out of bits and pieces of complaint, you will not be able to use, as a sufficiently complete justification, *this* matter to do it with"—"this matter" referring to Caesar's accusation that Antony's "wife and brother / Made wars" against Caesar on Antony's behalf (ll. 42–44). Editors explain the passage in two ways, both misleading and unnecessary: a) Some read "As" to mean "Even though"—"If you will make a quarrel out of bits and pieces even though you have a complete and substantial reason to quarrel . . . ." b) Some follow Rowe in emending "you have" to "you have not" or "you've not"— "If you will make a quarrel out of bits and pieces, since you have got no complete and substantial reason to quarrel . . . ." But if we understand the phrase "as matter whole you have to make it with" to modify the phrase "with this" in the next line, the meaning is clear and simple enough without emendation: "It must not be with *this* matter [that

you patch up a quarrel] as [if it were] sufficient matter with which to make [i.e., justify] a quarrel."

7. II.v.1–2: Compare "Give me some music; music, moody food / Of us that trade in love" with "If music be the food of love, play on" (*Twelfth Night*, I.i.1).

8. II.v.8–9: Compare "And when good will is show'd, though't come too short, / The actor may plead pardon" with "For never any thing can be amiss, / When simpleness and duty tender it" (etc.) (*A Midsummer Night's Dream*, V.i.82–105).

9. II.vi.71–73: When Pompey asks Enobarbus, "how far'st thou, soldier?" Enobarbus replies, "Well, / And well am like to do, for I perceive / Four feasts are toward." There is a pun here on the two senses of "fare": to get along and to eat. In other words, "How are you doing?" "I am doing well" and "I am likely to eat well since there are to be four feasts."

10. Compare the suggestion of Menas to Pompey at II.vii.64–73 to kill his guests with Antonio's temptation of Sebastian in *The Tempest* (II.i.204–294).

11. IV.xi.1: "But [= except for] being charg'd, we will be still [= quiet, inactive] by land"—i.e., Unless we are charged at (by the opposing army), we will not fight by land.

12. IV.xii.25–29: Antony says, "O this false soul of Egypt . . . / Like a right gipsy, at fast and loose / Beguil'd me to the very heart of loss." The word "gipsy" is a common corruption of *Egyptian* and here makes for a pun. "Fast and loose" is a cheater's (by stereotype a gipsy's) betting game: "A leathern belt is made up into a number of intricate folds, and placed edgewise upon a table. One of the folds is made to represent the middle of the girdle, so that whoever should thrust a skewer into it would think he held it fast to the table; whereas, when he has so done, the person with whom he plays may take hold of both ends, and draw it away."[2] This commonplace phrase for cheating also appears in *Love's Labour's Lost* (I.ii.155–57 and III.i.103) and *King John* (III.i.242).

---

[1] Thompson adds: "In a typical sonnet of the period, the elements' actions can be seen as responses to the charms of the poet's beloved, but here the woman speaks on her own behalf, her myth containing realistic portraiture instead of sonneteering statuary, and what is 'conceit' in poetry becomes a passionate state of mind, a reality."—From "Reflections (Literary and Philosophical)" in Philip Thompson, *Dusk and Dawn: Poems and Prose of Philip Thompson*, ed. Gideon Rappaport (San Diego: One Mind Good Press, 2005), p. 187.

[2] Sir I. Hawkins, quoted in M.R. Ridley, ed., *Antony and Cleopatra*, The Arden Shakespeare (Cambridge, MA: Harvard University Press, 1954, reprint 1956), p. 180, note to IV.xii.28.

Histories

Introduction to the History Plays

Assuming that he is the author of *Edward III* (see Chapter 13 of Part 1), Shakespeare wrote eleven plays based on English history. The first (*Edward III*) and last (*Henry VIII*), constructed as pageants, bracket two tetralogies (from the Greek *tetra*, four). These eight plays are historical dramas that record the history of the Wars of the Roses. *King John*, about a king who lived a century and a half before Edward III, is thus the one English history play unrelated to those wars. Though the date of *King John* is debated, it was most probably written in 1590, around the time of the three Henry VI plays of the earlier tetralogy.

It is important to remember that the first tetralogy written (composed c. 1589–93) treats of the later period of the Wars of the Roses, and the second tetralogy written (composed c. 1595–99) treats of the earlier period. One may read the plays in order of composition, with an eye to the growth of Shakespeare's mastery of the medium, or in order of the plot, with an eye to the unfolding of the long conflict in historical time.

The sources of Shakespeare's history plays are the chronicle histories of England, in particular Edward Hall's *Union of the Two Noble and Illustrate Famelies of Lancastre and York* (1548), and Raphael Holinshed's *Chronicles of Englande*, 2nd ed. (1587), both of which included redacted versions of many earlier historians. By our standards, Shakespeare's use of his sources is striking: in some ways faithful, in others cavalier. In studying the history plays one must distinguish not only between history as record and history as drama, but also between post-nineteenth-century standards of academic historical accuracy and the standards of historical writing of Shakespeare's time and earlier. No history written by human beings can ever be untainted by point of view, but modern history, unless tainted by ideology, generally aims at hard factual evidence regardless of theme. The earlier view was that history should be instructive, that the significance of facts is dependent on the general truths revealed by them. Hence Shakespeare's history plays, like the chronicles on which they are based, subordinate factual detail to thematic purposes. Shakespeare's goals are a) to make English history come alive for his audience, and b) to reveal in that history the moral structure of historical reality. To serve these purposes, Shakespeare will often add or subtract the details and characters and adjust the timelines of his sources. As the poet Philip Thompson writes, "Government and its actions are moral and religious functions and comprehensive allegories in all of Shakespeare, and his political scenes always embody a moral and religious drama."[1]

Together the two tetralogies dramatize an image of England as having fallen into a period of corruption and tribulation followed by expiation and redemption. The corruption and deposing of Richard II are England's fall, resulting in an entire age of rebellions and civil wars that bedevil the nation. The corruption and tribulation are temporarily interrupted by the glorious rule of Shakespeare's short-lived hero-king, Henry V, after which England descends deeper than ever into evil and chaos, which climax in the rise to power of the arch-villain Richard III, seen in part as a scourge of God. When he is finally defeated and killed, England is reborn under Henry VII, the founder of the Tudor line, whose descendants ruled during Shakespeare's own time. Philip Thompson describes as follows that sweep of history as Shakespeare depicts it:

> Richard [II] is the Adam who through frivolity, greed and despotism literally unmade himself and his country, and from his time on, England is a fallen world (though briefly, in the state of Henry V, she has health and glory). Finally, after the long "tribulation" of Henry VI's rule, the arrival of Antichrist, who meets his destruction at the hand of the redeemer. . . .

> The fall of Richard II is original sin, a fall deserved but tragic on both the individual and the public plane—before he is overthrown, nothing appears in Richard but tyranny and insolence. Richard III's fall is pure redemption; before the battle of Bosworth there is only one just man in the court of England. [Laurence] Olivier's movie [of *Richard III*, 1955] powerfully expressed this image of England as a world utterly dominated by villains—John of Gaunt's prophecy [*Richard II*, II.i.31–138] fulfilled to the letter.[2]

As an example of Shakespeare's allegorizing of history, one can look at his treatment of deformity and of illegitimacy. Adjusting the Neoplatonic tradition, in which inward quality must show itself outwardly, as ideally it would, Shakespeare demonstrates that it is the free will rather than external show by which human beings are to be judged. This principle is embodied in the characters who are born illegitimate or physically deformed. Philip the Bastard, renamed Richard, in the play *King John*, is presented as virtuous despite his illegitimacy, just as later Edmund in *King Lear* can say, as he is dying, "Some good I mean to do, / Despite of mine own nature" (*King Lear* V.iii.244–45). Every choice of Richard III causes his character to conform to his physical deformity, as does that of Caliban in *The Tempest*, "a savage and deformed slave," the lowest of natures in human form, until the latter, his will corrected, can say, "I'll be wise hereafter, / And seek for grace" (*Tempest*, V.i.295–96). Like Edmund's, that is a conversion that Richard III never achieves, but the obstacle lies in his will rather than in his native deformity.

Shakespeare's first histories, the three parts of *Henry VI*, burst upon the English stage with a bang. Whereas previous plays about English history had been either didactic morality tales or pageants, Shakespeare brought to the moralizing of history a method and a language that were revolutionarily alive, real, and fresh. As Robie Macauley writes, "The novelist of history offers us a kind of mystery-play in which the great mass of ideas and events are concentrated into a sharp and comprehensible drama. Shakespeare's historical cycle and [Tolstoy's] *War and Peace* are such mystery-plays . . . almost the grandest of their kind."[3] Shakespeare's invention of historical drama was unlike anything previously seen (or indeed anything seen since). We may look upon the *Henry VI* plays as Shakespearean apprentice work, and so they are in light of the dramatist's steadily increasing mastery. But in the context of the time, they were seen as a thrilling and triumphant new kind of drama, and when well-acted, they remain compelling and moving to us.

The first tetralogy written ends with *Richard III*. Richard's bloody achievement of the throne and his following overthrow conclude the Wars of the Roses. A few years after writing that play, Shakespeare returned to the subject to tell how those wars began, the subject of *Richard II*. In the two *Henry IV* plays Shakespeare examines the relation of right and merit in a king and depicts the coming of age of the best king he could imagine. The second tetralogy is completed with *Henry V*, in which Shakespeare offers us his image of the ideal king and that king's ideal government. As we know from the earlier tetralogy, that hiatus in the Wars of the Roses was short-lived, but Shakespeare does his best to make it nonetheless glorious.

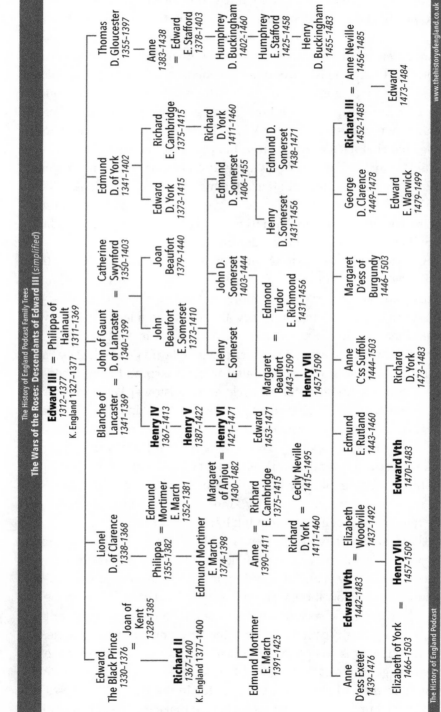

The History of England Podcast Family Trees
The Wars of the Roses: Descendants of Edward III (simplified)

www.thehistoryofengland.co.uk

The History of England Podcast

"Wars of the Roses: Descendants of Edward III (simplified)." Diagram reprinted with thanks courtesy of David Crowther https://thehistoryofengland.co.uk/resource/wars-of-the-roses-family-trees/.

—∞∞∞—

Notes to the Diagram of the Wars of the Roses:
(English monarchs are in **Boldface**)

The symbol of the House of Lancaster, descendants of John of Gaunt, Duke of Lancaster, was the red rose. The symbol of the House of York, descendants of Edmund Langley, Duke of York, was the white rose. Hence the conflicts among the descendants of the two houses were called the Wars of the Roses.

The first son and heir apparent of **Edward III** was Edward the Black Prince. Since the Black Prince died a year before his father, **Richard II**, son of Edward the Black Prince and **Edward III**'s grandson, became king.

The second son of **Edward III** was William of Hatfield (not in the diagram), who died young.

The third son of **Edward III**, Lionel, Duke of Clarence, had no sons. His daughter married Edmund Mortimer and their granddaughter married into the House of York (see below).

The fourth son of **Edward III**, was John of Gaunt, Duke of Lancaster and founder of the House of Lancaster. His son, Henry, called Bullingbrook (or Bolingbroke) deposed **Richard II** and became **Henry IV**. **Henry IV**'s son was **Henry V**, whose own son was **Henry VI**. These are the Lancastrian kings. John of Gaunt married a second wife and their great grand-daughter was the mother of **Henry VII** (whose name appears in two places in the diagram). However, between the reigns of **Henry VI** and **Henry VII** came the reigns of the Yorkist kings.

The fifth son of **Edward III** was Edmund of Langley, Duke of York and founder of the House of York. His great grandson (whose mother was the great granddaughter of Lionel, Duke of Clarence, **Edward III**'s third son and Edmund of Langley's older brother) was Richard, Duke of York. The descendants of Richard (whose name appears in two places in the diagram) became the three Yorkist kings: **Edward IV** (Richard Duke of York's eldest son), **Edward V** (**Edward IV**'s son), and **Richard III** (Richard Duke of York's youngest son and younger brother of **Edward IV**). **Richard III** was defeated in the battle of Bosworth Field by **Henry VII**.

The sixth son of **Edward III** was Thomas of Woodstock, Duke of Gloucester, murdered (as his widow claims in *Richard II*) by henchmen of **Richard II**.

Henry VII (whose name appears in two places in the diagram), founder of the House of Tudor, was the son of Edmund Tudor and of the great granddaughter of John of Gaunt, Duke of Lancaster. By marrying the daughter of the Yorkist king **Edward IV**, **Henry VII** united the two houses of Lancaster and York, putting an end to the Wars of the Roses.

Not in the diagram:

The son of **Henry VII** was **Henry VIII**, who fathered three monarchs, **Edward VI**, **Mary Tudor**, and **Elizabeth I**.

The daughter of **Henry VII**, Margaret, married James IV, King of Scotland. Their son was James V of Scotland. His daughter was Mary Queen of Scots. Her son was James VI of Scotland who, on the death of **Elizabeth I**, became **James I** of England.

Shakespeare lived during the reigns of **Elizabeth I** and **James I**.

---

[1] From "Notes on Shakespeare" in Philip Thompson, *Dusk and Dawn: Poems and Prose of Philip Thompson*, ed. Gideon Rappaport (San Diego: One Mind Good Press, 2005), p. 221.

[2] Thompson, p. 227.

[3] Robie Macauley, Introduction to Ford Madox Ford, *Parade's End* (New York: Knopf, 1961), p. ix.

Richard III

Richard III is the fourth play in the first-written of Shakespeare's two tetralogies on English History. It records the rise and fall of the brilliant but deformed and villainous Richard, Duke of Gloucester. Brazen and subtle, he labors to eliminate all the Lancastrian (Red Rose) and Yorkist (White Rose) claimants that stand between himself and the throne until he is crowned Richard III. Unintentionally serving as a scourge of God, Richard purges England of the thoroughgoing political corruption and consequent civil wars that have characterized it since the original sin of the justifiable but tragic deposing of Richard II. The purge is completed with Richard's own death.

The defeat of Richard III at the Battle of Bosworth Field is accomplished by Henry Tudor, Earl of Richmond, the great-great grandson of John of Gaunt, Duke of Lancaster. Henry marries Elizabeth, the great-great granddaughter of Edmund Langley, Duke of York. He thereby unites the houses of Lancaster and York. In assuming the throne as Henry VII, he puts an end to the Wars of the Roses and establishes the royal House of Tudor. It was his granddaughter, Elizabeth I, who was England's monarch when the play was performed.

Even audiences wowed by the three Henry VI plays would have been astonished by the compelling power of *Richard III*. In addition to its more sophisticated poetic style and its fast-moving plot, the character of Richard is both a thoroughly Machiavellian demon of immoral self-interest and a clever, subtle, and highly entertaining wit. We are elated and entertained by his brilliance even as we are horrified by his evil. He prefigures both Iago (in *Othello*) and Macbeth.

Shakespeare had begun to develop that character of Richard in the soliloquies of *Henry VI, Part 3*, when Richard, Duke of Gloucester, later Richard III, considers that "between my soul's desire [i.e., the crown] and me . . . / Is Clarence [Richard's older brother], Henry [descendant of John of Gaunt and future Henry VII], and his [Edward IV's] young son Edward [briefly later Edward V], / And all the unlook'd-for issue of their bodies [i.e., their offspring]" (*3 Henry VI*, III.ii.128–31). Richard contemplates his own body, rejecting the idea of finding "heaven in a lady's lap" (*3 Henry VI*, III.ii.148):

> O miserable thought! and more unlikely
> Than to accomplish twenty golden crowns!
> Why, love forswore me in my mother's womb;
> And . . . did corrupt frail nature with some bribe,
> To shrink mine arm up like a wither'd shrub,
> To make an envious mountain on my back,
> Where sits deformity to mock my body;
> To shape my legs of an unequal size,
> To disproportion me in every part,
> Like to a chaos . . . .
> And am I then a man to be belov'd?
>
> (*3 Henry VI*, III.ii.151–63)

These characteristics of Richard's body (hunchback, withered arm, unequal legs that caused him to limp), like Richard's wit and capacity for deceit, Shakespeare inherits from his sources. They were John Rous's *History of the Kings of England* (*Historia Regum Angliae*), Polydore Vergil's *English History* (*Anglicae Historiae*), and Thomas More's *History of King Richard III*, all of which were redacted in various ways and read by Shakespeare in Edward Hall's *Union of the Two Noble and Illustrate Famelies of Lancastre and York* (1548) and in Raphael Holinshed's *Chronicles of England* (1587). These sources were themselves based on long-standing tradition among earlier writers on Richard. Rous reports that Richard was born with teeth (cf. *3 Henry VI*, V.vi.75 and *Richard III*, IV.iv.49), was two years in his mother's womb before birth, and had uneven shoulders. More describes Richard as "little of stature, ill-featured of limbs, crook-backed." From More Shakespeare also inherited the idea that Richard's deformities were external representations of his inner character. More had "set out to present his tyrant in a satiric light, maximizing his villainy, but treating it always with irony and detachment."[1] Shakespeare preserves the villainy and increases the irony, brilliantly injecting the latter into the character of Richard himself.

In the same soliloquy from *Henry VI, Part 3*, Richard turns from considering what he cannot enjoy to what he does enjoy:

Then since this earth affords no joy to me
But to command, to check, to o'erbear such
As are of better person than myself,
I'll make my heaven to dream upon the crown . . . .

(3 Henry VI, III.ii.165–68)

Like Macbeth later, he wants to be the ultimate commander, the king.

Richard goes on to revel in his gift for duplicity by comparing himself to a list of classical archetypes of betrayal and one important modern one:

Why, I can smile, and murther whiles I smile,
And cry "Content" to that which grieves my heart,
And wet my cheeks with artificial tears,
And frame my face to all occasions.
I'll drown more sailors than the mermaid shall,
I'll slay more gazers than the basilisk,
I'll play the orator as well as Nestor,
Deceive more slily than Ulysses could,
And like a Sinon, take another Troy.
I can add colors to the chameleon,
Change shapes with Proteus for advantages,
And set the murtherous Machevil to school.

(3 Henry VI, III.ii.182–93)

(See Specific Note 1 for glosses on the classical references.) The modern archetype, "Machevil," is Machiavelli, already thought of in England at this time as the incarnation of amorality in the name of self-serving political gain (see Chapter 7 in Part 1). To "set to school" means Richard is claiming to be able to teach Machiavelli a thing or two about murder for political expediency.

Richard concludes the speech thus:

Can I do this, and cannot get a crown?
Tut [= tsk], were it farther off, I'll pluck it down.

(3 Henry VI, III.ii.194–95)

Richard's character is thus already present in *3 Henry VI*. What remains to be told is the story of how that character achieves his successful rise and meets his inevitable fall.

That rise and fall are the business of the highly rhetorical tragedy *Richard III*. The play is almost all in verse, the one significant exception being the conversation of the two murderers of Clarence (I.iv). The verse is almost all end-stopped lines, as is characteristic of the early period of Shakespeare's work. And the use of rhetorical devices, as in the other plays of Shakespeare's early period, is elaborate and obvious, indeed almost operatic. An example is the threnody in which the old Queen Margaret (widow of Henry VI), the Duchess of York (mother of the three brothers Edward IV, George, Duke of Clarence, and Richard III), and Queen Elizabeth (widow of Edward IV) lament those whom Richard has murdered on his way to the throne (IV.iv).

The use of rhetoric is not merely decorative. The rhetorical elaboration serves the multi-layered purposes of the drama, conveying meaning through the medium of the three forms of rhetoric according to Aristotle: *logos* (information and argumentation), *ethos* (attitude, moral character), and *pathos* (emotion). For example, Richard, who has just murdered Henry VI and the Prince his son, heir to the throne, woos the Lady Anne, the Prince's widow. He does so in the presence of the dead body of the king he has killed, her father-in-law, even as—in keeping with the folklore tradition—the wounds of the murdered bleed again in the presence of the murderer. And, amazingly to us and to himself, Richard succeeds in that wooing. Alone again, Richard says to the audience,

> Was ever woman in this humor woo'd?
> Was ever woman in this humor won?
> I'll have her, but I will not keep her long.   (I.ii.227–29)

One can enumerate the figures of speech in these three lines: anaphora, antithesis, assonance, consonance, alliteration, diacope, erotesis, isocolon, meiosis, etc. But here the repetitions, rhetorical questions, and balanced antithesis of "have" and "not keep" are more than punctuation. By their very nature they convey the combination of glee and murderous self-glorification that are the essence of Richard's character. In a sense, Richard is seducing us, the audience, even as he seduces Lady Anne, and even as we retain awareness of his thoroughly evil will.

The play is also built upon a series of parallel but contrasting scenes—the turning against Hastings (III.iv) and the turning against Buckingham (IV.ii); the successful wooing of Lady Anne (I.ii) and the failed wooing of Elizabeth for her daughter (IV.iv); the dream of Clarence before his death (I.iv) and the dream of Richard before his death (V.iii); the ghosts' appearance to Richard and then their appearance to Richmond (V.iii). And one by one the characters of the drama discover Richard's perfidy and fall away.

Richard is given also a series of highly theatrical performance bits: In the first wooing scene, he hands Lady Anne a sword pointed toward his own breast and invites her either to kill him or to marry him (I.ii); he disarmingly sends the Bishop of Ely out of the room for strawberries (see Specific Note 2) before reentering in a rage and ordering the execution of Hastings (III.iv); he repeatedly avoids Buckingham's request for a promised reward for his help (IV.ii, see Specific Note 3); he plays at religious piety for the London crowd by having Buckingham beg him to take up the crown and pretending to resist out of holy humility (III.vii). His smarmy pseudo-religiosity in that scene is exquisite:

> Buckingham: Come, citizens. 'Zounds, I'll entreat no more.
> Richard: O, do not swear, my lord of Buckingham.
>
> (III.vii.219–220)

Himself a cheerful breaker of at least eight of the Ten Commandments, he pretends to be offended at Buckingham's taking the name of the Lord in vain. (The exclamation "Zounds" is an oath, a shortened form of "by His [i.e., Christ's] wounds." Buckingham is pronounced "BUCK-ing-um.")

The play also makes repeated use of prophecies and omens: Richard has spread it around that "G" will murder the heirs of Edward IV (I.i.39–40) and uses it to do away with his brother George, Duke of Clarence, whose name begins with the letter G. The prophecy comes true when Richard himself, Duke of Gloucester, which also begins with the letter G, becomes the murderer. Clarence dreams of drowning in the sea before he awakes and is actually drowned in a butt of malmsey wine (I.iv); Richard reports on a prophecy about Richmond that plays on the name of a castle called Rouge-mount (IV.ii.103–107); the many bitter prophecies of the old Queen Margaret (I.iii) all come true; the Duchess of York utters curses on her son that also come true (IV.iv.184–96). Dramatic ironies are repeatedly present in the fates of nearly every member of the court, including Hastings, Buckingham, the brothers of Queen Elizabeth, the young princes, and Richard himself. By the end of *Richard III*, all the prophecies of the corruption of England that John of Gaunt will utter in *Richard II* (written later) have been fulfilled.

The extremely well-constructed plot and evocative power of *Richard III* take shape in a masterful combination of elements that Shakespeare inherited from Senecan tragedy, from the revenge play tradition, from the medieval and earlier Renaissance morality play and its Vice character, from the influence of Machiavelli, and from the Christian belief in the perennial likelihood of the appearance on earth of *the*, or *the spirit of*, or *an* anti-Christ. (The sources for the latter are 1 John 2:22 and 4:3 and 2 John 7.) All these elements are joined with vitality into the twofold nature of Richard, thoroughly, deceitfully evil, and at the same time thrillingly witty, inventive, and therefore attractive. As easily as he seduces Lady Anne he wins over the audience, though our seduction is subtler and dawns on us more slowly. And it happens even as we are perfectly aware of Richard's demonic villainy. In making Richard attractive to us, Shakespeare implicates us, along with every Englishman on the stage, in the drama of good vs. evil. Then, having revealed the war between good and evil to be within us as psychomachia as well as outside us in the world, he shows us in Richard's fall the inevitable catastrophe fated to those whose self-worship remains unrepented. Its names are despair, death, and damnation.

KEY LINES:

1. Part of what makes the character of Richard so compelling is that he repeatedly tells us in soliloquies and asides what he is and what he is doing. "I am determinèd to prove a villain" (I.i.30); "if I fail not in my deep intent, / Clarence hath not another day to live" (I.i.149–50); "I'll have her, but I will not keep her long" (I.ii.229); "And thus I clothe my naked villainy / With odd old ends stol'n forth of holy writ, / And seem a saint, when most I play the devil" (I.iii.335–37); "Thus, like the formal Vice, Iniquity, / I moralize two meanings in one word" (III.i.82–83, see Key Line 2); "I am in / So far in blood that sin will pluck on sin. / Tear-falling pity dwells not in this eye" (IV.ii.63–65); "I shall despair" (V.iii.200).

2. One of the sentences in the previous list calls for more attention. At III.i.82–83, Richard says, in an aside to the audience, "Thus, like the formal Vice, Iniquity, / I moralize two meanings in one word." The first "meaning" is in Richard's immediately previous aside to the audience, "So wise so young, they say, do never live long" (III.i.79), implying that he is already contemplating the murder of the princes. The second "meaning" he speaks aloud to the other characters: "I say, without characters fame lives long" (III.i.81); that is, *even* without written records,

fame will live on. The "one word" of two meanings is the phrase "live long." The doubleness of the two meanings is perceived only by the audience.

To "moralize" is also used in two senses: a) Literally it means to find in a phrase the moral or symbolic meaning that is different from its literal meaning. In this case, the moral meaning of "live long" in line 81 is directly opposite to the literal meaning implied in line 79: precocious boys do *not* live long; fame *does* live long. b) To "moralize" suggests a reference to the older morality plays, in which the character called the "Vice," who embodied all vices and was sometimes named "Iniquity," drove the plot. In the phrase "formal Vice," the word *formal* means conventional or typical, referring to the stock character of the Vice in the old morality plays. Antony Hammond, quoting Bernard Spivack, writes,

> in the earlier moralities the several vices which afflict mankind were individually personified; in the mid-sixteenth century a single representative figure of evil came to be called 'the Vice', who 'acquired distinctive theatrical personality and status far beyond the allegorical features'. . . . He is 'homiletic showman, intriguer extraordinary, and master of dramatic ceremonies'; . . . He displays the 'trick of tears and laughter. His weeping feigns his affection and concern for his victim; his laughter, for the benefit of the audience, declares the triumph of his subtle fraud and his scorn for the puny virtue of humanity.'[2]

Compare with Richard the references to the Vice in *Twelfth Night*, IV.ii.124, in *1 Henry IV*, II.iv.453, and in *Hamlet*, III.iv.98. Shakespeare makes of Richard more than merely a morality-play Vice. He is also a kind of devil, an anti-Christ figure, and a scourge of God. But his tone and style come from the morality play tradition.

3. In IV.ii, after spreading the rumor that the boys are illegitimate, Richard proposes murdering the two sons of his brother, Edward IV, who take precedence over Richard as heirs to the throne. The murderer Tyrrel, who has arranged for the murder of the boys, calls it "The most arch deed of piteous massacre / That ever yet this land was guilty of" (IV.iii.2–3). This is in keeping with the general attitude of Shakespeare's England that infanticide is one of the worst imaginable crimes. The same attitude stands behind the intended effect of the murder of the family of Macduff in *Macbeth* (IV.ii.83–84, IV.iii.193–219). The language of these

passages confirms the principle of J.V. Cunningham that "foreground is background" (see Chapter 7 in Part 1). Shakespeare has his characters express explicitly the background attitudes needed for the audience to appreciate the point.

4. In V.iii, on the night before the last battle, the ghosts of Henry VI, his son Prince Edward, Clarence, Rivers, Grey, Vaughan, the two young princes, Hastings, and Buckingham all appear successively to Richard in his dream and then to Richmond in his, cursing the former and encouraging the latter. The curse on Richard by all is "despair and die." When Richard awakens he accuses himself, shows he is aware of all his crimes, realizes that all his sins cry "guilty!" (V.iii.199), but at no point then or later in battle does he repent. The curse of the ghosts is therefore entirely fulfilled in the ultimate and theologically complete damnation of Richard's soul. Richard says, "I myself / Find in myself no pity to myself" (V.iii.202–203). That is, there is nothing in him that can desire forgiveness or ask for it. This is the literal meaning of despair, the conviction that one's soul cannot be saved, even by God. In Richard's case, there is nothing in him that can even *want* to be saved. The only possible consequence of this condition is damnation. Shakespeare will bring the same condition to an even higher pitch in the end of the tragedy *Macbeth*.

5. V.iv.7, 13: Richard's last line "A horse, a horse! my kingdom for a horse!" is a complex fabric of rhetorical devices, including alliteration, antithesis, assonance, consonance, diacope, ellipsis, epanalepsis, epimone, epizeuxis, hyperbole, meiosis, optatio, and symploce. Yet it strikes us with powerfully direct simplicity. Its great significance lies in its meiosis—a belittling reduction through the use of a small term for a great thing—that is both rhetorical and thematic. Having given up everything of value—family, friends, love, honor, virtue, and his own soul—in order to achieve the kingdom, Richard is now desperately willing to give up his kingdom for a mere horse. This meiosis is Shakespeare's brilliant embodiment in Richard, and in a line of verse, of the principle of all his history plays: to this pathetic end must come all pretentions to rule that divorce themselves from the universal moral principles of virtue and commitment to the common good.

SPECIFIC NOTES TO HELP IN YOUR READING:

1. In Richard's soliloquy from *3 Henry VI* discussed above (III.ii.186ff.)
   • The "mermaid" is a reference to the sirens, whose singing draws sailors to their death (Homer, *Odyssey*, XII).

- The "basilisk" was a serpent that could kill by merely looking at its victim.
- "Nestor" was the oldest of the kings that sailed to Troy to recover Helen. Homer mentions and Ovid reinforces Nestor's gift for oratory (Homer, *Iliad*, II.372, IV.293, etc.; Ovid, *Metamorphoses*, XII.63).
- "Ulysses" (Odysseus) was famed for his wiles and inventiveness (Homer, *Odyssey*).
- "Sinon" is a double agent who convinces the Trojans to accept the fatal horse into the city, because of which Troy was finally captured and destroyed (Virgil, *Aeneid*, II).
- The "chameleon," as noted by Ovid (*Metamorphoses*, XV.411–12) as well as modern science, is famously able to change its colors to disguise itself in its environment.
- "Proteus," a minor sea god with prophetic powers, also known as the "Old Man of the Sea," could change his shape when captured (Homer, *Odyssey*, IV.365–570).

2.   When Richard sends the Bishop of Ely for strawberries (III.iv.31ff.), the audience is no doubt meant to be aware of some such proverb as this, from Paradin's *Historical Devises* of 1591: "In gathering of flowers and strawberries that grow low upon the ground we must be verie carefull for the adder and snake that lieth lurking in the grass."[3]

3.   In IV.ii, to secure himself on the throne Richard asks Buckingham to consent in the deaths of Richard's nephews, the sons of Edward IV (Edward V, right heir to the throne, and his younger brother, York). The proposal is an outrage, and Buckingham wants to think it over. Buckingham's hesitation turns Richard against him. Later in the scene, Buckingham asks Richard for the earldom of Hereford, which Richard had promised him in return for his help (III.i.194–95). Richard ignores Buckingham four times. The fifth time, Richard asks "what's a' clock?" meaning what time is it, and when Buckingham repeats his request again, Richard repeats the question (IV.ii.109–111). When Buckingham says, "Upon the stroke of ten," Richard replies "Well, let it strike." Buckingham doesn't understand and asks why. Richard then says,

> Because that like a Jack thou keep'st the stroke
> Betwixt thy begging and my meditation.
> I am not in the giving vein to-day.   (IV.ii.114–16)

When Richard says, "Thou troublest me, I am not in the vein" (IV.ii.118), Buckingham realizes he is doomed to die at Richard's hands and leaves him.

In the automaton striking clocks of the Renaissance, the "jack" was the small human figure that swiveled to strike the bell on the hour. Richard is saying that Buckingham's repeated request is like the repeated clockwork striking of the bell. "Let it strike" probably means let it complete its striking of the hour and stop. In short, stop nagging me. There is also a pun on "jack" meaning lout or ill-mannered knave.

---

[1]   Anthony Hammond, Introduction to *King Richard III*, The Arden Shakespeare (London: Methuen, 1981), p. 78.

[2]   Hammond, p. 100, quoting Bernard Spivack, *Shakespeare and the Allegory of Evil* (New York: Columbia Univ. Press, 1958), pp. 135, 151, 157, 161–62.

[3]   Quoted in Hammond, p. 339 (Appendix II, n. to III.iv.32).

Richard II

The doctrine of the Two Bodies of the King, body personal and body politic, was discussed in Chapter 7 of Part 1. In *Richard II*, Shakespeare conveys an additional pair of qualities that ought to belong to a king, namely right and merit. A king rules by right only when he has inherited the throne legitimately from his predecessor. That is true even in a state like Denmark where the king must be chosen from the royal family by electors. In *Hamlet*, Claudius has forfeited his right to rule because he wrongly murdered his brother in order to become king. That being the case, Hamlet is the only legitimate heir to the throne. Illegitimacy of rule in a king implies both an immoral monarch and a precarious state.

But even a king who rules by right must also have merit. That is, he must have the abilities, the character, and the judgment to be a good king. Only thereby can he fulfill his function as the embodiment of the state. Selfishness, illegality, pride, abuse of power—these can turn even a rightful king into a tyrant.

In *Richard II*, Shakespeare depicts the deposing of one king by another. The first, Richard, is the rightful king. He is the direct and legitimate heir of his grandfather, Edward III, whose eldest son, Edward the Black Prince, Richard's father, had already died. However, Richard is a self-indulgent, unjust, and at times tyrannical man, using his position for his own gain and pleasure at the cost of his realm and his subjects. In the middle of the play, he is deposed—forced to renounce the crown and leave his office— by Henry Bullingbrook (sometimes spelled Bolingbroke), son of the Duke of Lancaster, Richard's first cousin, and a very competent, responsible, careful man, whose aim is to put England back on a solid footing. Should Richard die without an heir, Henry would be the next male in line for the throne—by descent through the male line. And England needs just such a competent and responsible king. However, Henry's right to the throne is questionable not only because Richard is alive but also because, by descent through the female, the next in line would be Edmund Mortimer,

Fifth Earl of March (great-grandson of Lionel Duke of Clarence through his daughter Philippa), whom (after the death in 1398 of Edmund's father Roger Mortimer, Fourth Earl of March) Richard himself recognized as heir presumptive.

Because, under the doctrine of the Two Bodies of the King, England and the king of England are one, John of Gaunt is right to observe that under Richard "That England that was wont to conquer others / Hath made a shameful conquest of itself" (II.i.65–66). Richard has abandoned royal duties in favor of personal self-indulgence, which he imagines his inherited right is sufficient to justify. Thus splitting right from merit and the natural man from the royal within himself, Richard splits apart England. His own fall, as Shakespeare depicts it, is also the fall of England into nearly a century of civil war.

The unfolding of the plot presents us with this tragic agony of England, moving from the government of a bad but rightful king to that of a good king whose legitimacy is in question. And this motion is embodied in the structure of the play by an expansion of the figure of speech called *chiasmus*—from the Greek letter *chi*, which is shaped like an X. It is the a-b-b-a or mirror-image structure of a line of verse. (This figure is called *antimetabole* when it repeats the same words in transposed order.) Here are some examples:

> Some **rise by sin**, and some **by virtue fall**.
> (*Measure for Measure*, II.i.38)

> Suit the **action to the word**, the **word to the action**.
> (*Hamlet*, III.ii.17–18)

> **Fair is foul**, and **foul is fair**. (*Macbeth*, I.i.11)

The structure of the whole play *Richard II* is a chiasmus of the plot: Richard (right) falls as Henry (merit) rises. This will be reversed at the play's end when Richard briefly rises in merit and Henry's right is challenged by rebellion in the kingdom. In addition, at the very moment when Richard hands the crown to Henry and they are both holding it as it passes from the one to the other, Richard speaks a verbal chiasmus (technically an antimetabole) that is the turning point of the play:

> Bullingbrook: Are you contented to resign the crown?

Richard: **Ay, no, no, ay,** for I must nothing be;
Therefore no no, for I resign to thee.   (IV.i.200–202)

"Ay, no, no, ay" has several levels of meaning, but the fundamental one is "yes, no, no, yes." It can also be heard as "I know no I," and "I know no ay." "Therefore no no" means since I know no "I," I cannot even answer "no" because I have resigned and am in no position to say "no" to your question. With this chiasmus the crown and the government of England shift from the rightful Richard to the meritorious Henry—the verbal chiasmus articulates the historical.

Because the distribution of the two qualities of right and merit is split between the two kings, the other characters in the play face a quandary: to which king are they duty-bound to be loyal—the rightful king or the competent one—and when? At the extremes, the Earl of Northumberland is one of the first to turn against Richard in favor of Henry. The Bishop of Carlisle, his antithesis, publicly denounces Bullingbrook for deposing Richard. Inside the imaginary brackets of those two, Aumerle, York's son, remains loyal to Richard too long and only rushes across to Henry at the last moment, saved by his mother and Henry's mercy from punishment for treason. One of the great portrayals in the play is that of Edmund of Langley, Duke of York, the uncle of both Richard and Henry, being the younger brother of Richard's father (Edward the Black Prince) and of Henry's Father (John of Gaunt, Duke of Lancaster). He begins in loyalty to the rightful nephew, Richard, but slowly moves through neutrality toward loyalty to the meritorious nephew, Henry. Shakespeare portrays these characters as a spectrum of loyalties to convey the dilemma into which England is thrown by the splitting of merit from right in Richard, which calls forth the answering split of right from merit in Henry.

The shift from Richard to Henry is associated with the historical movement from medieval to Renaissance concepts of kingship and the downward trajectory of history. The play begins in medieval-style ceremony and ends in Renaissance-style practical politics. Early in the play Richard sets up an old-fashioned medieval trial by combat between the opponents Bullingbrook and Mowbray, whose conflict arises from contrary claims of loyalty and betrayal (I.i and I.iii). That conflict remains unsettled when Richard prevents its resolution, and it erupts again in the beginning of IV.i. At the end of the play, Henry is threatened by rebellions and strives to consolidate his rule through force, abetted by the practical but unwelcome murder of Richard by Sir Pierce of Exton (V.iv and V.vi). Richard rests on right, and his doing so is represented by the formalities of scenes I.i and I.iii. Henry rests on merit, and the practical concerns of establishing his rule and the peace of England are represented by the throne-room deliberations and planning of scenes V.iii and V.vi.

This movement from medieval to Renaissance political action is associated with the clash of two concepts of kingship: Does the king have absolute rule by divine right or is he limited by feudal law, custom, and contract? Under the influence of the former idea, Richard believes he can do anything he wants and so appropriates the lands and wealth of Lancaster after the death of John of Gaunt. Under the influence of the latter idea, Bullingbrook believes that peers of the realm are entitled to their inheritance by the same laws and customs that justify the royal inheritance of kings and so claims his rights to Lancaster.

The shift from Richard to Henry also illustrates Shakespeare's awareness of the historical changes from what C.S. Lewis called "the medieval synthesis" to the disintegrations of the Renaissance brought on by the Reformation, the religious wars, Machiavelli, and Bacon's new science (see Disintegrating Forces in Chapter 7 of Part 1). Shakespeare's treatment of these changes illustrates the Renaissance idea that universal human history constitutes a decline from the initial perfection of the created world (imaged as the Garden of Eden in Genesis and as the Golden Age by the ancient Greeks) toward the final dissolution of the world expressed in line 12 of Sonnet 55: "That wear this world out to the ending doom."

The play's governing structure of chiasmic rise and fall is embodied in little in Act III, Scene ii, when Richard returns to England from his Irish war and Henry is gathering forces against him and executing Richard's corrupting sycophants. Here Richard alternates between joy and despair as his followers alternately attempt to cheer him and then announce that yet another of his forces has abandoned him for Henry. Richard's moments of joy are characterized by a self-indulgent and egotistical sentimentality of right. Richard imagines that his followers, his name, the natural world, angels, and God will fight for him against Henry, despite his own utter failure to govern properly or to take any responsibility for his predicament, merely because he is the rightful king. He likens himself to the sun, and imagines that his mere appearance, like the sun driving thieves into hiding, will scatter Henry's forces. He imagines that Henry's armies will be defeated by the earth of England, its spiders and toads, nettles and snakes, merely because he, Richard, rules by right (III. ii.10–26, 36–62, 83–90, 188–93). To this list of supposed defenders Richard later adds divine armies of pestilence (III.iii.85–90). Interrupting these fantasies are the reports that one force after another has gone over to Henry. These reports drive Richard into intermittent bouts of despair (III.ii.76–81, 93–103, 144–177, 204–214). The alternating rise and fall of Richard's emotions exemplify the larger pattern of rising and falling that is tied to the chiasmic structure of the play. Richard falls as Henry rises. Right falls as merit rises. At the end, as we shall see, Richard's body falls as his soul rises.

Written in the same period as *Romeo and Juliet* and *A Midsummer Night's Dream, Richard II,* like them, is dense with figures of speech in a highly wrought poetic style used to convey complexities of idea, emotion, and character, or, in Aristotle's terms, *logos, pathos,* and *ethos.* Because of this style of his verse some critics have characterized Richard as a poet. This characterization misses the point. The poetry of Richard's alternations between his self-serving claims to metaphysical right and his self-serving renunciations depicts Richard as essentially a sentimentalist—i.e., one who worships his own emotional states rather than channeling or subduing them in the name of reason and of the good government of himself and of England. Shakespeare makes Richard's poetic imagery convey not aesthetic gifts but sentimentality, a form of moral blindness.[1] Richard entertains himself with his own imagery of himself as king, as if the fact of being the rightful king were sufficient when what is called for from a king is also effective and just government. John of Gaunt's criticism of Richard's rule is accurate:

> A thousand flatterers sit within thy crown,
> Whose compass is no bigger than thy head,
> And yet, incagèd in so small a verge,
> The waste is no whit lesser than thy land.   (II.i.100–103)

Richard is a flatterer of himself, as if the fact of being the rightful king could relieve him of the duty to govern England rightly. And if England's king is corrupted, England is corrupted.

Richard's sentimental self-worship and the consequent failure to take responsibility for his kingdom is illustrated in the conversation of the gardener in III.iv, which was discussed in Chapter 6 of Part 1 as an example of how Shakespeare can use such small scenes unrelated to the main plot to contribute to the unity of theme. In that scene the metaphor of trimming and pruning a garden illustrates what is happening to England, which Gaunt has called "this other Eden, demi-paradise" (II.i.42).

Richard's moral failure is dramatized one final time in the depiction of its opposite—not now the opposite represented by Henry's practicality, but the opposite contained in Richard's first and only moral success, his own moral transformation in prison at the end of the play. In his great soliloquy (V.v.1–94) Richard, confronted with the inevitable fact of his failure, is at last moved to take responsibility. Once again there is a series of rising and falling:

> Sometimes am I king;
> Then treasons make me wish myself a beggar,
> And so I am. Then crushing penury
> Persuades me I was better when a king;
> Then am I king'd again, and by and by
> Think that I am unking'd by Bullingbrook,
> And straight am nothing. (V.v.32–38)

He concludes that he will never be eased with *having* nothing until he *is* nothing (V.v.38–41), another example of his self-indulgence in despair.

But then a significant breakthrough occurs. Someone from outside the prison tries to comfort Richard with music, the symbol of the moral, spiritual, and structural harmony built in to God's creation and longed for within the fallen and therefore conflicted self. But the music is played badly, out of time. It thus becomes, like the garden in III.iv, a symbol of Richard's life:

> How sour sweet music is
> When time is broke, and no proportion kept!
> So is it in the music of men's lives.
> And here have I the daintiness of ear
> To check time broke in a disordered string;
> But for the concord of my state and time
> Had not an ear to hear my true time broke.
> I wasted time, and now doth time waste me . . . (V.v.42–49)

That last line is yet another chiasmus (in the form of antimetabole), revealing the birth of self-knowledge in Richard. The music itself is a gift, but the more significant gift is that it is played badly, a metaphor for Richard's bad government, of which his imprisonment is the consequence. Only suffering could bring Richard to see in himself the truth of Gaunt's critique of him in II.i. In response to this suffering, Richard rises to the occasion of his imprisonment and, with the help of the badly played music, realizes the truth of his life: his failure to merit what he was given by right.

This breakthrough in Richard's knowledge of himself then leads to a moral breakthrough, a turning of his will:

> This music mads me, let it sound no more,
> For though it have holp mad men to their wits,
> In me it seems it will make wise men mad.
> Yet blessing on his heart that gives it me!
> For 'tis a sign of love; and love to Richard
> Is a strange brooch in this all-hating world. (V.v.61–66)

For the first time in his life, Richard has considered the good intention of another human being and in gratitude has uttered a blessing on someone other than himself. For once, thanks to his recognition of his own responsibility, he is able to set aside his own ego and to bless the intention of the giver of even badly played music. He regresses to habit for a moment in blaming his horse for not stumbling when Henry was on his back, but then immediately says,

> Forgiveness, horse! why do I rail on thee,
> Since thou, created to be aw'd by man,
> Wast born to bear? I was not made a horse,
> And yet I bear a burthen like an ass,
> Spurr'd, gall'd, and tir'd by jouncing Bullingbrook. (V.v.90–94)

And then, when the jail-keeper refuses to test Richard's food for poison as he usually does, Richard says, "Patience is stale, and I am weary of it" (V.v.103) and acts. He beats the jail keeper and resists his murderers. His final rise and fall are expressed in his last words:

> Mount, mount, my soul! Thy seat is up on high,
> Whilst my gross flesh sinks downward, here to die.
>
> (V.v.111–12)

In this final action Richard has at last joined merit to right. His appropriate epitaph is spoken by his murderer, Sir Pierce of Exton: "As full of valor as of royal blood" (V.v.113). "Royal blood" implies right; "valor" implies merit. In dying Richard has finally united the two in himself and in this way, at the last moment, redeemed his broken time.

Philip Thompson writes that "The murder of Richard II removes the metaphysical problem: England's anointed king is not England's king—does England exist?" The death of Richard leaves Henry now as England's anointed king, but though Richard's last act somewhat healed the split between right and merit in himself, his death cannot heal the split he initiated between right and merit in England. In V.iii we see that Henry's rise through merit will be attended by difficulties because of his questionable right. Rebellions in the land (V.iii.140–41) and the apparently dissolute behavior of Henry's son and heir (V.iii.1–12) threaten the stability of Henry's rule. In the final scene Henry laments the death of Richard, acknowledging that he must now bear the guilt of both the deposing and the murder of the rightful king:

> I'll make a voyage to the Holy Land,
> To wash this blood off from my guilty hand. (V.vi.49–50)

The end of the play is thus a completion of the chiasmic structure. Richard falls by trusting to right without merit. Henry rises by trusting to merit with questionable right. At the end, Richard rises into merit and heaven and Henry sinks into guilt and worry. From this time England will not be at peace until right and merit are united again in one king, temporarily in Henry V, and finally (for the purposes of Shakespeare's history plays) in Henry VII.

KEY LINES:

1. Using the royal plural, Richard says, "We were not born to sue, but to command" (I.i.196). This encapsulates Richard's image of himself. Because he is born to command, he assumes that all his commands, however self-indulgent and harmful to England, are justified.

2. J.V. Cunningham's dictum that in Shakespeare "foreground is background" (see Chapter 7 in Part 1) is illustrated by John of Gaunt's important observation at I.ii.37–41:

> God's is the quarrel, for God's substitute [i.e., the King],

His deputy anointed in His sight,
Hath caus'd his [i.e., Gloucester's] death, the which if wrongfully,
Let heaven revenge, for I may never lift
An angry arm against His minister.

(Gloucester, Richard's uncle, was the younger brother of John of Gaunt and of York.) Here both the reinforcement of Richard's right to rule and the principle that forbids harming the rightful king are expressed by the father of the man who will later depose Richard and become king in his place. The tragedy lies in the fact that Henry's deposing of Richard, though forbidden, is needed.

3.   At the point of death, characters in Shakespeare often speak true prophecy. This is the case with the eloquent prophecy of John of Gaunt at II.i.31–66. Gaunt predicts not only the fall of Richard but the utter corruption of England, a result of Richard's disastrous government of right without merit, which cannot be expiated by his necessary but tragic overthrow at the hands of merit without right. This tragic fall of England will be redeemed, as Shakespeare portrays its history, only after eighty-five years of civil strife ending with the death of Richard III and the accession of Henry VII.

4.   As his subjects gradually turn their loyalties from Richard toward Henry, the virtuous Duke of York is caught in the dilemma. At II.iii York is at a turning point:

I have had feeling of my cousin's [i.e., Henry's] wrongs,
And labour'd all I could to do him right;
But in this kind to come, in braving arms,
Be his own carver and cut out his way,
To find out right with wrong—it may not be;
And you that do abet him in this kind
Cherish rebellion and are rebels all. . . .
I cannot mend it, I must needs confess,
Because my power is weak and all ill left;
But if I could, by Him that gave me life,
I would attach [= arrest] you all, and make you stoop
Unto the sovereign mercy of the King;
But since I cannot, be it known unto you
I do remain as neuter [= neutral].   (II.iii.141–159)

York then invites Henry and his followers to repose in his castle for the night:

> It may be I will go with you, but yet I'll pause,
> For I am loath to break our country's laws.
> Nor friends, nor foes, to me welcome you are . . . . (II.iii.168–70)

By the end of the play, York will accuse his own son (historically his wife's son), Aumerle, of treason against Henry. The tide of events has carried York's loyalty from one king to another without harm to his own character. He is the last representative of the generation of virtue, innocent of participation in the corruption that engulfs England through the next three generations.

5. Like the deathbed prophecy of Gaunt, the conversation in II.iv between a Welsh Captain and the Earl of Salisbury prophesies Richard's fall: "I see thy glory like a shooting star / Fall to the base earth from the firmament" (II.iv.19–20). The image will be echoed by Richard himself in III.iii: "Down, down I come, like glist'ring Phaëton, / Wanting the manage of unruly jades" (III.iii.178–79). "Jades" is a demeaning term for horses, insulting to the horses of the sun. Richard fails to notice that not the horses but Phaeton's pride was to blame for the disaster. (Phaeton, son of the sun-god, Apollo, in doubt about his father's identity, journeyed to the east, where Apollo offered to fulfill any wish of Phaeton as proof of his paternity. Phaeton asked to drive the chariot of the sun for one day. The horses were too much for him and wildly went off course, first upward, scorching the sky in a swath that became the Milky Way, then downward, scorching the earth in a swath that became the Sahara Desert and turning the men of the region black. Zeus put an end to the disaster by killing Phaeton with a thunderbolt. See Ovid, *Metamorphoses*, 1.750–2.339.)

6. The metaphor of England as garden, first heard from John of Gaunt at II.i.42, is developed in III.iv when the king's gardener says,

> O, what pity is it
> That he had not so trimm'd and dress'd his land
> As we this garden! . . .
> Had he done so, himself had borne the crown,
> Which waste of idle hours hath quite thrown down. (III.iv.55–66)

The word *waste* will reappear in Richard's final soliloquy: "I wasted time, and now doth time waste me" (V.v.49). There may also be an intended hint in the phrase "thrown down" of the sense "throne down" or "thrown down from his throne."

7. The prophecy of the Bishop of Carlisle echoes that of John of Gaunt (see Key Line 3). The Abbot of Westminster has called the deposing of Richard a "woeful pageant" (IV.i.321). Carlisle responds,

> The woe's to come; the children yet unborn
> Shall feel this day as sharp to them as thorn.   (IV.i.322–23)

The woe to come will be the eighty-five years of civil wars.

SPECIFIC NOTES TO HELP IN YOUR READING:

1.   At II.ii.120–122, most editors print the lines thus:

> I should to Plashy too.
> But time will not permit. All is uneven,
> And every thing is left at six and seven.

This is in keeping with the general editorial principle of regularizing lines into pentameters. Here, however, doing so is an editorial error, made at the cost of having to invent a half-line and two empty feet. Both Q1 and F print the three lines as two lines thus:

> I should to Plashy too. But time will not permit.
> All is uneven, and every thing is left at six and seven.

The editors have missed Shakespeare's bit of witty prosody: The first line is intentionally six metrical feet, making a hexameter. The second line is intentionally seven metrical feet, making a heptameter. This disordering of the normal pentameters embodies in the two irregular lines the very disorder and confusion implied by the phrase "at six and seven" (or, as we would say, "at sixes and sevens"), a phrase already long in use by Shakespeare's time.

2.   This is a historical note related to the play:

On February 8, 1601, Robert Devereux, Second Earl of Essex, led a band of supporters and malcontents into London in an attempted rebellion against Queen Elizabeth I. On the day before the uprising, there was an unusual performance of *Richard II* by Shakespeare's company, the Chamberlain's Men. The performance had been commissioned by Sir Gelli Merricke, a devoted supporter of Essex, in the hopes that seeing the play would influence the populace to support the rebellion. The Chamberlain's Men objected that they would lose money since the play was so old that no one would likely show up. But they were offered forty shillings beyond their normal charge to perform a play, and so the play was performed. The rebellion of the next day failed, and both Essex and Merricke were executed by the end of the month. Augustine Phillips, a representative of the Chamberlain's Men, had to give a deposition to explain why the company had agreed to perform that play about the deposing of a king on the day before a rebellion against the Queen. The examiners were satisfied that the company had not been privy to the plot. The Queen's archivist, William Lambarde, reports that, reading about King Richard II in the archives, and having in mind the Essex rebellion, Elizabeth said, "I am Richard; know ye not that?" The day before Essex was executed, the Chamberlain's Men performed *Richard II* before the Queen at Whitehall. We owe some of these details to Francis Bacon in his *Declaration of the Practises and Treasons . . . by Robert late Earle of Essex.*

---

[1]   Cf., the discussion of sentimentality in the chapter on *Twelfth Night.*

Henry IV, Part 1

In *Richard II*, the first play of Shakespeare's second tetralogy on English history, Henry Bullingbrook deposed the king and became King Henry IV. *Henry IV, Part 1*, the second play in the tetralogy, opens and closes with the King's efforts to secure the stability of England and his hold on the crown. Given Henry's effective practical ability to counteract the depravities of the previous reign, the question of the play becomes what kind of man will inherit from Henry the government of the realm. In inventing three kinds of competitors for that role, Shakespeare reveals the natures of both honor and justice through his extraordinary mastery of the unity-in-variety that characterize his greatest plays. And he does so in a play that is also dramatically entertaining and, thanks to the invention of the character of Falstaff, contains some of the most hilariously witty comedy ever written.

The three characters who are implicitly in competition for the rule of England are Prince Hal, Hotspur, and Falstaff. Hal is the literal heir apparent. The other two, though not literal pretenders to the throne, seek to control England, Hotspur through war and division of the kingdom, and Falstaff through his personal influence upon the prince. Together they represent three distinct principles of government—different kinds of internal government of themselves and consequently different conceptions of the government of England. Upon the resolution of their competition will depend the justice and integrity of the state.

The long tradition coming to Shakespeare from Plato's *Republic* articulates three parts of man—mind, heart, and body—whose functioning is expressed respectively as thought, emotion or will, and physical need and desire. Plato imagined these three functions to be governed by three souls, the intelligible, the sensible, and the vegetable. The characteristic virtue called for from the intelligible soul or mind is wisdom. The characteristic virtue called for from the sensible soul or heart is courage. And the characteristic virtue called for from the vegetable soul, responsible for physical life and growth, as well as from the others, is temperance. Each of these three parts of man can also exhibit the vices opposite to these virtues: folly opposite to wisdom, cowardice opposite to courage, and self-indulgent sensuality opposite to temperance.

But none of these three parts of the human being is autonomous. Following Plato, the tradition recognizes a proper hierarchy among them. As concluded in the *Republic*, when the mind trains the heart to help bring the body under its government, that is, when wisdom directs courage in temperance, then order is achieved and justice appears. For this principle Plato offers the image of a charioteer driving one obedient and one wild horse. This conception of Plato's is the source of the four cardinal virtues of Western tradition: wisdom, courage, temperance, and justice, to which Christianity added the three theological virtues of faith, hope, and love. According to the tradition, in a just man the mind controls the actions of the body through the well-trained emotions. When either the passions of the heart or the desires of the body rebel against the wisdom of the mind, or when the mind forgoes its function and allows passions or sensual desires to overrule it, internal chaos and consequent injustice inevitably result.

Shakespeare's Prince Hal, while he is clearly a dramatization of the historical prince, also represents the well-integrated man whose wisdom of intellect governs his passions and his actions. This virtuous man is not what outsiders see at the beginning of the play. For Prince Hal has intentionally misled all of England into believing in the truth of his reputation as a self-indulgent wastrel hanging out in the taverns of the London slums. But the audience knows that the prince has constructed that bad reputation by design. We know it because he tells us in the crucial soliloquy at the end of I.ii.

Why has the Prince chosen to sacrifice his reputation in order to create this false picture of himself? The answer is that he faces a difficult problem: As the eldest son of Henry IV, he is clearly the rightful heir to the throne. But Henry IV himself, as we know from *Richard II*, came to the throne by power rather than by right. Despite his having saved England from the self-indulgent and irresponsible King Richard II, Henry's reign has been characterized by self-serving rebellions against him, rebellions whose justification is rationalized on grounds of Henry's questionable legitimacy. How can Prince Hal reunite in himself both his father's merit and Richard's right—the merit of his own good character and his right to inherit the throne from his father—such that the unity of England is restored under his rule?

Prince Hal's answer is given in the soliloquy at I.ii.195–217 (see Variation in Speech in Chapter 4 of Part 1 for a detailed discussion of the structure of the speech). He will create the illusion that the heir to the throne has a character very like that of Richard II, frightening the nation with the prospect of yet another self-indulgent king. Then, when he actually does inherit, he will reveal himself to be a wise and just ruler. The great surprise and relief of the nation will unify it in loyalty to him. This plan comes to fruition at the end of *Henry IV, Part 2*. In *Henry V* he supplements that success with the plan of unifying the nation through the war to regain England's possessions in France won by his great-grandfather Edward III.

Hal's plan is so effective that even the King and court, along with some modern critics of the play, are taken in by it. However, interpreters of this play who see it as either a promotion or a critique of Machiavellian cynicism or as a "coming-of-age" story of moral transformation in the prince are misguided by their own modern concerns (see Chapter 8 in Part 1). The Prince's reputation as self-indulgent wastrel is an illusion purposely created by the Prince himself. In fact the play gives us no instance of Prince Hal's behaving in any way but morally and honorably. He never robs except from the thieves in order to return the money; there is no textual authority for picturing him as engaging in compromising relations with prostitutes—just the opposite: "what a pox have I to do with my hostess of the tavern?" he says (I.ii.47–48); when he drinks with the tapsters it is to learn their language and win their love, which he does (II.iv.4–20). Among other things, Prince Hal is a representation of the perfect blending of the humors, harmonized in him to make an exemplary man and king. The audience is never fooled, as the other characters are, into thinking of the prince as being in rebellion with himself, subject to sensualities. All his apparently low-life activities are mere show, except in his using them to win the loyalty of the commoners who will eventually be his subjects.

The effect of this show is that we find Prince Hal sacrificing the *appearance* of honor in order to achieve true honor. And in him true honor lies in his fulfillment of his function as heir apparent: to unify England as best he can under a king both honorable and honored. The irony of Henry IV's accusing his son of being too much like Richard II (III. ii.93–128) is that the Prince, with complete self-control and the highest of motives, is outwardly imitating Richard only in order to "[redeem the] time when men think least I will" (I.ii.217). That time comes at the end of *Henry IV, Part 2*, the third play of the tetralogy.

As the Prince represents the wise man, the Prince's foil, Hotspur, also based on a historical personage, represents the passionate man, specifically a choleric man ("What? drunk with choler?" says his father at I.iii.129). Hotspur is governed by his desire to achieve glory at all costs, and his method of achieving it is the winning of battles. He is a fighter in every context: his relation with his wife is cat-fighting; he will "cavil on the ninth part of a hair" (III.i.138) in competing with his fellow conspirators; and of course he rebels against the King. He would even "divide myself and go to buffets" with himself when he feels he has erred (II.iii.32). All this life of conflict leads to his actively attempting to divide England itself, into the three parts drawn on a map in III.i and thence into two opposing armies in civil war. These last conflicts put him squarely in the wrong. Shakespeare's two history tetralogies are performed only slightly more than a century since Henry VII unified England after the century of the civil wars depicted in them. Even in Shakespeare's time the threat of rebellions against Queen Elizabeth was never absent. Shakespeare's audience cannot have felt anything but repulsion at the prospect of the civil wars that must result from Hotspur's attempt to split England into three kingdoms. Later, in *King Lear*, Shakespeare makes similar use of that perennial fear, a fear we may comprehend if we imagine some faction today wishing to cause a coalition of states to secede from the union that is the United States of America.

Hotspur's goal in all his divisions is not destruction but honor. Yet he cannot find honor in loyalty or duty or serving the good of England. His concept of honor is nothing but the personal glory of winning in battle, regardless of whom or why he fights. His only goal is the glory of his reputation, and his only means of achieving that glory is through conflict. Dying, he says,

> I better brook the loss of brittle life
> Than those proud titles thou hast won of me.
> They wound my thoughts worse than thy sword my flesh.
>
> (V.iv.78–80)

Prince Hal's eulogy offers a precise assessment of Hotspur's character:

Fare thee well, great heart!
Ill-weaved ambition, how much art thou shrunk!
When that this body did contain a spirit,
A kingdom for it was too small a bound.   (V.iv.87–90)

Hotspur's "great heart," what Plato called the "spirited part" of man, lived in rebellion against wisdom of mind which ought to have governed it. His ambition to remake England in his own image is also the ambition of the heart to govern the head. That ambition of his spirited part repeatedly breaks out against reason—against the King's messenger, the King himself, and even his uncle Worcester in I.iii; against the critic of his plans, himself, and his wife in II.iii; against Glendower and nature itself (in the desire to turn the course of the Trent River) in III.i; against destiny with his willful misreading of the failure of allies to show up to the battle in IV.i and iii; and against the King again in the final battle in V.ii–iv.

The Prince's other main foil, Falstaff, a character entirely of Shakespeare's own invention, lives by the principle of indulging his lowest self. In terms of the humors he is the sanguine type—fat, red-faced, and cheerful. In terms of stock characters, he is the latest and greatest incarnation of the braggart soldier combined with elements of the Vice character from the old morality plays. But Falstaff is much more. He is a realistic, believable, and huge personality. He also is in his rotundity an embodiment of the world, and in his actions an embodiment of worldliness. His superbly witty intellect and his emotions are all in the service of his own sensual pleasures. There is no limit to the joy we take in Falstaff's wit and the wit practiced upon him thanks to his inventive self-indulgence—"I am not only witty in myself, but the cause that wit is in other men," he says (*2 Henry IV*, I.ii.9–10). But this supremely entertaining wit is accompanied by utter irresponsibility and immorality. "Do not thou, when thou art king, hang a thief," he counsels the Prince (*1 Henry IV*, I.ii.62), hoping the Prince as king will abolish all gallows, meaning abolish justice in favor of Falstaff's own lower will. "I would to God thou and I knew where a commodity of good names were to be bought" (I.ii.82–83)—bought, not earned. Thieving is "my vocation" (I.ii.104), as if God, in spite of the eighth commandment, would call a man to be a thief. When Prince Hal reports "I am good friends with my father and may do anything," Falstaff replies, "Rob me the exchequer the first thing thou doest" (III.iii.181–84). (The use of "me" in "Rob me the exchequer" is an ethical dative, not a direct object, and means "rob for me." The exchequer is the King's treasury.) Finally, Falstaff concludes his "catechism of honor," which articulated his rejection of honor as a value, by saying "I'll none of it, honor is a mere scutcheon" (V.i.140). *Scutcheon*, short for escutcheon, is the coat of arms hung upon a coffin as a body is carried to burial. Falstaff means that honor has no substance in itself but is only an external sign associated with the dead, to whom it is useless (see Specific Note 16).

All of these highly entertaining attitudes of Falstaff, turned to practice, prove vicious. Given a leadership role to redeem himself from his thieving, Falstaff instead proves disastrous in that role. He takes money to release from the draft any men fit to be soldiers and drafts instead "slaves as ragged as Lazarus" (IV.ii.25). In the battle itself, he tells us, "I have led my ragamuffins where they are pepper'd; there's not three of my hundred and fifty left alive" (V.iii.35–37). Later, in the next play, when Falstaff hears that King Henry IV is dead and Prince Hal is to be crowned, he says, "Let us take any man's horses, the laws of England are at my commandement" (*2 Henry IV*, V.iii.135–137). Thus if Falstaff were ever to have actual influence over the heir apparent when Hal becomes king, as Falstaff fully expects he will have, that influence would be thoroughly destructive, like that of the parasites that once surrounded Richard II.

But Prince Hal is not actually in danger from Falstaff's vanity, though he allows his father and all England to fear that he is. In all the witty exchanges with Falstaff, Prince Hal is constantly jabbing at and criticizing and satirizing Falstaff's corruptions. From Hal's first accusation of Falstaff's being "fat-witted" with drinking, eating, and wenching (I.ii.2–12) to his eulogy for the supposedly dead Falstaff—"O, I should have a heavy miss of thee / If I were much in love with vanity" (V.iv.105–106)—we are aware that while it is fun and useful for now for the Prince to play with Falstaff, and immensely entertaining to us, the Prince knows perfectly well that it would be fatal for the governor of England to remain under the influence of Falstaff's vanity. "Banish plump Jack, and banish all the world," says Falstaff, in the role of the Prince in their hilariously enjoyable tavern drama (II.iv.479–80). To this the Prince, in the role of his father, says "I do." And then, coming out of character and speaking as himself, the Prince adds, "I will." In *Part 2*, as soon as he is king, Hal does just what here he predicts he will do—he banishes from his presence Falstaff, Falstaff's self-indulgent worldliness, and his own bad reputation.[1]

Both Hotspur and Falstaff have false conceptions of honor. For Hotspur honor lies in self-glorification through winning battles (I.iii.

194–98, 201–208). For Falstaff honor is nothing but a word (V.i.133–34). It is in Prince Hal that we find true honor, which lies in the Platonic idea of justice. Justice appears in the individual man in whom the wisdom of the intellect rules over the passions of the heart and the desires of the body. It appears in the state when the wise man governs it, the army is courageous in its defense in obedience to that wisdom, and the workers temperate in service to it. It lies in the Aristotelian fulfillment of one's function. God is not in fact calling Hotspur to be a rebel and to divide England. Nor is he calling Falstaff to be a thief. He *is* calling Prince Hal to serve the good of the whole with all his gifts, including the virtue of wisdom (revealed in the cleverness he inherited from his father), the virtue of courage (as great as Hotspur's and inherited from his grandfather John of Gaunt as well as from his father), and the virtue of temperance (revealed in his actual behavior and in his ongoing critique of the self-indulgence of Falstaff). In answering that call with virtue, Prince Hal embodies Shakespeare's ideal of good kingship.

The tripartite structure of foil characters is joined in this play by an elaborate structure of plot foils founded on the principle that the rebels against the King are like the Eastcheap thieves: they "prey on [the commonwealth]" (II.i.79–82). The higher thieving is represented in Hotspur, the man of courageous heart but no wisdom, and the lower thieving by Falstaff, the man whose only wisdom lies in wit and in the satisfactions of his corpulent body. Prince Hal moves between these two worlds, wittily needling Falstaff for his vices and at last courageously defeating Hotspur in battle. He is the wise, courageous, and temperate man, who will become England's most just king.

KEY LINES:

1. At I.iii.127–28 Hotspur says, "I will ease my heart, / Albeit I make a hazard of my head" (*albeit*, pronounced as three syllables, means "although"). As one of my students has pointed out, "this is the quintessential Hotspur." The meaning he intends is that he will be satisfied in his emotions even if it costs him his life, which in the end it does. But we can also hear in it an inversion of the right hierarchy. Hotspur is all about serving the passion of the heart at the cost of being blind to the reason of the head.

2. II.i, like the gardener scene in *Richard II*, offers a homely foil scene to the main conflicts of the play. The carriers complain that the inn has been ruined "since Robin ostler died" (II.i.10–11). An ostler (from *hosteler*)

is the person in a roadside inn that looks after the horses. The disorder of
the inn after the death of Robin offers a parallel to the disorder of England
after the death of Richard II. Thieves like Gadshill and the Chamberlain
(an inside man), and fleas, haunt it as Worcester and his faction haunt
England. Gadshill's claim that his companions "do the profession [of
thieving] some grace" (II.i.71) is a punning reference to Prince Hal, who
is addressed as "Your Grace."

3. In II.iv the trick played on Francis the drawer (meaning waiter
or tapster, who "draws" beer or wine from its cask) may seem somewhat
forced and perhaps not very funny to us, but the thematic implication
is significant and lies in the Prince's description. Francis, though human
("son of a woman"—II.iv.99), does nothing but carry ale upstairs and
downstairs, speaks few words, and uses numbers only for reckoning
tavern bills. That is, he is nearly subhuman in having no ambition and
no capacity to reason. Offered a thousand pounds for a pennyworth of
sugar "when thou wilt" (II.iv.67), Francis can say nothing but "Anon"
(= soon, right away). His opposite, according to the Prince, is Hotspur,
who "kills me some six or seven dozen of Scots at a breakfast, washes
his hands, and says to his wife, 'Fie upon this quiet life! I want [= lack]
work'" (II.iv.102–105). (The "me" in "kills me some . . . Scots" is again
an ethical dative.) The point is that neither is the Prince himself of
the mind of Francis nor "I am not yet of Percy's mind" (II.iv.101–102),
neither pusillanimous nor foolhardy, neither under-ambitious nor over-
ambitious. He lives within Aristotle's golden mean, unlike the opposite
extremes of Francis and Hotspur.

4. The matter of central importance in III.i is the willingness of the
factions, under the instruction of the mastermind Worcester, to divide up
England. Given the horrors of the civil Wars of the Roses, Shakespeare's
audience would immediately recognize this effort at division to be an
evident evil. Ironically, the dividers of England are also divided among
themselves, and we are reminded of Falstaff's comical "A plague upon
it when thieves cannot be true one to another!" (II.ii.27–28). In this scene,
Hotspur and Glendower, each in different ways a man of pride and self-
assurance, conflict over the turning of the boundary line formed by the
Trent River. Glendower is full of vainglory: "I say the earth did shake
when I was born" (III.i.20). Hotspur "in the way of bargain . . . will cavil
on the ninth part of a hair" (III.i.137–38). Each wants to be granted honor,
but both are determined to act in fundamentally dishonorable ways in
order to achieve it, Glendower by bragging and Hotspur by fighting. To

his credit, Hotspur will exhibit bravery in actually fighting in the final battle, from which Glendower will absent himself. In the meantime Mortimer, who turns out, as the King has called him, to be "revolted" indeed, having gone over to the side of the rebels and Glendower, is more concerned about the difficulties of communicating with his non-English-speaking Welsh wife than with the stability of England. When the fundamental loyalty to the King is broken, loyalty itself dissolves in self-serving.

5. In III.ii.93–108, the King makes explicit his concern that the behavior of his son and heir will recreate the disastrous behavior of his predecessor, Richard II. Prince Hal's response moves the King to recognize that his son's character, despite the reputation he has cultivated, is entirely to be trusted (III.ii.129–59). The end of the play will show the Prince precisely fulfilling the vow that he makes to his father here.

6. Vernon's glorious description of Prince Hal at IV.i.97–110 and his description of Hal's modesty at V.ii.51–68 demonstrate that the shining truth of Prince Hal's character, "so much misconstrued in his wantonness" (V.ii.68), is become visible even to his enemies. Vernon's prophecy, "let me tell the world . . . / England did never owe so sweet a hope" (V.ii.65–67), will come true.

7. The villainy of Worcester is confirmed in V.ii when he withholds from Hotspur the King's offer of peace: "O no, my nephew must not know, Sir Richard, / The liberal and kind offer of the King" (V.ii.1–2). The irony is that Worcester's reason for not accepting the King's offer is that the King will never in future trust Worcester not to be a traitor. In saying so, he reveals that the King would be right not to trust him, for Worcester is here being treacherous not only to the King but to his own nephew.

8. At the end of the play Prince Hal asks the king for permission to dispose of the prisoners (V.v.23–24). This is a direct contrast with Hotspur's refusal at the beginning of the play to obey the King in the matter of his prisoners (I.i.92–95, I.iii.77). As soon as the King does give Prince Hal permission, the Prince demonstrates two forms of magnanimity: to his friends and to his enemies. He gives his brother Prince John the "honorable bounty" of freeing the Douglas without ransom because

> His valors shown upon our crests to-day
> Have taught us how to cherish such high deeds
> Even in the bosom of our adversaries. (V.v.29–31)

Prince John then says, "I thank your Grace for this high courtesy, / Which I shall give away immediately" (V.v.32–33), i.e., John will immediately share with the Douglas the courtesy that Prince Hal has shared with John. The magnanimous spirit of this exchange is precisely the opposite of self-serving spirit shown by Hotspur and Glendower in their argument over boundaries in III.i and by all the rebels in their arguments of IV.iii.

SPECIFIC NOTES TO HELP IN YOUR READING:

1. I.i.96–97: Westmoreland (pronounced WEST-mer-lind) says, about Hotspur's refusal to send his prisoners to the King, "This is his uncle's teaching; this is Worcester, / Malevolent to you in all aspects." Notice how Shakespeare uses an introductory trochee instead of an iamb to throw extra stress upon the fourth syllable ("unc-"), and then makes the stresses fall upon the second "this" and the first syllable of "Worcester" (pronounced "Wooster"), so that the three heaviest stresses of the line reinforce the sense that Worcester is the evil plotter behind Hotspur's disobedience to the King. In the second of these lines the word *aspects*, stressed on the second syllable here, refers to the astrological influences of the planets. Showing one aspect, a planet may have a positive influence; showing another, a negative. The planet Worcester, moving around the sun that is King Henry, exerts a negative influence ("malevolent" = bad-willing) no matter what "aspect" he turns toward the King.

2. I.ii.46: "buff jerkin"—the kind of jacket worn by law officers or jailers.

3. I.ii.62—68: "hang a thief"—Falstaff and the Prince play on four senses of the phrase:

   a) l. 62: "Do not thou, when thou art king, hang a thief"—do not enforce the law against theft, for which the punishment is hanging.

   b) l. 63: "No, thou shalt [hang a thief]"—you will hang (i.e., be hanged) as a thief.

   c) ll. 64–65: "O rare . . . I'll be a brave [= fine, splendid] judge"—O wonderful . . . As a judge I will be responsible for applying to thieves the law that says they must be hanged.

   d) ll. 66–68: "Thou judgest false already [hinting at the kind of judge Falstaff would be]. I mean thou shalt . . . become a rare hangman"—become an unusual example of the officer responsible for the physical hanging of thieves. This sense leads to the two senses of "obtaining of suits" in l. 71: being granted a request by the king and inheriting the clothing of the hanged criminal, which was the prerogative of the hangman.

4. I.ii.88–89: "wisdom cries out in the streets, and no man regards it"—referring to Proverbs 1:20–24.

5. I.ii.: Gadshill—Gadshill is both a hill between London and Canterbury, famous for the highway robberies that occurred there (I.ii.125), *and* the name of a character, nicknamed for the place (I.ii.129).

6. I.iii.92, 93: "revolted Mortimer." Following Samuel Daniel's *Bookes of the Ciuile Wars Between the Two Houses of Lancaster and Yorke*, one of his sources for this play, Shakespeare, knowingly or not, conflated two historical Mortimers: Sir Edmund Mortimer (who was a younger brother of Hotspur's wife, allied with Glendower, and was refused ransom by, and raised an army against, Henry IV) and his nephew, Edmund Mortimer, Fifth Earl of March (heir-designate to Richard II on the death of his father, Roger Mortimer, Fourth Earl of March, younger brother to Hotspur's wife and elder brother to Sir Edmund). As A. R. Humphreys writes in Appendix VIII to his Arden edition of the play, "Shakespeare did not notice, or did not care, that one and the same person cannot call Hotspur's wife 'aunt Percy' [III.i.194] and be called by her 'my brother Mortimer' [II.iii.81]."[2]

7. I.iii.230, 233: "sword-and-buckler . . . pot of ale"—demeaning images directed at Prince Hal alluding to his reputation for slumming. The sword and buckler were used by low class soldiers as opposed to the rapier and dagger of aristocrats. The pot of ale is a drink of the taverns, not of the palace. These are examples of the figure of speech called meiosis, the use of belittling terms.

8. II.ii.4: "Poins! Poins, and be hang'd! Poins!"—To me this is one of the funniest lines ever written. As my students know, after it cracks me up—every time—I have attempted to explain why. The harder I try, the more my students laugh—at me. Here is a final attempt:

In the adventure of the thieves, Poins has taken and hidden Falstaff's horse. Falstaff, having to walk on his own two feet, huffing and puffing, is shouting at Poins to return the horse to him. "And be hang'd" is an automatic colloquialism often repeated by Falstaff. It is the equivalent of "and be damned" or "and to hell with you." As a common colloquialism it generally follows a verb, as in Falstaff's "tarry at home and be hang'd" (I.ii.132–33), or the First Carrier's "come away and be hang'd" (II.i.22), or Falstaff's "give me my horse, and be hang'd" (II.ii.29–30). In *Measure for Measure* Lucio says, "Show your sheep-biting face, and be hang'd an hour!" (V.i.354–55); in *Antony and Cleopatra*, Menas says about drums, trumpets, and flutes, "Sound and be hang'd, sound out!" (II.vii.133); and in *Timon of Athens* Timon in his misanthropy says, "Speak and be hang'd" (V.i.131).

Here the funny part is that Falstaff, in his outburst of frustration, mechanically adds "and be hang'd" not to a verb but to the mere name Poins, as if to his existence itself. Technically, the figures of speech of which the line is built are epizeuxis, diacope, epanalepsis, and others, the key one being ellipsis, the omission of a word or phrase that is nevertheless understood, the omission here being of the verb or rather the whole phrase "give me my horse" as at ll. 29–30. The line is funny because it is a) mindlessly mechanical, b) completely irrational grammatically and logically, c) thematically apt because hanging is the standard punishment for thieves, and Poins has robbed Falstaff of his horse, even as they are all trying to rob the travelers, and d) perfectly expressive of Falstaff's emotion. This is the best I can do to explain *why* it is funny. *That* it is funny you must hear for yourself.

9.   II.iv.239: "If reasons were as plentiful as blackberries"—Falstaff is playing on the similar sounds of *reasons* and *raisins*, which in Shakespeare's time were probably closer in sound if not exact homonyms, though Shakespeare is not loath to play such verbal games even when the sounds are not so very close. Modern audiences have less tolerance for the stretch than the Elizabethans had.

10.   At II.iv.391–481, it is important to understand that in the little drama performed by the Prince and Falstaff, Falstaff begins by playing at being the King, and Prince Hal is playing at being himself. When Falstaff as the King vulgarly calls Hal a "naughty varlet," Hal asks "Dost thou speak like a king?" and changes places with Falstaff. Then Prince Hal plays his father and Falstaff plays Prince Hal. Part of the humor lies in the fact that whatever role Falstaff plays he uses to justify himself. Falstaff's comical "Depose me?" (l. 435) alludes to Henry IV's fateful deposing of Richard II.

11.   II.iv.535ff.: In the list of Falstaff's debts read by Peto, *s.* stands for shillings; *d.* stands for penny or (in the plural) pence (from Latin *denarius*, an ancient Roman coin worth ten of the smaller coin called the *as* or *assarius* and derived from the sense "containing ten"); and *ob.* (from the Latin *obolus*, Greek *obolos*, meaning a nail or spit of metal, the name of an ancient Greek coin) stands for half a penny, pronounced hā'p'ny.

12. III.i.49: When Hotspur says about Glendower "I think there's no man speaks better Welsh," the implication, as a student of mine pointed out, is that "Glendower's claims are naught but excellent Welsh," a demeaning assertion that the *content* of Glendower's speech is negligible.

13. IV.i.122–23: "Harry to Harry shall, hot horse to horse, / Meet and ne'er part till one drop down a corse."—The alliteration on the five initial *H*'s and the repetitions in the first line express the breathlessness of Hotspur's eagerness to win glory from his rival. The word "corse" is our word *corpse*.

14. IV.iv: This short scene shows us the turning of the tide from the forces of rebellion toward the forces of the King, and also the fear beginning to develop among the rebel faction and within the minds of many of them. It prepares us to find truth in the King's words at the end: "Thus ever did rebellion find rebuke" (V.v.1). The external "rebuke" of defeat in battle is prepared for by the internal dissension and fear that illegitimate rebellion inevitably generates both among and within the rebels. In *King Lear* and *Macbeth* Shakespeare will push to the poetic extreme this correspondence of realms, disorder echoed within the individual mind, in the body politic, and in the whole natural world.

15. V.i.101–103: The King first seems to agree to venture the life of Prince Hal in single combat with Hotspur but then changes his mind with "No, good Worcester, no" before he offers the terms for peace. The single combat happens nonetheless in V.iv within the context of the general battle.

16. V.i.140 "I'll none of it, honor is a mere scutcheon": Because honor has no material substance, cannot set a broken arm or leg, it means nothing to Falstaff. In his conclusion Falstaff espouses the nominalist heresy according to which abstractions are merely names signifying no reality behind them. Prince Hal embodies the contrary doctrine of idealism, incarnating in his nature and actions the non-material reality of honor, which expresses itself in his every word and deed.

V.iv.121–23: Falstaff, contemplating the corpse of Hotspur, says, "'Zounds, I am afraid of this gun-powder Percy though he be dead. How if he should counterfeit too and rise?" Falstaff's hilarious idea that Hotspur could, like himself, be so cowardly as to pretend to be dead is absurd in itself and punctuates the difference between the two men's contrary conceptions of themselves—the cowardice of the sensual man vs. the bravery of the passionate-choleric man.

[1] Philip Thompson writes, "It is Hal's relation to [Falstaff] that allows us to put aside moral questions and simply enjoy him—Hal's presence prevents him from arousing fear or disgust. When he and Hal are effectively separated at the end of *Part II* and he roars "The Laws of England are at my commandment," we suddenly see him as a real force for corruption, and of course we regret losing him as a "court jester" nonpareil whose vices are turned to fun by the prince's direction. The episode of the ragged recruits has prepared us for this final declaration of misrule, but in our "enjoyment" of the sole source of wit (and because of the tone of caricature) we didn't really notice."—from "Notes on Shakespeare" in Philip Thompson, *Dusk and Dawn: Poems and Prose of Philip Thompson*, ed. Gideon Rappaport (San Diego: One Mind Good Press, 2005), p. 221, 227.

[2] A. R. Humphreys, ed., *The First Part of King Henry IV*, The Arden Shakespeare (London: Methuen, 1960, reprinted 1967), p. 202.

Henry IV, Part 2

Henry IV, Part 2, brings to dramatic completion the plan of Prince Hal for his public transformation on his accession to the throne. In verse and prose that richly represent the mastery of the incarnational style of Shakespeare's mature period (see Universal Realism in Chapter 1 of Part 1), the play takes us inexorably toward the triumph of the good Prince and the bending of all England toward justice under his government. This movement is prepared for by a variety of pictures of uncertainty in all main characters but the Prince, all reinforcing the need for a strong and just leader to restore and secure the health of the commonwealth of England. The play is built on the movement from these initial uncertainties to their resolution in four dramatic confrontations: Prince John's bloodless defeat of the rebels, the final reconciliation of King Henry and Prince Hal, the new King Henry V's surprise approval of the Chief Justice, and his just-but-merciful banishment of Falstaff from his presence.

The uncertainty to which the accession of Prince Hal to the throne puts an end is conveyed in several ways. First, the play begins with an induction (which we would call an introduction) by the abstract character "Rumor," whose costume is painted with tongues. Rumor, called "a pipe / Blown by surmises, jealousies [= suspicions], conjectures" (Ind. 15–16), serves a triple function. It reminds us that at the end of *Part 1* Prince Hal defeated Hotspur's rebellion; it announces that it will be sending false news of that defeat to Northumberland and others; and it conveys the confusion of the time by being itself the bearer of both truth and falsehood.

Uncertainty and confusion govern Northumberland in his effort to continue the rebellion against Henry IV. He flies into a desperate passion on hearing that Hotspur is dead (I.i.136–60), then determines to gather forces to fight the King (I.i.212–15), then is said to be an uncertain prop for the rebellion fostered by the Archbishop of York (I.iii.18–33), and finally, though he says he wants to join the Archbishop's forces, instead chooses to escape to Scotland (II.iii.67). He is joined in these uncertainties by the Archbishop and those of his faction—are they sufficient with Northumberland to stand against the King's forces? Are they sufficient without him? Will the King bring all his forces against them or divide his armies? etc. (I.iii). In his own expression of uncertainty the Archbishop includes all the people of England, who, he says, once rejected Richard and are now fed up with Henry:

> The commonwealth is sick of their own choice,
> Their over-greedy love hath surfeited. . . .
> What trust is in these times? . . .
> Past and to come seems best; things present worst.
>
> (I.iii.87–108)

The King himself is also filled with uncertainty and confusion, concluding his meditation on his own lack of repose due to care with the famous line "Uneasy lies the head that wears a crown" (III.i.31). He laments that Northumberland, who supported him in deposing Richard II, has now, eight years later, turned against him, fulfilling Richard's prophecy:

> "The time will come, that foul sin, gathering head,
> Shall break into corruption." (III.i.76–77)

"Gathering head" means gathering up armed forces. Then he introduces the question of to what degree the events of history are a function of necessity. He observes about his deposing Richard and becoming king,

> Though then, God knows, I had no such intent,
> But that necessity so bow'd the state
> That I and greatness were compell'd to kiss. (III.i.72–74)

Warwick (pronounced WAR-ick) adds that Richard might well have prophesied correctly because events of the past determine by necessity events yet to come (III.i.80–92). To this the King replies, "Are these things then necessities? / Then let us meet them like necessities" (III.i.92–93). This universal question whether our own actions and historical events are functions of will or of necessity is laced through the play. Its focus here is the effects of political uncertainty in the absence of a God-established monarch, whom it is every man's duty to obey, and of a clear picture of where virtue lies. Necessity may be appealed to by both the virtuous (like King Henry IV) and the self-indulgent (like the Archbishop of York or Falstaff). The quandary of the Duke of York in *Richard II*—how long to remain loyal to the rightful but destructive king, when to switch loyalty to the competent but usurping king—becomes the universal quandary of England, now divided by civil wars. In his confusion King Henry, too, like Richard in *Richard II*, is England in little. In IV.iv the King's inner conflict reaches its peak, taking the form of physical sickness even as he hears good news of the success of his troops against the rebels.

The witty self-indulgence that fills the Falstaff scenes of the play reinforces the confusion and uncertainty of England in its riffraff as in its aristocrats. The wit of Falstaff is of wider scope than in *Part 1* but rings with less joyful hilarity, partly because of the distance from him of Prince Hal. (The two appear together in this play only in II.iv and in the great rejection scene of V.v.) Falstaff is as witty as ever but exercises his wit no longer under the protective covering of the Prince's plan to appear dissolute. Instead he is set against such sober and unsusceptible men as the Chief Justice, Westmoreland (pronounced WEST-mer-lund), and Prince John of Lancaster—that is, the forces of justice in the realm and the true company of the future King Henry V. This change from *Part 1* builds in to the structure the sense that as the King sickens, the Prince is moving away from Falstaff toward assuming with virtue the royal mantle of his destiny.

The passage of time and aging hang more threateningly over Falstaff in *Part 2*, as they do over the King. Falstaff says, "I am old, I am old" (II. iv.271), and the King says "More would I [say], but my lungs are wasted so / That strength of speech is utterly denied me" (IV.v.216–17). There are many references to the past in the play: to scenes from *Richard II*—the interrupted trial by combat, the corruption and deposition of the King, the shady paths of Bullingbrook—to the battle at Shrewsbury in *Part 1*, to Falstaff's and Shallow's youths. And the future the King intended—to fight for the Holy Land and die in Jerusalem as prophesied—shrinks to a room in the palace (historically a hall next to Westminster Abbey) called "Jerusalem." Time in this play leads us inexorably toward the inevitable disappointment of Falstaff's perverse hopes and the fulfillment of the King's good hopes in the dramatic triumphs of the Prince.

To return to Falstaff: His scenes are a riot of wit devoted to the self-indulgent corruption of himself and his cronies: the braggart Pistol, the foolish Hostess Quickly, the immoral Doll Tearsheet, the alcoholic thief Bardolph, and in the later scenes the unethical self-indulgences of the King's justice of the peace Shallow and his time-pleasing servant Davy. The events involve brawling, drinking, fornicating, sentimentality, wishful thinking, and corruption of the king's press (the commissioned power to draft men for the army).

Falstaff observes about Shallow,

> It is a wonderful thing to see the semblable coherence of his men's [= servants'] spirits and his. They, by observing him, do bear themselves like foolish justices; he, by conversing with them, is turned into a justice-like serving-man. Their spirits are so married in conjunction with the participation of society that they flock together in consent, like so many wild geese.
> ... It is certain that either wise bearing or ignorant carriage is caught, as men take diseases, one of another. (V.i.64–77)

This observation is partly true: the company one keeps influences one's character and behavior. It is also true of himself and those with whom *he* keeps company. In fact, in duping Shallow Falstaff will be as venal as Shallow, though more clever. But the mutually corrupting influence of Falstaff and Shallow and their fellow dissolutes is the shadow of Prince Hal's mission to influence his subjects in a positive direction by his own behavior.

At the same time, the influence of society is not merely a function of necessity. That man still has free will is illustrated by the few examples of virtue amidst the vice-ridden. Among the foolish, venal, and cowardly Shallow and Falstaff and their army recruits, one man stands as a contrast with them despite his unprepossessing stature: When the stout Bullcalf buys his way out of military service, it is ironically the weakling Feeble, of all people, who submits to being drafted, saying:

> a man can die but once, we owe God a death. I'll ne'er bear a base mind. And't be my dest'ny, so; and't be not, so. No man's too good to serve 's prince, and let it go which way it will, he that dies this year is quit for the next. (III.ii.234–38)

This simple philosophical humility shows virtuous courage to be the antidote to the tyranny of necessity. Note the use of oxymorons—"wrathful dove or most magnanimous mouse" (III.ii.160)—about Feeble, who is himself an oxymoron: strength of character in a weak body.

Thanks to the similar if more savvy virtues of Prince Hal and his brother Prince John, all of these confusions—Rumor, Northumberland's vacillations, the rebel leaders' uncertainties, the King's troubles and illness, and the corruption among the commoners—are healingly resolved by the four dramatic triumphs of the play.

The first is the triumph of Prince John and Westmoreland over the rebels at Gaultree Forest. Modern critics have had a field day in accusing Prince John of Machiavellian larceny, injustice, immorality, and cynicism in seeming to swear to redress the wrongs of the Archbishop and his fellow rebels and then seeming to go back on his word. It is true that Prince John equivocates with "My lord, these griefs shall be with speed redressed" (IV.ii.59) and "my love to ye / Shall show itself more openly hereafter" (IV.ii.75–76). But the rebels have evoked his treatment of them: Being traitors they can experience justice only as treachery—a principle also explicit in Dante's *Inferno* and implicit in Milton's *Paradise Lost*—and John's equivocation, like Prince Hal's low-life disguise, is justified by his higher purpose. The criticism of the critics is just that of the rebels themselves:

> Mowbray: Is this proceeding just and honorable? . . .
> Archbishop: Will you thus break your faith?   (IV.ii.110, 112)

To these accusations Prince John replies with perfect honesty:

> I pawn'd thee none.
> I promis'd you redress of these same grievances
> Whereof you did complain, which, by mine honor,
> I will perform with a most Christian care.
> But for you rebels, look to taste the due
> Meet for rebellion.   (IV.ii.112–17)

He is completely justified. The legitimate grievances the rebels put forward in the negotiations Prince John will indeed redress. But no such grievances justify the taking up of arms against the King. And the critics ignore the actual outcome: John has concluded a peaceful resolution of the conflict without the loss of a drop of blood except that of the rebel leaders, who are properly executed for treason against the King, as they knew they would be if the battle were fought and lost. As John says, confusion and folly lay in the very plan to oppose an army against the King, and that folly was completed in the folly of sending the rebel armies away (IV.ii.118–19). When he says, "God, and not we, hath safely fought to-day" (IV.ii.121), we are meant to agree with him. Prince John is an instrument of the good of the commonwealth, and his mastery of the day without bloodshed is a major turning point toward the just government of Henry V.[1]

The second major dramatic triumph comes with Prince Hal's contemplation of the crown in the presence of the sleeping Henry IV, who he thinks has died, and the following reconciliation between father and son. First Prince Hal acknowledges that the crown is a "polish'd perturbation" (IV.v.23), just as Henry IV had felt in III.i. Then the prince, thinking his father is dead, puts the crown on his head, not in eagerness or pride, but a)

> To try with it, as with an enemy
> That had before my face murdered my father   (IV.v.166–67)

—that is, to test himself against its physical, political, and moral weight, and b) to acknowledge that he inherits it, and will pass it on to his heirs, legitimately:

> Lo where it sits [i.e., on his own head],
> Which God shall guard; and put the world's whole strength
> Into one giant arm, it shall not force
> This lineal honor from me. This from thee
> Will I to mine leave, as 'tis left to me.   (IV.v.43–46)

("Put the world's whole strength" means "let the whole world's strength be put," i.e., "even if it were put . . ." .) With these words Prince Hal expresses the determination to expiate any illegitimacy in his father's taking the crown from Richard II. When the King awakens and once again (as in 1 *Henry IV*, III.ii) accuses the prince of having the dissolute behavior and character of Richard II (IV.v.92–137), the prince movingly proclaims "The noble change that I have purposed!" (IV.v.154). The King is persuaded and advises his son to "busy giddy minds / With foreign quarrels" (IV.v.213–14) in order to distract the nation from any remaining doubts about Lancastrian legitimacy. The prince then confirms his intention "rightfully" to "maintain" his hold on the crown (IV.v.220–24).

The third major triumph takes place in V.ii when the new king's brothers and courtiers, including the Chief Justice, who once had put Prince Hal in jail for striking him, express fear about Henry V's character and likely behavior. Will he be another Richard II, dissolute and destructive to the realm and to justice, governing under the influence of Falstaff and his ilk? We are then treated to the great pleasure of seeing those fears melt away with the honorable and healing words of Henry V.

> This is the English, not the Turkish court,
> Not Amurath and Amurath succeeds,
> But Harry Harry.   (V.ii.47–49)

In the exchange with the Chief Justice we experience the birth of the wise and just ruler we have all along known to be gestating in Prince Hal.

The justice tempered with mercy of Henry V is confirmed and dramatized in the final triumph of this play: the ten-mile banishment of Falstaff from the King's presence (V.v.63–65). It is important to remember, lest we jump on the bandwagon of critics who disapprove of Henry's behavior, that the moment Falstaff has learned of the death of Henry IV, he says,

> I am Fortune's steward . . . Let us take any man's horses, the laws
> of England are at my commandement. Blessed are they that have
> been my friends, and woe to my Lord Chief Justice!
> (V.iii.130–38)

In other words, Falstaff believes that his misrule will be the rule in England now that his supposed protégé will be king. When the newly crowned King Henry V says "I know thee not, old man, fall to thy prayers" (V.v.47), we empathize with Falstaff's disappointment, but we must not be surprised or disapproving. We must, like all the virtuous of England, be relieved and uplifted. Henry is not being cruel. He has warned Falstaff again and again what the "old white-bearded Satan" (*1 Henry IV*, II.iv.463) is facing if he doesn't mend, and promised to banish him with his "I do. I will" in *1 Henry IV* (II.iv.481). Henry mercifully provides Falstaff a stipend to live on, so

That lack of means enforce you not to evils,
And as we hear you do reform yourselves,
We will, according to your strengths and qualities,
Give you advancement.   (V.v.66–70)

But banish Falstaff from his own presence Henry must, and in his doing
so his transformation before the eyes of the court and the multitudes is
complete. His disguise of dissipation is shed, and the king under it is
revealed to be the wise and just ruler for whom England has longed.

KEY LINES:
1.   In II.ii.45–47 Prince Hal reminds us of what was revealed about
his purposes in his important soliloquy in *Henry IV, Part 1* (I.ii.195–217),
namely that his apparently dissolute behavior among the riffraff is a
ruse. Here he says to Poins, "By this hand, thou thinkest me as far in
the devil's book as thou and Falstaff, for obduracy and persistency. Let
the end try the man"—that is, let him be judged by his ends, meaning
a) his purposes, and b) the end of the story (when he becomes king).
Later in the scene, after calling to mind Jupiter's disguising himself
as a bull, he says of his own descent into disguise, "From a prince to a
prentice? A low transformation! That shall be mine, for in every thing
the purpose must weigh with the folly" (II.ii.174–76)—that is, the folly
will be justified when weighed in the balance against his ultimate
purpose. Whereas Jupiter's descent was for the sake of self-indulgent
lust, Hal's has been for the sake of the kingdom's good. Finally, the
Prince reminds us when speaking for the last time with his dying father
that his supposed moral transformation will be a performance that he
has always intended:

If I do feign,
O, let me in my present wildness die,
And never live to show th' incredulous world
The noble change that I have purposèd!   (IV.v.151–54).

("Feign" means pretend, i.e., to sorrow at thinking the King was dead.)
Nothing in his actual character has needed transformation; it is only his
outward behavior, which itself was a ruse, that will seem to change when
he becomes king.

SPECIFIC NOTES TO HELP IN YOUR READING:

1.   II.i.74: "He hath eaten me out of house and home"—The phrase and others like it have been found earlier, but its wide popularity can be attributed to this use of it by Hostess Quickly

2.   At I.ii.66ff. Falstaff had pretended to be deaf and engaged in a contest of wits with the Chief Justice. Then in II.i.166ff., after the Chief Justice, discussing important matters with Gower, pays no attention to Falstaff's attempt to horn in on the conversation, Falstaff in turn pretends to ignore the Chief Justice when the latter speaks to him. At ll. 191–93 Falstaff implies that he has learned this impolite behavior from the Chief Justice and concludes, "This is the right fencing grace, my lord, tap for tap, and so part fair" (II.i.192–93)—that is, he has given the Chief Justice as good as he's gotten in the way of being ignored, and so they are even. All of this brazen disrespect for his superior, an outrage against hierarchy of both rank and character, is founded on Falstaff's belief that when Prince Hal becomes king, Falstaff will be able to do what he pleases, as summed up when he presumptuously predicts "woe to my Lord Chief Justice!" (V.iii.138).

3.   At III.ii.36–38 Justice Shallow, after his commonplace observation on death, "'tis certain . . . all shall die"—referring to Psalm 89:48: "What man liveth, and shall not see death?"—ironically asks "How [= how much is] a yoke [= pair] of bullocks at Stamford fair?" unwittingly referring to the book of Ecclesiasticus (Sirach): "How can he get wisdom that holdeth the plough, and . . . whose talk is of bullocks?" (38:25 KJV). The implication is that wisdom will forever escape Shallow, who moves so quickly from contemplating death in trite terms to discussing the price of cattle.

4.   At IV.i.69, the Archbishop of York says that the rebels "find our griefs heavier than our offenses." He means the grievances against the King justify the offense of mounting the rebellion. Prince John, though he will strive to redress the grievances, will properly disagree that they justify plunging the country into civil war.

5.   At IV.iii.86, after Prince John has said that he will speak about Falstaff better than he deserves, Falstaff hilariously replies (after the prince exits), "I would you had but the wit"—that is, if only you had the wit to speak of me better than I deserve. He means a) facetiously, that he deserves so much that it would be hard to exaggerate it, and b) seriously, that he would stand to gain if only the prince would recommend him. Falstaff goes on to complain that Prince John cannot be made to laugh,

as his brother Prince Hal can—or anyway could in *Part 1*—because John drinks no wine. Drinkers among us may sympathize with Falstaff's assessment of Prince John, but we are certainly not meant to approve of it (see Endnote 1).

6. V.iii.134–35: "Boot, boot, Master Shallow!"—The line is a triple pun. "Boot" can mean a) footwear: put on your boots because I am in a hurry to get to the new king; b) benefit, service: provide for me, perhaps in the form of the thousand pounds that Falstaff borrows from Shallow; and c) booty: you will reap advantages for being my crony when I come to London and get the new king to do my bidding.

---

[1] Philip Thompson refutes the erroneous critical stance thus: "Here, as in the case of *Measure for Measure*, the critical habit of opposing 'sympathetic' characters to 'unsympathetic' ones (Falstaff vs. Prince John, Prince Hal vs. King Henry V, the deposed Richard to Bolingbroke—and Claudio vs. Isabella) implies the notion that Shakespeare should have been celebrating modern sympathies, which are with 'unyoked humors' [(*1 Henry IV*, I.ii.196)] and emphatically not with the 'commonwealth' that is his theme in these plays—the result is that their action as a whole is ignored and their incidents are used merely to judge individual characters in the way acquaintances might be judged (Does he read? Is he funny? Does he see both sides of a question? Is he all business? etc.). When Prince John by a ruse spares both armies and then executes the rebel leaders, he is judged to be an unworthy tavern-companion! The tavern is not Shakespeare's ideal world, and he means what Prince John says about traitors. Liberation from battle is what the verse emphasizes. ('Mine ease at mine inn' [(*1 Henry IV*, III.iii.80–81)] is a pleasure, not an ideal.)"— from "Notes on Shakespeare" in Philip Thompson, *Dusk and Dawn: Poems and Prose of Philip Thompson*, ed. Gideon Rappaport (San Diego: One Mind Good Press, 2005), p. 221, 227.

Henry V

Henry V, the last play in Shakespeare's second tetralogy, was briefly mentioned in Chapter 10 of Part 1 as falling into the category of pageant. That is because the play is built of a succession of scenes whose through-line is simply the triumphant kingship of Henry V, ending with his successful conquest of France and marriage to Katherine, daughter of the French King Charles VI. The pageant quality of the play is reinforced by the introduction of each act by a Chorus, exhorting us to use our imaginations and filling in gaps in the unfolding story.

In the first of the choral speeches, called "Prologue," Shakespeare gives both a description and an example of the playwright's method of bringing his story to life through words, the central medium of Shakespearean drama:

> Think, when we talk of horses, that you see them
> Printing their proud hoofs i' th' receiving earth . . . . (Prol. 26–27)

And we do, so irresistible is Shakespeare's art. For example, the alliteration on the two plosive *p*'s and the troche on "Printing" leading to the spondee on "proud hoofs" become a force that lands on the softness of the four unstressed syllables of "'i' th' receiving" and the non-plosive sound of "earth," just as the hoofs of the horses print themselves into the earth in the image—a subtle and compelling use of the figure of speech called onomatopoeia. The invitation sets us up to "piece out" the entire pageant with our "thoughts" (Prol. 23).

But as always with Shakespeare, no category can hold him in. In addition to being a pageant, *Henry V* is also a thrilling dramatization of what makes for excellence in a good king. In Henry, Shakespeare's ideal king, we find virtue, justice, self-knowledge, wit, the power to inspire his followers, and humility before God.

In the subplot scenes, we have the report of the last-minute repentance and the death of Falstaff, ending the era of Henry's youth, whose dissoluteness (in Shakespeare's version of history) was always an illusion. We also have the interactions of representatives of the four peoples that make up what would later become the United Kingdom: Gower, the Englishman; Fluellen, the Welshman; Macmorris, the Irishman; and Jamy, the Scotsman. (Wales was joined to England by law in 1535 and 1542. Under King James I, England, Scotland, and Ireland were joined in 1603.) There is some friction among the four characters, implying the same among the four nations, but they are united in loyalty to Henry and in brave fighting for him in the wars against the French, proving the validity of the advice of Henry's dying father:

> Be it thy course to busy giddy minds
> With foreign quarrels, that action, hence borne out,
> May waste the memory of the former days
>
> (*2 Henry IV*, IV.v.213–15)

—that "memory" being of Henry IV's coming to the throne by deposing Richard II and the consequent rebellions against him.

With that overview in mind, let's look at some of the key scenes in the play.

After the stirring prologue, the play begins by giving us a picture of the court gossip and intrigue that invariably surround a king. Here the Archbishop of Canterbury and the Bishop of Ely share with us high praise of the virtuous transformation of the wild Prince Hal into the virtuous King Henry V, realizing that the Prince had intentionally "obscur'd his contemplation / Under the veil of wildness" (I.i.63–64). That conversation is bracketed by their concern over a bill that would strip the Church of half its property, a bill they try to counteract by offering to donate a vast sum of money from the Church to fund the King's intended war in France.

In the next scene, the Archbishop engages in a long discourse on European royal history to justify Henry's right to the throne of France (see Specific Note 1 below). Satisfied that he is indeed justified, the King admits the French Ambassador, who delivers from the Dauphin (literally "dolphin," the name for the French heir apparent to the throne) the mocking gift of tennis balls. Henry responds,

> We are glad the Dolphin is so pleasant with us . . . .
> When we have match'd our rackets to these balls,

We will in France, by God's grace, play a set
Shall strike his father's crown into the hazard.   (I.ii.259–63)

And we are reminded again that Henry's earlier wildness was a ruse:

we understand him well,
How he comes o'er [= taunts, scoffs at] us with our wilder days,
Not measuring what use we made of them.   (I.ii.266–68)

This scene has settled Henry's determination to unite England and its allies in a legitimate war to recover the former English dominions in France.

Before Henry can lead his forces to France, however, he must deal with a secret plot against his life in England. In II.ii, the traitors Lord Scroop, the Earl of Cambridge, and Sir Thomas Grey advise Henry not to forgive a drunken man for railing against him. Henry forgives the man against their advice and then, handing the three their own indictments for treason, says,

The mercy that was quick in us but late,
By your own counsel is suppress'd and kill'd.   (II.ii.79–80)

After a powerful speech about how deeply surprising and hurtful the treachery of these three men has been, he sends them to be executed as they deserve, praying that "God acquit them of their practices [= plots]" (II.ii.144), i.e., may God forgive them. The scene is important in revealing both that Henry will not tolerate the kind of rebellions that his father had to war against all his reign, and that Henry, in his judgments, tempers justice with mercy. He is merciful when real danger to the state is not involved, but he metes out justice in response to dangerous treachery. And he distinguishes between his own responsibility for earthly justice enacted upon the subjects' lives and God's responsibility for heavenly justice upon their souls. This theme will return on the night before the battle of Agincourt.

In II.iii we have the description by Hostess Quickly (now married to Pistol) of the death of Falstaff. Her ignorance (substituting "Arthur's bosom" for Abraham's at II.iii.9–10) is funny, but from her speech we gather that Falstaff has gone to his maker in a state of penitence, for "'a babbl'd of green fields" and "'a cried out, 'God, God, God!' three or four times" (II.iii.17–19). The green fields are probably the "green pasture" of Psalm 23:2 (Geneva Bible, "pastures" in KJV). If so, Falstaff, experiencing himself to be in the valley of the shadow of death, must be trying to recite that psalm in a deathbed repentance (see Specific Note 2 below). In any case, that Falstaff calls out on God tells us what we are meant to know. It is both funny and painfully ironic that the Hostess "bid him 'a should not think of God; I hop'd there was no need to trouble himself with any such thoughts yet" (II.iii.20–22) when such thoughts are precisely what he ought to be thinking at the last possible moments for him to think them.

In II.iv the French court is depicted, with its weak king and its proud and overconfident lords, as ripe for defeat by the brave and virtuous Henry followed by a united England. That unity is expressed in the scenes with Fluellen, Gower, Macmorris, and Jamy, when the proprieties and improprieties of behavior in battle are debated. Through his Welsh pronunciation of the English language, Fluellen is revealed as a noble-minded true liegeman to the King. His own subordinate form of justice, mirroring the King's, is played out in the matter of the leek against the "rascally, scald [= scurvy, scabby], beggarly, lousy, pragging [i.e., bragging] knave, Pistol" (V.i.5–6). The braggart soldier, representing the depraved cronies of Prince Hal's past, is put in his place by the upright and principled comrades of Henry's mature kingship.

The depravities of the French aristocracy before and during battle are contrasted with Henry's two great speeches before the walls of Harfleur in Act III, which show him to be both an inspiring leader in battle ("Once more unto the breach, dear friends" etc.—III.i.1–34) and a master of peacemaking ("How yet resolves the governor of the town?" etc.—III.iii.1–43). The latter speech is unfortunately and erroneously used to justify the critique of Henry as a bloodthirsty warmonger. This utterly misreads the point of the speech. As Philip Thompson writes,

> Our film critics are very happy that Kenneth Branagh's *Henry V* [film of 1989] restores the speech of Harfleur which Olivier had deleted [in his film of 1944]. This is because it reveals a "different" Henry, whose many sides include one that is capable of the utmost brutality. As in the case of Prince John's despised deception in *Henry IV, Part 2*, the event [= outcome] does not enter into their response: Harfleur is threatened with the utmost brutality in order that none will occur. And none does—[Henry] orders mercy for all. The critics confuse the power of oratory

to horrify men out of war with a lust for the action described in order to prevent it; they speak as though the massacre had happened and added a "dark" aspect to Henry's character.[1]

There is no "dark" aspect to Henry's character, and the Branagh film is utterly misleading in giving us a *Henry V* of blood and mud and nasty *realipolitik*. Branagh even has Henry hard-heartedly standing by to watch as his former crony Bardolph is hanged. In Shakespeare's play, Fluellen reports that Bardolph, serving under the Duke of Exeter, is "like [= likely] to be executed for robbing a church" (III.vi.100–101). Fluellen adds, "his nose is executed, and his fire's out" (III.vi.105–106), and later the Boy confirms that indeed both Bardolph and Nym have been justly hanged for theft (IV.iv.72–73). But that execution takes place offstage and is not directly of Henry's doing, except insofar as Henry has forbidden his army to engage in plundering the French. Henry's comment on hearing this report is

> We would have all such offenders so cut off; and we give express charge that in our marches through the country there be nothing compell'd from the villages; nothing taken but paid for; none of the French upbraided or abus'd in disdainful language; for when lenity and cruelty play for a kingdom, the gentler gamester is the soonest winner. (III.vi.107–113)

There can be no good reason for thinking that Henry should be sentimentally sorrowful over the death of Bardolph, who in life had many opportunities and good cause to change his drunken, thieving ways and has not done so. Where kingdoms are at stake, it would be foolish to spend time on sorrowing for the likes of Bardolph, whose punishment, like that of the traitors in II.ii, is just. Henry's supposed friendship with Falstaff, Bardolph, and the others was never truly friendship, and our attachment to the jollities of the comic scenes in the Henry IV plays ought not to evoke more compassion for the banishment of Falstaff or the execution of Bardolph than admiration for the seriously responsible King, who is nothing like the imaginary cold-hearted politician that modern critics invent and that Branagh portrays—against Shakespeare's obvious intention.

Another supposed excuse for portraying an imaginary dark aspect to Henry is his order to kill the French prisoners during the battle at

Agincourt. But again, though he gives this order at IV.vi.37, apparently because "The French have reinforc'd their scatter'd men" (IV.vi.36), we find out at the beginning of the next scene that the King's decision is a punishment for the depravity of the French, who, during the battle have circled behind the English and attacked their boy servants and supplies. As Fluellen fumes,

> Kill the poys [= boys in his Welsh pronunciation] and the luggage! 'Tis expressly against the law of arms. 'Tis as arrant a piece of knavery, mark you now, as can be offert; in your conscience, now, is it not? (IV.vii.1–4)

And Gower reports,

> 'Tis certain there's not a boy left alive, and the cowardly rascals that ran from the battle ha' done this slaughter. . . . wherefore the King, most worthily, hath caus'd every soldier to cut his prisoner's throat. (IV.vii.5–10)

There is no justification for bringing modern sensibilities to bear in accusing the King's action here, nor for doubting the validity of the opinion of the trusty Gower. Henry's own response to this French outrage, when next we see him, is "I was not angry since I came to France / Until this instant" (IV.vii.55–56). In giving the order to execute the prisoners, the King is not damning their souls but trying to win a battle against injustice. Guilt for the death of the French prisoners is on the heads of the French, and the disposition of the prisoners' souls by God, as we will see, is on their own heads.

The contrast to the French is further developed in the scenes portraying the eve of the battle of Agincourt. In the French tents, the lords are nervously awaiting the dawn: The Dauphin is bragging about his horse, and the others are variously backbiting (III.vii and IV.ii). At the same time, in the English camp, we get first the comical moral uplift of Fluellen:

> It is the greatest admiration in the universal world, when the true and aunchient prerogatifes and laws of the wars is not kept. . . . If the enemy is an ass and a fool and a prating coxcomb, is it meet, think you, that we should also, look you, be an ass and a fool and a prating coxcomb, in your own conscience now? (IV.i.66–80)

And then a great philosophical conversation takes place. About King Henry the Chorus tells us,

> forth he goes, and visits all his host,
> Bids them good morrow with a modest smile,
> And calls them brothers, friends, and countrymen. . . .
> That every wretch, pining and pale before,
> Beholding him, plucks comfort from his looks.
> A largess universal, like the sun,
> His liberal eye doth give to every one,
> Thawing cold fear, that mean and gentle all
> Behold, as may unworthiness define,
> A little touch of Harry in the night.　　　　　(IV.Chor.32–47)

("Mean" means of the lower classes, and "gentle" means of the gentility, here including aristocrats.) Henry then disguises himself and brings that "little touch" to three typical English soldiers.

When the disguised King claims that the King's "cause [is] just and his quarrel honorable" (IV.i.127–28), Williams says, "That's more than we know" (IV.i.129). Bates then asserts that

> we know enough, if we know we are the King's subjects. If [the King's] cause be wrong, our obedience to the King wipes the crime of it out of us.　　　　　(IV.i.131–33)

But Williams fears that

> if the cause be not good, the King himself hath a heavy reckoning to make. . . . if these men do not die well, it will be a black matter for the King that led them to it.　　　　　(IV.i.134–45)

To this Henry replies in a long prose speech that offers two analogies to the king-subject relation: father-son and master-servant. His point is that

> The King is not bound to answer the particular endings of his soldiers, the father of his son, nor the master of his servant; for they purpose not their death when they purpose their services. . . . Every subject's duty is the King's, but every subject's soul is his own.
> 　　　　　(IV.i.155–77)

Henry's argument satisfies the soldiers. But Williams' initial concern evokes from Henry the great verse soliloquy on ceremony, which compares the sound sleep of the subject to the uneasy watchfulness of a king, echoing his father's speech that ended "Uneasy lies the head that wears a crown" (2 *Henry IV*, III.i.4–31). Here Henry says,

> The slave, a member of the country's peace,
> Enjoys it; but in gross brain little wots [= is little aware]
> What watch the King keeps to maintain the peace,
> Whose hours the peasant best advantages.   (IV.i.281–84)

("To keep watch" means both to stay awake and to guard.) Then Henry prays,

> Not to-day, O Lord,
> O, not to-day, think not upon the fault
> My father made in compassing the crown!   (IV.i.292–94)

and he lists the forms of penance he has done for the soul of Richard II.

The next morning, after we hear the French engaging in more of the foolish pride that goeth before destruction, King Henry gives his inspiring and justly famous speech to his minuscule English army, encouraging them to bravery despite the overwhelming odds against them. He does so by inviting them to imagine looking back on this St. Crispin's Day—October 25, the feast of the Christian brother-saints Crispinus and Crispianus, martyred in 287 A.D.—from the vantage point of having won the battle:

> And Crispin Crispian shall ne'er go by,
> From this day to the ending of the world,
> But we in it shall be rememberèd—
> We few, we happy few, we band of brothers;
> For he to-day that sheds his blood with me
> Shall be my brother; be he ne'er so vile,
> This day shall gentle his condition;
> And gentlemen in England, now a-bed,
> Shall think themselves accurs'd they were not here;
> And hold their manhoods cheap whiles any speaks
> That fought with us upon Saint Crispin's day.   (IV.iii.57–67)

("Shall gentle his condition" means to raise his rank to that of gentleman.) In the phrase "with us," Henry entirely unites himself with his army: the word "us" refers both to himself in the royal plural and to the band of brothers. And then the miraculous happens: King Henry's forces defeat the French.

It is one of the striking qualities about this play that at crucial moments Henry exhibits an intense and repeated reverence before God. When he reads the list of the French dead (many) and the English dead (four men of name, meaning of higher rank, and only twenty-five others), he says,

> O God, thy arm was here;
> And not to us, but to thy arm alone,
> Ascribe we all! (IV.viii.106–108)

alluding to the *"Non nobis"* of Psalm 115:1 ("Not unto us, O Lord, not unto us, but unto thy Name give the glory"), which a few lines down he will order recited along with the hymn *Te Deum* ("We praise thee, O God"). (See a partial list of further examples of Henry's reverence under Key Lines below.)

In Act V, through the formal and ceremonious agency of the Duke of Burgundy, Henry comes to terms with the French king, is named the heir to his throne, and marries Katherine, the French king's daughter, after some wooing in his broken French and her broken English. When he tries to kiss her and she objects, Henry translates, "It is not the fashion for the maids in France to kiss before they are married, would she say?" (V.ii.265–66). Then he replies,

> O Kate, nice customs cur'sy to great kings. Dear Kate, you and I cannot be confin'd within the weak list of a country's fashion. We are the makers of manners, Kate. (V.ii.268–71)

The final Chorus mentions the glory of "This star of England," Henry V, and tells us that of England and France he

> left his son imperial lord.
> Henry the Sixt, in infant bands crown'd King
> Of France and England, did this king succeed. (V.Epi.8–10)

However, "so many had the managing" of his state,

> That they lost France, and made his England bleed;
> Which oft our stage hath shown   (V.Epi.12–13)

i.e., in the first tetralogy—the three parts of *Henry VI* and *Richard III*.

The play as a whole makes use of the patriotism of his audience, its anti-French disposition and fear of internal civil strife, to inspire unity under the monarch. At the same time, it challenges every succeeding monarch to rise to the standard of justice and empathy for his subjects that Henry sets. England would not find a comparably heroic leader until the days of Winston Churchill, when the Battle of Britain was survived and World War II won partly because the words of this play lived in the minds and hearts of Shakespeare's twentieth-century audience.

KEY LINES:

1.   Here are some further examples of Henry's expression of awareness of and reverence for God:

> We charge you, in the name of God, take heed   (I.ii.23)

> But this lies all within the will of God   (I.ii.289)

> for, God before,
> We'll chide this Dolphin at his father's door   (I.ii.307–308)

> God quit you in his mercy!   (II.ii.166)

> Let us deliver
> Our puissance into the hand of God   (II.ii.189–190)

> O God of battles, steel my soldiers' hearts   (IV.i.289)

> And how thou pleasest, God, dispose the day   (IV.iii.133)

> Praised be God, and not our strength, for it   (IV.vii.87)

> Take it, God,
> For it is none but thine   (IV.viii.111–12)

And be it death proclaimed through our host
To boast of this, or take that praise from God
Which is his only.   (IV.viii.114–16)

Yes, captain; but with this acknowledgment,
That God fought for us.   (IV.viii.119–20)

SPECIFIC NOTES TO HELP IN YOUR READING:

1. I.ii.38–39: "'*In terram Salicam mulieres ne succedant*,' / 'No woman shall succeed in Salique land'"—The Archbishop's discourse recounts European royal history to refute the French claim that Henry has no right to the French throne because of the "law Salic" (*Loi Salique*), according to which females in Salic lands cannot inherit. The French claim the Salic lands to be in France; the Archbishop claims them to be in Germany. The issue matters because Henry claims France through his great-grandmother, Isabella of France, wife of Edward III and sister to Charles IV of France. When Charles IV died in 1328, Edward claimed the French throne as Charles's nephew and his nearest adult male relative and renewed the claim in 1340 when the French appropriated Edward's lands in Aquitaine. That exchange initiated the Hundred Years' War. The Archbishop adds that several earlier French kings themselves—Pepin, Hugh Capet, Lewis X—claimed the crown of France by virtue of descent through a female.

2. II.iii.17: "'a babbl'd of green fields"—It was the editor Theobald (pronounced TIB-ald) who emended the Folio's "a Table" to "'a babbled," a reading justified by script analysis and followed by almost all editors. (Even if "Table" was the intended word, the corrupted line may still refer to the same psalm—see Psalms 23:5.)

3. In III.iv, the French princess, destined to become Henry's queen, is trying to learn English, beginning with the names of the parts of the body. Some of those words, as pronounced by Alice, her waiting gentlewoman, sound immodest, "non pour les dames de honneur d'user" ("not for honorable women to use"—III.iv.54). Specifically, at III.iv.51 the English word *foot* sounds to Katherine like the French word *foutre*, the exact equivalent of the English f-word for sexual intercourse. Alice pronounces the English word *gown* as *count*, which sounds like the French word *con*, which is the equivalent, though derived differently, of the English c-word for the female pudendum.

4.   IV.i.93-94: "Under Sir Thomas Erpingham"—Henry equivocates: He implies that he is a soldier serving under the command of Sir Thomas Erpingham, but he is not lying because in fact he is at the moment sitting "under" the cloak belonging to Sir Thomas, which he had borrowed back at l. 24.

---

[1]   Philip Thompson, "Notes on Shakespeare" in Gideon Rappaport, ed., *Dusk and Dawn: Poetry and Prose of Philip Thompson* (San Diego: One Mind Good Press, 2005), p. 228.

Satire

Troilus and Cressida

Troilus and Cressida is unique among Shakespeare's plays for not being a comedy, a history, or a tragedy. Like the comedies it has many comical elements, like the histories it tells a historical tale, and like the *de casibus* tragedies it involves the fall of princes. But it lacks the happy ending of the comedies, the relative authenticity of the histories, and the profound personal engagement of the tragedies. If we are to categorize the play at all, given its plot, language, and tone, it must be as a satire, as mentioned in Chapter 10 of Part 1. Even at that the play is not a typical satire of the period, or indeed of any period, based as it is on an imaginative recreation of the famous heroes of the ancient Trojan War.

Because of its uniqueness as Shakespeare's only satire, the play has suffered from critical attempts to force it into one of the more familiar categories of plays. Some have tried to see it as a tragedy by imagining Troilus as a tragic hero. Some have read it as a failed comedy to be included among the so-called "problem plays." Some have seen it as the diatribe of a disillusioned Shakespeare-turned-cynic like Timon in *Timon of Athens*. These attempts falsify the play's real subject and its actual effects. A careful study of the language of the play in the context of the background discussed in Chapter 7 of Part 1 will reveal the reality: *Troilus and Cressida* is a dramatic evocation of a morally benighted civilization in the process of collapse as seen from the perspective of an audience for whom redemption, by contrast, is available.

The matter of Troy, the great topic of the ancients from Homer on, was very familiar to Shakespeare and his audience. The tradition of often retold tales combined veneration for the heroes of the Trojan War and horror at the destruction of the famous ancient city of Asia Minor. In other places Shakespeare himself alludes to the greatness of the ancient Greek and Trojan heroes. The tradition was not pristine: in various versions it includes flaws in the heroes. But in general the heroic reputation of the warriors on both sides at Troy prevailed.

In this play, however, Shakespeare detaches himself and us from such veneration in order to serve his satirical purposes. In fact, it is precisely the universal fame of those heroic tales and the more or less permanent invulnerability of the traditional treatment of the matter of Troy that permit Shakespeare to use the Trojan War to achieve the effects he wanted—namely to expose his audience to a biting analysis of the corruption and inevitable collapse of a whole civilization. (To set such a depiction of the collapse of human society in a time and place closer to home would be to distract the audience with topical allusions—and to risk government censorship, or worse.) To accomplish his task, Shakespeare takes the whole matter of Troy and turns it on its head. Though he keeps to the external facts, the famously great ancient heroes are here riddled with major character flaws, their self-promotion but so much empty swagger and their love but a pretense for lust. Thersites becomes the true oracle of this play, in whose view the entire matter of Troy is summed up in the phrase "still [= always] wars and lechery, nothing else holds fashion" (V.ii.194–95).

The structure of *Troilus and Cressida* is built of a masterful complexity of Shakespeare's familiar use of foils, parallels, and antitheses. The characters Troilus and Cressida are a perfectly matched couple, opposite but equal in their respective errors. The same is true of the Trojans and Greeks generally. The play as a whole dramatizes two opposite but equally corrupt forms of moral blindness: misplaced idealism and cynicism. Together these two characteristic forms of moral blindness account for the self-caused fall of the civilization depicted in the play.

The play is named for the lovers whose story came to Shakespeare from Homer via a line of descent including Benoît de Sainte-Maure's *Roman de Troie* and Boccaccio's *Il Filostrato* and culminating in Chaucer's *Troilus and Criseyde* (c. 1385) and Robert Henryson's *Testament of Cressid* (later 15th c.). From the Middle Ages into Shakespeare's time Troilus was an archetype of faithful love betrayed and Cressida of feminine infidelity (which makes it highly ironic that Toyota named a modern automobile for her). Shakespeare keeps to the tradition with Cressida, but instead of taking Troilus as received, Shakespeare makes him into a lover equally, though differently, at fault.

Cressida, appropriately enough, is the daughter of a Trojan priest who has gone over to the Greeks. Her own words show Cressida to be calculating, hypocritical, and unchaste from the start, well before she betrays Troilus with Diomedes. Her banter with Pandarus is risqué, and she is guileful in manipulating him into manipulating Troilus. With "wit" she will defend her "wiles," and with "secrecy"— not virtue—she will defend her "honesty" (I.ii.261–62). While her following soliloquy expresses her love for Troilus (I.ii.282–95), it also expresses her cynicism about the love of Troilus for her. Her false character is then embodied in her willingness to go to bed with Troilus without his first marrying her and in her later betrayal of him with Diomedes. Unlike the besotted Troilus, Ulysses in the Greek camp sees through Cressida's external beauty to her falsity: she is a "wanton" "daughter of the game" (IV.v.54–63), a niece befitting her uncle the pander.

Troilus, who unlike Cressida is naïve, is nevertheless also guilty of betraying her before she ever betrays him. First of all we see that he himself is changeable. When the play opens, he is in arms. Then he says he will "unarm again" (I.i.1) because of his love longing. Then he goes to the field of battle after all. In the meantime, Troilus has abased himself in begging for the aid of the go-between Pandarus to get into Cressida's bed, making Pandarus "Our doubtful hope, our convoy and our bark" (I.i.104). He subjects himself to a salesman who praises Cressida to Troilus and Troilus to her in order to tantalize the already converted, and Troilus cannot imagine that the resistance of both Pandarus and Cressida is merely contrived, as in fact it is. When he does get into Cressida's bed, he does so without benefit of marriage. His highest goal is not marital but merely sexual union, as we will see in his arguments in the debate among the Trojan leaders. At the end of the play, he says about himself, "Never did young man fancy / With so eternal and so fix'd a soul" (V.ii.165–66), a perfectly ironic expression of Troilus's foolish devotion to notoriously changeable "fancy" rather than to love. In short, Troilus betrays Cressida by treating her as a mere object of his desire, and his pleasure in her bed as the ultimate good. For this betrayal he is then repaid by Cressida's betrayal of him in the arms of Diomedes.

Troilus is foolishly ardent and ingenuous; Cressida is cynically designing and disingenuous. Troilus fights for Troy; Cressida goes over to the Greeks. Like the lovers who give their name to the play, the warriors of the two armies are depicted as suffering from a similarly complementary corruption of values. Their respective betrayals of the heroic ideal are explicitly conveyed in the two great debates—one among the Greek leaders (I.iii), one among the Trojan leaders (II.ii)—and in their conclusions.

Like Cressida, the Greeks are cynically debunking of all ideals. Their debate is about the law of political relations (hierarchy vs. insubordination). Like Troilus the Trojans are foolishly ardent about false ideals. Their debate is about the law of personal relations (marriage vs. lechery). Ulysses' speech to the Greeks voices the truth of the external order, opposite to the chaos of war; Hector's speech to the Trojans voices the truth of the personal order, opposite to the chaos of lechery. These opposite general faults form the two halves of the supposed "age of heroes"—two forms of corruption of the one set of universal truths that Shakespeare and his audience believed to be built in to the nature of things (see Chapter 7 of Part 1).

The Greek debate in I.iii begins with Agamemnon and Nestor, who both speak to the fact "That after seven years' siege yet Troy walls stand" (l. 12). What the forces call "shames" (l. 19) Agamemnon calls "But the protractive trials of great Jove" to test the warriors' "constancy" (ll. 20–21). Nestor reiterates the idea by saying, with many examples, that "In the reproof of chance / Lies the true proof of men" (ll. 33–34). That is, their failures are merely tests of their mettle. But then Ulysses gives a very long and justly famous speech to analyze the *cause* of the failures. He locates that cause in the overturning of rule, insubordination to the general, the "untuning" of the string of "degree."

Ulysses' speech on "degree" is a detailed evocation of the principle of hierarchy discussed in Chapter 7 of Part 1. Only by keeping their places in the hierarchy of the universe are the natural and human worlds—planets, elements, communities, schools, brotherhoods, commerce, "Prerogative of age, crowns, scepters, laurels" (I.iii.107)—sustained. The stability of all things depends upon "degree, priority, and place, / Insisture, course, proportion, season, form, / Office, and custom, in all line of order" (ll. 86–88). "Take but degree away" (l.109), he says, and nothing but discord follows until

> Each thing meets
> In mere oppugnancy . . .
> Strength should be lord of imbecility,
> Force should be right, or rather, right and wrong . . .
> Should lose their names, and so should justice too!
> Then every thing include itself in power,
> Power into will, will into appetite,
> And appetite, an universal wolf . . .
> Must make perforce an universal prey,
> And last eat up himself.　　　　　　　　　　(I.iii.110–24)

This is all quite right. Ulysses' analysis is accurate and apt. It applies specifically to Achilles, who has refused to participate in battle and has spent his time mocking Agamemnon and the other leaders. And without Achilles the Greeks have no hope of defeating Hector, the prop of Troy. But it also applies to Agamemnon himself, whose previous speech turns decorum on its head:

> Speak, prince of Ithaca, and be't of less expect
> That matter needless, of importless burthen,
> Divide thy lips, than we are confident,
> When rank Thersites opes his mastic jaws,
> We shall hear music, wit, and oracle.   (I.iii.70–74)

This crabbed and overwrought rhetoric, with its inverted word order, double negatives, and chiasmus of images, is inappropriate in the speech of the chief leader of the Greeks, and its compliment to Ulysses is made through a base comparison to the reviled Thersites.

So Ulysses' denunciation of the insubordination of the Greek forces, and specifically of Achilles, is quite correct. But then what follows it? Ulysses himself, joined by Agamemnon, the general of all the forces, Nestor, the oldest and most experienced of leaders, and other Greek heroes all abase their own "degrees" by stooping to play a cynical schoolyard trick on Achilles. They decide to use Achilles' pride to force his return to battle by pretending to promote the equally proud but not so capable Ajax into Achilles' place as a match for Hector. In other words, no sooner has Ulysses identified and articulated the behavior that has caused the Greeks' ongoing failure than he and those he is advising rush to engage in precisely that behavior. In this way Shakespeare illustrates how throughout a society the habit of cynicism blinds the will to the dictates of reason.

In the debate among the Trojans we see that the will of men may be similarly blinded to right reason by false idealism. Nestor has sent Troy an offer: "Deliver Helen" and the Greek forces will forego every other claim and depart (II.ii.3–7). The only wise man in Troy, the counterpart to Ulysses among the Greeks, is Hector, who argues that Helen "is not worth what she doth cost / The keeping" (II.ii.51–52).

Troilus, the voice of youth and passion, asks "What's aught but as 'tis valued?" (II.ii.52), one of the pithiest expressions of corrupt relativism in our literature.[1] The value of anything, he implies, lies only in what people are willing to pay or do to have it. To this absurdity, Hector wisely replies,

> But value dwells not in particular will,
> It holds his estimate and dignity
> As well wherein 'tis precious of itself
> As in the prizer. 'Tis mad idolatry
> To make the service greater than the god.   (II.ii.53–57)

That is, true value lies not only in the opinion of the valuer but in the reality of the thing valued. But Troilus argues for keeping Helen, despite the cost and the injustice of doing so, because they have all agreed to value her for her beauty's sake and to keep her for their honor's sake.

There is significant irony in the argument of Troilus and in the example he uses to illustrate it. He says, speaking hypothetically,

> I take to-day a wife, and my election
> Is led on in the conduct of my will,
> My will enkindled by mine eyes and ears,
> Two traded pilots 'twixt the dangerous shores
> Of will and judgment.   (II.ii.61–65)

The example is ironic because though Troilus will in fact take a lover, he will *not* make her his wife. He then argues that his will (meaning not only free will but also willfulness and sexual desire) are enkindled by his eyes and ears. This is not wrong. It is characteristic of young lovers (and others) that their desire follows the lead of the external senses. But then Troilus calls the eyes and ears "traded pilots" (i.e., experienced intermediaries) between will and judgment, which he calls "dangerous shores." Judgment a "dangerous shore"? Eyes and ears to be trusted as go-betweens? The irony of his argument is that his image is directly opposed to what Shakespeare and his audience believed to be the more accurate picture of man's condition: It is the judgement that ought to mediate between eyes and ears on the one hand and the choices of the will (in all senses) on the other, judgment that ought to govern the will's pursuit of what the eyes and ears value. True danger lies in the will's following the eyes without reference to the judgment.

Troilus then blames Hector for counseling a change of mind: "O theft most base, / That we have stol'n what we do fear to keep!" (II.ii.92–93), failing to realize that a dishonorable theft cannot be made honorable by persisting in it. When Cassandra then enters to prophesy, "Troy burns, or else let Helen go" (l. 112), Troilus rejects her prophecies as brainsickness and, along with the besotted Paris, argues for keeping Helen at all costs. So that Hector is quite right to accuse Troilus of arguing

> but superficially, not much
> Unlike young men, whom Aristotle thought
> Unfit to hear moral philosophy.   (II.ii.165–67)

(Shakespeare's use of anachronism in the reference to Aristotle, who lived long after the Trojan War, takes nothing away from the point.)

In response to the "superficial" chop logic of Troilus, Hector argues rightly as follows:

> Nature craves
> All dues be rend'red to their owners: now,
> What nearer debt in all humanity
> Than wife is to the husband? . . .
> If Helen then be wife to Sparta's king,
> As it is known she is, these moral laws
> Of nature and of nations speak aloud
> To have her back return'd. Thus to persist
> In doing wrong extenuates not the wrong,
> But makes it much more heavy.   (II.ii.173–88)

The aptness of Hector's speech sounds much like that of Ulysses' speech in I.iii. However, again, as with Ulysses' speech, what follows completely betrays the uttered wisdom:

> Hector's opinion
> Is this in way of truth; yet ne'er the less,
> My spritely brethren, I propend to you
> In resolution to keep Helen still,
> For 'tis a cause that hath no mean dependence
> Upon our joint and several dignities.   (II.ii.188–93)

In other words, he caves in. He jettisons his rational and virtuous loyalty to the laws of nature and of nations in favor of pursuing a superficial idea of honor. Since we have stolen her, our dignity requires that we should keep her. Dignity, not virtue.

Hector's moral collapse here prefigures that which will occasion his own death. Later in the play, ignoring his sister Cassandra's prediction and the dreams and entreaties of his wife, Andromache, and his father, King Priam, Hector goes into battle, where he chases after a Greek for his shiny armor. Having killed the man and observing "Thy goodly armor thus hath cost thy life" (V.viii.2), an epitaph that unintentionally applies to himself, Hector says, "Now is my day's work done" (V.viii.3) and takes his own armor off. He is immediately surrounded and killed by Achilles' Myrmidons. Hector's valuing of armor over life leads to his losing his own life for the sake of a goodly armor. Of course he loses it to the utterly reprehensible and unheroic choice of Achilles to have his men surround an unarmed man and kill him because Achilles himself has been physically weakened by his idleness. But this is the point: one morally corrupt army is warring against another, the anti-heroic wishful thinkers against the anti-heroic cynics. Both exhibit a benighted disregard of fundamental moral principles.

In both the debates, then, true value is articulated, then betrayed. As in the supposed love relation between Cressida and Troilus, so in the war relation between Greeks and Trojans, moral blindness leads to destruction. People betray others because they have betrayed themselves. The play demonstrates what the world is like when the essence of the advice of Polonius in *Hamlet* (written at about the same time) is rejected:

> This above all: to thine own self be true,
> And it must follow, as the night the day,
> Thou canst not then be false to any man. (*Hamlet*, I.iii.78–80)

Immoral in himself, one cannot be true to others.[2]

Beyond the major contrasting foils of Cressida and Troilus, Greek and Trojan, Greek debate and Trojan debate, a partial list of the many parallels and antitheses of the play would include the following: The vicious mascot of the Greeks is the cowardly biting dog Thersites, and that of the Trojans the sexual go-between Pandarus. The prophecies of the Greek Calchas are used to gain his own advantage; the true prophecies of Cassandra are met with disbelief. Ulysses the Greek speaks the truth about value and then betrays it; Hector the Trojan speaks the truth about value and then betrays it. Agamemnon, the leader of the Greeks, is reduced to a cheap trick to entice Achilles to fight; King Priam of Troy is reduced to begging his son Hector not to fight. The great Greek hope Achilles, weakened by inaction, runs away from Hector and then has his men surround and kill the unarmed hero; Hector, the prop of Troy, chases after a shiny armor, unarms, and is killed in an unfair fight. Achilles, against the will of his people, declines to go to battle so he may keep an oath made to the enemy Trojans for love of the Trojan girl Polyxena; Hector, against the will of his people, goes into battle in order to keep an oath made to the enemy Greeks to fight them for his honor. Patroclus begs Achilles to fight; Andromache begs Hector not to fight. Cressida is a calculating Trojan held by the Greeks; Helen is a flighty Greek held at Troy. The whole war turns on the broken marriage of the feckless cuckold Menelaus and the beautiful nitwit Helen.

Hector's words about Helen—"she is not worth what she doth cost / The keeping (II.ii.51–52)—are validated by what we see of her in Act III, Scene i. In that scene Pandarus comes to get Paris to make excuses to Priam for Troilus's absence from court. (Troilus is absent because he will be spending the night in Cressida's bed.) Helen engages with Pandarus in naughty verbal byplay and persuades him to sing a naughty song called "Love, love, nothing but love" (III.i.113, 115). Shakespeare has made Helen a perfect focal point of the drama of corruption by overturning her mythic reputation for beauty and showing her to be a shallow, frivolous ditz. Paris's love for her is seen to be an equally frivolous sensuality with no hint of the "marriage of true minds" of Sonnet 116. As with Cressida and Troilus, there can be no true love in this Greek/Trojan couple because she is an empty vessel and he is a worshipper of her shell.

To sum up, the Greeks are cynics, debunking every ideal and believing in nothing. The Trojans are fools, rushing in without the rational capacity to govern passion with reason or weigh competing ideals—too young for moral philosophy. Achilles responds to the chivalric challenge from his ideal opposite with "'tis trash" (II.i.126) and kills Hector in cynical cowardice. Hector believes that whatever he does is right because he is the hero Hector and dies chasing a shiny armor. Ulysses schemes to pit Achilles and Ajax against one another in a pride that supplants all possibility of heroism; Pandarus schemes to unite Troilus and Cressida in a lust that supplants all possibility of love. Troilus foolishly idealizes sexual love while Cressida cynically uses it. Hector foolishly idealizes his own heroism while Achilles cynically squanders his. To paraphrase Yeats in "The Second Coming" (ll. 7–8), the knowing Greeks lack all conviction while the foolish Trojans are full of passionate intensity.

Because of these corruptions of the true order of values, all fall prey to the universal wolf appetite, the concluding image in Ulysses' great speech on degree (I.iii.121). The play begins with the Prologue's minimizing the matter of Troy: "The ravish'd Helen, Menelaus' queen, / With wanton Paris sleeps—and that's the quarrel" (Prol. 9–10). This reductive sentence is an example of the belittling figure of speech called meiosis, of which, in a sense, the whole play can be read as an instance. The play ends with Pandarus bequeathing to the go-betweens in the audience his own venereal disease (V.x.56), a perfect image of appetite, the universal wolf, eating up itself (I.iii.124).

KEY LINES:

1.   In III.i there is a telling passage that is easily overlooked. Amidst the double meanings in the banter that opens the scene, we find in the Servant a character otherwise nonexistent in this play, namely one who "depend[s] upon the Lord." "You know me, do you not?" asks Pandarus. "Faith, sir, superficially" (III.i.9–10), says the Servant. His "Faith, sir" (i.e., "in faith" or "by my faith") implies (with another anachronism) a faith in God that, held by others in the play if it were available to them, would light a path out of their moral benightedness. And he uses "superficially" in three senses: a) he knows Pandarus not very well; b) he knows him by his outward show, which is different from his inward reality; and c) he knows him to be superficial. When Pandarus says, "know me better," the Servant says, "I hope I shall know your honor better" (III.i.13). In calling him "your honor" he is giving him an epithet he does not deserve. But the greater sense is not merely know *you* better but have reason to know that you have gained some *honor* that so far I don't see in your character. Finally, Pandarus, after implying that his niece Cressida is more attractive than Helen, says, "my business seethes," meaning is about to boil over, implying that he is in a hurry. To this the Servant responds with "Sodden business! There's a stew'd phrase indeed!" (III.i.41–42). *Sodden*, the past participle of *seethe*, also implies what is meant by *stewed*, from the metaphor *stews*, that is, brothels. (Compare the puns on "stewed prunes" in *Measure for Measure*—II.i.90 ff.) In other words, the Servant recognizes that Pandarus is about the business of a sexual go-between, taking his own advantage from the lust of others.

2.   The fecklessness of Menelaus, in keeping with the play's overall satirical intent, is illustrated in IV.v.28–46 when Cressida comes to the Greek camp and allows every one of the Greek heroes to kiss her. When it is the turn of Menelaus, Patroclus jumps in and kisses her twice, once for himself and once for Menelaus, mocking the way Paris jumped into

Menelaus' place in Helen's bed (IV.v.28–29). This mock is in keeping with Thersites' mocking of the Greek leaders that Achilles and Patroclus have so enjoyed (II.iii etc.). When Cressida says to Menelaus, "you are odd, and [Paris] is even with you" (IV.v.44), Menelaus answers "You fillip me a' th' head" (IV.v.45), meaning (literally) flick your fingernail against my head and (figuratively) allude to my cuckold's horns. (Horns on his own forehead, visible to everyone but himself, are the symbol of the cuckold.) Ulysses says, "It were no match, your nail against his horn" (IV.v.46). That is, the fingernail of a Cressida is minute compared to the size of Menelaus' horn, the implication being that Cressida's entertainment of the heroes' kisses (i.e., her loose character) is insignificant compared to the cuckolding of Menelaus. A few lines earlier, Ulysses has given voice to why: "O deadly gall, and theme of all our scorns, / For which we lose our heads to gild his horns!" (IV.v.30–31). The "argument" [= point of dispute] of the entire war is, as Thersites has said, "a whore and a cuckold, a good quarrel to draw emulous factions [= the competitive rival armies] and bleed to death upon" (II.iii.72–74), "good" here being bitterly ironic in keeping with Thersites' savage wit.

3.   The two parallel oaths mentioned above reinforce Shakespeare's theme and structure. Achilles is engaged by oath to the enemy queen for love of her daughter (Troilus's sister), Polyxena. Achilles says,

> My sweet Patroclus, I am thwarted quite
> From my great purpose in to-morrow's battle.
> Here is a letter from Queen Hecuba,
> A token from her daughter, my fair love,
> Both taxing me and gaging me to keep
> An oath that I have sworn. I will not break it.
> Fall Greeks, fail fame, honor or go or stay,
> My major vow lies here; this I'll obey.
> Come, come, Thersites, help to trim [= decorate] my tent;
> This night in banqueting must all be spent.   (V.i.37–46)

He has taken an oath not to fight against the Trojans, fighting whom ought to be his only mission. His opposite, Hector, is engaged by oath to fight the Greek enemy. He says to his father Priam,

> Aeneas is a-field,
> And I do stand engag'd to many Greeks,

Even in the faith of valor, to appear
This morning to them . . .
I must not break my faith.
You know me dutiful, therefore, dear sir,
Let me not shame respect, but give me leave
To take that course by your consent and voice,
Which you do here forbid me, royal Priam.   (V.iii.67–75)

However, given the prophecy of his sister Cassandra and the pleading of his wife Andromache and of his father King Priam, his real duty lies in *not* going out to battle that day.

Both speeches use the word *gage* (as "gaging" and "engag'd") about their oaths. Neither hero chooses to break his oath, the one not to fight, the other to fight. Both choices, putting oaths to the enemy before loyalty to friends, result in disaster. Because Achilles does not fight, his friend Patroclus dies. Because Hector does fight, he himself dies, and Troy falls. The defeat and fall of Troy are seen, then, not as a great triumph of one heroic army over another, or one hero over another, but as the result of moral collapse on both sides.

SPECIFIC NOTES TO HELP IN YOUR READING:

1.   In myth, Cassandra was a priestess of Apollo to whom the god gave the gift of true prophecy. When she refused his love, he cursed her with never being believed.

---

[1]   As the poet Philip Thompson, whose understanding of the play was the original inspiration for this chapter, writes, "The true corruption of Troilus' question is 'who values nothing is nothing' or 'who nothings value, Value nothings' (verbs)." Philip Thompson, "Notes on Shakespeare" in *Dusk and Dawn: Poems and Prose of Philip Thompson*, ed. Gideon Rappaport (San Diego: One Mind Good Press, 2005), p. 223.

[2]   Philip Thompson puts it thus: "In his speech about 'degree' [I.iii.75–137] Ulysses means to rebuke the military paralysis caused by insubordinate 'factions,' but what his words really give is a full description of the world in which the play takes place: a world lacking ['degree, priority, and place,' etc. (ll. 86–88, 103–107)], in which ['Each thing meets / In mere oppugnancy,' etc. (ll. 110–124)]. Like the worlds of Coriolanus and Timon, it is a world in which no good can arise because the moral devastation stemming from radical disorder is its permanent condition. And because the good is powerless to be born, annihilation is the only possible destiny for these worlds."—Thompson, p. 224. The phrase "powerless to be born" intentionally echoes ll. 85–86 of Matthew Arnold's "Stanzas from the Grande Chartreuse."

Late Romances

The Winter's Tale

The Winter's Tale, the next to last of the four romance plays Shakespeare wrote before he retired, bears special comparison with *Othello*. Both plays turn on the main character's jealousy of his wife. (For Shakespeare and his audience, the word *jealousy* also meant suspicion.) But the differences are telling. *Othello* is a tragedy that ends in death and damnation whereas *The Winter's Tale*, essentially a comedy, ends in joyful redemption. But there is also a significant dramaturgical difference. Othello's fall into jealousy takes place during a long and complex seduction by the demon-villain Iago in a painstaking psychological study of the way a self-important mind can fall, step by step, into destructive jealousy. By contrast, jealousy in *The Winter's Tale* happens instantly, without cause, without reason, without ulterior motive. If there is a demon of jealousy in this play, it remains hidden from sight—except in its effects. In the first scene and a half of the play Leontes is in a state of harmony with his wife, Hermione, and his best friend, Polixenes. Then, without warning, Leontes suddenly falls into a violently jealous rage starting at I.ii.108: "Too hot, too hot!" This sudden and mysterious onslaught of a wrong idea is in keeping with the characteristics of the four last plays, which all involve self-born villainies, supernatural mysteries, divine revelations, and surprise redemptions. Here we are in a world in which the veil between the natural facts of human lives and the spirit invisibly at work in the world is grown thin, a world in which the invisible is dramatically revealed in events with the immediacy of myth, or of an "old tale," as the Gentlemen call it (V.ii.28 and 61).

Leontes' jealousy, which explodes with such suddenness, falls into the calm and lovely courtly life at Sicilia like a rock thrown with violence into a peaceful pond, and its rings of negative influence spread inexorably wider. In his soliloquy at I.ii.108–207 Leontes reveals his jealousy to the audience first. Then he attempts to bring Camillo under its influence. The poison spreads to attack Polixenes, who escapes with Camillo from the King's murderous intent. The lords of the court are one by one dragged by the King toward suspicion of Hermione. All of them object to his accusations, but being the king, he overrules them. Even Leontes' own innocent newborn child suffers under his suspicion and is sent off to be exposed and die in a deserted land. Finally, the god Apollo is called to testify in court. In his delusion, Leontes fully expects the god to justify his suspicions.

When through his oracle Apollo asserts Hermione's innocence, even he is accused of participation in the conspiracy of adultery that is in fact the product of nothing but Leontes' jealous imagination. When Leontes says, "There is no truth at all i' th' oracle" (III.ii.140), the outward-spreading effects of Leontes' error reach their limit. A servant enters and announces that the King's son and heir, Mamillius, is dead. With a suddenness equal to the onset of his jealousy, Leontes' eyes are instantly opened: "Apollo's angry, and the heavens themselves / Do strike at my injustice" (III.ii.146–47). Hermione, too, as it appears to everyone, including the audience, has died on hearing the news of Mamillius. Thus from here on Leontes must live in penitence and sorrow, knowing that his inexplicable jealous suspicion is responsible for the death of his son and of his wife, hence of his whole future, for the oracle has said that "the King shall live without an heir, if that which is lost be not found" (III.ii.134–36). (In Latin the infant's name, Perdita, means "lost.") Later we find the wise Paulina causing Leontes to swear that he will not marry again without her permission (V.i.69–71) and saying that that permission will never be given "Unless another, / As like Hermione as is her picture, / Affront his eye" (V.i.73–75). And so we leave Leontes to his lifetime of repentance.

Balancing the suddenness of both the onset and the vanishing of Leontes' jealousy, the play now invites us to imagine a surprisingly long expanse of time. We are taken to Bohemia, where Antigonus, to fulfill his oath and in obedience to a vision of Hermione, leaves the infant Perdita to the mercy of nature. Once he does, he is devoured by a bear as the ship that carried him sinks in a storm. At the same time that the young shepherd (called "Clown," meaning unsophisticated country fellow) watches the old man die, the old shepherd finds the baby: "thou met'st with things dying, I with things new-born" (III.iii.113–14). Being good men, the shepherds bury the remains of Antigonus and take up the infant Perdita. This is the explicit turning point of the play, the transition from the old to the new, from Sicilia to Bohemia.

It is also the transition from winter to spring and from tragedy to redemption. To punctuate this transition, Shakespeare brings onto the stage the allegorical figure of Time, the Chorus, who tells us that sixteen years have passed. Such a passage of time exemplifies independence of Elizabethan playwrights, and especially Shakespeare, from the rigid adherence to the unities of time, place, and action derived from Aristotle's *Poetics* and insisted on by Sir Philip Sidney in his *Defence of Poesy*. This chorus of Time splits the play into two halves. The first half depicts the widening tragic consequences of Leontes' sudden jealousy, which has taken place in winter, as we know from Mamillius' observation "A sad tale's best for winter" (II.i.25), which gives the play its title. The second half of the play is the mysterious weaving together of those consequences into a healing redemption in an atmosphere of spring and summer.

The actual time of Act IV is late June, the usual time of the sheep-shearing festival mentioned by the Clown (IV.iii.37), which was a standard practice of English country life. But Autolycus has begun the scene by singing of daffodils (IV.iii.1), which appear in early spring, and Perdita's speech of welcome to the visitors include references to flowers of early spring (IV.iv.113), which she lacks now, flowers of May (the time of the Whitsun pastorals mentioned at IV.iv.134), and the flowers of late summer (IV.iv.79–82). Florizel, whose name itself contains the idea of flowers, likens Perdita to Flora, the goddess of flowers (IV.iv.2). Thus Act IV is suffused with the atmosphere of springtime and summer, as befits the developing love of the young lovers.

The idyllic pastoral world of Act IV is not without its conflict. The comic jealousy in the song sung by Autolycus and the shepherd girls (IV.iv.306–307) harmlessly echoes the tragic jealousy of Leontes. More threateningly, Polixenes breaks up the joy of the festival in an attempt to break up the young lovers. As in the first half of the play Polixenes was the unwitting occasion of the ruination of the court of Sicilia, so here he is the unwitting driver of everyone's return to Sicilia. He reasonably opposes Florizel's love for a shepherd girl because he cannot know that Perdita is in fact a royal princess, a perfect match for Florizel and a perfectly natural object of his love, who was led to her by divine intention under the guise of a natural event:

> I bless the time
> When my good falcon made her flight across
> Thy father's ground. (IV.iv.14–16)

Polixenes' obstruction unintentionally drives the couple to flee, and, thanks to Camillo's ulterior motive, they flee to Sicilia. All the strands of motivation—the oracle of Apollo, the lovers' love, the shepherds' virtue, the King's devotion to the good of the commonwealth, the longing of Camillo to return home, even the vice of Autolycus—are woven together to make possible the great final reunion.

And then Shakespeare shocks the audience with two utterly surprising theatrical devices. First, he relegates the actual reunion and recognition scene to a third-person prose narration. The revelation of who Perdita really is, the fulfillment of the oracle, the reconciliation of the two kings, the rewarding of the shepherd, the report of the death of Antigonus—all of these happen off-stage, described movingly but simply in court-gossip prose (rather than high dramatic verse) by three random gentlemen. At this point the audience is caught between joyous fulfillment and theatrical outrage. "This is all wonderful, of course, but why aren't you *showing* us this reunion, which is obviously the end of the play? Why are you just telling us *about* what we have been longing to see with our own eyes?" These questions must have been the more pressing for those who had read Robert Greene's *Pandosto*, the very popular prose romance that is the source of the plot of *The Winter's Tale*. That story ends with the reunions described in V.ii of the play. But here the entire denouement is only reported, and the scene containing what ought to have been the dramatic conclusion of the play ends with everyone marching off to look at a statue. Where is our fulfillment to come? From some dumb statue (dumb in both senses)? Has the playwright lost his mind?

Well, the statue is a masterpiece, we are told by Third Gentleman,

> many years in doing and now newly perform'd by that rare Italian master, Julio Romano, who, had he himself eternity and could put breath into his work, would beguile Nature of her custom [= put her out of business], so perfectly he is her ape [= imitator]. He so near to Hermione hath done Hermione that they say one would speak to her and stand in hope of answer. (V.ii.96–102)

The First Gentleman adds, "Every wink of an eye some new grace will be born" (V.ii.110–11). (If you follow the word *grace* through the play, you will discover how Shakespeare infuses the literal story with layer upon layer of spiritual implication—see Key Line 1.) As it turns out, the third-person report of V.ii sets us up for the second radical theatrical surprise in V.iii, the great statue scene, which achieves nothing less than an experience of the meaning of resurrection.

In *Pandosto* the Hermione character, who has died (as we are told in the equivalent of our Act III of the play), really is dead. In this final scene of the play, looking at the statue of Hermione, we watch her come back to life. Of course in the play it is not that a statue is literally being brought to life, like Galatea by Pygmalion. At the literal level, Hermione has not in fact died but has remained in hiding for the fourteen years until the oracle is fulfilled and that which was lost is found. But in the empathic experience of the audience, as of Leontes, it is as if Hermione is rising from the dead.

The scene then becomes a reunion scene beyond anything that could have been depicted of the reunions described in the prose conversation of V.ii. The Gentlemen in the previous scene described the joy of the reunions and reconciliations of this world. And Shakespeare intentionally distances them from us in order to prepare us for the greater reunion yet to come. Here, in V.iii, the reunion with the living Hermione becomes an image of that reunion promised by the Christian's faith in resurrection and hope for heaven. Paulina, the wise woman of virtue, pretends to be engaging in the very kind of white magic that Prospero will actually wield in Shakespeare's next play, *The Tempest*, saying "It is requir'd / You do awake your faith" (V.iii.94–95). But she does so to protect the others from dying of shock. In reality, though not a magician, she has been setting them up, as Shakespeare has set us up, to experience and be able to bear the unimaginable joy of living reunion with those whom the "wide gap of time" and apparent death have "dissever'd" (V.iii.154–55). As she says to Hermione, from death "Dear life redeems you" (V.iii.103).

The young Mamillius had asked whether his mother wanted a tale "Merry, or sad." She answers "As merry as you will," whereupon he says that "A sad tale's best for winter" (II.i.23–25). And so it is for the world of time, space, error, and death. The sadness is real: unlike his mother, Mamillius has actually died. But this sad "winter's tale" is also suffused with grace. And grace, if we are penitent, redeems us from time and space and error and even death. Depicting that grace at work and wedded to virtue, *The Winter's Tale* ends by being a tale far beyond "As merry as you will," a tale of transcendent joy.

KEY LINES:

1.   The word *grace*, with its cognates (*graces, gracious*), is particularly associated with Hermione, who both depends on grace and, like her daughter, embodies it: Both are often called "gracious." With "Grace to boot!" (I.ii.80) Hermione asks for heavenly grace in introducing the

distinction between unmarried sexual love and innocent married love. A few lines later she hopes "would her name were Grace!" (I.ii.99) and "'Tis Grace indeed" (I.ii.105) about her having said yes to marriage with Leontes. When she has been falsely accused by Leontes, she tells her women not to weep:

> When you shall know your mistress
> Has deserv'd prison, then abound in tears
> As I come out; this action I now go on
> Is for my better grace. (II.i.119–22)

Dion, about the "something rare" that will "rush to knowledge" when the oracle is read, says, "gracious be the issue [= outcome]!" (III.i.20–22). Hermione appeals to Leontes' conscience to admit "how I was in your grace, / How merited to be so" (III.ii.47–48). Time, the Chorus, tells us that Perdita, after sixteen years, has "now grown in grace / Equal with wond'ring" (IV.i.24–25), and Perdita herself wishes "Grace and remembrance" (IV.iv.76) to Polixenes and Camillo (both in disguise). Autolycus sarcastically accuses the Shepherd of offering "to have his daughter come into grace" (IV.iv.777–78), meaning marry into the royal family. Of course in this sense Perdita is "in grace" already, being herself the daughter of a king. As quoted above, the First Gentleman observes that "Every wink of an eye some new grace will be born" (V.ii.110–11). Paulina mentions the "surplus of [Leontes'] grace" (V.iii.7), which we read in two senses: Leontes is doing a favor (= an act of grace) to Paulina by visiting her house to see the statue of Hermione, and Leontes has a surplus of heavenly grace descending upon him, as he is about to find out. Leontes observes about Hermione that "she was as tender / As infancy and grace" (V.iii.26–27), uniting in our minds the images of Hermione and Perdita. Finally, Hermione calls upon the gods to "pour your graces / Upon my daughter's head" (V.iii.122–23). The grace associated with virtue characterizes both Hermione and her daughter throughout, and the grace that descends as the unmerited gift of heaven suffuses the second half of the play with its healing.

    2.   In the midst of his access of jealousy, Leontes observes, "Affection! . . . Thou dost make possible things not so held, . . . With what's unreal thou co-active art, / And fellow'st nothing" (I.ii.138–42). Leontes asserts that *affectio*, a sudden invasion of the mind by passion, can join itself ("fellow" used as a verb) to unrealities ("nothing") and make things seem

real that are not. This is exactly what is happening to him: his sudden jealousy makes him see infidelity where there is none. But he cannot recognize that this principle applies to him. Rather he uses it to reinforce the delusions of the *affectio* itself: "Then 'tis very credent [= believable] / Thou mayst co-join with something, and thou dost" (I.ii.142–43). The stress here is on the word *something* in antithesis with *nothing* in the previous line. If the passion can invent things that are not real, then how much more credible is it that the passion can attach itself to real things. He concludes, falsely, that that is the case with him, that the infidelity he imagines has actually happened.

3. At II.ii.58 Paulina says that Perdita is freed from the prison of the womb "By law and process of great Nature." At IV.iv.88, Perdita herself rejects the human art that attempts to share with "great creating Nature." These phrases point to the unseen forces at work in nature and human life, forces before which Hermione, Paulina, and Perdita are humble and with which they are especially in touch. Perdita rejects the horticultural art that would modify nature itself, just as she would not want Florizel to desire her only because of superficial cosmetics (IV.iv.79–103). Her commitment to what is natural reinforces our awareness that, though neither of them knows it, Perdita is in fact Florizel's natural equal. Great creating Nature is arranging things better than human beings can know, and virtue lies in letting that great Nature take its course. This idea of "Nature" is not the modern idea of unconscious material processes subject to nothing but physical laws and accident. For Shakespeare and his audience, "Great creating Nature" is itself the creation of God and the incarnation of his will.

4. The words used by Cleomenes and Dion in III.i—"celestial," "reverence," "ceremonious," "solemn," "unearthly"—and the description of their journey to Delphi as "rare, pleasant, speedy" evoke complete faith in the authenticity and validity of Apollo's oracle, which will be read out at court in the next scene (III.ii.132–36).

SPECIFIC NOTES TO HELP IN YOUR READING:

1. The name Polixenes (which replaces the name "Egistus" in Greene's *Pandosto*, the source of the story) originally comes from Homer: Polyxeinus led some forces of Elis to Troy in *Iliad*, Book 2, lines 615-24. Shakespeare had used the name in *Troilus and Cressida* for one of the Greek forces killed in battle (V.v.11). But it comes from the Greek *polyxenos*—the *x* being not the Greek letter Chi but the letter Xi (Ξ, ξ), the *gs* or *ks* sound—meaning "very hospitable," "entertaining many guests,"

from ξενος (*xenos*), meaning stranger, but probably more significantly from ξενοω (*xenou*), which means to entertain, to make into a guest, or to make a treaty of hospitality with someone. The emphasis of I.i is the mutual hospitality of Leontes and Polixenes. Based on their names, one could think of Polixenes meeting Leontes as Hospitality meeting Lion. And to Shakespeare's ear, perhaps the contrast in sounds was as important as the meanings of the root words. The sounds of their names make them not only brothers in containing each an *l*, but also contrasting in the difference between the sharpness of the *x* in "Polixenes" and the nasal *n* in "Leontes."

2. I.ii.108–208: Leontes' soliloquies are characterized by language spinning out of control to illustrate the wild disorder in his mind spurred by his sudden jealousy. His words leap from topic to topic, repeat, interrupt themselves, exhibit passion mangling reason. This chaotic language bursts into the calm, peaceful, and playful language of warm affection and celebration of friendship with which the play and this scene began.

3. I.ii.148: The line "What cheer? How is't with you, best brother?" is assigned to Leontes in F, the only authoritative text, but must in fact be said by Polixenes as a continuation of his "How? My lord?" in the previous line. It is Leontes who is looking "unsettled" and distracted and "mov'd," evoking the queries from both Polixenes and Hermione about what is bothering him.

4. In I.ii the words "brows" (l. 119), "neat" [= tidy and cattle] (l. 123), "steer," "heckfer" [heifer] and "calf" (l. 124), "pash" and "shoots" (l. 128), "hard'ning of my brows" (l. 146), and "fork'd" (l. 186) all refer to the idea of horns, based on the common notion that a cuckold, a man whose wife was unfaithful to him, grew horns on his forehead visible to everyone but himself.

5. At V.i.75 F assigns the phrase "I have done" to Cleomenes. It should be assigned to Paulina (as the Riverside edition assigns it) thus:

> Paulina: Unless another,
> As like Hermione as is her picture,
> Affront his eye.
> Cleomenes: Good madam—
> Paulina: I have done.
> Yet if my lord will marry . . .

The Tempest

The Tempest is the last of the four so-called romances of Shakespeare's final period of work and the last play Shakespeare wrote before retiring from the theater and probably from London to Stratford. (It was followed after his retirement only by *Henry VIII*, the lost play *Cardenio*, and his part in *The Two Noble Kinsmen*.) The only early text is that of the First Folio (F). The plot of *The Tempest* is, so far as we know, Shakespeare's own, though many elements of the play in plot and theme can be traced to a large variety of sources including:

- Montaigne's essay "Of Cannibals" (around 1580) and Florio's translation of it (1603);
- Book VI of Spenser's *Faerie Queene*;
- Various English and possibly Italian pastoral romances;
- Ovid, *Metamorphoses* (VII.197–209) and Golding's translation of it (1567); and
- The Bermuda pamphlets, about a 1609 shipwreck on the Bermuda Islands, specifically,
    Sylvester Jourdain, *Discovery of the Bermudas* (1610),
    Richard Rich, ballad of *News from Virginia* (1610),
    William Strachey, *True Reportory of the Wrack* (dated 15 July 1610, first published in *Purchas His Pilgrimes*, 1625), and
    Council of Virginia, *True Declaration of the state of the Colonie in Virginia, with a confutation of such scandalous reports as have tended to the disgrace of so worthy an enterprise* (1610).

The Tempest, while not explicitly allegorical in a political or historical sense, is in some ways Shakespeare's most mystical play. For one thing, the plot unfolds in the same amount of time that the play takes in performance—the now in the theater is the now in the story—and all the action, apart from Prospero's exposition of events of twelve years previously, takes place on an island or on shipboard just off the coast of the island (I.i). This is an example, unusual in Shakespeare, of an approximation to the classical ideal of the unities of time, place, and action, sharply contrasting with the sixteen-year gap of time in Shakespeare's immediately previous play, *The Winter's Tale*. Moreover, the tempest of the title that takes place in the first scene is tied by the language to the tempest on the Sea of Galilee described in Matthew 8:23ff. It thereby becomes a metaphor for life itself, and for any one person's life, just as the island is a metaphor for the world (see Key Line 1). The language of the play in general is Shakespeare's most translucent, the fruits of the poet's two and a half decades of composition and performance. It is both simple and profound, as obedient a medium of the poet's intentions as Ariel is for Prospero.

The play weaves together thematically the contrasting principles of nature and art, nature and nurture, outward appearance and inward reality, sin and forgiveness, justice and mercy, sexual desire and chastity, and the limitations of time and space in the context of eternal values. The introduction of white magic in an island world inhabited by two non-human rational beings raises the simple plot to the level of myth, so that the emotional and moral movement of the play carries serious metaphysical implications. Lastly, the epilogue and the applause at its end, as discussed at the end of Chapter 6 of Part 1, unite four levels of meaning in a single speech, much in the manner of the levels of allegory in scriptural interpretation and in Dante's *Divine Comedy*. The epilogue unites in one experience the roles of character, actor, playwright, and audience. In the third of those roles, that of the playwright, the epilogue has been read—quite reasonably—as Shakespeare's farewell to the stage. The more significant level, however, is that of the audience, whose applause becomes both approval of and participation in the sacrament of forgiveness.

Let us look at the characters of the drama as a way of organizing the discussion of this profound and complex play. In the tempest of I.i the character of the characters is revealed. The sailors are striving to fulfill their functions by saving the ship (see Specific Note 1 for explication of the nautical language); "the King and Prince [are] at prayers" (I.i.53); Gonzalo accepts the will of heaven but keeps hope; Sebastian and Antonio can only curse the seamen who are trying to save their lives. When Antonio says, "Let's all sink wi' th' King," Sebastian replies, "Let's take leave of him" (I.i.63–64). In II.i the two switch roles when Antonio becomes the tempter to evil and Sebastian the tempted, but their characters are consistent in their drawing one another toward vice. The Boatswain's speeches convey that the hierarchy of land is temporarily suspended on board ship in a storm. "What cares these roarers for the name of king?" he asks Gonzalo, and "if you can command these elements to silence, and work the peace of the present, we will not hand a rope more. Use your authority" (I.i.16–23). Aboard ship the authority of king and counselors must submit to the will of the boatswain, for in a storm only nautical authority can save the king's life and with it his political authority. Similarly, the authority of Prospero's virtue, seconded by his magic, will oversee the survival of the moral storm in the higher-ranking Alonso, a storm caused by Alonso's evil actions of twelve years earlier.

Those shipwrecked on the island are divided into three groups, making three parallel stories in relation to Prospero and unfolding three versions of the same themes. Alonso King of Naples, his brother Sebastian, Prospero's brother Antonio, old Gonzalo, and the other lords form one group. Ferdinand, joined by Miranda, forms the second. Stephano and Trinculo, joined by Caliban, form the third. The three groups must undergo various kinds of transformation on the island, and Prospero's and Ariel's work is not accomplished until those transformations are complete. Alonso must repent; Sebastian and Antonio must be thwarted in their evil designs and forced to submit to virtuous power; Ferdinand and Miranda must fall in love but remain chaste until their wedding; Stephano and Caliban must learn the unpleasant consequences of self-indulgence and untoward ambition. The "good old lord" Gonzalo's virtue serves as a contrast to the corruption of Alonso, Sebastian, and Antonio; the jester Trinculo's simple skepticism contrasts with the folly of Stephano and Caliban.

Ferdinand's mission is to love rightly—that is, to fall in love with his right match, as he does, and then to restrain his desires until marriage sanctifies the union, as he also does. But he must be tested before trusted, as Prospero says, "lest too light winning / Make the prize light" (I.ii.452–53). Like Ariel, Ferdinand puts up some manly resistance to apparent tyranny: "I will resist such entertainment till / Mine enemy has more pow'r" (I.ii.466–67). But overpowered by Prospero's art, he willingly submits to lowly service in the name of his love.

Miranda, whose name means "to be wondered at," in her innocence, having known no other man but her father and Caliban and seeing the handsome Ferdinand for the first time, expresses the belief in the Neoplatonic ideal that outward beauty must express inward virtue:

> There's nothing ill can dwell in such a temple.
> If the ill spirit have so fair a house,
> Good things will strive to dwell with't. (I.ii.458–60)

Her famous line "How beauteous mankind is! O brave new world / That has such people in't" (V.i.183–84), expressing the same attitude, calls for Prospero's mild correction: "'Tis new to thee." She is yet to learn, as we have learned from Alonso, Sebastian, and Antonio, that outward beauty may hide inward ugliness. But despite her innocence, she is not wrong about Ferdinand, whose virtue, by his good will, harmonizes with his outward beauty, as does Miranda's. Caliban will end by refuting the oneness of outward and inward in the opposite way. Whereas for most of the play his outward ugliness does express his inward vice, by the end he will seek an inward grace invisible in his outward form. Outward beauty may correspond with inward virtue or not; outward ugliness may correspond with inward vice or not. What counts is the free will's choice of virtue whatever the outward show may be.

At the end the lovers are revealed not embracing their mutual outward beauties in lust but playing intellectually at chess. That they do so to the tune of sweet "wrangling" must not be misunderstood.

> Miranda: Sweet lord, you play me false.
> Ferdinand: No, my dearest love,
> I would not for the world.
> Miranda: Yes, for a score of kings you should wrangle,
> And I would call it fair play. (V.i.172–75)

Miranda is not actually doubting Ferdinand's honesty or relativizing the concept of fair play. Her pretended accusation of cheating leads only to Ferdinand's protestation of love for her and her declaration of faith in him. The apparent conflict, as with opposites fighting a pretended "war" in the game of chess, is but a game of love existing only to emphasize how thoroughly the couple is at one.[1] Their sexual gratification will be postponed until their wedding, which will unite not only the two people but also their higher and lower natures. The sacrament of marriage redeems the lower desires by raising them into the service and celebration of love.

Ariel is called an "airy spirit" in the list of characters in the Folio. His name in Hebrew, as the Geneva Bible notes, means "lion of God," but his character and qualities derive not from biblical sources. Ariel is Shakespeare's imaginative composite of traditions about what, in *The Discarded Image*, C.S. Lewis calls the *Longaevi*,[2] long-lived ones (from the Latin *longus*, long, and *aevum*, age, lifetime). Those traditions include a) the great variety of "Ariel" characters in the magical tradition, e.g., Cornelius Agrippa's *Occult Philosophy* and various versions of the Faust legend, themselves influenced by the fallen angels of the Christian tradition who came to be known as demons; b) classical stories of nymphs, fauns, dryads, etc.; and c) English folk traditions about fairies of the kind seen in *A Midsummer Night's Dream*. Though a spirit of air, Ariel has powers to work in the other three elements as well (I.ii.190–92, 255). Being a spirit he is unconstrained by the physical world. As Frank Kermode writes, he can be "invoked and indeed maltreated, by a goetist [like] Sycorax; but the theurgist [i.e., Prospero] commands him by 'reason of affinity.'"[3] (A goetist is a sorcerer of the dark arts. A theurgist is a magician of white—i.e., natural or sympathetic—magic. See below.)

What Ariel wants most is his freedom to follow his own whims, and he is promised that by Prospero in return for a short period of labor. Symbolically, Ariel represents that immaterial part of the human being which longs for freedom from all limitations, including the constraints of time, space, and every form of moral and social duty. A part of all of us wants to do what we want. Another part of all of us wants to serve something higher than ourselves. Only in that do we find lasting meaning. Thus before Ariel can have his desire, he must serve. In return for submission of his will to the higher will of Prospero, he is finally given that freedom to return to his merely elemental being. In this he is representing the Augustinian principle that perfect freedom lies only in perfect service to God. The promise of freedom inspires Ariel to utter his desire to serve in one of the simplest and most moving expressions in all literature: "That's my noble master! / What shall I do? say what? what shall I do?" (I.ii.299–300). (See Key Line 1 for what is here echoed in the word *master*.)

In the character list in the Folio, Caliban is called a "savage and deformed slave." Each of these words is intended precisely: "Savage" means merely natural, untutored, wild, and amoral. "Deformed" means corrupt (from the human) in both shape and quality, the outward repulsive ugliness figuring his inward vice. That correspondence reflects Miranda's belief in the Neoplatonic idea of correspondence of inner to outer. "Slave" is the lowest possible condition of the human being because, while God's greatest gift to man is the free will, the slave's will is not his own. Caliban is a slave by nature—that is, appropriate to be a slave because of his character—not because he is enslaved by Prospero. Prospero's enforced restraint on Caliban is but a just form of punishment arising from Caliban's initial vicious behavior toward Miranda. It is the external form of Caliban's enslavement to his own lowest nature: his sense of injured merit and his lust. His desire to be free from rule is like Ariel's, but the path to freedom he chooses is obedience not to higher will or virtuous master but to merely natural desire. He attempts to tyrannize over Miranda by raping her and over the island by killing Prospero because he himself is tyrannized over by his lower self.

One of the great questions of the play is whether such a nature as Caliban's is redeemable through nurture. Caliban is invented in part as an instance in a debate among two traditions about the "natural man." As Frank Kermode explains, there were "two opposing versions of the natural; on the one hand, that which man corrupts, and on the other that which is defective, and must be mended by cultivation." "[T]he reports of the voyagers upon whom Montaigne and Shakespeare both depend . . . tended to describe the natives as purely virtuous or purely vicious."[4] In Montaigne's essay and elsewhere, the merely savage man was thought to be naturally good, corrupted from natural virtue only when he comes under the influence of a fallen civilization. This idea of man is expanded to monstrous proportions with the burgeoning of Romanticism in the late eighteenth and early nineteenth centuries. The other attitude is that the merely savage man, unilluminated by civilization and the Christian gospel, must perforce be morally deformed, slavish, and vile. In the former notion, that of Rousseau, all nurture is corruption. In the latter, nurture is redemptive. (The two notions are directly debated by Polixenes and Perdita in *The Winter's Tale*, at IV.iv.79–103.)

Shakespeare has Caliban representing something of each view. The virtuous Prospero and Miranda at first treat Caliban with "humane care" (I.ii.345–46) and do nothing to corrupt him. Stephano, on the other hand, selfishly abuses Caliban for his own advancement, claiming to be a god and corrupting him with liquor, as was reported, notes Kermode, about some Europeans in the West Indies.[5] But well before Stephano appears, Caliban has tried to rape Miranda, and he remains unrepentant despite punishment. When he then tries to kill Prospero, he is spoken of by Prospero, in his rage, as irredeemable: "A devil, a born devil, on whose nature / Nurture can never stick" (IV.i.188–89).

However, we are given hints of Caliban's potential for redemption in his response to beauty:

> Be not afeard: the isle is full of noises,
> Sounds and sweet airs that give delight and hurt not.
> Sometimes a thousand twangling instruments
> Will hum about mine ears; and sometime voices
> That, if I then had waked after long sleep,
> Will make me sleep again; and then, in dreaming,
> The clouds methought would open and show riches
> Ready to drop upon me, that, when I waked,
> I cried to dream again.   (III.ii.135–43)

By the end nurture makes inroads in Caliban's nature once he has experienced the difference between the effects of the rational government of the higher over the lower (Prospero's) and the effects of the irrational government of the lower over the higher (Stephano's). At the end he movingly observes, "I'll be wise hereafter / And seek for grace" (V.i.295–96).

Caliban represents the merely natural, physically desiring part of the human being who cannot at first see any value in restraining or channeling his desire in the name of higher values. His submission to Prospero's higher will must be forced. In Caliban's case nurture must take the form of punishment. But punishment can be merely punitive or purgatorial, depending upon the will of the one punished. Caliban at last benefits from punishment, and his will is shown to be capable of correction thanks to the joining of his will to the grace hidden within the punishment. Thus Shakespeare shows us that the nature/nurture controversy itself may be redeemed by grace.

The "good old lord Gonzalo," as Ariel calls him quoting Prospero (V.i.15), is known to be good from the beginning. It was he who provided Prospero and the infant Miranda with food, water, clothing, and books. His attitude in the tempest is patient—in the old sense of that word: willing to bear affliction—and hopeful. On the island he is not included among those condemned by Ariel dressed as a harpy in III.iii.

In II.i Gonzalo voices a utopian vision of society, and during his exposition of it he is constantly made fun of by the cynical Antonio and Sebastian. There is a superficial illogic in Gonzalo's vision. As the two carpers point out, he begins by saying "Had I plantation of this isle, my lord . . . And were the king on't" (II.i.144–46) and later says there would be "No sovereignty" (II.i.157). However, we are not to join Antonio and Sebastian in their carping, for Gonzalo's vision, like Ariel's longing for freedom, is a longing in all of us: a life without toil, conflict, the need for trade, laws, riches or poverty, without any evil, but with all needs and desires provided for by nature. It is an ideal world, a combination of the classical "golden age" (II.i.169) and the biblical Garden of Eden.

That vision of Gonzalo is seen against the backdrop of the corrupt societies of Milan and Naples, the fallen world of society (Alonso, Antonio, Sebastian, and Stephano) and nature (Caliban) that Prospero strives to correct. It would be foolish to take Gonzalo's utopian vision as actually possible to be achieved by merely human beings, even on an island that provides food and water and is governed by a virtuous master of magic. But it would be equally foolish not to recognize the goodness of the heart that longs for such a world, in contrast with the evil of the hearts that would murder for power or rape for pleasure.

At the end, it is the good-hearted Gonzalo who recognizes the larger meaning of the tempest and shipwreck:

> Was Milan thrust from Milan that his issue [= offspring]
> Should become kings of Naples? O, rejoice
> Beyond a common joy, and set it down
> With gold on lasting pillars: in one voyage
> Did Claribel her husband find at Tunis,
> And Ferdinand, her brother, found a wife
> Where he himself was lost; Prospero, his dukedom
> In a poor isle; and all of us, ourselves,
> When no man was his own. (V.i.205–213)

("Was Milan thrust from Milan" means the duke from the city.) Life in the world is like a tempest on an island governed invisibly by a benign ruler. Our sufferings may be gifts of grace that draw us toward finding ourselves, which means finding that we belong to ourselves only in the sense that we are called to serve—in virtue, patience, and humility—something beyond ourselves, namely love, in the form of right eros, right obedience, right government of ourselves and of others, right caring for others, and forgiveness of the penitent for their errors.

In the late 1580's Christopher Marlow wrote a popular play called *Doctor Faustus* about a man who sold his soul to the devil for twenty-four years of magical power and then, because he would not repent, was haled off to hell. The Latin word *faustus* (from *faveo*, meaning to favor, help, support, be favorable) means lucky, favorable, auspicious. It is a synonym for the Latin word *prosperus* (from *pro spero*, meaning according to one's hope), which means fortunate, favorable, lucky, prosperous. Shakespeare chose to tell the story of a magician named Prospero as an explicit antithesis to the story of Faustus.[6] Faustus was a *goetist* (from the Greek *goēs*, sorcerer), that is, a magician commanding evil powers, using what was called black magic. (The term *black magic* was erroneously derived from *necromancer*, mistakenly thought to be derived from the Latin *niger*, black. Actually *necromancer* derives from the Greek *nekros*, dead body, and *manteia*, divination.) By contrast with Faustus the goetist, Prospero is a *theurgist* (from the Greek *theos*, god, and *ergos*, worker), a miracle or wonder worker, master of what was called white magic, with divine approval commanding good metaphysical powers by the force of his own virtue informed by mystical knowledge. The Church in medieval times, following St. Augustine, treated both categories as sinful magic, but the Neoplatonic tradition, revived in the Renaissance, preserved the distinction, and Shakespeare makes use of it here.

The Tempest has suffered somewhat in modern times because of the misreading of the course Prospero takes through the play. Such misreading has resulted partly from applying anachronistically the distracting screens of recent ideologies related to American slavery and European colonialism. More damaging has been critics' determination to see Prospero as needing moral transformation. It is Alonso and Caliban, not Prospero, who must be morally transformed in the play. Prospero is virtuous from the beginning to the end. He does, however, have a moment of desperate anger, justified by the attempt on his life by Caliban. And he has a moment of choice, when all his "enemies" are in his power. But his consistent virtue brings him triumphantly through those moments, without any change in his character.

The moment of anger comes in IV.i and evokes Prospero's great speech about the ultimate dissolution of everything. Some have taken that speech as Shakespeare's final word on reality. This is nonsense. Such a reading results from taking the speech out of its context, as misguided as treating Gloucester's "As flies to wanton boys are we to th' gods, / They kill us for their sport" (*King Lear*, IV.i.36–37) or the "Tomorrow" speech of the desperate and self-damned Macbeth (*Macbeth*, V.v.19–28) as if they were the poet's own final judgments on life. The context here is Prospero's rage at "that foul conspiracy / Of the beast Caliban and his confederates / Against my life" (IV.i.139–41). Both Ferdinand and Miranda are startled by Prospero's unusual anger: Ferdinand says, "This is strange. Your father's in some passion /That works him strongly" (IV.i.143–44), and Miranda says, "Never till this day / Saw I him touch'd with anger, so distemper'd" (IV.i.144–45). Prospero then says that

> like the baseless fabric of this vision,
> The cloud-capp'd tow'rs, the gorgeous palaces,
> The solemn temples, the great globe itself,
> Yea, all which it inherit, shall dissolve,
> And like this insubstantial pageant faded
> Leave not a rack [= wisp of cloud] behind. We are such stuff
> As dreams are made on; and our little life
> Is rounded with a sleep.   (IV.i.151–58)

("The baseless fabric of this vision" is the spirits' performance of the masque. The "great globe itself" may allude to the Globe Theatre, in which the play may have been performed after its initial presentation to King James at Whitehall in 1611.) This speech, which serves as a kind of *memento mori*, a reminder that nothing in the created world is eternal, is not the last word of the play. It conveys a common human experience of even the most virtuous, a sudden awareness that our existence and the world's are limited. All worldly things are mutable, and worldly time itself as perceived by human beings will end, as Christianity and modern science agree. But the dark emptiness of the vision lasts but a moment and passes. Such a vision cannot be relevant to the real purpose of human beings living life in the present moment and eternally in the mind of God. Prospero himself says,

> Sir, I am vex'd;
> Bear with my weakness, my old brain is troubled.
> Be not disturb'd with my infirmity.   (IV.i.158–60)

In other words, the speech is a sign of temporary infirmity. We are to take it in the context of Prospero's entirely understandable vexation as a moment of weakness, not as a final word. The speech does not represent either a final despair or even a character flaw that needs correcting. It is the way even the wisest might feel when suddenly recalled from celebration to the threat of destruction by evil.

Prospero's moment of choice is also not a sign of any break in his virtue. When Ariel announces that all his tasks are accomplished and the lords are all either "distracted" (= mad) or "mourning over" those who are (V.i.12–13), he and Prospero have the following exchange:

> Ariel: Your charm so strongly works 'em
>   That if you now beheld them, your affections
>   Would become tender.
> Prospero: Dost thou think so, spirit?
> Ariel: Mine would, sir, were I human.
> Prospero: And mine shall.   (V.i.17–20)

Ariel's hypothetical sentiment is not schooling Prospero but bringing out what has been in him all along:

> Though with their high wrongs I am strook to th' quick,
> Yet, with my nobler reason, 'gainst my fury
> Do I take part. The rarer action is
> In virtue than in vengeance. They being penitent,
> The sole drift of my purpose doth extend
> Not a frown further.   (V.i.24–30)

This conclusion is not a new moral breakthrough but a fulfillment. Prospero could never have been the theurgist he is without being virtuous. It is here that the virtue always in him comes through as mercy tempering justice. As Frank Kermode explains, virtue here is Christian virtue, including the virtue of forgiveness, rather than Machiavellian *virtù*, which would, in an aristocrat, include vengeance. "'The rarer action is / In virtue than in vengeance' would be to [the Machiavellian] Antonio an utterly meaningless phrase."[7] As Antonio says about conscience, "Ay, sir; where lies that? . . . I feel not / This deity in my bosom" (II.i.276–78). Like Antonio, Sebastian, Caliban, Sycorax, and Stephano are all devoted to their own self-aggrandizement and power, even at the cost of corrupting their souls with evil. Their opposites are Prospero, Miranda, Ferdinand, and Gonzalo, who are filled with love of others and of the good.

But then there *is* a transformation in Prospero's life, though not his character: he renounces magic. After a speech that is a close imitation of the passage in Ovid's *Metamorphoses* (VII.197–209) in which Medea describes what she has been able to do with her magical art, Prospero says,

> But this rough magic
> I here abjure; . . . I'll break my staff,
> Bury it certain fathoms in the earth,
> And deeper than did ever plummet sound
> I'll drown my book.   (V.i.50–57)

Why? I have often asked professional actors in rehearsal for this play and my students studying it to ask themselves for what reason, if they had magical powers to stop accidents and floods or to cure diseases and prevent crimes, they would give up those powers. Prospero has used his magic for good, not evil. He has healed his world by disarming the villains Sebastian, Antonio, and Caliban; he has brought Alonso to repentance and atonement; he has arranged a perfect marriage for his daughter. Why stop now? Why not go back to govern Milan with magic?

After considering what your own answer to this question would be, you may think of Prospero's decision in the following several ways. First, it is through Ariel that Prospero has worked his magic on the island, and Prospero has promised Ariel his freedom. Second, as Lord Acton was later to phrase the idea, "power tends to corrupt, and absolute power corrupts absolutely." Prospero knows that this supernatural power has been permitted him for the purpose of accomplishing a task at the precise moment when it can be accomplished, the "zenith" of his fortunes (I.ii.181). That task accomplished, he must not keep hold on the tool needed to accomplish it. To do so would imply the very motives of self-aggrandizement and ambition that he has successfully defeated in Alonso, Sebastian, Antonio, Caliban, and Stephano. Shakespeare is very likely also making a parallel between Prospero's art of magic and his own art of poetic theatrical drama, from which he is about to retire.

Finally, Shakespeare remains a believing Christian. He recognizes that ultimately the condition of the soul before God must overrule the ambition to master the world that characterizes all magic, whether white or black (and also much of the modern science touted by Francis Bacon). What Prospero is renouncing is the goal of extending his power over "all things possible," as C. S. Lewis calls it in *The Abolition of Man*.[8] Prospero knows that power itself is not his purpose or his desire, and to pursue it would be to become Faustus. Doctor Faustus is forced to give up his magic when the devils come to take his soul to hell. Prospero forestalls the temptation that might lead to such an eventuality for him. His renunciation of magic is an explicit rejection of the self-deifying motives of Faustus in favor of retiring to Milan "where / Every third thought shall be my grave" (V.i.311–12). ("Every third thought" simply means often, an expression of humility in the face of mortality; but one may imagine him having a *memento mori* thought for each thought about Milan and about Miranda.) Prospero's renunciation of magic is thus a demonstration of the essential virtue of humility. His virtue, having mastered the art of magic and used it for the good of the world, renounces it for the good of his soul. The spiritual significance of that renunciation is then dramatized in the Epilogue (see Unity Joins Us in Chapter 6 of Part 1). The end of the Epilogue not only concludes the play but evokes from the audience a moment of approval of, and willing participation in, the great Christian principle of forgiveness of others as we would be forgiven. Prospero, as himself, as the actor playing him, and as the playwright inventing him, engages us in the simple gesture of clapping. That momentary theatrical gesture, evoked by the mere words of the magician Shakespeare, becomes in us, through our clapping, a joyful and undeniable incarnation of divine mercy.

KEY LINES:

1. In I.i, the use of the term "master" (ll. 2 and 12) alludes to Matthew 8:23–27 (Geneva Bible):

> 23 And when he was entered into the ship, his disciples followed him. 24 And behold, there arose a great tempest in the sea, so that the ship was covered with waves; but he was asleep. 25 Then his disciples came, and awoke him, saying, Master, save us; we perish. 26 And he said unto them, "Why are ye fearful, O ye of little faith?" Then he arose, and rebuked the winds and the sea, and so there was a great calm. 27 And the men marveled, saying, "What man is this, that both the winds and the sea obey him?"

The tempest here echoes the tempest on the Sea of Galilee, and the master, who appears only here and never again in the play, becomes an image of someone of greater and mysterious power governing events: at various levels of interpretation a) the invisible captain of the ship, b) Prospero on land, c) Jesus on the Sea of Galilee, and d) God in heaven.

2. Ariel's song at I.ii.397–405 provides for Ferdinand a magical consolation for the supposed death of his father. The bones that become coral, the eyes that become pearls, and everything that is "sea changed" "Into something rich and strange" evoke a beautiful but mysterious image of the meaning of death—not what we think it is—an image consoling despite the loss. From one point of view, the entire play is a lesson in recognition that a) things are not only what they seem; b) someone more powerful and with good motives is in charge of them; and c) the ultimate meaning is better than we could have hoped. Gonzalo expresses another version of the same ideas in his speech at V.i.205–213 beginning "Was Milan thrust from Milan, that his issue / Should become kings of Naples?"

3. When the lords come to land on the island, Gonzalo sees the grass as "lush," "lusty," and "green" (II.i.53–54) and their clothes as "hold[ing] . . . their freshness and glosses, being rather new dy'd than stain'd with salt water" (II.i.63–65) and "as fresh as when we put them on first in Afric" (II.i.69–70). At the same time Antonio and Sebastian see the grass as "tawny" (II.i.55), meaning dried up, yellow or brown, and the clothes as ruined (II.i.66–68, 105). The entire passage, as in I.i, contrasts Gonzalo's positive attitude with the satirical cynicism enjoyed by the villains. The magic of the island thereby reflects to each his own character. This reflection will be made explicit in Ariel's speech as harpy in III.iii (see Key Line 4).

4. The "Shapes" in the stage directions of III.iii, who bring in the banquet and then remove it, are spirits, Ariel's "quality" (I.ii.193), that is, his fellow spirits, his cohorts. They perform a role here just as they perform the roles of the goddesses Iris, Ceres, and Juno and of the nymphs and shepherds in IV.i. These are masques, performed by spirits, which Prospero arranges as performances to fulfill his purposes. The latter masque is for the delight and entertainment of the young couple.

Here the masque dramatizes the difference between the fruits the lords might enjoy if they practiced virtue and the punishments they will suffer if they fail to repent. Ariel's speech as harpy accuses Alonso and Antonio of their sin of supplanting Prospero, and by implication accuses Antonio and Sebastian of the echoing sin of attempting to murder Alonso. He proclaims that "destiny," "fate," "the powers," their "ministers," and nature itself have turned against the villains because of their sins and will continue to torment them unless they repent ("heart's sorrow"—III. iii.81) and do penance ("a clear life ensuing"—III.iii.82).

Ariel's language here is convoluted in syntax, expressing the strangeness of the vision and the ugliness of the sins, until the last line, which offers the lords the better choice in phrases of simple clarity.

5. At V.i.129, Prospero has let Antonio and Sebastian know that he knows of their attempt to kill Alonso. Since they are now disarmed, and know it, he refrains from further punishing them. Sebastian, in keeping with his cynical character in I.i. and II.i, says "The devil speaks in him." Prospero offers no argument and no proofs. He simply says, "No." From his position, that is all he needs or wants to say. To enter into discussion with Sebastian would be simply to "minister occasion" to his negativity (as Gonzalo said at II.i.173). Prospero's "No" is also the answer to any suspicion that his art was of the black magic kind.

6. At V.i.275–76, Prospero says, about Caliban, "this thing of darkness I / Acknowledge mine." At one level, this is simply Prospero claiming to be the liege lord of Caliban as Alonso is that of Stephano and Trinculo. A ruler is in part responsible for the behavior, good or bad, of those whom he rules, and so must "know and own" "these fellows" (V.i.274–75). At another level, however, "this thing of darkness" is an aspect of every man. The Caliban within us—the lower self, tempted to serve only itself—must be acknowledged in order to be mastered. Only then may it learn to be "wise hereafter / And seek for grace" (V.i.295–96).

SPECIFIC NOTES TO HELP IN YOUR READING:

1. Some of the language at I.i.1–35 is nautical idiom:
    1. 1. "Boatswain" (pronounced BŌ-sun): officer in charge of the physical ship
    1. 2. "master": captain of the ship (and see Key Line 1 above)
    1. 3. "Good": probably short for "goodman"; "yarely" = smartly, briskly, hop to it
    1. 6. "take in" = furl, take down and roll up the sails
    1. 8. "room enough" = sea room, the distance from shore needed to navigate the ship without running it aground
    1. 34. "Down with the topmast" = take down the additional higher and smaller mast that in good weather extends upward the length of the mast and supports the topsail
    1. 35: "Bring her to try with main-course" = "to try" is to lie to, that is, to bring the ship around to head into the wind to

stop its headway or forward motion, here by using the main sail ("course"); "with" is probably a contraction of "with th'" (i.e., with the).

---

[1] Like the playful wrangling of Portia and Bassanio and of Lorenzo and Jessica at the end of *The Merchant of Venice*.

[2] C.S. Lewis, *The Discarded Image* (Cambridge: Cambridge University Press, 1964, repr. 1967), Chapter VI.

[3] Frank Kermode, ed., Arden edition of *The Tempest* (Cambridge, MA: Harvard University Press, 6th ed., 1958), Appendix B, p. 143.

[4] Kermode, Introduction pp. xxxv–xxxvii.

[5] Kermode, Introduction p. xxxvii.

[6] The antithesis of Faustus and Prospero was first pointed out to me in private conversation by James Kirsch, Jungian analyst and author of *Shakespeare's Royal Self* (New York: Putnam, for the C.G. Jung Foundation for Analytical Psychology, 1966).

[7] Kermode, Introduction pp. liii–liv.

[8] In *The Abolition of Man* (New York: HarperCollins, 2001, orig. copyright 1944), pp. 77-78, C. S. Lewis writes (here not distinguishing between goetism and theurgy),
    There is something which unites magic and applied science while separating both from the 'wisdom' of earlier ages. For the wise men of old the cardinal problem had been how to conform the soul to reality, and the solution had been knowledge, self-discipline, and virtue. For magic and applied science alike the problem is how to subdue reality to the wishes of men: the solution is a technique; and both, in the practice of this technique, are ready to do things hitherto regarded as disgusting and impious—such as digging up and mutilating the dead.
    If we compare the chief trumpeter of the new era (Bacon) with Marlowe's Faustus, the similarity is striking. You will read in some critics that Faustus has a thirst for knowledge. In reality, he hardly mentions it. It is not truth he wants from the devils, but gold and guns and girls. 'All things that move between the quiet poles shall be at his command' and 'a sound magician is a mighty god'. In the same spirit Bacon condemns those who value knowledge as an end in itself: this, for him, is to use as a mistress for pleasure what ought to be a spouse for fruit. The true object is to extend Man's power to the performance of all things possible. He rejects magic because it does not work; but his goal is that of the magician.

Sonnets

Selected Sonnets

For a discussion of the general characteristics of Shakespeare's 154 sonnets, see Chapter 11 of Part 1. What follows here are notes on selected individual sonnets. There is no substitute for reading a sonnet aloud both before and after studying it.

SONNETS 1–17

The first seventeen sonnets in the sequence exhort the young man to whom the poems are directed to marry and beget children as a way of preserving his virtues and his beauty, which must inevitably pass away in time. Sonnet 15 prefigures a theme to which Shakespeare will return in later sonnets, starting with Sonnet 18, immortalizing the beloved in poetry. But Sonnet 15 is paired with Sonnet 16, which again urges the young man to marry.

Some have thought that Shakespeare was commissioned to write these poems by the young man's mother in an effort to get her son to marry and to carry on the family line. They argue that Shakespeare began by fulfilling this commission but then came to know and love the young man in himself and continued writing sonnets to convey his unfolding experience of love as the friendship developed. This is speculation; the facts are not known.

SONNET 18

The first line of the sonnet ("Shall I compare thee to a summer's day?") is a yes or no question to which the rest of the poem answers both yes and no. It can do so because of the double sense of the word *compare*. Shall I make a comparison of you to a summer's day? Yes—the rest of the poem makes that comparison. Do you bear comparison with a summer's day in the sense of being equal to it? No—because "Thou art more lovely and more temperate" (l. 2). The next six lines list the potentially intemperate qualities of a summer's day. The season of summer days may be late in arriving or early in departing (ll. 3–4); any given summer's day may be too hot or too cloudy (ll. 5–6); and every summer's day, like every form of beauty, declines with time (ll. 7–8).

The volta or turning point comes at the beginning of the third quatrain with the word "But" (l. 9, "But thy eternal summer shall not fade") and the proclamation that the beloved's beauty, by contrast with a summer's day, is eternal, surviving even death. Line 12 ("When in eternal lines to time thou grow'st") makes a play on words, distinguishing between temporal lines, the wrinkles that in time ruin a beautiful face, and eternal lines, the lasting lines of verse.

The couplet concludes the poem with the assertion that "this"—i.e., the poem itself—will survive in its unchanging form so long as there are human readers of poems. The beloved is immortalized by living on within the lines of the poem.

This power of poetry to bestow immortality on the poet and on his subject is an ancient theme, appearing in Horace (*Odes*, III.30.1–5) and Ovid (*Metamorphoses*, XV.871–79, *Amores*, I.10, I.15) and in many Renaissance poets including Spenser (*Complaints*: "The Ruins of Time," ll. 253–59, 358–64, 400–406). Shakespeare partly depends upon the awareness of that tradition for his effects in the sonnets. He is also, of course, aware that the better the poem, the likelier it is to survive through time.

SONNET 20

This is the one sonnet in which sexual, as opposed to romantic, attraction to the young man is hinted at, and in it the possibility of sexual satisfaction with the man is denied.

The sonnet figures the beloved friend as originally intended by Nature to be a woman because of his qualities: a beautiful face but painted so by Nature herself, rather than with the cosmetics used by women; a heart that is gentle (implying both gentleness and gentility) but not fickle and inconstant as women (governed by the moon, or perhaps only false women) were in general thought to be; a bright eye (from which light beams were thought to emanate, sight being produced by the reflection of those beams back to the eye); a manly combination of temperament and form that, however, compels the gaze of men and amazes the souls of women. (As editor G. Blakemore Evans writes, "In Neoplatonic terms, the eyes were thought of as the 'windows of the soul.' Men, therefore, may be thought of as viewing the youth intellectually, women, emotionally."[1]) In keeping with the feminine qualities of the young man, Sonnet 20, says Evans, "is the only one of Shakespeare's sonnets to use feminine rhyme throughout."[2] This is true, though Sonnet 87 has feminine rhymes in all but two of its lines. (See What Are Masculine and Feminine Endings? in Chapter 4 of Part 1).

However, as Nature was making this would-be female, she fell in love with her creation, and, being female herself, added one "thing" to turn him into a male. The word "thing" is common in Shakespeare as a euphemism for both the male and the female genitalia, and the implication is confirmed in the couplet with the triple pun "pricked thee out," meaning "chosen you," "decorated you," and "added a penis to your anatomy."

That one thing, however, added for the pleasure of women, is "to my purpose nothing." In other words, having that "thing," the beloved cannot fulfill the speaker's erotic purpose. Hence the addition of it, turning the intended woman into a man, "me of thee defeated": deprived me of the ability to enact the erotic relation with you that *might* have been had you been a woman as Nature originally intended. The added "thing" is, for the speaker's purposes, "nothing," i.e., useless, because it is "no thing," that is, not a woman's "thing."

The couplet's conclusion employs the noun "use" in three senses: a) interest or increase on an investment of capital, b) sexual intercourse in general and specifically use of the penis in sex, and c) increase, in the sense of producing offspring. Since nature has "pricked out" the young man for the sexual pleasure of women and the production of offspring, let his love itself be the speaker's "treasure," and let the "use" of that love—sexual intercourse and the pleasure and the increase it produces—be the treasure of women.

Hence, though the poet's love of the young man is romantic and often passionate, it is almost certainly not homosexual. By contrast, the poems to the "dark lady" are explicitly, even graphically, sexual at times, e.g., Sonnets 135 and 151. (See Was Shakespeare Gay or Not? in Chapter 11 of Part 1.)

SONNETS 29–30

These two sonnets dramatize the transformation of mood inspired in the speaker by the thought of the beloved friend.

In Sonnet 29 the transformation is embodied in the shift from the series of end-stopped lines, each a kind of sigh, to the elation expressed in the enjambment of ll. 11–12 ("Like to the lark at break of day arising / From sullen earth").

In l. 1 ("When in disgrace with fortune and men's eyes") the twofold "disgrace" refers to rejection by Fortune (see Fortune in Chapter 7 of Part 1) and the disapproval of men. "Bootless" (l. 3) means fruitless, useless. "Wishing me like to one" (l. 5) begins a list of five kinds of people who are better off, of which the first, "more rich in hope," is the general category into which the next four fall and means having a greater likelihood of future success. The second ("Featured like him," l. 6) has better looks and other personal qualities. The third ("like him with friends possessed," l. 6) has supporters of various kinds and degrees. The fourth ("this man's," l. 7) has better "art," meaning a focused gift for making some specific kind of valuable thing. The fifth ("that man's," l. 7) has "scope," implying the capacity to be successful in a wide variety of arenas. "Features" and "friends" (l. 6), in addition to being alliterative, make a contrast between that which one has in oneself and that which one has in others. Likewise "art" and "scope" (l. 7) are contrasting, art being narrow and focused and scope being wide-reaching.

Line 8 ("With what I most enjoy contented least") is a superb example of the unity of form and content. The four last words of the line form a chiasmus, a mirror image structure, with two verbs in the center ("enjoy" and "contented") flanked by their respective antithetical modifiers ("most" and "least"). But even as that balance is struck ("most enjoy contented least"), the content of the words forms a series of three against one and also six against one: three positive words ("most" "enjoy" "contented") followed by a word that overturns these positives and transforms them into negatives ("least"), so that the last word entirely reverses the effect of the previous three words, and thereby also of the previous six words ("With what I most enjoy contented—least"). The phrase expresses just how one feels when, depressed and frustrated, one turns to the one activity sure to console or please and that, too, turns to dust in the moment. (Pick a day when everything has gone wrong at school or at work, with friends, with your beloved, with your parents or your children, with your prospects, and you sit down to play the guitar to console yourself in your misery. If, then, the strings won't be tuned and your fingers won't do what you tell them, your last hope for uplift is dashed. The thing that you most enjoyed now contents you least.)

Line 9 ("Yet in these thoughts . . .") promises to be a volta, a turning point, with the word "Yet," but instead the word leads to the lowest point in the poem: "myself almost despising." The real turning point comes with "Haply I think on thee" (l. 10). "Haply" means perhaps or by chance, though it puns on "happily." The sound of the word "thee," which picks up the assonance from "beweep," "me," "Featured," "least," "these," and the *y* in "Haply" and sends it on toward the word "sweet" in l. 13, changes everything. The lark in l. 11–12 ("Like to the lark at break of day arising / From sullen earth") refers to the European skylark, which rises into the sky at dawn too high to be seen but which can be heard singing its beautiful melody. (It reappears in Shelley's poem "To a Skylark.") In l. 3 heaven is "deaf," but in l. 12 the speaker's "state" is, like the lark, singing hymns at heaven's gate. "State" means both state of mind and condition in the world, as in l. 2, and "hymns" makes a pun on "him," the beloved.

Repeating the word "state," the couplet asserts that the speaker would not exchange ("change") his state now *even* with kings, who represent possession of all that the speaker lacks in the first eight lines: smiled on by Fortune and men and able to command all that gives one richness of hope, features, friends, art, and scope. Such is the power of the "love rememb'red."

Sonnet 30 makes a similar transformation, this time from memories of previous woes, but not until the last line.

The sonnet begins with two law court metaphors ("sessions," l. 1, and "summon," l. 2). Into the court of memory are summoned "lack," "old woes," "time's waste," dead friends, lost love, "many a vanished sight," and old "grievances." The poet repeats the sounds of woe through the poem by associating long *o*'s, *w*'s, *s*'s and -*or*'s with words implying sorrow: "woes," "wail," "waste," "drown," "flow," "weep," "woe" again, "moan," "foregone," "woe" twice more, "o'er," "fore-bemoanèd," "moan," and "before"—twelve lines of old miseries recalled and recounted over and over in similar sounds. ("Tell" and "account" are accounting metaphors; bank clerks are called *tellers* because they *tell*—meaning count—cash.) In contrast to those sounds, the word "thee" in l. 13 ("But if the while I think on thee, dear friend"), assonant with the long *e* of "sweet" in l. 1, makes a total reversal in sound and feeling.

In the final line the poet joins all the sounds of woe into the words "restored" and "sorrows" and then puts an end to them with the word "end." Unlike the words of sorrow and woe, in which that long *o* can be drawn out endlessly, the pronunciation of the word "end" must actually end on the *d*. And what does "end" rhyme with? "Friend." The thought of the friend equals the end of the sorrows. Thus the form of the words and their senses become a single experience of love, the redeemer of moods.

SONNET 42

Sonnet 42 also involves a reversal in the couplet. The three quatrains express the speaker's frustration with the suspicion that the beloved friend and the "dark lady" girlfriend are having an affair. He is jealous of the friend over the girlfriend, and even more jealous of the girlfriend over the friend.

The reversal comes with the assertion that since he and his friend are one, the girlfriend loves only him after all. The reversal is embodied in the alteration of sounds as well as of sense: All those long *e*'s in ll. 1–5 and 7 ("grief," "be," "dearly," "she," "thee," "chief," "me," "nearly," "ye") turn into the *o-n-e* sounds ("one," "alone") at the end, the transformation reiterated in the sounds of the last line ("she . . . me alone"). The unity of the friends outweighs and at the same time redeems the love relationship with the girlfriend. "She loves but me alone" (l. 14) abolishes not only any distance between the speaker and his friend but also any betrayal by either the friend or the girlfriend.

One may wonder whether such an apparently satisfactory emotional resolution is actually possible to one who loves two people in these two ways. The poet challenges all previous categories of friendship, love, and jealousy and asserts an ideal unimaginable—until we have read this poem, which makes it irresistibly real.

SONNET 55

Like Sonnet 18, Sonnet 55 seeks to immortalize the beloved, here by presenting itself as a surer way of doing so than any physical monument can provide. One of the marvels of this sonnet, as of many others, is again the use of sound to convey and reinforce sense.

The first two lines ("Not marble nor the gilded monuments / Of princes shall outlive this pow'rful rhyme") make a strong contrast between the last word of l. 2 ("rhyme") and all the previous words. The series "marble," "gilded," "monuments," "princes," and "pow'rful" repeat the consonant sounds *l*, *m*, *n*, and *r* (consonance) and the vowel sounds *o*, *a*, *u*, and short *i* (assonance) to build up a sense of gravity, weighty monumentality, that is then exploded by the contrasting long *i* sound of "rhyme." This sudden contrast is assisted by the fact that all that monumentality is introduced by the negating words "Not" and "nor" in l. 1.

The next two lines pick up the long *i* of "rhyme" (l. 2) in the words "shine" and "bright," adding the sharp *t* sound in "bright" and "contents." These make a contrast with the mushy, slushy sounds of l. 4 ("unswept stone besmear'd with sluttish"), in which the wearing away of "stone," a word that picks up the long *o* and the *n* and thus the monumentality of ll. 1–2, again negates the value of physical monuments, and within the word "time" itself, the hard *t* from l. 3 is dissolved in the *m* from ll. 1–2.

The result is a four-line chiasmic series which expresses a) the smearing of monuments in time, and b) the sharp brightness of the beloved preserved in the poem (see the discussions of chiasmus in Chapter 4 in Part 1). Here the chiasmus (a-b-b-a or mirror image structure) is

a) "Not marble nor the gilded monuments / Of princes shall outlive this pow'rful"

b) "rhyme"

b) "But you shall shine more bright in these contents"

a) "Than unswept stone besmeared with sluttish time."

Line 4 creates in sound the equivalent of the smudging of lettering that time works upon stone, making a smeary fuzziness of sound corresponding to the smeary fuzziness of sight and contrasting with it the vowel sound of "rhyme" and the sharp *t* sound of "bright" that together represent the ever crisp and clear effect of the poem and of the beloved in it.

In l. 9 ("'Gainst death and all-oblivious enmity") the added unstressed (or perhaps elided) syllable (on the second *i*) in the word "ŏblívĭŏŭs" contrasts with the two spondees that begin l. 10 ("Sháll yoú páce fórth"). Against the smudging, smearing oblivion (felt in the four short vowels in "oblivious"), which the "enmity" of time works upon physical monuments and consequently upon the memory of those recorded on them, we have "Shall you pace forth," the stride of those four equally stressed syllables reinforcing the meaning of the word "pace." And those two spondees are followed by two and a half lines whose enjambment makes the reader of the poem run almost out of breath by the last word, "doom," which itself can be drawn out until the breath is gone ("your praise shall still [= always] find room / Even in the eyes of all posterity / That wear this word out to the ending doom"). So we have the beloved pacing forth through the long declining history of the world to its end represented in the long declining breath of the reader of the lines. (Again, there is no substitute for reading this poem aloud.)

"Ending doom" and "judgment" refer to the end of the world on the day of the Last Judgment, when, according to Christian doctrine, all the dead will be resurrected and judged by God. The final contrast of the poem, giving sound to the contrast between the wearing out of the world until doomsday and the perpetual living and shining of the beloved, is that between the *m* and long *o* sounds of "room . . . posterity . . .world . . . out . . . doom," which pick up the sounds of the first two lines ("marble . . . monuments . . .outlive . . . pow'rful"), and the long *i* of "arise" and "eyes," which pick up the sound of "rhyme" in l. 2.

Until doomsday then, the beloved will live in "this," the poem itself that we are reading, living in the eyes of its readers, who are lovers of their own beloveds and, reading the poem, become lovers of the speaker's beloved too.

SONNET 60

In Sonnet 60, as in Sonnets 18 and 55, the poem itself becomes the vehicle of the beloved's survival in the face of the passage of time that slowly but surely eats away at every beauty.

Line 1 begins with two trochees alternating with iambs to give a sense of forward motion: "Líke ăs thĕ wáves máke towards [pronounced *tŏrds*] thĕ pébblĕd shóre." Then l. 2 and l. 3 each begins with a trochee followed by all iambs ("Só dŏ̌ oŭr mín-" "Eách chănğĭng pláce"). The trochees feel as if they are trying to slow or stop our motion forward, putting the weight of the stresses early, but the force of time (and of meter in the verse) drives us forward to the end of the line as waves follow one after another at the shore and as time drives us forward toward our ends. The trochees in ll. 1–3 cannot stop the forward motion of the meter, and l. 4 ("In sequent toil all forwards do contend") is all regular iambic feet, punctuating the irresistible forward motion of time.

The same contrast happens in the second quatrain. The trochees are "ónce in" in l. 5, "Cráwls to" (and possibly "whérewith") in l. 6, and "Croóked" in l. 7. By l. 8 ("And Time that gave doth now his gift confound") we are back in irresistibly regular iambic rhythm again. The same happens with the trochee "Feéds on" in l. 11 followed by the regularly iambic l. 12 ("And nothing stands but for his scythe to mow"). The "parallels in beauty's brow" of l. 10 refer to wrinkle lines in the forehead.

The couplet reverses the relation, giving us a regular iambic l. 13 ("And yet to times in hope my verse shall stand") and beginning l. 14 with a trochee, "Práising." By contrasting it with trochees, the poem sets up the iambic as the forward motion of time, and then it uses the contrast of trochee and iamb to place the beloved outside time's "sequent toil."

SONNET 65

Sonnet 65 similarly makes "black ink" (l. 14) the miracle that has the "might" (l. 13) to "forbid" the "spoil of beauty" by Time (l. 12). The power of mortality that "o'ersways" the "power" (l. 2) even of "brass," "stone," "earth," and "boundless sea" (l. 1) is contrasted with the weakness of the rhyming word "flower" (l. 4). The battering of the hard consonants in "wrackful," "batt'ring," "rocks," "stout," "gates of steel," and "strong" (ll. 6–8) is contrasted with the drawn out sound of "decays" in l. 8, so that all strengths and hardnesses are finally eroded in sound as in sense. Against this decay of the vowels and consonants in the first twelve lines of the poem stands the crisp vowel-consonant combination in the rhyme "might" and "bright," which reverses the order of sound in the word "Time" (from *tī-* to *-īght*) and makes the miracle of the poem overrule with "-īght" the decaying power contained in the "Tī-" of Time.

SONNETS 73–74

In Sonnets 71–74 the speaker depicts his own coming death and its effects on his beloved friend. Sonnet 73 is rightly considered one of Shakespeare's greatest. Anyone who has been aware of the approaching death of a loved one, even of a pet, knows the intensification of love that the impending loss of the beloved evokes. In Sonnet 73 the speaker calls upon that phenomenon to strengthen the beloved's love for him.

The sonnet's three quatrains give three images of the nearing of death in the speaker:

The first is the image of the declining year. The beloved may see in the speaker the season of fall. Line 2 ("When yellow leaves, or none, or few, do hang") gives us a non-chronological series of images of the leaves on a tree: "yellow," "none," "few." To understand why the series is non-chronological, do the following thought experiment. Close your eyes and picture in your mind a large tree in full green leaf. Then picture that same tree when all the leaves have turned yellow. Then picture that same tree with all the leaves fallen to the ground. And then picture that same tree with all the leaves fallen to the ground except two or three of them. Which of these four images in the mind is the most poignant? Why? The answer explains Shakespeare's order of images. The saddest and most poignant image is that of the tree still holding those few yellow leaves that we know must inevitably fall, and soon. That is the feeling the beloved is to have about the speaker's nearness to death. The boughs, almost barren of leaves, are then imagined as the "bare ruin'd choirs" from which, because it is fall, the singing birds have departed for the south. Imagine choir stalls in a ruined church from which the human singers have departed. (Still in Shakespeare's time there were many such ruins in England following the suppression and expropriation of the monasteries by Henry VIII.) As singers have departed from ruined churches, as the birds and the leaves have departed from the trees, so youth has departed from the speaker.

The second quatrain presents the image of the ending of a day and its turning into night, also to be seen in the speaker. The remarkable use of consonants in l. 8 ("Death's second self, that seals up all in rest") gives us a sound to correspond with the image, a multiple repetition of the letter *s* ending in the *t* of "rest." The sound of *s* may be drawn out as long as one has breath. The sound of *t* may not; it puts an abrupt stop to all the *s*'s, as night silences the sounds of daytime and death the final breath of a life. This sound carries over into the image in the next quatrain.

The third quatrain produces an image, again to be seen in the speaker, of a dying fire. The fire is not blazing or flaming but "glowing" (l. 9), lying on the "death-bed" of its ashes (l. 11). Line 12 ("Consum'd with that which it was nourish'd by") inverts chronological order again, beginning with "Consum'd" and ending with "nourish'd." The fire is about to be consumed, put out, by the ashes which were once the wood that fueled the fire. What feeds the fire, wood, the fire converts to what will smother it in the end, namely ashes, the "ashes of his youth" (l. 10), just as the passage of time eventually turns youth to age and then to death. The sound that carries over from the previous quatrain is that of l. 8—*ssssst*—now the sound of the final extinguishing of a glowing fire.

The three quatrains and their three images are linked by the shortening of time. The first quatrain evokes the fall season of the year ending in winter, the second quatrain a day ending in night, and the third quatrain the few hours that a fire burns until it dies. Time is shortening through the poem as the speaker's time in life is running out. An additional link is that as in the first quatrain the weather turns cold, in the second the sun sets, and in the third a fire built for heat is dying. The wood of the boughs in the first quatrain, once night comes in the second, is burned in the fire of the third.

The couplet makes the volta or turning point, changing the sadness of approaching death to a kind of strength. Shakespeare takes the ending -*st* sound of l. 8 and of the dying fire, repeats it in "perceiv'st" (l. 13), and then reverses it, turning it into a beginning in the word "strong." In the last line we must not mistake the sense in the inverted word order: in "To love that well which" we must understand "To love well that which."

The sense is "to love well that which thou must leave ere [= before] long." Lastly, the word "leave" in l. 14, meaning depart, separate from, ties back to the "leaves" of l. 2, which themselves were leaving the tree in the first quatrain.

Sonnet 74 picks up where Sonnet 73 leaves off, turning to a different metaphor of separation, namely death as a sheriff arresting the speaker and carrying him away without possibility of bail. Once again we have the immortality of verse, but here the poem preserves not the beauty or life of the beloved but the love of the speaker himself. The worth of the speaker's physical body, which will eventually decay into the "prey of worms" (l. 10), is that it contains a spirit. And the spirit of the speaker, which has inhabited his body in life, has taken up residence in a second, more lasting body, namely "this" (l. 14), the poem we are now reading. The poem, which cannot decay, remains with the beloved. Hence the beloved is to be "contented" (l. 1) when death arrests the speaker and carries him away, for "this with thee shall stay" (l. 14). This poem, to me one of the most moving, not only remained with the beloved but remains with us, and through it, in us, lives the spirit of the poet.

SONNET 94

This sonnet comes in the center of a group in which the speaker fears that the beloved, whose "virtue" may not correspond with his "show" of beauty (93:14), may have betrayed or may forsake the speaker. This particular sonnet turns from the more personal language of "thou" to a more general complaint: "They that . . ." (l. 1).

The contrast is drawn in the first two quatrains between two kinds of men: a) those who have the power to hurt others but do not do so (ll. 1–2), who are the rightful heirs to "heaven's graces," including outward beauty (l. 5), who are not easily tempted to waste their gifts (ll. 4 and 6), who therefore can be considered the lords of the gifts they have been given by behaving in ways consistent with their outward beauty; and b) those who use their gifts to hurt others, who are easily tempted, who do not deserve "heaven's graces," whose outward gifts and inward character are not in harmony because, though beautiful on the outside, they are guilty in their character or behavior, and who therefore are merely stewards of their outward beauty but don't own it, are not one with it. The former are to be praised; the latter are repulsive.

The third quatrain then supports the distinction with a metaphor. The summer's flower, even though it lives and dies only to or for itself, that is, unseen by anyone, nevertheless by virtue of the sweet odor it exudes contributes sweetness to the summer generally. (In l. 10—"Though to itself it only live and die"—the word "only" modifies "itself" rather than "live and die." The sense is "though it live and die only in and for itself," such transposition of adverbs being fairly common in Shakespeare.[3]) But if the flower is infected from within, it comes to smell worse than weeds.

Lines 1 and 13 are both proverbial: "To be able to do harm and not to do it is noble," from the Latin "*posse et nolle, nobile*," and "The corruption of the best is worst," from the Latin *optimi corruptio pessima*."[4] But the poet's expression of the idea in the two lines of the couplet raises the proverbial to the sublime.

Here in ll. 13–14 ("For sweetest things turn sourest by their deeds; / Lilies that fester smell far worse than weeds") Shakespeare is at his marvelous best at uniting the sounds of words and their senses into an experience of meaning in form. The alliteration, assonance, and consonance of these lines and their use of antithesis and rhythm were discussed in Chapter 4 of Part 1. To these we may add that the first line of the couplet gives a general rule and the second a specific instance, leaving us the impression of a particularly illustrated universal. Here is a précis of some of the mechanics:

Alliteration:
> on *f*: For/fester/far
> on *s*: sweetest/sourest/smell
> on *th*: things/their/than
> on *w*: worse/weeds

Assonance:
> on long *e*: sweet-/deeds/weeds
> on short *e*: sweetest/sourest/their/fester/smell
> on short *i*: things/Lil-
> on the schwa plus *r*: sour-/worse

Consonance:
> on *r*: For/turn/sour-/their/fester/far/worse
> on *w*: sweet-/worse/weeds
> on *st*: sweetest/sourest/fester

Antithesis:
> sweetest/sourest, things/deeds, Lilies/weeds,
> Lilies/fester, sweet/fester, sweet/smell worse

Rhythm:
Line 13 is in regular iambic meter (rhythm and meter are
the same)
Line 14 is punctuated with a trochee ("Líľĭes") and a
spondee ("fár wórse"):
Líľĭes thăt féstĕr sméll fár wórse thăn wéeds.
Generalization:
"sweetest things turn sourest by their deeds"
Specific instance:
"Lilies that fester smell far worse than weeds"

The overall effect of this combination of figures of speech is
achieved not through construction brick by brick but by knack—the
phenomenal gift Shakespeare had for thinking in the medium of figures
of speech, of word-sound that we call poetry. In this case the effect is to
build disgust through the three *-est* words ("sweetest" to "sourest" to
"fester"), the last of which takes a very heavy stress, being preceded by
two unstressed syllables, the effect of starting the line with a trochee
(Líľĭes thăt fést-). The spondee ("fár wórse") builds upon the stress on
"sméll" to strike home the point with three stresses together, whereupon
the stress lets up on the iamb "thăn wéeds," which is thereby felt to be
less disgusting, embodying in the sounds the idea that weeds are less
offensive than festering lilies. In the context there is no more powerful
force than the word "fester" where it comes, and its meaning, placement,
and sound evoke just the repulsion against betrayal that the poem exists
to condemn.

SONNET 116

Justly Shakespeare's most often recited sonnet, Sonnet 116 make a
universal claim about the nature and meaning of love and then punctuates
and enforces the claim with a witty conditional assertion in the couplet.

"Let me not to the marriage of true minds / Admit impediments"
(ll. 1–2) refers to the Anglican marriage ceremony, in which, in the Book
of Common Prayer of 1559, the priest "requires" and "charges" "if either
of you doe knowe any impedyment, why ye may not be lawfully joyned
together in Matrimony, that ye confesse it."[5] Here, however, the marriage
is not between a man and a woman but between "true minds." The word
"true" implies fidelity as well as honesty (cf., Polonius's "to thine own self
be true" in *Hamlet*, I.iii.78). "Mind" is the highest of the three divisions of

the self in Platonic and subsequent philosophical thought, so that while the marriage of man and woman is a uniting of minds, hearts, and bodies, here the marriage is of one mind (intelligible soul) with another, leaving out of consideration the sensible soul (the heart and its feelings) and the vegetable soul (the body and its needs and desires). The speaker hints that there may be impediments to joining hearts and to joining bodies, or to joining minds that are not "true," but he will not "admit" (= "permit in" and "allow that there may be") any impediment that can obstruct the union of true minds.

Then comes a statement that is a startling explication of *why* the speaker will not "admit" impediments. The reason is that "Love is not love" (l. 2)—which would be a paradox if it were not for the enjambment that leads on to the next line, "Which alters when it alteration finds" (l. 3), that is, that changes when love finds some change in one with whom it has united. The "Which" clause modifies the first of the two words "love" in the previous line, not the second: i.e., love that alters when it alteration finds is not love. Similarly, love does not alter just because one of the lovers leaves, or betrays, or dies ("bends with the remover to remove" in l. 4).

"Mark" (l. 5) refers to a sea mark, akin to a landmark, by which we navigate because it is fixed and therefore can be trusted as a guide. "Bark" (l. 7) means ship, and the quatrain in general uses the metaphor of navigation. Ships navigated by the stars, and particularly by the North Star or Polestar, by which the ship's position at sea (in the Northern Hemisphere) can always be determined. At least for the purposes of poetry, the stars in Shakespeare's time were still thought of as turning in perfect motion upon the perfectly created and incorruptible crystalline spheres (see Chapter 7 in Part 1). The function of the stars, in addition to making navigation possible, was to receive God's grace and distribute it variously upon the world. As C. S. Lewis explains, to look up toward the heavens at night was not to look out into a vast emptiness punctuated by random fires but to look in to the center of true reality presided over by the mind of God, whose perfect creation was symbolized and illustrated by the heavenly lights.[6] We cannot measure the essential meaning or value of a star (its "worth," l. 8) because only God can do that, but we can measure its "height" (l. 8) from the horizon, and by that measurement know where *we* are. As the Polestar is the constant by which a ship is piloted, so love is the measure and guide of all our earthly motions.[7]

Love cannot be made a fool or victim by time, unlike the beauty of the physical body ("rosy lips and cheeks") and the body itself, which in time decay (ll. 9–10). There is a powerful use of onomatopoeia in ll. 9–11. Anyone who has ever cut grass or weeds with a sickle knows the sound it makes: *ssssk!* Shakespeare creates that kind of sound with the *ps* and *ks* sounds of "lips," "cheeks," and "weeks," and that exact sound three times with the *sk* sound in "sickle's compass come." With the hard *sk* sound of the cutting sickle is contrasted the long-drawn-out sound of "doom" in l. 12. So that the love of the marriage of true minds is associated with lasting until the end of time, in contrast with the body, which must soon be cut down by the blade of time. The "bending sickle" (l. 10) or scythe is associated with time and with death, the "grim reaper." The image is ancient: Chronos, the god of time, was conflated with the god of the harvest, who carried a sickle; the Bible images man as being cut down and withering like grass (Psalms 90:5–6, Isaiah 40:6–7).

The couplet ("If this be error and upon me proved, / I never writ, nor no man ever loved") presents an if/then conditional conclusion to the argument ending in another paradox. The phrase "upon me proved" (l. 13) means both proved against my argument and proved in my case. Thus, if these claims about love are proved wrong, by logic and by his own failing to love his beloved unalterably, then, the speaker asserts, he has never written and no man, including the reader, has ever loved. Well, we have just read the words the speaker has written, and no one reading the poem will admit to never having loved. Hence the logic of the couplet demands that the reader confirm the truth of the first twelve lines of the poem. If we admit that we have just read a poem—we have— and that we have loved truly—we believe we have—then love must be the unalterable, guiding, eternal reality that the poet claims it is. By virtue of the logic of the couplet, we ourselves witness that the poem's claims about true love are true.

SONNET 129

Sonnet 129 is a classic outcry against the illusory happiness that is promised by indulgence in lust, any kind of lust, but in particular that of sexual intercourse outside the context of sacramental marriage.

The poem begins with a double pun: "spirit" (l. 1), in addition to implying the non-physical part of the self, is also a term for semen, and "waste" (l. 1) puns on "waist," so that a man's acting out his lust is, mentally, the shameful waste of his psychic energy and, physically, the expending of semen in shameful sexual intercourse with an unchaste woman.

After the initial generalization, the poem launches into how lust behaves before its desire is accomplished in "action" (l. 2). In l. 4 "not to trust" means not to be trusted; in ll. 6–7 "Past reason" means irrationally, leading to "mad," meaning insane, in ll. 8 and 9.

In l. 5, to the evils of lust before it is fulfilled in action the poet begins adding the evils that characterize lust after it has achieved its goal. Line 10 ("Had, having, and in quest to have, extreme") reverses the chronological order of lust to punctuate its exaggerated or excessive ("extreme") nature after ("Had"), during ("having"), and before ("in quest to have") sexual intercourse. Line 11 restores chronology: "in proof" means in the act of experiencing, and "proved" means having been experienced. In l. 12 ("Before, a joy propos'd, behind, a dream") "behind" is simply the opposite of "Before"—before sexual intercourse, the fulfillment of one's desire promises joy; after it, that joy has evaporated into a mere dream.

Having listed the universal negatives of lust that apply to all men at all times, the couplet then shocks us with the equal truth of a different but equally universal view of lust: that "none knows well" how to shun it. As in the first lines of the poem, so here there is a double play on words: "heaven" (possibly read *haven*) and "hell" are both terms for the female genitalia. The chiasmic reversal (here as the figure antimetabole) of "well knows" to "knows well" and the internal rhyme of "none" and "shun" enforce the universality of the opposite truths: as negative as the evils of lust are, its irresistibility is an equal and opposite force. "The world well knows" the evils, but equally, "none knows well / To shun" the pleasure that is attended by them.

SONNET 130

Sonnet 130 makes use of a double-reverse that plays on the long tradition of the sonnet as a medium for the kind of poem called a blazon. The word *blazon* originally meant "shield," came to mean a heraldic description (cf., "fivefold blazon" in *Twelfth Night*, I.v.293), and was imported by the poets as a term for a detailed description of the beloved that likened her parts to various natural phenomena. In *Epithalamion* Spenser writes about his beloved that "Her goodly eyes [are] like sapphires shining bright, / Her forehead [is] ivory white . . . / Her lips [are] like cherries . . ." (ll. 171–74). Sir Philip Sidney writes about his beloved that "Her hair [is] fine threads of finest gold . . . her forehead [is] more white than snow." There was also a tradition of the comical *contreblazon* or anti-blazon, in which the parts of the beloved are satirically mismatched to the natural phenomena, as in a Sidney poem in which the beloved's lips are "sapphire blue."

Sonnet 130 becomes the pinnacle of both traditions by turning both on their heads. In the first twelve lines the clichés of the blazon tradition are overturned in what promises to become a complete anti-blazon. It is important to remember that the standard description of the ideal woman in Shakespeare's time included blond hair, blue eyes, and fair peaches-and-cream skin. The beloved here has dark hair and dark eyes and olive or brownish skin.

In l. 3 "dun" means grayish brown. "Wires" in l. 4 is not itself a negation—we are not to think of electrical wires, which did not yet exist in Shakespeare's time, but of fine filaments of gold, a cliché for the ideal woman's blond hair. In contrast the beloved here has dark hair ("black wires"). In l. 5 "damasked" (pronounced with the stress on the first syllable, "DAM-asked") means multicolored, here red (blush of modesty) and white (fair skin). It is a reference to a near-eastern species of flower called the damask rose, which has fragrant pink and white flowers from which the perfume attar of roses is made. The image may also refer to the colorfully embroidered and soft silk fabric called damask (originating in Damascus, Syria), from which the flower apparently took its name. In l. 8 "reeks" means is breathed out, emitted. The word does not have the extreme sense of stink that it later took on, but it was already associated with negative sources of odor. In l. 11 "go" means not only move in general but also, specifically, walk, so that the same word can apply to the goddess's floating along in the air and the woman's walking "on the ground."

In l. 9 the speaker has hinted that despite his mistress' less than ideal qualities, he still loves her, but after the hint he returns to the anti-blazon in describing her voice and her movement. Thus by the end of l. 12 the speaker has established two things: a) that his beloved is not an ideal beauty, and b) that he is an honest describer and therefore can be trusted.

The brilliance of the sonnet is capped in the couplet. Having established his credentials as an honest poet, unlike all those in the previous tradition who have engaged in exaggerated praise of their beloveds—the figure of speech is called hyperbole—the speaker then says, "I think my love as rare / As any she belied with false compare" (ll. 13–14). Here "as rare" means as rare a beauty. And the grammar of the last line is not "she belied," as if those words were subject and verb. "As any she" here means as any woman, and "belied" is a participle meaning who has been lied about, i.e., in the false comparisons of the previous poets. So "I think my love as rare a beauty as any woman about whom any previous poet has told lies."

Because we have come to believe the speaker after his twelve lines of telling the truth, we believe him when he tells us that his beloved is a rare beauty nonetheless. This anti-anti-blazon thus uses surprise and wit to accomplish what the previous poets strove to accomplish with hyperbolical praise.

SONNET 135

Sonnets 135 and 151 are perhaps the most sexually explicit among the poems to the "dark lady," 135 being the more complex in its structure. Where Sonnet 151 has "my flesh" "rising" to "stand in thy affairs" (referring to male and female genitalia respectively), Sonnet 135 (along with Sonnet 136) makes an elaborate play on the word "will."

The main idea of Sonnet 135 is the speaker's requesting the lady to welcome his sexual advances even though she may be sleeping with others too. About the form of the poem, G. Blakemore Evans writes that here and in Sonnet 136 "Shakespeare abandons himself (and his readers) to two frankly bawdy and frenetically witty exercises in which he obsessively exploits (and exhausts) various denotative and connotative shades of meaning that Elizabethans associated with the word 'will', both as noun and verb."[8]

The word "will" must be understood in this poem as having at least six senses, any combination of which may be layered into a particular use of the word: a) the poet's name, short for William, (possibly the name of the beloved male friend and also, based on pure speculation, of the hypothetical husband or perhaps another lover of the "dark lady"); b) the future tense expressing intention, as in "wilt thou" (l. 5); c) the free will, the human capacity to make choices; d) willfulness, determination to have one's way; e) sexual desire, as "to have one's will with someone" can mean to possess him or her sexually; f) the male and female sexual parts, as in "hide my will in thine" (l. 6) and "add to thy Will / One will of mine" (ll. 11–12). (In some places the word *willy*, derived from the name William, still means penis, as does the word *dick*, derived from the name Richard.)

In Q the word "will" is capitalized and italicized in seven of its twelve uses in the poem. We cannot know whether or not the graphics were Shakespeare's, and in any case they may mislead us into reducing the six senses of the word to two. It is better to ignore the graphics here and to pursue on your own the complex implications of Shakespeare's punning art.

SONNET 138

In Sonnet 138 the speaker's complaint about the infidelity of the dark lady and his desire to continue their liaison is built up through the fundamental antithesis of their respective dishonesties.

In l. 1 ("When my love swears that she is made of truth") "made of truth" implies both honesty and sexual fidelity. In l. 2 ("I do believe her, though I know she lies") "she lies" means both that she is telling lies and that she is lying with another man or other men. How it is that the speaker can both "believe her" and "know she lies" is the paradox that energizes the poem. In l. 4 ("Unlearnèd in the world's false subtilties") "the world's false subtilties" refers to the lies or tricks or falsehoods with which people beguile others. In l. 5 ("Thus vainly thinking that she thinks me young") "vainly" means both with vanity and in vain. In l. 7 ("Simply I credit her false-speaking tongue") "Simply" means both entirely (completely, absolutely) and like a simpleton. In ll. 9–10 ("But wherefore says she not she is unjust? / And wherefore say not I that I am old?") "Wherefore" means why, and "unjust" means both unfaithful and dishonest. In l. 11 ("O, love's best habit is in seeming trust") "habit" means both repeated practice and clothing or attire, and therefore disguise. And "seeming trust" means both the appearance of trust and seemly or superficially appropriate trust. In l. 12 ("And age in love loves not t' have years told") "told" means not only spoken but counted (as a bank teller "tells" or counts money).

In the couplet ("Therefore I lie with her, and she with me, / And in our faults by lies we flattered be") "lie" and "lies" both work both ways. We tell lies to one another so that we may be pleased ("flattered") by lying in bed together, and we lie in bed together and are deceived or tricked by the lies we tell one another.

SONNET 144

In this poem the speaker contrasts his two beloveds, the young man and the dark lady, figuring them respectively as angel and devil in a kind of *psychomachia*, a battle between good and evil within the psyche (see the essay on *Othello* in Part 2).

In l. 2, to "suggest" means to tempt, to draw the speaker respectively toward good ("The better angel") and toward evil ("The worser spirit"). The crisis of the poem lies in the speaker's suspicion that the woman has succeeded in seducing the friend, making both guilty of betrayal of the speaker. In l. 11 ("But being both from me, both to each friend") "from" means both absent or away from and divided or alienated from; "both to each friend" means each of them is a friend to the other, and "friend" can imply either a platonic or an erotic relationship. Line 12 ("I guess one angel in another's hell") once again, as in Sonnet 129, depends on "hell" as a pun on the euphemism for the female genitalia. "To fire out" (l. 14) has the double meaning of a) to drive out with the burning of venereal disease, and b) to cast out, as foxes are driven out of their holes with firebrands and smoke (cf., *King Lear*, V.iii.23).

SONNET 146

This is perhaps the most philosophical of all the sonnets. Following in a long tradition, the poet presents a dialogue between the soul and the body. (The Christian version of the tradition begins with St. Paul and is elaborated in St. Augustine's *Confessions*. Neoplatonic and humanist versions appear in Castiglione, Sidney, and others.) Addressing his own soul, the speaker challenges it to learn detachment from the wealth and pleasures of the physical body in favor of storing up spiritual wealth.

In l. 1 the "center of my sinful earth" is a composite image. The earth is the center and lowest point of the universe, and the "center" is that point at the center of the earth about which the heavenly spheres turn in circular motion. The earth is "sinful" because it is cursed since the fall of Adam and Eve from the Garden of Eden (Genesis 3:17). The soul is the center about which turns the "earth" that is the "sinful" human body. Like the earth itself, from which Adam was made, the body is sinful because of inborn original sin.

In l. 2 there is a typographical error in the original Q edition that has plagued every editor since. The typesetter erroneously repeated the last three words of the previous line and skipped the word or words actually written in the manuscript, so that ll. 1 and 2 in Q read

> Poore soule the center of my sinfull earth,
> My sinfull earth these rebbell powers that thee array

We know that this was an error because, in addition to being nonsensical, the repetition turns the second line into an awkward hexameter. Nearly a hundred possible emendations have been suggested by editors over the years to supply the missing iamb or trochee. All have proven the impossibility of imitating Shakespeare's genius for the space of even a single foot of verse. Some of the many efforts include "Fooled by," "Spoiled by," "Foiled by," "Pressed by," "Feeding," "Rebuke," "Bearing," "Fenced by," "Gulled by," "Thrall to," and "Lord of." The editor G. Blakemore Evans, setting a good example, says, "Rather than privilege any one of these emendations, it is better, I think, to indicate a textual hiatus at the beginning of the line."[9]

The more the speaker spends on the "fading mansion" (l. 6) that is his body, the more the soul is impoverished within. The metaphor is of a householder impoverishing himself by spending a fortune to decorate the "outward walls" of a mansion (the body) on which he has a short lease and of which the heirs ("inheritors") will be worms.

The third quatrain offers the contemplation of physical death as the way of feeding the soul spiritually. This is in keeping with the long tradition of *memento mori* ("remember that you will die"), which stands behind the many paintings depicting saints and monks contemplating human skulls and behind the contemplation of Yorick's skull in Act V, Scene i, of *Hamlet*. The speaker urges his soul to reverse the habit of l. 3 and instead to let "that" (the body) "pine" in order to increase the soul's store of spiritual wealth. The word "aggravate" means add weight to, from the Latin *gravis*, meaning heavy. The sense of l. 11, "Buy terms divine in selling hours of dross" depends on understanding "terms" to mean long-term interest in an estate, contrasting with mere "hours," so that the antitheses of the line are "Buy"/"selling," "terms"/"hours," and "divine"/"dross." By "selling" the few hours one has to live in the body one will "buy" eternal life.

The poet then extends the images of pining and dearth in l. 3 and eating in l. 8 to the feeding of the soul itself. And the food is now death. Instead of letting itself be eaten away by death in focusing on the material concerns of the physical body, which death is eating away inevitably, the soul may instead contemplate ("feed on") death and thereby tie itself to immortality.

The last line of the couplet ("And Death once dead, there's no more dying then") is one of the most remarkable lines in all Shakespeare. It uses three versions of the same word (the figure of speech is called polyptoton): "Death," "dead," "dying." All but one of the line's words are monosyllables, and it uses but one metaphor (of death being dead).

Where it comes, the final phrase ("there's no more dying then") is as simple, profound, and moving as any phrase in Shakespeare. It bears comparison with Lear's "Pray you undo this button" (*King Lear*, V.iii.310) and with Leontes' "O, she's warm!" (*The Winter's Tale*, V.iii.109). The couplet of this poem causes us to experience the very simplicity that the poem as a whole is advocating: the heavenly calm of its final phrase is as close as words can come to giving us an experience of the reward of contentment promised to those who let go of their attachment to the things of this world in favor of the things of the spirit.

---

[1]   G. Blakemore Evans, ed., *The Sonnets* (Cambridge: Cambridge University Press, 1996, reprinted 1998), p. 133, n. 20:8.

[2]   Evans, p. 132, n. 20:1.

[3]   For the transposition of the adverb see E. A. Abbott, *A Shakespearean Grammar* (London: Macmillan, 1874), §420.

[4]   Morris Palmer Tilley, *A Dictionary of the Proverbs in England in the Sixteenth and Seventeenth Centuries* (Ann Arbor: University of Michigan Press, 1950), H170 and C668, quoted in Evans, p. 201–202, n. 94:1,13.

[5]   Book of Common Prayer, 1559 at http://justus.anglican.org/resources/bcp/1559/Marriage_1559.htm.

[6]   C. S. Lewis, *The Discarded Image* (Cambridge: Cambridge Univ. Press, 1964, reprinted 1988), p. 119.

[7]   Cf., Dante's *Purgatorio*, Canto XVII, ll. 103–105, the center tercet of the *Divine Comedy*.

[8]   Evans, p. 252–53, n. 135:headnote.

[9]   Evans, p. 265, n. 146:2.

Appendix 1: Suggestions for Further Reading

Editions

Facsimiles of Early Editions:

Quarto: Michael J. B. Allen and Kenneth Muir, *Shakespeare's Plays in Quarto* (Berkeley: University of California Press, 1981)

First Folio: Charlton Hinman, *The Norton Facsimile: The First Folio of Shakespeare* (New York: Paul Hamlyn, 1968)

The Sonnets: Robert Giroux, *The Book Known as Q: A Consideration of Shakespeare's Sonnets* (New York: Atheneum, 1982), pp. 227–95; *Shakespeare's Sonnets: The First Quarto, 1609, a Facsimile in Photo-Lithography from the copy in the British Museum* (Forgotten Books, 2018)

Complete Works:

G. Blakemore Evans and J. J. M. Tobin, eds., *The Riverside Shakespeare* (Boston: Houghton Mifflin, Second Edition 1997), republished as *The Wadsworth Shakespeare*

Alfred Harbage, ed., *William Shakespeare: The Complete Works* (New York: Viking Press, 1969, reprinted 1984)

Scholarly Editions:

The Arden Shakespeare, Second Series. (The Arden Shakespeare is now an imprint of Methuen Drama; the Second series is preferable to the Third.)

G. Blakemore Evans, *The Sonnets* in The New Cambridge Shakespeare Series (Cambridge: Cambridge University Press, 1996, 2006)

Popular Edition Series:

The Pelican Shakespeare

The Penguin Shakespeare

The Folger Shakespeare Library

Signet Classics

Shakespeare's Life

Samuel Schoenbaum, *William Shakespeare: A Compact Documentary Life* (Oxford: Oxford University Press, 1978)

Samuel Schoenbaum, *Shakespeare's Lives* (Oxford: Clarendon Press [Oxford University Press], New Edition, 1991), facts and myths about Shakespeare

Background

E. M. W. Tillyard, *The Elizabethan World Picture: A study of the idea of order in the age of Shakespeare, Donne and Milton* (New York: Vintage, 1959)

C. S. Lewis, *The Discarded Image* (Cambridge: Cambridge University Press, 1964, reprint edition, Canto Classics, 2012)

Shakespeare's Theatre

C. Walter Hodges, *The Globe Restored: A Study of the Elizabethan Theatre* (New York: W. W. Norton, 1973)

Shakespeare's Language

Dictionaries:

The Oxford English Dictionary

David Crystal and Ben Crystal, *Shakespeare's Words: A Glossary and Language Companion* (New York: Penguin, 2002)

Eric Partridge, *Shakespeare's Bawdy: A Literary and Psychological Essay and a Comprehensive Glossary* (New York: E. P. Dutton, 1960)

Alexander Schmidt, *Shakespeare Lexicon and Quotation Dictionary* (New York: Dover, 1971, reprint 2015), a republication of Alexander Schmidt, *Shakespeare Lexicon*, 3rd ed. revised and enlarged by Gregor Sarrazin, (Berlin: Georg Reimer, 1902)

Grammar:

E. A. Abbott, *A Shakespearean Grammar: An Attempt to Illustrate Some of the Differences Between Elizabethan and Modern English* (London: Macmillan, New Edition 1874), reprinted in hardcover by Palala Press, 2016, in paperback by Sagwan Press, 2018

Rhetorical Figures of Speech:

Sister Miriam Joseph, *Shakespeare's Use of the Arts of Language* (1947) reprinted (hardcover: Paul Dry Books, 2005; paperback: Martino Fine Books, 2013; Kindle: Ravenio Books, 2016)

Gladys Willcock, "Shakespeare and Elizabethan English," *Shakespeare Survey*, 7 (1954), pp. 12–24.

Richard A. Lanham, *A Handlist of Rhetorical Terms: A Guide for Students of English Literature* (Berkeley: University of California Press, 1969)

Brian Vickers, "Shakespeare's Use of Rhetoric" in *A New Companion to Shakespeare Studies*, ed. K. Muir and S. Schoenbaum (Cambridge: Cambridge University Press, 1971), pp. 83–98

Classical Rhetoric in English Poetry (New York: St. Martin's Press, 1970; reprint: Southern Illinois Univ. Press, 1989)

Pronunciation:

Louis Scheeder and Shane Ann Younts, *All the Words on Stage: A complete Pronunciation Dictionary for the Plays of William Shakespeare* (Hanover, NH: Smith and Kraus, 2002)

Theodora Ursula Irvine, *How to Pronounce the Names in Shakespeare* (originally New York: Hinds, Hayden & Eldredge, 1919, reprint London: Forgotten Books, 2015)

Louis Colaianni, *Shakespeare's Names: A New Pronouncing Dictionary* (New York: Drama Publishers [Quite Specific Media Group], 1999)

Shakespeare's Sources

Geoffrey Bullough, ed., *Narrative and Dramatic Sources of Shakespeare* (New York: Columbia University Press, 1966), 8 volumes

Stuart Gillespie, *Shakespeare's Books, A Dictionary of Shakespeare Sources*, Arden Shakespeare Dictionaries (London/New York: Bloomsbury, The Arden Shakespeare, Second Edition, 2016)

Literary Criticism:

Plays:

See the Selected Bibliography in G. Blakemore Evans and J. J. M. Tobin, eds., *The Riverside Shakespeare* (Boston: Houghton Mifflin, Second Edition 1997), pp. 2021–2034

Sonnets:

Stephen Booth, *An Essay on Shakespeare's Sonnets* (New Haven: Yale University Press, 1969)

C. S. Lewis, *English Literature in the Sixteenth Century Excluding Drama* (Oxford: Clarendon Press, 1954), pp. 502–508

Appendix 2: A List of Shakespeare's Sources

Here is a list of some of the works Shakespeare must have read. We know he read them because he used them as sources for his own works, in which many of them have left clear traces. For more on sources see Appendix 1.

For English History Plays:
> Fabyan, *Chronicle*
> Foxe, *Acts and Monuments*
> Geoffrey of Monmouth, *Historia Regum Britanniae*
> Hall, *The Union of the Two Noble and Illustre Families of Lancaster
>   and York*
> Holinshed, *Chronicles*
> Several anonymous plays on English history

For Comedies:
> Anonymous, *Gl'Ingannati*
> Ariosto, *Orlando Furioso*
> Bandello, *Novelle*
> Belleforest, *Histoires Tragiques*
> Cinthio, *Hecatommithi*
> Gascoigne, *Supposes*
> Lodge, *Rosalynde*
> Ovid, *Metamorphoses* (in the original Latin and translated by
>   Golding—Shakespeare's most often used source)
> Painter, *The Palace of Pleasure*
> Plautus, *Menaechmi, Amphitruo*
> Rich, *His Farewell to Military Profession*
> Spenser, *The Faerie Queene*
> Earlier English plays by Lyly, Marlowe, and Whetstone

For Tragedies:

Anonymous, *The Chronicle History of King Leir*

Appian, *Civil Wars*

Belleforest, *Histoires Tragiques*

Blenerhasset and Higgins (editors), *Mirror for Magistrates*

Brooke, *The Tragical History of Romeus and Juliet*

Caxton, *The Ancient History of the Destruction of Troy*

Chaucer, *The Canterbury Tales, Troilus and Criseyde*

Cinthio, *Hecatommithi*

Daniel, *The Tragedy of Cleopatra*

Holinshed, *Chronicles*

Homer, *Iliad* (translated by Chapman)

Lydgate, *The Ancient History and Only True Chronicle of the Wars [of Troy]*

Montaigne, *Essays* (possibly the original French and as translated by Florio)

Ovid, *Metamorphoses*

Pliny, *The History of the World*

Plutarch, *Lives* (translated by North)

Seneca, *Thyestes, Hercules Furens, Agamemnon*

Sidney, *Arcadia*

Tacitus, *Annals*

For Romances:

Blenerhasset and Higgins (editors), *Mirror for Magistrates*

Boccaccio, *Decameron*

Chaucer, *The Canterbury Tales* (The Knight's Tale)

Gower, *Confessio Amantis*

Greene, *Pandosto, the Triumph of Time*

Holinshed, *Chronicles*

Jourdain, *A Discovery of the Bermudas*

Montaigne, *Essays* (translated by Florio)

Ovid, *Metamorphoses*

Richard Rich, ballad of *News from Virginia* (1610)

Strachey, *True Repertory of the Wrack and Redemption of Sir Thomas Gates*

[Virginia Council], *True Declaration of the Estate of the Colony in Virginia*

For Poems:
Apuleius, *The Golden Ass* (translated by Adlington)
Daniel, *Delia, The Complaint of Rosamond, A Funeral Poem upon the Death of the late noble Earl of Devonshire*
Livy, *Historia*
Marlowe and Chapman, *Hero and Leander*
Ovid, *Metamorphoses, Fasti*
Sidney, *Arcadia, Astrophel and Stella*
Spenser, *Ruines of Rome: By Bellay, The Ruines of Time*
Wilson, *The Arte of Rhetorique*

Appendix 3: Chronology of Shakespeare's Plays and Poems[1]

The following chronology of the dates of composition should be considered roughly correct based on the facts of publication that we know, on the best scholarly conjectures founded on them, and on internal evidence, subject always to the findings of further research. Some of the dates, as for the Sonnets, can be given only as ranges.

Q = Quarto; F = Folio; Ms = Manuscript.

Year	Play	Authoritative Early Editions
1589–90 (revised 1594–95)	*1 Henry VI*	F1
1590–91	*2 Henry VI*	F1
1590–91	*3 Henry VI*	F1
1592–93	*Richard III*	F1
1592–93 (possibly late 1580s)	*Venus and Adonis*	Q1
1592–94	*The Comedy of Errors*	F1
1592–95	*Edward III*	Q1
Composed 1580s–1609? Printed 1609	*Sonnets*	Q1
1593–94	*The Rape of Lucrece*	Q1
1593–94	*Titus Andronicus*	Q1, F1

Year	Play	Authoritative Early Editions
1593–94	*The Taming of the Shrew*	F1
1594	*The Two Gentlemen of Verona*	F1
1594–95 (revised 1597)	*Love's Labour's Lost*	Q1, F1
1594–95	Additions to *Sir Thomas More*	Ms
1594–96	*King John*	F1
1595	*Richard II*	Q1, F1
1595–96	*Romeo and Juliet*	Q2, F1
1595–96	*A Midsummer Night's Dream*	Q1, F1
1596–97	*The Merchant of Venice*	Q1, F1
1596–97	*I Henry IV*	Q1, F1
1597 (revised 1600–1601)	*The Merry Wives of Windsor*	F1
1598	*2 Henry IV*	Q, F1
1598–99	*Much Ado about Nothing*	Q, F1
1599	*Henry V*	F1
1599	*Julius Caesar*	F1
1599	*As You Like It*	F1
1600–1601	*Hamlet*	Q2, F1
1601	*The Phoenix and the Turtle*	Q1
1601–1602	*Twelfth Night*	F1
1601–1602	*Troilus and Cressida*	Q, F1
Composed 1602–1608? Printed 1609	*A Lover's Complaint*	Q

Year	Play	Authoritative Early Editions
1602–1603	*All's Well That Ends Well*	F1
1604	*Measure for Measure*	F1
1604	*Othello*	Q1, F1
1605	*King Lear*	Q1, F1
1606	*Macbeth*	F1
1606–1607	*Antony and Cleopatra*	F1
1607–1608	*Coriolanus*	F1
1607–1608	*Timon of Athens*	F1
1607–1608	*Pericles*	Q1
1609–1610	*Cymbeline*	F1
1610–11	*The Winter's Tale*	F1
1611	*The Tempest*	F1
1612–13	*Henry VIII*	F1
1612–13	*Cardenio* (a lost play)	—
1613	*The Two Noble Kinsmen*	Q

[1] Based on the Chronology and Sources table in G. Blakemore Evans and J. J. M.Tobin, ed., *The Riverside Shakespeare* (Boston: Houghton Mifflin, Second Edition, 1997), pp. 77–87.

CPSIA information can be obtained
at www.ICGtesting.com
Printed in the USA
LVHW110523030622
720156LV00003B/28